English-Spanish & Spanish-English

GLOSSARY OF THE PETROLEUM INDUSTRY

Third Edition

Inglés-Español y Español-Inglés

GLOSARIO DE LA INDUSTRIA PETROLERA

Tercera Edición

Inglés-Español e Español-Inglés

GLOSARIO DE LA INDUSTRIA PETROLERA

Tercera Edición

Contiene más de 20,000 vocablos y expresiones de uso corriente en todas las fases de las industrias petrolera y del gas— exploración, perforación, producción, transporte, refinación, procesamiento del gas y mercadeo—y actividades afines.

PennWell Books

PennWell Publishing Company
Tulsa, OK

English-Spanish & Spanish-English

GLOSSARY OF THE PETROLEUM INDUSTRY

Third Edition

Contains more than 20,000 technical terms and idioms commonly used in all phases of the oil and gas industry—exploration, drilling, production, transportation, refining, gas processing, and marketing—and ancillary fields.

PennWell Books

PennWell Publishing Company
Tulsa, OK

Copyright © 1996 by
PennWell Publishing Company
1421 South Sheridan/P.O. Box 1260
Tulsa, Oklahoma 74101

Library of Congress
Cataloging-in-Publication Data
Main entry under title:

Glossary of the petroleum industry
ISBN 0-87814-616-4

Printed in the United States of America

1 2 3 4 5 00 99 98 97 96

PREFACE

This book is a comprehensive English-Spanish and Spanish-English glossary of terms of the oil industry originally compiled and published in 1947 by editors of PennWell Publishing Co., publishers of *Oil & Gas Journal Revista Latinoamericana* (and formerly of *Petróleo Internacional*).

The third edition of the *Glossary* revises the previous version by more than 20 percent. Included are new technical and general terms used in the oil and gas industry as well as recurrent words from ancillary and related fields such data processing, electricity, navigation, geology and geophysics, construction, soldering, commerce, and others. The contents have been extensively revised and reorganized for the third edition, and new terminology compiled and inserted by María-Dolores Proubasta, former managing editor of *Petróleo Internacional* and translations editor of *Revista Latinoamericana*.

Abreviaturas para las Secciones de Español e Inglés
ABBREVIATIONS FOR SPANISH AND ENGLISH SECTIONS

a.	adjetivo/adjective
a	automóvil/automobile
abr.	abreviación/abbreviation
aero	aeronáutica/aeronautics; aviación/aviation
Ar	Argentina
adv.	adverbio/adverb
angl.	anglicismo/anglicism
bl	barril/barrel
bm	bomba/pump
Bo	Bolivia
ca	cable/cable
carp	carpintería/carpentry
cl	caldera/boiler; calor/heat
cm	comercio/commerce
Co	Colombia
contr	contrato/contract
cn	construcción/construction
CR	Costa Rica
Cu	Cuba
CH	Chile
dp	proceso de datos/data processing
ec	ecología/ecology
Ec	Ecuador
e.g.	por ejemplo/for instance
Es	España/Spain
el	electricidad/electricity
eq	equipo/equipment
expl	explosivos/explosives; voladura/blasting
fl	fluidos/fluids
frn	horno/furnace
g	geología/geology
gas	procesamiento del gas/gas processing
gf	geofísica/geophysics
gravim	gravimetría/gravimetry
hd	hidrología/hidrology
in	instrumentos/instruments
insur	seguros/insurance
la	laboratorio/laboratory
ma	maquinaria/machinery

mar	costafuera/offshore
mc	mecánica/mechanics
Me	México
mn	minería, mining; minerales/minerals
mo	motores/engines
mt	matemáticas/mathematics
mu	metalurgia/metallurgy
n.	nombre/noun
nav	navegación/navigation
nt	náutica/nautic
o	o/or
oc	ocupación/occupation
op.	contrario de/opposite
p	oleo-gasoluctos/pipelines
paleo	paleontología/paleontology
Pe	Perú
perc	perforación a percusión/percussion drilling
pr	producción/production
PR	Puerto Rico
pref.	prefijo/prefix
prf	perforación/drilling
qm	química/chemistry
q.v.	véase también/see also (*quo vide*)
r	río/river
rd	caminos/roads
rf	refinación/refining
rr	ferrocarril/railroad
sd	soldadura/soldering
stats	estadística/statistics
tk	tanque/tank
tl	herramienta/tool; taller/shop
tr	turbinas/turbines
trans	transporte/transportation
tp	topografía/topography; levantamiento de planos/surveying
tu	tubería/tubing and pipe
Ur	Uruguay
va	válvulas/valves
Ve	Venezuela
vlc	volcanología/volcanology
vol	volumen/volume
wt	peso/weight

Glossary of the Petroleum Industry

A

a (annum), año: símbolo del SI; q.v.
atto
A (ampere), amperio: unidad de
corriente eléctrica;(argon)argón
A (Ångstrom), angstrom
A frame, cabria en A, mástil en
forma de A, cabrestante (o
caballete, armazón) en A, poste
en A
A mast, mástil en A
abandon, v. abandonar;
abandonment, n. abandono
abandoned beach, (g) antigua playa
(de la cual se ha retirado el mar)
abate, v. reducir, disminuir, rebajar;
anular, eliminar; (nt) amainar;
abatement, n. reducción,
disminución, rebaja,
eliminación
abbreviation, abreviatura
Abel tester, probador Abel
abiosis, n. (g) abiosis; abiotic, a.
abiótico
ablation, ablación; desgaste (de
rocas), reducción por
derretimiento (de heleros)
aboard, a bordo
abort, abortar (un proceso), poner
término, suspender, interrumpir
abrade, bruñir, desgastar, raer
abrasion, abrasión, desgaste,
raspadura
abrasive, n. abrasivo; a. abrasivo,
rayante
abroad, en el exterior, en el
extranjero
abs (absolute), absoluto
— address, (dp) dirección absoluta

— alcohol, alcohol absoluto
— electrometer, electrómetro de
balanza
— galvanometer, galvanómetro de
unidad absoluta
— open flow, (pr) flujo abierto
— permeability, permeabilidad
absoluta
— porosity, porosidad absoluta
— temperature scale, escala de
temperatura absoluta
— warranty, garantía de título
— viscosity, coeficiente de
viscosidad, viscosidad absoluta
— zero, cero absoluto
abscissa, abscisa
absorb, v. absorber, (mc)
amortiguar; absorbent, a. n.
absorbente
absorber, (gas) absorbedora; (mc)
amortiguador; (rf) torre de
absorción
— capacity, (gas) capacidad de
absorbedora (o de absorción)
absorbtion, (mc) amortiguamiento,
amortiguación; (qm) absorción,
absorbencia; (el) absorción
— column, torre (o columna) de
absorción
— gas, gas de absorción
— gasoline, gasolina de absorción
— oil, aceite de absorción
— plant, planta (o instalación) de
absorción
— spectrometer, espectrómetro de
absorción
— tester, probador de absorción
— tower, torre de absorción,
absorbedor
abut against, empotrar en, apoyarse
en, estribar en, adosar a
abutment, remate, contrafuerte;
(mc) tope
abutting property, propiedad
limítrofe, terreno lindante
abyss, abism, abismo, despeñadero

1

abysmal, abyssal, *a.* abisal,
insondable
— **rocks,** rocas abisales, rocas
profundas (o plutónicas)
— **sea,** mar abisal
ac (alternating current), corriente
alterna (ca)
accelerate, acelerar
acceleration, aceleración
accelerator, acelerador; (qm)
catalizador
— **pump,** bomba del acelerador,
bomba acelerante
— **rod,** varilla del acelerador
accelerometer, (gf) acelerómetro
access, acceso
— **time,** (dp) tiempo de acceso
accesories, accesorios, aditamentos
accessory, *a.* accesorio
— **mineral,** mineral secundario
— **shaft,** eje accesorio
accident, accidente, desgracia, (nt)
siniestro
acclivity, contrapendiente
account, (cm) cuenta; relato,
informe
accountant, (oc) contador,
contable
accretion, (g) acrecimiento,
acrecentamiento, acrecencia,
acumulación, yuxtaposición,
aumento por yuxtaposición
accruals, (cm) acumulaciones
accumulator, (el) (mc)
acumulador; (mc) amortiguador
— **battery,** batería de acumuladores
accuracy, *n.* exactitud, precisión;
accurate, *a.* exacto,
preciso,correcto, cabal
acenaphthylene, acenaftileno
acetal, acetal
acetaldehyde, acetaldehido
acetate, acetato
acetone, acetona
acetyl, acetilo
acetylation, acetilación

acetylene, acetileno
— **black,** humo de acetileno
— **burner,** quemador (o mechero)
de acetino
— **gas,** gas acetileno
— **generator,** generador (o
gasógeno) de acetileno
— **series,** serie acetilénica
— **torch,** soplete oxiacetilénico
— **welding,** soldadura autógena (o
con acetileno, oxiacetilénica)
**acfm (actual cubic feet per
minute),** pies cúbicos reales por
minuto
acicular, acicular
aciculum, acículo
acid, ácido
— **brittleness,** fragilidad ácida
— **cell,** (el) acumulador ácido de
plomo
— **core solder,** soldadura con
núcleo ácido
— **corrosion,** corrosion causada por
ácidos
— **dissociation constant,** (ec)
constante de disociación
— **fracture,** fracturamiento con
ácido
— **gas,** gas ácido (o amargo)
— **gun,** inyector de ácido
— **heat,** (rf) calentamiento por
ácido
— **heat test,** prueba ácida en
caliente, (Ar) ensayo de
reacción exotérmica por ácido
— **inhibitor,** supresor (o inhibidor)
de ácido
— **jet gun,** inyector de ácido
— **metal,** aleación antiácida
— **number,** índice de acidez
— **oil ratio,** relación ácido-petróleo
— **process,** proceso ácido
— **rain,** lluvia ácida
— **reaction,** reacción ácida
— **recovery plant,** planta para la
recuperación de ácido

— **refining**, refinación ácida (o con ácido)

— **resistent**, resistente al ácido

— **restoring plant**, (rf) planta regeneradora (o restauradora) de ácidos

— **rock**, roca ácida

— **sludge**, lodo (o cieno, sedimento) ácido

— **stimulation**, estimulación con ácido (q.v. **acidize**)

— **steel**, acero ácido

— **tank**, (rf) tanque inyector de ácido

— **tar**, alquitrán ácido

— **treating head**, cabezal para inyección de ácido

— **treatment**, tratamiento con ácido

— **wash color**, (rf) color después del lavado con ácido

— **washing**, baño antiácido

acidic lava, lava ácida

acidify, acidificar

acidity, acidez

— **coefficient**, (g) coeficiente de acidez, relación de oxígeno

acidize, acidizing, acidificación, tratamiento ácido (de pozos), acidulación, tratar (o cargar) con ácido

acidproof, a prueba de ácidos

acidulate, acidular; mezclar con una pequeña cantidad de ácido

aclinic, (g) aclínico, sin inclinación (o buzamiento)

— **line**, línea aclínica, ecuador magnético

acme thread, rosca de 29°, filete acme (de tornillos)

acmite, acmita

acorn nut, tuerca (o ciega) ovalada

acoustic, acústico

— **doppler navigator**, piloto (acústico por efecto) Doppler

— **horizon**, (g) horizonte acústico

— **impedance**, impedancia acústica

— **log**, registro sónico

— **position reference**, orientación por medio de ondas acústicas

— **signatures**, señales acústicas

— **survey**, registro sónico (q.v. **sonic logging**)

acre, acre (40,47 áreas)

acre-foot, acrepié, acre-pié: volumen de un pie de espesor por un acre de extensión

acreage, área en acres, extensión de terreno (en general)

acrolein, acroleína

acrometer, oleómetro, acrómetro

a-cropping, hacia el afloramiento

across, *adv.* a través, transversalmente

across-the-line valve, válvula de cierre

acrylic, acrílico

acrylonitrile, acrilonitrilo

ACT, q.v. **automatic custody transfer**

act of God, fuerza mayor, caso fortuito

acting manager, (cm) gerente suplente (o interino)

actinograph, actinógrafo

actinolite, (g) actinolita, actinota

actinometer, actinómetro

action, funcionamiento, movimiento; acción; impulsión

— **zone**, (g) zona herítica

activated, *a.* activado

— **carbon**, carbón activado

— **clay**, arcilla activada

activation, activación

active, *a.* activo

— **component**, (el) componente vatada

— **current**, corriente activa, vatada

— **power**, potencia activa (o efectiva)

actual, *a.* real, verdadero, efectivo

3

English - Spanish

— **absolute gravity**, gravedad
absoluta real
— **cost**, coste efectivo
— **gradient**, gradiente real
— **horsepower**, caballos de fuerza
efectiva
— **parameter**, (dp) parámetro
efectivo
— **power**, potencia real (o activa)
— **value**, valor en plaza (o del
mercado)
actuate, impulsar, accionar, actuar,
activar, mover
actuating, impulsor, accionador,
activador, de mando
— **pressure valve**, válvula
excitadora de presión
actuator, impulsor, accionador,
actuador, activador, servomotor
ACU (automatic calling unit),
(dp) unidad automática de
llamada
acuiclude, (g) acuiclusa
acute, agudo
— **angle**, ángulo agudo
— **bisectrix**, bisectriz aguda
acute-angled, acutángulo
acyclic, (el) acíclico, unipolar
A/D (analog-to-digital), (dp)
(conversión) de analógico a
digital
ad valorem, ad valorem
adamantine, *a.* adamantino,
diamantino
— **drill**, barrena adamantina (o de
diamantes), sonda de
municiones
— **spar**, corindón
adamellite, (g) adamelita
adamite, adamita
adapter, adaptador
— **plug**, tapón adaptador
adapter-type ball bearing, cojinete
de bolas con adaptador
addition, suma, adición

additive compound, (rf) aditivo,
elemento de adición
address, dirección, domicilio
addressee, destinatario
adduct, aducto
adelfotype, adelfotipo
ader wax, ozoquerita cruda
adhere, adherir, adherirse
adherence, adhesión
adhesive, adhesivo, adherente
adiabatic, *a.* adiabático; curva (o
línea) adiabática
— **bulk modulus**, módulo
adiabático de volumen
— **change**, proceso adiabático
— **compression**, compresión
adiabática
— **expansion**, expansión adiabática
— **gradient**, gradiente adiabático
adiagnostic, adiagnóstico
adipic acid, ácido adípico
a-dipping, en la dirección del
buzamiento
adit, socavón, tiro inclinado, pozo
de arrastre; (mn) galería de
extracción, contramina
aditive, aditivo
adjacent, adyacente
adjoining rock, roca vecina (q.v.
country rock)
adjust, *v.* ajustar, regular, graduar,
poner en punto, corregir
adjustable, *a.* ajustable, que puede
regularse (o ajustarse)
— **choke**, estrangulador (o válvula)
graduable, cebador ajustable
— **speed motor**, motor de velocidad
regulable (o ajustable)
— **voltage control**, control por
tensión regulable
adjuster, ajustador, regulador; (cm)
asesor, ajustador
— **board**, tabla ajustadora (del
vástago pulido); guía para el
cable

4

adjusting, *a.* ajustador, de
regulación; (in) de corrección
— **clamp**, abrazadera graduable,
grapa retén, agarradera de
tornillo
— **clasp**, abrazadera de tornillo
— **eyebolt**, perno de ojo para ajuste
— **nut**, tuerca ajustadora
— **pin**, clavija de corrección
— **screw**, tornillo de ajuste (o de
corrección)
— **tool**, ajustador
adjustment, reajuste, ajuste,
regulación, reglaje; (in)
corrección, verificación
admiralty constants, (nt)
coeficientes del almirantazgo
para la potencia requerida en
máquinas marinas
admiralty metal, aleación de 88%
cobre, 10% estaño, 2% cinc
admission, admisión; aspiración
— **cam**, leva de admisión
— **lead**, avance de la admisión
— **port**, lumbrera de admisión,
orificio de aspiración
— **stroke**, carrera (o período) de
admisión; tiempo de aspiración
— **valve**, válvula de admisión (o de
aspiración, de toma)
admixture, mixtura, agregado
coloidal
adolescent, (r) adolescente
adsorb, *v.* adsorber; **adsorbent**, *n. a.*
adsorbente
adsorption, adsorción
— **gasoline**, gasolina de adsorción
aduncity, *n.* encorvadura, comba,
torcedura
aduncous, *a.* encorvado, curvo,
combado, torcido
advance, *n.* avance, mejora,
adelanto, progreso; (mc) avance;
(ec) anticipo, provisión de
fondos; *v.* avanzar, mejorar,
adelantar, progresar

adventive crater, cráter advenedizo
adverse grade, pendiente en subida
advertisement, anuncio,
propaganda, aviso
adviser, advisor, (oc) asesor,
consejero
advisory, *a.* consultivo
adz, adze, *n.* azuela; *v.* azolar,
desbastar, aparar
AEM, q.v. **airborne**
electromagnetics
aeolian, eólico
— **rock**, roca de origen eólico
aerate, *v.* airear, aerar, aerear;
aerator, *n.* aereador; aerador
aereal mapping,
aerofotogrametría, cartografía
aérea
aerial, *a.* aéreo; *n.* antena
— **bridge**, puente colgante (para
tubería)
— **mapping**, aerofotogrametría,
cartografía aérea
— **spud**, cable de draga
— **survey**, estudio aerotopográfico
— **tramway**, tranvía aéreo,
andarivel, funicular aéreo, cable
teleférico, (Ar) alambrecarril
— **triangulation**,
aerotriangulación
aerify, aerificar; gasificar
aerobe, *n.* aerobio
aerobic, *a.* aeróbico
aerogene gas, gas pobre, gas de aire
(q.v. **producer gas**)
aerogenic, aerógeno
aerolite, (g) aerolito
aeromagnetic survey,
levantamiento aeromagnético
aerometer, aerómetro, densímetro
aerosphere, aerosfera
aerostatics, aerostática
aeruginous, (g) ruginoso
affidavit, (cm) declaración jurada,
testimonio, afidávit

5

affiliated company, compañía asociada (o afiliada)

affluent, afluente, tributario

afflux, aflujo

AFL (abstract family of languages), (dp) familia abstracta de lenguajes

aft, (nt) hacia la popa

afterburning, combustión retardada, postcombustión

aftercooler, n. (gas) (rf) postenfriador, postrefrigerador

aftercooling, postenfriamiento, postrefrigeración

aftergases, (mn) gases de explosión (o de incendio)

aftershock, temblor secundario, sismo final, (Es) réplica

against the current, a contracorriente

agate, ágata

AGC, q.v. automatic gain control

age, (g) edad, piso

agenda, orden del día, programa, temaria, puntos a tratar, agenda

agent, agente; (cm) gestor, representante, encargado; apoderado, mandatario

agglomerate, (g) aglomerado

agglutinate, aglutinado

aggradation, (g) agradación, adición (o modificación) por sedimentación (o por deposición sedimentaria)

— plain, planicie de deposición uniforme (de regiones áridas)

aggrade, (g) elevarse (mediante deposición uniforme)

agreement, convenio, acuerdo, pacto, avenencia, trato

aggregate, agregado

aggregate-handling plant, instalación para el manejo de agregados

aging test, prueba (o ensayo) de envejecimiento

agitate, agitar; agitator, agitador, batidora

Agnotozoic, agnotozoico (q.v. Algonkian, Proterozoic)

agonic line, (g) línea agónica

agreed value, (cm) valor entendido

agreement, (cm) acuerdo, convenio, trato

aground, (nt) varado, encallado

ahead, adelante

A-hr (ampere-hour), amperio-hora

AI (artificial intelligence), (dp) inteligencia artificial

aim, apuntar; (nt) enfilar

air, aire

— balanced unit, unidad contrapesada neumáticamente

— bleed, extracción del aire

— blower, soplador, ventilador

— borne, llevado por el aire

— box, tubo rectangular de ventilación

— brake, freno neumático

— chamber, cámara (o campana) de aire (o neumática)

— chuck, mandril neumático

— cell covering, revestimiento aerocelular

— circuit breaker, disyuntor al aire

— cleaner, depurador (o limpiador, purificador) de aire; filtro de ire

— clutch, embrague neumático (o de aire)

— cock, llave de alivio de aire, válvula purgadora de aire

— compressor, compresor de aire (o neumático)

— condenser, (el) condensador de aire; (mc) condensador de enfriamiento por aire

— conditioning plant, planta de acondicionamiento de aire

— cooled, a. enfriado por aire

— cooling, n. enfriamiento por aire

— cooler, enfriador de aire

— core, núcleo de aire

Glossary of the Petroleum Industry

— **coupling**, conexión para tubo (o manguera) de aire
— **cushion**, colchón de aire
— **density**, densidad del aire
— **displacement meter**, medidor de desplazamiento de aire
— **drain**, conducto de aire (o de ventilación)
— **dried, dry**, secado al aire
— **drill**, barrena neumática (o accionada por aire), taladro neumático, perforadora de aire, sonda neumática
— **drilling**, perforación con aire
— **drive**, (pr) inyección de gas (o aire comprimido)
— **duct**, conducto de ventilación (o de aire)
— **ejector**, eyector de aire
— **engine**, motor neumático; motor enfriado por aire
— **filter**, filtro (o depurador, purificador) de aire
— **flooding**, (pr) inyección de aire (o gas)
— **furnace**, horno de aire, (mu) horno de tiro natural
— **gage**, manómetro de aire
— **gas**, gas de aire
— **gun**, (gf) pistola neumática
— **hammer**, martillo neumático
— **hoist**, elevador (o malacate) neumático, dispositivo neumático de elevación, torno de aire
— **hose**, manguera de aire
— **injection**, inyección de aire
— **intake**, toma de aire, respiradero
— **level**, nivel de burbuja de aire
— **lift**, (pr) extracción por aire
— **lock**, *n*. (ma) bolsa de aire; (tunnel) esclusa de aire
— **motor**, motor neumático
— **operated**, neumático, de funcionamiento neumático
— **oven**, horno secador de aire

— **pocket**, bolsa de aire
— **port**, respiradero, sopladero, orificio de ventilación; (nt) ojo de buey, porta
— **pressure**, presión del aire (o neumática)
— **rate**, (cm) tarifa aérea
— **receiver**, tanque receptor de aire, tanque de compresión (o de aire comprimido), (CH) campana de aire
— **removal**, saca de (o remoción del) aire
— **sampling**, (ec) muestreo de aire
— **scrubber**, depurador de aire, tanque limpiador de aire
— **shot**, explosión amortiguada por aire
— **shaft**, (mn) pozo (o caja) de ventilación, tiro ventilador, tragante, chimenea de aire
— **slaked**, apagado al aire; (g) descompuesto en el aire
— **space**, hueco, espacio vacío
— **spade**, zapadora (o pala) neumática, martillo de pala, (Co) guataca, (Ve) palín
— **starter**, arrancador neumático
— **station**, (photogrammetry) punto aéreo de exposición
— **sweetening**, desulfurar (o endulzar) por aire
— **switch**, interruptor al aire
— **tempering**, atemperación del aire
— **terminal**, (el) terminal aéreo
— **tight**, hermético
— **tools**, herramientas neumáticas
— **transformer**, transformador de aire
— **trap**, colector (o trampa, interceptor) de aire; cierre de sifón
— **valve**, válvula de aire, ventosa
— **vent**, respiradero, escape de aire, ventilación

7

— **vessel**, cámara de aire
— **wave**, onda sonora
— **well**, pozo de ventilación
— **winch**, malacate neumático
air-acetilene welding, soldadura aeroacetilénica
air-actuated, impulsado (o accionado) por aire comprimido
air-actuated remote recorder, teleregistrador neumático
air-blast transformer, transformador enfriado por soplo de aire
air-cooled exchanger, radiador enfriado por aire
air-hardened, endurecido al aire
air-line oiler, aceitera de línea
air-locked, *a.* obturado por aire
air-operated recording regulator, regulador registrador neumático
airborne electromagnetics, (gf) aéreo-electromagnetismo
airborne magnetometer, magnetómetro aéreo
airfoil, superficie aerodinámica
airometer, aerómetro, contador de aire
airproof, hermético
airtight, hermético
Ajax metal, metal antifricción (de cobre, estaño, plomo y arsénico)
akerite, aquerita
alabandite, alabandina, alabandita
alabaster, alabastro
alarm relay, (el) relai avisador (o de alarma)
alaskite, alasquita (granito)
albertite, albertita (q.v. **asphalt rock**)
Albian, albiense
albite, (g) albita, feldespato
alcaline, alcalino
alchemy, alquimia
alcohol, alcohol
aldehyde, aldehido
alembic, alambique

Alemite fittings, accesorios para engrase Alemite
ALF (airborne laser fluorosensor), laser fluoroscópico aerotransportado
algae, algas
algal, (g) algal
Algol (algorithmic language), lenguage algorítmico
Algonkian, algonkiano, algonquín (q.v. **Agnotozoic**)
alidade, alidada, (Ar) dioptra
alien, *n.* extranjero, forastero; *a.* extraño, desconocido
alignment, alineación, alineamiento, enderezamiento
— **chart**, nomograma
— **gage**, calibrador (o indicador) de alineación
aliphatic, *a.* alifático, graso
— **diolefin**, diolefina alifática (o grasa)
alive, (el) cargado
alizarin, alizarina
alkadiene, alcadieno
alkadiyne, alcadiino
alkalescence, *n.* alcalescencia;
alkalescent, *a.* alcalescente
alkali, *n.* álcali; *a.* alcalino
— **metal**, metal alcalino
— **soil**, tierra (o suelo) que contiene sales solubles
— **test**, prueba alcalina
alkali-proof, a prueba de álcalis
alkalimeter, alcalímetro
alkaline, *a.* alcalino; **alkalinity**, *n.* alcalinidad
— **cell**, (el) acumulador alcalino
— **earth**, tierra alcalina
— **flooding**, inyección de fluidos alcalinos
alkalize, alcalizar
alkaloid, alcaloide
alkane, alcano
alkene, alqueno
alkyl, alquilo; *pref.* alquil-

— **quinoline**, quinolina alquílica
— **radical**, radical alcohilo, alquilo, radical alcohólico
— **sulfide**, sulfuro alquílico
alkylate, alquilato, alkilato
alkylation, alcohilación, alquilación
alkylbenzene, alquilbenceno (q.v. **phenylpropene**)
alkylene, alquileno
alkylize, alquilar, alquilizar
all levels sample, muestra de todos niveles, muestra compuesta
all thread, roscado enteramente
all welded construction, construcción enteramente soldada
allanite, alanita
Allan's metal, aleación de cobre y plomo
alley arm, (el) cruceta excéntrica
alliaceous, aliáceo
alligation, aleación, liga
alligator grab, pinzas de lagarto, atrapador de mandíbulas, (Ar) pescador cocodrilo, (Ve) pescador de caimán
alligator wrench, llave dentada (o de mordaza)
allocation, asignación, cuota
allochromatic, (g) alocromático
allochtonous, alóctono
allogenic, alógeno
allophane, (g) alofana
allothigenic, alotígeno
allotriomorphic, alotriomorfo (q.v. **xenomorphic**)
allotrope, *a.* alotrópico; **allotropy**, *n.* alotropía
allowable, permisible
— **load**, carga límite (o admisible) de seguridad
allowance, tolerancia, sobreespesor
alloy, *n.* aleación, liga, (Ur) aleaje; *v.* alear, ligar

— **casting**, pieza de aleación fundida
— **cast iron**, aleación de hierro fundido (o colado)
— **pipe**, tubo de aleación
— **steel**, acero de aleación
alluvia, tierras de aluvión
alluvial, *a.* aluvial, (Co) aluvioso
— **deposit**, aluvión, depósito aluvial, terreno de acarreo, acarreo fluvial, (Pe) terreno de transporte
— **fan**, abanico (o cono) aluvial, abanico de deyección (q.v. **talus fan**)
— **terrace**, terraplén aluvial
alluviation, acumulación aluvial
alluvium, aluvión, tierra aluvial
allylacetylene, alilacetileno (q.v. **pentenyne**)
almandite, almandita
alongside, al costado, (nt) abarloado
along the bedding, (g) a lo largo de la estratificación
alpha, alfa
— **brass**, aleación de cobre y cinc
— **methyl naphthalene**, alfametilnaftalina
— **particle**, partícula alfa
— **ray**, rayo alfa
alpha-naphtylamine acetate, acetato de alfanaftilamina
Alpine, alpinense, alpino
altazimuth, altazimut
— **instrument**, teodolito altacimutal
alteration, alteración
— **switch**, (dp) conmutador (o llave) de alteración
altered rock, roca alterada
alternance, alternancia
alternate, *a.* alterno, alternante, substitutivo, variante; optativo, opcional

alternating current, corriente
alterna
alternating motion, movimiento
alternativo
alternator, alternador
— **transmitter**, alternador-
transmisor
altimeter, altímetro
altimetry, altimetría
altitude, altitud, elevación, cota,
altura
— **valve**, válvula controladora de
nivel
ALU, q.v. **arithmetic and logic
unit**
alum, alumbre; sulfato de aluminio
— **earth**, alcilla piritobituminosa (o
aluminosa)
— **schist**, esquisto aluminoso
— **shale**, lutita aluminosa
— **stone**, alunita, piedra de alumbre
alumina, alúmina
aluminite, aluminita
aluminothermic welding,
soldadura aluminotérmica (o de
termita)
aluminum, aluminium, aluminio
— **base grease**, grasa a base de
aluminio
— **bronze**, bronce de aluminio
— **hydroxide**, hidróxido de
aluminio, gibbsita
— **oxide**, óxido de aluminio,
alúmina
— **silver**, aleación de plata y
aluminio
— **solder**, soldadura de aluminio
alundum, alundo
alunite, alunita (q.v. **alum stone**)
amalgam, amalgama
amalgamation process, beneficio
por amalgamación
amber, ámbar
ambient, *a.* ambiental; del
ambiente

— **concentrations**, (ec)
concentraciones del ambiente
— **temperature**, temperatura
ambiental
amethyst, amatista
amianthus, (mn) amianto
amine, amina
ammeter, amperímetro
ammonia, amoníaco
— **compressor**, compresor de
amoníaco
— **dynamite**, dinamita amoniacal
— **oil**, lubricante para máquinas
frigoríficas
ammonite, amonita
ammonium, amonio
— **acetate**, acetato amónico (o de
amonio)
— **carbonate**, carbonato de amonio
— **chloride**, cloruro amónico
amorphous, amorfo
amortization, (cm) amortización
amount, cantidad; suma; total
amperage, (el) amperaje
ampere, amperio
— **turn**, amperio-vuelta,
amperivuelta
ampere-hour, amperio-hora
amperemeter, amperímetro
amphibious, anfibio
amphibole, (g) anfíbol
amphibolite, anfibolita
amplifier, amplificador
— **stage**, etapa amplificadora
amplify, amplificar
amplitude, amplitud
— **compass**, brújula de azimut
— **control**, control de la amplitud
— **curve**, curva de amplitud
— **variation with offset**,
— **meter**, vibrómetro
(gf) variación de amplitud
— **ratio**, relación de amplitudes
— **response**, (gf) respuesta en
amplitud

— **variation with offset**, (gf) variación de amplitud con apartamiento (o offset)

amygdaloid, *n*. roca amigdaloide; **amygdaloidal**, *a*. amigdaloide

amyl, amilo, alcohol amílico; *pref.* amil-

amylacetylene, amilacetileno (q.v. **heptyne**)

amylbenzene, amilbenceno (q.v. **phenylpentane**)

amylene, amileno (q.v. **pentene**)

amylheneicosane, amilheneicosano

anaclinal, opuesto al buzamiento, anaclinal

anaerobic, anaeróbico, aneróbico, sin (o carente de) oxígeno

analcite, analcita

— **basalt**, basalto analcítico

analcitite, (g) analcitita

analog, analogue, analógico

analysis, *n*. análisis; **analytical**, *a*. analítico; **analytically**, *adv*. analíticamente

analyst, (oc) analista

analtical balance, balanza de precisión, balanza analítica

analyzer, (in) analizador

anamorphism, (g) anamorfismo

anamorphosis, anamorfosis

anatase, anatasa; octaedrita

anchor, *n*. ancla, áncora, amarre; anclaje; (cn) sujetador, trabilla, afianzador, muerto, fijador; *v*. anclar, fondear; afianzar, sujetar, trabar, asegurar

— **base**, base de ancla

— **bolt**, perno remachado, perno de anclaje (o de sujeción), perno prisionero

— **buoy**, boya de anclaje

— **clamp**, abrazadera (o grapa) de anclaje

— **guy**, retenida con ancla de tierra

— **hitch**, enganche de vuelta, vuelta (o eslinga) estranguladora

— **hole**, hoyo (o antepozo) para ancla de la tubería

— **ice**, hielo de fondo (o de anclas)

— **log**, macizo de anclaje, muerto, morillo

— **packer**, empaquetadura para el ancla del entubamiento, empaquetador de anclaje

— **pile**, pilote de anclaje

— **piles**, ancla de pilotes hincados (q.v. **drilled-in anchor**)

— **pin**, pasador de anclaje

— **pole**, poste de anclaje

— **shackle**, grillete para ancla

— **stop**, tope de ancla

— **tower**, columna (o torre, mástil) de anclaje

— **washpipe spear**, pescante de la tubería lavadora

— **winch**, malacate para ancla

anchorage, (nt) fondeadero

ancillary, auxiliar, complementario; (cm) subordinado, subsidiario

— **platform**, plataforma auxiliar

andalusite, andalusita

andesine, andesina

andesite, andesita

andradite, andradita

anemometer, anemómetro

aneroid barometer, barómetro aneroide

angle, ángulo; (nt) apertura

— **back-pressure**, válvula angular de contrapresión

— **beam**, viga angular

— **butt weld**, soldadura a tope en ángulo

— **check valve**, válvula angular de retención

— **compressor**, compresor de ángulo

— **coupling**, acoplamiento angular

— **dozer**, niveladora de empuje angular (q.v. **bullgrader**)

— **iron,** hierro angular, ángulo de
  hierro, (Ar) perfil de hierro,
  (Es) cantonera; (nt) esquinal
— **meter,** goniómetro; clinómetro
— **of deflection,** ángulo de
  desviación (o de desvío)
— **of depression,** ángulo
  descendente
— **of dip,** ángulo de inclinación; (g)
  ángulo de buzamiento
— **of elevation,** ángulo ascendente
  (o vertical)
— **of emergence,** (gf) ángulo de
  salida
— **of incidence,** ángulo de
  incidencia
— **of repose, rest,** ángulo de talud
  natural (o de reposo)
— **of seat,** ángulo (o conicidad) de
  un asiento (de válvula)
— **of sight,** ángulo de la visual
— **of slide,** ángulo de deslizamiento
— **of strike,** ángulo de rumbo (o
  direccional)
— **pillow block,** caja de chumacera
  angular
— **prism,** escuadra prisma
— **station,** puesto (o estación) de
  ángulo
— **target,** mira (o corredera)
  angular
— **tower,** (el) torre de ángulo
— **upon the bow,** (nt) marcación
— **valve,** válvula angular (o de
  codo)
— **vise,** tornillo ajustable
— **weld,** soldadura en ángulo
— **wrench,** llave acodada
angle-type compressor, compresor
  de tipo angular
angled hoop, abrazadera de codos
angling, sesgar, poner oblicua una
  cosa
anglesite, anglesita
angular, *a.* angular, anguloso

— **displacement,** calaje, desviación
  angular
— **lead,** ángulo de avance
— **magnification,** ampliación
  angular
— **parallax,** paralaje angular,
  ángulo paraláctico
— **perspective,** perspectiva angular
  (o de dos puntos)
— **pitch,** (el) avance angular
— **slide,** cursor en ángulo
— **unconformity,** (g) discordancia
  angular
— **velocity of rotation,** velocidad
  angular de rotación
angular-contact bearing, cojinete
  de contacto angular
angularity, angulosidad
— **correction,** corrección para
  compensar la angulosidad
anhydride, anhídrido
anhydrite, anhidrita, sulfato
  anhidro de calcio
anhydrous, *a.* anhidro, anhídrico,
  sin agua
— **aluminum chloride,** cloruro de
  aluminio anhidro
— **ammonia,** amoníaco anhidro (o
  seco)
— **calcium chloride,** cloruro de
  calcio anhidro
— **hydrofluoric acid,** ácido
  fluorhídrico anhidro
— **hydrogen fluoride,** ácido
  fluorhídrico anhidro (o seco)
— **phenol,** fenol anhidro
anhysteretic, (magnetics)
  anhisterético
aniline, anilina
— **equivalent,** equivalente anilínico
— **point,** punto de anilina
anion, anión
anisometric, anisométrico
anisotrope, anisótropo
anisotropic, anisotrópico,
  anisótropo

anisotropy, anisotropía
ankaramite, ancaramita
ankaratrite, ancaratrita
ankerite, ankerita
annealing, *v.* (mu) recocer,
destemplar, (Es) revenir
— **box**, caja (o horno) de recocer
— **color**, color de recocido
— **point**, punto de recocido
announcement, anuncio; aviso
annual, anual
annuity, anualidad
annular, *a.* anular
— **blowout preventer**, preventor
anular (o esférico)
— **borer**, barrena sacamuestras
— **velocity**, (prf) velocidad anular
annulus, espacio anular
anodal, anódico
anode, ánodo, polo positivo
— **battery**, batería anódica (o de
placa)
— **converter**, convertidor para
voltaje anódico
— **copper**, cobre bruto
— **dissipation**, disipación de placa
— **drop**, diferencia del ánodo, caída
de tensión al ánodo
— **voltage**, tensión anódica (o de
placa)
anomalous, anómalo
anomaly, anomalía, singularidad,
irregularidad
anorthic, (crystallography)
triclínico
anorthite, anortita, feldespato
anoxic, *a.* (g) carente de oxígeno
(q.v. **anaerobic, OAE**)
Antarctic, *n.* Antártica; *a.*
antártico
antecedent stream, (g) río
antecedente
anthophyllite, antofilita
anthracene, antraceno, antracina
anthracite, antracita
— **coal**, (coal) antracita

anthracitous, antracítico
anthraconite, antraconita; calcita
bituminosa
anthraciferous, antracífero
anthraxolite, elaterita bituminosa
anthopogenic, (ec) antropogénico
antialias filter, (gf) filtro antialias
anticlinal, *a.* anticlinal
— **axis**, eje anticlinal
— **blowing nose**, nariz arqueada
anticlinal
— **bulge**, protuberancia anticlinal
— **closure**, cierre de anticlinal
— **fold**, pliegue (o plegamiento)
anticlinal
— **ridge**, cresta (o filo) de anticlinal
— **trap**, trampa anticlinal
anticline, *n.* anticlinal
anticlinorium, anticlinorio;
anticlinal compuesto
anticorrosive, anticorrosivo
antifoam agent, antiespumante,
antiespuma
antifreeze, anticongelante
antifriction, antifricción
antiknock, *n.* antidetonancia; *a.*
antidetonante
— **fuel**, supercarburante,
combustible antidetonante
antilog (antilogarithm),
antilogaritmo
antimony, antimonio
antioxidant, antioxidante
antiskid, antideslizante
antitrust, antimonopolio
anvil, yunque, bigornia, (Me)
ayunque; (in) tope, quijada fija
— **block for dressing bits**, yunque
con sujeción para afilar
barrenas
— **vise**, yunque de tornillo, (Ve)
morsayunque
AOF, q.v. **absolute open flow**
apatite, apatita
aperiodicity, aperiodicidad
aperture, abertura, orificio, hueco

apex, ápice, vértice, clave; cima
— **of anticline**, ápice del anticlinal
aphanite, *n.* afanita; **aphanitic**,
   a. afanítico
aphthitalite, aftitalita, glaserita,
   arcanita
a-pinene, pineo alfa
**API (American Petroleum
   Institute) gravity**, gravedad (o
   densidad) API
aplitic rock, aplita
apogean tide, marea muerta (o de
   apogeo)
apongin, espongina
apophysis, (g) apófisis
aporhyolite, aporiolita
apparatus, aparato
apparent, aparente
— **dip**, buzamiento aparente
— **gravity**, gravedad aparente
— **horizon**, horizonte sensible (o
   visible)
— **inductance**, (el) inductancia
   aparente
— **power**, potencia (o vatiaje)
   aparente
— **time**, tiempo aparente (o solar)
appeal, apelación, alzada, recurso
appliance, dispositivo, aparato,
   artefacto, artificio
application, *n.* (cm) propuesta,
   solicitud, aplicación
apply, aplicar
appraisal, tasación, avalúo,
   valuación, aforo
appraiser, (oc) tasador, apreciador,
   avaluador, justipreciador,
   aforador
approach, *n.* acceso, aproximación;
   v. aproximar(se), acercar(se);
   (nt) embocar, acostar
appropriation, (cm) suma
   presupuestada, asignación,
   consignación, (Cu) apropiación
appurtenances, accesorios,
   aditamentos

apron, (mc) mandril, placa
   delantal; zócalo, chapa
   protectora; (g) cono aluvial;
   (hd) zampeado, platea,
   acolchado, derramadero,
   escarpe, (Cu) vertedero,
   paramento exterior; caja
   delantera (de la pala de
   arrastre)
— **ring**, (tk) anillo inferior, fondo y
   primer anillo
approval, *n.* visto bueno,
   aprobación; **approve**, *v.*
   aprobar; **approved**, *a.* aprobado
Aptian, aptiense
apyrous, infusible, refractario
aqua, agua
— **ammonia**, agua amoniacal;
   hidrato de amonio
— **fortis**, ácido nítrico, agua fuerte
— **regia**, agua regia
aquagel, acuagel, arcilla coloidal
aqueduct acueducto, conducto
aqueous, acuoso
— **rocks**, rocas sedimentarias
aquiclude, acuicierre, acuiclusa
aquifer, capa acuífera (o freática),
   depósito de agua subterráneo,
   (Me) acuífero
aquifuge, acuifuga
aragonite, aragonita
arbitration, arbitraje
— **clause**, cláusula compromisoria
arbitrator, (oc) arbitrador, tercero
arbor, árbol, eje; portaherramientas
arc, arco
— **brazing**, soldadura fuerte al arco
— **of meridian**, arco de meridiano
— **quencher**, apagador de arco
— **stream**, flujo de arco
— **welding**, soldadura al arco
Arcadian, arcadiense
arch, arco; bóveda; (g) anticlinal en
   arco
— **anticline**, anticlinal en arco
— **truss**, armadura en arco

14

Glossary of the Petroleum Industry

Archean, arcaico
arched, arqueado, abovedado,
curvado, combado
Archeozoic, arqueozoico
Archimedean screw, (fl) tornillo de
Arquímedes
arcifinial point, punto arcifinio
area, área, superficie
— sampling, muestreo por áreas
areal, de área, superficial
areation, aireación, aereación
arenaceous, arenoso, arenáceo
argentite, argentita, argirosa, plata
gris
argillaceous, argillous, a. arcilloso
— sandstone, arenisca arcillosa
argillite, argilita, (Ve) arcillita
argon, argón
argyrite, argirita, argirosa,
argentita
arid, árido
ariegite, ariegita
arithmetic, n. aritmética; a.
aritmético
— and logic unit, (dp) unidad
aritmética y lógica
— mean, media aritmética
— shift, (dp) desplazamiento
aritmético
Arkansan, arkansiense
arkose, arcosa
arm, brazo; palanca
armature, (el) armadura; (mo)
inducido
— core, núcleo del inducido
— winding, devanado (o
arrollamiento) del inducido
Armco iron, hierro dulce Armco
armored, blindado, acorazado
aromatic, n. substancia aromática;
a. aromático
— blend, mezcla aromática
— compound, compuesto
aromático
— hydrocarbons, hidrocarburos
aromáticos

— series, serie aromática
aromatization process, proceso de
aromatización
arosorb process, proceso arosorb
arrangement, arreglo; disposición
array, conjunto, fila, hilera; serie
homogénea; matriz
— processor, (dp) procesador de
matrices (o matricial)
arrested, interrumpido
— anticline, anticlinal terraza (o
interrumpido)
arrester, (el) chispero, parachispas;
(mc) detenedor
arrival, llegada
arrow, flecha
arsenic, arsénico
arsenopyrite, arsenopirita, pirita
arsenical
artesian, artesiano, surgente
— flow, corriente (o pluma) de agua
artesiana
— head, carga artesiana
— spring, fuente artesiana,
manantial artesiano (o
surtidor), (Ar) manantial
ascendente
— well, pozo artesiano (o surgente)
articular, articular
— loading arm, brazo articulado
para carga
articulated joint, articulación,
unión articulada (o de rótula),
(Cu) cardán
artificial, a. artificial, fabricado;
artificial, falso
— graphite, grafito fabricado
— horizon, (in) horizonte artificial
— lift, bombeo artificial
artifinial point, punto artifinio
asbestos, n. asbesto, amianto; a.
asbestino
— packing, empaquetadura (o
guarnición) de asbesto
— ribbed gasket with inner lap,
empaquetadura con nervadura

15

English - Spanish

de asbesto y borde interno
arrollado
ascending grade, pendiente en
subida
aschistic, (g) asquístico
**ASCII (American standard code
for information interchange)**,
(dp) código americano
normalizado para el
intercambio de la información
aseismic, asísmico
ash, (vlc) ceniza; escoria
— **bed**, depósito de ceniza
(volcánica)
— **content**, contenido de ceniza
— **pit**, cenicero industrial
asiderites, (g) asideritas
**ASME (American Society of
Mechanical Engineers)**
— **boiler code**, código para calderas
ASME
— **specifications**, especificaciones
ASME
asphalt, asfalto
— **coating**, capa preservativa de
asfalto
— **enamel**, esmalte asfáltico (o de
asfalto)
— **felt**, fieltro asfaltado
— **mixer**, mezclador de asfalto
— **paper**, papel asfáltico
— **paver**, asfaltador
— **penetration**, (rf) asfalto de
penetración determinada
— **rock**, roca asfáltica (o
impregnada de asfalto) (q.v.
albertite)
— **stripping**, (rf) separación del
asfalto
asphalt-base oil, petróleo (o crudo,
aceite crudo) de baseasfáltica,
petróleo asfáltico (o nafténico)
(q.v. **naphtene-base oil**)
asphalt-base petroleum, petróleo
de base asfáltica

asphalt-coated, revestido (o
bañado) de asfalto
asphaltene, asfalteno, (Es) asfaltina
asphaltic, *a.* asfáltico
— **concrete**, hormigón (o concreto)
asfáltico
— **limestone**, caliza asfáltica
— **macadam**, macádam asfáltico (o
asfaltado)
— **mastic**, mástique asfáltico (o
asfaltado), (Ve) masilla
asfáltica
— **pyrobitumen**, pirobitumen
asfáltico
— **sheet**, lámina asfáltica
asphaltite, asfaltita
asphyxiate, asfixiar, sofocar
aspirator, aspirador
assemble, *v.* montar, armar,
agrupar, ensamblar
assembler, (oc) ensamblador
assembly, montaje, montura,
armadura, ensamblaje;
conjunto, grupo, ensamblado;
(cm) asamblea, reunión,
junta
— **jig**, patrón (o plantilla) de
montaje
— **language**, (dp) lenguage
ensamblador
— **line**, cadena (o línea) de montaje
(o de producción), tren de
ensamblaje
— **room**, sala de sesiones
assets, (cm) activo, capital activo;
bienes, haberes, valores, riqueza
assignee, cesionario; apoderado
assigner, assignor, cedente,
transferidor
assignment, asignación; cesión;
(contr) traspaso, transferencia
assimilate, *v.* asimilar,
assimilation, *n.* asimilación
assistant, adjunto, ayudante,
auxiliar, asistente, segundo, *pref.*
sub-

16

— **chief**, subjefe, segundo (e.g.,
segundo ingeniero), en jefe
— **engineer**, ingeniero auxiliar,
subingeniero
— **manager**, subgerente,
subdirector, gerente adjunto
— **secretary**, subsecretario
associate, socio, consocio, asociado
assorted, *a.* variado, surtido;
assortment, *n.* surtido
assurance, (dp) tasa de servicio
astatic, *a.* (gf) astático
— **pendulum**, péndulo astático
astatizing force, fuerza de
astatización
**ASTM (American Society for
Testing Materials)**
— **cloud and pour point**, prueba
para los puntos de opacidad y
fluidez ASTM
— **distillation**, destilación de
norma ASTM
— **test**, prueba según normas
ASTM (q.v. **fifty percent point,
mid-boiling point**)
astringent, astringente
astronomic, astronomical,
astronómico
asymmetric, asymmetrical, *a.*
asimétrico, no simétrico
— **fold**, (g) pliegue asimétrico
asymmetry, *n.* asimetría
asymptotic, asintótico
asynchronous, asincrónico,
asíncrono
athermic, atérmico
athwart, (nt) atravesado
ATL (automated tape library),
biblioteca automatizada de
cintas, cintoteca automatizada
ATM, q.v. **automatic teller
machine**, cajero automático,
máquina de cambio
atm (atmosphere), atmósfera:
unidad de presión atmosférica
(q.v. **pascal**)

atmospheric, *a.* atmosférico
— **burner**, quemador atmosférico
— **condenser**, condensador
atmosférico
— **cooling tower**, torre de
enfriamiento atmosférico
— **pressure**, presión atmosférica
— **relief valve**, válvula de desahogo
a la atmósfera
— **reservoir**, depósito a la
intemperie
atoll, atolón, arrecife de coral
atom, átomo
atomic, *a.* atómico
— **hydrogen**, hidrógeno atómico
— **hydrogen welding**, soldadura
oxhídrica al arco, soldadura con
soplete de hidrógeno atómico
— **number**, número atómico
— **weight**, peso atómico
atomization, *n.* pulverización,
atomización; **atomize**, *v.*
pulverizar, atomizar
atomizer, pulverizador, atomizador,
disparador
at sight, (cm) a la vista
attached, *a.* adherido, unido,
pegado, en contacto; sujetado
— **ground water**, agua subterránea
adherida (o fijada)
attachment, accesorio, pieza
accesoria, aditamento; (cm)
embargo
— **plug**, (el) clavija de conexión (o
de contacto)
attainment area, (ec) área de
alcance
attapulgite, (prf mud) atapulguita
attenuation, (gf) atenuación
— **constant**, constante de
atenuación
— **distortion**, distorsión de
atenuación-frecuencia,
deformación de amplitud-
frecuencia

17

English - Spanish

— **equalizer**, igualador de
  atenuación
— **ratio**, relación (o razón) de
  atenuación
attenuator, atenuador
attitude, actitud, postura
atto (a), *pref.* SI = 10^{-18}
attorney, abogado, consejero,
  procurador; apoderado,
  mandatario
attrition, desgaste, frotamiento,
  roedura
at wt (atomic weight), peso atómico
atylolite, estilolita
auction, subasta
audio, *a.* audio; vocal, oral
— **amplifier**, audioamplificador,
  amplificador de audiofrecuencia
— **frequency**, audiofrecuencia
— **peak limiter**, limitador de
  máximo de audiofrequencia
— **signal**, audioseñal
— **system**, sistema audiofrequente
  (o de audio)
— **transformer**, transformador
  para audiofrecuencias
— **voltage**, voltaje de audio, tensión
  de audiofrecuencia
audit, *n.* (cm) revisión,
  intervención de cuentas; *v.*
  revisar, intervenir, repasar,
  comprobar
— **gas**, (ec) gas de auditoría
auditor, (oc) interventor,
  controlador, revisador, revisor
  de cuentas, (Me) auditor
auganite, auganita; auganita-
  andesita
augen structure, (g) estructura
  ojiforme
auger, barrenador, barrena, broca,
  taladro
— **bit**, barrena espiral (o de
  caracol), mecha de barrena
— **handle**, mango de barrena

— **sinker-bar guide**, guía para
  plomada de vástago de barrena
— **stem**, vástago de barrena (o de
  perforación), (Ar) barra
  maestra
augite, augita, piroxena
augitophyre, pórfido augítico
augmenter, (condenser)
  aumentador
aureole, (g) aureola
auriferous, aurífero
austenite, *n.* austenita; **austenitic**,
  a. austenítico
authentication of signature,
  reconocimiento de firma
authigenic, (g) autigéno
autocatalytic, autocatalítico
autochthonous, autóctono
autoclastic, autoclástico
autoclave, (la) autoclave, marmita
  hermética
autoconverter, (el)
  autoconvertidor
autocovariance, autocovariancia
autogenic, autogenous, autógeno
autoignition, autoencendido
autoinduction, autoinducción
automatic, *a.* automático
— **brakes**, frenos automáticos
— **choke**, válvula automática,
  estrangulador automático
— **coding**, (dp) codificación
  automática
— **controller**, regulador
  automático
— **custody transfer**, medición y
  muestreo automático
— **driller**, perforador automático
— **drilling-control unit**, unidad de
  perforación de control
  automático
— **feed**, alimentación automática
— **frequency control**, control
  automático de frecuencia
— **gain control**, control automático
  de ganancia (o de volumen)

18

— **pumping station**, estación automática de bombeo
— **reset**, reposición automática
— **slips**, cuñas automáticas
— **teller machine**, (cm) cajero automático
— **time switch**, interruptor cronométrico (o automático de reloj)
— **volume control**, control automático de volumen
automation, automatización
automobile, automóvil
automotive, *a.* automotor, automotriz, automóvil
autostarter, arrancador automático
autotransformer, autotransformador
Autunian, autuniense
auxiliary, *a.* auxiliar, secundario, ayudante
— **relay**, relai auxiliar
available energy, energía utilizable (o disponible)
availability, disponibilidad
avalanche, alud, avalancha, lurte
AVC, q.v. **automatic volume control**
avdp (avoirdupois), peso avoirdupois: cuya unidad es la libra de 16 onzas, en vez de 12 onzas como la libra corriente
average, *n.* promedio; (insur) avería; *a.* medio, promedio, de término medio; *v.* promediar
— **boiling point**, punto promedio de ebullición
— **bond**, fianza de avería
— **loss**, (insur) pérdida parcial
— **policy**, (insur) póliza de averías
— **pressure**, presión media
— **velocity**, velocidad media
average-case analysis, (dp) análisis del caso medio

average-end-area formula, fórmula de la sección media
avgas, aviation fuel, gasolina de aviación, (Ar) nafta de aviación
AVO, q.v. **amplitude variation with offset**
award, *n.* (contr) adjudicación; *v.* adjudicar
awash, a flor de agua
awl, lesna, alesna, subilla
awning, toldo
ax, axe, hacha, segur
axial, *a.* axil, axial, del eje, (Es) áxico
— **compression**, compresión axial
— **flow compressor**, compresor de flujo axial
— **flow fan**, ventilador axial
— **line**, línea axial
— **plane**, plano axial
— **thrust**, empuje axial
axinite, axinita
axis, eje, línea central, pivote, centro de oscilación
— **of collimation**, línea de colimación
— **of coordinates**, eje de coordenadas
— **of tilt**, eje de inclinación
axle, (mc) eje, árbol
— **box**, caja de engrase (o de chumacera, o del eje)
— **bushing**, camisa (o buje) de eje (q.v. **axle sleeve**)
— **casing**, envoltura del eje
— **clamp**, abrazadera de eje
— **grease**, grasa para ejes
— **housing**, caja del eje
— **I beam**, vigueta del eje, viga I de eje
— **load**, carga sobre un eje
— **nut**, tuerca de eje
— **pin**, pasador (o clavija) de eje
— **pinion**, piñón (o chaveta) de eje
— **shaft**, árbol de eje, flecha para ejes; (a) semieje; eje propulsor

— **sleeve**, manguito (o camisa, buje)
del eje (q.v. **axle bushing**)
— **tilt**, inclinación del eje
azeotropic distillation, destilación
aceotrópica (o azeotrópica)
azimuth, *n*. acimut, azimut
azimuthal, *a*. acimutal, azimutal
— **compass**, brújula (o aguja)
acimutal
— **dial**, cuadrante azimutal
— **grid**, cuadrícula de acimut
— **of epicenter**, acimut de epicentro
azoic, (g) (qm) azoico
azurite, azurita, cobre azul

B

B (Bel), bel: unidad no dimensional
para expresar regímenes de
intensidad o energía (q.v.
decibel)
B (boron), boro
babbitt, metal blanco, metal de
antifricción
babbitted bearing, cojinete de (o
reforzado con) metal blanco
back, parte posterior, espalda, dorso
— **brake**, (perc) freno del
cabrestante de la cuchara
— **firing**, contraexplosión,
encendido prematuro
— **filling**, relleno
— **jack post box**, chumacera del
poste de la rueda motora
— **land**, (g) postpaís
— **lash**, juego, desajuste, juego
inverso, efecto de reacción
— **legs**, patas traseras, pilares
traseros
— **off**, (prf) desenroscar
— **pressure**, contrapresión
— **pressure valve**, válvula de
contrapresión

— **slope**, (g) menor pendiente; (rd)
talud del corte, talud exterior de
la cuneta
— **stroke**, carrera (o golpe) de
retroceso del émbolo
— **up**, *v*. (tu) aguantar, sostener
(mantener firme un tubo
mientras se le enrosca otro)
— **way**, (nt) reculada
back-end processor, (dp)
procesador especializado (o de
fondo)
backfill, *n*. relleno; *v*. rellenar
back-in unit, (prf) equipo de
reparación (q.v. **carrier pig**)
back-side crank pump, bomba
conectada al cigüeñal auxiliar
backdraft, contratiro
background level, (ec) nivel
antecedente
background samples (ec) muestras
antecedentes
backhoe, *n*. pala mecánica,
excavadora; *v*. excavar
backing, respaldo
backoff joint, unión de seguridad,
junta desenroscable (provista de
rosca inversa) (q.v. **release
couple**)
backplane, plano posterior; panel (o
placa) dorsal
backplug, *n*. retrotaponamiento; *v*.
retrotaponar
backsight, *n*. (tp) visual inversa,
retrovisual; *v*. retrolectura,
nivelada de atrás
backtracking, búsqueda de
retroceso, vuelta atrás
backup, *n*. equipo de reserva; (dp)
copia de seguridad (o de reserva)
— **post**, poste de retención (o de
soporte)
— **tongs**, llaves de contrafuerza
backwash, retrolavado;
contracorriente
backwater, remanso, cilanco

Glossary of the Petroleum Industry

BACT, q.v. **best available control
technology**
bad air, aire viciado
baffle, deflector, desviador, chicana
— **collar,** collar obstructor
— **plate,** (rf) placa desviadora,
placa deflectora
— **tile,** ladrillo para tabiques
interceptores
— **tower,** torre de desviadores
— **wall,** tabique interceptor, pared
desviadora, muro de
obstrucción, atajadizo
bag, bolsa, saco
bail, asa, manija, grillete, cogedero;
estribo; *v.* achicar
bailer, (prf) achicador, cuchara
— **bottom,** fondo del archicador
— **dart,** dardo de la válvula de
fondo del achicador, (Ar) lanza
de la válvula del fondo de la
cuchara
— **grab,** gancho pescacuchara,
pescador de cuchara
— **valve,** válvula en el fondo del
achicador
bailing, achique, acción de achicar,
(Ar) cuchareo
— **and swabbing block,** motón para
achique y limpieza de un pozo
— **drum,** tambor de la línea de
achicar
— **line,** línea de achicar
— **reel,** torno (o carrete) del cable
del achicador, (Ar) tambor de
cuchareo (q.v. **sand reel**)
Bajoccian, bajocciense
bake, hornear
bakelite, bakelita
balance, *n.* balanza; balancín,
equilibrio; (cm) saldo, balance;
v. contrapesar, equilibrar, saldar,
— **bob,** contrabalancín
— **of payments,** (cm) balanza de
pagos

— **tank,** tanque de compensación,
tanque igualador (q.v. **floating
tank, surge tank**)
— **weight,** contrapeso, estabilizador
de equilibrio (o de
compensación)
balancer-booster, (el) compensador
elevador
balancing point, centro de
gravedad
balata belt, correa de balata
balboa, balboa: moneda de Panamá
ball, bola
— **and seat valve,** válvula de bola y
asiento, (Ve) guasa
— **and socket joint,** articulación
esférica
— **bearing,** cojinete de bola,
cojinete a bolilla
— **bearing cage,** jaula (o armazón)
portabolas de cojinete
— **bolt,** perno de cabeza esférica
— **cock,** válvula de flotador
— **dropping device,** dispositivo
para dejar caer la bola (en la
tubería)
— **float trap,** trampa con flotador
de bola
— **governor,** regulador de bolas,
regulador de contrapesos
esféricos, regulador centrífugo
— **grinder,** amoladora (o afiladora,
esmeriladora) de bolas
— **gudgeon,** cojinete, muñón
esférico
— **housing,** caja esférica
— **joint,** unión esférica, junta de
bola, (Ve) rodilla; articulación
esférica
— **sealers,** sellos de bolas
— **up,** embolar
— **valve,** válvula de bola
ball-peen hammer, martillo de
bola, martillo con boca esférica
ballast, *n.* lastre, balasto, balastro;
(el) resistencia; (nt) lastre, *v.*

lastrar, alastrar; (rr) balastar,
embalastar
ballistite, variedad de pólvora sin
humo
band, *n.* zuncho, fleje, banda, (Me)
cincho; (g) estrato, capa; *v.*
zunchar, enzunchar, cinchar
— **brake,** freno de banda (o de
cinta)
— **clutch,** embrague de banda
— **pass,** (gf) paso de banda
— **saw,** sierra sin fin, aserradora de
banda
— **shaft,** eje de la rueda motora
— **tug rim,** canto de la polea de
remolque
— **wheel,** (perc) rueda motora
band-limited channel, (dp) canal
de banda limitada
band-pass filter, (dp) filtro de paso
de banda
band-stop filter, (dp) filtro de
banda eliminada
banding metal, recalcado exterior
bandwidth, anchura (o ancho) de
banda
bank, *n.* (r) orilla, ribera, margen;
(nt) bajo, bajío, banco,
encalladero; cantera de grava (o
arena); (rd) peralte; talud,
terraplén, escarpa; *v.* (cl)
amontonar, cubrir con carbón
— **draft,** giro bancario
bar, (tl) palanca, alzaprima; barra,
varilla; (nt) banco, bajío, arenal,
barra; *abr.* barómetro
— **and-chain tool tightener,**
apretador de herramientas tipo
palanca y cadena
— **stock valve,** válvula de hierro de
barra
barchan, (g) barcana
bare electrode, electrodo desnudo
(o lavado)
barefoot completion, terminación
en agujero abierto (o

descubierto) (q.v. **open hole
completion**)
barge, barcaza, lanchón, gabarra,
(Co) planchón, (Me) chalán
barite, barita, sulfato de bario
barium, bario
— **sulphate,** sulfato de bario
barnacle, (mar) lapa, escaramujo
barograph, barógrafo
barometer, barómetro
barometric, barométrico
— **condenser,** condensador,
barométrico
— **correction,** corrección
barométrica
barrel (bl, bbl), barril: medida de
volumen para petróleo (equivale
a 42 galones E.U. o aprox. 159
litros). Un metro cúbico =
6,2897 bl; tambor; cilindro de
bomba
— **compressor,** compresor de barril
barren, improductivo, estéril, seco
barrier, barrera; valla
— **basin,** (g) cuenca de represa
— **beach,** banco, bajío, barra (q.v.
bar)
— **lake,** (g) lago endicado
— **reef,** arrecife barrera
barter, *n.* (cm) trueque
barysphere, (g) barisfera
baryte, barita; sulfato de bario
basal, (g) basal, de fondo
— **complex,** complejo basal;
fundamento (q.v. **basement**)
— **conglomerate,** morena de fondo
basalt, basalto
— **tuff,** toba basáltica
basaltic, basáltico
— **layer,** capa basáltica
basanite, basanita
base, *n.* (g) (gf) (qm) base; a base de;
(cn) zócalo, fundamento;
plancha de fondo (o de base)
— **correction,** corrección de base
— **difference,** diferencia de base

— **gravity,** gravedad de la base
— **level,** nivel de referencia (o de equilibrio)
— **levelled profile,** perfil de equilibrio
— **map,** mapa de referencia
— **number,** índice de base
— **of weathering,** base de la capa intemperizada
— **pressure,** presión base
— **station,** (tp) estación de base
— **steel,** base de acero
— **stock,** (rf) material base, material de base
— **tie,** (tp) valor de la referencia a la base
— **value,** (gravim) valor de la gravedad en la estación de base
baseline, (tp) línea de base, (Ve) base de triangulación
basement, (g) basamento; (prf) sótano, (Ar) antepozo (q.v. basal complex)
— **rock,** roca de basamento (o basamentaria)
basic, básico
— **magma,** magma básico
— **sediment and water,** contenido de agua y sedimento
— **steel,** acero de proceso básico
Basic (beginners all-purpose symbolic instruction code), (dp) código de instrucciones simbólicas de carácter general para principiantes
basin, estanque, pileta, alberca, depósito; (g) cuenca, hondonada; (tp) hoya, cuenca, (Co) artesa; cubeta cerrada; (harbor) dásena
basis, base
basket, cesta, cesto, canasto; (ca) casquillo, taza
— **bit,** barrena de cesto, (Ar) trépanocanasto

batch, (rf) tanda, lote, cochada, (Ar) camada, (Me) bache; (cement) carga, colada, (Me) amasada, (Pe) templa; v. dosificar, proporcionar, (Ve) tercear
— **cementing,** (prf) cementación parcial
— **distillation,** (rf) destilación por tandas, (Ar) destilación intermitente
— **processing,** (dp) proceso por lotes
— **sphere,** esfera para separar tandas
— **treatment,** (pr) tratamiento por tandas
— **vaporization,** vaporización intermitente
batching, (p) bombeo de densidad dispar (para prevenir la mezcla), (Me) bacheo
bath, baño
batholith, (g) batolito
bathyal, a. (g) batial, (mar) de gran profundidad
— **zone,** zona nerítica
bathymetry, batimetría
batter, talud
battery, (tk) grupo, batería; (el) pila batería; acumulador
— **acid,** electrólito
— **box,** caja de acumulador
— **carrier,** portaacumulador
— **ignition,** encendido por acumulador
— **overcharge,** sobrecarga de un acumulador
— **plate separator,** separador (o aislador) de las placas de un acumulador
Baumé gravity, gravedad Baumé
baud rate, velocidad en baudios
bauxite, bauxita
bay, bahía

bayonet gauge, indicador del nivel de aceite tipo bayoneta

BDU (benchmark data unit), (dp) unidad de datos de referencia (q.v. **benchmark**)

Bé, q.v. **Baumé gravity**

beach, playa (q.v. **shore**)

— **barrier,** barra

beacon, (nt) baliza, radiofaro

bead, (sd) cordón; (tu) reborde, anillo centrador; moldura, filete, nervio

— **weld,** cordón, soldadura de un solo cordón

beaker, (la) redoma, cubilete, vaso picudo

— **tongs,** tenacillas (o pinzas) para cubilete

— **with lip and spout,** cubilete de vertedero

beam, (ma) balancín, viga, tirante; (balance) brazo, mástil; (light) rayo, haz de luz; (nt) manga

— **balance,** balanza de contrapeso (para medir la densidad del lodo)

— **counterbalance,** (prf) contrapeso del balancín

— **hanger,** colgadero, suspensor (o colgador) de varillas de bombeo, (Me) cable colgador

— **head,** (bm) cabezal de balancín

— **pumping unit,** unidad de bombeo mecánico

— **spacer,** (bm) espaciador del balancín

— **type counterbalance,** (prf) contrapeso de balancín

Beaman stadia arc, arco estadimétrico Beaman

bean, tubo reductor de inserción, (Ar) estrangulador a orificio, (Me) estrangulador

bear market, (cm) mercado bajista

bearance, punto de apoyo de la palanca

beard, rebaba, rebarba, barba del metal fundido

bearding, chaflán, rebajo

bearer, apoyo, sostén, soporte, caballete, gancho; (cm) portador

bearing, (mc) cojinete, chumacera; (compass) rumbo; (g) rumbo del filón (o estrato); apoyo, asiento, soporte

— **adjustment nut,** tuerca de ajuste de cojinete

— **ball,** bolilla de cojinete (o de apoyo)

— **bar,** barra de apoyo (o de sostén)

— **bracket,** sostén de cojinete

— **brushing,** buje de cojinete

— **cage,** encaje de cojinete, jaula de cojinete

— **cap,** tapa (o sombrerete, concha) de cojinete (q.v. **bearing shell**)

— **cover,** tapa (o sombrerete, concha, cubierta) de cojinete (q.v. **bearing shell**)

— **cup,** cubeta de cojinete

— **flange,** brida de cojinete

— **insert,** guarnición de cojinete (q.v. **sleeve**)

— **metal,** metal blanco, babbitt, metal de cojinete

— **of epicenter,** (gf) azimut (o orientación) del epicentro

— **pilot,** cojinete de guía

— **pump,** bomba montada sobre cojinetes

— **retainer,** retén de cojinete

— **shell,** tapa (o sombrerete, concha) de cojinete (q.v. **bearing cup**)

— **sleeve,** guarnición de cojinete; camisa (o casquillo) del eje (q.v. **insert**)

— **surface,** superficie de cojinete, (Ar) pista de cojinete

24

bed, (r) cauce, lecho, alveo, fondo;
(g) estrato, capa, lecho; (sand)
banco, lecho, bajo, capa
bedded, *a.* estratificado
— **conglomerate,** (g)
conglomerado estratificado
bedding, (g) estratificación (o
disposición) de los estratos
— **fault,** falla paralela al
buzamiento y rumbo del estrato,
falla estratigráfica
— **plane,** plano de estratificación
bedrock, lecho (o estrato) de roca
beetle, aplanadora, pisón, maza
behavior, comportamiento;
funcionamiento
bell, campana; timbre
— **hole,** (sd) hoyo del soldador,
hoyo de campana
— **metal,** metal de campana
— **nipple,** niple de campana (o de
botella), (q.v. **swaged nipple)**
— **screw,** enchufe de pesca,
pescador de campana
— **socket,** enchufe de campana
provisto de cuñas dentadas
bell-hole welding, soldadura de
rodeo
bellied, acombado, convexo
bellows, fuelle; insuflador
belly brace, abrazadera de caldera
belt, *n.* (ma) correa, cinta, banda;
(g) zona, faja; *v.* instalar una
correa, accionar por correa
— **clamp,** abrazadera (o amarra,
garra) de correa
— **cutter,** cortadora de correa
— **dressing,** pasta para correa de
transmisión
— **drive,** mando (o transmisión)
por correa
— **fastener,** asegurador de correa
— **guard,** protector de correa
— **house,** casilla de la correa
— **idler,** polea volante (o loca)

— **lacing,** costura de la correa;
hebras de cuero para coser
correas; tiento
— **punch,** punzón para correas
— **saw,** sierra sin fin, sierra
continua
— **stretcher,** estirador de correa,
atestador de correas
belt-driven compressor, compresor
accionado por correas
belt-reduction pumping unit,
unidad de bombeo con poleas
reductoras de la velocidad
belting, correaje, sistema de correas
de mando
bench, banco, banqueta; (g) terraza
de roca, banco; (nt) bajío, bajo,
(tp) banco de nivel, banco de
cota fija; *v.* escalonar
— **level,** nivel de banco
— **saw,** sierra circular de torno
— **shears,** cizallas
benchmark, (tp) punto de
referencia (o de cota), banco de
cota fija; (dp) prueba (o
programa, punto) de referencia,
prueba patrón
bend, (tu) codo, comba, doblez,
unión acodada, curva; *v.* doblar,
encorvar, combarse, pandearse
— **test,** prueba de doblez, prueba de
flexión
bending, *n.* dobladura, flexión; *v.* de
doblar
— **chain,** cadena de doblar
— **machine,** máquina dobladora (o
de curvar)
— **stress,** esfuerzo de flexión
Bendix drive, mando Bendix
bent sub, sub ponderado
bentonite, bentonita
benzene, benceno
benzine, (*archaic*) bencina
benzoic acid, ácido benzoico
benzol, benzol

benzol-ketone dewaxing,
desparafinación al benzol
ketona
benzole, benzol (q.v. benzol)
— **of cementation,** (prf) zona de
cementación
— **of weathering,** (g) zona de
desgaste (o disolución)
berea sandstone, arenisca de berea
berm, (g) berma, meseta sobre una
ladera
berth, (nt) borneadero
beryl, berilo, esmeralda verdemar
beryllium, berilio, glucinio
best available control technology,
(ec) la mejor tecnología de
control disponible
best fit, ajuste óptimo, adaptación
óptima
beta particles, partículas beta
beta rays, rayos beta
bevel, n. bisel, chaflán; falsa
escuadra, escuadra plegable; v.
biselar, chaflanar
— **differential,** diferencial cónico
— **gear,** engranaje cónico,
engranaje en bisel (o en ángulo)
— **protractor,** transportador de
ángulo
— **weld,** soldadura de bisel (o de
chaflán)
beveling machine, máquina
biseladora
BHA, q.v. **bottom-hole assembly**
BHGM, q.v. **borehole gravity**
meter data
BHP, bhp, q.v. **bottom-hole**
pressure; brake horsepower
BHT, q.v. **bottom-hole**
temperature
bias, al sesgo, oblicuidad; (mt) sesgo
biaxial, biaxial, diaxial
bibb, grifo, llave, espita
bicarbonate, bicarbonato
bichloride, bicloruro
bichromate, bicromato

bicyclodecane, biciclodecano (q.v.
decalin)
bicyclohexane, biciclohexano
bicyclononane, biciclononano (q.v.
hydrindane)
bid, n. (cm) puja, licitación; v. pujar,
licitar
— **bond,** aval de oferta
— **price,** precio ofrecido
bidder, postor
bidding, licitación
— **specifications,** pliego de
condiciones
bight, curva; (ca) vuelta, seno; (tp)
caleta
bilge, sentina
— **gunk,** sedimentos de sentina
bill, n. (cm) factura, cuenta; efecto,
letra de cambio; v. pasar la
cuenta
— **board,** cartel, letrero de anuncio,
mural de aviso
— **of exchange,** letra de cambio
— **of lading,** conocimiento de
embarque, (Ar) carta de porte
bin, (gf) celda
binary, binario
— **code,** código binario
— **coded decimal,** decimal
codificado en binario
— **digit,** dígito binario
binaural, binaural
binder, (rd) aglomerante, ligador,
recebo; (cm) documento
provisional de protección
(especialmente en seguros)
binding, amarre; traba (o sujeción)
debida a fricción; (cm) que
compromete (o vincula, obliga)
— **chain,** cadena de amarre
binning, (gf) partición en celdas
binocular, binocular
biochemical oxygen demand, (ec)
demanda bioquímica de oxígeno
bioherm, arrecife (de coral u otros
organismos)

biolith, (g) biolita (q.v. **biotite)**
bioreactor, biorreactor
bioremediation, biorremediación
biosphere, biósfera
biotite, (g) biotita (q.v. **biolith)**
bird, (gf) sensor aéreo
birefringence, (g) birrefringencia
bisect, bisecar
bisector, bisectriz
bisectrix, bisectriz
bismuth, bismuto
bisulphide, bisulfuro
bisulphite, bisulfito
bit, (prf) barrena, (Co) broca, (Ve) mecha, taladro, (Ar) trépano; (dp) bit (binary digit)
— **basket,** cesto de barrena, (Ar) canasto del trépano
— **breaker,** desconectador de barrena, soltador de la barrena, sueltabarrenas
— **cone,** cono (o fresas) de barrena (q.v. **bit cutters)**
— **cutters,** fresas de la barrena, (Ar) rolos del trépano
— **dresser,** máquina reparadora (o afiladora) de barrenas, amoladora de brocas
— **forge,** fragua para barrenas
— **gage,** calibrador de barrenas
— **head,** portafresas, portacuchillas, portaconos, (Ar) cuerpo del trépano
— **holder,** portabarrenas, (Ar) portatrépano
— **hook,** gancho pescabarrenas, (Ar) gancho enderezador del trépano
— **matrix,** matriz de la barrena de diamantes
— **ram,** ariete moldeador de barrenas
— **record,** registro de las barrenas (utilizadas)

— **sub,** portabarrenas, conexión entre la barrena y la tubería lastrabarrenas
bitter, amargo
— **earth,** magnesia calcinada
— **salt,** dolomita
bitumen, betún, bitumen
bituminous, bituminoso
— **coal,** carbón bituminoso
— **limestone,** caliza bituminosa
— **sandstone,** arenisca bituminosa
— **shale,** lutita bituminosa
bivalent, (qm) bivalente
blacking, carbón en polvo
black, negro
— **oil,** aceite negro, aceite de residuos
— **powder,** pólvora negra
— **waters,** aguas negras (o con desperdicios biológicos)
black-red head, calor al rojo oscuro
blacksmith, herrero
— **roll,** (sd) caldear, calda del herrero, calda a rodillo (o a martillo hidráulico) (q.v. **forge welding,** hammer roll)
blackstone, lulita carbonífera
blackwork, (mu) forjado bruto
blade, hoja, paleta, aleta
blank, *n.* llave ciega; *a.* liso, en blanco; *v.* punzonar
— **bolt,** perno ciego
— **determination,** determinación teórica, análisis preliminar
— **flange,** brida ciega, brida de obturación, brida lisa
— **form,** (cm) formulario, modelo, (Co) esqueleto, (Ar) fórmula
— **liner,** (prf) tubo revestidor sin perforaciones, revestidor auxiliar ciego, (Ar) caño ciego, (Me) tubería corta ciega
— **pipe,** tubo sin punzonar (o sin agujeros, perforaciones), (Ar) caño ciego, (Me) tubería ciega

blanket, (rd) capa de desgaste, pavimento bituminoso, (Ve) carpeta de asfalto
— sand, manto de arena
blanking plug, tapón obturador
blast, *n.* voladura, explosión, disparo, dinamitación; (wind) ráfaga; (sand) chorro; *v.* volar, hacer saltar, dinamitar
— furnace, alto horno, horno de fundición
— hole, perforación para voladura, taladro para explosivos
— hole drill, barrena para perforaciones de voladura
— tip burner, quemador de boquilla sopladora
— trap, interceptor de aire caliente, trampa depuradora de gases de horno
— wave, (gf) onda de la explosión
blaster, detonador
blasting, voladura, dinamitación
— cap, fulminante, cápsula explosiva
— cartridge, cartucho de voladura
— machine, (gf) disparadora, detonadora, máquina disparadora
— powder, pólvora para voladura (o barrenos)
blastoporphyritic, blastoporfirítico
blau gas, gas azul (q.v. blue gas)
bleaching, blanqueo
— earth, arcilla blanquedora
— powder, polvo blanqueador
bleed, drenar, liberar (líquido o gas lentamente)
— point, punto de purga
bleeder, grifo de purga
bleeding valve, purgador
blend, *n.* mezcla; *v.* mezclar
blende, (g) blenda
blended, mezclado
— gasoline, gasolina mezclada
— oil, aceite mezclado

blending, mezclante
— agent, (rf) agente mezclante (o de mezcla)
— gasoline, gasolina para mezcla
— valve, válvula mezcladora
blind, ciego
— flange, brida ciega
— ram, ariete ciego
blink, parpadeo
blizzard, nevasca
BL method, método BL
block, (rigging) motón, garrucha, polea; (g) bloque; *v.* obstruir, cerrar, bloquear; calzar una rueda
— and tackle, polipasto, aparejo de poleas
— cast cylinders, cilindros fundidos en bloque
— casting, fundición en bloque
— chain hoisting, aparejo de cadena, polipasto de cadena
— diagram, (g) diagrama estereográfico (o en bloque), estereograma; (dp) diagrama de bloques, esquema funcional
— storage, almacenaje en bloque
— valve, válvula de bloqueo
blockaxe, hachuela
blocker, azuela
blooey line, línea de desalojo
bloom of oil, fluorescencia del petróleo (q.v. cast of oil)
blow, *n.* golpe; *v.* soplar
— case, tanque inyector de ácido
blowback, soplo inverso, inyección de gas en dirección contraria para limpiar un filtro o un tubo
blowdown heat exchanger, (rf) calentador mediante vapor de sangría
blower, ventilador, soplador, insuflador, fuelle
blowoff valve, válvula de descarga (de escape, de desahogo)

blowout, (prf) reventón, brote imprevisto (Ar) erupción, surgencia a pozo abierto; (g) depresión eólica, (g) depresión formada por el viento en terrenos arenosos

— **preventer (BOP),** (prf) preventor de reventones, impiderreventones, (Ve) válvula de seguridad (o de emergencia), grampa cabeza, (Ar) armadura de seguridad

— **preventer stack,** conjunto preventor de reventones

blowpipe, (la) (sd) soplete

blowtorch, (sd) soplete de aire

BLPD (barrels of liquid per day), producción bruta (de petróleo y agua)

blue, azul

— **gas,** gas azul

— **iron,** vivianita, ocre

— **malachite,** azurita

— **ochre,** vivianita, ocre

— **oil,** aceite azul

— **print,** copia heliográfica, copia azul, fotocalco azul, impresión azul; (v) fotocopiar, fotocalcar

— **vitrol,** vitriolo azul, sulfato de cobre

bluestone, (cn) piedra azul; (qm) sulfato de cobre

bluff, risco, morro, farallón

bluish, azulado, azulino

blunt, embotado, sin punta, romo, sin filo, obtuso

board, (in) tablero, cuadro; (carp) tabla, tablón, plancha; (cm) junta directive, consejo; *v.* entablar, enmaderar

— **a ship,** abordar

— **foot (BF), pie cuadrado de tabla** (144 pg³)

— **member,** vocal

— **of directors,** junta directiva, consejo de administración

— **of governors,** junta sindical

— **of trustees,** patronato

boat, bote; lancha; barco

BOD, q.v. **biochemical oxygen demand**

body, cuerpo, armazón; caja, carroza, carrocería; (bit) fuste; (fl) espesor, consistencia

— **casting,** pieza fundida del cuerpo

bog, cenegal, región pantanosa

— **iron,** limonita (q.v. **limonite**)

— **manganese,** pirolusita (q.v. **pyrolusite**)

boiler, caldera

— **baffles,** tabiques de separación (en calderas)

— **compound,** desincrustante para calderas

— **feed-water heater,** calentador alimentador de agua para calderas, calentador del agua de alimentación

— **feed-water regulator,** regulador de agua de alimentación

— **fittings,** accesorios para calderas

— **horsepower,** caballos de fuerza de caldera

— **injector,** inyector para caldera

— **jacket,** camisa (o forro) de caldera

— **tube,** tubo de fuego

boiler-gage cick, grifo indicador de nivel

boiler-tube cleaner, limpiador de tubo de caldera

boiling, *n.* ebullición, cocción, *v.* hervir

— **point,** punto (o temperatura) de ebullición

— **range,** límite de ebullición

bolivar, bolivar: moneda de Venezuela

boll-weevil tongs, tenazas a cadena, llaves boll weevil

bolson, bolsón

bolster bolt, perno maestro

English - Spanish

bolt, *n.* perno, tornillo, bulón; cerrojo, pasador, pestillo; *v.* atornillar, empernar, bulonar; echar el cerrojo
— dies, dados para filetes de pernos, dados de terraja para pernos
— plate, placa de perno
— stud, perno prisionero, espiga roscada; (chain) travesaño, (Ar) espárrago
— threading machine, máquina de roscar pernos
bolted coupling, acoplamiento empernado, unión empernada
bolted steel tank, tanque de acero empernado, (Ar) tanque de acero bulonado
bomb, bomba (q.v. pump)
bond, trabazón, adhesión, ligazón; (qm) grado de afinidad; (cm) bono, fianza, título; (sd) liga
bonding drill, (tl) broca para conexión eléctrica de rieles
bone, hueso
— coal, carbón argiláceo, (Ar) carbón animal
bonnet, casquete, tapa, bonete
— guide pin, pasador guía del casquete
— seal ring, anillo sellador del casquete
bookkeeping, (cm) contabilidad, teneduría de libros
Boolean algebra, álgebra booleana
boom, (crane) aguilón, pluma, pescante, botalón; (harbor) barrera; (nt) tangón; *(figurat)* auge
— tractor, tractor grúa, tractor huinche (o guinche, con pluma)
boomer, atacargas
booster, *n.* (mc) reforzador, aumentador de presión; (el) elevador de potencial (o de tensión); calentador (de material bituminoso)

— pump, bomba reforzadora
— station, estación auxiliar (o de rebombeo), bomba auxiliar para aumentar el vacío
boosting, *n.* reforzante, *angl.* boosting; *v.* reforzar
boot, (tu) manguito; (a) parche
— jack, pescacuchara (q.v. latch jack)
— socket, pescacuchara (q.v. latch jack)
— vent, tubo del colector de gas
bootleg, (cl) hervidor, placa de agua; tubo separador (q.v. water-leg)
BOP, q.v. blowout preventer
boracite, boracita
borax, bórax, borato de sosa
border, borde, frontera; cuadro, marco, filete, reborde, ribete, límite, canto; *v.* colindar con
bore, *n.* taladro, agujero; (mc) calibre, diámetro interior; *v.* perforar, taladrar, barrenar, agujerear
borehole, hoyo, agujero (q.v. wellbore)
— gravity meter data, datos gravimétricos del pozo
borescope, (in) calibrescopio
boric acid, ácido bórico
boring, (prf) perforación de cateo, (p) perforar un túnel
— chuck, mandril (o portaherramientas) de la máquina de barrenar (o taladrar)
— head, (mu) cabezal de taladrar, corona cortante
borings, viruta de perforación
borium, boro (q.v. boron)
bornite, bornita
boron, boro (q.v. borium)
— trifluoride, trifluoruro de boro
boss, jefe, capataz, sobrestante; (g) macizo intrusivo, cuerpo

30

Glossary of the Petroleum Industry

magmático; (mc) protuberancia,
lomo
Boston inserted-joint casing,
tubería de revestimiento de
junta tipo Boston, (Ar) cañería
de entubación enchufada tipo
Boston
bostonite, bostonita
bottle, botella
— **gas,** gas comprimido en botellas
(o en cilindros)
— **test,** (la) prueba de la botella
bottleneck, gollete (o cuello) de
botella, paso angosto,
atascamiento
bottlenecking, (tu) reducción del
diámetro
bottom, *n.* fondo; (r) lecho;
(mountain, wall) pie; (nt) nave
de carga; *v.* inferior
— **choke,** estrangulador de fondo
— **dead center,** punto muerto
inferior
— **hold-down,** (well bm) ancla de
bomba
— **intermitter,** válvula
intermitente de la bomba en el
fondo del pozo
— **land,** tierra de aluvión
— **pressure,** presión de fondo
— **pressure bomb,** bomba de
presión (de fondo)
— **product,** producto residual,
residuo de fondo
— **sampler,** probador de fondo,
sacamuestras de fondo
— **scraper,** raspador o escariador de
fondo
— **settlings,** (tk) residuos de fondo;
sedimento
— **temperature bomb,** bomba de
temperatura de fondo
— **water,** agua de fondo
— **wiper plug,** (prf) tapón
limpiador
bottom-hole, fondo (del pozo)

— **assembly,** conexiones (o
conjunto) de fondo, mecanismo
de fondo del pozo, mecanismo
subsuperficial
— **choke,** estrangulador de fondo
— **pressure,** presión de fondo
— **temperature,** temperatura de
fondo (de pozo)
bottoms, residuos, asientos, fondos;
(tp) q.v. **bottom land**
bottomsets, cimiento sedimentario
Bouguer and free air correction,
correción combinada de
Bouguer y aire libre
boulder, canto rodado, (Ve) peñón
— **clay,** (g) limo de derrubios (q.v.
tillite)
— **conglomerate,** conglomerado de
cantos rodados
— **graben,** fosa de peñascos, (Ve)
peñonal
— **gravel,** grava de cantos rodados
grandes
bouldery ground, (g) pedriscal,
(Ar) canchal
bouncing pin, indicador de
golpeteo, aguja indicadora, (Ur)
aguja de rebote
boundary, lindero, límite
— **fault,** (g) falla marginal
— **formation,** formación de
contorno
— **wave,** (gf) onda limítrofe
bow lines, cables de proa
bowl, tazón, taza, caja, cucharón
box, *n.* caja, cajón; (ma) caja,
chumacera; (mail) apartado,
casilla; (smelter) bastidor; (tu)
conexión hembra (q.v. **tool
joint**)
— **and pin,** (tu) conexiones macho
y hembra
— **and pin substitute,** (tu)
reducciones macho y hembra
— **beam,** viga en forma de caja
— **canyon,** cañón encajado

— **condenser,** condensador de caja
— **frame,** bastidor tipo cajón, armadura en forma de cajón
— **metal,** metal de cojinetes
— **template,** calibrador de cajas
— **thread,** rosca de la conexión hembra
Boyle's law, ley de Boyle: el volumen de un gas disminuye en la misma proporción de aumento de la presión, a temperatura constante
bpd (barrels per day), barriles por día (b/d)
Bq (becquerel), becquerel: unidad de actividad de radionuclidos
brace, *n.* refuerzo; (cn) puntal, riostra, codal, adema; (nt) braza; (tl) berbiquí, taladro; *v.* apuntalar, arriostrar, acodar, apuntalar, entibar
— **and bit,** berbiquí y barrena, (Ar) taladro manual
— **bit,** barrena para berbiquí, (Ar) mecha para taladro manual
braced, ligado, reforzado
brachistochronic path, (gf) trayectoria braquistocrónica
bracing, amarre, traba, puntal, refuerzo
bracket, ménsula, consola, cartela, palomilla, (Ar) brazo, (Ve) pie de amigo
brackish, salobre, fluviomarino
— **water,** agua salobre
bradenhead, (q.v. **casing head**)
brake, freno, retranca
— **actuating rod,** varilla de mando del freno
— **adjuster,** ajustador del freno
— **adjustment,** ajuste (o regulación) de los frenos
— **assembly,** conjunto de freno
— **band,** banda (o cinta) del freno
— **block,** zapata (o almohadilla, calza, bloque) del freno

— **cable,** cable del freno
— **chamber,** cámara del freno
— **control,** gobierno (o control) del freno
— **cylinder,** cilindro del freno
— **dog,** fiador del freno
— **drum,** tambor del freno
— **equalizer,** igualador del freno
— **facing,** revestimiento del freno
— **flange,** brida del freno
— **fluid,** fluido (o líquido) del freno
— **horsepower,** potencia efectiva (o al freno), caballos de fuerza al freno
— **housing,** caja del freno
— **lever,** palanca del freno
— **lever friction latch,** pestillo de fricción de la palanca del freno
— **lining,** revestimiento (o forro) del freno, (Me) balata
— **linkage,** sistema de empalme del freno, conexiones del freno
— **master cylinder,** cilindro maestro del freno
— **pedal,** pedal del freno
— **quadrant,** sector dentado del freno
— **rim,** brida del freno (q.v. **brake flange**)
— **rod,** varilla del freno
— **shaft,** eje (o árbol) de freno
— **shoe,** zapata del freno
— **staple for bull wheel,** garfio del freno del malacate de las herramientas
— **staple for calf wheel,** garfio del freno del malacate de tuberías
— **wheel,** tambor del freno
brakeman, (oc) guardafrenos, frenero, (Co) brequero, (CH) palanquero
braking, frenaje
branch, bifurcación
— **fault,** ramal de falla
— **line,** (tu) ramal

Glossary of the Petroleum Industry

— **office,** (cm) sucursal, compañía afiliada
branched-chain hydrocarbon, hidrocarburo de cadena ramificada
branching fault, falla ramificada
brand, marca de fábrica
brass, latón
brasses, cojinetes de latón (o bronce)
braze, *n.* soldadura con latón; *v.* soldar con latón, soldar en fuerte
brazing, soldadura fuerte, soldadura con latón
brea, brea
breach, (g) rotura, fractura, grieta, raja
breached anticline, anticlinal fracturado
breadth, anchura; (nt) manga
break, *n.* rotura, fractura; (g) falla, hendidura; cambio de litología; (el) interrupción; *v.* romper, fracturar; (tu) desconectar; interrumpir, desconectar; (bm) comenzar a circular, iniciar un turno
— **in oil,** aceite de estreno
— **in sedimentation,** (g) interrupción en la sedimentación
— **out tongs,** tenazas para desconectar
— **point,** punto de quiebra (o de rotura)
breakage, (cm) pérdida debido a roturas
breakdown, avería, falla
breaker, (rf) separador de viscosidad; (el) interruptor automático, disyuntor; (a) ruptor; rompedor
— **strips,** tiras de ajuste
breaking, rotura, ruptura, fractura; (qm) descomponer

— **down,** (prf) desconectar tubería (q.v. **lay down pipe**)
— **strength (stress, strain),** resistencia a la rotura (o a la falla)
breakoff, rotura del tubo de perforación
breakout, *v.* (prf) desenroscar tubería
— **block,** soltador de la barrena (q.v. **bit breaker**)
— **cathead,** (prf) torno de las llaves, (Ar) carretel de afloje
— **plate,** placa de desconexión
— **plate for fish-tail bits,** placa desconectadora para barrenas cola de pescado, (Ar) aflojador de trépanos cola de pescado
— **post,** barra para desconexión
— **tongs,** llaves de desenrosque (q.v. **lead tongs**)
breakover, (prf) cambio de tipo de lodo
breaks, (g) fallas pequeñas; lechos blandos dentro de capas duras; (tp) cambios topográficos de llanuras a cerros
breakwater, rompeolas, tajamar
breast, pecho
— **auger,** barrena de pecho
— **drill,** taladro de pecho, berbiquí de herrero
breather, respiradero
breccia, breccia; brecha
breeching, tragante, humero, caja de humo
breeding fire, fuego espontáneo
brick, ladrillo
— **clay,** arcilla de alfareros
— **machine,** máquina para hacer ladrillos
bridge, *n.* puente; *v.* salvar con puente; pontear; conectar
— **anvil,** yunque tipo puente
— **circuit,** (el) circuito en puente

33

— **plug,** (prf) tapón intermedio (o
puente, retenedor)
— **toll,** (cm) pontazgo, pontaje
— **wall,** (frn) altar, tornallamas
bridging ball, válvula de la zapata
de cementación, (Ar) válvula de
cierre de zapata de cementación
bridging material, (prf) material
obturante (q.v. **lost circulation
material)**
bridle, (bm) brida (q.v. **sucker rod
pumping)**
Brigg's standard, especificaciones
Brigg para tubos
bright, pulido, bruñido,
pulimentado; luminoso
— **rope,** cable de acero desnudo
— **spot,** (gf) punto brillante
brightstock, aceite lubricante
brightstock
brimstone, azufre vivo (o fundido)
brine, salmuera
— **pit,** foso de agua salada
Brinell hardness number, dureza
según la escala Brinell
bring in a well, inducir a
producción
briquet, (coal) briqueta, losilla,
aglomerado combustible
brittle, frágil, quebradizo,
deleznable
broach, *n.* broca, mecha, terraja,
escariador, barrena; *v.* escariar
broadcasting, difusión
brochure, folleto
broker, (cm) corredor, agente
comercial, intermediario, gestor
brokerage, (cm) comisión
bromide, bromuro
bromination, adición de bromo a
una molécula
bromine, bromo
— **number,** número bromo
bromite, (qm) bromito
bromoform, bromoforma
bromophenol, bromofenol

— **blue indicator,** indicador de azul
de bromofenol
bronze, *n.* bronce; *a.* broncíneo
bonze-bushed bearing, cojinetes
con bujes de bronce
bronze-flanged fitting, unión con
reborde de bronce
bronzite, broncita
brook, arroyo, riachuelo
brookite, brookita
brow, (g) frente de pliegue
brown coal, lignito
brucite, brucita
Brunton compass, brújula Brunton
brush, escobilla, cepillo, brocha,
pincel; maleza
bs, q.v. **bottom settlings**
BSI (British Standards Institute),
Instituto Británico de Normas
bs&w (basic sediment and water),
sedimentos y agua
Btu (British thermal unit), unidad
termica británica
bubble, *n.* (rf) burbuja; *v.* burbujear
— **cap,** casquete (o campana) de
burbujeo
— **deck,** bandeja de burbujeo
— **plate,** bandeja (o plato) de
burbujeo
— **point,** punto de burbujeo
— **pulses,** (gf) pulsos de burbuja
— **tower,** torre (o columna) de
burbujeo
— **tray,** bandeja (o plato) de
burbujeo (q.v. **bubble deck)**
bucket, cubo, cubeta; álabe
— **pump,** bomba de cubo, bomba
vertical con válvula en el
émbolo
— **trap,** trampa tipo cubeta
bucking-on machine, máquina
para forzar empalmes a rosca en
tubos sin aterrajar
buckle, anilla, abrazadera, aro;
hebilla

Glossary of the Petroleum Industry

buckling stress, (prf) esfuerzo de pandeo
buckup tongs, llaves de enroscar, (Ar) llaves de retroceso
budget, presupuesto
— **cut,** recorte del presupuesto
buffer, tope, amortiguador, paragolpes; pulidor; (dp) memoria intermedia, tampón; (cm) colchón—**inventory,** existencias de seguridad
buffing oil, aceite para pulir
bug blower, (prf) ventilador espantainsectos
build, construir
building, *n.* edificio, casa; construcción
— **license,** permiso (o licencia) de obras
built-in tool wrench, llave de herramientas enteriza
built to specification, construido a la medida (o a pedido, a propósito, a especificación)
buildup test, (prf) prueba de incremento de presión
bulb, ampolla; bombilla eléctrica
bulk, *n.* volumen, masa, macizo; *v.* abultar, hincharse; *a.* (cm) a granel, al por mayor
— **modulus,** módulo de volumen
— **station,** estación (o almacén) de ventas a granel
bulkhead, (nt) mamparo
bull, (prf) llenar de barro la barrena
— **line,** (nt) cable de ladeo
— **plug,** (tu) tapón ciego (o macho); (Ve) tapón de huevo
— **pump,** (mn) bomba a vapor de acción simple
— **quartz,** cuarzo bastardo
— **rope,** cable de herramientas
— **reel,** tambor del cable de perforación

— **wheel,** (perc) torno (o malacate) de herramientas
bull-wheel
— **bearing,** chumacera del torno de herramientas
— **braces,** tornapuntas del poste del torno de herramientas
— **brake,** freno del torno de herramientas
— **gear,** engranaje principal
— **girt,** larguero del torno de herramientas
— **gudgeon,** muñones del torno de herramientas
— **market,** (cm) mercado alcista
— **post,** poste del torno de herramientas
— **rope,** cable del torno de herramientas
— **shaft,** eje del torno de herramientas
— **spool,** tambor del torno de herramientas
— **tug,** polea del torno de herramientas
bulldog, (prf) arpón pescatubos
— **spear,** cangrejo pescador
— **wrench,** llave dentada
bulldozer, topadora, hoja de empuje, empujadora niveladora, (Ec) trompa, (Me) escrepa de empuje, bulldozer
bullet, bala
bulletin board, pizarra, tablero de avisos (o anuncios)
Bullgrader, niveladora de empuje angular (q.v. **angle dozer**)
bumper, tope, paragolpes, parachoques, cabezal de choques, amortiguador de choques
— **hill,** (g) morro del subsuelo
— **housing,** estuche (o cartucho) para la dinamita
— **jar,** destrabador, (Ar) tijera golpeadora, (Me) martillo

35

— **post,** poste amortiguador
— **sub,** compensador de movimiento vertical (q.v. jar)
buna-S, buna S
bundle, atado, haz, manojo; grupo
bunker fuel, combustóleo para barcos
bunkering, suministro de combustible
Bunsen burner, quemador (o mechero) Bunsen
buoy, boya
— **rope,** orinquete
— **tender,** balizador
buoyancy, flotabilidad, flotación; (hd) subpresión
— **correction,** correción por flotabilidad
— **tank,** tanque de flotación
buoyant power, fuerza de flotación
bur, arandela, virola, cincel de desbastar
burden, (el) carga; (nt) porte, tonelaje; (mn) volumen de roca por cada tiro
Bureau of Standards, negociado de normas de la Secretaría de Comercio de EU
buret, burette, (la) bureta, probeta
— **clamp,** portabureta
buried, enterrado, sepultado
— **hill,** morro (o cerro) sepultado
— **fault,** falla de subsuelo (q.v. compressional fault, concealed fault)
burn, *n.* quemadura; *v.* quemar, calcinar; arder
burner, quemador; mechero; estufa
burning, de quemar
— **oil,** aceite de lámpara kerosina, kerosene
— **pit,** quemadero, presa del quemador
— **point,** punto de ignición
— **test,** prueba de combustión

burnish, bruñir, pulimentar, lustar, pulir
burst mode, (dp) modalidad en ráfagas
bus, (dp) bus, enlace (o conductor) común, vía omnimbus
bush, *v.* revestir, encasquillar, forrar, (Co) embujar
bushing, buje, casquillo, manguito
— **extractor,** extractor de bujes
business, negocio
— **card,** tarjeta comercial
— **day,** día laborable
— **hours,** horario comercial
— **year,** ejercicio social
buster, (pr) separador (q.v. separator)
butadiene, butadieno
butadiyne, butadiino (q.v. diacetylene)
butane, butano
— **air plant,** planta de butano-aire
— **drilling engine,** motor de butano para perforación
butene, buteno, butileno (q.v. butylene)
butenyne, butenino
butte, monte aislado
butt, tope, culata
— **cleat,** (mn) plano secundatio de clivaje
— **hinge,** bisagra de tope
— **howel,** doladera, tajadera
— **joint,** (sd) junta a tope
butt-welded joint, junta soldada al tope
butt-welded pipe, tubo empalmado con soldadura al tope
butterfly, mariposa
— **nut,** tuerca mariposa
— **valve,** válvula de mariposa (o de aletas)
button, botón
— **bit,** barrena de botón (o de inserciones de carburo de tungsteno)

— head fitting, grasera tipo botón
— screen, botón colador
butyl acetate, acetato butílico
butyl formate, butil fórmico
butylacetylene, butilacetileno (q.v.
    hexyne)
butylbenzene, butilbenceno
butyldocosane, butildocosano
butyleicosane, butileicosano
butylene, butileno, buteno (q.v.
    butene)
butylnonane, butilnonano
butyne, butino
butyric acid, ácido butírico
buzzer, zumbador, (Ar) chicharra
    eléctrica
BWPD, bw/d (barrels of water per
    day), barriles de agua diarios
BWPH (barrels of water per
    hour), barriles de agua por hora
byheads, cabezadas, flujo
    intermitente al brotar del pozo
bylaws, estatutos sociales
bypass, *n.* comunicación lateral,
    desvío, derivación, tubo de paso,
    (Me) desviación; *v.* desviar
— valve, válvula de derivación (o
    de paso, derivación)
byproduct, subproducto, producto
    accesorio (o secundario)
— coke, coque producido con
    subproductos
byte, (dp) byte, octeto

C

c, q.v. centi
C, q.v. celsius, centigrade;
    coulomb; carbon
C link, eslabón en C
C_3's, símbolo para propano y
    propileno

C_4's, símbolo para butanos y
    butenos
C_5's, símbolo para pentanos,
    pentenos y pentadienos
C_6's, símbolo para hexanos,
    hexenos y hexadienos
C_7's, símbolo para heptanos,
    heptenos, heptadienos y tolueno
C_8's, símbolo para octanos, octenos,
    octadienos y xilenos
cab, cabina, caseta, casilla
cabinet projection, proyección
    exométrica
cable, cable
— coating compound, compuesto
    para preservar cables de acero
— drilling bits, barrenas
    percutentes, (Ar) trépanos para
    cable
— slide, descensor, cablecarril
— splice, empalme de un cable
— system, sistema de perforación a
    percusión, sistema de cable
— tools, (perc) herramientas de
    cable
cable-tool jars, percusores para
    equipo de cable, (Ar) tijeras
    para cablecablegram,
    cablegrama, cable
CAD, q.v. computer-aided design
cadmium, cadmio, óxido de zinc
caesium, cesio
cage, (ma) anillo portabolas, aro de
    rodillos; (va) cámara, jaula
caisson completion system, (mar)
    terminación con cámara
    impermeable
cake, costra, aglutinación,
    aglomerado, (Ar) revoque;
caking, aglutinación,
    endurecimiento,
    apelmazamiento,
    encostramiento, (Me) enjarre
calamine, calamina
calaverite, calaverita

            ▲

calc-alkali, alcalino-cal
calcareous, calcáreo
calcic, cálcico
calcine, calcinar
calcite, calcita
calcium, calcio
— **carbonate,** carbonato de calcio
— **chloride,** cloruro de calcio
— **hydrate,** hidrato de calcio, hidróxido de cal
— **hypochlorite,** hipoclorito cálcico
— **sulfate,** sulfato de calcio, yeso
calcium-treated mud, lodo cálcico
caldera, (vlc) caldera
Caledonian, caledoniense
calendar day, día del calendario
calf reel, tambor del cable de entubación (o maniobras)
calf wheel, (perc) torno (o malacate) de las tuberías, (Ar) tambor de maniobras
— **arms,** rayos de la rueda del malacate de las tuberías
— **bearing,** chumacera del malacate de las tuberías
— **brake,** freno del malacate de las tuberías de producción
— **cant,** llanta del malacate de la tubería de producción
— **gudgeons,** muñones del malacate de las tuberías de producción
— **posts,** postes del malacate de las tuberías de producción, soporte del tambor de maniobras
— **rim,** llanta acanalada del malacate de las tuberías de producción
— **shaft,** flecha (o eje) del malacate de las tuberías de producción
— **sproket,** rueda dentada del malacate de las tuberías de producción
caliber, *n.* calibre; **calibrate,** *v.*calibrar

calibrating solution, (ec) solución de calibración
calibration, calibración, ajuste
caliche, caliche
caliper, calibrador, compás de espesores
— **log,** registro de calibración
calking, calafateo, calafateadura (q.v. **caulking**)
— **tool** cincel de recalcar (o de calafatear)
— **chisel,** cincel de recalcar (o de calafatear)
call for bids, (cm) llamar a concurso, anunciar la licitación
CALM, q.v. **catenary anchor leg mooring buoy**
calorie, caloría
calorific power, potencia calorífica, poder calorífero
calorific value, potencia calorífica, poder calorífero
calorimeter, calorímetro
CAM, q.v. **computer-aided manufacturing**
cam, leva, parte saliente de una rueda excéntrica
— **lever,** palanca de leva
— **shaft,** árbol de levas
Cambrian, (g) cámbrico, cambriano
camera, cámara
— **lucida,** cámara lúcida
camp, campamento
Campanian, (g) campaniense
camphane, canfano
camphene, canfeno
camshaft, árbol de levas
— **bearing,** cojinete del árbol de levas
can, *n.* vasija, lata, envase de lata, bote; *a.* **canned,** envasado
Canada balsam, bálsamo del Canadá
candle-power, poder iluminate

cannel coal, carbón mate (o de
bujía), (Me) carbón de ampelita
cant, *n.* chaflán, inclinación, canto,
llanta; *v.* inclinar, inclinarse
— **file,** lima triangular
cantalite, (g) cantalita (q.v.
pitchstone)
canted leg, (mast) pata inclinable
cantilever, cantilever, voladizo,
volado
— **arm,** brazo (o tramo) volado
— **beam,** viga voladiza (o
acartelada)
— **bridge,** puente cantilever (o
volado)
— **mat jackup,** plataforma
autoelevadiza de volada (o
voladiza) con plancha de apoyo
— **slab,** placa volada
canvas, lona
—**stitched belt,** correa de lona
pespuntada
canyon, (g) cañon, (Ar) cajón,
cañadón
cap, (expl) cápsula, detonador; (tu)
tapa, casquete, hembra,
sombrerete, casco; travesaño,
cabezal, cepo; (pilon) carguero,
travesero; *v.* encepar, adintelar;
unir con largueros, encepar
— **a well,** dominar (o tapar) un
pozo (q.v. blowout)
— **jet,** inyector de casquete
— **nut,** casquillo roscado
— **plate,** (derrick) plancha de
coronamiento
— **rock,** (g) roca (o estrato)
impermeable de cobertura, capa
sello, cresta de domo salino,
(Me) sombrero
— **screw,** perno de precisión,
tornillo de cabeza
capacitor, capacitor; condensador
capacity, capacidad
cape, (g) cabo, punta

— **chisel,** cortahierro de ranurar,
cortafrío ranurador
capillarity, capilaridad
capillary, *n.* (g) fisura, grieta; *a.*
capilar
— **action,** capilaridad
— **fringe,** franja capilar, orla
freática
capital assets, (cm) bienes de
capital
capital stock, (cm) acciones de
capital
capstan, cabrestante, cabria, grúa,
malacate
capture, (g) captación, *v.* capturar
— **cross section,** sección transversal
de captura
— **gamma rays,** rayos gama de
captura
capuchine, abrazadera
car load, vagonada, furgonada:
9.100 a 15.000 kg
carbene, carbeno
carbide, carburo
carbolic acid, ácido carbólico
carbon (C), (qm) carbono, carbón
— **arc welding,** soldadura de carbón
al arco
— **black,** negro de humo, negro de
carbón
— **chain,** cadena de hidrocarburos
— **dioxide,** ácido carbónico, (Me)
bióxido de carbono
— **formation,** carbonización,
formación depósitos carbonosos
— **log,** registro del carbón
— **monoxide,** óxido carbónico,
monóxido de carbono
— **ratio,** relación (o proporción) de
carbono
— **regenerating unit,** (ec) unidad
regeneradora de carbón
— **steel,** acero al carbono
— **tetrachloride,** tetracloruro de
carbono
carbonaceous, carbonoso

carbonate, carbonato
— reef, arrecife calizo
— rock, roca carbonatada
Carboniferous, carbonífero
carbonyl sulfide, carbonilo
sulfúrico, sulfuro de carbonilo
carborundum, carborundo
carboxymethyl cellulose,
carboximetilo de celulosa
carburate, v. carburar
carburet, carburo
carburetor, carburador
— float, flotador (o flotante) del
carburador
— nozzle, boquilla de carburador
— throttle, mariposa del
carburador, acelerador
carburizing box, horno cuadrado
para carburación
cardan joint, articulación (o junta)
universal, junta de cardán
careen, v. (nt) carenar
cargo, cargamento
carnallite, carnalita
Carnot's cycle, ciclo de Carnot
carp, empalme, empalmadura
carpenter's brace, berbiquí (q.v.
brace and bit)
carriage control tape, (dp) cinta de
control de carro
carrier, (mc) conductor, portador;
(cableway excavator) carrito;
(cm) transportador, empresa
transportadora, acarreador; (nt)
buque tanque
— bar, barra portavarillas
— carrier, (rf) gas portador
— rig, (prf) equipo de reparación
carryall, traílla, excavadora
acarreadora
carrying bars, barras portatubos, (o
portacañería)
carrying rollers, rodillos
transportadores
carrying tongs, tenazas para
transportar tubería

carryover, sobrante, exceso
cartographic, cartográfico
— correction, corrección
cartográfica
cartridge, cartucho
case, caja; (in) estuche; (mu)
superficie endurecida
— hardening, temple superficial,
endurecimiento superficial
cased, revestido, (Me) ademado
cash, (cm) pago anticipado, en
efectivo, al contado
— on delivery (COD), cobro
contra entrega
— sale, venta al contado
— with order, pago al contado,
pago con el pedido
cashier, (oc) cajero/a
casing, tubería de revestimiento,
tubo revestidor, tubería de
ademe, (Ar) cañería aisladora
(o de entubación)
— adapter, adaptador para tubería
de revestimiento
— anchor packer, empaque de
anclaje para tubería de
revestimiento
— and tubing spider, crucetas (o
arañas) para tubería de
revestimiento y de producción
— bridge plug, tapón de retención
para tubería de revestimiento
— burst pressure, presión de
ruptura de la tubería de
revestimiento
— bushing, buje de reducción para
grapa de anillos
— center, centrador de tubos de
revestimiento
— centralizer, centrador de tubería
de revestimiento
— clamp, abrazadera de tubería de
revestimiento
— coupling, unión de rosca, (Me)
cople
— cutter, cortatubos

Glossary of the Petroleum Industry

— **dollies,** rodillos para tubería de revestimiento

— **elevator,** elevador para tubería de revestimiento

— **equipment,** accesorios para tubería de revestimiento

— **handling tools,** herramientas para manipulación de tubería de revestimiento

— **hanger,** colgador de tubería de revestimiento

— **head,** cabezal de tubería de revestimiento

— **head gas,** gas húmedo

— **hook,** gancho de aparejo para tubería de revestimiento

— **jack,** gato para tubería de revestimiento

— **landing flange,** brida para sostener la tubería de revestimiento durante su inserción en el pozo

— **landing spider,** cruceta (o araña) para tubería de revestimiento

— **line,** cable de la tubería de revestimiento

— **mandrel,** molde que se introduce en el tubo para tubería de revestimiento

— **nipple,** niple para tubería de revestimiento

— **packer,** obturador de la tubería de revestimiento

— **perforator,** perforador de tubos de revestimiento

— **plug,** tapón de tubería de revestimiento

— **pressure,** presión en el interior de la tubería de revestimiento

— **protector,** protector de tubería de revestimiento, (Me) guardarroscas

— **pulley,** polea de la tubería de revestimiento

— **pump,** bomba de producción por la tubería de revestimiento

— **rack,** muelle de tubería (q.v. **pipe rack**)

— **reel,** tambor de cable de entubación

— **ripper,** tajatubos

— **roller,** rectificador de la tubería de revestimiento

— **scraper,** raspatubos, diablo

— **setting,** colocación de la tubería de revestimiento, entubación

— **shoe,** zapata de cementación de la tubería de revestimiento, (Me) zapata guía (q.v. **cementing hose**)

— **slip,** cuña para tubería de revestimiento, (Me) araña

— **snubber,** encajadora de tubería de revestimiento

— **socket,** enchufe para tubería de revestimiento

— **spear,** cangrejo pescatubos, cangrejo (o arpón) de tubería, arpón pescatubos, (Me) machuelo

— **spider,** cruceta (o araña) para tubería de revestimiento

— **spider bowl,** anillo de suspensión

— **splitter,** (fishing tl) rajatubos, tajatubos

— **string,** sarta de revestimiento

— **support,** suspensor de tubería de revestimiento

— **suspender,** suspensor de tubería de revestimiento

— **swab,** limpiatubos, escobillón para tubería de revestimiento

— **swedge,** manguito (o niple) de reducción para tubería de revestimiento

— **swivel,** conexión articulada para tubería de revestimiento, niple giratorio

— **tester,** probador de tubería de revestimiento, pruebatubos

— **tongs,** tenazas (o llave) para
tubería de revestimiento
— **wagon,** carretilla para tubería de
revestimiento (q.v. **conductor
pipe, drive pipe**)
casinghead, cabezal de tuberías
— **gas,** gas húmedo; gas de boca de
pozo
— **gasoline,** (rf) gasolina natural
(q.v. **natural gasoline**)
cassiterite, casiterita
cast, *n.* (g) impronta, calco;
(smelter) molde; *v.* fundir,
moldear, colar, viciar
— **iron,** hierro fundido (o colado),
fundición
— **flange,** brida de hierro fundido
(o colado)
— **flanged fitting,** (tu) conexión de
hierro colado con reborde
— **screwed fitting,** (tu) conexión
roscada de hierro colado
— **tungsten,** tungsteno fundido
cast-steel screwed fittings, pieza de
acero fundido para enroscar
castellated nut, tuerca castillo,
tuerca de corona
caster, rueda apivotada, inclinación
del eje delantero; rodaja
casting, fundición, pieza fundida
castor oil, aceite de castor
CAT, q.v. **computer-aided testing**
cataclastic, (g) cataclástico
catalysis, catálisis
catalyst, catalizador
— **case,** caja del catalizador
— **chamber,** cámara de
catalización
— **cooler,** enfriador del catalizador
— **regenerating system,** sistema de
regeneración de catalizadores
— **stripping,** despojar (o
despetrolizar) el catalizador
catalytic, catalítico
— **alkylation,** alquilación catalítica

— **cracking,** crácking (o craqueo)
catalítico (q.v. **cracking**)
— **dehydrogenation,**
deshidrogenación catalítica
— **desulfurization,** desulfuración
catalítica
— **medium,** agente catalítico
catamaran, balsa con cabria
catch, fiador, pestillo, retén, aldaba
— **bowl,** (fishing tl) tazón de
mordaza (o de agarre)
catchment, captación; desagüe
— **area,** cuenca (o hoya) de
captación (o colectora),
superficie de desagüe
**catenary anchor leg mooring
buoy,** (mar) monopodio de
carga con ancla catenaria
caterpillar, locomotora de orugas
— **tractor,** tractor de orugas (o
carriles), (Cu) tractor de esteras
— **tread,** rodado tipo oruga
cathead, cabrestante (o torno)
auxiliar, (Me) cabeza de gato
cathode, cátodo, polo negativo
— **ray,** rayo catódico, rayo negativo
cathodic protection, protección
catódica
cation, catión
catline, cable de cabrestante
auxiliar, (Me) cable de la cabeza
de gato
catshaft, eje del cabrestante
auxiliar, (Me) eje de la cabeza
de gato
catwalk, pasillo; rampa
caulk, *v.* calafatear; **caulking,**
calafateo, calafateadura (q.v.
calk, calking)
caustic, cáustico
— **alkali,** álcali cáustico
— **soda,** sosa cáustica, hidróxido de
sodio
— **wash tower,** tolumna de lavado
cáustico, columna inyectora de
solución cáustica

Glossary of the Petroleum Industry

CAV, q.v. constant angular velocity

cave, *n.* cueva, caverna; *v.* derrumbarse, hundirse
— catcher, recogederrumbes
— packer, guardaderrumbes
cave-in, derrumbe, hundimiento
cavern, caverna
cavernous, cavernoso
— limestone, caliza cavernosa
cavey formation, formación susceptible a derrumbes
caving, (prf) derrumbe
cavings, material de derrumbe
cavitation, (gf) cavitación
cavity, cavidad
CCW, q.v. constituent concentrations in wastes
cd (candela), candela: unidad de intensidad luminosa
CDP, q.v. common depth point
CE, q.v. combustion efficiency
cell, celda, célula; (el) pila, par, elemento
cellar, sótano, bodega; (prf) sótano, (Ar) antepozo, (Me) contrapozo
— control gates, válvulas de compuerta instaladas en el sótano
— control valve, válvula de control instalada en el sótano
— deck, cubierta inferior (q.v. main deck, Texas deck)
cellophane, celofán
cellulose, celulosa
celsius (C), celsius: unidad de temperatura expresada en grados (*archiac*: centígrados) (q.v. Farenheit, kelvin)
cement, cemento
— band, adherencia del cemento
— band survey, registro sónico de la cementación
— binder, aglomerante, ligador (o endurecedor) de cemento

— casing, cementar la tubería de revestimiento
— dump bailer, (prf) cuchara vertedora de cemento
— float collar, collar de flotación para cementar
— guide shoe, zapata guía para cementar
— lined, revestido con cemento
— mixer, mezcladora de cemento (q.v. cementing unit)
— plug retainer, retenedor del tapón de cementación
— retainer, retenedor (o fijador) del cemento (q.v. cementing tool, cementing packer, cementer)
— setting accelerator, acelerador de fraguado del cemento
— system, cemento especial, lechada específica
cementation, cementación
cementer, cementador
cementing, cementación
— basket, cesto de cementación
— channeling, canalizaciones del cemento
— collar, collar de cementación
— head, cabezal (o cabeza) de cementación
— hose, manguera de cementación
— packer, retenedor de cemento (q.v. cement retainer)
— plug, tapón de cementación
— shoe, zapata de cementación (q.v. set shoe, casing shoe)
— tool, retenedor de cemento (q.v. cement retainer)
— truck, mezcladora de cemento portátil (o montada en camión)
— unit, mezcladora de cemento (q.v. cement mixer)
cementite, cementita
Cenomanian, cenomaniense
Cenozoic, cenozoico
center, centro

43

— **drill**, (tl) broca de centrar
— **irons**, (perc) soportes del balancín
— **line**, (rotary prf) línea de centro
— **of gravity**, centro de gravedad
— **punch**, punzón centrador
centi (c), *pref.* SI = 10^{-2}
centigrade (C), q.v. **celsius**
centigram, centígramo (cg)
centiliter, centilitro (cl)
centimeter, centímetro (cm)
centimeter-gram-second, centímetro-gramo-segundo (cgs)
centipoise, centipoise (cp)
centistoke, centistoke
central, central
— **core**, núcleo, corazón central
— **geared power**, central de bombeo de engranaje de fuerza mecánica
— **latch elevator**, elevador de cierre central
— **processing unit (CPU)**, unidad central de proceso (UCP)
— **pumping station**, estación central de bombeo, central de bombeo
centralizer, centrador (q.v. **casing centralizer**)
centrifugal, centrífugo
— **acceleration**, aceleración centrífuga
— **blower**, soplador (o insuflador) centrífugo
— **clarifier**, clarificador centrífugo
— **compressor**, compresor centrífugo, compresora centrífuga
— **force**, fuerza centrífuga
— **governor**, regulador centrífugo
— **pump**, bomba centrífuga
— **purifier**, purificador (o depurador) centrífugo
centrifuge, *n.* centrífuga
— **test**, prueba de la centrífuga

CERCLA (Comprehensive Environmental Response, Compensation, and Liability Act), Decreto Ambiental Comprensivo para Respuesta, Compensación y Responsabilidad
ceresin, ceresina
certificate of insurance, certificado de seguro
certificate of origin, certificado de origen
certification, certificación
certified check, cheque intervenido (o certificado, aprobado)
certified environmental specialist, (oc) especialista ambiental certificado
cerussite, cerusita
cesium vapor magnetometer, (gf) magnetómetro de vapor de cesio
cetane, cetano (q.v. **hexadecane**)
— **number**, número cetano
— **rating**, graduación cetánica
CFB, q.v. **circulating fluid bed**
CFCs, q.v. **chlorofluorocarbons**
CFG, q.v. **cubic feet of gas**
CFR fuel-testing unit, unidad CFR para prueba de combustibles, aparato para detectar las características detonantes de la gasolina y otros combustibles (q.v. **knock-testing apparatus**)
CGA (color graphics adapter), (dp) adaptador gráfico en color
CGL (comprehensive general liability), responsabilidad general comprensiva
chain, cadena
— **and gear drive**, cadena y engrane impulsor (q.v. **chain drive**)
— **code**, (dp) código en cadena
— **drive**, transmisión por cadena, mano de cadena

— **hoist,** montacargas de cadena, grúa de cadena
— **idler,** polea loca de cadena, rodillo tensor para cadena
— **link,** eslabón de cadena
— **pitch,** paso de cadena
— **pump,** bomba de cadena
— **reaction,** (qm) reacción en cadena
— **tongs,** tenazas (o llaves) de cadena
chain-reduction pumping unit, equipo de bombeo con cadenas reductoras de la velocidad
chalcedony, calcedonia
chalcocite, calcosita
chalcopyrite, calcopirita
chalk, tiza; creta
chamber, (mc) cámara, caja, cuerpo; (rf) torre, columna; (sluice) cuenco; (mn) anchurón, salón
— **of commerce,** cámara de comercio
chamfer, *n.* bisel, chaflán, estría; *v.* estriar, acanalar, formar moldura de media caña, achaflanar, biselar
chamfering machine, máquina de chaflanar
Champlainic, champlainiense
channel, *n.* (mc) ranura, canaleta, garganta, acanaladura; (mar) canal, estrecho; (r) cauce, canal; (gf) circuito sismográfico (q.v. **filter circuit**); (cn) viga canal (o en U); *v.* acanalar, ranurar; encauzar, canalizar
— **baffle,** desviador de canal
— **coding,** (dp) codificación de canal
— **flange,** brida de la cámara de encauzamiento de un termopermutador

— **iron,** hierro de canal, hierro en U, vigueta de canal, hierro acanalado
— **steel,** acero acanalado
— **wave,** (gf) onda confinada, onda de canal
channeling, canalización (o encauzamiento) de gases (o condensados) en las bandejas de burbujeo
chap, grieta, abertura, rajadura, hendidura
chaps, muescas, quijadas de un tornillo
char value, capacidad de calcinación
character density, (dp) densidad (de grabación) de caracteres
charcoal, carbón de madera
charge, *n.* (rf) (el) (vol) carga; *v.* cargar; (cm) cargar en cuenta
Charles' law, ley de Charles: el volumen de cualquier gas bajo cualquier condición de presión constante es proporcional a la temperatura absoluta
chart, diagrama, esquema; carta hidrográfica; (stats) gráfica
— **drum,** tambor de la cinta de registro gráfico
chasm, abismo, sima
chassis, chasis, armazón, bastidor
— **lube,** lubricante para chasis
check, *n.* verificación, comprobación; prueba; (cm) cheque; *v.* comprobar, verificar, revisar
— **digit,** (dp) dígito de verificación, cifra clave
— **nut,** contratuerca, tuerca de retén (o de seguridad)
— **point,** punto de control
— **valve,** válvula de retención; válvula de cierre
checkered brick, ladrillo jaquelado (o cuadriculado)

chemical, *n.* substancia química; *a.*
químico, reactivo
— **compound,** compuesto químico
— **oxygen demand,** (ec) demanda
química de oxígeno
— **engineer,** (oc) ingeniero químico
— **feeder,** alimentador de
substancias químicas
— **hazard information profile,**
(ec) perfil de información sobre
peligros químicos
— **pump,** bomba de substancias
químicas, bomba de inyección
— **reaction,** reacción química
chemist, (oc) químico
chemistry, química
chert, horsteno, lidita, pedernal,
chert, (Me) roca cuarzosa
cherty limestone, caliza córnea
chicken hook, vara con gancho
chief engineer, (oc) primer
ingeniero, ingeniero en jefe
chill ring, anillo protector para
conexiones soldadas
chilled, (iron) resfriado, acerado,
templado superficialmente
— **casting,** fundición endurecida,
(Ar) arrabio
chiller, enfriador
chilling
— **coil,** serpentín de enfriamiento
— **effect,** (g) fundición parcial de
una roca, (Ar) fritamiento,
fritura
— **machine,** máquina enfriadora
— **plate,** plancha enfriadora
chimney, chimenea, (vlc) canal de
erupción
China clay, caolín
chip axe, azuela
CHIP, q.v. **chemical hazard
information profile**
chisel, (tl) cortadora, cortafrío,
tajadera; (carp) escoplo, formón
— **bit,** barrena de cincel, escoplo
perforador

chloracetone, cloroacetona
chlorex, clorex
chloride, cloruro
chlorinated hydrocarbons,
hidrocarburos clorinados
chlorination, clorinación
— **system,** sistema de cloración (o
de clorinación)
chlorinator, clorador, aparato de
clorar
chlorine, cloro
chlorite, clorita
chloritoid, cloritoide
chloroaniline, cloroanilina
chlorofluorocarbons (CFCs),
clorofluorocarburos
chloroform, cloroformo
choke, *n.* (prf) estrangulador,
obturador, (Ar) cebador; (el)
reactor; (a) estrangulador (o
regulador) de aire, cebador del
carburador, obturador; (q.v.
flow nipple, flow plug, bean)
— **and kill lines,** líneas de
estrangular y matar
— **manifold,** múltiple de
estrangular (o de
estrangulamiento)
choker, estrangulador, reductor
chondrodite, condrodita
chordal pitch, paso alternado
Christmas tree, (pr) árbol de
conexiones (o de navidad, de
válvulas), (Ve) armadura de
surgencia, cruz
chrome, cromo
— **plated,** cromado, enchapado
chromel, cromel
chromic acid, ácido crómico
chromic oxide gel catalyst,
catalizador de gel de óxido de
cromo
chromite, cromita
chromium, cromo
— **steel,** acero al cromo
chromometer, cromómetro

chromophore, cromóforo
chronograph, cronógrafo
chronolite, cronolito
chronometer, cronómetro
chrysene, criseno
chrysocolla, (g) malaquita
chrysolite, (g) crisolita, serpentina
chrysotile, (g) crisotilo
chuck, (lathe) mandril; (light drill) portavástago
churn, batir; agitar
CIF, q.v. **cost, insurance, and freight**
C&F, q.v. **cost and freight**
cinder, ceniza
cinnabar, cinabrio
circle jack, (perc) gato circular
circuit, circuito
— **board,** placa (o panel) de circuito
— **breaker,** cortracircuito, interruptor automático
— **switching,** conmutación de circuitos
circular, *a.* circular; (cm) carta circular
— **fault,** (g) dislocación periférica
— **saw,** sierra circular
circulate, circular
circulate-and-weight method, (prf) método de circulación y densidad
circulating, circulante
— **fluid bed,** (rf) lecho fluido circulante
— **head,** cabeza de circulación, válvula controladora de circulación
— **pump,** bomba de circulación
— **register,** (dp) registro circulante
— **water treatment,** aplicación (o uso) de agua en circulación
circulation, circulación
— **joint,** unión de circulación, unión con válvula para regular la circulación

circulatory system, sistema circulatorio (o de circulación)
circumference, circunferencia
cirque, (g) circo, anfiteatro de paredes rectas al costado de una montaña (q.v. **corrie, glacier circus**)
CISC (complex instruction set computer), ordenador de juego de instrucciones complejas
cistern, cisterna
claim, reclamación
clamp, abrazadera; grapa, grampa; (carp) cárcel; afianzador; (dp) circuito de retención (o de bloqueo)
— **hubs,** cubos de mordaza
clarifier, clarificador
clarify, clarificar; aclarar
claroline, clarolina
clasp, abrazadera
clastic, (g) clástico, fragmentoso
— **grain,** grano clástico
— **rock,** roca clástica
— **sediments,** sedimentos clásticos (o mecánicos) (q.v. **mechanical sediments**)
Claus process, proceso Claus para convertir sulfuro de hidrógeno en azufre elemental
clause, cláusula
claw, (mc) garra, uña
— **end,** extremo de garra
clay, arcilla; barro
— **activation,** (rf) activación de la arcilla
— **burner,** quemador de arcilla
— **chamber,** cámara de la arcilla
— **contacting,** hacer contacto con la arcilla
— **filtration,** filtración a través de arcilla
— **ironstone,** arcilla ferruginosa
— **shale,** lutita floja
— **treating,** tratamiento por arcilla
claystone, argilolita, arcilita

cleanout, *n.* limpieza de pozo
— **bailer,** cuchara limpiapozos
— **door,** portezuela (o boca) de limpieza
— **rig,** equipo de limpieza de pozos
cleansing oil, aceite para limpiar
clear, despejar, liberar; restablecer a un estado anterior; borrado, puesta a cero
clearance, (mc) espacio libre, despejo, luz, holgura, juego, distancia libre
cleavage, (g) clivaje, hendedura; (mn) crucero
— **fracture,** fisibilidad
— **plane,** plano de clivaje
clevis, grillete, clavijero
cliff, risco, barranco, precipicio, acantilado, paredón
climate, clima
climatic, climático
clingage, (tk) embarre
clinker, escoria
clinograph, clinógrafo
clinometer, clinómetro
clip, abrazadera, sujetador, grapa
clock-driven, accionado por reloj
clocking, sincronización
clockwise, de izquierda a derecha, en la dirección de las manecillas del reloj, en sentido cronométrico
clog, clogging, *n.* obstrucción, atascamiento; *v.* taponar, obturar, tapar
clone, (dp) clon
close nipple, (tu) niple de rosca corrida, niple de largo mínimo
closed, (g) cerrado
— **anticline,** anticlinal cerrado
— **basin,** cuenca cerrada
— **circuit,** circuito cerrado
— **contour,** curva de nivel cerrada
— **cycle,** ciclo completo (o cerrado)
— **fold,** pliegue cerrado
— **loop,** (dp) bucle cerrado

— **tester,** (la) probador cerrado
closed-in pressure, presión a pozo cerrado (q.v. **formation pressure**)
closed-type sample container, portamuestra cerrado
closing-unit pump, bomba de la unidad de cierre
closure, cierre definitivo; (g) cierre, distancia vertical entre la parte superior de un anticlinal (o domo) y el fondo; (tp) cierre del trazado
cloud, nube
— **point,** punto de opacidad (q.v. **pour point, cold test, cold setting**)
— **test,** prueba de opacidad
cloudiness, opacidad, nebulosidad
cloudy, nublado
clover-leaf duct, conducto en orma de hoja de trébol
cluster, grupo, racimo, agrupamiento; piña de terminales
— **analysis,** análisis de conglomerados (o de grupos)
clutch, embrague
— **assembly,** conjunto de embrague
— **back plate,** placa de respaldo de embrague
— **brake,** freno de embrague
— **case,** caja de embrague
— **cone,** cono de embrague
— **countershaft,** contraeje de embrague
— **cover,** tapa de embrague
— **dog,** garra (o fiador) de embrague
— **disc,** disco de embrague
— **driving disc,** disco de mando de embrague
— **facing,** revestimiento del embrague
— **friction,** embrague de fricción

— **friction ring,** placa friccional del
embrague
— **housing,** caja de embrague
— **lever,** palanca de embrague
— **lining,** revestimiento (o forro) de
embrague
— **pedal,** pedal de embrague
— **pedal stop,** tope del pedal de
embrague
— **pressure plate,** placa de presión
de embrague
— **release,** desacople de embrague
— **release fork,** horquilla de
desacople de embrague
— **release lever,** palanca de
desacople de embrague
— **shaft,** eje de embrague
— **spring,** resorte de embrague
CLV, q.v. **constant linear velocity**
CNG, q.v. **compressed natural gas**
coagulation, coagulación
coagulator, coagulador
coaking, endentado de piezas por
medio de machos (o dados),
colocación de dados de bronce a
los motores, ajuste, empalme
coal, carbón de piedra, hulla
— **bed,** estrato carbonífero,
yacimiento de carbón
— **gas,** gas de carbón
— **oil,** kerosina
— **tar,** alquitrán de hulla, brea
coal-bearing, carbonífero
coal-tar enamel coating, capa de
esmalte de alquitrán
coalesce, v. unirse, fundirse,
conglutinarse
coalescence, (g) soldadura, fusión,
coalescencia, conglutinación
coarse, grueso; basto; áspero
— **gravel,** grava gruesa
— **screen,** criba gruesa, tamiz de
malla ancha
coarse-grained, (g) de grano grueso,
de fibra gruesa
coast, costa

— **line,** línea costera, costa
coastal plain, llanura costanera
coastline effect, efecto de litoral
coastwise shipping, cabotaje
coat, n. (paint) mano, capa;
revestimiento; v. forrar, revestir,
aplicar una capa de pintura
coated pipe, tubería revestida
coating, baño; recubrimiento,
revestimiento, recubridor; mano
de pintura, capa
cobalt, cobalto
cobaltite, cobaltita
cobble, guijarro, canto rodado,
chinas, (Ve) peñas
— **conglomerate,** conglomerado de
cantos rodados (o de peñas)
— **gravel,** grava de cantos rodados
medianos, (Ve) peñascal
— **stone,** piedra guijarrosa
Coblentzian, coblentziense
**Cobol (common business-oriented
language),** (dp) lenguaje de
proceso de datos que utiliza el
idioma inglés común
cock, grifo, espita, llave, canilla
— **and bind,** retroceso y atasco
cocurrent operation, operación de
corrientes en la misma dirección
COD, q.v. **cash on delivery**
coda, fase de la coda, fase final (q.v.
final phase)
code, clave; código
codimer, codímero
coding, codificación
coefficient, coeficiente
— **of elasticity,** coeficiente de
elasticidad
— **of expansion,** coeficiente de
expansión
— **of linear expansion,** coeficiente
de dilatación lineal
coercive force, fuerza coercitiva
(q.v. **hysteresis**)

English - Spanish

coffer dam, *n.* (cn) ataguía, dique
provisorio, (Ar) atojo; *v.*
ataguiar, encajonar
cog, diente de rueda, leva
cogen (cogeneration) plant, planta
co-generadora (de electricidad y
vapor), planta generadora
combinada
coherence, coherencia
cohesion, cohesión
coil, *n.* (tu) serpentín, (Me) espiral;
(ca) rollo, aduja; (el) bobina,
carrete; *v.* enrollar, adujar,
enroscar
— **clutch,** embrague espiral
— **spring,** resorte espiral
coil-in-box condenser, enfriador de
serpentín en caja
coil-in-box cooler, enfriador de
serpentín en caja
coil-type feed-water heater,
calentador de serpentín
coiler, enrollador
coincidence method, (g) método de
coincidencia
coke, *n.* coque, cok; *v.* coquificar,
coquizar
— **drum,** tambor (o cilindro) de
coquificación
coker, coquificadora, coquizadora
cokestill, alambique de coque
coking, coquificación
— **drum,** cilindro de coquificación
cold, frío
— **bend,** doblez hecho en frío
— **chisel,** cortafrío; cincel para
cortar en frío, cortafierro
— **drawn,** estirado en frío
— **end drive,** (tr) impulso de
arranque en frío
— **expanded pipe,** tubería estirada
en frío
— **pressing,** prensar en frío
— **reserve,** (el) capacidad de
reserva fuera de funcionamiento
— **rolling,** laminado en frío

— **room,** salón refrigerador
— **settling,** asentamiento de la
parafina cuando el petróleo se
somete a baja temperatura
— **starting,** (mt) arranque en frío
— **test,** prueba de congelación (q.v.
pour point, cloud point)
— **working pressure,** (va)
resistencia a la presión en frío
colic sediment, sedimento cólico (o
anemógeno)
collapse pressure, presión de
derrumbamiento
collapsed pipe, tubo caído
collapsible, plegadizo, desarmable
— **tap,** macho de terraja plegable (o
desarmable)
collar, collar, cuello, collarín, (Me)
cople; anillo, aro, argolla
— **buster,** rompecollares,
rompecuellos
— **pipe,** tubería lastrabarrena (q.v.
drill collar)
— **plate,** arandela
— **socket,** enchufador de collar,
enchufacollar
— **flange,** brida de collar (o de
cuello)
— **weld joint,** acoplamiento con
collar a soldadura
— **welding jig,** sujetador de guía
para soldar collares en tubos
collar-leak clamp, collar (o
abrazadera) para fugas de
tubería
collating sequence, (dp) secuencia
de intercalación
collection, (cm) cobro; recolección
— **agency,** agencia de cobros
— **basin,** cámara colectora
— **efficiency,** (ec) eficiencia de la
recolección
collector, colector; (gf) receptor de
ondas
collimation, colimación
collimator, colimador

colloid, coloide
colloidal, coloide
— **mud,** lodo coloidal
— **solution,** solución coloidal
— **state,** estado coloidal
colon, colón: moneda de Costa Rica
  y El Salvador
color graphics adapter, (dp)
  adaptador gráfico en color
color test, prueba del color
colorimeter, colorímetro
columbite, columbita
column, columna, torre
— **binary,** (dp) binario en columna
— **contactor,** (rf) torre de contacto
— **split,** (dp) divisor de columna
column-stabilized
  semisubmersible drilling rig,
  equipo semisumergible de
  perforación estabilizado por
  columnas
columnar, (g) (mn) columnar,
  prismático
— **joint,** disyunción prismática
— **basalt,** basalto prismático
— **section,** (gf) columna
  estratigráfica (o geológica)
Comanchean, comancheano
combination, combinación
— **drive,** empuje natural
  combinado (de gas y agua) (q.v.
  reservoir drive mechanism,
  gas-cap drive, water drive)
— **oil and gas burner,** quemador de
  gas y petróleo combinados
— **pull-rod clamp,** abrazadera de
  combinación para varillas de
  tracción
— **rig,** equipo de combinación,
  equipo combinado de
  perforación
— **socket,** compana de pesca en
  combinación, pescacasquillos
— **string,** sarta combinada (con
  tramos de distintas
  características)

— **trap,** (g) trampa combinada
  (estructural y estratigráfica)
combustion, combustión
— **boat,** (la) vasija de combustión
— **chamber,** cámara de combustión
— **control,** control de combustión
— **efficiency,** eficiencia de
  combustión
— **heat,** capacidad calorífica (q.v.
  heating valve)
command, (dp) mandato,
  instrucción de canal (en
  lenguaje de máquina)
commingling, (p) mezclar
commissary, proveeduría
commission, junta, consejo,
  comisión; (cm) comisión
common, corriente, común
— **carrier,** empresa de transporte de
  servicio público
— **depth point,** (gf) punto de
  reflejo común
— **midpoint,** (gf) punto intermedio
  de reflejo común
— **shot gathers,** perfiles sísmicos
  horizontales
— **stock,** (cm) acciones votantes
commutator, (el) conmutador,
  colector
compaction, compactación,
  compresión
companion flange, brida gemela
company (Co), compañía (Cía)
compass, brújula
— **saw,** serrucho de punta
compensated neutron log, registro
  de neutrón compensado
compensation, compensación
competent, (g) competente
— **bed,** lecho competente
— **folds,** pliegues armónicos (o
  competentes)
competition, competencia
competitor, competidor
complaint, queja

complete shut off, paro (o cierre) completo
completion, terminación, acabamiento, finalización
— **fluid**, (prf) fluido de terminación
complex, complejo
— **fault**, falla compleja
compliance, (mc) deformación
component, componente
composite joint, (sd) junta compuesta
composite stream, corriente compuesta (de petróleo y gas)
compositing, (gf) composición, mezclado (q.v. **mixing**)
composition, composición
— **cup**, capa de cuero sintético para el émbolo de la bomba; copilla de bomba
— **disc**, (va) disco de composición
compound, *n.* compuesto; *a.* compuesto, combinado, mezclado; *v.* combinar
— **engine**, máquina compound, máquina de vapor de doble expansión; (el) motor de devanado compuesto
— **pressure and vacuum gage**, indicador de presión y vacuómetro combinados
compounded oil, aceite mezclado
compounding, (el) compoundaje; (mo) en combinación
— **kettle**, caldero (o marmita) de mezclar
— **operation**, operación de mezclar
— **unit**, (mc) unidad combinada (o en combinación)
— **valve**, válvula de relevo (o de compoundaje)
comprehensive general liability, (insur) responsabilidad general comprensiva
compressed air, aire comprimido
compressed natural gas (CNG), gas natural comprimido (GNC)

compressibility, compresibilidad
— **factor**, factor de compresibilidad
compression, compresión
— **factor**, factor de compresión
— **fault**, (g) falla compresional (q.v. **buried fault**)
— **ignition**, (ma) ignición por compresión
— **joint**, (g) piezoclasa
— **ratio**, relación de compresión
— **refrigeration cycle**, ciclo de refrigeración por compresión
— **stress**, esfuerzo por compresión
— **stroke**, carrera de compresión
compressional wave, onda compresional (q.v. **primary wave, longitudinal wave**)
compressive basin, cuenca compresiva
compressive strength, fuerza compresora, resistencia a la compresión
compressor, compresor
— **clearance**, holgura (o espacio libre) del compresor
— **strength**, fuerza compresora
comptroller, (oc) auditor
computation, cómputo, cálculo, computación
computer, (dp) ordenador, *angl.* computadora, computador
— **graphics interface**, interfaz de gráficos informáticos
— **hardware description language**, lenguaje de descripción de hardware informático
— **logic**, lógica informática, lógica de ordenador
— **network**, red informática, complejo de ordenadores
— **power**, capacidad de cálculo de ordenador
computer-aided design, diseño asistido por ordenador, *angl.* diseño computarizado

computer-aided manufacturing, fabricación asistida por ordenador

computer-aided testing, prueba asistida por ordenador

concave, cóncavo

concealed fault, falla de subsuelo (q.v. buried fault)

concentrate, *n.* concentrado; *v.* concentrar

concentration, concentración

concentric, concéntrico

— fold, pliegue concéntrico

— structure, estructura concéntrica

concession, concesión, otorgamiento gubernativo a favor de particulares

conchoidal fracture, fractura concoidea (o curvilínea)

concordant, (g) concordante

concrete, hormigón, concreto

— mixer, mezcladora de concreto (o de hormigón)

— platform, (mar) plataforma de concreto (o hormigón)

concretion, (g) concreción

concurrent, concurrente, coexistente

— method, método concurrente (q.v. circulate-and-weight method)

condensate, condensado

— reservoir, yacimiento de gas y condensado

condensation, condensación

condense, condensar; condensarse

condenser, condensador

— jacket, caja refrigerante

— tube, tubo condensador

condition, *v.* acondicionar

conditioning pit, foso de acondicionamiento

conductance, conductancia

conduction, conducción, transmisión

conductive method, método de conducción

conductivity, conductividad

conductor, conductor

— casing, tubo conductor

— pipe, primera tubería de revestimiento, primer tubo revestidor, (Me, Ve) tubo conductor, (q.v. surface casing, drive pipe)

conduit, tubería, cañería, acueducto, conducto; (el) tubo conducto, conducto portacables, conducto celular

cone, cono

— bit, barrena de conos

— coupling, acoplamiento cónico

— pulley, polea escalonada (o de cono)

cone-in-cone structure, (g) estructura cono entre cono

confirm, confirmar

confirmation, confirmación

conformable, (g) concordante

— beds, capas de contactos paralelos

— faults, fallas conformes

conformity, concordancia

conglomerate, conglomerado, pudinga

conglomeration, conglomeración

conic projections, proyecciones cónicas

conical, cónico

— beaker with lip and spout, (qm) vaso cónico con vertedero y pico

— seal joint, acoplamiento cónico

conjugate faults, fallas conjugadas

connate water, agua innata (o connata, juvenil), agua de formación (o sinergética), agua congénita

connection, conexión

connecting rod, biela

— bearing, cojinete de biela

— link, eslabón común

connector, conector, conexionador, unión

consequent stream, (g) arroyo consecuente

conservation, conservación; reparación

consignee, (cm) consignatario, depositario

consignment, (cm) consignación

consignor, consignador

consistency, consistencia

consistometer, consistómetro

consolidated, consolidado

— **sediments,** sedimentos consolidados

constant, *n. a.* constante

— **angular velocity,** velocidad angular constante

— **choke-pressure method,** (prf) método de presión constante

—**linear velocity,** velocidad lineal constante

— **pit-level method,** (prf) método de nivel constante en las presas

constantan, (mu) constantano, constantán

constituent, componente, elemento, ingrediente

— **concentrations in wastes,** (ec) concentraciones de componentes en desperdicios

consular visa, (cm) visado consular

consumer, consumidor

contact, contacto, (g) (prf) pase (de un sedimento a otro)

— **action,** (g) fenómenos de contacto

— **curve,** curva de contacto

— **filtration,** filtración por contacto

— **jaw,** (sd) prensa de contacto

— **metamorphic zone,** zona de metamorfismo por contacto

— **metamorphism,** metamorfismo por contacto

— **minerals,** minerales de contacto

— **treatment,** tratamiento con ácido por el método de contacto

contacting, (rf) contacto del ácido y el petróleo; poner en contacto

contactor, contactor

— **treating process,** tratamiento por contacto de substancias inmiscibles

container, recipiente

contaminate, contaminar

contemporaneous, contemporáneo

continental, continental

— **deposits,** depósitos continentales

— **drift,** deriva continental

— **fringe,** borde continental (o orla) continental

— **layer,** capa continental

— **shelf,** plataforma epicontinental

continuity equation, ecuación de continuidad

continuous, continuo

— **correlation,** correlación continua

— **gasoline treating plant,** planta para el tratamiento continuo de gasolina

— **phase,** fase continua

— **profiling,** (gf) perfilaje continuo

continuous-flow gas lift, bombeo neumático contínuo

contorted, contorsionado

contortion, contorsión; plieque

contour, curva (o línea) de nivel; (tp) (gf) contorno, perfil

— **datum,** curva de nivel de referencia; nivel de referencia (q.v. **datum plane**)

— **interval,** intervalo entre curvas, distancia vertical entre los planos de nivel

— **line,** curva de nivel, (Ar) curva hipsométrica

— **map,** plano topográfico (o acotado), (Me) plano de curvas de nivel

— **mapping,** planimetría

contract, contrato
contracting parties, partes
  contratantes
contraction, contracción,
  disminución
— **factor,** (pr) factor de
  contracción
contractor, contratista
control, *n.* control, gobierno,
  regulación; *v.* controlar,
  gobernar, regular, mandar
— **arm,** brazo de gobierno (o de
  mando)
— **board,** tablero de control (o de
  mandos, de regulación)
— **casinghead,** cabezal de seguridad
  para tubería de revestimiento,
  cabeza de seguridad
— **equipment,** (rf) accesorios de
  gobierno
— **instrument,** instrumento de
  gobierno (o de control)
— **point,** (tp) punto dominante (o
  obligado), punto de
  comprobación
— **room,** sala de mando (o de
  control)
— **station,** estación de control (o de
  cierre)
— **switch,** interruptor de mando
— **valve,** válvula de control (q.v.
  **blowout preventer, master
  gate, control head, etc.**)
control-head packer, cabezal
  obturador de control
controlled pressure gage,
  manómetro para la presión
  controlada
controller, regulador
convection, convección
— **bank,** batería de tubos de
  convección
convector, convector
conventional, corriente,
  convencional, común

— **gas-lift mandrel,** mandril de
  bombeo neumático
— **signs,** signos convencionales
convergence, convergencia
conversion, conversión; (hd)
  transición
— **constant,** (rf) constante de
  conversión
— **per pass,** (rf) conversión de la
  carga por cada recorrido a
  través de la torre de
  reformación
— **table,** tabla de conversión
converter, convertidor
convertible engine, motor
  convertible
convex, convexo
conveyor, transportador mecánico,
  conductor
— **furnace,** horno de conductor
convolution, (mt) convolución
coolant, líquido enfriador,
  refrigerante
cooler, enfriador, refrigerador
cooling, enfriamiento
— **coil,** serpentín enfriador
— **control,** regulador del
  enfriamiento
— **plate,** plancha de enfriamiento
— **system,** sistema de enfriamiento
— **tower,** (rf) torre de enfriamiento,
  torre enfriadora
— **unit,** unidad de enfriamiento
coordinate, coordenada
— **axes,** ejes de coordenadas
— **paper,** papel cuadriculado
coping saw, serrucho calador, sierra
  de calar
copolymer, copolímero
copolymerization,
  copolimerización
copper, cobre
— **bearings,** cojinetes de cobre
— **bottomed,** con fondo de cobre
— **dish gum,** goma en plato de
  cobre

— **dish test,** (la) prueba en platillo de cobre
— **nickel,** (mn) niquelina
— **number,** número (o índice) de cobre
— **plate,** plancha de cobre
— **pyrite,** pirita de cobre, calcopirita
— **strip,** tira (o lámina) de cobre
— **strip test,** prueba con tira de cobre
— **sulfate,** sulfato de cobre
— **sweetening process,** procedimiento de desulfuración con cloruro de cobre
— **vitriol,** vitriolo azul, sulfato de cobre
copper-bearing steel, acero al cobre, acero encobrado
copper-clad, cobrizado por soldadura
coprolites, (g) coprolitos
copyright, propiedad intelectual, título de propiedad, derecho de autor
coquina, coquina
coral, *n.* coral; *a.* coralino
— **limestone,** caliza coralina
— **reef,** arrecife (o banco) coralígeno, banco de coral
— **rock,** roca coralina
— **sand,** arena (o arenisca) de coral
cord, cuerda, cordón, cordel
cordage, cordaje, cordelería
— **oil,** aceite para cordaje
cordierite, cordierita
cordillera, cordillera
cordoba, córdoba: moneda de Nicaragua
core, núcleo, corazón, (Me) alma, (Ar) testigo
— **analysis,** análisis de núcleos (o de muestras)
— **barrel,** sacanúcleos, sacamuestras, tubo estuche para núcleos, (Me) muestrero

— **bit,** barrena sacanúcleos (o sacamuestras)
— **catcher,** atrapanúcleos, recogemuestras
— **cutterhead,** corona cortadora de núcleos
— **drill,** barrena sacamuestras (o sacanúcleos)
— **drilling rig,** equipo de perforación para sacar núcleos
— **extractor,** sacanúcleos
— **head,** cabeza de sacanúcleos; grupo de cortadoras colocados en el fondo del sacanúcleos
— **image library,** (dp) biblioteca imagen de la memoria
— **pusher,** expulsanúcleos
— **recovery,** recuperación (o obtención) de núcleos rescatados
— **retainer,** atrapanúcleos, atrapamuestras
— **samples,** muestras de núcleos
— **storage,** (dp) memoria de núcleos magnéticos
— **waves,** (gf) ondas centrales
core-testing equipment, equipo para probar núcleos (o muestras) de formaciones
corindum, corindón
coring, extraer núcleos, corazonar, extracción de muestras
— **equipment,** equipo para sacar núcleos
— **reel,** tambor del cable del sacanúcleos
— **time,** tiempo consumido en el trabajo de extraer núcleos
cork, corcho
— **borer,** perforacorchos
— **gasket,** empaquetadura de corcho
corkscrew, *a.* de tirabuzón, en espiral
corner, esquina
— **cramp,** grapa angular
— **joint,** (sd) junta esquinada

cornice, cornisa

corporate name, (cm) razón social

corrasion, (g) corrasión, remoción

correction, corrección

— curve, curva de correción

— factor, factor de corrección

— for curvature, correción de curvatura

correlate, v. poner en correlación, (Me) correlacionar

correlation, (gf) correlación

— horizon, horizonte de correlación

— shooting, tiro de correlación

correlogram, correlograma

corrie, circo glaciar (o glaciárico) (q.v. cirque, glacier circus)

corrode, v. corroer, desagastar, oxidar

corrosion, corrosión; desgaste

— cap, casco anticorrosión

— coupon, testigo de corrosión

— fatigue, fatiga del metal causada por la corrosión

— resisting steel, acero resistente a la corrosión

— test, prueba de corrosión

corrosive, corrosivo

corrugated, corrugado, acanalado, ondulado

— friction socket, pescasondas corrugado de fricción

— metal gasket, empaquetadura de planchas de metal corrugadas

— sheet metal, lámina corrugada de metal

— socket, campana de pescar corrugada

corundum, corindón

cosine, (mt) coseno

cosmogenetic, cosmogenético

cost, coste, costo

— accounting, contabilidad de costes

— and freight, costo y flete

— insurance and freight (CIF), costo, seguro y flete (CSF)

cost-benefit analsis, análisis de costo y beneficio

cotter pin, pasador hendido, chaveta (o clavija) hendida

cotype, (paleo) cotipo

coulisse, bastidor, corredera

coulomb (C), culombio: unidad de electricidad

counterbalance, contrapeso, equilibrio, (Me) contrabalanceo

— crank, manivela de contrapeso

— weights, pesas de contrapeso

counterbore, n. abocardo de fondo plano; v. abocardar con fondo plano

counterbored, perforación abocardada, orificio abocardado, (o avellanado, fresado)

— tool joint, unión abocardada de tubería vástago

counterboring, abocardado, ensanchamiento de la entrada de un tubo

counterclockwise, contrario, en sentido contrario a las agujas del reloj, a la izquierda

countercurrent, contracorriente

— operation, operación de corrientes contrarias

counterflow, (rf) contracorriente

countershaft, contraeje, eje auxiliar (o secundario), (Me) eje de transmisión intermedio

countersink, n. avellanador; v. fresar (o avellanar); abocardo;

countersunk, a. embutido, abocardado, avellanado, fresado

counterthrust, contraempuje

countervein, (mn) contrafilón, contravena

counterweight, contrapeso

country rock, (mn) roca madre, (Bo) roca encajonante, (Me)

piedra bruta, tepetate; roca
vecina (q.v. **adjoining rock**)
couple, *v.* unir, ensamblar,
engranar, acoplar; *n.* **coupler,**
acoplador; unión
coupling, (tu) manguito,
acoplamiento, (Me) cople; (mc)
empalme, unión, acopladura,
acoplamiento, (Ar) acople,
(CH) copla, (Cu) acoplo; (el)
acoplamiento
— **box,** manguito de acoplamiento
— **clamp,** abrazadera de unión
— **joint,** acoplador
— **pin,** pasador de enganche
— **puller,** tirador de uniones
coupon, muestra de acero para
ensayo
course-elastic, línea elástica en el
cálculo de las reacciones y de los
momentos de flexión de una
viga
covariance, (gf) covarianza,
covariancia
cove, *n.* ensenada, caleta, cala,
ancón, abra; *v.* abovedar,
arquear
covellite, covelita
cover, *n.* tapa, cubierta; *v.* tapar,
cubrir
covered, cubierto
cps (cycles per second), ciclos por
segundo
CPU, q.v. **central processing unit**
crab, cabrestante, malacate, cabria,
(Ar) torno, noria, molinete
crack, *n.* grieta, hendedura, raja,
rendija, cuarteadura; *v.* agrietar,
rajar, quebrajar, resquebrar;
agrietarse, cuartearse, (Ar)
fisurarse; (rf) craquear,
fraccionar, desintegrar
— **a valve,** hacer gotear una válvula
crack-per-pas, (rf) crácking por
recorrido, cantidad de producto

obtenida en cada recorrido de la
carga
cracked, cuarteado, rajado,
agrietado, estrellado, hendido
— **distillate,** destilado reformado (o
de crácking) (q.v. **cracking,
reforming**)
— **distillate rerun plant,** planta de
redestilación de crácking, planta
de repaso para destilado de
crácking (q.v. **crácking,
reforming**)
— **gasoline,** gasolina reformada (o
de crácking) (q.v. **crácking,
reforming**)
cracker furnace, horno para planta
de reformación térmica
cracking, (rf) crácking, craqueo
(*ambos angl. usados en
refinación*), descomposicón
térmica, desintegración por
calor, reformación, (Es) rotura
— **plant,** instalación (o planta) de
crácking
— **process,** procedimiento (o
método, proceso) de crácking,
craqueo, descomposición de los
hidrocarburos
— **still,** alambique de crácking
— **still gas,** gas de alambique de
crácking
— **unit,** instalación (o planta,
unidad) de crácking
cradle, armazón, marco, cuña
crag, (g) risco; marga fosilífera de
origen marino
cramp, grapa, montante, brida
crane, grúa, grúa corrediza,(o
giratoria), (Ar) guinche
— **boom,** aguilón de grúa
— **derrick,** grúa giratoria con
aguilón horizontal y trole
corredizo
— **post,** poste de grúa
crank, manivela, cigüeña,
manubrio, codo de palanca

— **and counterbalance assembly,** conjunto de manivela y contrapeso

— **disk,** disco de manivela, contrapesos del cigüeñal

— **hole reboring machine,** máquina fresadora para ensanchar el agujero de la manivela

— **throw,** codo de manivela (o de cigüeña)

— **pin,** pasador de manivela

crankcase, cárter, caja del cigüeñal

— **oil,** aceite para el cárter

crankpin, gorrón de manivela, muñón (o muñequilla, clavija) del cigüeñal

crankshaft, cigüeñal, árbol cigüeñal, eje acodado, árbol motor

crash, choque

crater, cráter

cratered well, pozo con cráter

crawler, vehículo con rodado a carriles, carril, oruga

— **belt,** llanta articulada (o de oruga), banda de esteras

— **tractor,** tractor de carriles (o de orugas)

crawler-mounted, montado sobre orugas

creak, crujir, rechinar

crease, estría, acanaladura, pliegue, doblez

credit, *n.* (cm) crédito; *v.* abonar, acreditar

— **balance,** saldo acreedor (o al haber)

— **insurance,** seguro de crédito

— **rating,** límite (o índice) de crédito

— **risk,** riesgo de falta de pago

creditor, acreedor

creek, caño, arroyuelo

creep, *n.* (g) derrubio, movimiento paulatino del terreno; (mu) flujo; (belt) resbalamiento; (hd) **percolación,** filtración; *v.* deslizarse, correrse

— **ratio,** (hd) factor de percolación (o filtración)

— **strength of steel,** resistencia del acero al flujo

creeping sediment, sedimento resbalante (o escurridizo, corrido)

crenulation, (g) arrugamiento en forma de diente (q.v. **crumpling)**

creosote, creosota

crescent, *n.* lúnula; *v.* cortar en medialuna

crescentic, en forma de media luna (o de lúnula)

cresol, cresol, ácido acetílico

crest, (tp) cresta, cima, cumbre, crestón

— **line,** charnela anaclinal

— **of anticline,** cresta de anticlinal

Cretaceous, cretáceo, cretácico

Cretaceous-Tertiary (K/T) boundary, límite cretáceoterciario

crevasse, grieta de glaciar, diaclasa

crevice, grieta, hendidura

crew, cuadrilla de trabajadores, personal, dotación (q.v. **party**)

crewboat, bote para transportar personal

critical, crítico

— **angle of incidence,** ángulo crítico de incidencia

— **aquifer protection area,** área crítica de protección de depósitos subterráneos de agua

— **damping,** amortiguamiento crítico

— **dip,** inclinación crítica, echado crítico

— **path method**, (dp) método del camino crítico

— **pressure**, presión crítica

crocetane, crocetano

crocket, gancho

crocoite, crocoita

crocus, rojo de pulir

crook, gancho, garfio

crooked hole, pozo desviado, agujero curvo (o torcido), hoyo tuerto

crooked pipe, tubo doblado (o curvado)

crop out, *v.* (g) aflorar, (Ar) arrumbar

cross, cruz; transversal; cruceta

— **coupling**, acoplamiento cruzado (o en cruce)

— **feed**, interferencia

— **hairs**, retículo, hilos cruzados

— **section**, corte transversal

— **spread**, (g) despliegue en cruz

— **valve**, válvula de cruz

crossbar, traviesa

cross-bearing box, caja de cojinete de la cruceta

cross-bedded conglomerate, conglomerado cruzado

cross-bedding, estratos (o capas) entrecruzados, (Ar) estratificación diagonal

crosscorrelation, (gf) correlación cruzada

crossflow, (g) flujo transversal; corriente transversal

cross-folding, (g) plegamiento entrecruzado, plieques cruzados

cross-laminated, láminas cruzadas

crossed belt, correa cruzada en forma de 8

crosshead, cruceta, cruceta de cabeza

— **guides**, guías de la cruceta, (Ar) paralelas de cruceta

— **pin**, pasador de cruceta

— **shoe**, patín de cruceta, zapata de la cruceta

crosslaminated, de láminas cruzadas

crossline, (gf) contralínea

crossover, (tu) curva de paso, cruce en arco; (gf) crucero; (el) cruce de conductores

— **joint**, tubería de combinación

cross-section, (gf) sección transversal

cross-spread, (gf) tendido cruzado (o en cruz)

crosstalk, interferencia

crossthreading, rosca cruzada, tuerca trasroscada

crotonic acid, ácido crotónico

crowbar, pie de cabra, alzaprima, barreta, palanca, (CH) chuzo

crown, *n.* cima, corona; copa; (g) frente de pliegue; (Ve) (derrick) cornisa; *v.* coronar; redondear

— **block**, (derrick) bloque de corona, travesero (o caballete) portapoleas, poleas de corona; (Ar) corona

— **block beam**, solera del caballete portapoleas

— **block bearing**, cojinete de poleas de corona

— **pulley**, (perc) polea de las herramientas; polea del cable de las herramientas; polea principal

— **sheave**, roldana de las poleas de corona

— **sheet**, (cl) cielo del hogar

— **valve**, (bm) válvula de corona (o de jaula)

crowning of pulley, *n.* gábilo de polea, curvatura de la cara de la polea

crow's nest, (prf) plataforma de corona, (Ar) plataforma de seguridad, (Me) nido del cuervo

crucible, crisol

Glossary of the Petroleum Industry

— **furnace**, horno de crisol
— **steel**, acero al (o de) crisol
— **tongs**, (la) tenacillas (o pinzas) para cápsulas
crude, *n.* petróleo crudo; *a.* crudo, bruto
— **assay**, evaluación del petróleo crudo
— **naphtha**, nafta cruda (o bruta)
— **oil**, petróleo crudo; aceite bruto
crude-oil pipeline, oleoducto para petróleo crudo
crumble, desmoronarse, desmenuzarse
crumbly, deleznable, desmoronadizo
crumple, arrugar
crumpling, (g) arrugamiento de un estrato entre dos estratos competentes (q.v. **crenulation**)
crushing face of the bit, cara triturante de la barrena, cara activa, superficie de trituración de la barrena
crushing strength, resistencia a la compresión
crust, costra, corteza, capa; corteza terrestre
cryogenic plant, planta criogénica
cryolite, criolita
cryptocrystalline, criptocristalino
crystalline, cristalino, claro, transparente
— **aggregate**, agregado cristalino
— **compound**, compuesto cristalino
— **dolomitic limestone**, caliza dolomítica cristalina
— **limestone**, caliza cristalina
— **rock**, roca cristalina
crystallizable, cristalizable
crystallization, cristalización
— **systems**, singonía cristalográfica
crystallize, cristalizar
crystalloblastic, (g) cristaloblástico
crystallography, cristalografía
crystographic, cristográfico

CSO, q.v. **complete shut off**
cube, *n.* cubo; *v.* cubicar; elevar al cubo
cubic, cúbico
— **centimeter**, centímetro cúbico
— **feet of gas**, pies cúbicos de gas
— **yard**, yarda cúbica
cuesta, (g) cuesta
cumulative, acumulado, cumulativo
— **production**, producción acumulada
cumene, cumeno (q.v. **isopropylbenzene**)
cumulites, cumulitos
cumulophyric, cumulofírico
cup, *n.* taza, copa, cubeta; (la) vaso, cubeta; (bm) empaquetadura para émbolo de bombeo; *a.* acopado, forma U
— **packer**, empacador de copa
— **spacer**, (bm) espaciador de empaquetaduras de émbolo buzo
— **valve**, válvula de copa (o de campana)
— **washer**, arandela acopada
— **weld**, soldadura de enchufe
curl, comba, curvatura, bucle, alabeo, ondulación
currency, moneda corriente (o acuñada)
current, corriente, (g) (Ar) correntada
— **account**, (cm) cuenta corriente
— **bedding**, estratificaciones cruzadas
— **density**, densidad eléctrica
— **drain**, (el) consumo
— **instruction register**, (dp) registro de instrucción en curso
— **tap**, (el) toma de corriente
— **transformer**, transformador de corriente (o de intensidad)
cursor, cursor
curvature, curvatura
curve, *n.* curva; *v.* curvar, encorvar

English - Spanish

— **for the stripped earth,** gráfica
para la tierra sin las capas
superiores
— **of flexure point,** curva de punto
de flexión
cushion chamber, cámara de
amortiguamiento
cusp, cúspide
cuspate, en forma de cúspide
customer, cliente
custom built, fabricado a la orden
(o a pedido, a medida)
customs, aduana
— **agent,** agente aduanal
— **clearance,** despacho de aduana
— **duties,** derechos de aduana
— **inspector,** aforador de aduana
CUT (coordinated universal time),
hora de Greenwich
cut, (la) porcentaje de agua y sólidos
en suspensión en el análisis de
petróleo; (rf) producto o
fracción derivada de petróleo;
corte; cortadura, incisión; *a.*
cortado
— **oil,** aceite emulsificado
cutaway view, corte transversal
cutback asphalt, asfalto diluido en
un destilado ralo (q.v. **asphalt
liquid bitumen**)
cutoff, nivel de corte (o de cierre),
fin, término
— **coupling,** unión de quitapón
— **frequency,** frecuencia crítica
— **line,** (tp) línea de acortamiento
(o de cierre provisional, de
comprobación)
cutoff valve, válvula de cierre
automático
cutter, cortadora, tajadora
— **bit,** fresa cortadora
— **dredge,** draga de succión con
cabezal cortador
— **head,** cabeza de barrena;
fresadora; portacuchilla

cutting, cortadura, corte, recorte,
tajadura; tala; cantería;
desmonte
— **machine,** máquina cortadora
— **oil,** aceite para corte (o para
fresar)
— **rate,** (prf) velocidad de
penetración de la barrena
— **torch,** soplete cortador (o para
corte)
cuttings, (prf) cortes, virutas,
cortaduras, (Ar) detrito
CWP (cold working pressure)
resistencia a la presión en frío
cycle, (mo) ciclo, tiempo; (el) ciclo,
período
— **condensate,** condensado de
reinyección
— **gas,** gas reinyectado
— **index polynomial,** polinomio de
índice de ciclo
— **of erosion,** ciclo de erosión
— **plant,** planta de recirculación
cycle-time efficiency, eficiencia del
tiempo consumido por un ciclo
cyclic, cíclico
— **hydrocarbon,** hidrocarburo
anular (q.v. **ring hydrocarbon)**
— **redundancy check,** prueba (o
código) de redundancia cíclica
— **series of hydrocarbons,** serie
cíclica de hidrocarburos
— **shift,** desplazamiento cíclico
cycling, (pr) reinyectar (q.v.
recycling)
cyclization, (rf) ciclotización
cyclo, *pref.* ciclo-
cyclo-olefins, hidrocarburos
cicloolefínicos
cyclohexane, ciclohexano,
hexametileno (q.v.
hexamethylene)
cyclohexene, ciclohexeno
cyclone, *n.* (mc) centrífuga; *a.*
centrífugo, ciclónico

62

— **separator,** (rf) separador
ciclónico (o centrífugo)
cycloparaffins, hidrocarburos
cicloparafínicos
cyclopentane, ciclopentano (q.v.
pentamethylene)
cyliner, cilindro
— **barrel,** cuerpo de cilindro
— **block,** bloque de cilindros
— **block assembly,** conjunto de
bloque de cilindros
— **bore,** diámetro interior del
cilindro
— **capacity**, cilindrada
— **head,** culata del cilindro
— **head gasket,** guarnición de
culata de cilindros
— **hone,** rectificador de cilindro
— **liner,** forro del cilindro, camisa
interior del cilindro
— **oil,** aceite para cilindros
— **sleeve,** manguito de cilindro
— **stock,** (rf) aceite para cilindros
— **stock solution,** solución de
aceite para cilindro
— **valve**, válvula cilíndrica
— **water jacket,** camisa de agua
cyprite, ciprita

D

d, q.v. **deci**
da, q.v. **deka**
DAC, q.v. **digital-to-analog
converter**
dacite, dacita
daily, diario, por día
daisychain, (dp) cadena tipo
margarita, conexión en batería
dam, *n.* (hd) represa, presa; (mn)
cerramiento; *v.* represar,
tranear, embalsar, (Es)
remansar
damage, avería, perjuicio, daño

damp, dampen, damping, *v.* (ma)
(gf) amortiguar; hacer menos
violentas las vibraciones (o
golpes); humedecer; humectar
damped period, período
amortiguado
dampener, amortiguador
damper, (mc) registro, regulador de
tiro, compuerta de tiro; (el)
(mo) amortiguador, desviador
silenciador
damping vane, aleta
amortiguadora
dangling sheave, roldana libre
Danian, daniense
darcy, darcy, medida de
permeabilidad
dart, *n.* dardo, saeta, flecha; *v.*
lanzar, tirar, flechar; lanzarse,
arrojarse
— **bailer,** achicador de dardo (o de
lanza)
— **valve,** válvula de dardo
dart-type BOP, preventor de
reventones tipo dardo
dashboard, guardafango; tablero de
instrumentos
DAT, q.v. **digital audio tape**
data, información; (dp) datos
— **adapter unit,** unidad adaptadora
de datos
— **capture**, captación (o captura,
obtención, recogida) de datos
— **compaction**, condensación de
datos
— **element,** elemento de datos
— **entry,** entrada (o introducción)
de datos
— **file,** fichero de datos
— **gathering,** centralización (o
recopilación) de datos
— **item,** unidad de información de
datos
— **link,** enlace (de transmisión) de
datos

English - Spanish

— **logging,** registro (secuencial) de datos,
— **management,** gestión de datos
— **network,** red informática
— **path,** camino (o bus) de datos
— **processing,** proceso de datos
— **reduction,** conversión (o reducción) de datos
— **retrieval,** recuperación
— **selector/multiplexer,** selector/multiplexor de datos
— **set,** conjunto de datos, fichero, archivo; convertidor de señal, modem
— **sheet,** cuadro de características, ficha técnica
— **transfer rate,** velocidad de transferencia de datos
data-driven design, diseño articulado en torno a la base de datos
databank, banco de datos
database, base de datos
dataflow, flujo (o circulación) de datos
datolite, datolita
datum, nivel de comparación; cero normal; base de operación; plano de referencia (o comparación)
— **horizon,** horizonte guía
— **level,** nivel (o plano) de referencia
— **plane,** plano de referencia (o de cota cero, de nivel)
— **point,** punto de referencia
davit, pescante
day shift, turno de día
DBMS, q.v. **database management system**
DCN (document control number), número de control del documento
DCR (document control register), registro de control del documento

dead, muerto; apagado; mate; falso, simulado; fijo
— **axle,** eje fijo (o muerto)
— **blow,** golpe seco
— **center,** (mo) punto muerto
— **load,** peso muerto
— **oil,** aceite de creosota, (Ar) petróleo sin gas, (Me) aceite muerto
— **point,** punto muerto
— **sheave,** polea muerta
— **tight,** hermético
— **weight,** peso muerto
— **weight ton (dwt),** toneladas muertas, toneladas de peso muerto
— **well,** pozo muerto
— **wood,** (tk) volumen muerto
— **wraps,** (ca) vueltas muertas
deadline, (prf) cable muerto, línea muerta; (cm) plazo (o fecha) límite
— **tie down anchor,** ancla del cable muerto
deadlock, (dp) bloqueo, impasse, interbloqueo, enlace fatal, abrazo mortal
deadman, macizo de anclaje, punto de atadura, anclaje, morillo, (Ar) taco de rienda, (Me) muerto
deaerator, desaereador
deasphalted oil, petróleo desasfaltado
deasphalting, desasfaltación
debit balance, (cm) saldo deudor (o al debe)
debouncing, eliminación de rebote
debris, escombros, despojos
debug, *n.* depuración; *v.* depurar; eliminar fallos
debugger, instrumento de depuración (o de puesta a punto)
debutanize, desbutanizar
debutanizer, desbutanizador, desbutanizadora

64

decadiene, decadieno
decadiyne, decadiino
decalin, decalina (q.v. biocyclodecane)
decane, (qm) decano
decanter, ampolla de decantación
decarbonizing, decarbonización
decay time, tiempo de extinción, intervalo de decadencia (de impulso)
decelerate, desacelerar
deceleration, aceleración negativa, desaceleración, deceleración
decene, deceno
deci (d), *pref.* SI = 10^{-1}
deck, (rf) placa, bandeja; (derrick) piso; (nt) cubierta
declination, declinación (q.v. meridian)
— **compass,** declinatorio, brújula de declinación
decline curve, curva de declinación
declivity, declive, pendiente, talud, inclinación
decoder, decodificador
decompose, descomponer
decomposition, descomposición
decompression, descompresión
— **chamber,** cámara de descompresión
decontaminants, descontaminantes
deconvolution, deconvolución
decrease, rebajar, reducir, disminuir
decrement, decremento
decylacetylene, decilacetileno (q.v. dodecyne)
decyne, decino
dedicated, dedicado, especializado, específico, exclusivo
— **mode,** (dp) modalidad dedicada (o especializada)
deep, *n.* abismo oceánico; *a.* profundo, hondo
— **focus earthquake,** terremoto de foco profundo

— **well pump** bomba de profundidad
deep-seated folds, (g) pliegues profundos
deep-seated salt dome, domo salino profundo, cúpula salina profunda
defect, defecto, imperfección
deflation, (g) denudación eólica
deflecting blades, aletas desviadoras
deflection, desviación, desvío, flexión, comba
— **of the vertical,** desviación de la vertical
— **point,** punto de desviación
deflector, desviador
deflocculation, defloculación
defoamer, antiespumante
deforestation, deforestación
deformation, deformación
— **without shearing,** transformación anaclástica
degasser, desgasificador, (Me) desgasador
— **tower,** torre desgasificadora
degradation, degradación, disminución; descenso
degrade, degradar, disminuir, rebajar
degree, grado
dehumidify, deshumedecer
dehydrate, deshidratar
dehydration, deshidratación
dehydrator, deshidratador; deshidratante
dehydrogenation, deshidrogenación
DEIS, q.v. **draft environmental impact statement**
deisobutanizer, desisobutanizador
— **tower,** torre desisobutanizadora
deka (da), *pref.* SI = 10^{1}
delay line, (dp) línea de retardo

delay differential equations, (dp)
ecuaciones diferenciales de
retardo
delayed, atrasado, retardado
— **branch,** (dp) bifurcación diferida
— **coking,** coquificación retardada
— **explosion,** explosión atrasada (o
retardada)
— **ignition,** encendido atrasado (o
retardado)
deletion, borrado, eliminación,
supresión
deliver, entregar, hacer entrega
delivery, reparto, entrega, de
reparto, de entrega, descarga,
conducto, salida
— **on field,** engrega en el campo
— **order,** orden de entrega
dell, (g) cañada
delta, *n.* delta; **deltaic,** *a.* deltaico
deluxe, de lujo
demagnetize, desimantar,
desmagnetizar
demagnetized, desimantado
demand, *n.* demanda; *v.* demandar,
exigir
— **side of process,** porción regulada
del proceso
demethanizer tower, torre
desmetanizadora
demonopolization,
desmantelamiento del
monopolio
demulsification, demulsificación
— **test,** prueba de emulsificación a
vapor (q.v. **SE number)**
demulsifier, desmulsificador
demulsify, desemulsionar
demultiplexer, desmultiplexador,
demultiplexor, demultiplexador
demultiplication,
desmultiplicación
dendritic, dendrítico
— **drainage,** drenaje dendrítico
densimeter, densímetro
density, densidad

— **contrast,** contraste de densidades
— **determination,** determinación
de la densidad
— **difference,** diferencia de
densidad
— **log,** registro de densidad
— **variation,** variación de densidad
dent, abolladura, mella
denudation, (g) remoción, (Ar)
lavaje (q.v. **washing)**
denuded oil, petróleo despojado de
fracciones livianas (q.v.
stripped oil)
deoiling, (rf) descaptación
deoxidized copper, cobre
desoxidado
departure, (tp) desviación, punto de
partida, partida, salida
depentanize, despentanizar
depentanizer, (rf) despentanizador
dephlegmator, desflemador
depletion, agotamiento, depleción
deploy, instalar; desplegar
depolarizing electrode, electrodo
despolarizante
deposit, depósito; yacimiento
deposition, *n.* (g) depósito,
acumulación; **depositional,** *a.*
depositado
— **environment,** ambiente de
depósito
depot, depósito, almacén, estación
depression, (g) hondonada,
depresión, hoya
depropanizer, despropanizador
depth, profundidad
— **penetration,** profundidad de
penetración
— **point,** punto de profundidad
derivative, (qm) derivado; (mt)
derivativo
derrick, torre de perforación,
cabria, faro; grúa
— **braces,** riostras de la torre
— **cornice,** cornisa de la torre
— **floor,** piso de la torre

Glossary of the Petroleum Industry

— **floor sills,** largueros (o soleras) del piso, durmientes

— **foundation,** cimientos de la torre

— **foundation posts,** pilotes de base de la torre

— **girts,** travesaños de la torre

— **guy-line anchor,** ancla de contraviento

— **ladder,** escalera de la torre

— **legs,** patas de la torre, (Me) pilares

— **man,** torrero, (Me) chango, farero, (Ve) encuellador

— **substructure,** subestructura de la torre

— **V front,** abertura en V del frente de la torre de perforación

desalters, desaladores

desalting plant, planta de desalación

desander, desarenador

descent, descenso, caída, bajada, pendiente, inclinación

desert, desierto

— **valley,** valle en el desierto

desiccant, desecante

desiccation, desecación

desiccator, desecadora; secador

design, diseño, dibujo, plano, proyecto

— **capacity,** capacidad calculada

— **factor,** (ca) factor de seguridad (q.v. **safety**)

— **pressure,** presión de diseño

— **water depth,** tirante de diseño

desilter, eliminador (o removedor) de lodo, (Me) deslimizador

desorption, deadsorción

desulfurization, (rf) desulfurización, endulzamiento

desuperheater, desrecalentador

detachable, desmontable

detail mapping, cartografía detallada

detector, detector, sensor, transductor (q.v. **geophone**)

determination, determinación

detonation, detonación, explosión

— **characteristic,** característica de detonación, número octano (q.v. **octane number**)

detonator, fulminante; detonador

detrital, detrítico

— **material,** material detrítico

detritus, detrito

deuteron, deuterón

development, desarrollo; fomento; producción; explotación

— **well,** pozo de desarrollo

deviation, desviación, desvío, deriva

— **survey,** medición de la desviación

device, dispositivo, aparato, mecanismo, ingenio, unidad

devil, terraja para roscar madera

Devonian, devoniano, devónico

dew point, punto de rocío

dewater, desecar, desaguar

dewax, desparafinar

dewaxed oil stripper, alambique para destilar la nafta del petróleo desparafinado

dewaxing, desparafinación

DHI, q.v. **direct hydrocarbon indications**

diabase, (g) diabasa

diacetylene, diacetileno (q.v. **butadiyne**)

diaclasse, (g) diaclasas

diaftoresis, (g) diaftoresis

diagenesis, diagénesis

diagonal fault, falla diagonal

diagram, diagrama, croquis

dial, cuadrante; esfera

— **unit,** unidad de cuadrante

dialkyl sulfate, sulfato de dialcohilo

diallylene, dialileno (q.v. **hexenyne**)

dialysis, diálisis

diamagnetic, (g) diamagnético

English - Spanish

diameter, diámetro
diamond, diamante
— drill, barrena con puntas de
diamante, barrena de diamantes
— point, punta rómbica (o de
diamante)
— point rotary bit, barrena con
punta de diamante
diaphragm, diafragma, membrana
— burner, quimedor de diafragma
— case, caja del diafragma
— control, control de diafragma
— control valve, válvula de
control, tipo de diafragma
— gage, indicador (o manómetro)
de diafragma
diaphragm-type blowout
preventer, impiderreventones
tipo de diafragma
diaschistic, diaesquistoso
diaspore, diásporo
diastem, diástema
diastrophism, diastrofismo
diatom, diatomea
diatomaceous earth, tierra
diatomácea, tierra de diatomeas,
diatomita, harina fósil
diatomaceous shale, lutita
diatomácea
diatomic, diatómico
diatomite, (g) diatomita (q.v.
diatomaceous earth, infusorial
earth)
dibenzyl, dibencilo
dibromopropyl alcohol, alcohol
dibromopropilo
dibutyldecane, dibutildecano
dibutylnonane, dibutilnonano
dibutyl phthalate, ftalato
dibutílico
dichroism, (g) dicroísmo
dicyclic, dicíclico
die, dado, matriz, cuño, troquel,
cojinete de terraja
— collar, collarín de dado, (Me)
tarraja

— nipple, niple de dado, (Me) niple
(o manguito) tarraja
— stock, terraja, portadado
dielectric constant, constante
dielétrica
dielectric strength, fuerza
dieléctrica (q.v. disruptive
strength)
diesel, diesel
— electric power, fuerza diesel-
eléctrica
— electric unit, grupo electrógeno
diesel
— engine, motor diesel
— engine oil, aceite para motores
diesel
— diesel fuel, diesel
— oil, aceite diesel
diethyl, pref. dietil-
— carbinol, dietil carbinol
diethylene glycol, glicol dietileno
difference in potential, diferencia
de potencial
differential, diferencial
— compaction, (g) consolidación,
compactación diferencial
— erosion, erosión diferencial
— fill-up collar, collarín (o cople)
diferencial de llenado
— gauge, manómetro diferencial
— normal moveout, (gf)
sobretiempo diferencial normal
por distancia
— pressure, presión diferencial
— weathering, (g) desgaste
diferencial
diffraction, difracción
diffuse, difundir
diffusion, difusión, propagación
dig, v. cavar, excavar, socavar
digital, (dp) digital
— audio tape, cinta magnética
digital de registro sonoro
— computer, ordenador digital
— differential analyzer,
analizador diferencial digital

68

— **filtering**, filtrado digital, filtro aritmético
— **signal processing**, proceso de señales digitales, elaboración de señales numéricas
— **sorting**, clasificación digital
digital-to-analog converter, convertidor de digital a analógico
diisoamyl, diisoamilo
diisobutyl, diisobutilo
diisopropyl, diisoproilo
dike, *n*. (g) dique, (Ar) filón; (hd) dique, caballón, atajo, (CH) pretil, (Me) barraje; *v*. endicar, atajar
— **rock**, roca filoniana
dilatational wave, onda de dilatación (q.v. **longitudinal wave**)
dilation, (g) dilatación
diluent, diluyente
— **gas**, (la) gas diluyente
dilution, dilución, desleimiento
— **and attenuation factor**, factor de atenuación y dilución
diluvial, (g) diluvial
diluvium, diluvión
dimension, dimensión
dimethyl, *pref*. dimetil-
— **mercury**, mercurio dimetilo
— **sulfate**, sulfato dimetilo
dimmer switch, conmutador reductor (o amortiguador) de luz
dimorphism, dimorfismo
di-n-butyl mercury, mercurio dibutílico normal
diode, diodo
diolefin, diolefina
— **hydrocarbons**, hidrocarburos diolefínicos
— **series**, serie diolefínica
diopside, diópsido
diorite, (g) diorita
— **quartz**, cuarzo diorítico

diozonide, biozónido
dip, *n*. (g) buzamiento, inclinación, caída, (Me) echado; (mn) recuesto; inmersión, baño; *v*. meter, sumergir; buzar, inclinarse; (paint) bañar
— **fault**, falla paralela a la inclinación, falla perpendicular (o transversal), (Ar) dislocación rumbeante
— **fold**, pliegue buzante
— **of the horizon**, (tp) depresión del horizonte
— **needle**, brújula de inclinación
— **pipe** tubo de inmersión
— **shooting**, tiro para determinar buzamientos, tiro de echados
— **slip**, desplazamiento vertical
— **slope**, pendiente estructural, pendiente del buzamiento
— **stick**, regleta
— **vector**, vector de inclinación (o del echado)
dip-slip fault, falla de buzamiento
dip-slip diagonal fault, falla diagonal de buzamiento
dip-slip dip fault, falla transversal de buzamiento
dip-slip strike fault, falla longitudinal de buzamiento
diphenyl, *pref*. difenil-
— **oxide**, óxido de difenilo
— **sulphone**, difenilsulfona
dipmeter, inclinómetro
dipole, bipolo, dipolo
dipole-dipole array, (gf) distribución (o arreglo) dipolo-dipolo
dipping, (g) buzante, inclinado
dipropyl, *pref*. dipropil-
direct, directo
— **acting pump**, bomba de acción directa
— **current**, (el) corriente continua
— **drive**, mando directo, propulsión directa

English - Spanish

— **driven rotary,** perforadora
rotatoria de propulsión directa
— **fired,** de fuego directo
— **hydrocarbon indications,**
indicaciones directas de
hidrocarburos
— **injection,** inyección directa
— **memory access,** (dp) acceso
directo a la memoria, acceso de
memoria directo
direct-coupled machines,
máquinas de acoplamiento
directo, máquinas en toma
directa
direct-fire air heater, calentador de
aire a fuego directo
direction, dirección, sentido;
instrucción
— **of rotation,** sentido de rotación
directional drilling, perforación
direccional, perforación de
desviación controlada
**directional drilling orientation
tool,** herramienta de
orientación direccional
directional survey, medición de la
desviación
dirt, tierra; viruta; suciedad
disable, (dp) neutralizar, desactivar,
inutilizar, poner fuera de
servicio
disc, disk, disco
— **and doughnut,** fraccionadora
con discos y roscas
— **bit,** barrena de discos
— **clutch,** embrague de disco
— **clutch facing,** revestimiento de
embrague de disco
— **valve,** válvula de disco
— **wheel,** rueda de disco
discard, descartar
discharge, (bm) descarga,
expulsión, derrame, desagüe,
escape, vaciamiento
— **end of pump,** extremo de
descarga de una bomba

— **monitoring report,** (ec) informe
del control de descargas
— **valve,** válvula de descarga (o de
escape)
discharger, disparador,
descargador, excitador
disconformity, discordancia
discoloration, descoloramiento
discoloring, descoloramiento
disconnect, v. desconectar, desunir,
desacoplar, desengranar,
desembragar
discontinuity, discontinuidad
discordance, n. discordancia;
discordant, a. discordante
discount rate, tasa de (o tipo de)
descuento
discovery, descubrimiento
— **well,** pozo descubridor
di-sec-butyl, dibutilo secundario
di-sec-butyl mercury, mercurio
dibutílico secundario
disengage, desembragar,
desengranar, desacoplar
dish, reborde de llanta, combadura
dish-bottom tank, tanque de fondo
cóncavo
disintegration, disgregación,
desintegración
disjoint, a. no consecutivo, disjunto
disjunction, disyunción, disjunción
disjuntor, disyuntor
disk drive, (dp) unidad de discos
diskette, (dp) disco flexible
dislocation, dislocación; falla
— **mountain,** montaña de
dislocación
dismantled, a. desarmado,
desmontado
dismount, v. desmontar, desarmar
dispersant, dispersante
dispersing agent, agente
dispersador
dispersion, dispersión

70

displacement, desplazamiento; desalojamiento; dislocación, cilindrada
— **fluid,** (cement) fluido de desplazamiento
— **meter,** contador (o medidor) de desplazamiento
— **plunger,** émbolo de bomba de desplazamiento, (Me) émbolo buzo de desplazamiento
— **pumping,** bombeo a base de desplazamiento (del fluido inyectando otro agente)
displacer, émbolo auxiliar de compresión
display, (dp) representación visual
— **tube,** tubo de rayos catódicos, pantalla de representación visual
disposal, disposición; (water) eliminación, desecho
— **well,** pozo de desechos
disruptive strength, fuerza dieléctrica (q.v. **dielectric strength**)
dissected peneplain, penilladura encañada
disseminated, diseminado
dissipate, disipar
dissociation, disociación
dissolve, disolver
dissolved gas drive, empuje por gas disuelto
dissolved oxygen, oxígeno disuelto
distance, distancia
— **curve,** curva dromocrómica, curva de tiempo y distancia
distillate, destilado, condensado
distillation, destilación
— **curve,** curva de destilación. (q.v. **true-boiling-point curve**)
— **of petroleum,** destilación de petróleo
— **plant,** planta de destilación
distilled water, agua destilada
distort, *v.* deformarse, retorcerse

distortion, deformación, distorsión
distributable, repartible
distributary, distributivo
distributive faults, fallas (o fracturas) escalonadas
distribution, distribución
— **law,** ley de distribución
— **line,** oleoducto distribuidor; manguera (o tubo) distribuidor
distributor, distribuidor
disturbance, (g) perturbación; (legal) disturbio
disturbed, (g) perturbado
— **area,** área transformada (o perturbada)
— **bed,** estrato perturbado
disulfide, bisulfuro
ditch, zanja, cuneta de desagüe, foso (q.v. **trench**)
ditcher, (ma) zanjadora (Ar) cuneteadora
diurnal, diurno, diario
— **change,** cambio diurno
— **variations,** (gf) variaciones diurnas
diver, buzo
— **assist,** con ayuda de buzos
— **lock-out submersible,** submarino de salida (o de acceso) de buzos
divergent, divergente
diverless reentry system, sistema de reentrada sin ayuda de buzos
divert, *v.* desviar, rodear; **diverter,** *n.* desviador
divide, (g) divisoria de aguas, (Me) parteaguas
dividers, compás de puntas secas
divider drum, separador del cable, guía separadora del cable
diving bell, campana de buceo
divinylacetylene, divinilacetileno
DO, q.v. **dissolved oxygen**
dock, muelle
dockyard, astillero
docosane, docosano

71

docosene, docoseno
doctor,
— plant, equipo para el
tratamiento doctor
— solution, solución doctor
— test, prueba doctor
doctor treating, tratamiento
doctor, tratamiento con óxido
de plomo (o con plumbito)
documents against acceptance,
documentos contra aceptación
documents against payment, pago
contra documentos
dodecadiene, dodecadieno
dodecadiyne, dodecadiino
dodecane, dodecano
dodecene, dodeceno
dodecylbenzene, dodecilbenceno
dodecyne, dodecino
dog, detenedor, trinquete (para
evitar que algo gire en dirección
contraria); fiador, pestillo, retén
— house, caseta
— leg, doblez pata de perro
dohexacontane, dohexacontano
dolina, (g) dolina (q.v. sink)
dollar ($), dólar: moneda de
Bahamas, Barbados, Belize,
Bermuda, Canadá, Islas
Caymán, Estados Unidos,
Guyana, Jamaica, Puerto Rico,
Trinidad y Tobago
dolly, carretilla de rodillo, carrito,
vagoneta, (Me) rol; (rr)
locomotora pequeña para
maniobras; (a) gato rodante;
(cn) sufridera, estampa,
cazoleta, doile, boterola;
aguantadora, contraestampa,
contrarremachador,
contraboterola
dolomia, dolomía (q.v. dolomite)
dolomite, dolomita, (Me) dolomía
dome, (g) cúpula, domo, (Ar)
tumor; bóveda, techo
— fold, pliegue abovedado

domestic demand, demanda del
comercio interior
domestic supply, abastecimiento de
la demanda interior
donkey engine, motor auxiliar
donkey pump, bomba auxiliar
doodlebug, (oc) geofísico de campo
dope, (tu) grasa para rosca; (ca)
suavizador; (expl) material
absorbente
— machine, (tu) máquina de
barnizar tubería
dopentacontane, dopentacontano
doping, acción de cubrir la tubería
con capa protectora de asfalto o
brea
DOT, q.v. directional orientation
tool
dot chart, carta de puntos
dot matrix printer, impresora por
puntos, impresora matricial de
puntos
dotetracontane, dotetracontano
dotriacontane, dotriacontano
double, doble
— beam torsion balance, balanza
de torsión de doble brazo
— bending, (rf) mezcla de
chorreaduras de condensados;
acción de mezclar chorreaduras
de condensados
— block and bleed system, sistema
de doble bloqueo y desfogue
— bonded hydrocarbon,
hidrocarburo de doble enlace
— case pump, bomba de caja doble
— drum, tambor doble
— drum service rig, perforadora de
servicio de dos tambores
— end heater, calentador con
calefacción a ambos extremos
— extra-strong pipe, tubería doble
extrafuerte
— gear reduction, reducción de
doble engranaje

— **jointing,** soldar tubería en secciones de dos juntas
— **pin tool joint,** unión de tubería vástago de doble conexión macho
— **pipe chiller,** enfriador de tubos doble
— **punch,** doble registro
— **reduction,** de reducción doble, de desmultiplicación doble
— **refraction,** refracción doble
— **row bearing,** cojinete de doble hilera
— **seat valve,** válvula de doble asiento
— **solvent extraction,** extracción por dos disolventes
double-acting, de doble efecto
— **brake,** freno de doble efecto
— **pump,** bomba de doble acción
— **pull,** fuerza en la barra de tiro, fuerza de tracción
double-strap hanger, colgador (o sujetador) de tubería de dos tirantes
double-width roller chain, cadena de rodillos de doble ancho
double-wing Christmas tree, árbol de conexiones de dos ramas
doughnut, anillo colgador
dovetail, *v.* ensamblar a cola de milano, empalmar
dowel, espiga, clavija, perno, media caña
— **screw,** espiga roscada, perno roscado
down, abajo
— **pipe,** tubo de bajada, (Ar) caño de descarga
— **structure,** estructura abajo
downdip, buzamiento abajo
— **apparent velocity,** velocidad aparente buzamiento abajo
downdraft, contratiro
— **carburator,** carburador de corriente descendente

— **convection section,** sección de convección de tiro hacia abajo
downhill, cuesta abajo
downhole, fondo del pozo; *a.* pozo abajo, de fondo
download, (dp) teleenvío, carga (o transmisión) por teleproceso, transferencia de un ordenador a otro
downspout, bajante, tubo (o caño) de bajada, (Ar) bajada pluvial
downstream, circuito posterior, corriente abajo, río abajo
downstructure, estructura abajo, hacia abajo
downthrown, (g) movido hacia abajo
— **block,** fosa tectónica (q.v. **fault trough, sunken block**)
downtime, tiempo muerto (o improductivo), período inactivo; tiempo de mantenimiento (o reparación); período de paralización
downward continuation, (gf) continuación descendente
draft, *n.* (mc) tiro, succión, aspiración, tiraje; (air) corriente; (nt) calado, cala; (cm) giro, letra de cambio, libranza; *v.* (design) dibujar
— **control,** control de tiro
— **damper,** registro (o regulador) de tiro
— **environmental impact statement,** declaración preliminar de impacto ambiental
— **hood,** pantalla (o cubierta) de tiro
— **recorder,** registrador de tiro
— **regulator,** regulador de tiro
— **stabilizer,** regulador de tiro
— **tube,** tubo de aspiración
drafting room, sala de dibujo (o de proyectos)

English - Spanish

draftsman, (oc) dibujante, delineante, delineador

drag, *n.* arrastre, traba, oposición, resistencia, retardo, fricción; (rd) rastra, narria; (nt) rastra, draga; *v.* arrastrar

— **anchor,** ancla flotante (o de capa) (q.v. **floating anchor**)

— **bit,** barrena de arrastre (o de fricción) (q.v. **fishtail bit**)

— **fold,** pliegue de arrastre, pliegue sobreescurrido

— **link,** barra de dirección

— **scraper,** trailla de arrastre

dragline, dragalina, excavadora de arrastre; cable de arrastre

drain, *n.* desagüe, desaguadero, (Me) drene; *v.* desaguar, purgar, drenar, escurrirse, sanear

— **cock,** grifo de drenaje

— **opening,** orificio de purga

— **plug,** tapón de purga (o de evacuación, de drenaje), purgador

— **spade,** pala lengua de buey

drainage, desagüe; drenaje; seneamiento

— **divide,** línea divisoria de aguas, divorcio de aguas

drainator, purgador, trampa de agua (q.v. **stream trap**)

drastic pyrolysis, pirólysis, pirólisis drástica

draught, tiro, aspiración; tracción (q.v. **draft, draw**)

draw, *n.* (tp) arroyo, quebrada; (mn) hundimiento; *v.* (bm) aspirar, chupar; (design) trazar, dibujar; (chimney) tirar; (ca) estirar; (nail) arrancar; (nt) calar; (magnet) atraer; (contr) redactar; (cheque) girar, librar

— **key,** chaveta de tracción

— **works,** (prf) malacate, (Ar) cuadro de maniobras, (Ve) la máquina

— **works drum brake,** freno del tambor del malacate

— **works drum socket,** receptáculo del tambor del malacate

drawbar, barra de tiro

— **horsepower,** caballos de fuerza en la barra de tiro

— **pin,** pasador de la barra de tiro

drawdown, (prf) abatimiento

— **potential,** producción potencial determinada por medición del nivel y la presión del fluido en una serie de intervalos en que se permite al pozo producir lentamente

drawee, girado

drawer, girador

drawing, dibujo

drawoff valve, válvula (o grifo) de desagüe

dredge, *n.* draga, *v.* dragar

dredging, dragado; acción de dragar

dress, (bit) afilar; acondicionar herramientas de perforación

dressing, revestimiento, preparación mecánica

— **tool,** herramienta alisadora

drift, *n.* desviación, falta de coincidencia (de orificios), movimiento lateral; (gf) (nt) deriva; (g) terreno de acarreo, material depositado por un glaciar, morena; (derrick) alcance; *v.* impeler, ir a la deriva, amontonarse (arena o nieve), (mn) perforar

— **angle,** ángulo de deriva

— **correction,** corección de deriva del gravímetro, corrección instrumental

— **indicator,** indicador de desviación

— **meter,** desviómetro

— **punch**, punzón mandril
— **recorder**, desviómetro registrador
— **sand,** (g) arena movediza (q.v. **quicksand)**
drill, *n.* barrena (q.v. **drill bit**); *v.* perforar, barrenar, taladrar
— **bit,** barrena, perforadora, (Ar) trépano, sonda, broca, (Ve) mecha
— **collar,** (prf) cuello de tubería vástago, cuello de perforación, (Ar) barra maestra, (Me) tubo lastrabarrena
— **collar sub**, substituto del tubo lastrabarrena
— **column**, sarta de perforación
— **cuttings,** viruta de perforación, ripio
— **ejector**, sacabarrena
— **extractor,** sacabarrena (Ar) arrancasondas
— **gage,** calibrador de barrenas
— **holder,** portabarrena
— **hole,** hoyo, agujero, perforación, (Pe) hueco, (Ve) taladro, hoyo
— **pipe,** tubería de perforación, tubería, (Ar) caños para vástago de perforación, barras de sondeo (o de perforación)
— **press,** prensa taladradora
— **sleeve,** boquilla para barrenas
— **stem,** tubería de perforación
— **stem test**, prueba de formación
— **string compensator,** compensador del movimiento de la sarta
drill-in a well, *v.* perforar la formación productiva de un yacimiento petrolífero
drill-out bit, barrena trituradora
drill-pipe
— **elevator,** elevador para tubería de perforación
— **float,** válvula flotadora para tubería de perforación

— **safety valve**, válvula de seguridad de la sarta de perforación
drill-pipe slips, cuñas
drill-stem formation tester, recogemuestras del contenido del estrato (o formación) (q.v. **rathole formation tester**)
drill-stem testing, examen de pruebas del contenido de la formación por medio de la tubería de perforación
drillable, perforable
— **alloy,** aleación perforable
— **casing,** tubería triturable de revestimiento
— **liner,** tubería triturable
drilled, perforado; horadado (cuando no es un pozo)
drilled-in anchor, ancla de pilotes hincados
driller, (oc) perforador
driller's log, informe (o registro) de perforación
drilling, perforación
— **barge,** gabarra de perforación
— **break,** incremento en la velocidad de penetración (al encontrar un estrato menos duro que el anterior)
— **cable,** cable de perforación
— **clamp,** abrazadera de perforación
— **clay,** arcilla para lodo de perforación
— **contract,** contrato de perforación
— **control,** control de la perforación
— **cycle,** ciclo de perforación
— **engine,** motor de perforación
— **equipment,** equipo de perforación
— **fluid desander,** desarenador del lodo (o del fluido) de perforación

— **head,** cabezal de perforación
— **jars,** percusores
— **line,** cable de perforación (o de la barrena)
— **line measurement,** profundidad medida por medio del cable
— **mud,** lodo de perforación
— **platform**, plataforma de perforación
— **rate,** velocidad de penetración
— **rig,** cabria de perforación (q. v. **derrick**)
— **spool,** carrete espaciador
— **unit,** equipo de perforación
— **weight indicator,** indicador del peso que empuja la barrena
drilling-in unit, equipo de terminación de pozos
drillship, buque de perforación
drillsite, localización, ubicación
drinking water standards, normas para el agua potable
drip, purgador, goteadero, escurridor
— **box,** caja colectora
— **oil,** aceite condensado
— **oiler,** aceitera de goteo
— **pocket,** colector de condensación
— **raiser,** tubo colector
— **well,** colector de condensación (q.v. **drip, drip pocket**)
drive, *n*. (ma) transmisión, propulsión, impulsión, accionamiento; *v*. impulsar, accionar, mover, impeler, actuar; (well) perforar; (pilon) hincar, clavar; (a) conducir, manejar, guiar
— **axle,** eje de mando
— **bushing,** buje de trasmisión
— **chain,** cadena de mando
— **clamp,** abrazadera de golpeo (o de martillo), abrazadera encajadora
— **gear,** engranaje de mando
— **head,** cabeza de golpeo

— **pinion,** piñón de mando
— **pipe**, primera tubería de revestimiento (q.v. **surface casing, conductor pipe**)
— **shaft,** eje de mando (o de transmisión), eje cardán (o propulsor, motriz, motor)
— **shaft bearing,** cojinete del eje de mando
— **sproket,** rueda dentada de mando, rueda motriz dentada
— **shoe,** zapata de hincar
drive-down socket, enchufe de empuje
driven, accionado, impulsado, movido, mandado, secundario
— **cone,** cono secundario
— **shaft,** árbol secundario, eje secundario (o loco)
driver, (dp) programa (o rutina) de gestión, conductor
driving, conducción, manejo; impulso, mando; acción de impulsar
— **cap,** casquillo de protección
— **chain,** cadena de mando (o de propulsión)
— **disc,** disco de mando
— **flange,** brida de mando
— **pinion,** piñón de mando
— **wheel,** rueda de mando
drop, *n*. gota; baja, caída, descenso; *v*. dejar caer; bajar, descender
— **center rim,** llanta de centro cóncavo, llanta acanalada
— **forging,** forjadura a martinete, pieza forjada a martinete
— **hammer,** martinete
— **point,** punto de goteo
— **press,** martinete
— **valve,** válvula de caída
dropped axle, eje acodado
drowned well, pozo ahogado
drum, (prf) tambor (q.v. **reel**)
— **brake,** freno del tambor
— **flanges,** bridas del tambor

— **line,** cable del tambor
— **shaft,** eje del tambor
drum-drive chain, cadena primaria
de transmisión del tambor
druse, (g) drusa
dry, seco
— **air,** aire seco
— **bed,** absorbente, adsorbente
— **chamber,** cámara seca
— **Christmas tree,** árbol de
navidad (en) seco
— **cleaning,** limpieza en seco
— **completion,** terminación en seco
— **disc clutch,** embraque de disco
seco
— **drilling,** perforación en seco
— **gas,** gas seco (o no asociado)
— **hole,** pozo seco (o improductivo)
— **ice,** hielo seco
— **natural gas,** gas natural seco
— **oil,** aceite deshidratado
— **oven,** horno de secar
— **point,** punto seco
— **run,** ejecución seca (o de
prueba), puesta a punto
— **sand,** arena seca
— **submersible,** submarino de
ambiente seco (o de una
atmósfera)
— **well,** pozo seco
dry-cell battery, batería de pilas
secas, batería (o pila) seca
dry-hole plug, tapón para pozo
improductivo
drydock, dique seco (o de carena)
DSDP (deep sea drilling project),
proyecto de perforación en
aguas profundas
DST q.v. **drill stem test**
dual, doble, gemelo
— **completion,** terminación de un
pozo a dos zonas, terminación
doble
— **completion packer,** obturador
para pozos a dos zonas
— **flash,** (el) "flasheo" doble

— **fuel engine,** motor para dos
combustibles
— **induction focused log,** registro
enfocado de doble inducción
(q.v. **induction survey**)
— **inlet manifold,** mútiple de doble
admisión
dual-purpose, *a.* de doble
aprovechamiento
dual-zone well, pozo que produce
de dos zonas simultáneamente
duck nest, receptáculo
duct, conducto, tubo, canal, ducto
ductile, dúctil, maleable
ductility, ductilidad, maleabilidad,
flexibilidad
dummy keyway, ranura falsa para
chaveta
dump, *n.* descarga; (dp) volcado,
copia (o vaciado) de memoria,
vaciado; *v.* descargar, volcar
— **bailer,** cuchara vertedora,
achicador vertedor, cubeta
— **cable,** cable de descarga
— **valve,** válvula de descarga
dune, duna
dunnite, dunita
duo servo, duoservo
— **brake,** freno duoservo
duplex, duplex, gemelo, doble
— **corrugated gasket,**
empaquetadura corrugada doble
— **pump,** bomba doble (o duplex),
bomba de doble efecto
dust, polvo
— **cap,** tapa (o taza, casco)
guardapolvo
— **seal,** sello guardapolvo
duster, pozo improductivo
dustproof, a prueba de polvo
dutchman, (tu) ragón, pedazo de
rosca macho atascado dentro de
una rosca hembra
duty, (ma) servicio, trabajo;
redimiento; (cm) derechos de

aduana; (hd) dotación, alema, coeficiente de riego

DWS, q.v. **drinking water standards**

dwt (deadweight tons), toneladas de peso muerto, toneladas muertas

dye, tinte, tintura

dynagraph, dinágrafo

dynamic, dinámico

— **balance**, equilibrio dinámico

— **gravimeter**, gravímetro dinámico

— **magnification**, amplificación dinámica

— **memory relocation**, (dp) reubicación dinámica de la memoria

— **metamorphism**, metamorfismo dinámico (o de dislocación)

— **positioning**, emplazamiento (o posicionamiento) dinámico

— **range**, (gf) rango dinámico

— **viscosity**, viscosidad dinámica

dynamic-static metamorphysm, metamorfismo dinámicoestático (o local)

dynamics, dinámica

dynamite, dinamita

— **cap**, fulminante de dinamita

dynamiting, dinamitación, torpedeamiento

dynamo, dínamo

dynamometer, dinamómetro

— **card**, carta dinamométrica

— **well survey**, estudio dinamométrico de un pozo

dynamometrical brake, freno dinamométrico

dyne, dina

E

E, q.v. **exa**

EA, q.v. **environmental assessment, environmental auditing**

ear, mango, asa, oreja, orejera, espiga

early spark, chispa avanzada, avance del encendido

early strength, resistencia temprana

earphone, auricular, audífono

earth, tierra; globo terrestre; (el) tierra, masa

— **body**, macizo (o bloque) continental, cuerpo terrestre

— **currents**, (gf) corrientes terrestres (o naturales)

— **dam**, presa (o dique) de tierra, presa de terraplén, (CH) tanque de tierra, (Me) cortina de tierra

— **density**, densidad de la tierra

— **discontinuity**, (g) superficie de discontinuidad de la tierra

— **fall**, hundimiento de tierra

— **fill**, terraplen, relleno, (Ur) erraplenado

— **flax**, amianto, asbesto

— **inductor**, inductor terrestre

— **magnetism**, magnetismo terrestre

— **moving**, movimiento (o traslado, remoción) de tierra

— **observing satellites (EOS)**, satélites de observación terrestre

— **oil**, petróleo

— **pitch**, brea mineral

— **tilt**, inclinación de grandes bloques de tierra

earth-inductor compass, brújula de inducción

earthen pit, foso de tierra

earthen reservoir, represa de tierra

earthen sump, represa de tierra

earthquake, terremoto, temblor de tierra, sismo

— **seismograph,** sismógrafo para terremoto (q.v. **long-period earthquake seismograph**)
— **wave,** onda sísmica
ease, adelgazar los bordes, desahogar, aflojar
east, *n.* este; *a.* del este, oriental; *adv.* al este
— **by north,** este cuarta al nordeste (E 1/4 al NE)
— **by south,** este cuarta al sudeste (E 1/4 al SE)
— **northeast,** este nordeste (E N E); lesnordeste
— **of north,** este del norte (E del N)
— **southeast,** essudeste (E S E)
easy fit, ajuste libre
ebb, *v.* menguar, decrecer, refluir
— **tide,** marea menguante, reflujo, bajamar
ebb-and-flow structure, estratificación resultante del flujo y reflujo
ebonite, ebonita
ebullioscope, ebullioscopio
ebullioscopy, ebullioscopía
eccentric, *n.* excéntrica; *a.* excéntrico
— **bit,** barrena excéntrica
— **key,** cuña para excéntrica
— **load,** carga excéntrica
— **releasing overshot,** enchufe excéntrico de pesca, pescasondas de enchufe
— **rod,** varilla de la excéntrica
— **strap,** abrazadera (o anillo) de la excéntrica
— **trapered reducer,** reductor cónico excéntrico
— **wear,** desgaste excéntrico
eccentric-piston rotary pump, bomba rotativa de pistón excéntrico
eccentricity, excentricidad
echelon, q.v. **en echelon**
echo, eco

— **sounding,** (gf) sondeo acústico
— **suppression,** supresión del eco
echometer, ecómetro
echosounder, ecosonda, ecosondador
eclimeter, eclímetro
ecolgite, eclogita
ecology, ecología
economic geology, geología económica
economizer, economizador
EDA, q.v. **extensive dilatancy anisotropy**
edafology, edafología
EDC, q.v. **error detection and correction**
eddy, remolino, torbellino; contracorriente, contraflujo
— **currents,** corrientes parásitas, corrientes de Foucaula, corrientes turbulentas
— **loss,** (hd) pérdida por remolino; (el) pérdida por corrientes parásitas
edge, *n.* canto, borde, reborde; arista; orilla, margen; (tl) filo; *a.* de borde, de canto, lateral, marginal
— **cam,** leva de disco
— **joint,** junta de canto
— **water,** agua marginal (o suyacente), agua de fondo
— **weld,** soldadura de cantos
— **well,** pozo marginal
edger, canteador, canteadora
edge water, agua marginal
edge well, pozo exterior
edgewise conglomerate, (g) conglomerado de canto; conglomerado de filo
EDI, q.v. **electronic data interchange**
edit, (dp) editar, revisar, compaginar; seleccionar por no igualdad
eduction, educción, descarga

— **pipe,** tubo de descarga
— **tube,** tubo de escape (o de
   expulsión)
eductor, eyector, eductor
**EDVAC (electronic discrete
   variable automatic computer),**
   ordenador automático
   electrónico de variables
   discretas
effect, efecto
effective, efectivo
— **address,** (dp) dirección real (o
   efectiva), dirección modificada
   (o calculada)
— **head,** presión hidrostática
   efectiva; (hd) carga (o caída)
   efectiva, salto neto
— **horsepower,** energía neta en
   caballos
— **language,** (dp) lenguaje de
   ejecución
— **output,** (mc) potencia efectiva;
   producción neta
— **porosity,** porosidad efectiva
— **pressure,** presión real o efectiva
— **size,** tamaño efectivo (o real),
   diámetro eficaz
— **volts,** voltaje efectivo, tensión
   virtual
efficiency, eficacia, eficiencia;
   rendimiento; (cm) economía
— **curve,** curva de rendimiento
efflorescence, eflorescencia
effluent, efluente
effusion, efusión
— **bottle,** botella de efusión (o de
   efluvio)
effussive period, (g) período efusivo
   (o de efusión)
EFTS, q.v. **electronic funds
   transfer system**
eggshelling, *n.* (tu) deformación,
   aplastamiento; *v.* deformar,
   aplastar
eicosadiene, eicosadieno
eicosadiyne, eicosadiino

eicosane, eicosano
eicosene, eicoseno
eicosyne, eicosino
eigenfunction, función propia
eigenvalue valor propio
EIS, q.v. **environmental impact
   statement**
ejector, eyector; eductor
— **condenser,** condensador a
   chorro
— **pump,** bomba a chorro
— **tailgate,** mandril trasero
   expulsor
eking, empalme, zapata, talón
elapsed time, tiempo transcurrido,
   intervalo real
elastic, elástico
— **coefficient,** coeficiente elástico
— **constant,** constante elástica
— **deformation,** deformación
   elástica
— **discontinuities,** (gf)
   descontinuidades elásticas
— **flow,** fluencia elástica
— **impulse,** impulso elástico
— **limit,** (gf) límite elástico (o de
   elasticidad)
— **modulus,** módulus de elasticidad
— **rebound,** (gf) rebote elástico,
   reacción elástica
— **resilience,** elasticidad, rebote
   elástico
— **strength,** resistencia elástica
— **waves,** (gf) ondas elásticas (o
   sísmicas)
elasticity, elasticidad
elastomer, elastómero
elaterite, elaterita
elbow, (tub) codo, ele, codillo,
   ángulo
— **pipe,** tubo acodado
— **connector,** conector angular (o
   ele)
electric, eléctrico
— **arc welding,** soldadura eléctrica
   al arco

Glossary of the Petroleum Industry

- **blaster,** explosor eléctrico
- **blasting cap,** fulminante eléctrico
- **blow-pipe,** soplete eléctrico
- **brazing,** soldadura fuerte eléctrica
- **buzzer,** zumbador eléctrico, (Ur) chicharra eléctrica
- **cable,** cable eléctrico
- **canned motor,** motor eléctrico envasado (o en armazón)
- **circuit,** circuito eléctrico
- **circuit breaker,** interruptor automático, desconectador
- **column,** pila voltáica
- **condenser,** condensador eléctrico
- **conductivity,** conductividad
- **conduit,** conducto portacables, tubo conducto
- **current,** corriente eléctrica
- **dehydration,** deshidratación eléctrica
- **dehydrator,** deshidratador eléctrico
- **deslating,** desalación eléctrica
- **desander,** desarenador eléctrico
- **drill,** taladro eléctrico
- **drive,** impulso eléctrico, accionamiento eléctrico
- **fan,** ventilador eléctrico
- **field,** campo eléctrico
- **furnace,** horno eléctrico
- **fuse,** fusible eléctrico, cortacircuito
- **generator,** generador de energía eléctrica
- **horsepower,** caballo de fuerza eléctrica (746 vatios)
- **induction,** inducción eléctrica, densidad de flujo dieléctrico
- **insulator,** aislador
- **latern,** linterna eléctrica
- **light plant,** planta eléctrica, planta de energía eléctrica, (Ar) usina
- **log,** perfil eléctrico, registro electrográfico
- **logging,** perfilaje eléctrico, estudio por registros eléctricos
- **meter,** contador eléctrico, medidor
- **moment,** par eléctrico
- **motor,** motor eléctrico
- **power,** potencia eléctrica
- **precipitator,** precipitador eléctrico
- **prospecting,** prospección eléctrica
- **pump,** bomba eléctrica
- **relay,** relevador, relai
- **resistance,** resistencia eléctrica
- **resistance thermometer,** termómetro a resistencia eléctrica
- **resistivity,** resistividad eléctrica
- **rig,** equipo de perforación eléctrico
- **seismograph,** sismógrafo eléctrico
- **sounding,** (gf) sondeo eléctrico
- **steel,** acero de horno eléctrico
- **submersible pump,** bomba eléctrica sumergible
- **survey,** levantamiento con método eléctrico, perfilaje (o registro) eléctrico
- **switch,** interruptor, cortacircuito, commutador, (Co) suiche
- **tape,** cinta aisladora
- **transformer,** transformador eléctrico
- **varnish,** barniz aislador
- **wave,** onda eléctrica (o hertziana)
- **welder,** soldador eléctrico
- **welding,** soldadura eléctrica
- **well survey,** perfilaje eléctrico, registro electrográfico de un pozo
- **wire,** alambre eléctrico

— **wiring conduit,** tubo aislante para alambres eléctricos

electrical, q.v. **electric**

electrician, (oc) electricista

electricity, electricidad

electrochemical, electroquímico

— **phenomena,** fenómenos electroquímicos

— **properties,** propiedades electroquímicas

electrochemistry, electroquímica

electrode, electrodo

— **basis,** base del electrodo

— **clamps,** grampas del electrodo

— **distribution,** distribución de electrodos

— **holder,** portaelectrodo

— **point,** (sd) boquilla (o casquillo) del electrodo

— **polarization,** polarización electródica

— **resistance,** resistencia electródica

— **spacing,** espaciamento de electrodos

— **tip,** (sd) boquilla (o casquillo) del electrodo

electrodynamics, electrodinámica

electrofiltration, (gf) electrofiltración

— **potential,** potencial de electrofiltración

electrogalvanic, electrogalvánico

electroluminescent, electroluminiscente

electrolysis, electrólisis

electrolyte, electrólito

electrolytic, electrolítico

— **conduction,** conducción electrolítica

— **current conduction,** conducción de corriente electrolítica

— **phenomena,** fenómenos electrolíticos

electromagnet, electroimán

electromagnetic, electromagnético

— **damping,** amortiguamiento electromagnético

— **field,** campo electromagnético

— **interference,** interferencia electromagnética

— **seismograph,** sismógrafo electromagnético

— **stress,** tensión elecromagnética, esfuerzo electromagnético

— **wave,** onda electromagnética (o eléctrica, hertziana)

electromagnetics, n. (gf) electromagnetometría

electromagnetically dampened detectors, detectores de amortiguamiento electromagnético

electrometallurgy, n. electrometalurgia

electrometer, electrómetro

electromotive force, fuerza electromotriz

electron, electrón

— **drift,** flujo de electrones

— **logging,** perfilaje electrónico, registro electrónico

electron-coupled oscillator, oscilador de acoplamiento electrónico

electronegative, electronegativo

electronic, electrónico

— **conduction,** conducción electrónica

— **data interchange,** (dp) intercambio electrónico de datos

— **filing,** (dp) archivo (o archivamiento) electrónico, clasificación electrónica

— **funds transfer system (EFTS),** sistema electrónico de transferencia de fondos

— **numerical integrator and calculator,** calculador e integrador numérico electrónico

— **surveying,** levantamiento electrónico

electronics, *n.* electrónica, técnica electrónica
electroosmosis, electroósmosis
electrophone, electrófono
electropositive, electropositivo
electrophrometer, electropirómetro
electroscope, electroscopio
electroscopic, electroscópico
electrostatic, electroestático, electrostático
— **capacity,** capacidad electrostática, permitancia
— **coupling,** acoplamiento electrostático (o capacitivo)
— **disturbance,** disturbio electrostático
— **field,** campo electrostático
— **precipitator,** precipitador electrostático
— **stress,** tensión electroestática
— **treater,** tratador electrostático (q.v. **emulsion treating**)
electrotechnical, electrotécnico
electrothermometer, termómetro eléctrico
element, (qm) (el) (mt) elemento
elemental particle, (gf) partícula elemental
elemental sulfur, azufre puro (o elemental)
elevated tank, tanque elevado
elevating grader, niveladora-elevadora, motonivelador
elevation, (tp) elevación, cota; alzamiento, altura, altitud
— **angle,** ángulo de elevación
— **correction,** (gravim) correción de alturas
— **curve,** curva de altura, curva de elevación
— **head,** (hd) carga de altura, desnivel
elevator, elevador; montacargas
— **bails,** (prf) asas del elevador
— **links,** (prf) eslabones de elevador

— **plug,** tapón de elevadores
ell, ele, unión en forma de L , codo
— **swivel,** codo articulado, ele articulada
ellipse, elipse
— **area,** (tellur) área elíptica
ellipsoid, elipsoide
ellipsoidal, elipsoidal
elliptic, elíptico, de forma elíptica
— **body,** cuerpo elíptico
— **polarization,** polarización elíptica
elliptical, elíptico
elongation, elongación, alargamiento, prolongación
ELSBM, q.v. **exposed location single-buoy mooring**
elutriation, elutriación; lavado por decantación, (Ar) levigación
— **apparatus,** levigador
eluvial, (g) eluvial
eluvium, eluvión
emanation, emanación
— **chamber,** cámara de emanación
emanometer, emanómetro
embankment, terraplén, (Ec) embanque
embay, *v.* (r) (nt) ensenarse, aconcharse; **embayment,** *n.* ensenada, (Ar) embalse
embedded, empotrado, embutido, encastrado, incrustado
— **computer,** ordenador especializado integrado en un equipo
emblem, emblema, símbolo
embolite, embolita
embolus, émbolo
emboss, grabar, estampar en relieve, almohadillar
embrittlement, friabilidad, fragilidad, (Es) aquebradización
embryonic volcano, volcán en embrión
emerald, esmeralda

emerge, brotar, aflorar; emerger;
(groundwater) alumbrar
emergence, emergencia, (g)
levantamiento
— angle, ángulo de (o de
emergencia) salida
emergency, emergencia
— brake, freno de mano(o de
emergencia)
— drill pipe hang off tool,
colgador de tubería para
emergencias
— fuel tank, depósito auxiliar de
combustible
— gate valve, válvula esclusa de
emergencia
— kit, botiquín de primera cura
— lock, esclusa de emergencia
— pipe clamp, grapa tapafugas
para tubería
— spillway, aliviadero de seguridad,
descagadora
— stop valve, válvula de cierre para
emergencia
emery, esmeril
— cloth, tela esmeril
— grinder, esmeriladora
— paper, papel esmeril, papel de
lija
— stone, piedra esmeril
— wheel, rueda (o piedra) esmeril,
esmeriladora
EM, q.v. electromagnetic,
electromagnetics
EMI, q.v. electromagnetic
interference
emission standard, (ec) norma de
emisión
empirical formula, fórmula
empírica
empyreumatic oil, aceite
empireumático
emulsification test, prueba de
emulsionamiento
emulsified, emulsionada

— asphalt, asfalto emulsionado,
emulsión asfáltica
— medium breaking asphalt,
emulsión asfáltica de rotura
media
— quick breaking asphalt,
emulsión asfáltica de rotura
rápida
— slow breaking asphalt, emulsión
asfáltica de rotura lenta
— water, agua emulsionada
emulsifier, emulsionador, emulsivo
emulsify, emulsificar
emulsifying agent, dispersante
emulsion, emulsión
— breaker, desemulsificador
— test, ensayo (o prueba) de
emulsión
— treating plant, planta de
tratamiento de emulsiones
— wax deoiling process, proceso
para extraer aceite de parafina
emulsionándola con agua
emulsive, emulsivo
en echelon, en escalón
— faults, fallas escalonadas, fallas
al tresbolillo, fallas en filas
paralelas cruzadas en diagonal
(q.v. staggered faults)
— folds, pliegues escalonados
enable, activar, habilitar, poner en
servicio, facultar; capacitar,
validar
— pulse, impulso de activación (o
habilitación)
enamel, esmalte
— paint, pintura esmalte
enargite, enargita
encase, encajar, embutir, encajonar;
encerrar
enclosed, cubierto, encerrado,
blindado; adjunto
enclosure, cercamiento; recinto;
cercado; (cm) contenido,
inclusión

encode, *v.* codificar; **encoder,** *n.*
codificador (q.v. **code**)

encroachment, (g) intrusión, (Me)
invasión

encumbrance, (cm) gravamen

end, extremo; fin; (rf) fracción
final, (Ar) corte final

— **fraction,** corte final, fracción
final

— **cleat,** (mn) plano secundario de
clivaje

— **clevis,** eslabón grillete

— **dump,** volquete al extremo,
vaciado (o descarga) por el
extremo

— **joint,** (g) diaclasa transversal
(q.v. **dip point**)

— **measuring rods,** calibre normal,
(o esférico)

— **plate,** placa de extremo

— **play,** juego longitudinal

— **point,** (rf) temperatura límite (o
final) de destilación, (Ar) punto
seco

— **point gasoline,** gasolina de
destilación de punto seco

— **thrust,** empuje longitudinal

— **wrench,** llave de boca

end-around carry, (dp) acarreo (o
arrastre) circular, arrastre a la
posición extremo derecha,
acarreo en bucle

end-around shift, desplazamiento
(o permutación) circular

Endangered Species Act, Decreto
de Especies en Peligro de
Extinción

endless, *a.* sin fin, continuo

— **belt,** correa sin fin

— **chain,** cadena sin fin

— **flat belt,** correa plana sin fin

— **line,** cable sin fin

— **screw,** tornillo sin fin

endogenetic, endogenous, (g)
endógeno, endogenético

endomorphic, *a.* endomórfico;
endomorphism, *n.* endomorfismo

endorse, (cm) (cheque) endosar;
endorsement, endoso, (Ar)
endorso; (insur) aditamento que
modifica la póliza básica

endothermic, endotérmico

ends, productos livianos de petróleo,
fracciones livianas de primera
destilación cortes finales, (o
cortes terminados) (q. v. **cuts**)

endurance, resistencia, aguante,
duración

— **limit,** límite de resistencia

energize, (el) excitar; energizar,
acelerar

energy, energía, fuerza, potencia

— **balance,** balance de energía

engage, *v.* engranar, enganchar,
endentar, acoplar, embragar;
engagement, *n.* engrane, acople

engaging scarf, muesca de engrane

engine, motor; máquina

— **arrester,** chispero, sombrerete,
arrestallamas, (Ar) trampa de
llamas (q.v. **flame arrester**)

— **base,** base (o zócalo) de motor

— **block,** bloque del motor

— **cooling unit,** enfriador del
motor

— **distillate,** destilado para motores

— **driven compressor,** compresor a
motor

— **failure,** falla de la máquina

— **generator set,** conjunto de
motor y generador, equipo
motogenerador

— **house,** casa de máquinas

— **lathe,** torno mecánico (o
corriente)

— **mud sill,** vigas de asiento del
motor

— **muffler,** silenciador del motor

— **oil,** aceite de motor, aceite para
máquinas

English - Spanish

— **pony sills,** largueros de asiento
del motor
— **room,** sala de máquinas
— **setting,** montura del motor
— **speed governor,** regulador de
velocidad del motor
— **supports,** apoyos del motor
— **upper cylinder lubricator,**
lubricador del cilindro superior
del motor
engine-driven, a motor, impulsado
a motor
engineer, (oc) ingeniero;
maquinista
engineering, n. ingeniería
englacial, frente a un glacial
Engler distillation test, prueba
para determinar la volatilidad
de una gasolina
enhanced oil recovery (EOR),
recuperación mejorada (q.v.
**primary, secondary, tertiary
recovery**)
ENIAC, q.v. **electronic numerical
integrator and calculator**
enlargement, agrandamiento,
ensachamiento; expansión;
ampliación, aumento
enriching, v. enriquecer, aumentar
el calor de un gas
enstatite, enstatita
enthalpy, entalpía
entity, entidad, ente
**entity-relationship attribute
model,** modelo de entidades-
relaciones-atributos
entrained air, aire arrastrado
entrainment, (qm) (hd) arrastre
entrance head, (hd) carga de
entrada
entrapment, (g) entrampamiento
entropy, entropía
environment, cercanías; (ec) medio
ambiente
environmental, a. ambiental

— **assessment,** evaluación
ambiental
— **audit,** revisión (o intervención)
ambiental, (Me) auditación
ambiental
— **impact statement,** declaración
sobre el impacto ambiental
— **impairment liability,**
responsabilidad de perjuicio (o
daño) ambiental
— **priority implementation,**
implantación prioritaria
ambiental
— **protection,** protección al
ambiente
— **quality index,** índice de calidad
ambiental
— **sample,** muestra ambiental
— **study,** estudio de impacto
ambiental
environmentalist, ambientalista
Eocene, eoceno
eolian, eólico, eolio
— **deposits,** depósitos eólicos (o
eolios)
— **sediments,** sedimentos eólicos (o
anemógenos)
eon, (g) eón (q.v. **Phanerozoic,
Proterozoic, Archean**)
EOR, q.v. **enhanced oil recovery**
EOS, q.v. **earth observing
satellites**
Eötvös torsion balance, balanza de
torsión de Eötvös
Eötvös unit, unidad Eötvös: unidad
de gradiente gravimétrica 1 x
10^9 dinas/cm.
Eozoic, eozoico
epeirogeny, (g) epirogenia
epianticlinal fault, falla
epianticlinal, falla superpuesta a
un anticlinal
epicenter bearing, azimut del
epicentro
epicentral distance, distancia
epicentral

epicontinental sea, mar epicontinental
epidote, epidota
epigenetic, (g) epigenético
epirocks, (g) epirocas, epizona
epirogenetic movement, (g) movimiento epirogenético
epithermal neutron log, registro de neutrones epitérmicos
epoch, (g) época (q.v. **series,** e.g. **Pliocene**)
EPROM (erasable programmable read-only memory), memoria de sólo lectura programable borrable
equalizer arm, barra igualadora (o equilibradora)
equalizing gear, engranaje compensador
equalizing spring, muelle idualador, (Ar) elástico igualador; engranaje compensador
equation, ecuación
equatorial radius, radio ecuatorial
equilateral triangle, triángulo equilátero
equilibrium, equilibrio
— **condensation,** condensación equilibrada, condensación en equilibro
— **constant,** factor constante de equilibrio
— **contacting method,** método de contacto en equilibrio
— **curve,** curva de equilibrio termodinámico
— **flash vaporization,** vaporización en el instante de equilibrio
equipment, equipo
— **blanks,** (qm) (ec) blancos de equipo
equipoise, equilibrio; contrapeso
equipotential surface, superficie equipotencial, superficie de nivel

equispaced contouring, curvas de nivel equidistantes
equivalent direct radiation, equivalente directo de radiación
equivalent method, (ec) método equivalente
era, (g) era (e.g. **Cenozoic**)
ERA model, q.v. **entity-relationship attribute model**
erase, borrar
erg, ergio
Erlenmeyer narrow mouth flask, matraz Erlenmeyer de boca angosta
erosible, (g) degradable, gastable, deslavable
erosion, erosión, desgaste, derrubio, deslave, degradación; corrosión
— **cycle,** ciclo de erosión
— **drilling,** perforación erosiva
eroded, desgastado
erratic, errático
error
— **analysis,** análisis de errores
— **burst,** (dp) ráfaga (o avalancha) de errores
— **detection and correction,** detección y corrección de errores
— **of closure,** error de cierre (q.v. **misclosure**)
— **of the chronometer,** (nt) estado absoluto
errors excepted (EE), salvo error u omisión
eruption, erupción
eruptive, eruptivo, volcánico
erythrite, (mn) eritrina, flores de cobalto
escarpment, escarpa, escarpe
esker, cresta fluvioglacial
essential oil, aceite esencial (q.v. **volatile oil**)
essexite, esexita
established base, base establecida

estatizing force, fuerza de
estatización, sensibilización
ester, ester
esterellite, esterelita
estimated profits, (cm) utilidades
probables
estimated ultimate recovery, (pr)
producción total estimada
estuarine, *a.* estuarino,
fluviomarino
— **deposit,** tierra de aluvión,
depósito estuarino
— **flat,** planicie estuarina
estuary, estuario
ethane, etano; dimetilo
ethanol, etanol; alcohol etílico
ethene, eteno, etileno (q.v.
ethylene)
ether, éter
ethyl, etilo; *pref.* etil-
— **acetate,** etanoato de etilo; éter
acético
— **alcohol,** alcohol etílico (q.v.
ethanol)
— **benzene,** etilbenceno (q.v.
phenylmethane)
— **chloracetate,** etilo cloroacetato
ethylene, etileno, eteno (q.v.
ethene)
— **dichloride,** bicloruro de etileno
— **glycol,** etilenglicol
— **hydrocarbons,** hidrocarburos de
etileno
ethyne, etino (q.v. **acetylene**)
eudiometer, eudiómetro
EUE, q.v. **external upset ends**
EUR, q.v. **estimated ultimate
recovery**
eustatic cycle, (g) ciclo eustático
eutectic, *a.* eutéctico
evacuate, evacuar, vaciar
evacuation, evacuación
evaluate, avaluar, valorar
evaluation, evaluación
evaporable, evaporable
evaporate, evaporarse; evaporar

evaporation, evaporación
— **gage,** medidor de evaporación
— **loss,** pérdida (o merma) por
evaporación
— **test,** prueba de evaporación
evaporative cooling, enfriamiento
por evaporación
evaporator, evaporador
— **tower,** torre evaporadora
evaporite, evaporita
evaporimeter, evaporímetro,
atmómetro
even, *a.* par, llano, liso, del mismo
nivel; *v.* enrasar, nivelar, igualar,
emparejar
— **parity check,** (dp) verificación
(o control) de paridad par
— **step transmission,** transmisión
sin multiplicación
event, suceso, evento,
acontecimiento
everdur, metal everdur, aleación
con base de cobre
everglades, pantano
exa (E), *pref.* SI = 10^{18}
examination, examen, inspección
excavate, excavar, cavar, zapar,
(Me) vaciar
excavator, excavadora, zapadora
excess, exceso
— **profit,** exceso de utilidades,
excedente de granancias
— **pressure,** sobrepresión
— **weight,** sobrepeso
exchange, *n.* (cm) cambio;
intercambio; *v.* cambiar,
intercambiar
— **ions,** iones intercambiables
exchanger, (qm) (mc)
intercambiador
— **type steam generator,**
generador de vapor de tipo
intercambiador
excitator, excitador
exciter, excitador, excitatriz
excoriate, excoriar

excoriation, excoriación
excrescence, excrecencia
exemption, exención
exfoliate, *v.* (g) exfoliarse;
    exfoliation, *n.* exfoliación
exhalation, exhalación, emanación
exhale, exhalar, emitir vapores
exhaust, *n.* tubo de escape; *v.*
    descargar, vaciar
— **arrester,** silenciador de motor
— **curve,** curva de escape
— **chamber,** cámara de escape
— **draft,** tiro de aspiración (o de
    extracción)
— **fan,** ventilador aspirador (o
    extractor)
— **feed heater,** calentador de la
    carga con gas (o con vapor de
    escape)
— **gases,** gases del escape
— **heat,** calor de proceso (o
    compresión, expansión)
— **lead,** avance del escape
— **line,** tubo (o caño) de escape
— **manifold,** múltiple de escape
— **pipe,** tubo (o caño) de escape
— **port,** orificio de escape; tubo de
    escape
— **relief valve,** válvula de escape
— **silencer,** silenciador de la
    válvula de escape
— **steam,** vapor de escape (o
    agotado)
— **stroke,** carrera de escape
— **valve,** válvula de escape (o de
    descarga)
exhauster, aspirador; ventilador
    eductor, agotador
— **gas,** gas de aspirador
exhausting pump, bomba
    extractora (o aspiradora),
    bomba de vacío
exhumed dome, domo exhumado
exogeneous, (g) exógeno
— **dome,** domo exógeno
exogenetic, exogenético

exomorphic, exomórfico
exomorphism, exomorfismo
exothermic, exotérmico
expand, expandir, ensanchar, abrir,
    dilatar
expander, expansor, ensanchador,
    mandril expandidor
— **driven compressor,** compresor
    con motor a expansión de gas
— **stop,** limitador del ensanche
expanding, expandible,
    ensanchable
— **brake,** freno de expansión
— **casing mill,** fresa de cuchillas
    extensibles para tubería de
    revestimiento
— **cement,** cemento expansible
— **electrode system,** sistema de
    electrodo de expansión
— **pulley,** polea de diámetro
    regulable
— **tool,** ensanchador
expansible, expandible
expansion, expansión, dilatación
— **bearing,** apoyo de expansión,
    cojinete de expansión
— **bend,** curva de dilatación, codo
    compensador
— **bolt,** perno de expansión
— **brake,** freno de expansión
— **coil,** serpentín de expansión
— **curve,** curva de expansión, (o de
    dilatación)
— **dome**, cúpula de expansión, (Me)
    domo de expansión
— **end**, extremo móvil
— **engine,** máquina de vapor a
    expansión
— **joint,** junta de dilatación, (o de
    expansión)
— **line,** tubería de dilatación,
    cañería de expansión
— **loop,** curva de dilatación (o de
    expansión)
— **pulley,** polea de diámetro
    regulable

— **ratio,** relación de expansión
— **ring,** anillo de expansión, anillo de dilatación
— **roof tank,** tanque con techo de expansión
— **steam trap,** trampa de agua de expansión, purgador de expansión
— **stroke,** carrera de expansión
— **valve,** válvula de expansión
expansive bit, barrena de expansión
experiment, experimento
expiration, vencimiento, caducidad
expire, (cm) caducar, expirar, vencerse
exploder, detonante, fulminante
exploit, explotar, aprovechar
exploitation, explotación, desarrollo
— **tax,** impuesto de explotación
— **well,** pozo de explotación
exploration, exploración
explorationist, (g) (gf) explorador
exploring electrode, electrodo explorador
explosimeter, explosímetro
explosion, explosión
— **cone,** cono de explosión
— **crater,** cráter de explosión
— **engine,** motor a explosión
— **proof,** a prueba de explosión
— **wave,** onda explosiva
explosive, explosivo
— **limits,** límites de explosión
— **mixture,** mezcla explosiva
exponent, exponente
export, exportación
— **market,** mercado extranjero, mercado de exportación
— **oil,** petróleo de exportación
exporter, exportador
exposed location single-buoy mooring (ELSBM), monoboya de carga para mar abierta

exposed spring pop safety valve, válvula de seguridad con resorte descubierto
exposure, (g) afloramiento; (atmos) a la intemperie
explusion, expulsión
extended spread, (gf) tendido desplazado
extenders, (qm) alargadores
extension, extensión; prolongación; prórroga
— **bit,** trépano de extensión
— **fracture,** fractura de extensión
— **well,** pozo de extensión
extensometer, extensómetro
exterior, exterior
— **focussing,** de enfoque exterior
external, externo; exterior
— **coking method,** producción de coque por calentamiento externo de la cámara
— **contact,** contacto externo
— **cutter,** cortador exterior
— **diameter (ED),** diámetro exterior (DE)
— **drill-pipe cutter,** cortatubos (o cortatubería) exterior
— **flush,** diámetro exterior constante, exterior liso
— **flush tool joint,** unión de diámetro exterior a ras para tubería de perforación
— **upset,** tubería de recalcado (o de refuerzo, de resalto) exterior
— **upsed ends,** tubo con extremos exteriores de mayor espresor
extinction angle, (gf) ángulo de obscurecimiento
extinct volcano, volcán apagado (o extinguido)
extinguisher, extintor, extinguidor
extra, extra
— **hard steel,** acero extraduro, acero de herramientas
— **heavy pipe,** tubería extrapesada, cañería reforzada

90

— heavy valve, válvula reforzada
— strong pipe, tubería extrapesada, cañería reforzada
extract, *n.* extracto; *v.* extraer
— stripping stage, etapa en la operación de extraer el disolvente de un producto
extraction, extracción
— plant, (rf) planta de extracción
— process, proceso de extracción
— thimble, copa porosa para la extracción de substancias en solución
extractor, extractor
extraneous gas, gas extraño, gas exterior al yacimiento
extrapolate, *v.* extrapolar; extrapolation, *n.* extrapolación
extruded metal, metal estirado por presión
extrusion, estiramiento por presión; (g) efusión, erupción, extrusión
extrusive, efusivo, extrusivo
— body, roca efusiva, cuerpo efusivo
— rock, roca efusiva (o superficial, extrusiva)
— sheet, manto efusivo
exude, exudar
eye, ojo; ojal, argolla
— nut, tuerca de ojo, ojal con tuerca
eyebar, barra de ojo (o de argolla)
eyebolt, tornillo de ojo, perno de argolla, armella, cáncamo
eyebolt and key, perno de argolla con pasador
eyepiece, (in) ocular, lente ocular
— micrometer, ocular micrométrico

F

f, q.v. femto

F, q.v. farad, Fahrenheit, fluorine
f-k filter, (gf) filtro *f-k*
fabric, tela, tejido, género
fabricated piping, tubería preformada, (o adaptada)
face, superficie, cara, anverso
— plate, *n.* placa protectora, *v.* revestir, forrar, pulir, ajustar, cepillar, igualar, frentear
facet, faceta
faceted spur, contrafuerte labrado en facetas, contrafuerte facetado
facies, facies
facility, instalación
facing, capa de refuerzo; revestimiento, forro; paramento
facsimile, facsímil, telecopia
factor analysis, análisis de factores
factory-bent pipe, tubería acodada en la fábrica
fade, (gf) desvanecerse; atenuar (q.v. mute)
Fahrenheit (F°), grados Fahrenheit
fail-safe, protección en caso de fallos, de seguridad garantizada, fallo sin riesgo, seguro en caso de fallo, funcionalidad completa
— valve, válvula a prueba de fallo
fail-soft, (dp) tolerante al fallo, funcionalidad reducida, de degradación ligera
failure, avería, fallo, defecto; rotura; anomalía; (cm) quiebra; fracaso
— rate, tasa de averías (o de fallos)
fall, *n.* caída; descenso; inclinación, declive, pendiente; salto; *v.* caer; bajar; menguar, decrecer
— of a dike, vertiente de un dique
— of a river, declive (o inclinación, pendiente) de un río
fallback, (dp) recurso de emergencia
false, falso

— **bedding**, seudoestratificación, estratificación entrecruzada
— **bottom**, doble fondo
— **cleavage**, contrahendedura
— **equilibrium**, equilibrio inestable
— **galena**, esfalerita, blenda
— **key**, ganzúa, llave falsa
— **set**, (tunnel) entibación provisional
fan, ventilador; (g) abanico
— **belt**, correa de ventilador
— **blade**, paleta de ventilador
— **bracket**, sostén de ventilador
— **delta**, (g) abanico fandeltaico
— **drive**, mando de ventilador
— **fold**, pliegue en abanico
— **pulley**, polea de ventilador
— **shooting**, (gf) tiro de abanico
— **shroud**, cubierta de ventilador
— **spread**, (gf) despliegue en abanico (q.v. **fan shooting**)
fan-out, (dp) cargabilidad de salida, abanico de salida, factor piramidal de salida
fang, (tl) espiga, cola, rabo, garra, uña, diente
fanglomerate, (g) fanglomerado
Fanning's equation of flow, ecuación de Fanning para determinar la pérdida de presión debida a turbulencia del flujo en un conducto circular
farad, faradio, farad: unidad SI de capacitancia eléctrica
faradic path, (gf) trayectoria farádica
farnesan, trimetildodecano (q.v. **trimethyldodecane**)
FAS, q.v. **free alongside ship**
fast, firme, fijo, estable; rápido, ligero
— **Fourier transform**, (dp) transformación (o transformada) rápida de Fourier
— **sheave**, (prf) polea rápida
fasten, atar, unir, asegurar, apretar

fastener, broche, sujetador, apretador
fat oil, (rf) aceite enriquecido
fathom, (nt) braza, (mn) superficie de 6 pies en cuadro
fatigue, (mu) fatiga, agotamiento
— **breaks**, roturas por fatiga
— **failures**, roturas por fatiga
fatty, craso, graso
— **oil**, aceite graso (o craso)
faucet, grifo, canilla
fault, (g) falla, *obs.* paraclasa
— **block**, bloque de fallas, gleba tectónica
— **breccia**, breccia (o brecha) de falla
— **bundle**, grupo de fallas
— **complex**, complejo (o conjunto) de fallas, grupo de fallas cruzadas
— **dip**, buzamiento de falla
— **fissure**, fisura (o grieta) de la falla
— **limb**, (g) labio (o ala) de falla
— **line**, línea de dislocación, línea que sigue la falla
— **plane**, superficie de dislocación, (Me) plano de la falla (q.v. **fracture plane**)
— **scarp**, barranca de falla, (Me) falla escarpada, (Ar) escalón (o escarpa) de fractura
— **strike**, dirección (o rumbo) de una falla
— **surface**, plano (o superficie) de falla
— **system**, sistema de fallas
— **trap**, trampa por falla
— **trough**, cuenca de falla, (Ar) región de hundimiento, fosa tectónica (q.v. **graben**)
— **zone**, zona de fallas, zona fallada, (Bo) zona de dislocación
fault-pit, (g) dislocación circular
faulted

Glossary of the Petroleum Industry

— **anticline,** anticlinal fallado
— **block,** bloque limitado por fallas
— **monocline,** monoclinal fallado
FDM, q.v. **frequency division multiplexing**
FCC q.v. **fluid catalytic cracking**
feasibility study, estudio de factibilidad
feather, pluma
— **key,** cuña de corredera
— **pattern,** (gf) arreglo con sensibilidad distribuida
— **valve,** válvula de lengüeta
feathering, escalonamiento
features, características, rasgos, detalles; ventajas
feed, *n.* (cl) (el) (rf) alimentación; (frn) carga; (mc) avance; *v.* alimentar, cargar, avanzar
— **holes,** (dp) perforaciones de arrastre (o de alimentación)
— **inlet,** tubo (o entrada) de alimentación
— **off,** (prf) bajar la barrena
feedback loop, (dp) bucle de retroalimentación (o de realimentación)
feeder, alimentador
— **line,** oleoducto tributario
feeding screw, tornillo alimentador
feedstock, carga, materia prima
feed-water heater, precalentador de agua de caldera
feed-water injector, inyector de agua de caldera
feed-water pump, bomba alimentadora de agua
fees, (cm) honorarios
feet, q.v. **foot**
feldspar, feldespato
feldspathoid, feldespatoide
felsite, (g) felsita, petrosílex
felt, fieltro
— **washer,** arandela de fieltro
female connection, conexión hembra

femto (f), *pref.* SI = 10^{-15}
fen land, tierra pantanosa
fender, guardabarro, guardafango; (bridge) espolón; (dock) defensa
fenster, miradero
fergusite, ferrogusita
fermentation, fermentación
ferrate, ferrato
ferric, férrico, de hierro
ferrite, (g) ferrita; (qm) ferrito
ferro-magnesium minerals, minerales ferromagnesianos
ferro-prussiate paper, papel heliográfico
ferromagnetic, ferromagnético
ferromagnetism, ferromagnetismo
ferrous, ferroso
— **alloy,** aleación ferrosa
fetch, *n.* (dp) búsqueda y carga de instrucciones (o de programas); *v.* extraer datos de la memoria; buscar y cargar programas
fettling, desbarbadura, rebarbadura
FFT, q.v. **fast Fourier transform**
fiber, fibra
— **gasket,** empaquetadura de fibra
— **optics,** (sistema de transmisión) con fibras ópticas (o de óptica de fibras)
— **packing,** empaquetadura de fibra
fiducial, *n.* testigo, marca; *a.* fiduciario
— **time,** tiempo fiduciario
field, campo
— **balance,** magnetómetro
— **coil,** bobina del inductor (o de campo), arrollamiento
— **geology,** geología de campo
— **pressure,** presión subterránea
— **strength,** (g) intensidad de campo
— **winding,** (el) devanado (o arrollamiento) del inductor (o del campo)

English - Spanish

fifty percent point, punto medio de
ebullición (q.v. **mid-boiling
point**)
figure-eight blank, brida
ciegatubos, ciegatubos tipo
anteojos
file, lima
fill, *n.* terraplén, relleno; *v.*
terraplenar, rellenar; (mn)
atibar; (paint) aparejar
filler, (ca) núcleo de pasta
— **cap,** tapa de gollete
— **washer,** arandela suplementaria
fillet, filete, gusanillo de rosca
— **weld size,** tamaño de una
soldadura en ángulo
— **welded joint,** junta soldada en
ángulo
fillister head screw, tornillo de
cabeza cilíndrica
film, película; membrana
filter, *n.* filtro; *v.* filtrar
— **bowl,** (rf) vasija de filtro, tazón
de filtro
— **cake,** costra de lodo, revoque,
(Me) enjarre (q.v. **mud cake**)
— **circuit,** (gf) circuito de filtros
(q.v. **channel**)
— **clay,** (rf) arcilla de filtro, arcilla
para filtrar
— **cloth,** (rf) paño de filtro (o de
filtrar)
— **correction,** (gf) corrección por
filtro
— **curve,** (gf) curva de filtro de
sismógrafo, curva de selector de
frecuencia
— **leaf,** (rf) colador para filtro, hoja
de filtro
— **loss,** pérdida del filtrado
— **medium,** elemento filtrante
— **press,** (rf) filtro prensa; (prf)
prensa de filtrado
— **screen,** cedazo para filtro, hoja
de filtro (q.v. **filter leaf**)

filtering, (dp) filtrado, filtración,
enmascaramiento (q.v. **band-
pass, band-stop, high-pass, low
pass**)
— **bed,** estrato (o capa, lecho)
filtrante
filtrate, *n.* filtrado
filtration, filtración
fin, aleta, resalte; (sd) rebaba (q.v.
flash)
final drive, mando final
financial statement, balance,
informe del estado de cuentas
fine grained, de grano fino
fine products, productos de alta
pureza
fines, finos, polvo que pasa por los
filtros
finger, (mc) saliente, lengüeta, dedo
— **board,** astillero de torre, (Ar)
plataforma de enganche, (Me)
peine, (Ve) trabajadero,
encuelladero (q.v. **fourble
board, thribble board, pipe
rack**)
fingering, (prf) (fl) (inject)
digitación
finish, *n.* acabado; *v.* acabar
finishing bead, cordón de acabado
(q.v. **bead**)
finite-element method, (dp)
método de elementos finitos
finned tube, tubo aletado, tubo con
aletas (o nervaduras)
fire, fuego
— **box,** (frn) hogar, caja de fuego
— **box sheets,** planchas para caja de
fuego
— **brick,** ladrillo refractario
— **bridge,** (frn) altar de hornalla
— **clay,** arcilla infusible
— **clay brick,** ladrillo de barro
refractario
— **damp,** gas grisú
— **door,** puerta de horno de caldera

Glossary of the Petroleum Industry

— **escape,** escalera de escape, escalera de salvamento, escalera de incendio
— **extinguisher,** extinguidor de incendio
— **fighting apparatus,** aparato contra incendio
— **floats,** flotafuegos
— **flood,** combustión in situ
— **foam,** espuma apagadora
— **hazard,** riesgo de incendio
— **hose,** manguera de bombero
— **insurance,** seguro contra incendio
— **point,** punto de combustión (o de llama, de ignición), temperatura de combustión
— **pot,** (sd) hornillo de soldar; hornilla
— **stops,** parafuegos
— **test,** prueba para determinar la temperatura de combustión
— **wall,** pared cortafuego, muro refractario (o a prueba de incendio), parallamas
fireman, (oc) bombero; fogonero
fireproof, a prueba de fuego, resistente al calor, (Ar) ignífugo
firing, fogueo; encendido
— **chamber,** hogar
— **line,** (sd) línea de fuego; (gf) alambre que conecta el explosivo con el detonador
— **order,** orden del encendido
— **rate,** régimen de fogueo
— **time,** (gf) instante de la explosión
first-aid kit, botiquín de urgencia (o de primera cura)
first arrival, (gf) primeros arribos, primeras llegadas, primeras ondas que llegan al sismógrafo
first break, (gf) primer quiebre
firth, estrecho de mar; estuario
fiscal stamp, timbre fiscal
fiscal year, año fiscal, ejercicio

fish, n. (prf) pieza perdida; v. pescar, rescatar
fish-tail bit, barrena cola de pescado
fishing, (prf) pesca, salvamento, rescate
— **basket,** cesta de pesca
— **grab,** gancho de pesca, (Ve) pescador de gancho
— **head,** cabeza de pesca
— **jar,** percusor (o tijera) de pesca, (Ve) cimbra de pesca
— **magnet,** pescante magnético
— **socket,** campana (o empate, enchufe) de pesca
— **tap,** macho de pesca, machuelo
— **tool,** herramienta de pesca
fissile, hendible, rajadizo
fissure, grieta, hendedura, abertura, rajadura, fisura
— **vein,** mineral depositado por el agua en una grieta
fissured rock, roca resquebrajada
fit, n. ajuste, empalme, encaje; v. ajustar, montar, empalmar, encajar adaptar
fitting, ajuste, encaje; adaptación
fittings, piezas, accesorios, aditamentos, (tu) conexiones, auxiliares
five-spot flooding system, sistema de inyección de agua a cuatro pozos por un quinto para producir el petróleo por presión hidráulica
five-way cock, grifo de cinco vías
fix, n. (nav) posición definida; v. fijar; asegurar, asentar; arreglar, componer
fixed carbon, carbón estable (o fijo)
fixed choke, estrangulador con abertura fija (op. adjustable choke)
fixed-bed catalyst, catalizador de lecho fijo
fixtures, accesorios, artefactos

95

fjord, (g) fiord
flag, señalizador, indicador,
banderín; bandera
flagstone, (g) laja
flake, laminilla, escama, hojuela;
casquito
flaky, escamoso; floculento
flame, llama
— **arrester,** parallamas, (Ar)
trampa de llamas
— **cutting,** cortadura por llama de
gas, cortadura con soplete
— **detector,** detector de llama
— **front,** frente de llama
— **priming,** chamuscar
flange, *n.* (tu) brida, pletina,
platillo; (rail) base, patín; (mc)
oreja, pestaña, reborde, resalte;
(smelter) rebordeadora;
(beam) cabeza, cuerda,
cordón; *v.* rebordear, embridar,
bordear, bridar
— **adapter,** ajustador de brida
— **bolts,** pernos de brida
— **connection,** conexión en brida
— **orifice fitting,** portaorificio
embridado
— **union,** unión de brida, unión
embridada
— **up,** embridar
flanged, de reborde, embutido
— **fittings,** accesorios embridados
— **gudgeon,** muñón de disco (o
brida)
— **pipe,** tubo de bridas, tubería
embridada, (Ar) cañería
embridada
— **union,** unión embridada
— **valve,** válvula embridada
— **wheel,** rueda de pestaña
flangeway, canal (o vía) de pestaña,
carrilada, ranura de pestaña
flanging machine, pestañadora,
máquina rebordadora
flank, flanco, costado

flap valve, válvula de charnela (o
de chapaleta, de gozne) (q.v.
hanging valve)
flapper, chapaleta
flare, quema; tea
flared joint, junta abocinada
flash, *n.* relámpago; destello;
resplandor; fucilazo; fogonazo;
(sd) rebaba; *v.* encender; (expl)
quemar; relampaguear;
destellar; (cn) proteger con
planchas de escurrimiento
— **back,** llama interior; fogonazo
— **chamber,** (rf) cámara (o torre)
de destilación por expansión
instantánea, torre de expansión
instantánea (q.v. **flash drum**)
— **distillation,** (rf) destilación por
expansión instantánea
— **drum,** (rf) cámara (o torre) de
destilación por expansión
instantánea, torre de expansión
instantánea, (Me) tanque de
orear (q.v. **flash chamber**)
— **equilibrium evaporation,**
evaporación instantánea en
equilibrio
— **flood,** golpe de agua, inundación
repentina
— **point,** (rf) punto de deflagración,
punto relámpago, (Me) punto de
inflamación
— **set,** (cement) fraguado repentino
— **tank,** separador
— **test,** prueba de deflagración,
prueba de punto relámpago (q.v.
flash point)
— **tower,** torre de destilación
instantánea, (Ar, Ve) torre de
destilación relámpago
— **vaporization,** vaporización
instantánea (o relámpago)
— **weld,** soldadura de
recalentamiento
flask, (la) frasco, matraz, redoma

flat, *n.* (steel) planchuela, pletina; (tp) llanura; *a.* plano, chato, llano
— **bilge,** (nt) pantoque
— **car,** carro de plataforma, carro plano
— **curve,** curva plana
— **file,** lima plana
— **head,** *a.* de cabeza plana (o chata), achatado
— **seat valve,** válvula de asiento chato
— **spot,** (gf) punto plano
— **spring,** muelle fabricado de alambre aplanado, muelle de hojas
— **truck,** camión de plataforma
— **valve bailer,** válvula plana de cuchara
— **washer,** arandela plana
flathead screw, tornillo de cabeza perdida
flatland, llano, llanura
flattening, achatamiento
flaw, *n.* defecto, imperfección; grieta; *v.* estropear; agrietar
flawed, defectuoso; agrietado
flax, lino
— **packing,** empaquetadura de lino
flex joint, junta (o unión) flexible flexibility, flexibilidad
flexible, flexible, doblegable
— **array,** orden (o ordenamiento, matriz) flexible
— **ball-joint,** junta esférica flexible
— **binning,** (gf) partición flexible en celdas
— **connector,** conexión flexible
— **coupling,** unión flexible
— **tubing,** tubo (o tubería) flexible
flexible-band coupling, acoplamiento flexible a correa
flexible-disk coupling, acoplamiento de disco flexible
flexural, flexional
flexure, (g) flexura, pliegue

flint, *n.* pedernal; **flinty,** *a.* apedernalado
flip-out device, (el) dispositivo de disparo
float, *n.* (dp) flotador; (mc) leve desplazamiento del eje; (masonry) llana de madera, aplanadora, espátula, (Ar) fratacho, (Es, Me) talocha; *v.* flotar; poner a flote; (nt) desencallar, desvarar; aplanar, fratasar; (el) conectar como compensador
— **arm,** brazo del flotador
— **chamber,** cámara del flotador
— **collar,** collar flotador (o de flotación), (Me) cople flotador
— **hood,** cubierta del flotador
— **sand,** arena suelta en el pozo
— **shoe,** zapata flotadora
— **valve,** válvula flotante, válvula de boya (o de flotador)
float-operated valve, válvula controlada por un flotador
floater-type subsea template, plantilla submarina de tipo flotante
floating, flotante
— **axle,** eje flotante
— **barge,** barcaza insumergible
— **datum,** (tp) nivel de referencia variable
— **dock,** dique flotante
— **drilling vessel,** embarcación flotante de perforación
— **head,** cabeza flotante
— **head baffle,** desviador de la cabeza flotante
— **plug,** tapón flotante
— **point arithmetic,** (Ar, Bo, Br, CH, Es, Ve...) aritmética de coma flotante; (CR, EUA, Me...) aritmética de punto flotante
— **point operation,** (dp) operación en coma flotante; operación en

punto flotante (q.v. **floating point arithmetic**)

— **production system**, (mar) sistema flotante de producción

— **roof**, techo flotante

— **tank**, tanque de compensación, tanque igualador (q.v. **surge tank, balance tank**)

— **tube sheet**, placa portatubos (o tubular) flotante, placa de tubos flotante

flocculation, floculación

flocculating agent, agente floculador

flocculent, floculento

flood, *n*. inundación, crecida, creciente; *v*. inundar, anegar, apantanar

— **lamp**, lámpara proyectante (o inundante)

— **plain**, (g) lecho de creciente, área de inundación

— **tide**, (nt) marea creciente (o entrante), flujo de la marea; pleamar

flooded, inundado

floodlight, lámpara proyectante, flujo luminoso

floodlighting, iluminación proyectada

floor, *n*. (cn) piso, suelo, planta; (g) baja, bajo, reliz del bajo; (bridge) tablero; (mar) fondo; (dam) zampeado, platea; (canal) plantilla; *v*. entarimar, solar

— **block**, polea de servicio adherida al piso de la torre

— **grating**, emparrillado para pisos

floppy disk, (dp) disco flexible, disco floppy (q.v. **diskette**)

flops (floating-point operations per second), operaciones en coma (o punto) flotante por segundo

floridin, floridina

flotation, flotación

— **oil**, aceite de flotación

flour, *a*. en polvo

flow, flujo, corriente; descarga; (r) caudal, gasto, flujo, derrame; (mar) creciente, flujo; *v*. correr, fluir; subir, crecer

— **beam**, manguito de inserción para reducir el flujo

— **chart**, diagrama de flujo; organigrama; (dp) ordinograma

— **cleavage**, clivaje de flujo

— **controller**, regulador de flujo

— **diagram**, q.v. **flow chart, flow sheet**

— **drilling**, perforación mientras se produce, perforación en producción

— **formula**, fórmula de flujo

— **indicator**, indicador de flujo

— **line**, línea de flujo, (Me) tubería de descarga; (pr) tubería de producción, (Ve) tubería de disparo

— **line treater**, tanque desemulsionante

— **nipple**, estrangulador (q.v. **choke, flow beam, flow plug**)

— **packer**, obturador de flujo

— **pipe**, tubería flujo, (Ve) tubería de disparo

— **plug**, estrangulador (q.v. **choke, flow beam, flow nipple**)

— **proportioner**, dosificador de alimentación

— **rate**, velocidad del flujo

— **recorder**, registrador de flujo

— **sheet**, (rf) diagrama de flujo (o de circulación), (Ar) diagrama de elaboración (q.v. **flow chart**)

— **string**, tubería de producción

— **tank**, tanque de captación

— **valve**, válvula de descarga (o de paso)

flow-structure, (g) (Ar) textura fluidal

flowage, metamorfismo plástico
— **fold,** pliegue de flujo
flowhead, cabeza de descarga
flowing pressure, presión del flujo
flowing well, pozo productivo (o fluyente)
flowmeter, medidor de caudal (o de flujo)
fluctuate, fluctuar
fluctuating pressure, presión fluctuante
fluctuation, fluctuación
flue, tubo, flus; tragante, humero, respiradero, escape
— **beader,** bordeador de tubos de caldera
— **brush,** escobillón para limpiar tubos de caldera
— **cleaner,** limpiador de tubos de caldera
— **gas,** gas de chimenea
— **plate,** placa de tubos de caldera
fluid, *n. a.* fluido
— **catalytic cracking,** crácking (o craqueo) catalítico (tipo) fluido
— **coking,** coquificación fluida
— **column,** columna de fluido
— **contact,** contacto gas-petróleo (o agua-petróleo)
— **end,** (bm) sección de fluidos
— **film,** película fluida
— **flow operation,** operación fluido-líquida
— **level,** nivel del fluido
— **meter,** medidor de caudal
— **operated,** a impulsión hidráulica
— **pounding,** (well bm) choque del émbolo contra el fluido
fluid-loss additive, aditivo para la pérdida de fluido
fluidity, fluidez
flume, tubo separador de gas (q.v. **gas boot)**
fluorine, fluorina, flúor
fluorescence, fluorescencia
fluorescent, fluorescente

fluorite, fluorita, flúor espato
flush, *v.* nivelar, emparejar; baldear, mover por chorro de agua, limpiar por inundación; *a.* a ras, parejo, nivelado, en el mismo plano
— **bushing,** buje al ras
— **joint,** junta lisa, junta a ras
— **production,** producción afluente
— **valve,** válvula de limpieza automática (o de aspersión)
— **weld,** soldadura a ras
flush-joint casing, tubería de revestimiento de junta lisa, (Me) tubería de revestimiento flush joint
— **pipe,** tubería de junta lisa
— **sectional bailer,** achicador seccionado con uniones enrasadas (o lisas)
flushing, limpieza con chorro de agua, limpieza por inundación; baldeo
— **oil,** aceite de enjuagar, aceite de limpieza por inundación
flute, (g) acanaladura, estría
fluted, estriado, acanalado
— **drill collar,** lastrabarrena acanalado (q.v. **spirally grooved drill collar**)
— **swedge,** abretubos acanalado
fluvial, fluvial
fluviatile deposit, depósito fluvial
fluvioglacial, fluvioglacial
fluviomarine, fluviomarino
flux, *n.* (mu) fundente, flujo, fluidificante; (el) flujo; *v.* fluidificar
— **oil,** aceite fluidificante
fluxgate magnetometer, magnetómetro discriminador de flujo
fluxion, flujo; fusión; (mt) fluxión, derivada, diferencial
fluxional, (g) fluido

flying spot, (dp) punto móvil (o
volante)
— **scanner,** explorador de punto
móvil
flywheel, volante, (Co) rueda
voladora
— **governor,** regulador de volante
— **guard,** guardavolante
FM, q.v. **frequency modulation**
foam, espuma
foamite, espuma contra incendios
FOB, q.v. **free on board**
focal, focal
— **depth,** profundidad focal
— **length,** longitud focal
— **out time,** tiempo de origen en el
foco, hora de origen en el
epicentro
focus, foco, punto de origen,
epicentro
FOE, q.v. **fuel oil equivalent**
foil, *n.* (mu) hoja, lámina; oropel,
chapa; *v.* frustrar; embotar;
amortiguar
fold, *n.* (g) pliegue, plegamiento,
plisamiento, arrugamiento;
doblez; *v.* plegar; *suf.* (e.g.,
threefold, tenfold) triple (o tres
veces), diez veces etc.
— **belt,** cinturón de plegamiento
folded edge rubber-covered belt,
correa de caucho con borde
plegado
folded strata, capas plegadas
folding, (g) plegamiento
foliation, esquistosidad, exfoliación,
foliación
follower, (ma) rueda secundaria,
empujador
foot (*plur.* **feet**), pie (30,4799 cm);
(mc) pie, base, pata; (g) pie (de
monte, terraplén, etc.)
— **accelerator,** acelerador de pie
— **actuated,** accionado por pedal
— **oil,** aceite de parafina de
asentamiento

— **operated,** accionado por pedal
— **rest,** descansapié, apoyapié,
descansadillo
— **rule,** pie de rey
— **throttle,** acelerador de pedal
— **valve,** válvula de aspiración (o de
toma, de pie)
foot-pound, libra-pié
footage, (prf) profundidad en pies
foothill, estribación; ladera,
contrafuerte
footpiece, (pr) pie difusor (para
mezclar el gas inyectado con el
crudo)
footwall, (fault) muro, muro
colgante
foraminifera, *n.* foraminíferos;
foraminiferal, *a.* foraminífero
force, *n.* fuerza, potencia, energía; *v.*
forzar
— **feed,** alimentación forzada
— **of gravity,** fuerza de gravedad
force-feed lubrication, lubricación
a presión (o por alimentación
forzada)
forced draft, tiro forzado; corriente
forzada
forced vibration, vibración forzada
fore and aft, de proa a popa
forearch, (g) antearco
foredeep, *a.* de frente profundo
forehand welding, soldadura
directa
foreign exchange, (cm) cambio
extranjero
foreign material, materia extraña
foreland, (g) antepaís, (Ve) región
frontera
foreman, (oc) capataz, sobrestante,
cabo de cuadrilla, jefe, (Co)
capitán, (CH) mayordomo, (Ve)
caporal
foremast, (nt) palo de trinquete
forerunners, (gf) ímpetus previos
foreset bed, estrato frontal, capa
frontal deltaica

foreshock, temblor (o sismo) precursor (o preliminar)
foresight, (tp) vista (o visual) adelante, lectura frontal
forge, *n.* fragua, forja; *v.* fraguar, forjar
— **blower,** fuelle (o soplador) de fragua
— **steel,** acero forjado, acero de forja
— **welding,** soldadura de forja
forged-steel flange, brida de acero forjado
forging, forjadura, fraguado, forja; pieza forjada
fork, *n.* (rd) bifurcación; (mc) horca, horquilla; (r) confluencia; *v.* bifurcarse
forking, (g) bifurcación
formaldehyde, formaldehído
formation, (g) formación
— **dip,** echado de la formación
— **fracture pressure,** presión de fractura de la formación
— **fracturing,** fracturamiento de la formación
— **gas,** gas innato al estrato, gas de formación
— **plugging,** sellar (o obturar) la formación
— **formation strike,** rumbo de la formación
— **tester,** verificador del contenido de una formación
— **tester packer,** obturador del verificador del contenido de una formación
Fortran (formula translation), (dp) Fortran
forward, *a.* delantero; *adv.* adelante; *v.* remitir, transmitir
— **azimuth,** acimut de frente
— **of,** (nt) a proa de
— **tangent,** (tp) tangente de frente
forward-looking sonar, sonar de proyección delantera

forwarding agent, (oc) agente de fletes, agente expedidor
fossil, fósil
— **coral reef,** formación coralina
— **water,** (g) agua connata
fossiliferous, fosilífero
foul, *v.* (ma) ensuciarse, (rope) trabarse, enredarse; (nt) chocar, abordar
— **solution pump,** bomba para la solución eliminadora de suciedad
fouling resistance, (cl) resistencia a la transmisión de calor debida a la suciedad o condición de la superficie transmisora
foundation, base, cimiento, fundamento
— **bolt,** perno de anclaje (o de cimiento)
— **pipe,** sarta conductora, (Me) tubería superficial (q.v. **conductor pipe**)
foundry, fundición
four-pass, *a.* de cuatro pasos
four-phase, *a.* (el) tetrafásico
four-sided, *a.* cuadrilátero
four-stroke cycle, ciclo de cuatro tiempos
four-way, *a.* de cuatro pasos (o vías)
four-wheel
— **brakes,** frenos en las cuatro ruedas
— **drive,** impulsión por cuatro ruedas
— **trailer,** remolque de cuatro ruedas, (Ar) acoplado de cuatro ruedas four-wing rotary bit, de cuatro alas (o fresas)
fourble board, (prf) plataforma astillero para tramos de cuatro tubos, (Ar) plataforma de seguridad, (Ve) encuellader, trabajadero (q.v. **finger board, thribble board**)

English - Spanish

Fourier transform, transformación de Fourier
FP, q.v. **flowing pressure**
FPS, q.v. **floating production system**
frac, q.v. **formation fracturing**
frac fluids, fluidos de fractura
fraction, fracción
fractional
— **analysis,** análisis fraccionario
— **distillates,** destilados fraccionarios
— **distillation,** destilación fraccionada
fractionating
— **column,** (q.v. **fractionating tower**)
— **condenser,** condensador fraccionador, torre fraccionadora
— **tower,** torre fraccionadora, torre (o columna) de destilación fraccionadora (q.v. **stabilizing column**)
fractionation, fraccionamiento
fractionator, torre fraccionadora, fraccionador
fracture, (g) fractura, disyunción, fisura; rotura
— **cleavage**, clivaje de fractura (o disyunción)
— **plane,** superficie de fracturación, superficie de dislocación (q.v. *fault plane*)
— **prone,** propenso a las fracturas
— **spring**, manantial de fisura
— **zone,** (g) área de fracturación
fractured, fracturado
— **trend**, rumbo fracturado
fracturing, *n.* (g) agrietamiento; *v.* agrietarse
fragment, fragmento
fragmental, (g) fragmentario, fragmentoso
fragmentation, fragmentación

frame, *n.* (cn) armazón, estructura, tirantería, esqueleto; (ma) bastidor; (mt) armazón; (mn) cuadro de maderos; *v.* armar, ensamblar
framework, armazón, tirantería, armadura, entramado, esqueleto, reticulado
framing bits, (dp) bits de encuadramiento (o delimitadores)
franklinite, franclinita (mineral de manganeso)
free, libre
— **acid,** ácido libre
— **air,** aire atmosférico
— **air anomaly,** anomalía aire libre
— **air and Bouguer anomaly,** anomalía combinada de aire libre y Bouguer
— **air correction,** corrección de aire libre
— **alongside ship,** franco al costado del buque
— **carbon,** carbón libre
— **dock,** muelle libre
— **exhaust,** escape libre
— **fall,** caída libre
— **flowing powder,** polvo suelto
— **of all average,** exento de toda avería
— **of brokerage,** franco de comissión
— **of charge,** gratis
— **on board (FOB),** franco a bordo (FAB)
— **point indicator,** (prf) indicador del punto libre
— **port,** puerto libre
— **radical,** radical libre
— **water,** (prf) agua libre
free-water knockout, deshidratador
freeboard, (nt) francobordo; (tk) bordo libre
freewheeling, (prf) rodamiento libre

102

Glossary of the Petroleum Industry

freeze, congelar
— **point,** (prf) punto de pegado (q.v.
   free point indicator)
freezing, *a.* congelador
— **bath,** baño congelador
— **mixture,** mixtura congeladora
— **point,** punto de congelación;
   (oil) punto de fluidez
freight, *n.* (cm) flete; *v.* fletar
— **allowances,** bonificación sobre
   fletes
— **rates,** costo (o tarifa) de fletes
frequency, frecuencia
— **distribution,** distribución de
   frecuencia
— **division multiplexing,** (dp)
   multiplexión de división de
   frequencia
— **modulation,** frecuencia
   modulada
— **of oscillation,** frecuencia de
   oscilación
fresh
— **air,** aire puro
— **feed,** (rf) carga virgen
— **water,** agua dulce; agua fresca
fret, *n.* roce, raspadura, desgaste;
   relieve; calado; *v.* gastar, raer,
   corroer
— **saw,** sierra de calados, segueta
friable, desmenuzable, friable
friction, fricción
— **bearing,** cojinete de fricción
— **block,** almohadilla; calce de
   fricción
— **clutch,** embrague de fricción
— **cone,** cono de fricción
— **cone clutch,** cono de fricción
— **disc,** disco de fricción
— **disc clutch,** embrague de
   fricción de disco
— **drum clutch,** embrague de
   fricción del tipo de tambor
— **facing,** revestimiento de fricción
— **factor,** factor de fricción
— **loss,** pérdida por fricción

— **pull-rod clamps,** grapas de
   fricción para varillas de tracción
— **slip,** deslizadera del tipo de
   fricción
— **socket,** campana de pesca por
   fricción
frictional loss, pérdida por fricción
fringe, fleco, orla
— **water,** agua encima de la capa
   freática
fringing reef, arrecife costero (q.v.
   shore reef)
front axle, eje delantero
front-end
— **legs,** patas delanteras, pilares
   delanteros
— **power unit,** equipo motriz
   frontal
— **processor,** procesador frontal,
   procesador de formatos
front wave, (gf) frente de onda, (o
   avanzada) de onda
frontal, frontero, anterior, frontal,
   frental
— **moraine,** (g) morena terminal (o
   frontal)
froth, espuma; burbuja
frothing, espumar, echar espuma
ft, q.v. **foot**
fuel, *n.* combustible; *v.* aprovisionar
   de combustible
— **alcohol,** alcohol combustible
— **bowl,** tazón de combustible
— **cell,** pila combustible
— **control,** regulador de
   alimentación de combustible
— **cutoff valve,** válvula de cierre
   para el combustible
— **dope,** aditivo de combustible,
   antidetonante
— **drain,** drenaje de combustible
— **economizer,** economizador de
   combustible
— **feed,** carga de combustible
— **feed pipe,** tubo (o caño) de carga
   de combustible

103

— **filter,** filtro para combustible (o para fuel oil)
— **gage,** indicador de nivel de combustible
— **gas,** gas combustible
— **governor,** regulador de combustible
— **injector,** inyector del combustible; bomba de inyección del combustible
— **injection pump,** bomba de inyección de combustible
— **inlet,** entrada (o admisión) de combustible
— **line,** tubo del combustible
— **oil,** combustóleo, petróleo (o aceite) combustible, fuel oil
— **pipe,** caño de combustible
— **pump,** bomba de inyección del combustible
— **sensitivity,** sensibilidad de un combustible
— **strainer,** filtro de combustible
— **system,** sistema de combustible
— **tank,** depósito (o tanque) de combustible
— **value,** valor calórico
fuel-injection pump, bomba inyectora de combustible
fuel-transfer pump, bomba de alimentación de combustible
fulcrum, fulcro
fulfurite, (g) fulgurita
full, lleno; pleno, completo, total
— **admission,** (tr) admisión total, plena admisión
— **bore,** de pleno caudal (o abertura, calibre)
— **circle socket slip,** campana de pesca circular con aletas; campana de pesca con cuñas circulares
— **floating axle,** eje enteramente flotante

— **hole cementing,** cementación por la boca de fondo de la tubería
— **hole tool joint,** unión de tubería vástago con diámetro interior uniforme
— **load,** plena carga
— **pressure,** plena presión, presión máxima
— **steam,** a todo vapor
full-barrel tubing pump, bomba de cilindro enterizo introducida con el tubo de producción
full-face gasket, empaque de cara completa
full-gage bit, barrena de diámetro original
full-gage hole, agujero de diámetro correcto
full-load displacement, (nt) desplazamiento completo
full-load rating, capacidad nominal a carga completa
full-throttle, a plena admisión, a todo motor; (nt) a todo vapor
full-wave, plena onda, onda completa
full-way valve, válvula sin restricción, válvula de paso de sección complete
fuller's earth, greda, galactita, tierra de batán
Fullonian, fuloniense
fumaric acid, ácido fumárico
fumarole, (vlc) fumarola
fume, vapor, gas, vaho
— **duct,** conducto de ventilación
— **hood,** colector de emanaciones (o gases)
fuming acid, ácido pirofurfúrico, ácido humeante (o fumante)
fungible, a. mezclable
funnel, embudo
— **viscosity,** viscosidad Marsh
furfural, furfural

— **extraction,** extracción por furfural
— **lube oil plant,** (rf) planta para la refinación de aceites lubricantes mediante furfural
— **refining,** refinación con furfural
furnace, horno, fogón, fornalla
— **black,** negro de humo (de horno)
— **damper,** registrador (compuerta) de tiro
— **equilibrium,** equilibrio del horno
— **oil,** petróleo de horno (o de hogar), combustóleo de calefacción
furrow, *n.* surco; *v.* surcar, asurcar
furrowing, (g) surcamiento
fuse, *n.* (el) fusible, interruptor fusible; (expl) mecha, espoleta; *v.* fundir, derretir
— **plug,** tapón fusible
fused quartz, cuarzo fundido
fusible, fusible
— **plug,** tapón fundible de seguridad (q.v. **soft plug**)
fusion, fusión
fuzzy logic, (dp) lógica de conjuntos difusos, lógica poliequivalente

G

G, q.v. **giga**
gab, gancho
gabbro, (g) gabro
gad, cuña, punzón
gage, *n.* (in) manómetro, marcador, indicador de presión, calibrador; calibre; mira; cartabón; espesor; (rr) ancho de vía, entrevía; *v.* aforar, calibrar
— **cock,** grifo indicador de nivel
— **cutters,** fresas rectificadoras
— **glass,** tubo indicador, vidrio de nivel, nivel de caldera

— **hatch,** escotilla para introducir el medidor
— **pressure,** presión manométrica (o indicada)
— **protector,** protector de indicador
— **pulsation dampener,** amortiguador de vibraciones para indicador
— **table,** cuadro de medición
— **tank,** tanque medidor
— **valve,** válvula de manómetro
gager, aforador
gaging pole, varilla medidora (o graduada)
gain, *n.* beneficio; (el) amplificación, incremento; (gf) ganancia; *v.* ganar, beneficiarse; aventajar
— **trace,** (gf) traza de ganancia
gal, gal: unidad de aceleración gravitacional (1 cm/s^2)
galena, galena
gall, ludimiento
gallic acid, ácido gálico
gallon (gal), galón (inglés = 4,54 litros; EU = 3,78 litros)
galvanic
— **action,** acción galvánica
— **cell,** celda galvánica
galvanized, galvanizado
galvanometer, galvanómetro
galvanometric registration, registro galvanométrico
gamma, gamma: unidad de fuerza de un campo magnético
— **particles,** partículas gamma
— **rays,** rayos gamma
gang, cuadrilla, brigada, equipo, (CH) escuadra, (Me) parada (q.v. **crew**)
gangue, (mn) ganga
— **mineral,** mineral filoniano
ganister, (mu) arcilla refractaria
— **lining,** (frn) forro refractario
gap, espacio, hendidura, mella, laguna, solución de continuidad;

(tp) garganta, desfiladero, collado, angostura, brecha, hondonada; (el) (gf) intervalo
— **theorem,** (dp) teorema de los espacios intermedios
Garbutt rod, varilla arrastraválvula, (Me) pescante de la válvula de pie
garnet, granate
garnierite, garnierita
gas, gas
— **actifier,** activador de gas
— **anchor,** (pr) segregador de gas
— **bag,** talego de gas
— **balance,** balanza de gas
— **black,** negro de humo (de gas)
— **boot,** bota de gas
— **burner,** quemador de gas
— **cap,** casquete de gas, cúpula (o capa) gasífera, (Ve) cresta gasífera
— **cap drive,** (pr) empuje por gas libre, empuje por expansión del casquete de gas
— **constant,** factor constante de gas
— **cooler,** enfriador de gas
— **cut mud,** lodo cortado por gas
— **cutting,** (sd) corte con gas; (fl) mezclar con gas
— **cycling,** recirculación del gas
— **dehydration process,** proceso de deshidratación de gas
— **detector,** detector de gas
— **displacement meters,** contador de desplazamiento de gas
— **drilling,** perforación con gas (q.v. **air drilling**)
— **drive,** (pr) empuje por gas en solución
— **engine,** motor a gas
— **field,** campo de gas
— **feeding line,** tubo alimentador
— **furnace,** horno de gas
— **gage,** manómetro para gas
— **generator,** gasógeno
— **heater,** calentador del gas

— **holder,** gasómetro, tanque para gas (q.v. **gasometer**)
— **indicator,** indicador (o medidor) de gas
— **injection,** inyección de gas
— **injection well,** pozo inyector de gas
— **input well,** pozo inyector de gas
— **lift,** (pr) extracción artificial por gas, bombeo neumático, producción por presión de gas
— **lift mandrel,** mandril del equipo de bombeo neumático
— **line,** gasoducto, tubería para gas
— **liquids,** líquidos del gas
— **lock,** (bm) atasco (o traba) por gas, (Me) candado de gas
— **mask,** careta antigás
— **meter,** contador de gas
— **oil,** gasóleo, gas oil
— **plant,** planta (o fábrica) de gas
— **pocket,** (sd) cavidad (q.v. **blow hole**)
— **processing,** procesamiento (o proceso) del gas
— **proof,** a prueba de gas
— **pump,** bomba para gas
— **purification process,** proceso para purificación del gas
— **reversion,** inversión del gas
— **sand,** arena gasífera
— **scrubber,** depurador de gas
— **separator,** separador de gas
— **service,** derivación particular para gas
— **stack,** colector de gas
— **trap,** trampa de gas, colector de gas
— **turbine,** turbina de gas
— **volumen fractions,** fracciones del volumen de gas
— **welding,** soldadura a gas
— **well,** pozo de gas natural
— **zone,** zona gasífera
gas-fuel line, línea del gas combustible

gas-oil contact, contacto gas-petróleo, (Me) contacto gas-aceite

gas-oil ratio, relación gas-petróleo, (Me) relación gas-aceite

gas-pressure regulator, regulador de la presión del gas

gaseous, gaseoso, gaseiforme

— **hydrocarbons,** hidrocarburos gaseosos

— **olefins,** olefinas gaseosas

gasket, empaquetadura, empaque, arandela, zapatilla, guarnición

gasoline, gasolina, (Ar) nafta, (CH) bencina

— **charge,** carga de gasolina

— **engine,** motor a gasolina

— **storage,** depósito de gasolina

— **tester,** hidrómetro

— **trap,** separador de gasolina

gasoline-powered, con motor de gasolina

gasometer, gasómetro (q.v. **gas holder**)

gasser, pozo productor de gas

gastight, hermético (o estanco) al gas

gastrolith, gastrolito

gate, portón, puerta; (hd) compuerta; (tr) álabe giratorio (o director), paleta directriz;

— **array,** (dp) circuitos predifundidos (de puerta)

— **ring,** (tr) anillo regulador

— **valve,** válvula de compuerta, (Ur) válvula de esclusa

— **valve with bypass,** válvula de compuerta con llave auxiliar

gather, (gf) sección de trazas comunes

gathering, *a.* recolector, de colección

— **station,** (pr) estación recolectora

— **tank,** tanque de recolección

gauge, q.v. **gage**

gauss, gauss, gausio: unidad de intensidad magnética

Gaussian, *a.* (mt) (dp) gausiano, de Gauss

gauze, gasa

GCD (greatest common divisor), máximo común divisor

gear, *n.* engranaje, engrane, rueda dentada; *v.* engranar, encajar

— **box,** caja de engranajes (o de cambio)

— **case,** caja de engranajes

— **clearance,** luz (o distancia) libre en los dientes de un engranaje

— **compound,** compuesto para lubricar engranajes, grasa de engranajes

— **puller,** sacaengranajes

— **rack,** cremallera

— **ration,** relación de engranaje

— **reduction,** desmultiplicación (o redución) de engranajes

— **shifter housing,** caja de cambio de velocidades

— **shifting,** cambio de velociadades

— **tooth,** diente de engranaje

— **wheel,** rueda dentada

gear-reduction pumping unit, bomba con engranajes reductores de la velocidad del motor

geared hoist, aparejo a engranaje, garrucha de engranaje, huinche a engranaje, (Ar) guinche

geared pumping power, fuerza motriz a engranaje para bombeo

gearing, engranaje

gearshift fork, horquilla de cambio de velocidades

gearshift rail, barra (o corredera) de cambio de velocidades

geest, (g) (Ar) secadal, seguero

gel, gel, material gelatinoso formado por coagulación

— **strength,** esfuerzo gel

107

gelatin dynamite, dinamita
gelatinosa
gelatinous, gelatinoso
gelling agent, aditivo gelatinizador,
gel
general average, promedio general;
(cm) total de averías en tránsito
generalized linear inversion, (gf)
inversión lineal generalizada
generator, (el) generator
— **gas,** gas pobre
— **unit,** generador con máquina
impulsora
genotype, genotipo
gentle dip, buzamiento moderado
genus, género
geoanticline, anticlinal regional,
geoanticlinal
geochemistry, geoquímica
geocratic period, (g) período
geocrático
geode, (g) géoda
geodesy, geodesia
geodetic, geodético
geogeny, geogenia
geognostic map, plano geonóstico
geognosy, geonosia
geographic, geográfico
— **pole,** polo geográfico
geoid, geoide; geoidal
geologic, geológico
— **age,** edad geológica
— **column,** columna (o sección)
geológica
— **horizon,** horizonte geológico
— **mapping,** levantamiento de
planos geológicos
— **report,** informe geológico
— **section,** sección (o columna)
geológica
— **survey,** levantamiento de planos
geológicos, estudio (o
reconocimiento) geológico
— **time scale,** escala geológica de
tiempo
geological, q.v. **geologic**

geologist, (oc) geólogo
geology, geología
geomagnetic field, campo
geomagnético
geometric, geométrico
geometry, geometría
geomorphology, geomorfología
geophone, (gf) geófono; sismómetro
— **patch,** tendido de recepción,
parcela (o despliegue) de
geófonos
— **spread,** tendido de recepción,
haz (o despliegue) de geófonos
geophysical jetting bit, barrena de
circulación de agua para
perforaciones geofísicas
geophysical mapping,
levantamiento geofísico
geophysics, geofísica
Georgian, georgiense
geosyncline, geosinclinal
geothermal gradient, gradiente
recíproca de temperatura
geothermic, geotérmico
get afloat, *v.* (nt) desembarrancar
geyser, géiser
geyserite, geiserita
GHz (gigahertz), gigahertz: unidad
de frecuencia
gib, cuña, chaveta, contraclavija
gib-head key, chaveta de cabeza
gibbsite, gibsita, yesita
giga (G), *pref.* SI $= 10^9$
GIGO (garbage in, garbage out),
(dp) i.e. la calidad de los datos de
entrada condiciona la calidad de
la información de salida
gilsonite, gilsonita (q.v. **bitumen**)
gimbal, soporte cardán, balancín de
la brújula
— **joint,** junta universal
gimlet, barrena pequeña, barrenita,
gusanillo
gin, poste grúa; molinete, torno de
izar

— **block**, motón liviano de acero, motón sin cuerpo

— **pole,** poste grúa, pluma, grúa de palo, (Ar) pluma de cabria, travesero alzapoleas, (Ve) caballete

— **pole truck,** camión grúa

girdle, (g) estrato delgado

girt, (prf tower) travesaño; carrera, correa, cinta, larguero

GIS (geographic information system), sistema geográfico de información

glacial, glacial, helado

— **drift,** (g) acarreos de glaciar, derrubios glaciarios

— **meal,** polvo de roca

— **stream,** arroyo subglacial

— **tilt,** declive glacial (o glaciario), declive producido por acción glaciaria

glaciation, (g) glaciación

glacier, glaciar, helero, ventisquero

— **circus,** circo glaciar (o glaciario) (q.v. **corrie, cirque)**

— **outlet,** (Ar) portón de glaciar

— **table,** mesa glaciar (o glaciárica)

glan, collarín (q.v. **stuffing box**)

gland, (ma) casquillo (o collarín) del prensaestopas, caja estancadora

— **packing,** casquillo de prensaestopas, empaquetadura del casquillo

glass, vidrio

— **mat,** (tu) forro de tela de vidrio para tubería

— **paste,** (g) pasta vítrea

— **wool,** lana de vidrio

glauconite, glauconita

glazed, vidriado, glaseado, esmaltado

GLI, q.v. **generalized linear inversion**

glimmer, (mn) mica

glitch, ruido, interferencia, señal transitoria (o deformada)

globe valve, válvula de globo

globule, glóbulo

globulites, globulitos

glomeroporphyritic, glomeroporfirítico

glycol, glicol

— **amine gas treating,** tratamiento del gas por glicol-amina

— **type antifreeze,** anticongelante de tipo glicol

glyptoliths, gliptolitos

gneiss, neis, gneis

gneissic, néisico, gnéisico

GNP (gross national product), producto nacional bruto (PNB)

go-devil, (p) raspatubos, taco (o tarugo) de limpiar tubos, diablo, (Me) conejo, (Ve) chanchito (q.v. **pig**)

goggles, gafas protectoras, antiparras

gold bearing, aurífero

gonimeter, goniómetro

goodness-of-fit test, (stats) prueba del buen ajuste

gooseneck, tubo (o conexión) en S

— **siphon,** sifón cuello de cisne, sifón en S

— **yoke,** yugo cuello de ganso

GOR, q.v. **gas-oil ratio**

gorge, (g) garganta, quebrada, barranco

gouge, *n.* (tl) gubia; (g) salbanda; *v.* escoplear con la gubia

gourde, gourde: moneda de Haití

government anchor, (cn) ancla de pared

governor, (mc) regulador, controlador

gpm (gallons per minute), galones por minuto

gpM (gallons per 1,000 cubic feet), galones por 1.000 pies cúbicos

GPR, q.v. **ground penetrating
radar**
GPS (Global Positioning System),
(nav) Sistema de
Posicionamiento Global
grab, gancho de pesca, (Ve)
pescador de gancho
graben, graben, fosa tectónica,
zanja geológica, grabenfosa
gradation, (tp) graduación, (Co)
gradación
gradational, gradual
grade, *n.* grado, clase, calidad; (rd)
pendiente, gradiente, declive,
cuesta, rampa; rasante, nivel; *v.*
clasificar, graduar, tasar;
nivelar, explanar, emparejar,
allanar, aplanar, enrasar
graded string, (prf) sarta
combinada (q.v. **mixed string**)
grader, nivelador de caminos,
explanadora, (Ar) llanadora
gradient, gradiente
— **profile,** perfil de gradientes
gradienter screw, tornillo del
compás de nivelar
gradiometer, gradiómetro
graduate, *n.* probeta graduada
graduated, graduado
— **breaker with lip and double
spout,** vaso de precipitados
graduado con dos vertederos
— **cylinder,** stoppered, probeta
graduada con tapón
— **cylinder with spout,** probeta
graduada con pico
grahamite, grahamita, asfalto
Graham's law, ley de Graham: los
regímenes relativos de la
difusión de gases diferentes, bajo
las mismas condiciones, son
inversamente proporcionales a
la raíz cuadrada de la densidad
de los mismos
grain, (mu) textura; (g) clivaje
normal al crucero principal;

(wt) grano; (wood) veta, grano,
fibra, hebra; (abrasive) finura
— **alcohol,** alcohol etílico, alcohol
de cereales
— **tin,** caserita
grain-mole, grano-mol
gram, gramo
— **molecular weight,** peso
molecular en gramos
granite, granito
— **wash,** lavaduras de granito
granitic, granítico
granoblastic, granoblástico
granodiorite, granodiorita
granophyric, granofírico
grantee, (cm) concesionario
grantor, (cm) otorgante
granular, granular, granulado
granularity, granularidad
granulation, granulación
granule, gránulo, (Co, Ve) guija
— **conglomerate,** conglomerado de
gránulos
— **gravel,** gravilla, grava guijosa
granulite, granulita
granulose, granulosa
graph, esquema gráfico
graphic, gráfico
— **log,** registro (o informe) gráfico
graphical computation,
computación gráfica
graphite, grafito, plombagina
— **grease,** grasa de grafito
graphitization, conversión del
carbón amorfo en grafita
grasshopper counterbalance,
contrapeso saltón
grate, parrilla, rejilla
grating, emparrillado, rejilla,
parrilla, reja, verja, rejado
gravel, grava, gravilla, cascajo, (Ar)
rodados, ripio, (Ur) pedregullo
(q.v. **boulder, cobble, pebble,
granule gravel**)
— **packing,** relleno de cascajo;
empacador

Glossary of the Petroleum Industry

gravel-packed liner, tubo colador rodeado por grava para evitar que la arena se filtre en el pozo
graver, buril, concel, gradino
gravimeter, gravímetro (q.v. **gravity meter**)
— **period,** período de gravímetro
gravimetric, gravimétrico
gravitation, gravitación, gravedad
gravitational
— **attraction,** acción (o atracción) de la gravedad; acción gravitativa
— **compaction,** (g) compactación por gravedad
— **constant,** (gf) constante de gravitación
— **field,** (gf) campo de gravedad
— **potential,** (gf) potencial de gravitación
gravitative, gravitativo
gravitometer, gravitómetro
gravity, gravedad
— **anomaly,** anomalía gravimétrica
— **contour,** curva isogama
— **curve,** curva gravimétrica (o de gravedad)
— **drainage,** (pr) separación gravitacional
— **fault,** falla por gravedad
— **feed,** alimentación por gravedad
— **gradient,** gradiente gravimétrico (o de gravedad), vector principal de gravedad
— **maximum,** máximo de gravedad
— **meter,** gravímetro (q.v. **gravimeter**)
— **minimum,** mínimo de gravedad
— **observation,** observación gravimétrica
— **platform,** plataforma de gravedad (q.v. **pileless platform**)
— **profile,** perfil gravimétrico
— **reading,** lectura gravimétrica

— **recorder,** registrador de gravedad
— **settling,** asentamiento por gravedad
— **station,** estación gravimétrica
— **survey,** (gf) estudio gravimétrico
— **unit,** unidad gravimétrica (1/10 miligal)
gray iron casting, fundición gris, fundición de segunda fusión
gray water, (ec) aguas grises, aguas de desperdicios domésticos no cloacales
graywacke, graywacke, grauvaca
grease, n. grasa, (Ur) lubricante consistente; v. engrasar
— **box,** caja de grasa, engrasadora
— **cup,** grasera, (Ar) copilla grasera, (Ur) grasera de copa
— **gun,** pistola de engrase, engrasador a presión
— **kettle,** caldero (o marmita) de grasa
— **nipple,** grasera
— **pump,** bomba de engrase
— **reservoir,** depósito de grasa
— **retainer,** retén de grasa
— **seal,** empaquetadura contra grasa
green earth, glauconita
greenhouse effect, efecto invernadero
greensand, arena verde
greenstone, piedra verde
greisen, gres
grid, rejilla; (gf) malla
— **effect,** efecto por interpolación en malla
grief stem, (prf) vástago cuadrado de transmisión, junta cuadrada giratoria (q.v. **kelly joint**)
grillage, emparrillado, enrejado
grille, rejilla
grind, moler, amolar; (tl) afilar, amolar esmerilar;

111

pulimentar, refrentar; (mn) pulverizar

grindability, molibilidad

grinder, moledora; (mc) esmeriladera, rectificadora; amoladora, muela, afiladora

grinding machine, amoladora, moledora, esmeriladora; trituradora

grinding wheel, piedra de amolar (q.v. **grindstone**)

grindstone, piedra de amolar, muela, afiladora, asperón

grip, *n.* agarre, agarradero, cogedero, mango, puño; (mc) mordaza, garra; (rivet) agarre; *v.* agarrar

grit, *n.* arenilla; (g) arenisca; *a.*

gritty, arenoso, de granos angulosos

grommet, anillo protecter, orificio blindado

groove, *n.* ranura, muesca, gárgol, rabajo; *v.* ranurar, acanalar, estriar, muescar

groove-joint union, junta machihembrada (q.v. **tongue and groove joint**)

grooved, ranurado

— **pipe fittings**, conexiones para tubo acanalado

grooving, *n.* (g) acanalamiento; *v.* acanalarse

gross, *n.* (measure) gruesa (12 x 12); *a.* bruto

— **cost**, coste (o costo) total

— **income**, (cm) rentas brutas

— **production**, producción en bruto

— **ton**, tonela larga (o bruta)

— **tonnage**, tonelaje bruto

— **standard volume**, volumen bruto estándar

— **weight**, peso bruto

grossularite, grosularita

ground, *n.* tierra, terreno, suelo; (el) puesta a tierra; *v.* poner (o

conectar) a tierra; (nau) varar, encallar; *a.* molido; afilado

— **plate**, placa de cimiento

— **roll**, (gf) onda superficial (de largo período y poca velocidad), onda de tierra

— **strap**, (el) planchuela de contacto a tierra

ground-in-joint, unión rectificada (o pulimentada), conexión sin rosca y a fricción

ground-level concentration, (ec) concentración a nivel de tierra

ground-penetrating radar, radar de penetración terrestre

grounded circuit, (el) circuito a tierra

groundmass, (g) base vidriosa del pórfido, (Ar) pasta mineral (q.v. **matrix, gangue**)

groundwater, agua freática (o subterránea)

— **divide**, divisoria de las aguas freáticas

— **runoff**, escurrimiento subterráneo

— **table**, nivel freático

group interval, (gf) intervalo entre grupos

group roll, (gf) rodaje de grupos

grouser, agarradera, garra

growler, (lever) fulcro; (el) probador de inducidos

guarantee, *v.* garantizar, dar fianza;

guaranty, *n.* garantía

guarani, guaraní: moneda de Paraguay

guard, guardia, resguardo, (Ar) escudo, protector

— **band**, (dp) banda de guarda (o de seguridad) (q.v. **frequency division multiplexing**)

— **electrode log**, registro enfocado

— **stake**, (tp) estaca indicadora

guardrail, baranda, (Me) barandal

gudgeon, (mc) muñón, gorrón, macho, turrión, (Ar) pivote
guide, guía
— **formation,** estrato guía, (Ar) horizonte guía
— **fossil,** fósil índice
— **rib,** lomo de machihembrado
— **shoe,** guía de zapata, zapata guía
guidelines, cables guía; líneas de anclaje; pauta, directiva
— **tensioner,** tensor de las líneas de anclaje
guidelineless drilling system, sistema de perforación (flotante) sin líneas de anclaje (o sin anclas)
guiding ring, anillo guía, guiador
gulf, golfo
gullet, lima cilíndrica, gollete
gully, (g) quebrada, cárcava, arroyada, (Me) barranquilla
gum, *n.* goma; *v.* (petrol) engomarse
— **test,** (rf) prueba de gomosidad en platillo de cobre (q.v. **copper dish test**)
gumbo, (prf) gumbo, formación gelatinosa (o pegajosa)
gummy, gomoso, pegajoso, resinoso
gun, arma
— **barrel,** tanque de asentamiento, decantador
— **cotton,** fulmicotón, nitroalgodón
— **perforating,** (prf) perforar a bala un tubo de revestimiento, (Ar) punzado selectivo
— **perforator,** perforador a bala, (Ve) cañón, pistola de perforación
gunpowder, pólvora
gunite, gunita
— **lining,** revestimiento de gunita
gunk squeeze, taponamiento con bentonita
gusher, pozo surgente (o descontrolado)

gusset, codo de hierro, hierro angular de refuerzo
guy, retenida, contraviento, viento, tirante, (Ar) rienda, tensor; *v.* atirantar, contraventar, (Ve) ventear
— **cable,** cabo muerto
— **derrick,** grúa de contravientos de cable, grúa atirantada (o de retenidas)
— **hook,** gancho de retenida
— **ring,** anillo de retenidas
— **wire,** viento (o retenida) de alambre
guy-eye bolt, perno con ojo para retenida
guyed tower, torre retenida
guyline, cable contraviento (o de retenida), (Ar) cable tensor, (Me) cable de viento
— **anchor,** ancla para cable contraviento, (Me) ancla del viento
— **stakes,** estacas para contravientos
GVF, q.v. **gas volume fractions**
Gy, q.v. **gray**
gypsite, yesoide
gypsum, yeso
gyroscope, giroscopio

H

h, q.v. **hecto**
H, q.v. **henry; hydrogen**
H frame, (transmission line) caballete en H
H hinge, gozne en H
HA, q.v. **hazard assessment**
ha, q.v. **hectare**
hachures, sombreado, hachuras
hacker, (dp) intruso, pirata informático; computomaníaco, fanático de ordenador

English - Spanish

hacksaw, *n.* segueta, sierra para
metales; *v.* serrar (o aserrar)
metal
hade, (g) buzamiento, inclinación
de una vena (o estrato)
hair-pin-socket, (fishing tl) enchufe
ahorquillado
half, medio
— **bend,** (tu) curva de 180°
— **bearing,** medio cojinete
— **cell,** media celda
— **duplex,** semiduplex,
bidireccional alternativo
— **life,** media vida
— **life period,** semiperiodo de vida
— **round file,** lima media caña
— **skirt,** (fishing tl) mediacaña
guíadora
— **sole,** (tu) media suela
— **turn,** una revolución (o vuelta)
de 180°
— **turn socket,** pescabarrena de
media vuelta
— **wave,** semionda, media onda
half-angle, *a.* semiángulo
halide, haluro
halite, halita
halo, halo, corona
halogen, halógeno
haloid acid, ácido haloideo
haloid salt, sal haloidea
halt, parada, detención
hammer, (hand-held) martillo;
(two-hand) maza, macho;
(falling) pilón, martinete; *v.*
martillar, amartillar, machar;
(ma) golpetear
— **drill,** martillo de perforación
— **roll,** (sd) caldear, calda a
martillo hidráulico, calda a
rodillo, calda de herrero (q.v.
forge welding, blacksmith roll)
— **welding,** soldadura a martillo
hammer-lug union, unión provista
de orejas para ajuste a
martillazos

hand, *n.* asa, mango, agarradera,
manija, manivela; mano; (in)
aguja, manecilla, puntero; (oc)
operario
— **actuated,** accionado
manualmente
— **brake,** freno de mano
— **cart,** carro de mano, carretilla
— **cutter,** cortadora manual,
cortatubos de mano
— **drill,** taladro de mano, (Ve)
chompa
— **hole,** orificio de limpieza a mano
— **level,** nivel de mano
— **operated threader,** terraja
manual
— **pump,** bomba de mano
— **saw,** serrucho
— **wheel,** rueda de mano,
volantemanubrio
handhole, registro de mano, orificio
de limpieza, portezuela
handle, *n.* mango, cabo, astil;
cogedero, asa, agarradera;
maniqueta, manivela; *v.*
manejar, manipular, maniobrar
handrail, baranda, pasamano, (Me)
barandal
handshake, (dp) establecimiento de
comunicación, acuse de recibo,
intercambio de señales, saludo,
intercambio de indicativos y
señales de control
hands off, sin control manual
hands on, control manual
handy hoist, (prf) cabrestante
auxiliar de servicio
hanger, colgadero, barra de
suspensión
— **plug,** tapón aislador
hanging, colgante
— **tie,** (cn) colgante
— **glacier,** helero (o glaciar)
colgante
— **valley,** (g) valle colgante

— **valve,** válvula de gozne, válvula de charnela de disco exterior

— **wall,** (g) respaldo alto, cubierta del filón, (Ar) pendiente, yacente, (Bo) hastial de techo, (Co) muro colgante, (Me) reliz (o tabla) del alto (q.v. **roof**)

HAPs (hazardous air polutants), contaminantes de aire peligrosos

harbor, puerto

hard, duro

— **disk,** (dp) disco duro (o rígido, fijo, metálico)

— **emulsion,** emulsión estable

— **formation,** formación dura

— **water,** agua dura

hard-surfacing alloys, aleaciones duras para superficies

hardbanding, bandas de metal duro, banda dura

hardfacing, refrentado duro, recubrimiento

— **alloy,** metal de aleación dura para chapear (o refrentar)

hardening, temple, endurecimiento

— **of bits,** templado de barrenas

hardpan, (g) tosca, capa roscosa debajo de terreno blando

hardware, ferretería; máquinas; (dp), hardware, equipo físico, componentes físicos, dotación física (*counterpart of* **software)**

— **circuitry,** circuitos del hardware

hardwood, madera dura

harmonic balance, (gf) contrapeso antivibratorio, compensador

harmonic motion, (g) movimiento armónico, movimiento oscilatorio simple

HASINS, sistema submergible de alta presión para navegación submarina por inercia

hasp, pestillo de cerradura

hatch, (nt) escotilla; (tk) registro, escotilla de medición

hauling, transporte, acarreo

hay section, (cl) sección de filtrado

hay tank, (pr) tanque con heno

hazard, riesgo, peligro

— **assessment,** evaluación del peligro

— **index,** índice de peligro

— **ranking system,** sistema de clasificación de peligro

HDLC, q.v. **high-level data link control**

HDPE, q.v. **high density polyethylene**

HDS, q.v. **hydrodesulfuration**

He, q.v. **helium**

head, (well), boca, cabeza; (tu) cabeza, cabezal; (cylinder) fondo, tapa; (bl) fondo; (mt) culata; (fl) altura; (bm), altura de succión, (hd) carga, salto, caída, desnivel, altura; (g) cabeza de un pliegue terraplenado (o monoclinal), comba superior de un monoclinal (o terraplén); (cm) jefe, principal

— **fast,** (nt) proís, amarra de proa

— **gate,** compuerta de toma, boquera, (Es) templadera

— **guy,** (el) retenida final

— **pulley,** polea motriz

— **shaft,** árbol de cabezal, eje motor

— **to head,** derivación (o flujo) intermitente

— **wave,** (gf) onda precursora

headache post, (perc) poste para balancín, (Me) poste de apoyo

headend, extremo de cabeza (o de entrada)

header, (cl) cabezal, colector-cabezal, (Ar) cabeza de hervidores; (tu) cabezal de tubos, tubo múltiple; (el) canal transversal; (dp) cabecera, encabezamiento

— **bar,** barra cabecero

English - Spanish

— **box,** caja de unión, cabezal en U
(q.v. **return bend**)
— **record,** (dp) registro de cabecera
heart, núcleo, corazón, alma
— **cut,** corte del medio
hearth, hogar de forja, crisol de
horno
heat, calor
— **baffle,** deflector del calor
— **balance,** distribución de calor,
balance de caldeo
— **capacity,** capacidad térmica
— **content,** contenido de calor
— **decomposition,** descomposición
de calor
— **duty,** efecto útil (o rendimiento)
del calor
— **engine,** máquina térmica
— **exchange,** (rf) intercambio de
calor
— **exchanger,** (rf) permutador (o
intercambiador) de calor, (Ve)
termopermutador
— **input,** calor consumido
— **insulation,** aislamiento contra el
calor
— **liberation rate,** régimen de
liberación de calor
— **load,** carga de calor
— **of combustion,** calor de
combustión (q.v. **heating value**)
— **of formation,** calor de
formación
— **of fusion,** calor de fusión
— **of vaporization,** calor de
vaporización
— **prover,** calorímetro
— **transfer,** transferencia de calor,
termopermuta
— **treating,** tratamiento al calor,
tratamiento térmico
— **transfer coefficient,** coeficiente
de transmisión de calor
— **transfer oil,** aceite de
transmisión de calor

— **treating oil,** aceite para temple
(o para tratamiento al calor)
— **treatment,** tratamiento térmico
— **unit,** unidad de calor
heat-resisting steel, acero
resistente al calor
heat-treated, tratado al calor
heat-treating furnace, horno para
tratamiento térmico
heater, calentador; calefactor
heating, caldeo; calefacción; (ma)
calentamiento
— **surface,** superficie de caldeo (o
de calefacción)
— **plate,** plato calentador
— **value,** calor de combustión
— **valve,** (Me) capacidad calorífica
(q.v. **combustion heat**)
heave, (g) elevación, alzamiento;
(nt) oscilación vertical (de un
barco); henchidura (de una ola)
— **ahead,** virar sobre la popa
— **compensation,** compensación
del movimiento vertical
heaved block, (g) pilar tectónico,
gleba elevada (q.v. **horst**)
heaving shale, lutita desmoronable
(q.v. **shale**)
heavy, pesado; denso
— **crude,** petróleo crudo pesado (o
de alta gravedad API)
— **duty,** servicio pesado
— **end,** corte pesado final, residuo
pesado
— **fractions,** (rf) fracciones pesadas
de petróleo
— **hydrocarbons,** hidrocarburos
pesados
— **minerals,** minerales pesados
— **oil,** petróleo crudo, aceite espeso
— **oil plant,** planta de productos
pesados
— **spar,** sulfato de bario, baritina
— **water,** agua densa
heavy-weight drill pipe, tubería de
perforación extrapesada

116

hectare, hectárea
hectare-meter, hectárea-metro; superficie de una hectárea con un metro de espesor
hecto (h), *pref.* SI = 10^2
hedembergite, hedemburguita
heel, (nt) escora, inclinarse a la banda (q.v. **list**)
— **sheave,** roldana posterior; polea inferior
— **teeth,** dientes de la barrena (q.v. **gage cutters**)
height, altura
height-balanced, altura compensada (o equilibrada)
helical, helicoidal, hélico
— **gear,** engranaje helicoidal
— **scan,** (dp) exploración helicoidal
— **spooling,** (ca) enrollamiento helicoidal
helium, helio
helix, hélice (q.v. **propeller**)
helmet, casco
Helmholtz coil, bobina de Helmholtz
Helvetian, helvetiense
hematite, hematita
hemera, (g) hemera
hemimellithene, hemimeliteno
hemipelagic, (g) hemipelágico
hemp core, (ca) centro (o núcleo, corazón) de cáñamo (o de henequén)
heneicosane, heneicosano
heneicosene, heneicoseno
henheptacontane, henheptacontano
henry (H), henry: unidad de medida de inductancia
Henry's law, ley de Henry: la cantidad de gas disuelto por una cantidad dada de un líquido (con el cual no reacciona químicamente) a temperatura dada, es directamente

proporcional a la presión parcial del gas
hentetracontane, hentetracontano
hentriacontane, hentriacontano
hepta, *pref.* hepta-
heptadiene, heptadieno
heptane, heptano
heptene, hepteno
heptyl, heptil
heptyne, heptino (q.v. **amylacetylene**)
herbicidal oil, herbicida
hereinafter, en adelante
hermetical, hermético, a prueba de aire
herringbone gear, engranaje doble helicoidal, engranaje espina de pez
Herschel demulsibility number, índice de demulsibilidad de Herschel
Herschel oiliness machine, máquina Herschel de oleaginosidad
hertz (Hz), hercio: unidad de frecuencia
heterogeneous, heterogéneo
heulandite, heulindita
heuristic, heurístico
hexa, *pref.* hexa-
hexadecane, hexadecano (q.v. **cetane**)
hexadecene, hexadeceno
hexagon, hexágono
hexagonal, exagonal
hexane, hexano
— **(s) plus,** plushexanos
hexene, hexeno
hexyl, hexilo
hexyne, hexino (q.v. **butylacetylene**)
HF alkylation, alcohilación HF
HHC (highly hazardous chemical), compuesto (o producto) químico muy peligroso

hi-lead, mezcla de cobre y plomo
hiatus, (g) hiato
hickey, manguito sujetador
hidden layer, (gf) capa indetectable
(q.v. **blind zone**)
high, alto
— **angle fault**, falla gran angular,
falla con buzamiento mayor de
45°
— **blast furnace,** alto horno
— **boiling fraction,** (rf) fracción de
alta ebullición
— **density polyethylene,**
polietileno de alta densidad
— **frequency,** alta frecuencia
— **gravity,** máximo gravimétrico
— **low control,** control de alto y
bajo nivel
— **low frequency methods,**
métodos de inducción de alta a
baja frecuencia
— **molecular weight,** alto peso
molecular
— **pressure chamber**, cámara de
alta presión
— **resolution surveying,**
levantamiento geofísico de alta
resolución
— **torque**, alta torsión, fuerte
momento de torsión
— **water,** (mar) pleamar
high-level data link control, (dp)
protocolo de control de enlace
de datos de alto nivel
high-line interference, (gf)
interferencia de línea de alta
tensión
high-pass filter, filtro de paso alto,
(Ar) filtro pasa-altos, (Me)
filtraje de paso de altas
frecuencias
high-torque motor, motor de fuerte
momento de torsión
highway, carretera
hill, colina, cerro, loma
hillock, (g) altozano; otero

hillside, ladera, falda
hinge, *n.* (mc) charnela,
articulación; bisagra, gozne; *v.*
enquiciar, articular;
embisagrar, engoznar
— **fault,** (g) falla girada, falla en
espigación
— **jaw**, mordaza de articulación
— **pin**, pasador de bisagra
hinged joint, articulación, unión de
charnela, junta de bisagra,
rotulación
hip joint, (truss) junta de la cuerda
superior con el poste extremo
inclinado
hire, emplear
hi res (high resolution), alta
resolución
histogram, histograma
hit, acierto
— **on-the-fly printer,** (dp)
impresora al vuelo
— **hit rate**, tasa de acierto (o de
movimiento)
hitch, (mc) enganche; (mn) muesca
HLEM, q.v. **horizontal loop EM
system**
hoe, azada
hogback, (g) cuchilla, lomo de perro
hogging, (mar) distorsión (del casco
de un equipo marino de
perforación)
hoist, *n.* cabrestante, malacate,
montacargas, guinche, huinche,
aparejo; *v.* izar
hoisting block, motón de gancho
hoisting engine, malacate
hold, *n.* (nt) bodega, cala; *v.*
contener; aguantar; sujetar
hold-down anchor, (bm) ancla
holder, sujetador, fiador;
aguantador, sostenedor,
retenedor
— **clamp,** tornillo de fijación
holding

— **company,** compañía matriz (o dominatriz)
— **pond,** estanque
holdover post, brazo de sostén
holdup, q.v. **pull-rod holdup**
hole, agujero, perforación, barreno, hueco, pozo, cavidad, fosa
— **deflection with knuckle joint,** desviación del hoyo con herramienta de unión articulada
— **enlarger,** ensanchador de agujeros; escariador (q.v. **reamer**)
holiday, (tu) agujero (o raspadura, grieta) en la capa preservativa; (cm) día de fiesta
— **detector,** (tu) detector de huecos
hollow, *n.* hueco; (tp) hoyo, depresión; *a.* hueco, ahuecado
— **casing spear,** arpón pescatubos hueco
— **crankshaft,** cigüeñal hueco
— **reamer,** ensanchador (o escariador) hueco
— **stem valve,** válvula de vástago hueco
Holocene, holoceno
holocystalline, holocritalino
holohyaline, holohialino
holoeucratic, holoeucrático
holotype, holotipo
homing beacon, radiofaro direccional
homing device, indicador automático de ruta
homocline, homoclinal
homogeneity, homogeneidad
homogeneous, homogéneo
homologous series, serie homóloga
hone, rectificadora, pulidora, piedra de afilar
honeycomb formation, formación cavernosa
hood, capó, cubierta, capote; (mc) sombrerete, caperuza, cubierta

hook, *n.* gancho, garfio; *v.* enganchar
— **bolt,** perno de gancho
— **load capacity,** capacidad del malacate y mástil
— **pin,** pasador del gancho
— **shank,** espiga del gancho
— **up,** (el) acoplar; entrelazar
— **wrench,** llave de gancho, (Es) ganzúa
hook-off joint, q.v. **knock-off joint**
hook-wall packer, obturador de expansión que se agarra a la pared
Hooke's law, ley de Hooke
hookup, conexión, sistema de conexión, enganche, emplame; red de circuitos
hoop, *n.* aro, anillo, zuncho; (Ar) estribo, virola, (PR, Me) cincho; *v.* enzunchar, zunchar, anillar, cinchar
hopper, tolva, embudo
horizon, horizonte; (g) nivel, estrato
— **trace,** (tp) horizonte de imagen
horizontal, horizontal
— **component of magnetic field,** (gf) componente horizontal del campo magnético
— **directive tendency,** tendencia directiva horizontal
— **loop electromagnetic system,** sistema electromagnético de circuito cerrado horizontal
— **magnetic anomaly,** anomalía magnética horizontal
— **magnetic intensity,** intensidad magnética horizontal
— **offset,** desplazamiento lateral
— **pendulum,** péndulo horizontal
— **plan,** plano horizontal
— **throw,** desplazamiento horizontal
— **thrust,** (g) corrimiento horizontal

— **velocity gradient,** gradiente
lateral de la velocidad (q.v.
lateral velocity gradient)
horn, bocina
— **socket,** pescaherramientas
abocinado, campana de pesca
con garfios
hornblenda, (g) hornblenda,
anfíbol
horned nut, tuerca con salientes
hornfels, hornfelsa
hornstone, hornsteno, piedra
córnea
horse, (g) roca atrapada; (tl)
caballete, burro
horsehead, (pr) cabeza del balacín,
cabeza de mula; (cn) caballete
horsepower (hp), caballos de fuerza
(o de vapor), caballo, (Co)
caballaje
— **rating, (mt)** caballos de régimen
horsepower-hour (hp-hr), caballo-
hora
horseshoe, herradura
— **magnet,** imán de herradura
horst, (g) horst, pilar tectónico,
gleba (q.v. **heaved block**)
hose, manguera
— **coupling,** empalme (o conexión,
acoplamiento) de manguera
host computer, ordenador base (o
primario, principal, central)
hot, caliente
— **carbonate process,** proceso con
carbonato en caliente
— **riveting,** remachado en caliente
— **roll,** v. laminar acero
— **spot,** zona de calor, calefactor,
punto cálido
— **spring,** manantial termal
— **tap,** conexión a presión
— **wire detector,** detector térmico
Hotchkiss drive, mando tipo
Hotchkiss
hotel platform, plataforma de
alojamiento

hourglass structure, (g) estructura
reloj de arena, estructura en X
housing, vivienda, alojamiento;
(mc) bastidor, caja, envoltura;
cárter; casco
howel, doladera, dobladera, (Me)
tajadera
hp, q.v. **horsepower**
hp-hr, q.v. **horsepower-hour**
hub, (tu) campana, enchufe; maza,
cubo; copa; (dp) boca
huerfano, (g) huérfano, montañas
rodeadas (pero no cubiertas) de
depósitos sedimentarios
humic, húmico, relativo al humus
humidify, humedecer
humidity, humedad
hump, (g) giba
humus, (g) humus
hundred-year storm conditions,
(mar) condiciones de tormenta
de cien años, especificación para
instalaciones que deben resistir
vientos de 200 km/hora y las
condiciones de la tempestad más
violenta que se haya registrado
hundredweight, quintal: 100 libras
inglesas ó 454 kilogramos
hunting cog, diente suplementario
de una rueda dentada
Huronian, huroniense
hurricane deck, (nt) sollado
**HVAC (heating, ventilation, and
air conditioning system),**
sistema de calefacción,
ventilación y aire acondicionado
**HWDS (hazardous waste disposal
site),** sitio de disposición de
desperdicios peligrosos
hyalopilitic, hialopilítico
hybrid computer, ordenador
híbrido (o mixto)
hydatogenic, (g) hidatógeno
hydrate, hidrato
hydration, hidratación

hydrator, hidratador
hydraulic, hidráulico
— **coupling,** acoplador hidráulico
— **cylinder operator,** accionador
hidráulico de cilindro
— **drive,** mando hidráulico,
impulsión hidráulica (q.v.
hydraulic transmission)
— **gate,** compuerta
— **grade line,** línea piezométrica
— **gradient,** gradiente hidráulico (o
piezométrico)
— **jack,** gato hidráulico
— **lift pumping unit,** unidad de
bombeo que consiste de una
bomba de fondo accionada por
un fluido
— **mixer,** mezcladora hidráulica
— **motor actuator,** accionador a
motor hidráulico
— **oil,** aceite para mecanismo
hidráulico
— **packing,** empaquetadura
resistente al agua
— **pipe cutter,** cortatubos
hidráulico
— **press,** prensa hidráulica
— **pumping,** bombeo hidráulico
— **ram,** ariete hidráulico
— **similarity,** semejante hidráulico
— **slope,** pendiente hidráulica, línea
de carga
— **sluicing,** transporte (o acarreo,
laboreo) hidráulico
— **torque wrench,** llaves
hidráulicas
— **transmission,** transmisión
hidráulica (q.v. **hydraulic
drive**)
— **valve,** válvula accionada
hidráulicamente, válvula para
alta presión
hydraulics, *n.* hidráulica,
hidrotecnia
hydrindane, hidrindano (q.v.
bicyclononane)

hydrindene, hindrindeno
hydrocarbon, hidrocarburo
hydrochloric acid, ácido
clorhídrico (o hidroclórico)
hydrocodimer, hidrocodímero
hydrocracking, hidrocrácking,
hidrocraqueo,
hidrodesintegración (q.v.
cracking)
hydrocyclone, hidrociclón (q.v.
desander, desilter)
hydrodesulfuration,
hidrodesulfuración
hydrodynamics, hidrodinámica
hydrofining, hidrofining
hydroforming, (rf) hidroformación
— **plant,** planta hidroformadora
hydrogen (H), hidrógeno
— **sufide,** sulfuro de hidrógeno
hydrogenation, hidrogenación
hydrography, hidrografía
hydrolyzable acid esters, ester de
ácido hidrolizable
hydrolysis, hidrólisis
hydrometer, densímetro,
aerómetro
hydromatic brake, freno
hidroautomático
hydrophone, (g) hidrófono
hydrophylic, hidrófilo
hydrosilicates, hidrosilicato
hydrosphere, (g) hidrósfera
hydrostatic, hidrostático
— **bailer,** achicador hidrostático
— **head,** altura hidrostática
— **pressure,** presión hidrostática
hydrothermal, hidrotérmico
— **metamorphism,** metamorfismo
hidrotérmico
hydrotreater, (rf) hidrotratadora
hydroxide, hidróxido
hyetal interval, intervalo pluvial (o
hietal)
hygrometer, higrómetro
hygroscopic liquid, líquido
higroscópico

hyperbaric chamber, cámara
  hiperbárica
hypercube, hipercubo
hypersthene, hiperesteno
hypersthenite, hiperstenita
hypocenter, hipocentro, foco
  sísmico
hypochlorite, hipoclorito
— **sweetening,** endulzamiento por
  hipoclorito
— **treatment,** tratamiento
  hipoclorítico
hypocrystalline, hipocristalino
hypophosphorous, hipofosforoso
hypothesis, hipótesis
hypsometer, hipsómetro
hysteresis, (el) (mc) (gf) histéresis
— **lag,** atraso histerético
— **loss,** pérdida por histéresis
— **motor,** motor sincrónico (o de
  histéresis)
Hz, q. v. **hertz**

I

I, q.v. **iodine**
I beam, viga (o tirante) I
I-beam trolley, carretilla corrediza,
  trole
IC, q.v. **integrated circuit**
ice, hielo
— **age,** edad glacial (o del hielo)
— **breaker,** rompehielos
— **cap,** manto glacial
— **mill,** molino glaciárico
— **pack,** banco de hielo
— **screen,** barrera parahielos
— **worn,** raído por la acción glacial
iceberg, iceberg, témpano de hielo
Iceland spar, (mn) espato de
  Islandia
ichnite, pisada fosilizada
icicle, carámbano

ID (inside diameter), diámetro
  interior (DI)
idiostatic, idiostático
idle, v. (mt) andar (o trabajar) en
  ralenti, marchar en vacío; a.
  desocupado, inactivo
— **current,** (el) corriente
  desvatada, (Ar) corriente en
  vacío
— **speed,** velocidad baja sin carga
— **time,** tiempo de inactividad,
  tiempo pasivo
idler
— **gear,** engranaje loco (o
  secundario)
— **pinion,** piñón loco
— **pulley,** polea tensora (o muerta,
  loca), polea de guía
— **wheel,** rueda loca
idling nozzle, boquilla de velocidad
  sin carga
idocrase, (mn) idocrasa, vesuviana
IFR operation (certified for),
  (aero) para volar con
  instrumentos
igneous, ígneo
— **body,** cuerpo ígneo
— **rock,** roca ígnea (o volcánica,
  eruptiva), filón intrusivo
— **sheet,** hoja volcánica
ignite, inflamarse, encenderse
ignition, encendido, ignición
— **advance,** avance del encendido
— **delay,** retardo del encendido
— **quantity,** potencia de encendido
  (o de inflamación)
— **shorting switch,** interruptor por
  cortocircuito del encendido
**IGRF (international geomagnetic
  reference field),** campo
  geomagnético internacional de
  referencia
Illinoisan, illinoisiense
illuminant, n. iluminador; a.
  iluminante, iluminador

illuminating gas, gas rico, gas de alumbrado
ilmenite, ilmenita
image point, (gf) punto de imagen
imbibition, imbibición
imbricated, superpuesto, imbricado
imbrication, (g) imbricación
IMF (International Monetary Fund), Fondo Monetario Internacional
immersion, inmersión, sumersión
immiscible, inmiscible
impact, choque, impacto
impalpable powder, polvo impalpable
impedance, impedancia
— **meter,** impedómetro
impeller, impulsor, propulsor
impending blowout, reventón inminente
impervious, impermeable (q.v. **waterproof)**
— **bed,** estrato impermeable
impetus, ímpetu, impulsión
impingement, tropiezo, choque
— **nozzle,** tobera de choque
implosion, implosión
import list, (dp) lista importada (o transferida)
impounding, (g) agolpamiento, (Ar) endicamiento
impregnate, impregnar
impressed voltage, tensión aplicada, voltaje impreso (o de carga)
impression block, bloque de impresión
impsonite, impsonita; asfalto
impulse, impulso, impulsión; (el) onda
— **generator,** (el) generador de ondas
— **noise,** ruido de impulso (o de impulsión)
— **pump,** bomba de impulso

— **transformer,** transformador de impulso
— **turbine,** (hd) turbina de impulsión (o de chorro) libre
impurities, impurezas
in bulk, a granel
in field, en el campo
in kind, (cm) en especie
in situ, en el sitio, in situ
in stock, en existencia
inaccuracy, error; inexactitud
incandescent, incandescente
inch (in, "), pulgada (pg): 2,54 centímetros
incidence, (gf) incidencia
incident
— **angle,** (gf) ángulo de incidencia
— **compressional wave,** (gf) onda de compresión incidente
— **shear wave,** (gf) onda transversal, onda de cizallamiento
incineration, incineración
inclination, inclinación, declive, pendiente, talud, caída
inclined
— **fault,** falla inclinada, (Ar) falla diagonal
— **fold,** pliegue inclinado
— **plane,** plano inclinado
inclosed bodies, (g) cuerpos extraños incluídos (q.v. **enclosed)**
inclusion, (g) inclusión
income elasticity of demand, (cm) elasticidad consumo/ingreso
incompetent bed, estrato (o lecho) incompetente
incrustation, incrustación, escamación
indene, indeno
indentations, dientes; escotaduras
index, índice
— **die,** matriz de división

— **error**, (in) error de ajuste del
índice
— **fossil,** fósil indicador
— **mark**, (tp) marca de referencia
— **of refraction,** índice de
refracción
— **plane,** (g) plano de referencia
India ink, tinta china (o de dibujo)
indicating meter, manómetro
indicador
indications, indicaciones
indicator, indicador; medidor
— **cock**, llave indicadora
— **diagram**, diagrama del indicador
indigenous, autóctono
indigo copper, covelita, cobre
añilado
indraft, corriente hacia dentro
induced
— **draft,** tiro inducido (o aspirado)
— **feed-water heater**, calentador
inducido
— **magnetism,** magnetismo
inducido
— **polarization,** (gf) polarización
inducida
inductance, (el) (mo) inductancia
induction, inducción
— **flow,** flujo por aspiración
— **furnace**, horno de inducción
— **generator**, generador
asincrónico (o de inducción)
— **motor,** motor de inducción
— **period,** período de inducción
— **resistance welding**, soldadura a
resistencia por inducción
inductive methods, métodos de
inducción (de alta o baja
frecuencia)
inductor, (el) inductor, bobina de
indusctancia
indurate, *v.* endurecer; **indurated**,
a. endurecido, consolidado
industrial
— **crane,** grúa industrial

— **sewage**, aguas cloacales
industriales
— **wastes,** desperdicios (o aguas)
industriales
inelastic, no elástico, (Me)
inelástico
inert gas, gas inerte
inertia, inercia, fuerza de inercia
inertia-pressure gaging, (hd) aforo
por procedimiento inercia-
presión
inferential meter, contador tipo
ilativo
inferred fault, falla inferida (o
probable)
infilling well, pozo intermedio
infiltration, infiltración
— **index**, índice de infiltración
inflamation chamber, cámara de
inflamación
inflammable, inflamable
inflected curve, contracurva
inflection, inflexión
— **point,** punto de inflexión
influent, afluente, influente,
incurrente
— **ground water**, agua freática
afluente
— **seepage**, percolación afluente
influx, intromisión; afluencia
information storage and retrieval,
(dp) almacenamiento y
recuperación de información
information theory, (dp) teoría de
la información
infrared radiant heater,
calentador infrarrojo radiante
infusorial earth, tierra infusoria,
diatomita
ingot, lingote, barra de metal
ingredient, ingrediente
ingression, (g) ingresión
inhalator, inhalador; aspirador
inhaul, cable de aproximación,
cable de tracción de retorno

inhibitor, (qm) inhibidor, preventivo contra corrosión
— **sweetening,** endulzamiento por inhibidor
inhomogeneity, inhomogeneidad
initial, inicial
— **boiling point,** punto inicial de ebullición
— **daily production,** producción diaria inicial
— **dip,** buzamiento inicial
— **set,** fraguado inicial
— **stress,** esfuerzo inicial, prefatiga
— **vapor pressure,** presión (o tensión) inicial de vapor
injected igneous body, cuerpo ígneo inyectado
injection, inyección
— **gneiss,** (g) migmatita
— **mixer,** mezcladora de inyección
— **valve,** válvula de inyección
injector, inyector
inland waterway, vía de navegación interior
inlet, (hd) toma, boca de entrada (o de admisión), tomadero; (rf) admisor; (tp) caleta, estuario
— **cam,** leva de admisión
— **connection,** conexión de admisión
— **manifold,** mútiple de admisión
— **port,** orificio (o lumbrera) de admisión
— **valve,** válvula de admisión
inlier, (g) asomo; fenestra, ventana, miradero
in-line offset, (gf) desplazamiento en línea
in-line processing, (dp) proceso aleatorio, proceso lineal
innage, cubicación (o medición) directa; (tk) nivel
inner, interior
— **lap asbestos ribbed gasket,** empaquetadura con nervadura interior de asbesto

— **race,** pista interior
innocuous gas, gas inofensivo
inorganic, inorgánico
— **acidity,** acidez inorgánica
input, (rf) volumen de materia prima tratada; (dp) entrada
— **circuit,** circuito de entrada
— **filter,** filtro de entrada
— **/output,** (dp) entrada/salida
— **rate,** régimen de entrada
— **shaft,** eje impulsor
— **well,** pozo de inyección
insecticide, insecticida
insert, *n.* (mc) guarnición, pieza de inserción, (Me) inserto; *v.* (dp) insertar, intercalar
— **barrel,** cilindro insertado (o de inserción)
— **bowl,** tazón de cuñas (q.v. **spider, slip bowl**)
— **pump,** bomba de inserción
insert-type blowout preventer, impiderreventones de tipo de inserción
inserted-joint casing, junta de inserción para tubería de revestimiento
inserts, accesorios de inserción (en un pozo)
inside, *n.* interior; *a.* interior, interno; *adv.* dentro, adentro
— **calipers,** compás interior
— **diameter (ID),** diámetro interior (DI)
— **line-up clamp,** abrazadera interior de alineamiento
— **link plate,** plancha de eslabón interior (q.v. **impingement plate**)
— **location,** ubicación dentro del área probada del campo
— **tool,** gubia
insoluble, insoluble
inspection, inspección revisión, registro, fiscalización
— **plate,** placa de inspección

— **port,** orificio (o ventanilla) de inspección
instability, inestabilidad
install, instalar
installation, instalación, montaje, colocación
instantaneous velocity, velocidad instantánea
instrument, instrumento, aparato
— **blanks,** (la) blancos de instrumento
— **calibration,** calibración (o ajuste) de instrumentos
— **constant,** constante de instrumento
— **landing,** aterrizaje ciego
— **panel,** tablero de instrumentos
insulate, aislar; cubrir con material aislante
insulating brick, ladrillo refractario; ladrillo aislante
insulation, aislamiento; material aislante
insulator, aislador; material aislante
— **spool,** (el) roldana aisladora, aislador de carrete
insurable value, valor asegurable
insurance, seguro
— **policy,** póliza de seguro
intake, toma; (tu) admisión
— **air temperature,** temperatura del aire de admisión
— **manifold,** mútiple de admisión
— **pipe,** tubo de admisión
— **stroke,** carrera de admisión
— **valve,** válvula de admisión
integral stack, chimenea enteriza
integral tube sheet, placa enteriza para reunión de tubos
integrated circuit, circuito integrado
integrating meter, contador integrador
integrating orifice meter, medidor (o contador) integral de orificio

integration, integración
intensity, intensidad
— **anomaly,** (gf) anomalía de intensidad
interbedded, interestratificado
intercalated, intercalado
intercalation, intercalación
interchangeable, intercambiable
intercept time, (gf) tiempo de intercepción
intercooler, cambiador intermedio de temperatura, enfriador intermedio
interest, interés, (cm) rédito
interface, (dp) interfaz, interfase, junción; contacto interfacial, límite (o frontera) común (entre dos sistemas, elementos, etc.)
interfacial film, capa (o película) interfacial
interfacial tension, tensión interfacial
interference, interferencia
interferometer, interferómetro
interformational, interformacional
interglacial epochs, épocas interglaciales
intergranular, intergranular
interlaminated, interlaminado
interleave, *v.* (dp) interpolar; simultanear
interlocking, que traba, que enclavija; (gf) correlativa, energía contenida que ha viajado por la misma trayectoria en direcciones opuestas
intermediate
— **casing string,** tubería de revestimiento intermedia (q.v. **water casing**)
— **frequency,** frecuencia media
— **gear,** velocidad intermedia; engranaje intermedio
— **speed,** velocidad intermedia
— **rotary chain,** cadena intermediaria de transmisión

— **water,** agua intermedia

intermittent gas lift, producción intermitente por gas

intermitter valve, válvula intermitente

internal, interno; interior

— **combustion,** combustión interna

— **combustion engine,** motor de combustión interna

— **diameter (ID),** diámetro interior (DI)

— **erosion, (tu)** erosión interna

— **expanding,** expansión interna

— **expanding brake,** freno de expansión interna

— **expanding friction clutch,** embrague de fricción con expansión interna

— **flue,** humero (o tragante) interno

— **flush tool joint,** unión de diámetro interior a ras para tubería de perforción

— **gear transmission,** transmisión de engranaje interno

— **height,** altura interior

— **upset pipe,** tubo de resalto (o de recalcado) interior

international ellipsoid, elipsoide internacional

internet protocol, protocolo entre redes

interpolation, interpolación

interpretation, interpretación

interrupter, interruptor

intersection, intersección

interstage filter, filtro intermedio

interstice, intersticio (q.v. **pore**)

interstitial, intersticial

interstratification, interestratificación

interval, intervalo, espacio

— **timer,** (dp) cronómetro, registrador (o contador) de intervalos

— **velocity,** (gf) velocidad de intervalo

intrabasement anomaly, (g) anomalía intrabasamental

intraformational, intraformacional

intrusion, (g) intrusión

intrusive, intrusivo

— **fold,** (g) pliegue diapiro (o perforante)

— **rock,** rocas intrusiva

intumescence, (g) intumescencia (q.v. **swelling**)

invar, invar

inventory, inventario, existencias

inverse Fourier transform, (gf) transformada inversa de Fourier

inversely proportional, inversamente proporcional

inverted bucket trap, interceptor de cubo invertido

inverted emulsion mud, lodo de emulsión inversa

inverted pendulum, péndulo invertido

invoice, *n.* factura; *v.* facturar

I/O, q.v. **input/output**

iodide, yoduro

iodine (I), yodo

— **number,** índice de yodo

ion exchanger, intercambiador de iones

ionic, iónico

ionization, ionización

IOU (I owe you), (cm) vale, pagaré

IP (induced electric polarization), (gf) polarización inducida

IR drop, caída de potencial

IR incinerator, incinerador infrarrojo (o ultrarrojo)

iridescent film, película iridescente formada por el petróleo en el agua

iron, hierro, fierro

— **bosing,** viruta de hierro

— **carbonyl,** hierro carbonilo

— **casting,** fundición de hierro
— **clay,** arcilla ferrujinosa
— **foundry,** (tl) fundición de hierro
— **ore,** mineral de hierro
— **oxide,** óxido de hierro
— **plate,** plancha de hierro
— **roughneck,** llave doble
   automática
— **scrap,** hierro viejo, deshechos de
   hierro
— **sheet,** lámina de hierro, hoja de
   palastro
— **strap,** fleje (o zuncho, llanta) de
   hierro
— **work,** herraje, obra de hierro
iron-drawn, *a.* de hierro laminado
ironstone, mineral de hierro
irreversible steering gear,
   mecanismo de dirección
   irreversible
irrevocable, irrevocable
island, isla
— **mountain,** monte aislado,
   montículo de erosión
iso, *pref.* iso-, igual
**ISO (International Standards
   Organization),** Organización
   Internacional de Normas
isobars, (g) isobaras
isobath lines, (tp) isobatas
isobutyric acid, ácido isobutírico
isocarb, isocarbónica, línea que
   indica igual contenido de
   carbono
isochore, isocora
isochrones, isócronas, líneas que
   representan unidades iguales de
   tiempo
isochronism, isocronismo
isochronous, isócrono
isoclinal, isoclinic, isoclinal
— **contour,** curva de nivel isoclinal
   (o isóclina), línea isoclinal (o
   isóclina)
— **fold,** pliegue isoclinal
— **lines,** líneas isoclinales

isodynamic, isodinámico
— **lines,** líneas isodinámicas
isogal, isogala: línea de igual
   intensidad gravimétrica
— **lines,** (g) isógonas
isogram lines, líneas isogamas
isogeotherm, isogeoterma, líneas
   isogeotérmicas
isogonic, (tp) isógono, isogónico
— **chart,** mapa isogónico
— **contour,** curva de nivel isógona,
   línea isógona
— **lines,** líneas isogónicas, líneas de
   igual declinación
isogram, isograma, línea de igual
   intensidad magnética o
   gravimétrica
isogyres, isogiros
isohyetal, (g) isopluvial, isohieto
isolate, aislar
isolating shaft, eje separador
isolation, aislamiento
isomagnetic lines, (g) isodinas
isomer, isómero
isomeric, (qm) isomérico
— **butylene,** butileno isomérico
isomerization, isomerización
isometric, isométrico
— **projection,** proyección
   isométrica
isomorphic, isomórfico
isomorphism, isomorfismo
isopach, isopaca
isopachous, de igual espesor,
   isopaco
— **lines,** líneas isopacas
isopores, isoporas
isoparaffin, isoparafina
isoprene, isopreno
isopropyl alcohol, alcohol
   isopropílico
isorads, isoradioactivas
isoseismal line, (seismol) línea
   isosista, línea entre regiones de
   diferente intensidad

isoseismic lines, (gf) líneas isosísmicas, líneas de igual densidad sísmica
isostasy, (g) isostasia
isostatic, isoestático, isostático
isotherm, isoterma, línea isoterma
isothermal, isothermic, isotermo, isotérmico
— **expansion,** expansión isoterma (o isotérmica)
— **flow,** flujo isotermo
— **line,** (g) línea isoterma
— **surface,** superficie isoterma
isotime, de igual tiempo (q.v. **isochronous**)
isotope, isótopo
isotropic, (g) isótropo, isotrópico
itabirite, (g) itabirita
iterative, iterativo
isthmian, ístmico
isthmus, istmo
iteration, (mt) iteración
itinerary, itinerario

J

J, q.v. **joule**
J groove, ranura en J
J tool, herramienta con ranura de enchufe en forma de J
jack, *n.* (tl) gato, cric, (Ar) crique, (CH, Pe) gata; (oil bm) caballete (o burro) de bombeo; guimbalete; (el) receptáculo, (Ar) ficha hembra; (mn) esfalerita; (dp) tomacorrientes; *v.* levantar con gato
— **and circle,** gato de cremallera circular
— **board,** calza, poste aguantatubos (q.v. **jack post**)
— **box,** chumacera posterior del poste de la rueda motora

— **braces,** tornapuntas de los postes de la rueda motora
— **post,** (perc prf) poste de la rueda motora, soporte de la rueda motora
jacket, (bm) camisa, envoltura, (Me) barril
— **water,** agua envolvente
jacketed, enchaquetado
— **kettle,** paila enchaquetada
jackhammer, taladro neumático
jacknife, *v.* acodillarse
— **mast,** mástil abatible
jackscrew, gato (o cric) de tornillo
jackshaft, contraeje, eje intermedio
jackup, plataforma autoelevadiza, (Me) equipo autoelevable de perforación
Jacob's staff, (tp) vara portabrújula
jade, jade
jag bolt, perno arponado (q.v. **ragged bolt**)
jagged, dentado; dentellado, mellado
jam, *n.* atascamiento, apiñadura, atoramiento, *v.* atascarse, atorarse, (Me) agolparse; trabar, acuñar
— **nut,** tuerca de seguridad, contratuerca
— **weld,** soldadura de tope
Jamin effect, efecto de Jamin
jar, (prf) percusor, (Ar) tijera, (Ve) cimbra; choque, golpe; (acumulator) recipiente
— **socket,** receptáculo que se enchufa a golpes sobre la herramienta o pieza que se desea pescar
jar-down spears, arpones de pesca para percusoras
jarring, chirrido, sacudida, vibración
jasper, jaspe
jasperoid, jasperoide
jaspilite, jaspilita

jaw, (wrench) boca, quijada; (screw) mordaza; (grinder) mandíbula, quijada
— **clutch,** embrague de mordaza (o de quijada) (Ar) embrague a mandíbulas
jenny winch, grúa liviana de brazos rígidos
jerk, *n.* sacudida; latigazo; (nt) socollada de mar; *v.* sacudir, tirar violentamente
— **line,** (rotary prf) cable de las llaves, cable agitador, (Me) cable de apriete
— **pump,** bomba de émbolo buzo
jet, *n.* chorro, surtidor, pistola; (mn) azabache; *v.* perforar con chorro de agua (o lodo)
— **auger,** tubo inyector con barrena
— **bit,** barrena de chorro
— **blower,** soplador de chorro
— **carburator,** carburador de inyector
— **condenser,** condensador de chorro (o de inyección)
— **contactor,** contactor de chorro
— **fuel,** (mo) combustible de reacción (o de chorro), jet fuel
— **gun,** pistola de chorro
— **pipe,** tubo inyector
— **pump,** bomba de chorro
— **system,** sistema de chorro
jib crane, grúa de brazo, pescante, trucha
jig, *n.* (mc) gálibo, calibre, patrón, plantila; montaje, guía; (mn) clasificadora hidráulica; *v.* (mn) separar por vibración y lavado
— **saw,** sierra caladora, sierra para contornear
job, trabajo, tarea; empleo; obra, unidad de trabajo
— **scheduling,** planificación (o programación) de trabajos
jobber's drill, (tl) barrena corriente
jockey wheel, polea de tensión

join, unir, juntar, empalmar, acoplar
joint, (g) grieta; (tu) junta, acoplamiento, empalme, unión, conexión; tramo, tubo sencillo (q.v. **drill pipe, drill collar, casing, tubing, etc**.); (cm) conjunto, colectivo
— **agreement,** acuerdo conjunto
— **angle,** ángulo de empalme
— **bed,** estrato hendido que ha mantenido unidas las caras de la hendidura
— **inversion,** (gf) inversión simultánea de dos o más medidas relacionadas
— **plane,** (g) grieta (cuyos lados opuestos no han sufrido deslizamiento)
— **venture,** (cm) empresa colectiva (o conjunta)
jointing, junteo; articulado; (g) agrietamiento
joule (J), joule: unidad SI de energía (equivale a un newton-metro o un vatio-segundo)
Joule's law, ley de Joule: cuando un gas se expande no hay cambio de temperatura a menos que ejecute algún trabajo, o que reciba o rechace calor
Joule-Thomson effect, efecto de Joule-Thomson: el enfriamiento que ocurre cuando un gas comprimido se expande sin ejecutar trabajo y sin intercambio de calor
journal, (mc) muñón, gorrón, macho, pezón, muñequilla
— **angle,** (prf) ángulo del muñón
— **bearing,** chumacera
— **box,** muñonera, gorronera, chumacera
— **jack,** gato para muñones
joystick, palanca omnidireccional de mando (o de control)

Glossary of the Petroleum Industry

jug, q.v. **geophone**
jug line, q.v. **spread**
jumbo burner, quemador para el
  gas de desperdicio
jump, (dp) bifurcación, salto
— **correlation**, (gf) correlación
  defasada
— **weld**, soldadura de tope en
  ángulo recto
jumper, (el) alambre de cierre,
  puente, cable de empalme;
  barrena corta de mano
— **lead**, cable de empalme
— **switch**, (rr) cambiavía,
  saltacarril
junction, junta, unión; (el)
  empalme; (r) confluencia; (rr)
  entronque
— **box**, caja de empalmes (o de
  distribución)
junior orifice fitting, portaorificio
  sin bridas
junk, *n.* (prf) ripio; desperdicios,
  desechos; hierro viejo, chatarra;
  v. desechar; (prf) abandonar el
  pozo maquinaria o equipo viejo
— **basket**, cesto de pesca, cesta
  pescarripio, (Me) canasta
  chatarrera
— **ring**, anillo de retén (o de
  estopas)
Jurassic, jurásico
jute, yute, cáñamo
juvenile waters, (g) aguas juveniles
juxtapose, yuxtaponer

K

k, q.v. **kilo**
K (kelvin), kelvin: unidad de
  temperatura (273,15 K = 0° C)
K index, índice K: medida de la
  intensidad promedio de

  perturbaciones magnéticas en
  tiempo
K truss, armadura en K
Ka, q.v. **acid dissociation constant**
Kansan, kansaniense
kaolinite, kaolinita, kaolín
karst topography, karst, topografía
  en que todas las formas de
  erosión se relacionan con rocas
  calcáreas
katamorphism, catamorfismo
katazone, (g) catazona
Kater's pendulum, péndulo de
  Kater
KB, q.v. **kelly bushing**
KBPD (1,000 barrels per day),
  1.000 barriles diarios
keel, (nt) quilla
keeper, (magnet) retén, armadura
  de un imán artificial
kelly, (prf) junta (o barra) kelly,
  vástago cuadrado, barra
  cuadrada giratoria
— **bushing**, buje de junta kelly,
  (Me) buje de la flecha
— **bushing rollers**, rodillos del buje
  de junta kelly
— **cock**, válvula de tapón (q.v. **plug
  valve**)
— **driver**, accionador (o impulsor)
  de junta kelly
— **hose**, manguera de perforación
— **joint**, junta (o cuadrante) kelly,
  (Me) flecha
— **saver sub**, substituto de junta
  kelly
— **spinner**, rotor
— **valve**, válvula de junta kelly
kelvin (K), kelvin: unidad
  fundamental SI de temperatura
  (273,15 K = 0°C)
kerf, (sd) recorte; corte, ranura
kernel, núcleo
kerogen, kerógeno

kerosene, kerosine, kerosina, kerosene, kerosén, queroseno, petróleo (o aceite) de alumbrado
ketene, cetena
ketone, ketona
kettle, marmita, caldero; (rf) paila
— **hole**, (g) hoya glacial
key, chaveta; cuña metálica; llave; clave; tecla
— **bed**, (g) estrato índice
— **horizon**, (g) estrato índice, horizonte clave
— **puller**, extractor de chavetas (o cuñas), (Ve) sacacuñas
— **rock**, (g) roca determinante
— **seat**, asiento (o ranura) para chaveta, (Co) cuñero, (Me) ojo de llave, (Ur) chavetero
— **seat barge**, barcaza con mástil al costado
— **seat wiper**, escariador
keyboard, teclado
key-seating, (prf) enchavetamiento, ranura formada en el hoyo desnudo por la tubería vástago
keystone fault, falla en clave de arco, falla cuneiforme (o de cuña) (q.v. **wedge fault**)
kick, (prf) amago de reventón, surgencia imprevista de presión, (Me) manifestación
kickoff, (pr) inducir (el pozo) a producción por medio de gas o aire comprimido
— **joint**, codo escariador
— **point**, (horizontal prf) punto de arranque del desvío, punto de desviación de la vertical
— **pressure**, presión de arranque
— **valve**, válvula de arranque
kill, (prf) matar, dominar, controlar
— **a well**, dominar (o matar) un pozo
— **line**, línea de matar

— **slug**, tarugo de matar
killed steel, acero reposado
kiln, horno, horno de secar
kilo (k), kilo: unidad de peso; *pref.* kilo- equivale a un múltiplo de mil (10^3) e.g. kilómetro, kilovatio (q.v.), o (dp) un múltiplo de 2^{10} (1024) e.g. kilobit, kilobyte
kilocalorie (kcal), kilocaloría
kilocycle (kc), kilociclo
kilogram (kilo, kg), kilogramo
kilogram-meter (kg-m), kilográmetro
kiloliter (kl), kilolitro
kilometer (km), kilómetro
kilopascal (kPa), kilopascal
kilo-pound (kip), kilolibra
kilovolt (kv), kilovoltio, kilovolt
kilovolt-ampere (kva), kilovoltamperio
kilowatt (kw), kilovatio, kilowatt
kilowatt-hour (kw-hr), kilovatio-hora
Kimeridgian, kimeridgiense
kinematic viscosity, viscosidad cinemática
kinetic energy, energía cinética
kinetics, cinética
king pin, perno de pivote, gorrón
kink, (ca) ensortijamiento, coca, rectorcedura
kip, kilolibra
kit, estuche, caja
knee, codo, ángulo, escuadra, codillo
— **joint**, articulación, conexión articulada
knife edge, hoja cortante
knife switch, interruptor de cuchilla
knob, perilla
knock, golpe, *n.* (fuel) detonación, explosión; *v.* (ma) (mc) golpetear, cojear
knock off, *n.* desenganche; *v.* desenganchar

— **block**, bloque de desenganche
— **joint**, conexión de fácil desenganche
knock-rating test, prueba de detonación
knock-testing apparatus, aparato para probar las características detonantes de la gasolina (q.v. **CFR fuel-testing unit**)
knocking, cancaneo, golpeteo, retintín, detonancia
knockout, *n*. (pr) deshidratador mecánico para gas, cámara de expansión para deshidratar el gas
knot, (nt) nudo: unidad de velocidad que corresponde a una milla marina (1.852 m) por hora
knuckle, charnela, pivote, articulación
— **joint**, charnela, unión (o junta) articulada
— **pin**, perno vertical de charnela de dirección
knurled nut, tuerca estriada
KOP, q.v. **kickoff point**
kraft paper, papel de estraza
K/T boundry, frontera cretáceoterciaria
kyanite, (mn) cianita, distena

L

L head, (mo) culata en L
L spread, (gf) despliegue (o tendido) en L
label, etiqueta, rótulo, referencia, identificación
labilizing force, fuerza de labilización
labor union, sindicato obrero, asociación gremial, unión de trabajadores

laboratory, laboratorio
— **glassware**, envases de cristal para laboratorio
labradorite, labradorita
lac, lacquer, laca
laccolith, (g) lacolito (q.v. **plug**)
LACT (lease automatic custody transfer), relevo automático de custodia en arrendamientos
lacuna, (gf) ausencia de información (en el registro) (q.v. **gap**)
lacustrine deposit, (g) depósito lacustre
lacustrine facies, facies lacustre (q.v. **limnetic facies**)
ladder, escalera
ladle, cucharón de fundición
lag, *n*. (el) retraso, retardo, atraso; (ma) retardación, retardo; (elastic) retraso; *v*. (cl) forrar, revestir, aislar; (el) atrasarse
— **gravel**, gravilla de desierto
— **screw**, tirafondo, pija
lag-elastic action, (gf) acción elástica retardada
lag-thermal action, (gf) acción retardada termal
laggings, revestimientos
lagoon, laguna
laid length, longitud de tubería tendida
lake, lago
lamellar, laminado, laminar
lamina, (g) lámina, estrato delgado
laminar flow, corriente laminar (q.v. **stream-line flow**)
laminate, *a*. *v*. laminar
laminated, laminado, laminar, (Ar) hojoso
— **shims**, planchas de relleno laminadas, espesores laminados
laminating rollers, rodillos laminadores
lamination, laminación
lampblack, negrohumo, hollín

LAN (local area network), red de
área local

land, *n.* tierra, terreno; *a.* terrestre;
v. (airplane) aterrizar

— **bridge,** istmo

— **casing,** (prf) sentar la tubería de
revestimiento

— **disposal restrictions,** (ec)
restricciones para la disposición
en tierra

— **forms,** (g) formas fisiográficas

— **mass,** (g) tierra firme

— **rig,** (prf) equipo terrestre

— **surveying,** agrimensura,
levantamiento, topografía

landfill, (ec) relleno, depósito
dentro o sobre el terreno para
desechos peligrosos

landing, (cn) descanso, descansillo,
rellano; plataforma de carga;
(mn) vertedero; (aero)
aterrizaje

— **base,** base de tope

— **depth,** profundidad de la tubería
de revestimiento

— **head,** cabeza de tope

— **stage,** embarcadero flotante

landman, (oc) agente de tierras

landslide, derrumbe (o desplome)
de montaña, (Ar) deslizamiento
de faldeo

— **scar,** huella de derrumbe

lantern, farol, linterna, lámpara de
kerosina

lap, *n.* solapadura, cubrejunta, (Me)
traslape; *v.* solapar, revirar,
esmerilar, pulir

— **joint,** junta de solapa

— **welded casing,** tubería de
revestimiento (o de ademe)
soldada a solapa

lapilli, (g) lapilli

laptop computer, microordenador
portátil, ordenador de maleta

lapweld, soldadura a solapa

laser, láser

— **induced,** inducido por rayos láser

— **printer,** impresora de láser

lash, latigazo

lash-back, golpe de retroceso,
contragolpe; luz entre dientes de
engranajes

last-engaged thread, último filete
de la rosca

last-engaged-thread failures,
roturas debidas a desperfactos
del último filete en la rosca

latch, *n.* candado, pestillo, aldaba,
cerrojo, seguro; (dp) circuito de
retención, báscula electrónica; *v.*
sujetar con pestillo

— **bumper head,** cabezal
amortiguador de enganche

— **jack,** pescacuchara, (Ve)
pescador de pasador (q.v. **boot
jack, boot socket**)

— **jaw,** (wrench) quijada con aldaba

— **on,** conectar

late ignition, encendido retardado
(o atrasado)

late spark, chispa retardada

latency, (dp) latencia, tiempo de
espera (q.v. **seek time**)

latent heat, clor latente

lateral, lateral

— **formation drill,** barrena de
perforación lateral

— **moraine,** (g) morena lateral

— **offset,** (gf) desplazamiento
lateral

— **thrust,** empuje lateral

— **variation,** (gf) variación lateral

laterals, (p) ramales

laterite, (g) laterita

lathe, torno

latite, latita

latitude, latitud

— **anomaly,** anomalía de latitud

— **correction,** corección de latitud;
anomalía magnética

lattice, enrejado; (dp) retículo

Glossary of the Petroleum Industry

launch, lanzar; (nt) botar (un barco al agua)
Laurentian, laurentiense
lava, lava
— **block,** lava trabada
— **flow,** flujo (o corriente) de lava
— **stream,** corriente (o colada) de lava
lay, n. (ca) cableado, colchado, retorcido, trenzado, (Me) torcido; v. cablear, colchar, trenzar; (tu) tender, colocar
— **barge,** barcaza de tendido
— **days,** (nt) estadía
— **down pipe,** (prf) acostar tubería, sacar tubería del pozo y colocarla horizontalmente en el muelle
— **out,** v. (tp) trazar, localizar; proyectar
layer, (g) capa, estrato, lecho
laying-down pipe, (prf) retirar la tubería del interior de la torre durante la obra de perforación
layout chart, diagrama de distribución
LDPE, q.v. **low density polyethylene**
LDRS, q.v. **land disposal restrictions**
leach, leaching, n. lixiviación; v. lixiviar
leachate, (ec) líquido lixiviado
lead, n. (gf) adelanto; (mn) plomo; venero, filón; (thread) avance, paso; (sd) conductor; (el) conductor, avance; v. emplomar
— **clamp,** grampa contra fugas
— **line,** tubería de bomba a los tanques de almacenamiento; (prf) cable para levantar y mover utensilios
— **seal packer,** empaquetadura con sello de plomo
— **susceptibility,** aprovechamiento del antidetonante

— **tongs,** (prf) llave (o tenazas) de desenrosque
— **wool,** lana (o hilacha, fibra, estopa, filástica) de plomo
lead-coated, emplomado
lead-encased, revestido de plomo
lead-lined, forrado de plomo
leaded gasoline, gasolina de plomo
leader, rueda motriz
leading zeros, ceros a la izquierda
leads, (pile driver) guías del martinete, (Ar) cabriada
leaf, hoja, ala, aleta, lámina
leaf-type filter, filtro de hojas
leak, fuga, escape, filtración
— **clamp,** abrazadera contra fugas
— **clamp collar,** abrazadera para tapar fugas
— **detection system,** (ec) sistema de detección de filtración
— **proof,** a prueba de fugas
leakage, fuga, escape, filtración, pérdida
leaking modes, (gf) modos de dispersión
lean mixture, mezcla delgada (o pobre)
lean gas, gas seco
lean oil, (rf) aceite enjuto (o magro, pobre), gas absorbente
leapfrog test, (dp) programa de prueba de funcionamiento interno
lease, n. concesión, tierra (o parcela) arrendada; v. arrendar, alquilar
— **holder,** arrendatario
least squares fit, ajuste por mínimos cuadrados
least squares solution, solución de mínimos cuadrados
leave, hoja, lámina
lectotype, (paleo) lectotipo
ledge, (g) primera capa de roca consolidada, laja, cama (o lecho) de roca, roca viva, (Co)

135

roca fresca, (Me) roca fija, roca virgen

LeDuc's law, ley de LeDuc: el volumen de una mexcla de gas es igual a la suma de los volúmenes que cada componente de la mezcla ocuparía por sí solo a la misma presión y temperatura de la mezcla

lees, escorias, sedimento

leeward, sotavento

left hand thread, rosca de paso izquierdo

— **running tool,** herramienta viajera de rosca de paso izquierdo

left-lay cable, cable de torsión a la izquierda

leg, pata, soporte; ciclo

— **fender,** defensa de pata (en plataformas marinas)

— **of derrick,** pies derechos de la torre, patas de la torre

— **of fillet weld,** (sd) lado de la soldadura en ángulo

legal currency, moneda legal

legend, explicación; leyenda, signos

lempira, lempira: moneda de Honduras

length, largo, longitud

lens, (in) (g) lente

lensing, estratificación cuneiforme

lenticular, (g) lenticular

lepidolite, lepidolito

lessee, arrendatario

lessor, arrendador

let, alquilar, arrendar

lethal, letal

letter of credit, carta de crédito

leucite, leucita

leucitophyre, leucitrófiro

leucocratic, leucocrático

level, *n.* nivel, plano, llano, superficie; *v.* nivelar, aplanar, emparejar, igualar, allanar

— **gage,** indicador de nivel

— **rod,** (tp) mira de corredera, jalón de mira, (Me) estadal

— **sights,** pínulas para nivelar

levelling, (g) aplanamiento, estiramiento, nivelación

lever, palanca

— **arm,** brazo de palanca

— **jack,** gato de palanca

leverage, acción de una palanca; sistema de palancas, palanqueo

liability, riesgo; obligación, responsibilidad; (cm) pasivo

— **reserve,** reserva de pasivo

license, permiso, licencia

licensee, concesionario; tenedor de licencia; usuario de patente

licensing, expedición de licencias

lid, tapa, cubierta

lien, (cm) gravamen

life, duración en servicio; vida

lifeboat, bote salvavidas

lift, *n.* ascensor, montacargas; alza, elevación, altura de alzamiento; (cn) colada, hormigonada, (Ar) levante; (bm) altura de aspiración; *v.* levantar, alzar

— **above ground,** alce sobre el suelo

— **pump,** bomba aspirante

— **trap,** (steam) trampa de retorno

— **valve,** válvula de movimiento vertical

lifter, leva (o cama) de un eje (o árbol), brida, alzador

— **cog,** leva de un eje giratorio

— **pump,** bomba aspirante

lifting

— **jack,** gato mecánico (q.v. **jack**)

— **jar,** (perc) percusor de pesca (q.v. **jar**)

— **nipple,** niple elevador

— **sub,** niple elevador

lifting nipple, niple elevador o elevador de niple

lifting spider, elevador de araña

light, *n.* luz, alumbrado, iluminación; *a.* ligero, liviano;

claro; *v.* alumbrar, iluminar;
encender
— **displacement**, (prf) peso de
desplazamiento
— **draft**, (nt) calado sin carga, (Ar)
calado en rosca
— **duty**, *a.* de servicio ligero (o
liviano)
— **ends**, fracciones volátiles, cortes
livianos finales
— **fractions**, fracciones livianas de
petróleo
— **gasoline**, gasolina de alta
gravedad
— **naphtha**, nafta de alta gravedad
— **oil plant**, planta de productos
livianos
— **plant**, planta de luz eléctrica,
(Ar) usina
— **red silver ore**, plata roja clara,
proustita
light-water reactor, reactor de
agua ligera
lighten, aligerar, aliviar; (nt) zafar,
alijar
lighting load, carga de alumbrado
lightning arrestor, pararrayos
ligneous, leñoso
lignite, (g) lignito
limb, rama; (g) ala, flanco, lado;
(in) limbo
— **of anticline**, flanco de anticlinal
— **of fold**, flanco del pliegue
— **protractor**, transportador de
limbo
limber hole, (nt) agujero de desagüe
lime, cal
— **base grease**, grasa con base de
cal, (Ur) lubricante consistente
a la cal
— **mortar**, mortero de cal
— **mud**, lodo cálcico
— **water**, agua de cal
lime-coated, encalado
limestone, caliza
liming tank, alcalizador

limited partnership, (cm)
compañía en comandita
limit of error, margen mínimo de
error
limits, lindero, límites
limnetic facies, facies lacustre (q.v.
lacustrine facies)
limnic, (g) límnico
limnology, limnología
limonite, limonita, hierro fangoso
(o pantanoso) (q.v. **bog iron**)
limonitic, (g) limonítico
limy, calizo
linch pin, clavija, perno de
seguridad
line, *n.* (el) (tu) (rr) línea; cuerda;
cable; fila; (gf) trazado, traza,
línea; *v.* alinear; enderezar;
revestir; forrar
— **blind**, obturador de tubería
— **drive**, (water injection) línea de
inyección (q.v. **waterflood**)
— **electrode**, electrodo de línea
— **feed**, (dp) avance de una
interlínea, salto (o avance) de
línea
— **flood**, (pr) inundación (o
inyección) de un estrato en que
los pozos de inyección están en
línea y el agua inyectada va
progresando de línea en línea
— **of sight**, (tp) línea de mira
— **pipe**, tubería de línea
— **printer**, (dp) impresora por
líneas
— **pull**, fuerza de arrastre con cable
— **scale**, indicador de peso
— **shaft**, eje de transmisión, eje del
tambor auxiliar
— **shaft drive chain**, cadena del eje
del torno auxiliar
— **speed**, velocidad del cable
— **switching**, (dp) conmutacion de
líneas (o de circuitos)
— **valve**, válvula de paso

— **walker,** (oc) guarda de oleoductos
— **wiper,** (prf) limpiador de cable
line-roll, (gf) rodaje en líneas
line-setter adapter, adaptador para el colocador de tubería
linear, lineal, linear
— **codes,** (dp) código lineales
— **foot,** pie lineal
— **low density polyethylene,** polietileno de baja densidad lineal
— **polarization,** polarización lineal
— **scraper,** diablo (q.v. **go-devil, pig**)
— **spooler,** bobinador
— **travel,** trayectoria lineal
— **velocity,** velocidad lineal
linearity, linearidad
lined, forrado, revestido; marcado con líneas
liner, (ma) calza, calce; (cylinder) forro; (pr) tubería corta de revestimiento, tubo revestidor de fondo, revestidor auxiliar, (Me) camisa, (Ve) tubería calada, flauta de producción, liner
— **barrel,** camisa
— **catcher,** (prf) agarratubo de fondo, agarrador del revestidor auxiliar, pescador de tubo revestidor
— **completion,** terminación con tubería corta
— **hanger,** sujetador (o colgador) de tubería auxiliar de revestimiento, colgador del tubo revestidor de fondo
— **patch,** parche
— **puller,** (tl) extractor de camisa de cilindro
— **pump,** bomba con recubrimiento del cilindro de bombeo
liner-barrel, (bm) cilindro interior

— **pump,** bomba de cilindro interior, (Ve) bomba de madre de barril
liner-setter adapter, adaptador para el colocador de tubería revestidora de fondo
liner-setting tool, herramienta para colocar tubería revestidora de fondo
lineup, alineamiento
lining, forro, revestimiento, camisa
link, eslabón; enganche, engrane, varilla de conexión, argolla, anillo; enlace, unión
— **belt,** correa articulada
— **ear,** (prf) seguro del gancho de perforación
— **fuse,** fusible de cinta
link-type beam hanger, sujetador del tipo de eslabón (o de anillo)
linkage, sistema de conexiones, empalme
linker, (dp) montador de enlaces
lip, pico, boca, pestaña; labio
liparite, liparita
liquate, v. fundir, derretir, licuar
liquefaction, n. licuefacción, licuación
liquefiable, a. licuable, fusible
liquefied
— **natural gas (LNG),** gas natural licuado (GNL)
— **refinery gas (LRG),** gas licuado de refinería
— **petroleum gas (LPG),** gas licuado de petróleo (GLP)
liquid, n. a. líquido
— **assets,** (cm) activo circulante
— **dessicant,** secante líquido
— **level controller,** regulador de nivel para líquidos
— **level gage,** indicador del nivel de líquidos
— **petroleum gas (LPG),** gas licuado de petróleo (GLP), (Ar, Ur) supergás

— **phase process,** (rf) método de fase líquida
— **release test,** prueba de escape de líquido
— **seal,** sello líquido
— **sulphur dioxide,** anhidrido sulfuroso
— **to-liquid exchanger,** intercambiador de líquido
liquid-level gage, medidor del nivel de líquido
liquidate, liquidar
liquidation, liquidación
LISP (list processing), (dp) proceso (o tratamiento) de listas
list, *n.* filete, tira, listón; *v.* (nt) escora, dar carena, inclinarse a la banda
listric surface, (g) superficie lístrica de falla (o fractura)
liter (l), litro
litharge, litargirio, almártaga
lithic, lítico
lithification, litificación
lithified, litificado, petrificado
lithoclase, (g) litoclasa
lithogenesis, litogénesis
lithologic, litológico
lithology, litología
lithopysae, litofisuras
lithosiderite, litosiderita
lithosphere, litósfera
litmus paper, papel de tornasol
littoral deposits, (g) depósitos litorales (q.v. **shore**)
live load, carga viva, carga accidental, (Ar) sobrecarga; animales en pie
live steam, vapor vivo (o directo)
lixiviation, (g) lixiviación
LLDPE, q.v. **linear low density polyethylene**
LNG, q.v. **liquefied natural gas**
load, *n.* carga; *v.* cargar
— **allocation,** distribución de la carga

— **binder,** atacargas, (Me) perro
— **metamorphism,** metamorfismo de carga y descarga (q.v. **dynamic-static metamorphism**)
— **oil,** aceite fracturante
loading, cargar
— **arm,** (nt) brazo de carga
— **dock,** muelle de llenar
— **platform,** embarcadero
— **rack,** (tk) llenadera, cargadero
loam, barro, marga, (Me) migajón
loan, empréstito, préstamo
lobate delta shoreline, delta lobulado
lobe, (g) lóbulo
local, local
— **anomaly,** anomalía local
— **attraction,** (tp) perturbación de la brújula por la presencia de hierro
— **base level,** nivel de erosión local
— **current,** (gf) corriente local
— **gradient,** (gf) gradiente local
— **unconformity,** (g) discordancia local
locate, ubicar, emplazar, situar; localizar; (rd) trazar
location, localización, ubicación
lock, *n.* cerradura; (nav) esclusa, represa; *v.* cerrar con llave; (wheel) trabarse
— **nut,** contratuerca, tuerca de seguridad
— **screw,** tornillo de presión, de fijación
— **washer,** arandela de seguridad, arandela de presión
locking
— **arm,** brazo trabador (o complementario)
— **bar,** barra de fijación
— **gear,** engranaje trabador
— **pin,** perno de cierre (o de seguridad)

lockscrew, tornillo seguro (o de traba)

lodestone, piedra imán, magnetita, mena ferruginosa, calamita

loess, loes, marga

log, *n.* (prf) diario del perforador; (g) (gf) perfil, registro; (wood) tronco, troza, madero; (dp) registro de anotación de errores; (nt) corredera; *v.* registrar

— **anchor,** tronco de ancla, muerto

logarithm, logaritmo

logarithmic sine, seno logarítmico

logging, registrar, llevar anotaciones cronológicas de la perforación; (dp) anotación de errores

— **arch,** cabria transportadora de troncos

logic probe, (dp) verificador (o comprobador) lógico, exploración lógica

login, (dp) entrada en el sistema, identificación

logoff, logout, (dp) salida del sistema, cierre de sesión

long, largo; prolongado

— **path multiple,** múltiple de trayectoria larga

— **period earthquake seismograph,** sismógrafo para terremoto de largo periodo

— **residue,** (rf) residuo surtido

— **string,** tubería de explotación

— **stroke drilling jars,** percusores de carrera larga

— **threads and coupling joint,** acoplamiento de rosca larga con manguito

— **term,** (cm) largo plazo

— **ton,** tonelada larga

— **wave,** (gf) onda de largo periodo

longitude, longitud

— **correction,** corrección de longitud

longitudinal, longitudinal

— **fault,** (g) falla axial

— **parity check,** (dp) verificación de paridad longitudinal

— **waves,** (gf) ondas longitudinales

look box, caja de inspección

loom, forro de tela

loop, *n.* lazo, gaza; (tu) tramo (o desvío) suplementario; (el) empalme en bucles, conexión en circuito; (gf) circuito cerrado; *v.* enlazar; añadir tramos suplementarios

— **connection,** acoplamiento en bucles (o en vueltas)

— **gathering system,** sistema de oleoductos recolectores, oleoductos mallados

looping, tramo paralelo, desvío

loose, desatado, suelto, flojo

— **earth,** tierra floja

— **fit,** ajuste holgado; con holgura

— **pulley,** polea loca

LORAN (long range aid to navigation), sistema de radionavegación LORAN

loss of circulation, pérdida de circulación

lot, lote, partida; (land) solar, lote

Love wave, onda de Love

low, bajo

— **boy truck,** remolque de plataforma baja

— **coast,** costa playa

— **drum drive,** (hoist) marcha lenta del tambor

— **density polyethylene,** polietileno de baja densidad

— **frequency,** baja frecuencia

— **gear,** engranaje de baja (o primera) velocidad

— **molecular weight,** bajo peso molecular

— **pressure,** baja presión

low-angle fault, falla con ángulo cerrado, falla de ángulo menor

low-cut filter, (gf) filtro de corte bajo
low-pass filter, (gf) filtro de paso bajo, (Ar) filtro pasa-bajos
low-water mark, (r) estiaje, (mar) bajamar, (Ar) bajante
low-velocity layer, (gf) estrato (o zona, capa, horizonte) de baja velocidad (q.v. **weathering**)
lower
— **bridging,** (prf) tapón puente inferior
— **marine riser package,** conjunto de fondo del montante (marino)
— **kelly cock,** válvula de seguridad de la sarta de perforación (q.v. **drill pipe safety valve**)
lowering-in, (p) bajar (la tubería) a la zanja
lowest observed adverse effect level, (ec) nivel mínimo del efecto adverso observado
lowland, tierra baja, hondonada
LPG, q.v. **liquid petroleum gas**
lpm (lines per minute), (dp) líneas por minuto
LRG, q.v. **liquefied refinery gas**
lt, q.v. **long ton**
LTX (o LTS) (low temperature extraction unit), planta de extracción (o de separación) a baja temperatura
lube cut, corte para lubricante
lube oil blending, mezclar aceites lubricantes
lube oil plant, planta de aceites lubricantes
lube-contact filtering unit, planta de filtración por contacto para lubricantes
lubricant, lubricante
lubricating
— **cup,** grasera, copilla de engrase
— **grease,** grasa lubricante
— **oil,** aceite lubricante
— **pump,** bomba de lubricación

— **system,** sistema de lubricación
lubricating-oil filter, filtro del lubricante
lubrication, lubricación, engrase
lubricator, lubricador; engrasador
— **fitting,** grasera
Ludian, ludiense
lug, agarradera, muñón
lugging power, (diesel mo) par motor
lumber, madera aserrada, maderaje
lumen, lumen: unidad de flujo luminoso
Lumnite, cemento de alúmina de fraguado rápido
lump-sum bid, propuesta a suma alzada
luster, lustre, brillo
lutation, cementación
Lutetian, luteciense
LVL, q.v. **low-velocity layer**
lystric, q.v. **listric**

M

m, q.v. **milli**
M, q.v. **mega**
ma (milliampere) miliamperio
maar, (g) diatrema, maar (Ar) embudo de explosión
macadam, macádam
macaroni tubing, (pr) tubería macarrón
machine, *n.* máquina; *v.* fresar, tornear; pulir a máquina; taladrar
— **bolt,** perno común, perno ordinario, bulón, tornillo de máquina
— **screw,** tornillo para metales
— **shop,** taller macánico
— **tools,** herramientas de taller, herramientas mecánicas

machine-dressed bits, barrenas
afiladas a máquina
macroclastic, (g) marcroclástica
macroscale, macroescala
macroscopic, macroscópico
— **suspension,** suspensión
macroscópica (q.v. **coarse
suspension**)
macroseismic, macrosísmico
mafic, ferromagnesiano
Magdalenian, magdaleniense
magma, magma
magmatic, magmático
magnesite, magnesita
magnesium, magnesio
magnet, imán
— **wire,** alambre para imanes
magnetic, magnético
— **anomaly,** anomalía magnética
— **attraction,** atracción magnética
— **axis,** eje magnético
— **balance,** balanza magnética,
magnetómetro
— **bearing,** rumbo magnético,
marcación magnética
— **blade,** (magnetom) hoja (o
cuchilla) magnética
— **block,** (magnetom) bloque
magnético
— **bubble memory,** (dp) memoria
de burbujas magnéticas
— **chuck,** mandril
electromagnético
— **compass,** brújula
— **compensator,** (nt) neutralizador
de atracción local
— **conductivity,** conductividad
magnética, permeabilidad
— **core,** (dp) núcleo (o toro,
toroide) magnético
— **core storage,** memoria de
núcleos magnéticos
— **couple,** par magnético
— **creeping,** histéresis viscosa
— **curves,** curvas de fuerza
magnética

— **cycle,** ciclo de imanación
— **damping,** amortiguación
magnética
— **declination,** declinación (o
variación) magnética
— **dip,** inclinación magnética
— **dipole,** dipolo (o doblete)
magnético
— **doublet,** dipolo (o doblete)
magnético
— **drum,** tambor magnético
— **encoding,** (dp) codificación
magnética
— **equator,** ecuador magnético,
línea aclínica
— **field,** campo magnético
— **flux,** flujo inductor (o
magnético)
— **force,** fuerza magnética
— **gradient,** gradiente magnético
— **high,** (gf) máximo magnético,
anomalía magnética positiva
— **inclination,** inclinación
magnética (q.v. **magnetic dip**)
— **induction,** inducción magnética,
densidad de flujo magnético
— **intensity,** intensidad magnética
— **iron ore,** magnetita
— **iron oxide,** óxido ferrosoférrico
— **iso-anomaly lines,** líneas de
igual anomalía magnética,
líneas isogamas
— **lag,** atraso (o retardo) de
imanación
— **latitude,** inclinación de la
brújula
— **leakage,** dispersión magnética
— **limit,** límite de temperatura para
imanación
— **line,** línea magnética
— **low,** mínimo magnético,
anomalía magnética negativa
— **media,** (dp) soportes magnéticos
— **meridian,** meridiano magnético
— **moment,** momento magnético
— **needle,** aguja magnética

Glossary of the Petroleum Industry

— **north,** norte magnético
— **north pole,** polo norte magnético
— **north-seeking pole,** polo magnético atraído al norte
— **oxide,** óxido magnético (o ferrosoférrico)
— **parallel,** línea isóclina
— **permeability,** permeabilidad magnética
— **polarity,** polaridad magnética
— **pole,** polo magnético
— **profile,** perfil magnético
— **reluctance,** reluctancia magnética
— **remanence,** magnetismo remanente
— **repulsion,** repulsión magnética
— **resistivity,** reluctancia, resistencia magnética
— **resonance,** resonancia magnética
— **screen,** blindaje antimagnético, pantalla magnética
— **shielding,** blindaje magnético
— **slope,** (gf) pendiente magnética
— **south pole,** polo sur magnético
— **south-seeking pole,** polo magnético atraído al sur
— **storm,** tormenta magnética, tempestad (o perturbación) magnética
— **strip,** (dp) pista magnética
— **structure,** estructura magnética
— **survey,** estudio (o levantamiento) magnético
— **susceptibility,** susceptibilidad magnética
— **system,** conjunto magnético
— **tape cartridge,** (dp) cartucho (o cargador) de cinta magnética
— **tape reader,** lectora de cinta magnética
— **variation,** declinación (o variación) magnética
— **variometer,** magnetómetro

— **vector,** vector magnético
magnetism, magnetismo
magnetite, (g) magnetita, hierro magnético, piedra imán
magnetize, magnetizar, imantar
magneto, magneto
magnetometer, magnetómetro; balanza magnética
— **correction,** corección de base
— **force,** fuerza total del magnetómetro
— **scale division,** graduación del magnetómetro
magnetophone, magnetófono
magnetostriction, magnetostricción
magnification, amplificación, aumento
magnify, aumentar, ampliar
magnitude, magnitud
mail, *n.* correo; *v.* enviar por correo
main
— **deck,** (nt) cubierta principal
— **gear,** engranaje principal
— **shaft,** eje maestro, eje motor, eje principal
mainframe, (dp) procesador central, unidad principal (o central)
maintenance, conservación, manutención, mantenimiento, sostenimiento
make and model, marca y modelo
make hole, profundizar, continuar perforando
make-up, (tu) enroscar
— **pipe,** enroscar la tubería vástago (o de revestimiento) durante la perforación
— **time,** (dp) tiempo de puesta a punto
— **tongs,** llaves para conectar tubería (q.v. **lead tongs**)
— **wrench,** tenazas (o llaves) de montaje, llaves para enroscar las varillas en el pozo

143

— **water**, (cl) agua de reemplazo
maker, fabricante, constructor
malachite, malaquita
maleic acid, ácido maleico
malic acid, ácido málico
malfunction, fallo (o anomalía) de
    funcionamiento; avería
malleable, maleable, dúctil, flexible,
    forjable
— **castings,** piezas fundidas de
    metal maleable
— **flange,** brida de metal maleable
— **iron,** hierro maleable
mallet, maza, mazo, maceta,
    mallete
maltha, brea mineral
manager, gerente, administrador,
    jefe
manak, manak, brea de California
mandrel, mandril, polea de torno
    pequeño; husillo; (saw) árbol, eje
manganese, manganeso
— **steel,** acero al manganeso
manhole, pozo de visita (o de
    acceso), boca de inspección,
    (Ur) agujero de hombre, (Ve)
    boquilla
— **neck,** cuello de pozo de visita
manifold, múltiple, tubo múltiple
    para distribución, tubo
    distribuidor (con varias entradas
    o salidas), manifold; juego de
    válvulas; válvula de distribución
manila cable, cabo (o cable) de
    manila
manila cordage, cordaje de manila
manned underwater vehicle,
    vehículo submarino tripulado
manometer, manómetro
mantissa, (dp) mantisa, parte
    fraccionaria (q.v. **floating point
    notation**)
mantle rock, manto, roca suelta
    sobre la roca viva

manual shift type starting motor,
    motor de arranque del tipo de
    acople a pedal
manufacturer, fabricante
mapping, cartografía, planimetría,
    levantamiento (o relevamiento)
    de planos (o mapas)
marble, mármol
marcasite, marcasita
margin of safety, margen de
    seguridad
marginal fault, falla marginal
marginal well, pozo marginal
marine, *a.* oceánico, marino;
    marítimo
— **deposits,** depósito de sedimentos
    marinos
— **engine,** motor marino
— **facies,** facies marina
— **insurance,** seguro marítimo
marine riser, montante marino,
    tubo subiente, (Me) conductor
    marino
— **connector,** conector del
    montante
— **handling spider,** araña
    portamontantes
— **handling sub,** sub de manejo del
    montante
— **mandrel,** mandril del montante
marker, indicador; marcador
— **bed,** capa (o estrato) índice
marketing, *n.* comercialización,
    mercadeo, promoción de ventas,
    (Es) marketing; *v.*
    comercializar; mercadear, hacer
    marketing
marl, marga; greda
marlinespike, pasador de cabo,
    ajustadera, burel
marsh, pantano, marjal, ciénaga,
    bajial, aguazal, fangal
— **buggy,** carreta de pantano
— **gas,** metano, gas de pantano
mask, careta, máscara
masking, enmascaramiento

masonry, albañilería
mass, masa; promontorio
— **curve,** curva de volúmenes acumulados
— **specific gravity,** peso específico de masa
— **spectrometer,** espectrómetro de masa
— **storage,** (dp) almacenamiento masivo, memoria masiva
massive, macizo
mast, mástil; asta; árbol
masthead, cabeza de la torre de perforación; remate de la torre; extremo superior
master, maestro
— **bushing,** buje principal (o maestro)
— **clutch,** embrague maestro
— **cylinder,** cilindro principal (o maestro)
— **friction clutch,** embrague maestro de fricción
— **gate,** válvula maestra
— **joint,** junta principal (o mayor, maestra)
— **link,** eslabón maestro
— **tape,** cinta maestra (o duplicadora)
master-slave system, (dp) sistema combinado maestro/satélite, sistema principal/subordinado
mastic, mástique, masilla
mat, plancha de apoyo
— **jackup,** plataforma elevadiza con plancha de apoyo
— **supported drilling platform,** plataforma de perforación con plancha de apoyo
matched filtering, (gf) filtrado acoplado
material, material
matrix, (mc) (mt) (dp) matriz; (qm) aglomerante; (mn) ganga; (g) (Ar) pasta mineral, base vidriosa del pórfido

— **acidizing,** acidificación matricial
— **inversion,** (dp) inversión de matriz, inversión matricial
matter, materia
maturity, madurez
maul, mazo
maximize, realzar (o aumentar, elevar) a máximo rendimiento (o beneficio, capacidad, etc), *angl.* maximizar
maximum
— **amplitude wave,** onda de amplitud máxima
— **contaminant level,** (ec) máximo nivel de contaminantes
— **efficiency rate,** gasto de máxima aficiencia
— **gravity,** máximum gravimétrico, anomalía positiva
— **knock mixture,** mezcla de detonancia máxima
— **likelihood,** posibilidad (o probabilidad, verosimilitud) máxima
— **near offset,** (gf) máximo apartamiento cercano (q.v. **offset**)
— **offset,** (gf) apartamiento máximo (q.v. **offset**)
— **thermometer,** termómetro máximo, termómetro de máxima
— **water,** (prf mud) máximo de agua
maxwell, maxwell: unidad de flujo de inducción magnética
MBPD (million barrels per day), millones de barriles diarios
MCL, q.v. **maximum contaminant level**
MCS, q.v. **maximum combined seas**
md (millidarcies), milidarcias
MEA, q.v. **monoethanolamine**
mean, medio
— **deviation,** desviación media

— **temperature,** temperatura media
— **velocity,** velocidad
meander, (g) meandros
measure, medida, dimensión
— **in,** (prf) medir la tubería a medida que se inserta
— **out,** (prf) medir la tubería a medida que se extrae
measurement while drilling, medición al perforar
measuring, de medición
— **line,** (prf) cable de medición de profundidad
— **reel,** tambor del cable para medir profundidades
— **rule,** regla de medir
— **stick,** (prf) vara (o palo) de medir la profundidad penetrada por la barrena
— **measuring tank,** tanque de medición (o de aforo) (q.v. LACT)
— **tape,** metro; cinta de medir (o de medición)
mechanic, (oc) mecánico
mechanical, mecánico
— **contouring,** dibujo mecánico de curvas de nivel
— **draft,** tiro mecánico
— **drive rig,** equipo de perforación accionado mecánicamente
— **efficiency,** rendimiento, eficiencia mecánica
— **equivalent of heat,** equivalente mecánico del calor: factor de conversión para transformar unidades de calor a unidades mecánicas de trabajo (Btu 778 pies-lbs)
— **erosion,** erosión mecánica
— **jar,** percusor mecánico
— **octane number,** octanaje mecánico

— **sediment,** (g) sedimento mecánico (o clástico) (q.v. **clastic sediment)**
— **strain,** tensión mecánica, esfuerzo mecánico
— **stress,** tensión mecánica, esfuerzo mecánico
mechanics, *n.* mecánica
mechanism, mecanismo
median, del medio; mediana; punto medio
medicinal oil, aceite medicinal
mediterranean, *a.* (g) mediterráneo
medium, medio, mediano
mega (M), *pref.* SI $= 10^6$, e.g., MHz (q.v. MM); símbolo de 1.000, (e.g. Mcf); (binary system) múltiplo de 2^{20}, e.g. Mbyte
megajoule, megajoule: unidad métrica de servicio dada a una línea de izaje al mover 1.000 newtons de carga una distancia de 1.000 m
megohm, megohmnio
MEK (methyl-ethyl-ketone), (rf) metiletilketona
— **dewaxing,** desparafinación por MEK
melanocratic, melanocrático
melaphyre, (g) meláfero
melissane, melisano (q.v. **isotriacontane)**
mellite, melita
melt, derretir, fundir
melting, fusión, derretimiento, fundente
— **ladle,** cucharón de colada; caldero de colada
— **point,** punto de fusión; punto de derretimiento, (Ar) punto de escurrimiento
— **pot,** crisol
member, miembro, pieza, elemento; parte; socio, vocal

146

memory, (dp) memoria
— **data register,** (dp) registro de datos de la memoria
— **dump,** vuelco de memoria, vaciado de la memoria
— **guard,** custodia (o protección) de la memoria
— **reference instruction,** instrucción de referencias de memoria
meniscus, menisco
menthol, mentol
MER, q.v. **maximum efficiency rate**
mercaptan, mercaptano
mercaptide, mercáptida
mercury, mercurio
— **electrode,** electrodo de mercurio
— **freezing test,** prueba a punto de mercurio
— **switch,** interruptor (o conmutador) de mercurio
merge, fusionar, refundir; (dp) usionar, interclasificar, intercalar, mezclar
meridian, meridiano
mesa, mesa; meseta
mesh, *n.* malla; (el) triángulo; *v.* engranarse
mesitylene, mesitileno (q.v. **trimethylbenzene**)
mesorocks, (g) mesorocas, mesozona (q.v. **mesozone**)
mesosilicic rock, rocas mesosilícicas (o intermediarias)
mesothermal, mesotérmico
Mesozoic, mesozoico, era secundaria
mesozone, (g) mesozona, mesorocas (q.v. **mesorocks**)
metacenter, (nt) metacentro
metacryst, metacristal
metaigneous rock, roca metaígnea
metal, metal
— **alloy,** aleación metálica

— **arc welding,** soldadura al arco metálico
— **halides,** haluros metálicos
— **molding,** (el) conducto metálico superficial
metallic, metálico
— **arc cutting,** corte con arco metálico
— **arc welding,** soldadura al arco metálico (q.v. **metal arc welding**)
— **gasket,** empaquetadura metálica
— **oxide type catalyst,** catalizador del tipo de óxido metálico
— **packing,** empaquetadura metálica
metallized, revestido de metal
metallurgic, metalúrgico
metallurgy, *n.* metalurgia
metamorphic rock, roca metamórfica
metamorphism, metamorfismo
metaphosphoric, metafosfórico
metaphosphorous, metafosforoso
metasedimentary rock, rocas metasedimentarias
metasomatism, metasomatosis, substitución metasomática, metasomatismo
metasomatosis, (g) metasomatosis
metatype, metatipo
metaxite, metaxita
meteoric water, agua meteórica, agua de gravedad (q.v. **vadose water**)
meteorite, meteorito
— **impact theory,** (g) teoría de impactos meteóricos (*op.* continental drift)
meter, *n.* metro; (mc) contador, medidor; *v.* medir por contador
— **calibration,** calibración de medidores
— **flow,** contador de flujo, medidor de caudal
— **house,** caseta de los contadores

— **levelling saddle,** silla para
mantener a nivel instrumentos
medidores
— **run point,** (gas) punto de
medición
— **runs,** volumen medido por
contadores
metering
— **pin,** aguja dosificadora (o de
medición)
— **pump,** bomba contadora
— **separator,** separador medidor
methane, metano
— **series,** serie del metano, serie
parafínica de los hidrocarburos
methanol, metanol
method, procedimiento, método
methyl, metilo; *pref.* metil-
— **alcohol,** alcohol metílico,
metanol
methylacetylene, metilacetileno
(q.v. **propane**)
methylbenzene, metilbenceno (q.v.
toluene)
methylbutane, metilbutano (q.v.
isopentane)
methylene, metileno, nafteno
metric system, sistema métrico
metric ton, tonelada métrica: 1.000
kilogramos ó 2.204,6 libras
avoirdupois
mGal, q.v. **milligal**
**MGD (millions of gallons per
day),** millones de galones diarios
miarolictic, miarolítico
miascite, miascita
mica, mica
micaceous, micáceo
micaschist, (g) micasita
micro (1), *pref.* SI = 10⁻⁶ e.g.
microgramo (1g)
microcline, (g) microclino
microlites, microlitos
micrometer, micrómetro
micron, micra, micrón: una

millonésima de metro (0,001
milímetro ó 0,00003937
pulgada)
microphone, micrófono
microprogramming,
microprogramación
microrresistivity log, registro de
microrresistividad (q.v.
resistivity well logging)
microscope, *n.* microscopio;
microscopic, *a.* microscópico
microtexture, estructura
microscópica
mid-boiling point, punto medio de
ebullición
mid-percent curve, curva de
porcentaje medio
mid-stroke, punto medio de un
tiempo
midpoint, (gf) punto medio
middle distillate, destilado
mediano (o medio)
middle sample, prueba media
migmatites, (g) migmatitas
migration, (gf) migración; (g)
desplazamiento
mild steel, acero dulce
mile (mi), milla: 1.609 metros
mileage, millaje
milestone, mojón
mill, *n.* molino, fábrica; (tu)
molinillo; *v.* fresar, desbastar,
pulir, rectificar
— **defects,** defectos de fábrica
milled bit, barrena de conos
dentados (q.v. **steel-tooth bit**)
milli (m), *pref.* mili-, SI =10⁻³
milliammeter, miliamperímetro
milligal (mGal), miligal (*plur.*
miligales): equivalente a 1 x 10³
gal
milligram (mg), miligramo
milliliter (ml), mililitro
millimeter (mm), milímetro
milling

148

Glossary of the Petroleum Industry

— **cutter,** cortador rotatorio de metales, fresa
— **machine,** fresadora
— **shoe,** (tu) zapata fresadora
— **tool,** herramienta de fresar, fresadora (q.v. **mill**)
millivolt, milivoltio
mimetism, mimetismo
mine, mina
mineral, mineral
— **bed,** yacimiento mineral
— **crystals,** cristales minerales
— **deposit,** depósito mineral
— **gangue,** mineral filoniano
— **oil,** aceite mineral
— **seal oil,** aceite para señales, aceite mineral de foca
mineralization, mineralización
mineralize, mineralizar
mineralogy, mineralogía
minimum
— **gravity,** minimum gravimétrico, anomalía negativa
— **pendulum,** péndulo mínimo
— **phase,** fase mínima
— **thermometer,** termómetro mínimo (o de mínima)
— **time path,** trayectoria de tiempo mínimo
minimum-access programming, programación de tiempo mínimo de acceso (*compare with* **random-access programming**)
minute, *n.* minuto; *a.* diminuto
— **folding,** (g) arrugamiento, (Ar) plisamiento
Miocene, mioceno
misalignment, desalineamiento
miscible, mezclable, miscible
— **drive,** (pr) desplazamiento con miscibles
— **flood,** inyección de miscibles
misclosure, error de cierre (q.v. **error of closure, mis-tie**)
misfire, falla de encendido

Mississippian, misisipiense, carbonífero inferior
Missourian, misuriense
missourite, misurita
mis-tie, (gf) error de enlace
mist, niebla, neblina; (rf) niebla
— **drilling,** perforación con niebla
— **extractor,** extractor de neblina (o niebla)
mixed, mixto, mezclado
— **aniline point,** punto mixto de anilina
— **base crude,** aceite crudo de base mixta
— **phase cracking,** craqueo en fase mixta
— **phase process,** proceso de fase mixta
— **polymerization,** polimerización mixta
— **solvent extraction,** extracción por disolvente mixto
— **string,** (prf) sarta combinada (q.v. **casing string**)
mixer, mezcladora
mixing
— **circuit,** circuito de mezcladura
— **index,** índice de mezcladura
— **nozzle,** boquilla mezcladora
— **pit,** foso de mezclar
mixture, mezcla, mixtura
MM (million), millón, millones
mnemonic symbol, (dp) símbolo mnemotécnico
MO (moving out), (prf) sacando tubería
mobile, móvil, transportable
— **platform,** plataforma móvil
mobility, mobilidad
mode, modalidad
model, modelo, molde plantilla, patrón, muestra
modeling, modelling, modelado
moderator, regulador, moderador; (nuclear) moderador
modified cement, cemento tratado

modular-spaced workover rig,
(mar) equipo de reparación
modular
modulating control, control
modulador
module, módulo, coeficiente
modulus, módulo
— **of elasticity,** módulo de
elasticidad
— **of rupture,** módulo de rotura
mofette, (vlc) mofeta
**Moho (Mohorovicic)
discontinuity,** (gf)
discontinuidad de Mohorovicic
moisture, humedad
molal, molal
molasse, (g) molasa
mold, (g) molde, impronta
moldboard, vertedera
molded packing, empaque
moldeado
mole (mol), molécula-gramo, mol:
unidad fundamental SI de masa
de una substancia
— **percent,** porcentaje de moles
molecular, molecular
— **sieve,** tamiz molecular
— **weight,** peso molecular
molecule, molécula
Mollier's diagram, diagrama de
Mollier
mollusc, molusco
molten, materias en fusión
molybdenite, molibdenita
mole wt (molecular weight), peso
molecular
molybdenum, molíbdeno
— **steel,** acero al molíbdeno
moment of inertia, momento de
inercia
momentum, ímpetu, impulsión,
momento, cantidad de
movimiento, fuerza impulsiva
monadnock, (g) monadnock,
monte testigo
monel metal, metal monel

money order, giro postal
monkey, grapa, trinquete, maza de
martinete
— **board,** plataforma astillero,
plataforma del torrero (o del
chango) (q.v. **fourble board,
thribble board**)
— **spanner,** llave inglesa
— **wrench,** llave inglesa
monochromatic, monocromático
monoclinal, monoclinal
monocline, monoclinal, estructura
de buzamiento uniforme
monoclinic, monoclínico
monoethanolamine,
monoetanolamina
monomer, monómero
monovalence, *n.* monovalencia;
monovalent, *a.* monovalente
monument, mojón, hito
monzonite, monzonita
— **quartz,** cuarzo monzonítico
monzonitic, monzonítico
moonpool, escotilla de perforación,
(Me) contrapozo marino (en
barcos o estructuras flotantes)
mope, sobremango de llave
mooring, *n.* (nt) fondeo, atraque,
amarra; *v.* fondear, atracar,
amarrar
— **buoy,** boya de fondeo
— **lines,** cabos (o líneas) de anclaje
— **patterns,** patrón de fondeo
moraine, (g) morena
— **belt,** (g) cinturón morénico, (Ar)
anfiteatro morénico
morphology, morfología
mortar, (la) mortero, almirez; (cn)
argamasa, mexcla
mortise, *n.* contana, muesca; *v.*
ensamblar; enmuescar;
engargolar
mosaic, mosaico; mosaico
aerofotográfico
mosquito bill, tubo mosquito
moss, musgo

— **agate,** ágata musgosa
Mother Hubbard, chaqueta (q.v.
mud box)
— **bit,** barrena de paleta
motion, movimiento
— **compensation,** (mar prf)
compensación de movimiento
motive control, control a motor
motor, motor
— **fuel,** combustible para motores;
motogasolina
— **gasoline,** motogasolina
— **generator rig,** equipo de
perforación con
motogeneradores
— **grader,** motoniveladora
— **method,** método motor
— **mounting,** montura; base para
instalar un motor
— **oil,** aceite para motor
— **ship,** motonave
— **truck,** camión
— **valve,** válvula motor (o motriz)
mottled, moteado; abigarrado
mould, plantilla, molde, modelo,
matriz, horma; moho
moulding, moldura, moldeo;
enmohecimiento
mound, terraplén, malecón, dique
mountain chain, (tp) sierra,
cordillera
mounting, montaje, marco,
armadura
— **bolts,** pernos de montaje
mouse hole, (tu) hoyo del ratón
mousetrap, (prf) pescadespojos
mouth, boca
movable, movible, móvil
move mode, (dp) modalidad de
transferencia
movement, movimiento
moveout, (gf) sobretiempo por
distancia
moving system, (gravim) sistema
de mecanismo móvil

mpg (miles per gallon), millas por
galón
mph (miles per hour), millas por
hora
MR, q.v. **magnetic resonance**
MSP, q.v. **multiple shot processing**
MSV, q.v. **multipurpose service
vessel**
**MTBF (mean time between
failures)**, tiempo (o período)
promedio entre averías
mud, (prf) lodo de perforación,
(Ar) inyección, (Ve) fluido de
perforación
— **additive,** aditivo para el lodo
— **box,** artesa (o caja, encofrado)
del lodo, (Me) chaqueta
— **cake,** (prf) costra, (Me) enjarre,
(Ve) cáscara
— **collar,** collar para circulación de
lodo
— **conditioner,** acondicionador del
lodo
— **conveyor,** conductor del lodo
(q.v. **mud line**)
— **cracks,** hendiduras en el lodo
— **crib,** artesa (o caja, encofrado)
del lodo
— **ditch,** zanja (o canal) del lodo
— **end of pump,** extremo expulsor
de una bomba de lodo
— **flat,** llanura de lodo
— **flow,** flujo de barro, (o fango,
lodo)
— **guard,** guardabarro
— **gun,** inyector de lodo, (Me)
pistola del lodo
— **handling service,** servicio de
conservación, preparación o
mezcla del lodo
— **hose,** manguera de inyección
— **log**, registro del lodo
— **line,** tubo del lodo, manguera
(q.v. **mud conveyor**)
— **lubricator,** lubricador de lodo
— **mixer,** mezcladora del lodo

— **pit,** foso (o presa) del lodo
— **pump,** bomba del lodo
— **pump pressure gage,** indicador de la presión en la bomba para lodo
— **pump release valve,** válvula de purga de la bomba del lodo
— **return line,** tubo horizontal de retorno
— **return tank,** tanque de lodo devuelto
— **ring,** (rotary table) colector de lodo
— **saver,** economizador del lodo
— **screen,** colador (o criba) del lodo, (Ar) zaranda (q.v. **screen**)
— **shaker,** agitador de lodo
— **socket,** achicador de lodo
— **thinner,** diluyente (o adelgazador) del lodo
— **trap,** colector de barro
— **trough,** canaleta del lodo
— **up,** hacer lodo
— **volcano,** volcán de lodo
— **wave,** (mar) ola de fango
— **wiper,** abrazadera limpiadora de lodo (q.v. **mud saver**)
mud-gas anchor, segregador de gas y lodo
mud-laden fluid, lodo de circulación
mud-mixing gun, inyector mezclador de lodo
mud-off, segregar por medio de lodo, sellar con lodo
mud-pressure indicator, indicador de la presión del lodo
muddy, limoso, fangoso
mudline, fondo (o piso) marino
— **casing suspension system,** sistema de suspensión de la revestidora en el fondo
— **casing support system,** sistema de soporte de la revestidora en el fondo
mudsill, durmiente, larguero

mudstone, cieno endurecido; lutolita, (Co) litita, (Ve) lutita, (q.v. **shale**)
muffle, *n.* mufla; *v.* silenciar el escape, apagar el ruido; (rf) cámara de fusión (q.v. **combustion chamber**)
muffler, silenciador, válvula apagadora de sonido
mule-head hanger, colgadero (o suspensor) para varillas asido a la cabeza del balancín
mule shoe, pata de mula (q.v. **sub**)
mule-tail, desflecar el extremo de una soga (o cable)
multibore riser, montante multipozo
multibuoy mooring system, sistema de fondeo (o carga) multiboya
multichannel, *a.* multicanal, de canales múltiples
multicylinder engine, motor multicilíndrico
multieffect distillation, destilación de efecto múltiple
multigrid, multirred
multijet burner, quemador multichorro
multilayer, de capas múltiples
multilevel, multinivel
multilinked, multienlazado
multimedia, por medios múltiples
multimode, multimodal
multiple, mútiple
— **completion,** terminación múltiple
— **contact method,** método de contacto mútiple
— **coverage,** cobertura múltiple
— **detectors,** detectores mútiples
— **disc clutch,** embrague de discos mútiples
— **fault,** falla mútiple
— **integrator,** (gravim) integrador mútiple

— shot processing, (gf) procesamiento de fuentes múltiples
— stage cementing, cementación a intervalos (o en puntos distintos)
— stage cementing tool, aparato de cementación a varios niveles
— V-belt, banda (o correa) para roldanas de acanalado múltiple en V
— V-belt sheaves, roldana a polea de acanalado mútiple en V
— well pumping system, sistema múltiple de bombeo de pozo, (Me) sistema central de bombeo mecánico
— zone well completion, terminación a múltiples zonas
multiplexing, multiplaje, multiplexación
multiplex mode, modalidad múltiple
multiplexed, multiplexado
multiplexor, multiplexor de pozos en varias zonas
multiplier, multiplicador
— tube, válvula multiplicadora
multipurpose, *a.* de fines mútiples, multipropósito
— service vessel, embarcación de servicios
multistage
— cementing tool, herramienta de cementación múltiple
— compressor, compresor multietapa
— countercurrent extractor, extractor a contracorriente de etapas múltiples
— gas-lift, extracción por gas en varias etapas
multisystem mode, modalidad multisistema
multitasking, multitarea
multizone, zona múltiple

— completion, perforación a múltiples zonas
— production, producción procedente de varios horizontes petrolíferos
Muntz metal, metal Muntz
muriate, muriato
muriatic acid, ácido muriático
muscovite, moscovita
mushroom valve, válvula tipo hongo, válvula de obturador de manguito (q.v. poppet valve)
muskeg, tubera
mute, (gf) desvanecer, atenuar
mv (millivolt), milivoltio
mylonites, (g) milonitas
mylonitic, milonítico, cataclástico
mylonitization, milonitización
myricyl, miricilo (q.v. triacontane)

N

n, *pref. abr.* normal, e.g. n-butane, butano-n (o butano normal); q.v. nano
N, q.v. newton
nadir-point triangulation, triangulación nadiral
nail, *n.* clavo, punta; *v.* clavar
nano (n), *pref.* SI = 10^{-9} e.g. nanotesla (nT)
naphtha, nafta
— scrubber, desnaftadora
naphthalene, naftalina
naphthene, nafteno
— series, serie nafténica
naphthene-base crude oil, aceite crudo nafténico, crudo de base nafténica (q.v. asphalt-base oil)
naphthenic, nafténico
— acid, ácido nafténico
— hydrocarbons, hidrocarburos nafténicos

English - Spanish

nappe, (g) manto de corrimiento,
(Ar) manto sobreescurrido (q.v.
overthrust mass)

narrow, *a.* estrecho, angosto; *v.*
estrechar, angostar, hacer
estrecho; estrecharse
— **boiling range,** (rf) escala de
ebullición limitada
— **cuts,** (rf) cortes estrechos (o
cerrados)
— **pass,** (tp) desfiladero

narrowband, banda estrecha

narrows, (tp) garganta, angostura
desfiladero; estrecho

native, (g) nativo, metálico, virgen,
natural
— **clay,** arcilla nativa
— **coke,** coque natural

natrolite, natrolita

natural, natural
— **arch,** arco natural
— **binary-coded decimal,** (dp)
decimal natural codificado en
binario
— **bridge,** puente natural
— **draft,** tiro natural
— **gas,** gas natural
— **gas extraction plant,** planta de
gasolina natural, (Ar) planta
exhaustadora
— **gas liquids (NGL),** líquidos del
gas natural (LGN)
— **gasoline,** gasolina natural
— **gasoline plant,** planta de
gasolina natural
— **gas pipeline,** gasoducto
— **scale,** escala natural
— **state,** estado virgen (o natural)

navigation, navegación
— **systems,** sistemas de navegación
(o piloto)

near-trace gather, (gf) muestra de
las trazas cercanas

nearby shocks, temblores cercanos

neat cement, cemento puro

Nebraskan, nebraskiense

neck, (mc) cuello, gollete; paso;
istmo
— **down,** estrangular

needle, (in) aguja; (mc) aguja,
espiga, punzón
— **bearing,** cojinete de agujas
— **point valve,** válvula de punta de
aguja
— **valve,** válvula de aguja

needle-point globe valve, válvula
de globo con tapón de punta

negative, negativo
— **acceleration,** retardación,
deceleración
— **aniline equivalent,** equivalente
anilínico negativo
— **logic,** lógica negativa

Neocomian, neocomiense

neohexane, neohexano

neolithic, neolítico

neopentane, neopentano

neoprene, neopreno (o neoprene)

Neozoic, neozoico

nepheline, nephelite, (g) nefelina
— **syenite,** sienita nefelina

nephelinite, nefelinita, lencitita
(q.v. **lencitite**)

neptunium, neptunio

neritic, (g) nerítico, epicontinental

net, neto
— **balance,** (cm) saldo líquido
— **earnings,** (cm) utilidades
líquidas, ganancia neta
— **observed volume,** volumen neto
observado
— **opening,** luz (o abertura) libre (o
neta)
— **production,** producción neta
— **ton,** tonelada libre (o de 2.000
libras)
— **tonnage,** (nt) arqueo neto

network, red
— **database system,** (dp) sistema de
red de bases de datos
— **distribution,** (el) distribución
por parrilla

— **front end**, procesador frontal de red
— **transformer**, transformador para parrilla
neural network, (dp) red de nervios, red neural
neutral, neutral, posición neutral
— **alcohol**, alcohol neutro
— **flame**, llama neutral
— **oil**, aceite neutro (q.v. **pale oil, red oil**)
— **point**, punto muerto
— **salts**, sales neutras
— **zone**, (mc) huelgo positivo
neutralization value, valor neutralizador
neutralize, neutralizar
neutralized water, agua neutralizada
neutralizing clay, arcilla (o barro) neutralizador
neutron, neutrón
— **log**, registro de neutrón
— **curve**, curva de neutrones
neutron-gamma log, registro gama-neutrón
nevadite, nevadita
New York rod, (tp) tipo de mira de corredera
newt, unidad del sistema inglés para medir la viscosidad cinemática
newton (N), unidad SI de fuerza neta requerida para acelerar un objeto de 1 kilogramo de masa a una velocidad de 1 centímetro por segundo
NG (no good), no vale
NGL, q.v. **natural gas liquids**
Niagaran, niagarense
nickel, níquel
— **carbide**, carburo de níquel
— **iron**, hierroníquel
— **steel**, aceroníquel
nick-break test, prueba de mella
niccolite, nicolita
nicol prism, prisma de nicol

nife, (g) nife
night shift, turno de noche
nipple, (tu) niple, entrerrosca, boquilla; unión, acople, grasera, manguito
nippers, pinzas tenazas
niter, salitre (q.v. **saltpeter**)
nitrate, nitrato
nitric acid, ácido nítrico
nitride, nitruro
nitrile rubber, caucho nitrilo
nitrobenzene, nitrobenceno
nitrocellulose, nitrocelulosa
nitrocotton, nitroalgodón
nitrogelatin, nitrogelatina
nitrogen (N), nitrógeno
— **base**, base nitrógeno
— **dioxide**, dióxido de nitrógeno
— **fixation**, fijación de nitrógeno
— **oxides**, óxidos de nitrógeno
nitroglycerin, nitroglicerina
nitronaphthalene, nitronaftaleno
nitroparaffin, nitroparafina
nival, nival
niveau surface, superficie de nivel
NMO (normal moveout), q.v. **moveout**
NMR, q.v. **nuclear magnetic resonance**
nodal point, punto nodal
node, nodo, vértice
nodular, nodular
nodule, nódulo
nodulizer, tipo de pulverizador
noise level, nivel de ruido
nominal horsepower, potencia teórica
nomograph, nomograma
non-attainment area, (ec) área desatendida
nona, *pref.* nona-
nonadiyne, nonadiino
noncalcareous, no calcáreo
noncirculating period, periodo de circulación nula
nonconformity, discordancia

noncorroding liquid, líquido no corrosivo
nondestructive, no destructivo
— **read,** (dp) lectura no destructiva
— **test,** prueba no destructiva
nonene, noneno
nonenyne, nonenino
nonerasable storage, (dp) memoria imborrable, soporte indeleble
nonferrous alloy, aleación no ferrosa
nonfoaming, antiespumante
nonhazardous, no peligroso
nonlinear equations, ecuaciones no lineales
nonmetallic, no metálico
nonmethane hydrocarbons, hidrocarburos no metanos
non-Newtonian behavior, comportamiento no newtoniano
nonorogenic, (g) anorogenético
nonpiercement type salt dome, domo salino que no rompe a través de los estratos superiores
nonpolarizing electrode, electrodo impolarizable
nonporous, no poroso
nonpressure welding, soldadura sin presión
nonreturn valve, válvula de retención de vapor
nonreversible blade, cuchilla irreversible
nonrising stem gate valve, válvula esclusa de vástago estacionario
nonselective, no selectivo
nonsparking tools, herramientas a prueba de chispa
nontoxic, no tóxico
nonupset, (tubing and casing) (tubería de perforación y de revestimiento) sin recalque
nonvolatile memory, (dp) memoria remanente (o no volátil)

nonylnonadecane, nonilnonadecano
nonyne, nonino
norm, pauta; norma
normal, normal; (tp) perpendicular
— **circulation,** circulación normal
— **fault,** falla normal
— **fold,** pliegue normal (o parado) (q.v. **upright fold**)
— **gasoline range,** escala normal de gasolina
— **gravity,** gravedad normal
— **incidence,** incidencia normal
— **variation,** variación normal
north, norte
— **by east,** cuatro nordeste (1/4 NE)
north-northeast, nornordeste (NNE)
north-northwest, nornoroeste (NNO)
northeast, nordeste, nororiente (NE)
— **by east,** noroeste cuarto de este (NO 1/4 E)
— **by north,** nordeste cuarto al norte (NE 1/4 al N)
northern, del norte, septentrional, boreal
nose, (g) nariz, anticlinal abierto; (mc) oreja, talón, aleta
— **button,** (drill bit) punta de lanza
— **still,** solera de frente
nosepiece, (microsc) portaobjetos
notary public, (oc) notario
notch, muesca, corte, ranura, encaje, hendedura, mella, terraja
— **fatigue,** fatiga ocasionada por las mellas
— **filter,** (gf) filtro entonado; (dp) filtro de muesca (de hendidura) (q.v. **band-stop filter**)
notched beam, árbol dentado
notice, *n.* aviso; *v.* notar
novaculite, novaculita

nozzle, boquilla, inyector, (Me) tobera
— **neck,** cuello de tobera (o de boquilla)
nuclear magnetic resonance, resonancia magnética nuclear
nuclear precession magnetometer, magnetómetro de precesión nuclear
nucleus, núcleo, corazón (q.v. **kernel**)
null instrument, indicador de cero
— **method,** método del cero
— **point,** punto cero (o nulo)
number cruncher, superordenador, triturador de números (q.v. **supercomputer**)
number system, sistema numérico
nummulitic, (g) numulítico
nunatak, (g) nunatak
nut, tuerca, hembra de tornillo, (Me) rosca
— **lock,** contratuerca, fiador de tuerca
— **tap,** macho para tuercas
nutation, nutación

O

O, q.v. **oxygen**
OAE (oceanic anoxic event), evento oceánico anóxico
obducted, (g) obducido
object program, (dp) programa objeto (o ejecutable, generado)
objective lens, cristal (o lente) objectivo
oblique, oblicuo
— **fault,** falla oblicua (o diagonal)
— **incidence,** incidencia oblicua
— **perspective,** perspectiva oblicua (o de tres puntos)
— **triangle,** triángulo oblicuángulo
oblique-slip

— **fault,** falla oblicua, falla por desliz oblicuo en el plano de falla
— **dip fault,** falla transversal oblicua
— **oblique fault,** falla diagonal oblicua
— **strike fault,** falla longitudinal oblicua
oblong, oblongo, alargado
OBS, q.v. **ocean bottom seismometer**
obsequent stream, arroyo obsecuente
observation, observación
observed time, tiempo observado
observed traveltime, tiempo de propagación observado
observer, (oc) observador
obsidian, (g) obsidiana
obtuse bisectrix, bisectriz obtusa
occasional, ocasional, esporádico
occluded gas, gas absorbido (por algunas substancias porosas), (Ar) gas ocluido
occupational diseases, enfermedades laborales
occurrence, existencia, ocurrencia, presencia
ocean, océano, mar
— **bar,** banco submarino, bajío, arenal
— **basin,** cuenca marítima
— **bottom conditions,** condiciones de fondo (marino)
— **bottom seismometer,** sismómetro situado en el fondo marino
— **freight,** flete marítimo
— **rates,** tarifa de flete marítimo
oceanographic influences, influencias oceánicas
ocher, ochre, ocre
OCS (outer continental shelf), plataforma continental (o submarina)

octacosane, octacosano
octacosene, octacoseno
octadecadiene, octadecadieno
octadecadiyne, octadecadiino
octadecane, octadecano
octadecene, octadeceno
octadiene, octadieno
octadienyne, octadienino
octadiyne,octadiino
octagon, octágono
octahedron, octaedro
octamethyloctane,
    octametiloctano
octane
— index, índice octano
— number, número octano
— rating, grado de octano
— scale, escala de octanajes
octatriacontane, octatriacontano
octatriene, octatrieno
octene, octeno
octenyne, octenino
octet, (dp) octeto: ocho bits
    contiguos o un byte con ocho bits
octylbenzene, octilbenceno
octyldocosane, octildocosano
octylheptadecane,
    octilheptadecano
octylheptadecene,
    octilheptadeceno
OD (outside diameter), diámetro
    exterior (DE)
odd parity, (dp) paridad impar
odd-even check, (dp) control de
    paridad par-impar
odds, probabilidades
odometer, odómetro, cuentapasos
odorant, (gas) odorante
O/E (observed to expected ratio),
    relación de lo observado a lo
    esperado
oersted, oersted: unidad de
    intensidad magnética
OF, q.v. open flow
off-line processing, proceso fuera
    de línea, proceso autónomo

offset, excéntrico, sobresaliente; (gf)
    apartamiento, offset, distancia
    entre detectores (o geófonos) y
    puntos de disparo
— horizontal baffles, (rf)
    desviadores horizontales
    alternoescalonados (q.v. side-to-
    side pans)
— link, (chain) eslabón extra (o
    compensador, complementario),
    (Me) cadena de compensación
— link plate, plancha acodada de
    eslabón
— well, pozo contrarestante (o
    compensador)
offshore, costafuera, (Ve) costa
    afuera
ogive, (glacier) ojiva
OH, q.v. open hole
ohm, ohmio
ohmmeter, ohmímetro
ohm-meter (ohm-m), ohmio-metro
Ohm's law, ley de Ohm: resistencia
    = voltaje/corriente
oil, aceite; petróleo (*both terms used
    interchangeably for "petroleum"
    in some Spanish-speaking
    countries*)
— and gas, petróleo (o aceite) y gas
— and gas separator, separador de
    petróleo y gas
— base mud, lodo con base de (o a
    base de) petróleo
— bath, baño de aceite
— bearing, que contiene petróleo,
    petrolífero
— burner, quemador de petróleo
— can, aceitera
— cloth, hule, encerado
— coking drum, cilindro para
    coquificación
— cup, aceitera
— damped detectors, detectores
    con amortiguamiento de aceite
— deposit, yacimiento petrolífero,
    criadero de petróleo

Glossary of the Petroleum Industry

— **emulsion,** emulsión de petróleo
— **emulsion mud,** lodo de emulsión de petróleo
— **engine,** motor a petróleo (o a combustóleo)
— **equivalent,** equivalente de petróleo
— **feeder,** lubricador, alimentador de aceite
— **field,** campo petrolero; (g) campo petrolífero, criadero de petróleo
— **filler,** llenador de aceite
— **film,** película de aceite
— **filter,** filtro de aceite, depurador del aceite
— **gage,** indicador del nivel de aceite; manómetro, indicador de la presión del aceite
— **groove,** ranura para la circulación del aceite lubricante, pata de araña, estría de lubricación
— **heater,** calentador de aceite
— **in place,** petróleo remanente
— **level indicator,** indicador de nivel del aceite lubricante
— **line,** conductor del aceite lubricante, cañería de lubricación
— **line tube,** tubo del aceite
— **meter,** medidor de petróleo
— **migration,** migración de petróleo
— **mud,** lodo de petróleo
— **operator,** (oc) petrolero, individuo en negocios de producción o refinación de petróleo
— **originally in place,** petróleo en sitio al principio
— **pan,** colector (o bandeja) de aceite, (Ve) batea de aceite
— **patch,** campo petrolero

— **pool,** yacimiento (o campo) de petróleo (q.v. **oil deposit, oil field**)
— **producer,** (oc) productor de petróleo, petrolero; (well) pozo productivo
— **pulp,** jabón de alumino, pulpa de aceite
— **pump,** bomba del petróleo
— **reclaimer,** recuperador de aceite, depurador de aceite lubricante
— **recovery,** recuperación del petróleo
— **reservoir,** (mc) cámara de aceite; (g) yacimiento petrolífero
— **retainer,** retenedor de aceite
— **rights,** (cm) derechos minerales
— **sand,** arena petrolífera, (Me) arena aceitífera
— **saver,** (tu) economizador de petróleo, (Me) prensaestopas
— **saver rubber,** forro de caucho del economizador
— **seal,** (bm) cierre (o sello, obturador) de aceite
— **seep,** filtración de petróleo (q.v. **seepage**)
— **shale,** lutita petrolífera (o bituminosa)
— **slick,** película de petróleo
— **slinger,** esparcidor de aceite
— **spill,** derrame de petróleo
— **storage,** almacenamiento del petróleo; tanques de petróleo
— **string,** (prf) tubería de revestimiento final, (Ar) columna aisladora, (Me) tubería de explotación (q.v. **water string**)
— **sump,** colector de aceite, bandeja colectora del aceite, (Ve) batea del aceite
— **switch,** conmutador de aceite
— **tar,** alquitrán de petróleo
— **tempering,** templado al aceite

— **thief,** tomamuestras, muestreador, (Ve) ladrón de aceite

— **wax-solvent system,** sistema de disolvente para la extracción de parafina

— **well,** pozo de petróleo

— **zone,** zona (o región) petrolífera; (prf) horizonte petrolífero

oil-water contact, contacto petróleo-agua

oil-water emulsion, emulsión petróleo en agua (q.v. **reverse emulsion)**

oil-well cement, cemento para pozos

oil-wiper packing, empaquetadura del limpiavástago

oiliness, oleaginosidad

oiltight, hermético al aceite, resguardado del aceite

oily, aceitoso

old age, (ma) vejez; (g) senectud

old-age valley, valle senil

olefin, olefina

— **hydrocarbon,** hidrocarburo olefiínico

— **series,** serie olefínica (q.v. **ethyene series)**

olefinic content, contenido olefínico

oleum, ácido sulfúrico humeante, ácido Nordhausen

oligist, oligisto

Oligocene, oligoceno

oligoclase, (g) oligoclasa

olivine, (g) olivina, peridoto (q.v. **peridot)**

omission, omisión

— **of beds,** omisión de estratos

on board, a bordo

on edge, de canto

on end, de cabeza, de punta

on line, (dp) en línea, en directo, conectado al sistema y utilizable

on the flat, de plano

on-off control, control de encendido y apagado

on-the-fly error recovery, (dp) recuperación de errores al vuelo

once through, de un paso, de paso sencillo

one-man crosscut saw, sierra de través con mango para un hombre

onstream, en funcionamiento, en operación, (Ur) en corriente

— **time,** tiempo en funcionamiento, tiempo bajo carga

one-atmosphere (1-atm) diving suit, traje de buceo a una atmósfera

one-pass, *a.* de una sola pasada

one-way filter, filtro unidireccional

ontogenesis, ontogénesis, ontogenia

onyx, ónice, ónix

OOIP, q.v. **oil originally in place**

oolite, oolita

ooze, fango, limo

oozy, limoso, fangoso

op-amp (operational amplifier), (dp) amplificador operacional

op code (operation code), (dp) código de operación

opacity, opacidad

opal, ópalo

opalescence, opalescencia

opaque, opaco, obscuro

OPEC (Organization of Petroleum Exporting Countries), Organización de Países Exportadores de Petróleo (OPEP)

open, abierto

— **account,** cuenta abierta

— **cup,** (la) vaso abierto

— **dump,** (ec) vertedero (o botadero) abierto

— **ended,** (dp) susceptible de ampliación, ampliable, extensible

— **exhaust,** escape libre

— **flow,** flujo abierto
— **hearth process,** (mu) proceso Siemens-Martin
— **hole,** pozo franco, pozo sin tubería de revestimiento, (Me) agujero descubierto
— **flow,** a pleno flujo
— **flow potential,** producción potencial
— **sight alidade,** alidada de pínula (o mira) abierta
— **space deposits,** depósitos al aire libre
open-hole completion, terminación en pozo franco
opening, abertura, vano
operating
— **cycle,** ciclo (o período) de funcionamiento
— **pressure,** presión efectiva (o de trabajo)
— **rod,** varilla de mando
— **tool,** accionador
— **unit,** grupo operativo
operate, regir, conducir, manejar, *angl.* operar
operation, funcionamiento, operación
operator, (oc) (ma) operario; (dp) operador
ophicalcite, oficalcita
ophitic, ofítico
opposed flow, contracorriente
optic, óptico
— **angle,** ángulo óptico
— **axis,** eje óptico
— **normal,** normal óptico
— **orientation,** orientación óptica
— **plane,** plano óptico
— **sign,** signo óptico
optical density, densidad óptica (q.v. **true density**)
— **character recognition,** (dp) reconocimiento óptico de caracteres
— **scale,** densímetro
— **storage,** (dp) almacenamiento óptico, memorización óptica
optical lever, palanca óptica
optimize, mejorar, superar, aumentar; obtener máximo rendimiento (o provecho, etc.), (dp) optimizar
optimum, óptimo
optoelectronics, optoelectrónica
order, pedido, orden
— **acceptance,** (cm) aceptación de pedido
— **of precedence,** orden de precedencia (o de prioridad)
— **statistics,** estadística del orden (o de ordenamiento)
ordinate, ordenada, recta tirada desde un punto en una curva perpendicularmente a su eje
Ordovician, ordoviciano
ore, mineral; mena
— **assaying,** análisis de mineral
— **beds,** capas mineralíferas
organic, orgánico, producido por plantas o animales
— **amine,** ámina orgánica
— **deposit,** depósito de sedimento orgánico
— **remains,** restos orgánicos
— **rock,** roca orgánica
— **synthesis,** síntesis orgánica
organism, organismo
organogenic, organógeno
orientation, orientación
— **signaling,** instrumento señalador de orientación
oriented core, núcleo orientado
oriented drill pipe, tubo de perforación orientado
orifice, orificio
— **computation,** cómputo de orificio
— **fitting,** (gas tu) portaorificio
— **flange,** reborde (o brida) de orificio
— **meter,** contador de orificio

161

— **pipe tap**, toma de presión en tubería

— **plate**, placa (o disco) de orificio

— **well tester**, probador de orificio para pozos de gas

origin, origen

orle, orla, filete, listón

orogenesis, (g) orogénesis

orogenic, orogénico

orogeny, orogenia

orthoclase, (mn) ortoclasa, ortosa

orthocalsite, (g) ortoclasíta

orthoclastic, ortoclástic

orthogneiss, (g) ortogneis

orthogonal, ortogonal

orthonormal, ortonormal

orthophosphorous, ortofosforoso

orthophyre, (g) ortófiro

orthorhombic, ortorrómbico

orthose, ortosa

oscillate, oscilar, vibrar

oscillating wave, onda de oscilacíon

oscillation, oscilación, movimiento bascular

oscillator, oscilador

oscillograph, oscilógrafo

oscilloscope, osciloscopio

OSHA (Occupational Safety and Health Administration), Administración de Seguridad y Salud Laboral

osmotic pressure, presión osmótica

ostracoids, (paleo) ostracoides

O&SW (oil and salt water), petróleo y agua salada

ouija board, (prf engineering) (Me) uija

ounce (oz), onza: 28,3 gramos

outage, cubicación indirecta, merma, cantidad que falta para llenar, (Me) espacio libre; (el) parada, paralización; apagón

outboard, fuera de bordo

outconnector, (dp) conector de continuación, conector de salida

outcrop, (g) afloramiento, crestón, (Ar) asomo

outcropping formation, formación aflorante

outer barrel, cilindro exterior

outer race, (bearing) anillo exterior

outfit, *n.* equipo, habilitación, apero, apresto; *v.* equipar, habilitar

outlet, (rf) escape, salida; boca de salida, orificio de salida; (hd) emisario, boca de salida, escurridero, vano de descarga; (el) toma de corriente (o de derivación), caja de salida, conectador

— **temperature**, temperatura de salida

— **valve**, válvula de salida

outlier, (g) roca apartada (o extraña); (dp) valor atípico

outpost well, pozo de avanzada, pozo fuera de los límites del área probada, (Me) pozo exterior

output, rendimiento, volumen de producción; (dp) salida

— **circuit**, circuito de salida

— **filter**, filtro de salida

outrigger, contravientos, (Me) puntal

outside diameter (OD), diámetro exterior (DE)

outside location, ubicación externa, explazamiento exterior

outward axial thrust, empuje axial exterior

outwash plain, valle aluvial

overn, horno

overall efficiency, rendimiento total

overbalanced drilling, perforación sobreequilibrada (con presión del pozo superior a la de la formación)

overburden, *n.* (g) recubrimiento, cuerpo superyacente, estrato de

roca que se encuentra encima
del estrato de interés; *v*.
sobrecargar; oprimir
— **pressure,** presión de sobrecarga
overcharge, *n*. sobrecarga; (cm)
recargo de precio; *v*. sobrecargar;
recargar
overdraft, (cm) giro en descubierto,
adelanto en cuenta corriente
overflow, *n*. desbordamiento,
rebose, exceso, derrame;
sobreflujo; aliviadero; *v*. rebosar,
desbordarse, derramarse
— **duct,** tubo de rebose
— **position,** (dp) posición para
registros excedentarios
overflush, (prf) colchón adicional
(de fluido) (q.v. **matrix
acidizing**)
overfold, pliegue tumbado
overgage, overgauge hole, agujero
agrandado
overhand, (g) protuberancia
lateral, alero
overhaul, *n*. reajuste; desarme para
hacer reparaciones; *v*.
rehabilitar, reacondicionar,
componer, repasar
overhead, (cm) gastos fijos; (rf)
corriente (o producto) de cima
— **condenser,** (gas) condensador de
la corriente de cima
— **gas stream,** corriente de gases y
productos de evaporación
— **products,** productos de
evaporación
overheating, recalentamiento,
sobrecalentamiento
overlap, *n*. (g) superposición; *v*.
solapar, traslapar, sobreponer;
(dp) simultanear
— **fault,** falla sobrepuesta
overlapping, (g) transgresivo; (dp)
solapamiento

overlay, *n*. capa superpuesta,
recubrimiento, superposición;
(dp) simultaneidad
overlie, *v*. descansar sobre, yacer
encima de, sobreyacer
overload, *n*. sobrecarga; *v*.
sobrecargar
overprimed, excesivamente cebado,
sobrecebado
overpunch, perforación de zona
override, anular, contrarrestar
overrunning clutch, embrague de
rueda libre
overshot, enchufe de pesca, (Ar)
pescasonda, (Me) pescante de
cuñas, (Ve) pescador de cuello
— **guide,** guía del enchufe de pesca
oversize, sobremedida
overstrain, deformación excesiva
overthrust, (g) manto de
sobreescurrimiento, (Ar)
cobijadura, (Ve) corrimiento
— **fault,** falla acostada, (Ar)
sobreescurrimiento, (Me) falla
por empuje
— **mass,** (g) conjunto de estratos
superpuestos, (Ar) paquete de
mantos sobreescurrido
— **mountain,** montaña
sobreescurrida, montaña de
cobijadura
overtime, tiempo extra, horas
extraordinarias, sobretiempo
overturned, tumbado, invertido
— **anticline,** anticlinal tumbado
— **bed,** capa invertida
— **dip,** buzamiento invertido
— **strata,** estrato invertido
oxalic acid, ácido oxálico
oxbow lake, vega, brazo muerto; (r)
recodo
Oxfordian, oxfordiense
oxidation, oxidación
— **inhibitor**, inhibidor de oxidación
— **pond**, embalse (o laguna) de
oxidación

oxide, óxido
oxidizing flame, llama de oxidación
oxyacetylene, oxiacetileno
— blowpipe, soplete oxiacetilénico
— torch, antorcha de oxiacetileno,
    llama oxiacetilénica
— welding, soldadura con
    oxiacetileno, soldadura
    autógena
oxygen (O), oxígeno
— recorder, registrador de oxígeno
— regulator, regulador del oxígeno
ozokerite, ozocerita
ozone, ozono
— depleating chemicals, productos
    químicos que empobrecen el
    ozono

P

p, q.v. pico
P, p.v. peta; phosporus
P trap, sifón en P
P-low, presión baja
P wave, onda P, onda compresional
    (o longitudinal)
Pa, q.v. pascal
P&A, q.v. plug and abandon
pace, *n.* paso; *v.* medir a pasos
— counter, odómetro, cuentapasos
pacing, recorrer (o medir) a pasos
pack, (ma) empaquetar, estopar;
    (ice) banco; (shipping)
    empaquetar, embalar,
    encajonar, (fl) envasar; (dp)
    comprimir, condensar, formar
    lotes
— ice, banco de hielo, (Ar)
    banquisa
package, paquete, bulto; envase;
    conjunto; (dp) bloque, módulo,
    lote de programa
— deal, (cm) agrupación de varios
    artículos (o condiciones) en una

oferta (de venta, aceptación,
    etc)
packed-hole assembly, arreglo (o
    conjunto) de sarta para pozo
    desviado
packed tower, torre empacada para
    destilación
packer, obturador de empaque,
    (Me) empacador; tapón
— squeeze method, método de
    cementación con empacador
— test, prueba de la tubería de
    revestimiento con un fluido a
    presión
packet, (dp) paquete, grupo de bits
packing, embalaje, envase,
    encajonamiento; (ma) empaque,
    empaquetadura, guarnición
— box assembly, (va) conjunto de
    prensaestopas
— check valve, válvula de
    retención de la empaquetadura
— clamps, abrazaderas (o grapas)
    de empaquetadura
— density, (dp) densidad de registro
    (o de grabación)
— follower, casquillo del empaque
— gland, casquillo (o capillo) de
    presaestopas, (Ar) caja de
    prensaestopa, (Me) opresor,
    (Ve) pisaempaque
— head, cabezal obturador (q.v.
    packoff head)
— list, (cm) lista de embalaje (o de
    empaque)
— ring, anillo empaquetador
— ring retainer, anillo fiador de la
    empaquetadura
— screw, tornillo de la
    empaquetadura
— tool, herramienta de empacar el
    prensaestopas
— unit, unidad sellante
pack-off head, cabezal obturador
    (q.v. packing head)

Glossary of the Petroleum Industry

pad, (sd) relleno; cojín, almohadilla;
(saw) mango; (brace)
portabroca
padding, relleno
paddle, paleta
— mixer, mezcladora de paletas
padlock, candado
paint gun, atomizador de pintura,
(Ur) soplete de pintura
pale oil, aceite neutro (q.v. neutral
oil)
paleobiology, n. paleobiología
paleobotany, n. paleobotánica
Paleocene, paleoceno
paleogeography, n. paleogeografía
paleontologist, (oc) paleontólogo
Paleozoic, paleozóico, era primaria
(la que comprende los períodos
[o sistemas] cámbrico,
ordoviciano, silúrico, devónico,
carbonífero y pérmico)
paleozoology, n. paleozoología
pall, q.v. pawl
pallet, palette, (mc) paleta
paludal, palúdico, cenagoso
pantanoso, (Ve) paludal
pampa, pampa
pan, cuenco; paila; (mn) gamella
panel, panel, tablero
panel board, tablero de
instrumentos (o de distribución)
paraclase, (g) paraclasa, falla (q.v.
fault)
paradigm, (dp) paradigma
paraffin, parafina
— base oil, petróleo parafínico
— dirt, lodo parafínico
— distillate, destilador de parafina
(q.v. pressed distillate)
— inhibitor, inhibidor de parafina
— oil, aceite parafínico
— scraper, raspador (o escariador)
de parafina
— series, serie parafínica
— solvent, disolvente para parafina
— stock, petróleo parafínico

— wax, parafina, parafina sólida,
cera de parafina
paraffin-base oil, petróleo de base
parafínica, (Me) aceite
parafínico
paragenesis, paragénesis
paralic, (mar) (g) parálico
parallax, paralaje
parallel, paralelo
— access, (dp) acceso en paralelo
— computer, ordenador paralelo,
ordenador de funcionamiento
en paralelo
— contouring, acotación paralela
— faults, fallas paralelas
— folds, (g) pliegues paralelos
— of latitude, paralelo de latitud
— orientation, orientación
paralela
— perspective, perspectiva en
paralelo
— processing, proceso en paralelo,
tratamiento en simultaneidad
— running, (dp) ciclo de
funcionamiento en paralelo,
ejecución (o proceso) en
paralelo
— shooting method, (dp) método
de reparación (o corrección) de
errores en paralelo
— storage, (dp) memoria (o
almacenamiento) de acceso en
paralelo
— structures, estructuras paralelas
parallelogram, paralelogramo
paramagnetic, (g) paramagnético
parameter, parámetro
paramorphism, (g) paramorfismo
parasitic crater, cráter parasitario
(o adventicio, secundario)
paratype, (paleo) paratipo
parent rock, roca madre
parity, paridad
paroxysm, (vlc) paroxismo
parsing, (dp) análisis sintáctico
particle, partícula

particular average, avería parcial

particulates, (ec) partículas, particulados

parting, separación, fractura, rotura

partition ring, (rf) aro divisorio

parts catalogue, catálogo de piezas de repuesto

partly, en parte, parcialmente

pascal (Pa), pascal: unidad de presión equivalente a newton por metro cuadrado (N/m^2) (q.v. **atmosphere)**

Pascal, (dp) Pascal: lenguaje de programación

Pascal's law, ley de Pascal: la presión que se le aplica a un líquido encerrado se transmite igualmente en todas las direcciones a través del líquido

pass, (tp) paso, (Ar) congosto

passage, pasaje, conducto

passband, (dp) banda de paso, banda de transmisión libre

password, contraseña

paste, pasta

patch, parche, remiendo; (land) parcela; (gf) tendido de recepción (q.v. **spread)**

patchboard, panel (o tablero) de conexiones, cuadro de control abierto

patent, patente

path, camino, recorrido, trayectoria

— **of seismic wave,** trayectoria de la onda sísmica

— **testing,** (dp) comprobación de caminos (o ramas) de organigrama

pattern, *n.* modelo, esquema, disposición, pauta; ejemplar, muestra; patrón; molde, plantilla, escantillón; (g) configuración, forma, estructura; *v.* copiar; imitar

— **matching,** (dp) comparación de configuraciones (o formas, estructuras)

— **recognition,** (dp) reconocimiento de configuraciones

pavement, pavimento, empedrado

paver, pavimentadora

pawl, paul, pall, trinquete, retén, linguete, uña, seguro, crique

pay, *n.* (cm) sueldo, salario; (nt) embrear; *v.* pagar, liquidar; producir ganancia

— **sand,** arena productiva, horizonte (o intervalo) productor

— **seam,** (mn) venero

— **string,** tubería de explotación, última tubería de revestimiento

payment, pago

payroll, nómina

PBCs (polychlorinated biphenyls), bifeniles policlorados

PC clone, (dp) clon de ordenador personal, ordenador personal clónico

PDC, q.v. **polycrystalline diamond compact**

PDC (perforating depth control) log, registro de control de profundidad de perforación

peak, *n.* (tp) cima, cumbre; (gf) pico; vértice, cúspide; *a.* máximo

— **load,** carga máxima

— **observed reflection,** pico (o cresta) de reflexión

pearlite, perlita

peat, (g) turba

— **bog,** (g) turera, cenegal donde se forma la turba

pebble, guijarro, piedrecita

— **conglomerate,** conglomerado guijarroso

— **gravel,** grava guijarrosa

pectolite, pectolita

pediment, frontón, pedimento

peek, (dp) atisbar, leer, examinar
una posición para recuperarla
peeling, (g) descamación
peening, (sd) rebatido, martilleo
peephole, mirilla
peg, espiga, clavija, espárrago,
pernete
peg-leg multiple, (gf) múltiple
sucesivo
pegmatite, (g) pegmatita
— **texture,** textura pegmatítica
pelite, (g) pelita
pellets, granos, pelotillas
pendulum, péndulo
— **period,** período del péndulo
— **station,** estación de péndulo
— **stroke multiplier,** columpio
multiplicador del largo de la
carrera, columpio graduador de
carrera
penecontemporaneous,
semicontemporáneo
peneplain, (g) penillanura, (Ar)
llanura troncal
penetrating oil, aceite penetrante
penetration, penetración; (dp)
técnica de evaluación de
seguridad
— **rate,** velocidad (o tasa) de
perforación
peninsula, península
Pennsylvanian, pensilvaniano,
pensilvaniense, carbonífero
superior
pennyweight, escrúpulo (= 24
granos)
penstock, tubo de entrada, tubería
de carga
penta, *pref.* penta-
pentadiene, pentadieno
pentafining, pentafining
pentagon, pentágono
pentamethylene, pentametileno,
ciclopentano
pentane, pentano
— **insolubles,** insolubles de pentano

— **plus,** pluspentano, mexcla de
pentano y componentes más
pesados del gas natural
pentanol, pentanol
pentene, penteno (q.v. **amylene**)
pentenyne, pentenino (q.v.
allylacetylene)
pentriacontane, pentriacontano
pentriacontene, pentriaconteno
pentylheneicosane,
pentilheneicosano
pentyne, pentino (q.v.
propylacetylene)
pepper sludge, cieno pimienta
per-acre yield, producción por acre
percent (%), por ciento
— **frequency effect,** efecto del
porcentaje de frecuencia
percentage, procentaje
perch, pértiga
perched rock, roca transportada
por helero
Perco copper sweetening,
endulzamiento Perco por cobre
percolate, filtrar, percolar
percolating filter, (g) filtración,
percolación, coladura
— **filtration,** colación-filtración
percussion drilling, perforación
por percusión
percussive welding, soldadura de
impacto
perforated, (tu) agujereado, de
paredes perforadas, calado
— **completion,** terminación
abriendo agujeros en la tubería
— **liner,** tubo revestidor auxiliar
perforado, tubo calado, tubería
corta de revestimiento
perforada
— **pipe,** tubo colador, (Ar) caño
punzonado, caño filtro, (Me)
cedazo (Ve) tubo calado (q.v.
screen)
— **underbalanced,** perforación con
presión inversa

perforation, perforación
perforator, aparato perforador,
  (Ar) punzonador, (Ve) cañón
  perforador, pistola perforadora
performance, rendimiento,
  eficacia, desempeño
— **number,** índice de rendimiento
— **testing,** combrobación de
  rendimiento, prueba de
  funcionamiento (o de
  prestaciones)
peridot, (g) peridoto (q.v. **olivine**)
peridotite, (g) peridotita
perimeter, perímetro
period, período; (g) q.v. **system** (e.g.
  Tertiary)
— **of pitch,** (nt) tiempo de cabeceo
— **of roll,** (nt) tiempo de balanceo
— **resonance,** (el) resonancia
  natural
periodic motion, movimiento
  periódico
peripheral, periférico
— **buffer,** (dp) memoria intermedia
  periférica
— **interface adapter,** (dp)
  adaptador de interfaz para
  dispositivos periféricos
— **processor,** (dp) procesador de
  periféricos
— **speed,** velocidad periférica
perlite, perlita
permanency, estabilidad,
  permanencia
permanent
— **completion,** terminación
  permanente
— **guide structure,** bastidor (o base
  estructural) permanente
— **load,** carga muerta
— **magnetism,** magnetismo
  permanente
permeability, permeabilidad,
  porosidad
permeable, permeable
Permian, pérmico, permiano

permissible variations, variaciones
  aprobadas (o admisibles)
permit, permiso
Permo-carboniferous,
  permocarbonífero
permonophosphorous,
  permonofosforoso
peroxide, peróxido
personnel transfer submersible,
  sumergible para transferencia de
  personal
perspective, perspectiva
peseta, peseta: unidad monetaria de
  España
peso, peso: unidad monetaria de
  Argentina, Bolivia, Colombia,
  Cuba, Chile, México, República
  Dominicana y Uruguay
pestle, (la) mano de almirez
PET (polyethylene terephtalate),
  polietileno tereftalato
peta (P), *pref.* SI = 10^{15}
petcock, llave de purga (o de
  desagüe, de escape)
petrify, petrificarse
petrochemical, petroquímico
petrogenesis, petrogénesis
petrographic, petrográfico
petrography, petrografía
petrol, (England) gasolina
petrolatum, petrolato
petroleum, petróleo; nafta
— **asphalt,** brea, asfalto de petróleo
— **ceresin,** ceresina de petróleo
— **coke,** coque (o cok) de petróleo
— **ether,** éter de petróleo
— **jelly,** vaselina
— **pitch,** alquitrán de petróleo
— **refining,** refinación de petróleo
— **resources,** recursos petroleros,
  riqueza petrolífera
— **spirit, destilado ralo de
  petróleo,** espíritu de petróleo
  (q.v. **white spirit**)
— **still,** alambique de petróleo
petroliferous, petrolífero

Glossary of the Petroleum Industry

petroline, petrolina
petrolize, petrolizar
petrology, petrología
pH meter, medidor del pH
Phanerozoic, fanerozoico
phantom horizon, horizonte
   imaginario
phase, (el) (qm) (mu) (dp) fase; (tp)
   error aparente de dirección
— **angle,** ángulo de retraso de fase,
   ángulo de desfasamiento
— **change,** (dp) defasaje,
   defasamiento, desfase, cambio
   de fase
— **correction,** corrección de fase
— **difference,** desplazamiento (o
   avance) de fase, defasamiento
— **displacement,** desplazamiento
— **encoded,** (dp) de fase codificada
— **lag,** retraso de fase
— **lead,** avance de fase
— **meter,** fasómetro
— **relation,** relación de fase
— **rule,** regla de las fases
— **shift,** cambio de fase (q.v. **phase
   change**)
— **shifter,** decalador de fase
phenanthrene, fenantreno
phenocrysts, fenocristales
phenol, fenol
phenolate process, proceso con
   fenolato
phenolphthalein, fenolftaleína
phenyl, *pref.* fenil-
phenylmethane, fenilmetano,
   etilbenzol
phlogopite, flogopita
phonolite, fonolita
phosphate, fosfato
phosphor bronze, bronce fosforado
phosphoric acid, ácido fosfórico
phosphorite, fosforita
phosphorous (P), fósforo
photoelectric cell, celda
   fotoeléctrica

photographic recording, registro
   fotográfico
photometer, fotómetro
phrenite, frenita
phtalic anhydride, anhídrido
   ftálico
phyllite, (g) filita
phylogeny, (g) filogenia
physical constant, factor físico
   constante
physics, física
physiographic, fisigráfico
physiography, fisiografía
PI (productivity index), índice de
   productividad (IP)
picene, piceno
pick, *n.* pico, piqueta, alcotana; (gf)
   señal, marca; *v.* picar; (mn)
   separar mineral a mano;
   señalar, marcar
— **mattock,** zapapico, pico de punta
   y pala
pickup pump, bomba recogedora
pickup tool, herramienta de rescate
pico (p), *pref.* SI = 10^{-12} e.g. picofarad
   (pf)
picosecond, picosegundo,
   micromicosegundo
piedmont, pie de monte, formación
   piamontina
piercement-type salt dome, domo
   salino que rompe a través de los
   estratos superiores, domo salino
   penetrante
piezoelectric detector, detector
   piezoeléctrico
piezoelectricity, piezoelectricidad
piezometric level, nivel
   piezométrico, nivel hidrostático
pig, (p) taco raspatubos (q.v. **go-
   devil**)
— **iron,** lingotes de hierro, hierro en
   lingotes
— **launching trap,** trampa de
   raspatubos (o diablos)

169

pigging, (p) limpiar con taco (o diablo)

piggyback, *a.* (trans) en vagón de plataforma, a cuestas, (anchors) en tándem

pile, (cn) pilote; nuclear pila

— **driver,** martinete

piled platform, plataforma de pilotes hincados

pileless platform, plataforma de (apoyo por) gravedad, i.e. sin pilotes hincados

piling, amontonamiento; hincado de pilotes

pillow block, cojinete, descanso, tejuelo, cojín, caja de chumacera, cajera del eje

— **bearing,** bloque cojinete

pillow-lava, lava cordada (o elipsoidal)

pilot, piloto, guía

— **bearing,** cojinete de guía

— **bit,** barrena piloto

— **burner,** quemador piloto

— **joint,** unión piloto

— **mill,** (prf) molino piloto (o aguijón)

— **nozzle,** boquilla con válvula piloto

— **plant,** planta piloto

— **reamer bit,** escariador piloto

— **valve,** válvula piloto

pilot-operated valve, válvula piloto (o de maniobra)

pin, *n.* pasador; (mc) clavija, chaveta, pernete, espiga, macho, (Me) piñón; *v.* empernar, encabillar, enclavijar, apernar, espigar

— **bushing,** buje del pasador

— **drive,** movido por pernos

— **key,** chaveta de pasadores

— **link,** eslabón de pernos

— **link plate,** plancha de los pasadores de eslabón

— **packer,** empacador con pernos

— **punch,** punzón botador

— **shank,** cuerpo (o fuste) de pasador

— **shear,** perno rompible

— **socket,** pescaespigas

— **tap,** (fishing tl) pescante roscado, (Me) machuelo piñón

— **template,** calibrador de espigas

PIN (personal identification number), número de identificación personal

pinacoid, (g) pinacoide

pincers, pinzas, tenazas

pinch

— **bar,** pie de cabra, alzaprima, barreta

— **out,** *n.* (g) monoclinal, estructura acuñada; *v.* adelgazarse discordantemente; (mn) agotarse el filón

— **valve,** válvula de estrangulación

pinch-point crowbar, barra de punta de escoplo

pinchcock, apretadora para tubo flexible, abrazadera de compresión

pinching, (g) adelgazamiento

pinion, piñón

— **gear,** engranaje de piñón

— **shaft bearing,** cojinete del eje del piñón

pint, pinta: 1/8 de galón

pintle hook, gancho de seguridad

pipe, *n.* tubo, caño, tubería, (Ar) cañería; (g) formación cilíndrica vertical; (mu) bolsa de contracción; (earth dam) venero; *v.* entubar, (Ar) encañar; conducir por tubería; formar venero

— **and bolt dies and taps,** dados y machos de terraja

— **and bolt machine,** terraja, máquina de enroscar, roscadora

— **bend,** codo (o curva) de tubería

— **bender,** curvatubos

Glossary of the Petroleum Industry

— **clamp,** abrazadera para tubo
— **coupling,** unión (o acoplamiento) de tubos
— **cutter,** cortatubos
— **die,** tubo de inmersión
— **elevator link,** eslabón (o estribo) de elevador de tubería
— **expander,** ensanchatubos, (Ar) ensanchador de caños
— **fittings,** conexiones (o accesorios) para tubería
— **gang,** cuadrilla de tendedores de tubería
— **grip,** mordaza (o garra) para tubería
— **hanger,** colgador de tubería
— **hooks,** tenazas
— **jack,** alzatubos, gato para tubería
— **layer,** tractor tiendetubos, tractor grúa (q.v. **boom tractor**)
— **rack,** (tu) tarima para tubería, muelle de tubería, (Ve) panchada, casillero
— **racking fingers,** dedos de la tarima (o del muelle) de tubería (q.v. **finger board**)
— **ram,** ariete anular
— **ram preventer,** preventor anular
— **repair clamp,** abrazadera
— **saddle,** silleta para tubos, parche de remiendo
— **setback,** (derrick) haz de tubería en pie en el astillero (o plataforma de enganche)
— **skids,** patines (o polines) de tubos
— **still,** alambique de tubos (q.v. **tube still**)
— **straightener,** máquina para enderezar tubos
— **swedge,** abretubos
— **thread,** rosca de tubería, filete de tubo
— **thread die,** tarrajadora de dado
— **threader,** roscador (o aterrajador) de tubos

— **tongs,** llave de cadena para tubería, tenazas para tubería
— **trailer,** remolque para tubería
— **upset,** refuerzo
— **vise,** tornillo de banco para tubos
— **wiper,** limpiatubos
— **wrench,** llave de tubos
pipe-beveling cutter, cortatubos biselador
pipe-cleaning machine, máquina de limpiar tubos
pipe-cutting machine, máquina cortadora de tubería
pipe-fitting tongs, llave de cadena para tubería
pipe-joint clamp, abrazadera de unión para tubería
pipe-threading machine, roscadora de tubos
pipelaying barge, barcaza tiendetubos
pipeline, (p) tubería de conducción, conducto, (Me) ducto; (petrol) oleoducto; (gas) gasoducto; (water) acueducto; (products) tubería de productos
— **boom,** botalón para tubería
— **gas,** gas transportable
— **manifold,** múltiple de tuberías
— **oil,** petróleo limpio (o transportable)
— **processing,** (dp) proceso de encauzamiento (o tubular), proceso en pipeline
— **rates,** tarifa de oleoductos
pipette, pipeta, gotero
pirobituminous shale, lutita pirobituminosa (q.v. **shale**)
pisolite, pisolita
piston, émbolo, pistón
— **area,** superficie del émbolo
— **clearance,** espacio libre (o luz) del émbolo
— **displacement,** desplazamiento, cilindrada de émbolo
— **head,** cabeza de émbolo

171

— **pin,** pasador de émbolo
— **pin bushing,** buje de pasador de
  émbolo
— **pump,** bomba de émbolo
— **ring,** aro del émbolo (o de
  compresión), (Ar) anillo de
  pistón
— **stroke,** carrera del émbolo
— **rod,** vástago del émbolo, (Me)
  biela
— **valve,** válvula de corredera
pit, *n.* foso, hoyo, presa, cava; (mu)
  picadura, caracaña; *v.* picarse
— **gravel,** grava de cantera
— **head,** (mn) bocal
— **lathe,** torno con foso para obra
  grande
— **leaks,** fugas a través de
  cacarañas (o de picaduras)
— **level,** (mud) nivel en la presa
— **liner,** forro metálico del pozo de
  la turbina
— **volume totalizer,** totalizador de
  volumen de la presa
pitch, *n.* pez betún, brea, alquitrán;
  declive inclinación; (g)
  hundimiento de un eje de
  pliegue; (mn) buzamiento;
  espaciado, distancia; (ca)
  (chain) paso; (el) avance, paso;
  v. alquitranar, betunar, embrear;
  (nt) cabecear
— **and gather,** inclinación y
  convergencia
— **and circle gear,** paso del
  engranaje
— **of anticline,** buzamiento axial
  del anticlinal (q.v. plunge of
  anticline)
pitchblende, (g) pechblenda (q.v.
  uraninite)
pitchstone, piedra pez, cantalita
  (q.v. **cantalite**)
pitman, biela, barra de conexión,
  pitman, (Ve) brazo
— **bearing,** cojinete de la biela

— **stirrup,** (perc) estribo de la biela
pitting, picaduras, cacaraña
— **hammer,** martillo descostrador
pivot, *n.* pivote, muñón, gorrón; *v.*
  pivotar
pivotal fault, falla en pivote
pixel, (dp) pixel, elemento de
  imagen, punto
pH indicator, indicador de pH
placer, (mn) placer, mina de
  aluvión
plagioclase, plagioclasa
plagioclastic, (g) plagioclásica
plain, *n.* planicie, llano, llanura; *a.*
  llano, simple, sencillo, común,
  puro
— **cylinder with (without) spout,**
  probeta con (sin) pico
— **thermit,** (sd) termita simple
plain-end, (tu) sin rosca, de
  extremos lisos
plan, plan, heliografía, proyección
  horizontal
planar graph, grafo planar
plane, plano
— **boundary,** plano de contacto de
  dos capas
— **dilatational wave,** onda plana de
  dilatación
— **resection,** (tp) resección plana
— **surveying,** (tp) levantamiento
  plano (o ordinario), planimetría
— **table,** plancheta
— **table survey,** levantamiento a
  plancheta
planimeter, planímetro
plankton, plancton
plant, planta, instalación, fábrica
— **debris,** despojos de plantas
plasma display, (dp)
  representación visual por
  plasma
plasticizer, plastificante
plastotype, (paleo) plastotipo
plaster of paris, yeso
plastic, plástico

172

— **flow,** (g) flujo plástico
— **packing,** empaquetadura de material plástico
— **pipe,** tubería plástica
— **squeezing,** inyección de resinas (q.v. **sand consolidation**)
plasticity, plasticidad
plat, (tp) trazado, mapa
plate, (metal) plancha, lámina, placa; (el) placa
— **efficiency,** eficiencia de bandejas
— **gage,** calibrador de planchas
plateau, (g) meseta, altiplano, altiplanicie
platform, plataforma
— **complex,** complejo (o conjunto) de plataformas
— **jacket,** bastidor de plataforma, base de la plataforma
platforming, platforming, platformación
platinum, platino
platinum-iridium alloy, aleación de platino de iridio
platy, (g) escamoso, laminado
play, (ma) juego, holgura; (petrol) extensión productiva
playa, (g) playa
Pleistocene, pleistoceno, pleistocénico, comienzo de la era cuaternaria
PLEM, múltiple de tuberías
plenum chamber, cámara colectora de horno
pleochroism, pleocroísmo, pleocromatismo
plex, estructuras entrelazadas (o reticulares)
pliability, ductilidad, flexibilidad
plication, plegamiento
pliers, alicates, pinzas, tenazas, tenacillas
Plimsoll mark, (nt) línea de carga máxima
Pliocene, plioceno

plot, *n.* (land) solar, parcela; *v.* trazar, delinear
plotter, trazador de gráficos (o de curvas)
plotting, graficado
plow steel, acero de arado
plug, *n.* tapón, obturador; (el) enchufe, clavija de contacto; (va) macho; (tp) estaca de tránsito; (wood) taco, tarugo; (g) masa de roca ígnea intrusiva, lacolito (q.v. **laccolith**); *v.* tapar, taponar, atarugar; enchufar
— **and abandon,** taponar y abandonar
— **back,** *n.* (well) retrotaponamiento; *v.* retrotaponar, tapar el pozo en un punto intermedio entre el fondo y la boca
— **cock,** grifo, grifo de llave
— **flow,** flujo tapón
— **gage,** calibrador de macho, calibre cilíndrico
— **valve,** válvula macho
— **weld,** soldadura de tapón (o de cuña)
plug-in, *a.* acoplable
plug-type valve, válvula de tapón
plugged
— **bit,** barrena taponada, barrena con los agujeros de circulación obstruídos
— **well,** pozo taponado
plumb bob, plomada
plumb-line deviation, desviación de la vertical
— **of anticline,** inclinación del anticlinal (q.v. **pitch of anticline**)
plunge, *n.* (g) hundimiento regional, buzamiento; *v.* buzar, invertir; zambullir, sumergir

— **of anticline,** inclinación del
  anticlinal, buzamiento axial del
  anticlinal
plunger, émbolo buzo (o macizo),
  chupón (q.v. **sucker rod pump**)
— **cup,** casquillo (o copa) de
  émbolo
— **hanger,** colgadero del émbolo
  buzo
— **lift,** aspiración del émbolo
— **pump,** bomba de émbolo buzo
plutonic, (g) plutónico
plutonium, plutonio
ply, hoja, capa, pliegue, tela
plywood, madera laminada (o
  terciada), (Me) madera
  contrachapada
pneumatic, *a.* neumático
— **grinder,** moledora (o
  amoladora) neumática
— **logic,** (dp) lógica neumática,
  lógica de fluidos
— **pump,** bomba neumática
— **rubber fender,** defensas
  neumáticas de caucho
— **tire,** neumático, llanta
  neumática
— **wrench,** llave neumática
pneumatics, *n.* neumática
pneumatolytic, (g) neumatolítico,
  neumatológeno
pocket, bolsillo, cavidad, bolsa
pocketknife, cortaplumas, cuchilla
POD analysis, análisis de
  Podbielniak
podsol, podsol, tierra parecida a la
  ceniza
point, *n.* punto; (in) punta; *v.*
  apuntar; aguzar
— **electrode,** electrodo de punto
poise, poise: medida de viscosidad
poison, *n.* veneno; **poisonous,** *a.*
  venenoso
poke welding, soldadura de sello
poker, atizador; (pr tu) obturador

polar
— **compound,** compuesto polar
— **coordinates,** coordenadas
  polares
— **core orientation,** determinación
  de la posición original del núcleo
  en la formación por medio de la
  polaridad del núcleo
— **radius,** radio polar
polarization ellipse, elipse de
  polarización
polarizer, polarizador
polarizing microscope, microscopio
  de polarización
pole, palo, poste, asta, vara; (mt) (g)
  (el) polo; (tp) baliza, jalón
— **height viscosity index,** índice de
  viscosidad por altura de polo
— **mast,** mástil de poste
— **trailer,** remolque de tirante
poligonal, poligonal
polinomial form, forma
  polinómica
polish, *n.* pulimento, lustre; *v.* pulir,
  lustar
polished-rod, (bm) vástago pulido,
  (Ar) barra de sección cuadrada;
  (Me) varilla pulida, (Ve) barra
  lisa
— **clamps,** abrazaderas del vástago
  pulido
— **eye,** armella del vástago pulido
— **grip,** agarradera del vástago
  pulido
— **liner,** alineador del vástago
  pulido
pollutant, contaminante
polybutene, polibuteno
polyconic projections, proyecciones
  policónicas
**polycrystalline diamond compact
  bit,** barrena de compacto
  policristalino de diamante
polycyclic, policíclico
polyethylene, polietileno
polyester, poliéster

Glossary of the Petroleum Industry

polyform plant, (rf) planta
poliformadora
polyform process, proceso
poliforme
polygon, polígono
polyhedral projections,
proyecciones poliédricas
polymer, polímero
— gasoline, gasolina polímera
— mud, lodo con polímero
polymerization, polimerización
polymerized, (qm) polimerizado
polymethylene, polimetileno
polymorphism, (g) polimorfía;
(qm) (dp) polimorfismo
polynomial, n. (mt) polinomio; a.
polinómico
polypropylene, polipropileno
polysulfides, polisulfuros
polysynthetic, polisintético
polytropic expansion, expansión
politrópica
pond, estanque, alberca, charca
pontoon, pontón
pontoon roof tank, tanque con
techo de pontones, tanque de
techo flotante
pony rod, vástago pulido, varilla
corta (q.v. polished rod)
pool, (petrol) yacimiento, depósito
(q.v. reservoir)
pop valve, válvula de seguridad de
resorte (o de disparo)
poppet valve, válvula de disco con
movimiento vertical, (Ar)
válvula de asiento plano
pore, poro
— pressure, presión de poro
— volume, volumen de poro
porosity, porosidad
porous, poroso
— cake, costra porosa
— pot electrode, electrodo de vaso
poroso
— zone, zona porosa
porphyrite, (g) porfirita

porphyritic, porfídico, porfirítico
porphyry, pórfido
— quartz, cuarzo porfirítico
port, (mar) puerto; (ma) lumbrera,
orificio, abertura; (nt) babor;
(dp) puerta, puerto (o punto,
vía) de acceso
— captain, capitán de puerto
— pilot, práctico
portable, portátil
portland cement, cemento
portland
Portlandian, portlandiense
positive, positivo
— aniline equivalent, equivalente
anilínico positivo
— clutch, embrague positivo,
embrague de garras
— type choke, estrangulador de
tipo positivo
positive-displacement
— meter, contador de
desplazamiento positivo
— motor, motor de fondo del pozo
— valve, válvula de
desplazamiento positivo
possum belly, caja de recibo (o de
herramientas)
post, pilar, poste, montante
post-hole auger, barrena para
hoyos de poste
post-hole well, pozo somero
pot, marmite, caldero, olla; pote,
cacharro
potash, potasa
potassium, potasio
— hydroxide, hidróxido de potasio
— iodate solution, solución de
iodato potásico (o de potasio)
— iodide solution, solución de
yoduro de potasio
potential, n. potencial absoluto,
gasto máximo que la formación
puede aportar al pozo; a.
potencial

— **drop ratio,** relación de la caída
de potencial
— **electrode,** electrodo de potencial
— **production,** producción
potencial
potentiometer, potenciómetro
pothole, (g) marmita de gigante,
olla de remolino, molino glaciar;
(rd) bache, nido
pound, *n.* libra: unidad de peso; *v.*
golpear
— **sterling,** libra esterlina
pounding, golpeo; golpeteo
pour, verter
— **depressor,** rebajador de punto de
fluidez
— **point,** punto de fluidez,
temperatura más baja a que el
petróleo fluye cuando se somete
a enfriamiento progresivo, bajo
condiciones prescritas (q.v. **cold
test, cloud point**)
— **reversion,** inversión de fluidez
— **stability,** fluidez estable
pour test, prueba de fluidez a baja
temperatura (q.v. **cold test, cold
setting, pour point**)
powder, polvo; pólvora
power, (mc) potencia, fuerza
motriz; (el) energía, fuerza,
potencia; (cm) poderes
— **blower,** ventilador a fuerza
motriz
— **curve,** curva de potencia
— **electrode,** electrodo de potencia
— **factor,** factor de potencia
— **house,** casa de motores; central
eléctrica (q.v. **power plant**)
— **line,** línea de energía eléctrica
— **of attorney,** (cm) poder,
autorización legal
— **plant,** central eléctrica, planta
de energía eléctrica, (Ar) usina
— **pump,** bomba a motor, bomba
mecánica

— **pumping unit,** unidad de
bombeo a motor, (Ar) grupo
motobomba
— **rating,** potencia asignada
— **rod tongs,** llaves de potencia
— **shift,** transmisión automática
— **shovel,** excavadora mecánica,
pala mecánica, pala de motor
— **stroke,** carrera motriz, carrera
de impulsión
— **sub,** substituto rotatorio
— **take-off,** toma de fuerza,
tomafuerza
— **tongs,** llaves de potencia
— **unit,** unidad de fuerza,(o de
potencia)
powerforming, powerforming
ppb (parts per billion), partes por
billón (i.e. un millón de
millones); (*as intended in
English, however*) partes por
1.000 millones
ppm (parts per million), partes por
millón
Precambrian, precámbrico,
precambriano
precipitant, precipitante
precipitate, *n.* (qm) precipitado; *v.*
precipitar
precipitation, precipitación
— **naphtha,** nafta de precipitación
— **number,** índice de precipitación
precipitator, precipitador
precision, precisión
prefabricated piping, tubería
preformada
preferential absorption, absorción
preferencial
prefill, prellenado
prefilter, prefiltro
preflash tower, torre de destilación
primaria preliminar
preflush, colchón
preheater, precalentador
preignition, encendido anticipado
(o prematuro)

preliminary charge stabilizer, (rf) torre de destilación primaria preliminar (q.v. **preflash tower**)
preliminary seismic wave, (gf) onda precursora; (seismol) sismo precursor
premium gage, alto calibre
preplanning, anteproyecto
preservation, preservación
preservative, preservativo
press, *n*. prensa; *v*. prensar; apretar
— **drip**, goteo de prensa
— **roll**, rodillo compresor, cilindro laminador
pressed distillate, destilado de filtroprensa (q.v. **paraffin distillate**)
pressed steel, acero prensado
pressed-in, incrustado
pressure, presión, compresión
— **build-up**, fortalecimento de la presión
— **completion**, terminación a presión
— **control**, *n*. control de la presión; *v*. regular la presión
— **control setting**, posición del control de presiones
— **convertion constant**, factor constante para la conversión de la presión
— **curve**, curva de presión
— **differential**, presión diferencial
— **distillate**, destilado a presión
— **distillate rerun unit**, unidad de repaso a presión para destilados
— **drilling**, perforación con contrapresión del lodo
— **drop**, pérdida (o caída) de presión
— **gage**, manómetro, indicador de la presión
— **gage stabilizer**, estabilizador de manómetro
— **gradient**, gradiente de presión
— **gun**, pistola de engrase

— **loss**, pérdida de presión
— **lubrication**, lubricación a presión
— **maintenance**, conservación de la presión
— **parting**, fractura de la formación
— **reducer**, reductor de la presión
— **reducing valve**, válvula reductora de la presión
— **regulating station**, estación reguladora de presión
— **regulator**, regulador de presión
— **relief valve**, válvula de seguridad
— **still**, alambique de presión (q.v. **cracking still**)
— **storage tank**, tanque de almacenamiento a presión
— **type sand filter**, filtro de arena a presión
— **vessel**, recipiente a presión
— **welding**, soldadura a presión
pressurize, presurizar
prestressing, preestiramiento, pretensado
primary, primario
— **air**, aire primario
— **control**, control primario
— **decomposition**, descomposición primaria
— **dip**, inclinación principal
— **flash tower**, torre de expansión primaria
— **reference fuel**, combustible primario de referencia
— **separating chamber**, cámara de separación primaria
— **wave**, onda primaria (q.v. **longitudinal wave**)
prime mover, motor primario (o impulsor, primordial)
primer, (bm) cebador; (paint) imprimador, aprestador, tapaporos; (rd) aceite imprimador; (expl) cebo
priming valve, válvula de ceba

English - Spanish

prism, prisma
prismatic eye-piece, ocular prismático
private property, propiedad particular
privatization, *n.* privatización, (Bo) capitalización; **privatize,** *v.* privatizar, capitalizar
pro forma invoice, factura pro forma
probable fault, falla inferida (o probable)
probable misclosure, error probable de cierre
probe, *n.* sonda, tienta, cánula; *v.* sondear, explorar, tentar; *a.* exploratorio
procedure, procedimiento
— **oriented language,** (dp) lenguaje orientado hacia los procedimientos
process, *n.* procedimiento, método; (sequence of operations) proceso; operación, tratamiento; *v.* tratar, fabricar, elaborar
— **acetone-benzol,** desparafinación por acetona-benzol
— **coking,** (rf) método coquificante
processing, procesamiento, tratamiento, elaboración, manufactura; proceso de refinar, purificar o someter hidrocarburos a cualquier tratamiento
processor, (dp) procesador
producer gas, gas pobre, gas de aire (q.v. **aerogene gas**)
production, producción
— **casing,** tubería de revestimiento de explotación
— **ceiling,** tope de producción
— **curve,** curva de producción
— **island,** isla (artificial) de producción
— **platform,** plataforma de producción

— **run,** fase de ejecución (o de explotación), pasada de producción, proceso final (*op.* dry run)
— **sharing contract,** contrato de reparto de la producción
productivity, productividad
— **index,** índice de productividad
products pipeline, tubería para productos refinados
profile, perfil
— **paper,** papel cuadriculado
— **shooting,** (gf) disparo con detectores en línea recta
profiling, trazado de perfil
profit, ganancia; utilidad
— **worth rate,** (cm) relación de utilidad a capital
project, (future) proyecto, plan; (in progress) obra
projection, proyección; vuelo, resalte, saliente; (sd) resalto
promote, promover
prompt, (dp) indicación, petición de orden
prong drag bit, barrena de arrastre
prop, *n.* (cn) puntal, entibo, jabalcón; *v.* apuntalar, entibar, jabalconar
— **clasp,** abrazadera de puntal
— **strap,** abrazadera de puntal
propadiene, propadieno
propagation time, (gf) tiempo de propagación (q.v. **running time**)
propane, propano
— **deasphalting,** desasfaltación por propano
— **decarbonizing,** decarbonización por propano
— **dewaxing,** desparafinación por propano
propeller, hélice (q.v. **helix**)
— **shaft,** eje de propulsión, eje cardán, árbol de mando; (nt) eje de hélice

— **type agitator,** agitador tipo de hélice

propene, propeno, propileno (q.v. **propylene**)

property, (cm) propiedad; finca; (qm) propiedad, característica

— **tax,** contribución predial, impuesto real (o sobre bienes)

proportional, proporcional **proportionate variations,** variaciones proporcionadas

proportioner, dosificador

proportioning pump, bomba dosificadora

proppant, agente sustentante

propyl, *pref.* propil-

propyl alcohol, alcohol propílico

propylacetylene, propilacetileno (q.v. **pentyne**)

propylene, propileno, propeno (q.v. **propene**)

propylitization, (g) propilitización **propyne,** propino (q.v. **methylacetylene**)

prorate, prorratear, ratear

prospect, *n.* perspectiva; expectativa; situación; área potencial; *v.* catear, explorar

prospecting, exploración, búsqueda, (mn) cateo

prospective area, terreno con posibilidades (o indicios) de petróleo

protective coating, mano de pintura protectora

proterozoic, proterozoico (q.v. **agnotozoic**)

protogenic rocks, rocas protogénicas

protomylonite, (g) protomilonita

proton, protón

protractor, transportador

proven area, región con yacimientos de petróleo comprobados

province, provincia geológica, región con características geológicas semejantes

psammites, (g) psamitas

psephite, (g) psefita

pseudocode, (dp) seudocódigo

pseudocumene, seudocumeno (q.v. **trimethylbenzene**)

pseudomorphism, (g) seudomorfismo

pseudophenocrysts, seudofenocristales

pseudoporphyritic structure, estructura seudoporfirítica

pseudostratification, seudoestratificación

psi (pounds per square inch), libras por pulgada cuadrada

psig (pounds per square inch gage), libras por pulgada cuadrada manómetro

psilomelane, psilomelano

psychrometer, psicrómetro

puddling, (sd) mezcla del metal de aporte con el metal de base fundido

pucking, reboso, vómito

pull, *n.* tracción, tiro; *v.* halar, arrastrar, tirar; arrancar, (tu) sacar

— **apart basin,** (g) cuenca de desgarramiento

— **apart bed,** estrato de desgarramiento (o de pull-apart)

— **down,** de apretar

— **test,** ensayo de fuerza de tracción

pull-clown, equipo de trabajo a presión

puller, (tl) extractor

pulley, polea, roldana, garrucha, (Ar) motón

— **blocks,** motonería

pulling machine, máquina de tracción

English - Spanish

pulling unit, (prf) equipo de
servicio y reparaciones de pozos
petroleros (q.v. **servicing unit**)
pull-rod, varilla de tracción; tirante
— **carrier,** sostén de varillas de
tracción
— **clamps,** abrazaderas para
varillas de tracción
— **coupling,** acoplamiento de
varillas
— **hold-down,** sostén suspendido
para varillas de tracción
— **holdup,** estaca de sostén para
varillas de tracción
pulsating current, (el) corriente
pulsatoria
pulsating temperature,
temperatura pulsatoria
pulsation dampener, amortiguador
de vibraciones
pulse, pulso; (dp) impulso
pulverize, pulverizar, atomizar
pulverizer, pulverizador,
atomizador
pumice, púmice, piedra pómez
pump, bomba
— **adapter,** adaptador para bomba
— **barrel,** camisa, barril, cilindro
(q.v. **sucker rod pump,
working barrel**)
— **cage,** jaula de la bola de la
válvula de una bomba
— **down dart plug,** dardo
obturador que se inserta en el
pozo por medio del fluido
inyectado a bomba
— **down tool,** herramienta
inyectada a bomba
— **drive,** engranaje de mando de la
bomba
— **governor,** regulador de la
velocidad de la bomba
— **house,** casa de bombas
— **jack,** caballete de bombeo
— **liner,** camisa
— **manifold,** múltiple de bombeo

— **plunger,** émbolo de bomba
— **pressure,** presión de bombeo
— **seat,** asiento de la bomba
— **station,** estación de bombeo
pumpability, bombeabilidad (de
grasas lubricantes)
pumparound, retrobombeo
pumper, (oc) bombeador
pumping, bombeo
— **adjuster,** ajustador (o acoplador)
para bombeo
— **crank,** manivela de bombeo
— **dynamometer,** dinamómetro de
bombeo
— **head,** cabeza de bomba
— **jack,** caballete (o gato) de
bombeo
— **pressure,** presión de bombeo
— **tee,** (tu) conexión en T
— **well,** pozo a bomba
punch, punzón; (dp) perforación
pup joint, tubería de perforación,
producción o revestimiento de
menos de 9 metros (30 pies),
tubo corto
purchase, n. (cm) compra; (mc)
aparejo, palanca; v. comprar
purchaser, comprador
purge gas, gas de expulsión (o de
purga)
purging cock, grifo (o llave) de
purga
purification, purificación
purified, a. purificado; **purifier,** n.
purificador, depurador
purify, purificar
purlin, correa, carrera, larguero,
nervadura
push, n. empuje; v. empujar
— **rod,** varilla de empuje,
levantaválvula
push-button switch, interruptor de
botón
pushdown, a. de desplazamiento
descendente

PV diagram, gráfica de presión-volumen

PVT (pressure-volume-temperature), presión-volumen-temperatura; q.v. **pit volume totalizer**

PVC (polyvynil chloride), cloruro de polivinilo (o de vinilo), (Ar) policloruro de vinilo

pyknometer, pycnometer, picnómetro

pyrene, pireno

pyrex glass, vidrio pyrex

pyrite, pirita

pyritic, pirítico

pyroclastic, (g) piroclástico

pyroelectricity, piroelectricidad

pyrogenic, pirogénico, pirógeno

pyrolusite, pirolusita (q.v. **bog manganese**)

pyrolysis, pirólisis, descomposición química por el calor

pyrolytic, pirolítico

pyrometer, pirómetro

pyrope, piropo

pyrophosphorous, pirofosforoso

pyrophyllite, pirofilita

pyroxene, piroxena

pyroxenite, piroxenita

pyrrhotite, pirrotina

Q

q, fracción de la porosidad total ocupada por lutita dispersa

QA (quality assurance), garantía de calidad, (Ve) aseguranza de calidad

QC (quality control), control de calidad

QF (quality factor), factor de calidad

QL (query language), (dp) lenguaje de consulta

quad, quad: 10^{15} Btu; (el) unidad de cuatro cables aislados dentro de un cable

quadrant, cuadrante; (mc) codo de palanca, sector oscilante

quadrature, (mt) cuadratura, integración numérica

quadrilateral, cuadrilátero

quality, calidad; cualidad, característica

— **management system,** sistema de gestión de calidad

quantitative, cuantitativo

quantum, *n.* cuanto; *a.* cuántico

— **theory,** teoría cuántica (o de los tantos)

quarantine, *n.* cuarentena; *v.* poner en cuarentena

quarry, *n.* cantera, pedrera; *v.* sacar piedra de una cantera

quart (qt), cuarto de galón

quarter, *n.* cuarto, cuarta parte; trimestre; (nt) cuadra; *v.* cuartear

— **bend,** codo de un cuarto, acodado recto

— **deck,** (nt) alcázar

— **fast,** (nt) amarra de aleta

— **turn,** un cuarto de vuelta

quartering, cuarteo

quartz, cuarzo

— **bearing,** (magnetom) soporte de cuarzo

— **crystals,** cristales de cuarzo

— **grains,** granos de cuarzo

— **pebbles,** guijarros de cuarzo

— **rock,** cuarcita

— **sand,** arena cuarzosa

— **schist,** esquisto cuarzoso

— **tube,** tubo de cuarzo

— **wedge,** cuña de cuarzo, prisma de alumino

quartziferous, cuarcífero

quartzite, (g) cuarcita

— **granite,** granito con predominio de aluminio

quartzose, cuarzoso
quasi, *pref.* cuasi- e.g. cuasiestático
Quaternary, periodo (o sistema) cuaternario
quay, muelle
quench, templar, enfriar, apagar
quenched, templado
quenching oil, aceite para temple
quetzal, quetzal: moneda de Guatemala
queue, (dp) cola, fila de espera
quick-change link, eslabón de cambio rápido
quick-change union, unión de instalación rápida
quick-opening valve, válvula de acción rápida
quick-setting cement, cemento de fraguado rápido
quick-settling process, proceso de asentamiento rápido
quicklime, cal viva, óxido de calcio
quicksand, (g) arena movediza (o corrediza), (Co) arena fluida (q.v. **drift sand**)
quicksilver, mercurio, azogue
quiesce, (dp) inmovilizar, desactivar
quill, (mc) manguito
quintal, quintal (= 100 libras); quintal métrico (= 100 kilogramos)
quoin, piedra angular, clave, (Ar) cuña
quota, cuota, cupo, contingente; contribución
quotation, (cm) cotización
quotient, cociente
Q-**wave,** (gf) onda Love

R

R, roentgen: unidad de radiación; (seismol) onda Rayleigh;
Rankine: escala de temperatura del sistema inglés
rack, (tu) muelle, casillero, (prf) tarima; (mc) cremallera; percha (q.v. **pipe rack**)
— **and lever jack,** gato de cremallera y palanca
— **and pinion,** piñón y cremallera
— **jack,** gato (o cric) de cremallera
— **pipe,** *v.* arrumar (o estibar) tubería
radial
— **ball bearing,** cojinete de bolas radial
— **drainage,** desagüe, avenamiento radial
— **faults,** fallas radiales (o periféricas)
— **flow,** corriente radial
— **thrust,** presión (o empuje) radial
radial-thrust ball bearing, cojinete de bolas radioaxial
radian (rad), radián: unidad de velocidad angular
radiant, radiante
— **energy,** energía radiante
— **section,** sección radiante
— **tubes,** tubos radiantes
radiating cone, cone radiante
radiation, (cl) radiación, irradiación
— **chemistry,** química de las radiaciones
— **finned bonnet,** (va) bonete alado reductor de radiación
radiator, radiador
— **cap,** (mo) tapa de radiador
— **circulating system,** sistema de circulación por radiador
— **fan,** ventilador de radiador
— **filler cap,** tapa de gollete de radiador
— **guard,** protector de radiador
— **screen,** rejilla protectora de radiador
— **shell,** casco de radiador

Glossary of the Petroleum Industry

— **shutter,** persiana de radiador
— **tank,** tanque (o depósito) de radiador
radical, radical
radio, radio
— **beacon,** radiofaro
radioactive, radioactivo
— **material,** substancia radioactiva
— **methods,** métodos radioactivos
— **prospecting,** exploración por el método de radioactividad, prospección radioactiva
— **well logging,** informe (o histograma) radioactivo de un pozo
radiofrequency, radiofrecuencia
radiogram, radiograma; inalámbrico
radioisotope, radioisótopo
radiolaria, radiolarios
radiolarite, radiolarita
radius, radio
radon, radón
raffinate, refinado
ragged bolt, perno arponado (q.v. jag bolt)
rail rates, tarifa de embarque por ferrocarril
railing, baranda, barandal, guardacuerpo
railroad, ferrocarril
— **car oil,** aceite para chumaceras de vagones
— **freight,** flete férreo
railway valve oil, aceite para válvula y cilindros de locomotoras
rain forest, selva
rainbow, tornasol, iridescencia del petróleo crudo
raise, levantar; alzar
rake, *n.* rastrillo; (g) (cn) (mn) (ma) inclinación; *v.* rastrillar, inclinarse

ram, *n.* (prf) ariete empaquetador; (cn) pisón, martinete; *v.* apisonar, pisonear
— **blowout preventer,** preventor de reventones tipo arietes
— **gate,** compuerta de cierre total
— **head,** (tl) barreta
— **locking screw,** tornillo prisionero, tornillo afianzador del ariete
— **type blowout preventer,** impiderreventones de ariete
RAM (random access memory), memoria de acceso al azar
ram-rear seal ring, aro de empaque de la parte posterior de un ariete
ramjet, motor ramjet
ramp, (tp) rampa; (gf) cambio gradual
random
— **access,** (dp) acceso al azar, acceso aleatorio (o directo)
— **line,** (tp) línea perdida
— **noise,** (gf) ruido fortuito
— **numbers,** (dp) números aleatorios
— **sampling,** muestreo aleatorio, muestreo al azar
— **traverse,** (tp) trazado auxiliar
range, *n.* límite; escala; gama; serie; clase, rango; línea de productos; (winch) alcance; (mar) amplitud, carrera; (tp) línea de vista, enfilación; (tp) cordillera, sierra; (dp) ámbito, amplitud, alcance; (EU) faja de terreno de seis millas de ancho entre meridianos
— **finder,** telémetro
— **length,** (tu) rango, agrupamiento según longitud
— **pole,** jalón, vara de agrimensor
rangeability, (va) relación de flujo
rank, rango, jerarquía
rapids, (r) rápidos, (Ar) raudas

rarefaction wave, (gf) onda de
rarefacción (o de condensación)
raschig rings, anillos raschig,
anillos de material refractario
para torres de fraccionamiento
empacadas
rasp, *n.* escofina, raspa, limatón,
raspador, (Me) molino; *v.*
raspar, escofinar
raster-mode graphic display,
representación gráfica en forma
de trama
raster scan, exploración (o rastreo,
barrido) de trama
ratchet, trinquete, matraca, cric,
carraca, chicharra, (Ar) crique
— **lever hoist,** montacargas tipo
palanca con trinquete
— **stock and die,** terraja de
trinquete
— **type lifting jack,** gato de
trinquete
— **wrench,** llave de trinquete; llave
de roquete, (Ve) llave de broches
rate, *n.* razón, coeficiente; volumen
por unidad de tiempo; velocidad
por unidad de tiempo; (cm) tipo
de interés; (trans) tarifa; *v.* (ma)
fijar la capacidad (o potencia)
normal; valuar, justipreciar
— **of charge,** capacidad de carga,
régimen de carga
— **of flow,** régimen (o tasa) de flujo,
caudal
— **of penetration,** velocidad de
penetración
rated
— **capacity,** (mc) capacidad
nominal (o estimada),
capacidad de clasificación
— **horsepower,** potencia de
régimen
— **travel,** (va) carrera de
clasificación
rathole, ratonera, hoyo para
colocar provisionalmente

tramos de tubería, (Ve) hueco de
descanso; barreno de fondo,
hoyo que se perfora en el fondo
del pozo para estudiar el estrato
— **formation tester,**
recogemuestras del contenido
del estrato (q.v. **drill stem
formation tester**)
— **pipe,** tubo revestidor de la
ratonera
rating, (ma) (el) clasificación,
capacidad normal; tasación
ratio, relación; razón
rational ratio, razón racional
rattail file, lima rabo de rata
ravine, quebrada, cañada,
hondonada
raw, crudo, bruto
— **charge,** carga bruta
— **crude,** petróleo virgen, petróleo
no refinado
— **data,** datos en bruto, datos sin
procesar, datos a tratar
— **gasoline,** gasolina cruda,
gasolina estraída del gas natural
húmedo
— **material,** materia prima
— **oil,** aceite bruto
— **pressure distillate,** distilado a
presión no tratado
— **mix liquids,** líquidos crudos
mezclados
raw-edge rubber-covered belt,
correa de caucho con borde en
rústico
ray, rayo
Rayleigh wave, onda de Rayleigh
raypath, (gf) trayectoria
RCV (remote control vehicle),
vehículo teledirigido
R&D (research and development),
investigación y desarrollo
reactance, reactancia
reacting substance, substancia
reactiva
reaction, reacción

— **chamber**, cámara de reacción
— **by combination**, reacción por combinación
— **by substitution**, reacción por substitución
— **temperature**, temperatura de reacción
— **zone**, zona de reacción
reactivation, reactivación
reactive, reactivo
reactivity, tendencia reactiva
reactor, (rf) cámara de reacción, reactor
readability, legibilidad
reading, lectura registros; lectura de instrumentos
reagent, reactivo
— **circulation**, circulación del reactivo
real, verdadero, real, auténtico
— **estate**, bienes inmuebles (o raíces)
— **time processing**, proceso en tiempo real
real , real: moneda de Brasil
ream, escariar (o ensanchar, rectificar) una perforación
reamer, ensanchador, escariador, rectificador, (Ve) rima
reaming edge, arista ensanchadora, borde (o filo) ensanchador
rear
— **bucket**, caja trasera
— **end**, extremo trasero, parte trasera
rear-axle
— **housing**, caja de eje trasero
— **ratio**, relación de velocidades del eje trasero
— **reduction**, engranaje de reducción en el eje trasero
reassemble, rearmar
Reaumur's scale, escala de Reaumur
reboiler, (mc) rehervidor

rebound clip, abrazadera de rebote, grapa
receiver, receptor; depósito, recipiente; (air) tanque de compresión
— **line**, (gf) línea receptora
— **line interval**, (gf) intervalo entre líneas receptoras
recess, *n*. rebajo, caja, cajuela, escotadura, rebajada, (Co) receso, (Ur) encastre; *v*. rebajar, cajear
— **slip**, rebajo para cuñas
recessed coupling, acople de rebajo
reciprocal gradient, gradiente recíproco de temperatura
reciprocating
— **compressor**, compresor alternativo
— **duplex pump**, bomba alternativa doble
— **motion**, movimiento alternativo
— **plunger**, émbolo recíproco (de bomba)
— **reciprocating pump**, bomba alternativa (o recíproca)
reclaimed oil, aceite recuperado
reclamation, regeneración, recuperación; aprovechamiento
reclaimed pipe, tubería de segunda mano, tubería usada
recompletion, reconstrucción de un pozo
recondition, reacondicionar; rehabilitar
reconnaissance, reconocimiento, exploración preliminar
reconstitute, reconstruir
record, registro, diario, anotación; (gf) sismograma
recorder, registrador; el que registra
recording, *n*. registro; *v*. registrar
— **chart**, tabla de registro, cartilla de instrumento registrador
— **controller**, regulador registrador
— **gage**, manómetro registrador

— **truck,** (gf) camión de
instrumentos registradores
recoverable heat, calor recobrable
(o recuperable)
recovered acid, ácido regenerado (o
recuperado)
recovered oil, petróleo recuperado
(o regenerado)
recovery, recobro, recuperación
recrystallization, recristalización
rectangle, rectángulo
rectangular spacing pattern, (prf)
modelo de espaciado rectangular
rectification, (rf) fraccionación
(q.v. **fractionation**)
rectifier, transformador de
corriente alterna
recumbent fold, pliegue yacente (o
acostado, recumbente)
recycle, (rf) reciclo, repaso
— **ratio,** relación de reciclo
— **stock**, petróleo (o carga) de
repaso, carga de reciclo
recycling, (pr) recirculación de gas,
extracción de petróleos livianos
por recirculación de gas en el
yacimiento; (rf) repaso, reciclo
red, rojo
— **bed,** capa de arcilla roja
— **heat,** calor rojo
— **lead,** minio, albayalde rojo, (Me)
plomo rojo
— **oil,** aceite neutro (q.v. **neutral
oil**)
— **short iron,** hierro quebradizo al
rojo
redistillation, redestilación, (Ar)
desnatado
reduce, reducir
reduced crude, petróleo crudo
reducido, petróleo de la segunda
destilación (q.v. **topped crude**)
reducer, reductor
reducing, (petrol) reducción,
destilación hasta extraer la
kerosina

— **flame,** llama reducida
— **nipple,** manguito de reducción,
niple reductor
— **still,** alambique para destilación
preliminar
— **tee,** té de reducción
— **valve,** válvula de reducción
reduction, reducción
— **gear,** engranaje de reducción
— **table,** tabla de reducciones
redundancy, (gf) (dp) redundancia
redundant, repetido, adicional,
secundario, terciario
reef, arrecife, escollo, rompiente
— **barrier,** barrera adicional
reel, tambor, carrete, torno,
carretel, devanador (q.v. **drum**)
reeve, pasar el cable por las poleas
refacer, máquina esmeriladora
reference
— **ellipsoid,** elipsoide de referencia
— **fuel,** combustible de norma,
combustible aprobado por el
API
— **level,** nivel de referencia
— **station,** estación de referencia
refine, refinar, destilar
refined products pipeline,
oleoducto para productos
refinados
refinery, refinería, (Ar, Es)
destilería
refining, *n.* refinación, (Es) refino;
v. refinar
— **agent,** agente refinador,
substancia refinadora
reflected refraction, (gf) refracción
reflejada
reflected wave, (gf) onda reflejada
reflecting layer, (gf) capa de
reflexión
reflection, reflexión
— **dip**, reflexión de horizonte
inclinado; cálculo de
buzamiento por la reflexión
— **horizon**, horizonte de reflexión

Glossary of the Petroleum Industry

— **point,** punto de reflexión
— **profiles,** perfiles de reflexión
— **seismic,** sísmica de reflexión
— **shooting,** disparos para registro de ondas reflejadas
— **survey,** levantamiento por el método de reflexión
reflex gauge, manómetro de reflejo
reflux, reflujo
— **condenser,** condensador de reflujo
— **drum,** tambor de reflujo
— **ration,** (rf) relación de reflujo
— **valve,** válvula de reflujo
reformat, reformar, cambiar formato
reforming, reformación (q.v. **cracking, catalytic cracking, thermal cracking**)
— **furnace,** horno de reformación
refracted wave, (gf) onda refractada
refraction, (gf) refracción
— **horizon,** horizonte de refracción
— **profiles,** perfiles de refracción
— **shooting,** disparos para el registro de ondas refractadas
— **wave,** onda de refracción
refractive index, índice de refracción
refractivity, refractividad
refractometer, refractómetro
refractory, refractario
— **brick,** ladrillo refractario
— **cement,** cemento refractario
— **stock,** productos petroleros refractarios
— **wall,** pared de material refractario
refrigerant, refrigerante
refringence, refringency, refringencia
refuse-derived fuel, combustible derivado de desechos
regenerated catalyst, catalizador regenarador

regeneration, regeneración
regenerator, regenerador
regional disturbance, (gf) perturbación regional
registration, registro, matrícula
regression, (g) movimiento retrógrado, regresión
regular socket slip, campana de pesca sencilla con aletas
regulator, regulador
reimbursement, (cm) reembolso
reinforcement, refuerzo
rejuvenation, (g) rejuvenecimiento
relay, disyuntor, relai
release, *n.* alivio, descarga; (mc) disparador, escape, trinquete; *v.* soltar, aflojar, desembragar, desacoplar
— **couple,** unión desprendible (q.v. **backoff joint**)
— **time,** (gf) tiempo de recuperación
releasing and circulating spear, (fishing tl) arpón pescador desprendible y de circulación
releasing angle, ángulo libre
reliability, regularidad funcional, seguridad de funcionamiento
relic sea, mar antiguo
relief, (mc) relieve; (pressure) alivio
— **block,** mapa topográfico
— **crew,** cuadrilla de relevo
— **fitting,** (mc) orificio de alivio
— **grooves,** ranuras de alivio; conexiones macho
— **port,** (mc) orificio de escape
— **valve,** válvula de alivio (o de desahogo, de escape, de seguridad)
— **well,** pozo de alivio
relining mandrel, mandril para revestir cilindros
reluctance, (gf) reluctancia
remains, restos, residuos
remanent magnetization, magnetización remanente

187

remedial response, (ec) respuesta
correctiva
remedial workover, reperforación
correctiva
remediation, (ec) medidas
reparadoras
remittance, (cm) remesa, giro
remnant, remanente
remote, a distancia, remoto
— **access,** acceso a distancia
— **BOP control,** control remoto de
los preventores
— **installation,** instalación por
telemando
— **location,** emplazamiento a
distancia
— **sensing,** percepción remota
removable, de quita y pon,
removible, soltadizo, postizo,
desmontable
— **cementer,** tapón retenedor de
quita y pon para el cemento
— **head,** (cylind) culata removible
remover, (qm) disolvente
renew, renovar; (contr) extender,
prorrogar
renewable, renovable; prorrogable
rent, *n.* alquiler, renta; *v.* alquilar,
arrendar
repack, reempaquetadura
repair clamp, abrazadera para
reparar tubería
repair part, pieza de repuesto (o de
recambio), repuesto
repeatability, (la) repetición
repetition of beds, (g) repetición de
las capas
replacement, reemplazo,
substitución, reposición;
restitución
report, *n.* informe, parte; *v.*
presentar un informe, dar parte
represent, representar
representative, representante
repressive overlap, (g)
estratificación regresiva

repressuring, restaurar la presión
en un yacimiento, *angl.*
represionar
reproducibility, (la) reproducción
rerun, repetición de pasada, nueva
pasada
— **still,** alambique para
redestilación
— **unit,** unidad para redestilación
rerunning, redestilación
— **to coke,** (rf) elaboración hasta el
coque residual
resampling, remuestreo
resaturate, resaturar
research, investigación, estudio,
pesquisa
resequent stream, arroyo
resecuente
reserve buoyancy, flotación de
reserva
reservoir, yacimiento petrolífero;
depósito, estanque, represa
— **drive mechanism,** mecanismo
de empuje
— **energy,** energía del yacimiento
— **oil-gas ratio,** relación gas-aceite
en el yacimiento
— **pressure,** presión de yacimiento
— **rate,** régimen de reposición
— **rock,** estrato productivo, roca
productiva (o almacenadora),
(CR) roca reservorio
reset, poner a cero, restaurar,
reposicionar, despejar,
restablecer al estado anterior
residence time, tiempo de contacto
residual, *n.* residuo; *a.* (value)
residual, restante
— **anomaly,** anomalía residual
— **deposits,** depósitos residuales,
depósitos de residuos
— **disturbance,** disturbio residual
— **fuel oil,** combustóleo residual
— **mean square,** cuadrado medio
residual

— normal moveout, sobretiempo residual normal por distancia
— oil, petróleo (o aceite) residual
— stress, (sd) esfuerzo restante
residualize, (gf) residualizar, obtener residuales
residue bottoms, residuo
residue gas, gas residual
residuum, residuo
resilience, elasticidad, rebote, (Co) resiliencia, (Me) resorteo
resilient packing, empaquetadura elástica
resin, resina
resinous, resinoso
resistance, resistencia
— butt welding, soldadura a tope de resistencia
— flash butt welding, soldadura a tope de resistencia y por calentamiento
resistivity well logging, registro de resistividad
resolution, resolución, acuerdo; (qm) separación; (mt) descomposición; (gf) (dp) resolución
— of forces, descomposición de fuerzas
resonant circuit, circuito de resonancia
resource, recurso
respirator, máscara contra polvo, respirador
response, respuesta, sensibilidad, reacción
rest, encastre, apoyo, soporte, base
restart, reanudación, rearranque
restituting force, fuerza compensadora (o estabilizadora)
restored clay, arcilla restaurada, arcilla regenerada
restoring force, (gf) fuerza compensadora (o estabilizadora)

restrictor choke, estrangulador limitador
retail, al por menor, al detalle
retainer, fiador, retén, seguro
— production packer, obturador de producción
retaining wall, muro de sostén
retard of spark, atraso de la chispa (o del encendido)
retardation, retraso, retardo
retarded ignition, encendido atrasado
retention, retención
retinite, retinita
retort, retorta
retractable, retractable
retrieve, recuperar, recobrar
retroactive, retroactivo
retrograde condensation, condensación retrógrada
retrogressive, regresivo
return, *n.* regreso, vuelta; (cn) ala vuelta; *v.* regresar, volver
— bend, conexión en U, codo de 180°, (Ar) codo doble
— flame, llama de retorno
— header, conexión en U
— stroke, carrera de regreso (o de retroceso)
revamp, (cn) reformar, rehacer en parte, (Ar) reconvertir
revenue expenditures, (cm) gastos de explotación
reverberatory furnace, horno de reverbero
reversal, (g) inversión, buzamiento local en dirección contraria
— of dip, echado inverso
reverse, marcha atrás, retroceso
— bias, polarización inversa
— branch, (gf) rama inversa
— circulation, circulación inversa
— clutch, embrague de marcha atrás
— drive, transmisión de contramarcha

— **emulsion**, emulsión inversa
— **fault**, (g) falla invertida
— **gear**, engranaje de marcha atrás
reversed fault, falla inversa
reversed profiles, (gf) perfiles
    completos de refracción, perfiles
    invertidos
reversible, reversible
— **clutch**, embrague reversible
— **ratchet wrench**, llave reversible
    de trinquete
reversing
— **countershaft**, eje de
    contramarcha
— **gear**, engranaje inversor,
    engranaje de inversión de
    marcha
— **shaft**, árbol de cambio de
    marcha
— **switch**, interruptor de retroceso
— **transmission**, transmisión de
    marcha atrás (o de retroceso)
revolution, revolución, rotación;
    vuelta, giro; (mc) (g) revolución;
    (g) período completo de
    levantamiento de un sistema de
    montañas
— **counter**, cuentavueltas
revolving beam, árbol giratorio
revolving clamp, abrazadera
    giratoria
rewinding, rebobinado
rework, reparar, rehacer
rheology, reología
rheostat, reóstato
rhigolene, rigolina
rhodochrosite, rodocrusita
rhodinite, rodonita
rhombohedral, rombohedro
rhyolite, riolita
ria, (g) ría
rib, nervio, pestaña, costilla
rich mixture, mezcla rica (o crasa)
ridge, (tp) serranía, lomo de
    montaña, filo
rifle boring, orificio de lubricación

rifled pipe, tubo rayado
rift, (g) hendidura, grieta,
    cuarteadura
rifting, (g) agrietamiento, (CR)
    rifting
rig, equipo (o cabria) de perforación
    (incluye: torre, malacate,
    motores, bombas del lodo, árbol
    de transmisión y equipo
    auxiliar) (q. v. **derrick**)
— **front**, (perc) maquinaria fuera
    del perímetro de la torre de
    perforación
— **irons**, herraje de cabria (o de
    equipo)
— **up**, instalar el equipo de
    perforación
rigging, *n.* cabria, equipo de
    perforacion; *v.* aparejar,
    enjarciar, guarnir; instalar el
    equipo (o la cabria) de
    perforación
right angle, ángulo recto
right-angle fault, (g) falla con
    ángulo abierto
right-hand thread, rosca derecha
right-lay cable, cable de colchado
    (o trenzado) a la derecha
right-of-way, derecho de vía,
    servidumbre de paso
rigidity, rigidez
rig legs, refuerzos de las patas de la
    torre de perforación
rill mark, (g) huellas de riachuelos,
    estructuras dendríticas
    trenzadas
rill, surco, cava
rim, corona, llanta, aro
ring, anillo, aro, argolla, virola
— **and ball test**, prueba de anillo y
    bola
— **baffle**, desviador anular
— **gasket**, anillo de guarnición,
    empaquetadura anular
— **gear**, corona, corona dentada

— **hydrocarbon,** hidrocarburo anular (q.v. **cyclic hydrocarbon**)

— **joint assembly,** conjunto de unión anular

— **joint frange,** brida con junta de anillo

— **structure,** (molec) estructura anular

— **stand,** (la) soporte universal

— **tripod,** (la) trébedes

ringing, (el) oscilación transitoria (o amortiguada)

ringworm corrosion, corrosión anular

ripper, rasgador, escarificador

ripping chisel, cincel (o formón) dentado

ripple, (water) rizo, escarceo; (el) fluctuación

RISC (reduced instruction set computer), ordenador de grupos reducidos de instrucciones

riser, tubo de subida, tubo ascendente (o vertical, montante, conductor), (Ar) caño de subida, (Me) tubería de elevación; prolongación de la tubería de revestimiento (q.v. **marine riser**)

— **angle indicator,** indicador del ángulo del tubo conductor

— **cracking unit,** craqueadora catalítica de reactor en el montante espejo

— **tensioner line,** línea de tensión del montante

risk, riesgo

— **management,** administración de riesgos

river, río

— **bank,** ribera

— **bed,** lecho, cauce

— **clamp,** (p) ancla (o lastre) de tubería

— **crossing,** cruce de río, cruce fluvial

— **freight,** flete fluvial

— **system,** sistema hidrográfico

rivet, remache

— **plate,** arandela

riveted joint, junta remachada

riveted steel tank, tanque de acero remachado

rms, q.v. **root mean square**

roast, tostar, quemar, oxidar

robotics, robótica

robustness, fortaleza, robustez

rock, roca, piedra

— **arch,** (g) portal

— **a well,** activar el pozo, abrir y cerrar el pozo intermitentemente para aumentar la presión

— **bit,** barrena para roca

— **pressure,** (g) presión de formación

— **salt,** sal gema

— **shaft,** eje oscilante

— **wool,** lana de roca, lana pétrea

rocker, (mc) balancín, eje oscilante, brazo oscilante

— **arm,** balancín, brazo, palanca oscilante; (va) balancín

rocket fuel, combustible de chorro (o de reacción)

rocking the well, activar el pozo

Rockwell hardness machine, máquina Rockwell que indica la dureza de metales

rod, varilla, barra; (ma) vástago, varilla; (tp) baliza, mira de corredera, jalón de mira

— **anchor,** ancla para varilla

— **blowout preventer,** preventor para varillas

— **guide,** guía para varilla

— **hanger,** barra de suspensión

— **pump,** bomba de vástago, (o de varillas)

— **string,** serie (o sarta) de varillas

— **stripper**, limpiador de varillas
— **sub**, varilla corta
— **whip**, sacudidas (o latigueo) de las varillas de tracción
rod-hanger clamp, abrazadera de la barra de suspensión
rod-line counterbalance, contrapeso para varillas de tracción
rod-line hook-off assembly, juego de accesorios para desconectar varillas (q.v. **rod line knock-off assembly**)
rod-line pump, bomba conectada a varillas de tracción
roddle, (ca) garras
rodman, (tp) (oc) portamira
roll, *n*. balanceo; *v*. laminar, arrollar
— **along**, (gf) desplazamiento sucesivo
— **back**, (dp) repetir, reanudar
— **in routine**, (dp) rutina de reincorporación a la memoria
— **out routine**, (dp) rutina de descarga a disco
— **over scraper**, traílla volcadora de arrastre
— **up curtain**, cortina arrolladiza
— **welding**, soldadura a giratubo
roller, rodillo; cilindro laminador, cilindro arrollador
— **analysis**, análisis de finos
— **bearing**, chumacera (o cojinete) de rodillos, (Ve) balinera
— **bit**, barrena de rodillos, (Ve) mecha racha
— **chain**, cadena de rodillos
— **link**, eslabón de rodilo
— **type rod line**, transportador a rodillos
— **swedge**, abretubos de rodillos
rolling
— **country**, terreno undulado
— **mill**, taller de laminación
— **post**, poste de rodillo

ROM (read only memory), (dp) memoria sólo de lectura
roof, techo, cubierta; (g) pendiente, yacente, muro (q.v. **hanging wall**)
room, (mn) anchurón, salón, cámara; (ma) luz, espacio
roomy, espacioso
root mean square, raíz cuadrada de la media de los cuadrados, raíz cuadrática media
rooter, desarraigador, arrancaraíces, escarificador
ROP, q.v. **rate of penetration**
rope, soga, cuerda, cable, cordel, maroma, jarcia, cabo
— **chopper**, cortacables
— **clip**, grapa para cables
— **grab**, amarra de cable
— **socket**, casquillo sujetacable, portacable, (Ve) cabeza de cable
— **spear**, arpón pescacable
— **strand**, hebra, cordón, torón
— **thimble**, ojal para cable, guardacabos
ropy, fibroso
rose quartz, cuarzo rosado
rotameter, contador rotativo
rotary, *n*. (prf) mesa rotatoria, equipo rotatorio, (Me) rotaria; *a*. rotatorio, rotativo, giratorio
— **bit**, barrena para equipo rotatorio
— **bushing**, buje rotatorio (o principal, maestro) (q.v. **master bushing**)
— **chain**, cadena trasmisora de la mesa rotatoria
— **compressor**, compresor rotatorio
— **counterbalance**, contrapeso rotatorio
— **disc bit**, barrena giratoria de disco
— **drill**, barrena rotatoria, taladro rotatorio

Glossary of the Petroleum Industry

— **drilling hook,** gancho de perforación rotatoria
— **drilling hose,** manguera reforzada para equipo rotatorio
— **drilling swivel,** cabeza articulada para inyección de lodo con equipo rotatorio
— **drive,** mando rotatorio, rueda dentada de mando de la mesa rotatoria
— **drive clutch,** embrague de mando de la mesa rotatoria
— **fault,** (g) falla girada
— **filter,** filtro rotatorio
— **fishing tool,** (prf) herramienta rotatoria de pesca
— **head,** preventor rotatorio
— **hose,** manguera de perforación
— **jars,** percusores para pesca
— **milling shoe,** zapata cortatubos
— **pump,** bomba giratoria (o rotatoria)
— **rock bit,** barrena para roca, usada con equipo rotatorio
— **shoe,** zapata dentada
— **swivel,** acoplador giratorio, unión giratoria
— **tap,** (fishing tl)) macho rotatorio
— **table,** mesa rotatoria, (Me) mesa rotaria plataforma circular giratoria que hace girar el vástago de la barrena
— **table speed indicator,** taquímetro de la mesa rotatoria
— **tongs,** tenazas para perforación rotatoria
rotary-feed control, controlador de la presión sobre la barrena rotatoria
rotation, rotación, giro
— **ellipsoid,** elipsoide de revolución
— **gas lift,** bombeo neumático cerrado, extracción de crudo por recirculación de gas
rotational, rotatorio, rotativo

— **fault,** falla giratoria (o por rotación) (q.v. **hinge fault**)
rotor, rotor, pieza giratoria del motor
round trip, (prf) viaje de ida y vuelta, entrada y salida de la tubería de revestimiento (Me) viaje redondo
round nose rotary mill, fresa de punta redonda
rounding error, roundoff error, error de redondeo
route, ruta
routing, asignación de ruta
row, fila, hilera
— **binary,** (dp) binario en fila
royalties, (cm) regalías, derechos industriales
rpm (revolutions per minute), revoluciones por minuto
rub post, sostén de fricción
rubber, caucho, goma, (Me) hule
— **gasket,** empaquetadura de goma
— **packing,** empaquetadura de goma
rubbing, rozamiento, frotamiento, fricción
rubidium vapor magnetometer, magnetómetro de vapor de rubidio
ruby, rubí
rudder, (nt) timón
rudistic limestone, caliza rudística
rule, *n.* regla de medir; reglamento, regla; *v.* gobernar; reglamentar
run, (rf) tanda, jornada; período (o ciclo) de funcionamiento de una refinería, cochura, (Co) cochada
— **down,** embestir
— **high,** (well) la estructura petrolífera está en un alto
— **in,** meter (o insertar, introducir) tubería
runaround, plataforma de la corona
runback, repaso

193

rundown line, tubo a tanque, tubo
  bajante
running board, estribo
running gear, tren rodante
runoff, (hd) escurrimiento,
  derrame, aporte, afluencia,
  aflujo, (Co) rendimiento, (Pe,
  PR) escorrentía
runup, (mar) runup, máxima
  altura de ola registrada
rust, orín, herrumbre
— **prevention test,** prueba de
  anticorrosión
— **remover,** disolvente,
  quitaherrumbre
rusty, mohoso, oxidado
rutile, rutilo
Rvp (Reid vapor pressure), presión
  de vapor Reid
RZ (return to zero), (mag tape)
  vuelta a cero

S

s (second), segundo
S, q.v. **Siemens; sulphur**
S bend, acodado en S, contracodo
S trap, sifón en S
S wave, q.v. **shear wave**
S wrench, llave de doble curva
sabin, sabin: unidad de absorción
  acústica
saccharoidal, sacaróideo
sacrificial anode, ánodo de
  sacrificio
— **protection,** protección con
  ánodos de sacrificio
saddle, (mc) silleta, caballete, silla;
  (g) depresión
— **clamp,** abrazadera de silla
— **joint,** junta de doble bisel
safety, seguridad
— **cage,** plataforma colgante,
  puente de trabajo

— **glass,** cristal inastillable
— **head,** cabeza de seguridad (q.v.
  relief head)
— **hook,** gancho de seguridad
— **joint,** unión (o junta) de
  seguridad (q.v. **backoff joint**)
— **mud baffle,** desviador de
  seguridad para el lodo
— **tubing block,** motón de
  seguridad para tubería
— **valve,** válvula de seguridad
— **wall,** muro (o dique) de seguridad
sag, *n.* comba, doblegamiento; *v.*
  combarse, pandearse
salary, sueldo, salario
salband, (g) salbanda (q.v. **vein
  wall**)
saline, salino
salinity, salinidad
**SALM (single anchor leg
  mooring),** sistema de amarre de
  poste sencillo de anclaje
**SALS (single anchor leg storage
  system),** sistema de
  almacenamiento de poste
  sencillo de anclaje
salt, sal
— **dome,** (g) domo salino, cúpula
  salina
— **lake,** marisma, lago salado
— **residual,** (gravim) residual de sal
— **water,** agua salada (o salobre)
saltpeter, salitre, nitrato de potasio
  (q.v. **niter**)
salvage, (nt) salvamento
sample, *n.* muestra, (Me) testigo; *v.*
  muestrear, catear, probar
sampler, probador, extractor de
  muestras
sampling, recolectar muestras,
  muestrear
— **period,** período de muestreo
— **thief,** (tk) muestreador
samson post, poste maestro
sand, arena

— **bailing reel,** tambor para el cable de la cuchara. (q.v. **sand line spool**)

— **bank,** banco de arena, arenal

— **bar,** arenal, banco, bajío, barra

— **bed,** estrato arenoso

— **blast,** chorro de arena

— **casting,** colado en moldes de arean

— **cut,** pedazos de roca arenisca, muestras de roca subterránea

— **dry,** arena seca

— **dune,** duna

— **filter,** filtro de arena

— **gall,** (g) torca, dolina (q.v. **sand pipe, dolins**)

— **grain,** grano de arena

— **hog,** (tu) atrapadora de arena

— **line,** cable de la cuchara (o de cuchareo), cable para subir o bajar la cuchara o la bomba de arena

— **line spool,** tambor para el cable de la cuchara

— **oil,** arena petrolífera

— **out,** taponar con sustentante

— **pipe,** (g) torca, dolina (q.v. **sand gall, dolins**)

— **pump,** achicador (o bomba) de arena

— **pump pulley,** polea de la cuchara

— **reel,** malacate (o tambor, torno) de muestreo, carrete de cuchareo

— **reel lever,** palanca de presión del malacate de muestreo

— **reel reach,** vástago del malacate de muestreo

— **reel tail sill,** larguero subauxiliar

— **screen,** tubo colador, (Ar) filtro de pedregullo, (Ve) tubo calado

— **sheave pulley,** garrucha de la cuchara

— **trap,** trampa para arena

sandpaper, papel de lija

sandstone, arenisca

sandy clay, arcilla arenosa

saponifiable matter, materia saponificable

saponification, saponificación

saponify, saponificar

sapphire, zafiro

sapropel clay, arcilla sapropel

Sarmatian, sarmatiense

saturated, saturado

— **steam,** vapor saturado

saturation, saturación

— **diving,** buceo por saturación

saver sub, substituto de protección (q.v. **kelly saver sub**)

saw, sierra, serrucho

sawtooth, *n.* diente de sierra; *a.* forma en dientes de sierra

Saxonian, saxoniense

Saybolt Universal viscosity, viscosidad SU (q.v. **SUS**)

SBBM (tension leg supply boat mooring system), sistema de poste en tensión para amarre por la proa de botes abastecedores

SBK catalytic reforming, reformación catalítica SBK

SBM (single buoy mooring), monoboya de carga (y descarga)

SBMS (supply boat mooring system), sistema de fondeo para botes abastecedores

scaffolding, andamiaje, andamiada, castillejo, (Ve) burros

scale, *n.* (cl) incrustación, costras, escamas; (wt) báscula, balanza, romana; (mt) laminilla, cascarilla, (Ve) concha; escama, costra; (design) escala, regla; *v.* descamar, descostrar, descascarar, medir con escala

— **division,** divisiones de una escala

— **of intensities,** (gf) escala de intensidades

— **remover,** sacacosta, quitacosta

195

English - Spanish

— **wax**, parafina semirefinada
— **weight**, peso de báscula
scale-removing chemical, substancia química para eliminar incrustaciones
scaling, ajuste (o conversión, reducción) a escala
scan, (gf) barrer, muestrear
scanner, (dp) explorador, lector, escáner
scapolite, escapolita
scarf, *n*. (tl) rebajo, charpado; *v*. rebajar, charpar
— **joint**, junta biselada, junta charpada
— **weld**, soldadura al sesgo
scarp, (g) escarpa, talud, pendiente, inclinación
scatter read, (dp) lectura dispersa
scattering, *n*. (gf) dispersión; (mu) subida del metal al enfriarse
scavenging, barrido de gases de combustión
scfh (standard cubic feet hour), pies cúbicos estándard por hora (pies^3 est/hr)
scfm (standard cubic feet minute), pies cúbicos estándard por minuto
schedule, programa, horario, itinerario, (Ar) cronograma
scheduled, *a*. en fecha prevista, programado
scheduling, planificación, programación
scheelite, scheelita
schematic description, descripción esquemática
schematic flow sheet, cuadro esquemático del flujo
schist, esquisto
schistic rock, (g) roca esquistosa
schistose, esquistoso
scintillometer, cintilómetro

scissors fault, falla pivotal (o giratoria) (q.v. **rotational fault**)
scleroscope, escleroscopio
scoop, achicar
scope, ámbito; rango
score, *n*. muesca, rayadura, melladura; **scored**, *a*. rayado, mellado
scoria, escoria (q.v. **clinker**)
scour, desoxidar, desengrasar, limpiar, lavar
scrap, desechar, descartar
— **iron**, hierro viejo
scraper, (rd) pala de arrastre, traílla, cucharín de arrastre; (cl) limpiatubos, raspatubos; (tl) raspador, rasqueta
— **trap**, (p) trampa del raspatubos
— **trap closure**, (p) cerrojo de la trampa del raspatubos
— **trap pit**, (p) foso para trampa de raspatubos
scraper-loader, traílla cargadora
scraping, raedura, raspadura
scratch, rayadura ligera
— **awl**, lezna de marcar
screen, *n*. (tl) criba, colador, cedazo, tamiz; tela metálica; (dp) pantalla; *v*. cernir, cribar, tamizar
— **liner**, (tu) cedazo antiarena
— **pipe**, tubo colador (o calado) (q.v. **slotted pipe**)
— **wire**, tela metálica, tejido de alambre
screened liner, tubo colador
screw, *n*. tornillo; *v*. atornillar
— **connections**, conexiones de rosca
— **conveyor**, tornillo transportador, tornillo sin fin
— **coupling**, acoplamiento (o unión) atornillado
— **gauge**, calibre a rosca

196

— **grab,** machuelo arrancabarrena (o arrancasondas)
— **jack,** gato de tornillo
— **packer,** empacador de rotación
— **pump,** bomba de tornillo
— **pitch gauge,** calibrador de paso de rosca, juego de plantillas para rosca
screwdriver, destornillador
screwed end, (tu) extremo roscado
screwed valve, válvula atornillada, válvula de rosca
scroll, (dp) desplazar la imágen en dirección vertical
scrub, depurar, lavar
scrubber, (gas) depurador de gas; (air) tanque depurador de aire
sea, mar
— **current,** corriente marina
— **floor,** lecho (o piso, fondo) marino
— **level,** nivel del mar
— **suctions,** (nt) toma de agua de mar para lastre
— **surface temperature,** temperatura de la superficie del mar
seal, *n.* cierre, sello, hermeticidad; *v.* cerrar, tapar, sellar
— **off,** (prf) obturar con lodo
sealed pressure reservoir, depósito hermético a presión
sealing liquid, líquido obturador
seam, (g) hendedura, grieta, fractura, fisura; (tu) costura; (mn) filón, criadero, vena
— **weld,** soldadura de costura
seamless
— **pipe,** tubo sin costura (o soldadura)
— **roller,** rodillo sin costura
— **steel casing,** tubería de revestimiento de acero sin costura
— **tubing,** tubería sin costura

search electrode, electrodo explorador
searching, (dp) búsqueda, investigación lógica
seat, *n.* base, asiento; (va) asiento, (Ve) silla; *v.* asentar
— **protector,** protector de asiento de válvula
seating cup, copa de asiento
seaway, (g) ruta de invasión marina
sec-butylbenzene, butilbenceno secundario
second of arc, segundo de arco
second-derivative map, mapa de segunda derivada
secondary, secundario
— **compound,** compuesto secundario
— **recovery,** (pr) producción secundaria, (Ar) segunda recuperación, (Ve) recobro secundario
— **reference fuel,** combustible secundario de referencia
— **wave,** (gf) onda secundaria
section, *n.* corte, sección; (tu) sección, dos o más tramos de tubo unidos; *v.* seccionar
— **milling,** corte y recuperación de tubería
sectional, hecho en secciones, seccional; (land) regional
— **boiler,** caldera seccional
— **elevation,** alzada en corte
— **insulation,** forro aislante en secciones
— **liner-barrel pump,** bomba de cilindro interior seccionado
secular change, (gf) cambio secular
secular variation, (gf) variación secular
security clearance, acreditación de seguridad
security policy, normas de actuación sobre seguridad
sediment, sedimento

English - Spanish

— **oxygen demand,** demanda de
oxígeno de sedimentos
sedimentary, sedimentario
— **basin,** (g) cuenca sedimentaria
— **complex,** conjunto de estratos,
(Ar) paquete de estratos
— **rock,** roca sedimentaria
sedimentation, sedimentación
seeding, (dp) siembra de errores
seep, *n.* filtración, coladura;
manadero de petróleo; *v.*
filtrarse, colarse
seepage, coladura, filtración;
(petrol) emanación, manadero,
rezumadero, (Ar) brotadero,
(CR) lloradero, (Me)
chapopotera, (Ve) mene
segment, segmento
segregation, segregación,
separación; (g) secreción,
rellenamiento de huecos
redondeados en una roca
seismic, *n.* sísmica; *a.* sísmico/a
— **modeling,** modelado sísmico
— **prospecting,** prospección sísmica
— **ray,** rayo sísmico
— **recording,** registro sísmico (o
sismográfico)
— **velocity,** velocidad sísmica
seismogram, sismograma, registro
hecho por el sismógrafo
seismograph, sismógrafo
— **log,** sismograma, registro
sismográfico
— **party,** expedición (o cuadrilla)
de sismólogos (q.v. **crew**)
— **profile,** perfil sismográfico
— **recording unit,** equipo
registrador del sismógrafo
— **survey,** estudio sismográfico
seismographic record, sismograma
seismological station, estación
sismológica
seismologist, sismólogo
seismology, sismología
seismometer, sismómetro

seismotectonic, sismotectónico
seize, (ca) ligar
seizing, (ma) ligadura, aprieto,
adhesión
self-acting, automático
self-aligning
— **ball bearings,** cojinetes de bolas
de alineación automática, (Ar)
cojinete a bolilla de
autoalineación
— **coupling,** emplame de
alineación automática
— **roller bearing,** cojinetes de
rodillos de alineación
automática
self-centering, de alineación
automática, de centralización
automática
self-checking, autoverificador, de
autocomprobación
self-contained, enterizo
self-dual, autodual
self-elevating, autoelevadizo,
autoelevable
— **drilling unit,** (mar) equipo
autoelevadizo de perforación
self-energizing, de
automultiplicación de fuerza
self-equalizing, de compensación
automática, de igualamiento
automático
self-learning process, (dp) proceso
autoadaptable
self-locking, autotrabante, de ajuste
propio
self-lubricating, de lubricación
automática
self-oiling, de lubricación
automática
self-potential, autopotencial,
potencial espontáneo
self-starter, arranque automático
semiarid, semiárido
semicrystalline, semicristalino
semifloating, semiflotante
semi-flush joint, junta a semirás

semi-infinite horizontal plane,
plano horizontal semi-infinito
semi-ionization, semi-ionización
semimetallic gasket,
empaquetadura semimetálica
semiplant scale, planta
semicomercial
semisubmersible, (plataforma de
perforación) semisumergible
semitrailer, semiremolque, (Ar)
semiacoplable
semiwildcat, q.v. outpost well
sender-receiver terminal, terminal
emisor-receptor (o transmisor-
receptor)
Senonian, senoniense
sense light, luz de detección
sensibility, sensibilidad
sensible heat, calor sensible
sensitive stocks, productos
petrolíferos sensibles
sensitivity of instrument,
sensibilidad de instrumentos
SE (steam emulsification)
number, número de
emulsificación a vapor (q.v.
steam emulsification,
demulsification test)
separation, (g) separación
separator, separador, deflegmador
— **tower,** torre del separador
separatory funnel, (la) embudo
separador
septic tank, tanque séptico
septum, (g) septa
sequence, secuencia, orden sucesivo
— **control register,** registro de
control de secuencias
— **stratigraphy analysis,** (gf)
análisis secuencial estratigráfico
sequential, secuencial
sequestering agente, (qm) agente
secuestrante
serial processing, proceso en serie
sericite, sericita

series, (g) (mt) (el) serie (q.v.
epoch, e.g. Pliocene)
serpentine, serpentina
service, *n.* servicio, reparaciones; *v.*
reparar, hacer ajustes,
rehabilitar
— **engineering,** técnica de
mantenimiento, ingeniería de
funcionamiento
— **equipment,** equipo de servicio
— **station,** estación de servicio,
estación de gasolina, surtidor de
gasolina
servicing unit, maquinaria de
servicio y reparaciones. (q.v.
pulling unit)
servomotor, servomotor, motor
auxiliar
set, *n.* conjunto, juego, grupo;
activación, puesta a 1; (cement)
fraguado; *v.* fraguar; colocar;
(in) poner; (ma) montar
— **casing,** cementar tubería de
revestimiento
— **pipe,** cementar tubería de
revestimiento
— **screw,** tornillo de ajuste (o de
retén), tornillo graduador
— **shoe,** zapata de cementación
(q.v. **cementing shoe**)
— **up,** (mc) armar, montar;
colocar, poner; establecer,
preparar
setter, herramienta de ajuste (q.v.
setting tool)
setting, fraguado
— **point,** punto de fluidez (q.v. **pour**
point)
— **tool,** mecanismo de anclaje,
herramienta de inserción
settle, (fl) asentarse; (g)
sedimentarse, asentarse; (cn)
asentarse, bajarse, (cm) ajustar,
arreglar; saldar, liquidar
settled production, producción
regular (o asintótica)

settlement, asentamiento (humano)
settling, asentamiento
— **period**, período de asentamiento
— **pit**, foso (o presa) de asentamiento
— **tank**, tanque asentador
setup, arreglo, disposición
seven-spot flooding system, sistema de inyección de agua a seis pozos, por conductor de un séptimo pozo, con el fin de producir el petróleo por presión hidráulica
sewage, aguas negras
sewer, cloaca
shackle, grillete, gemelo, eslabón
shadow zone, zona sombreada
shaft, (ma) eje, árbol; (mn) pozo, (Me) tiro, lumbrera
— **collar**, cuello de eje
— **coupling**, empalme de eje
— **hanger**, soporte (o consola) colgante
shafting, transmisiones, juego de ejes
shake out, centrifugar
shaker, (prf) tamiz (o colador) vibratorio, sacudidor para remover los recortes del fluido circulante, (Ar) zaranda, (Me) temblorina
— **pit**, presa del colador
shale, lutita, (Ar) arcilla esquistosa, (Co) esquisto pizarroso, (Me) esquisto arcilloso, pizarra, (Pe) esquisto
— **break**, lutita intrusa, estrato intruso de lutita, interyacente de lutita
— **oil**, aceite de lutita
— **pit**, foso de ripio (o desperdicios)
— **shaker**, colador vibratorio
shale-like schist, esquistos lutíticos
shallow, poco profundo, somero

— **earthquake**, temblor a poca profundidad, temblor local
— **hole**, perforación de poca profundidad, pozo somero
— **salt dome**, domo salino achatado, cúpula salina achatada
— **well**, pozo somero, pozo poco profundo
shaly, lutítico
shank, *n.* (bit) mango, cuerpo, portabarrena, espiga, (CH) culatín; (rivet) fuste, cuerpo, vástago, (Ar) caña; (saw) media luna; *v.* espigar
— **nut**, tuerca de la espiga
sharp, afilado, aguzado, cortante; puntiagudo; (ang) agudo; (sand) angulosa, angular; (curv) cerrada, fuerte, forzada; (slope) fuerte, parada
— **thread**, rosca de ángulo agudo
sharpen, afilar; amolar
shatter, romper en pedazos
shear, *n.* corte, cizallamiento, esfuerzo cortante; tijera, cizalla, (Ar) guillotina; *v.* cizallar, recortar
— **action**, efecto cortante
— **ram**, ariete cortador, ariete de corte
— **ram preventer**, preventor con arietes de corte
— **relief valve**, válvula de descarga con pasador rompible, (Me) válvula de seguridad de clavo
— **secondary waves**, ondas transversales secundarias (q.v. **transverse secondary waves**)
— **stress**, esfuerzo cortante (o cizallante)
— **thinning**, adelgazamiento por esfuerzo cortante
— **wave**, (gf) onda transversal, onda de cizallamiento

200

— **wave anisotropy,** (gf) anisotropía de ondas transversales
— **zone,** (g) zona de deslizamiento cortante
shearing, (g) deslizamiento cortante
— **strength,** resistencia al corte, resistencia al cizallamiento
— **stress,** esfuerzo cortante, cizallamiento, cortadura
sheave, roldana, polea
— **bracket,** ménsula de garrucha
— **pin,** pasador de la roldana
sheet, *n.* (g) capa, estrato; (steel) chapa, plancha, lámina; *v.* forrar
— **iron,** hierro laminado, lámina de hierro, chapas de hierro, palastro
— **lead,** lámina de plomo, plomo laminado, plomo en láminas
— **metal,** metal laminado, chapa de metal, chapa metálica
— **packing,** empaque con láminas, empaque laminado
sheetflood, inundación de avenida
shelf, anaquel; (g) cama de roca, plataforma epicontinental
shell, concha, cáscara, vaina; (mc) casco; (tu) casco, pared; (cl) cuerpo, casco, cilindro; (pulley) cepo; (g) caparazón
— **rock,** roca de concha
— **still,** alambique acorazado, alambique de coraza
shellac, goma laca
shield, *n.* escudo protector; (g) núcleo, escudo; (el) pantalla; *v.* proteger
shielded, blindado, protegido
shift, *n.* (g) desplazamiento, salto (o desliz) horizontal; turno
— **of the fault,** desviación de una falla

shifter fork, horquilla de cambio de velocidades
shifter shaft, eje de cambio de velocidades
shifting
— **gage,** calibrador, gramil
— **shaft,** (mc) árbol de cambio de velocidades
— **wrench,** llave inglesa (q.v. **monkey wrench**)
shim, (mc) plancha de relleno, (Ve) suplemento, lámina de calzar; cuña delgada
— **stock,** (mc) material para láminas de calzar
shimmy, vibración
ship, buque, barco, embaración
shipment, embarque, envío, despacho
shipping, (cm) despacho, envío, embarque; barcos
shoal, banco de arena
shock, golpe, impacto; (seism) sacudida
— **absorber,** amortiguador
shoe, zapata, calzo; (auto) llanta, cubierta; (rr) patín
shoestring sands, (g) cordones estratigráficos, cintas estratigráficas de arena
shonkinite, shonkinita, tipo de roca ígnea negra y granulada
shoot, shooting, *n.* detonación, torpedeamiento, dinamitación, tiro; *v.* detonar
— **a well,** torpedeamiento (o dinamitación) de un pozo
— **box,** (expl) detonador
— **cable,** alambre de disparo
— **distance,** distancia de explosión
— **under,** tiro indirecto desplazado
shop-perforated pipe, tubo perforado en el taller
shore, orilla, (mar) litoral, costa, playa

English - Spanish

— **reef,** arrecife costero (q.v.
  fringing reef)
shoreline, línea costanera
— **deposition,** (g) sedimentación
  playera
short, corto
— **path multiples,** (gf) múltiples de
  trayectoria corta
— **residue,** residuo corto, petróleo
  crudo reducido
— **stroke drilling jars,** percusores
  de carrera corta
— **sweep,** curva cerrada
— **term,** tiempo (o plazo) corto
— **ton,** tonelada neta (o corta)
shortening, acortamiento
shorting switch, interruptor de
  corto circuito
shot, (gf) disparo, tiro; (prf)
  voladura
— **break,** instante de disparo
— **depth,** profundidad de disparo
— **downdip,** observación pendiente
  abajo
— **fan,** método de abanico (q.v.
  shot spread)
— **hole,** hoyo (o pozo) de la
  explosión
— **hole correction,** corrección por
  la profundidad de la explosión
— **hole disturbance,** perturbación
  ocasionada por la explosión
— **hole drill,** barrena para
  perforación de disparo
— **hole drilling rig,** equipo de
  perforación para pozos de
  explosión
— **instant,** instante de explosión
— **moment,** instante de detonación
  (q.v. **shot instant)**
— **updip,** observación pendiente
  arriba
shot-detector distance, distancia
  del detector
shot-receiver azimuth, acimut
  fuente-receptor

shotline, (gf) línea fuente, alambre
  disparador
— **interval,** intervalo entre líneas
  fuente
shotpoint, punto de disparo (o de
  tiro)
shoulder, hombro; (mc) resalto,
  espaldón; (rd) cuneta, berma
  lateral, (Me) acotamiento, (Co,
  PR) paseo, (Ve) hombrillo,
  banquina; (sd) hombro
— **bushing,** buje de resalto
shoulder-dressing tool, (tu)
  herramienta alisadora de
  rebordes
shovel, pala
show of oil, trazas (o indicios) de
  petróleo, vestigios (o rastros,
  muestras) de hidrocarburos
shower, chubasco, chaparrón,
  lluvia, (Ar) turbión
shrink, contraerse, acortarse
— **thread drill pipe,** tubería de
  perforación para enroscar en
  caliente
— **thread tool joint,** unión de
  tubería vástago para encaje en
  caliente
shrink-on tool joint, junta de ajuste
  por contracción, unión de
  tubería vástago empalmada en
  caliente
shrinkage, encogimiento,
  reducción, merma
shrinking, (g) contracción (q.v.
  contraction)
shroud, cubierta, anillo de refuerzo
  de una rueda dentada
shrouded jet nozzle, tobera con
  pestaña
shut, cerrado, (ma) parado
— **down,** n. cierre; v. parar,
  paralizar; a. cerrado, parado
— **down device,** dispositivo de paro
— **in,** cierre
— **off valve,** válvula de paso

shut-in bottomhole pressure, presión estática de fondo
shutter, obturador
— **and test flame control knob,** (la) botón de control para el obturador y la llama de prueba
shuttle valve, válvula tipo lanzadera
SI (Système International d'Unités), Sistema Internacional de Unidades de Medición
sial, (g) sial
Sicilian, siciliense
sickle bend, doblez en hoz
side, lado, costado, flanco; (flat) cara; (r) margen
— **bumpers,** paragolpes, esquineros, laterales
— **channel,** larguero acanalado
— **elevation,** elevación (o vista) lateral
— **piece,** montante, costado
— **rail,** larguero
— **rasp,** (perc) mediacaña escariadora
side-chain hydrocarbon, (qm) hidrocarburo de enlace de cadena lateral
side-cut stream, (rf) derivado lateral (o intermedio), (Ur) corte lateral
side-door elevator, elevador de cierre lateral
side-hole cutter, (prf) cortahoyos lateral, escofina cortapared
side-inlet T, T con toma auxiliar lateral
side-outlet T, T con salida lateral
side-to-side pans, (rf) desviadores horizontales alternoescalonados (q.v. **offset horizontal baffles**)
side-wall sampler, sacamuestras de pared
siderite, siderita

sidestream, corriente (o corte) lateral
sidetracking, (prf) desviación del hoyo
— **tool,** herramienta para desviar, herramienta desviadora
sidewall coring, tomar núcleos de pared
siemens, siemens: unidad SI de conductividad eléctrica
sieve analysis, análisis granulométrico
sieve plate, bandeja tamizadora
sight draft, giro a la vista
sight-feed lubricator, lubricador visible (o transparente), cuentagotas de engrase visible, (Ar) lubricador de gota visible
sigillaria, sigilaria
signal-to-noise ratio, (gf) relación señal-ruido
signature, (dp) signatura, identificación; (cm) firma
signature waveform, (gf) forma de onda característica
silencer, silenciador
silent chain, cadena de transmisión silenciosa
silica, sílice
— **fluor,** harina de sílica
— **gel,** gelatina (o gel) de sílice
silicate, silicato
siliceous, silíceo
— **oxides,** óxidos silíceos
— **sinker,** incrustación de sílice
silicon, silicio
— **carbide,** carburo de silicio, carborundo
— **chip,** chip (o pastilla) de silicio
sill, (derrick) durmiente, solera inferior; (g) capa intrusiva
sillimanite, silimanita
silt, cieno, limo
siltstone, limolita, cieno petrificado
silty, limoso
Silurian, silúrico

silver, plata
— nitrate, nitrato de plata
similar folds, pliegues semejantes (o
infratenuados) (*op.* pliegues
supratenuados)
simple harmonic motion, (gf)
movimiento armónico simple
simple multiple, (gf) múltiplo
simple
simplex, simple, sencillo, simplex
simulator, simulador
single, solo, sencillo, único
— beam torsion balance, balanza
de torsión de un solo brazo
— cylinder, monocilíndrico
— drum unit, tambor sencillo
— duty, función sencilla
— duty ejector, eyector simple
— leg, monopodio
— made, enterizo
— paddle stirrer, agitador con una
sola paleta
— plate clutch, embrague de
platillo único
— precision, (dp) precisión sencilla
— shell asbestos filled gasket,
empaquetadura con coraza
rellena de asbesto
single-acting pump, bomba de
acción simple
single-end pump, bomba de acción
simple
single-end heater, calentador con
fuego por un solo lado
single-phase fluid, (pr) fluido de
fase única, fluido homogéneo
single-speed floating control,
control flotante de velocidad
sencilla
single-stage
— centrifugal pump, bomba
centrífuga de una etapa
— compressor, compresor sencillo
(o de una etapa)

— fluid catalytic cracking,
crácking catalítico fluido de un
solo paso (q.v. cracking)
sink, *n.* (g) dolina; *v.* hundir (q.v.
dolina)
— funnel, (g) fosa de hundimiento
en forma de embudo
— hole, fosa causada por un
hundimiento; sumidero, hueco
sinker bar, (prf) barra de peso (o de
lastre), (Me) barretón
sinter, (mu) toba, incrustación,
(Me) concreción
— deposits, (g) goteras calcáreas,
estalagmitas, estalactitas
sintered glass plate, vidrio poroso
siphon, sifón
— bleeder, sifón de purga
skeleton, esqueleto
skew, *n.* oblicuidad, desfase, sesgo,
desalineamiento, desajuste; *a.*
oblicuo, sesgado, torcido
— bevel, rueda hiperbólica
skid, *n.* patín, polín; *v.* rodar,
arrastrar; (a) patinar
— frame, armazón de corredera (o
de polines, de patín)
— hoist, grúa con montaje en patín
skillet, crisol para acero
skim, (rf) desnatar
— pit, presa de asentamiento
skimmer, desnatador
skimming, (rf) desnatación,
desnatado, destilación primaria
inicial
— plant, planta atmosférica
skin, area expuesta de la formación
adyacente al pozo, (Me) daño
— effect, (el) efecto superficial
skirt, placa delantal
slab, losa, placa, (Me) dala; (mn)
laja, lámina
slack, *n.* (ca) seno; (coal) cisco,
carbón menudo; (tu) serpenteo,
tendido ondulante para
compensar el efecto de la

expansión y contracción, *v.*
aflojar, amollar
— **holder**, sujetador de cable
aflojable
— **off**, aflojar
— **wax**, parafina cruda (o bruta)
slacked lime, cal hidratada (q.v.
hidrated lime)
slag, escoria
**SLAR (side looking airborne
radar)**, radar aerotransportado
de barrido lateral
slate, pizarra
slaty, (g) esquistoso, apizarrado
— **cleavage**, (g) esquistosidad
transversal; (mn) clivaje
sledge hammer, almádena,
mandarria, macho
sleeve, manguito, camisa, casquillo
— **expansion joint**, junta con
abrazadera (o manguito) de
expansión
slice, (dp) elemento
slickenside, (g) espejo de fricción,
superficie de deslizamiento
slickensided, pulido
slide
— **bar**, guía
— **gauge**, calibre deslizable, pies de
rey
— **rule**, regla de cálculos
— **valve**, válvula de corredera,(o de
distribución)
sliding, *a.* corredizo
— **sleeve nipple**, junta de
circulación
slim-hole rig, equipo para
perforaciones de diámetro
reducido
slim-hole rotary drilling rig,
equipo de perforación para
hoyos de diámetro reducido
sling, *n.* eslinga, faja de lona para
sostener tubería; *v.* eslingar,
embragar

— **psychrometer**, psicrómetro
giratorio
slip, *n.* (g) (mt) deslizamiento; (bm)
escape; (earth) desprendimiento
v. resbalar, patinar, deslizarse;
desprenderse; (prf) mover
periódicamente el cable para
que se desgaste uniformemente
— **bowl**, tazón de cuñas
— **crushed pipe**, tubo abollado por
el uso impropio de las cuñas de
agarre
— **elevator**, (tu) elevador de cuñas
— **inserts**, segmentos dentados de
las cuñas
— **joint**, junta flexible, junta de
enchufe acampanado, (Me)
junta telescopiada
— **joint pliers**, alicates de
expansión
— **liner**, placa de cuña
— **marks**, marcas (o ranuras)
labradas por las cuñas de agarre
— **of a fault**, deslizamiento de una
falla
— **on flange**, brida de camisa
— **ring**, (el) anillo colector (o
rozante), anillo de frotamiento
— **ring motor**, motor de anillos
conductores, motor de inducido
devanado, motor de
anillos rozantes
— **seat**, asiento de cuñas
— **socket**, pescasondas de enchufe,
campana de pesca con aletas (o
con cuñas), (Ve) pescador de
cuña
— **stream**, entrada de fluido
— **type elevators**, elevadores tipo
cuña
slip-casing elevator, elevador a
mordazas para tubería de
revestimiento
slippage, resbalamiento; (mc)
pérdida; (gage) gasto no medido

slipping and cutoff, (ca) corrimiento y corte

slips, (prf) cuñas

slit, *n.* raja, hendidura, ranura; *v.* rajar, hender, tajar; ranurar

slop, (p) mezcla de contacto en el punto de unión de dos productos que se transportan sucesivamente por el mismo oleoducto

— **oil**, petróleo de desperdicio

slope, *n.* cuesta, pendiente; (rd) talud, declive; (tp) (g) ladera, falda, talud, vertiente, terreno en declive, (Ar) abajadero, rampa; *v.* inclinarse

— **wash**, lavaduras de falda

slotted, ranurado

slough, *n.* derrumbe, desprendimiento; *v.* derrumbarse, desprenderse

slow-curing asphalt, asfalto de fraguado lento

slow-opening valve, válvula de abertura retardada

sludge, cieno, barro, lodo; sedimento; (mn) fango mineral

— **acid**, ácido sucio (o lodoso)

— **conversion process**, refinación de residuo de petróleo

— **disposal process**, sistema para descarte del cieno

slug, (prf) sobrepeso, slug; (p) tarugo

— **the line**, colocar sobrepeso

sluice, *n.* esclusa; (mn) limpiadora; *v.* mover con corriente de agua

— **gate valve**, válvula esclusa, válvula de desagüe (o de compuerta)

slump, *n.* derrumbe; *v.* derrumbarse

— **test**, prueba de asentamiento

slurry, (prf) lechada, mezcla aguada

slush, lodo, barro (q.v. **mud**)

— **pit**, foso (o presa) del lodo de perforación

— **pump**, bomba para barro de circulación, bomba de inyección de lodo (q.v. **mud pump**)

— **pump manifold**, tubo múltiple de la bomba del lodo

— **pump rod packing**, empaquetaduras del pistón de la bomba de lodo

slushing oil, aceite para bañar piezas recién fresadas

smaltite, esmaltita

smearing, (gf) traslape

smelter, fundición, hacienda de benficio (o de fundición)

smelting, fundición, fusión

— **pot**, crisol, caso de fundir

smithsonite, smithsonita

smoke, humo

— **breeching**, tragante, humero

— **point**, punto de humo

— **stack**, chimenea

smokebox, (cl) caja de humos

smokeless powder, pólvora sin humo

smoky quartz, cuarzo ahumado

smoothed curve, curva compensada

smoothing, (mt) aproximación, nivelación, ajuste

S/N ratio, q.v. **signal-to-noise ratio**

snake, mordaza de la unión giratoria (q.v. **swivel connector grip**)

snap

— **head**, botador

— **lock**, cerradura de resorte, retén

— **ring**, aro de resorte, anillo de presión

snap-on wrench, llave de varilla de succión

snatch block, roldana (o polea) de maniobra, pasteca, (Me) polea viajera seccionada, (Ve) motón de combinación

Snell's law, ley de Snell: cuando una onda cruza de un medio a otro, la onda cambia de dirección en tal forma, que el seno del ángulo de incidencia (ángulo formado entre la normal a la onda y la normal al contacto) dividido entre la velocidad en el primer medio, es igual al seno del ángulo de refracción dividido entre la velocidad en el segundo medio (ley de la refracción)

snipe, madrina (q.v. **cheater**)

snips, tijeras de hojalatero

snow pinnacles, nieve penitente

snow-capped mountain, nevado, ventisquero

snowstorm, tormenta de nieve, nevasca

snub, intervenir en un pozo con presión

snubber, (prf) martinete, absorbedor de impactos, insertador de tubería contra presión; (mc) tambor de frenaje; (a) amortiguador

snubbing line, cable para frenado

snuffer, estinguidor, (Me) cortaflama

soaker, (rf) cámara de reacción (q.v. **reaction chamber**)

soaking drum, cámara de reacción

soaking time, (rf) tiempo de reacción

soap solution, solución de jabón, solución jabonosa

socket, (mc) casquillo, rangua, cubo, receptáculo; (el) tomacorriente, enchufe, pescatubos, pescabarrena

— **bowl,** casco de encastre, taza de enchufe

— **chisel,** escoplo, formón

— **joint,** articulación esférica

— **wrench,** llave tubular, llave de tubo (o de copa, de muletilla)

soda, sosa, soda, bicarbonato

— **ash,** carbonato de sodio calcinado, ceniza de soda

sodalite, sodalita

sodium, sodio

— **carbonate,** carbonato sódico

— **chloride**, sal común, cloruro de sodio

— **plumbite,** sodio plúmbico

— **sulphate,** sulfato de sodio

sodium-silicate mud, barro con silicato de sodio

soft, blando, dulce, maleable, dúctil, flexible

— **crossover**, (ca) patrón de enrollamiento de cruce suave

— **plug,** tapón fundible de seguridad (q.v. **fusible plug)**

— **steel,** acero dulce

softening, descarbonización del acero

— **point,** punto de reblandecimiento

software, (dp) software, soporte lógico, dotación lógica, componentes lógicos

soil, terreno, suelo, tierra

— **analysis,** análisis del gas del suelo

— **gas analysis,** análisis del gas del suelo

— **resistivity,** resistividad de la tierra

— **stress,** fuerza de adherencia, (Me) esfuerzo de adhesión

sol, sol: moneda del Perú

solder, *n.* soldadura; *v.* soldar

soldered joint, junta soldada

soldering, soldadura

— **copper,** soldador de cobre

— **iron,** soldador, cautín, hierro de soldar

sole, (g) yacente, muro, subestrato

solenoid switch, interruptor (o cortacircuito) de solenoide

solenoid valve, válvula de solenoide
solid, sólido
— **catalyst,** catalizador sólido
— **injection,** inyección sin aire, (Ar) inyección sólida
— **logic technology,** (dp) tecnología de la lógica de estado sólido
— **phosphoric acid catalyst,** catalizador sólido de ácido fosfórico
— **punch,** punzón romo
— **state,** semiconductor, estado sólido, transistorizado
— **wireline,** cable sólido de acero, línea piano
solid-liquid equilibrium, equilibrio entre sólido y líquido
solidification, solidificación
solifluction, solifluxión
solubility, solubilidad
— **curve,** curva de solubilidad
soluble, soluble
— **oil,** aceite diluíble en agua
solute, soluto
solution, solución
— **sump,** colector de solución
solution-gas drive, empuje por gas disuelto
solvent, disolvente
— **decarbonizing,** descarbonización por disolventes
— **extraction,** extracción por disolvente
— **neutral,** disolvente neutral
— **treated,** tratado con un disolvente
sonde, sonda
sonic delay line, (dp) línea de retardo sónico
sonic log, registro sónico
sonograph, sonógrafo
soot, hollín
sorbent, absorbente
sort, seleccionar, escoger; (dp) clasificar

sorter, (dp) clasificadora
sound damper, sordina, amortiguador de ruido, lenciador
sound wave, onda sonora
sour crude, petróleo crudo sulfuroso, (Ar) crudo agrio, (Me) crudo amargo
source location, (gs) emplazamiento de la fuente sísmica
source-receiver, (gf) fuente-receptor
source rock, roca productiva (o petrolífera, fuente)
south, sur
— **by east,** sur cuarta al sudeste (S 1/4 al SE)
— **by west,** sur cuarta al sudoeste (S 1/4 al SE)
— **southeast,** sursudeste (SSE)
— **southwest,** sursudoeste (SSO)
southeast, sudeste (SE), sur-oriente
— **by east,** sudeste cuarta al este (SE 1/4 al E)
— **by south,** sudeste cuarta al sur (SE 1/4 al S)
southwest, sudoeste (SO)
— **by west,** sudoeste cuarta al oeste (SO 1/4 al O)
— **by south,** sudoeste cuarta al sur (SO 1/4 al S)
SP, q.v. **self potential; steam pressure**
space lag, intervalo vacío
space velocity, velocidad-espacio
spacer, espaciador
spacing, espaciado, espaciamiento
— **clamp,** abrazadera espaciadora
spade, pala, garlancha; azada, azadón
spall, *n.* laja, astilla de piedra, lasca, (Ve) escalla, astilladura; *v.* salvar, franquear
— **of wrench jaw,** abertura de la boca de una llave inglesa

Glossary of the Petroleum Industry

spaghetti, tubería de producción de
diámetro muy reducido
spanner, q.v. wrench
spare parts, repuestos, piezas de
repuesto
spark, chispa; brillo
— advance, avance de la chispa
— arrester, arrestador de chispas,
chispero
— coil, bobina de chispa
— gap, abertura de chispa
— lever, palanca de la chispa
— plug, bujía
— plug tester, probador de bujías
spatial resolution, resolución
espacial
spatula, espátula
spear, (fishing tl) arpón, pescador
de gancho de cable
— bulldog, cangrejo pescador
— center, pescador de gancho
— tip, pescador de cuña para tubo
spearhead, q.v. preflush
species, especie
specific
— gravity, gravedad (o densidad)
específica
— heat, calor específico
— resistance, resistencia específica
specification, especificación
specimen, muestra, ejemplar,
espécimen
spectral analysis, análisis espectral
spectrometric, espectrométrico
spectroscope, espectroscopio
spectrum, espectro
speed, velocidad
— change gear, engranaje de
cambio de marcha
— indicator, indicador de
velocidad, velocímetro,
taquímetro
— kit, polea viajera doble
— layer, (gf) capa de velocidad
— recorder, taquímetro

— reducing gear, engranaje
reductor de velocidad
speed-reduction unit, caja de
engranajes de cambio (q.v. gear
box)
speedometer, velocímetro
spelaean, cavernoso
spent, usado, gastado
— catalyst stripper,
despetrolizador de catalizador
usado
spessartite, espersartita
sphere, esfera
spherical, esférico
— divergence, (gf) divergencia
esférica
spheroid, esferoide
spherometer, esferómetro
spherulites, esferulitas
spider, araña, cubo de garras;
(wheel) cruceta
— and slips, anillo y cuña de
suspensión
— casing landing, araña
centradora de la tubería de
revestimiento
— deck, (nt) sollado (q.v.
hurricane deck)
spigot, espita, grifo
spike, espiga, clavo largo
spill, clavija, broca;
derramamiento, rebose
spin, hacer girar, girar sin avanzar
spindle, muñón, gorrón, vástago,
broca
— oil, aceite para husillos
spinel, espinela
spinner, girador de junta kelly
spinning
— cathead, (prf) torno auxiliar de
enrosque y desenrosque
— chain, cadena enroscadora
— line torno manual, cable de
enroscar y desenroscar tubería
— wrench, llaves automáticas

209

English - Spanish

S-P interval, (gf) intervalo entre las
ondas
spiral, espiral
— **bevel gear,** engranaje
cónicohelicoidal
— **gear,** engranaje helicoidal
— **pipe,** tubo soldado en espiral
— **tear,** rotura espiral
— **welded casing,** tubería de costura
espiral
— **welded pipe,** tubo soldado en
espiral
spirifer, espirífero
spirit level, nivel de burbuja
spit, (g) lengua de tierra (o arena)
unida a la costa
splash box, chaqueta (q.v. **mud
box**)
splash lubrication, lubricación por
salpique
splatter loss, (sd) pérdida por
salpicadura
splice, n. juntura, empate; (el)
empalme; (ca) ayuste de cabos;
v. unir, empatar; empalmar;
ayustar
— **plate,** cubrejunta, brida,
sobrejunta, plancha (o chapa)
de unión
splicing, empalme, empalmadura
— **tool,** herramienta de empalmar
spline, ranura, estría
split, n. hendedura, cuarteadura,
raja, resquebrajo; (atom)
desintegración, escisión; v.partir,
hender, rajar, cuartear; rajarse,
resquebrajarse
— **beam,** (radio) haz partido
— **bearing,** cojinete bipartido,
cojinete en dos mitades
— **lock ring,** anillo de rosca partida
— **pin,** chaveta hendida, pasador de
aletas
— **ring,** aro partido, aro en dos
mitades
— **setup,** (gf) arreglo disperso

— **shaft,** eje partido
— **spider,** araña partida
— **spread,** tendido bilateral (o
simétrico)
split-dip shooting, disparo (o tiro)
simétrico para determinación de
echados
splitter, (tu) rajatubos
spm, q.v. **strokes per minute**
SPM (single point mooring),
monoboya de carga y descarga
spodumene, espodumen
spoke, rayo de rueda, cabilla
sponge, spiculae, espículas de
esponja, poros de esponja
spont, gollete, tubo, conducto
spontaneous combustion,
combustión espontánea
spontaneous polarization,
polarización espontánea
spool, n. tambor, carrete, carretel;
(flange) cuello; v. arrollar,
enrollar, devanar
spooler, guía que distribuye
uniformemente el cable al
arrollarse éste en el tambor
spooling flange, (winch) reborde
del tambor
spot correlation, (gf) correlación
discontinua
spot welding, soldadura por puntos
spotted, (g) noduloso
spray, rociar, regar
— **gun,** pistola pulverizadora
— **nozzle,** boquilla de regar, pico
regador, surtidor, pitón
atomizador
— **paint,** pintar a pistola (o con
pulverizador)
spread, distribución; (gf) tendido de
recepción (q.v. **geophone
patch**)
— **correction,** corrección por
tendido, sobretiempo normal
por distancia (q.v. **normal
moveout**)

spread man, (p) jefe de cuadrilla
spreader, (cn) viga de separación, travesaño, tornapunta
spring, (mc) resorte, muelle; ballesta; elasticidad, flexión; (water) manantial, fuente, ojo de agua, venero
— **loaded,** a resorte
— **seat,** asiento del resorte
— **spacer,** espaciador de resorte
— **steel,** acero para ballestas, acero de resortes
— **washer,** arandela de presión, (o e resorte)
sprinkler, rociador automático
sproket, rueda dentada, rueda de cadena, (Co) catilina
— **chain,** cadena para engranaje
— **wheel,** rueda dentada
SPS (submerged subsea production system), sistema submarino (integral) de producción
spud-in, (prf) iniciar la perforación de un pozo
— **bit** barrena de aletas
spudder, pulseta, martinete, barrena inicial; equipo portátil de pulseta
— **arm,** balancín tiracable para la barrena inicial
— **units,** equipos iniciadores de pozos
spudding
— **beam,** balancín de perforadora inicial
— **bit,** barrena tipo escoplo para perforación inicial
— **machine,** equipo para perforación inicial
— **shoe,** corredera para el cable de perforadora inicial
spur, trepadera, escalador; (g) contrafuerte, estribación; (p) ramal; (tl) puntal, codal, tornapunta; (rr) desvío

— **gear,** engranaje de dientes rectos (o de espuela), engranaje recto
— **line,** oleoducto auxiliar (o secundario)
squab, cojín, almohadón
square, (tl) escuadra, cartabón; (mt) cuadrado, segunda potencia
— **centimeter (sq cm),** centímetro cuadrado (cm^2)
— **drill collar,** tubo lastrabarrena cuadrado
— **inch (sq in),** pulgada cuadrada (pg^2)
square-drive master bushing, buje maestro de abertura cuadrada
squeak, chirrido, rechinamiento
squeeze cementing, (pr) inyección de cemento, cementación forzada
squeeze job, inyección de cemento en la formación geológica
squib, (expl) chartucho de nitroglicerina, (Ve) bomba
squiggle, señal de galvanómetro
squirrel cage, (el) rotor (o inducido) de jaula, rotor en circuito corto
squnch joint, junta (o unión) sin rosca
SS, q.v. **suspended solids; sand or sandstone**
SST, q.v. **sea surface temperature**
stab, (tu) centrar dos tubos para onectarlos a rosca
stabbing, conectar tubos roscados
— **board,** plataforma auxiliar mientras se corre tubería de revestimiento
— **protector,** protector centrador
stability, estabilidad
stabilize, estabilizar
stabilizer, estabilizador
stabilizing column, torre estabilizadora, torre de

fraccionación (q.v.
fractionating column)
stack, *n.* montón, pila, conjunto
apilado; arreglo en columna; (rf)
chimenea; (g) escollo de erosión,
peñasco, columna; (gf)
apilamiento; (cl) chimenea; (dp)
pila, lote;*v.* amontonar, apilar,
hacinar
— **blower,** insuflador de chimenea
— **draft,** tiro de chimenea
— **effect,** efecto de chimenea
stacking, (gf) apilamiento
stadia, estadía, taquímetro
— **arc,** arco taquimétrico
— **cross wires,** hilos de estadía,
alambres estadimétricos
— **hairs,** alambres estadimétricos,
hilos de estadía
— **rod,** mira taquimétrica
stage, etapa
stage-cementing equipment,
equipo para cementación por
etapas
staggered faults, (g) fallas al
tresbolillo (q.v. **echelon faults**)
staging, (dp) transferencia de cinta
a disco magnético
stain, *n.* mancha; *v.* teñir
stainless steel, acero inoxidable
stalactite, estalactita
stalagmite, estalagmita
stalk, tramo, sección de tubería
compuesta de varias juntas
stall, *n.* (mn) cámara; *v.* (ma)
parar, ahogarse, atascarse
stamping die, matriz de estampa,
estampa
stand, soporte, pie; (tu) parada,
lingada, tres tubos enroscados
— **of pipe,** haz de tubería en pie
stand-alone, *a.* autónomo,
independiente
standard, *n.* patrón, norma,
modelo; *a.* normalizado, de

norma, corriente, de tipo patrón,
standard, estándar
— **air,** aire normal (o estándar): a
temperatura de 20°C, presión de
1 kg/cm^{2}y
humedad relativa de 36%
— **cubic foot,** pie cúbico estándar:
0,02832 m^3
— **curve,** curva normal
— **error,** error típico (o estándar)
— **gage,** plantilla normal
— **interface,** (dp) interfaz
normalizada (o estándar),
interfase estándar
— **operating procedure,**
procedimiento corriente (o
estándar)
— **pressure,** presión estándar: 1,033
kg/cm^2 abs.
— **price,** precio corriente
— **product of sums,** producto
normalizado de sumas
— **rig band wheel,** rueda motora de
equipo de perforación corriente
— **rig irons,** herraje para torre de
perforación a percusión
standardization, normalización,
estandarización, unificación
standardize, uniformar,
estandardizar
standby equipment, equipo auxiliar
(o de relevo)
standby time, tiempo de espera,
tiempo de inactividad
standing
— **pressure,** (prf) (pr) presión
sostenida
— **valve,** válvula fija, (Ve) válvula
de abajo, perro
— **valve cage,** cámara de válvula
fija
standpipe, tubo vertical, bajante;
(hd) depósito regulador,
columna reguladora; (prf) tubo

Glossary of the Petroleum Industry

de la manguera, (Ar) caño-soporte de manguera
staple, *n.* armella, grampa, argolla; *v.* engrampar
star, estrella
— **bit**, barrena de cruz
starboard, (nt) estribor
starch indicator solution, solución de almidón para indicador
start, (ma) poner en marcha, echar a andar; arrancar
starter, motor (o mecanismo) de arranque (o prendedor, iniciador); (prf) barrena primera; (auto) arrancador
— **jet blower**, emisor de chorro de vapor, (Ur) puntero de vapor
— **jet ejector**, eyector de vapor para eliminar gases
— **jet pump**, bomba inyectora de chorro de vapor
— **line**, tubería de vapor
— **manifold**, mútiple para distribución de vapor
— **mixing**, mezclar al vapor
starting crank, manivela de arranque
starting gear, engranaje de primera velocidad, engranaje de arranque
startup, iniciación de operación, arranque
statement, (cm) estado de cuenta
static, estático
— **bottom-hole pressure**, presión estática
— **friction**, fricción estática
— **metamorphism**, metamorfismo estático
station, estación
stationary, estacionario, fijo
— **barrel pump**, bomba de cilindro fijo
— **full-barrel rod pump**, bomba de varillas con cilindro enterizo

— **tube sheet**, placa portatubos fija, placa tubular fija, (Ur) placa de tubos fija
statistics, estadística
stator, estator
— **slots**, ranuras de estator
— **winding**, arrollado del estator
staurolite, estaurolita
stave, duela
stay, estabilidad, soporte, fiador, apoyo, trinquete, nervio, amarre
— **bolt**, tornillo de separación y refuerzo, tornillo de fijación, estay, perno de puntal, tirante, espárrago
steady mass, masa inerte
steady state, régimen estacionario
steam, vapor
— **and oil separator**, separador de aceite y vapor
— **boiler**, caldera de vapor
— **cleanout rig**, equipo de servicio de limpieza de pozos a vapor
— **condenser**, condensador de vapor
— **cracking**, crácking con vapor (q.v. **cracking**)
— **distillation**, destilación a vapor
— **drain**, purgador (o desaguador) de vapor
— **emulsion test**, prueba de emulsificación a vapor (q.v. **SE number, demulsification test**)
— **engine**, máquina de vapor
— **flooding**, inyección de vapor
— **hammer**, martinete a vapor, (Ar) maza de vapor, (Me) pilón a vapor
— **hose**, manguera para vapor
— **jacketed valve**, válvula con camisa de vapor
— **pressure (SP)**, presión del vapor (PV)
— **pressure gage**, indicador a presión del vapor
— **refining**, refinación a vapor

213

— **scrubber**, interceptor (o separador) de agua; (Ur) trampa de vapor

— **trap**, interceptor (o separador) de agua, (Ur) trampa de vapor

— **stripping**, destilación al vapor

— **turbine**, turbina de vapor

stearic acid, ácido esteárico

steel, acero

— **building**, edificio de estructura de acero

— **channel**, pieza de acero en U

— **clad**, acorazado, cubierto (o revestido) de acero

— **gravity platform**, plataforma de acero de apoyo por gravedad

— **line measurement (SLM)**, medida con hilo de alambre

— **pig**, lupia de acero

— **sectional building**, edificio de acero desmontable

— **sheet**, plancha de acero, lámina de acero

steel-tooth bit, barrena de conos dentados

steep, empinado

— **dip**, buzamiento empinado

— **face**, (g) abismo, despeñadero (q.v. **abyss**)

steering, dirección, gobierno

stem, *n.* vástago; barra maestra, varilla; *v.* detener, contener

— **straightener**, enderezador de vástago

stemming, (expl) taco

step, *n.* paso; (ladder) escalón, peldaño; estribo; (mc) quicionera, rangua; (nt) carlinga; (g) escalón, escala; *v.* medir a pasos; escalonar

— **change**, cambio simple de valor

— **down**, reducción

— **faults**, fallas escalonadas (q.v. **distributive fault**)

step-thread flush joint, acoplamiento a ras con dos series de roscas

stepladder, escalera de tijera

stepout, (gf) corrimiento en tiempo, sobretiempo por distancia (q.v. **moveout**)

— **well**, pozo adyacente (o exterior) al yacimiento

stibnite, estibnita; antimonita

sticker, (tu) barra abreválvulas, barra llave

sticky, pegajoso

stiff-neck socket, portacable fijo, enchufe sólido para cable, enchufe rígido

still, alambique, destiladera destiladora

— **gas**, gas de alambique

stillbite, estilbita

stinger, aguijón, espolón; (prf) guía, cola

stipulation, estipulación

stirrer, agitador

stirring speed, velocidad de agitación

stirrup, estribo

stochastic matrix, matriz estocástica (o aleatoria)

stock, *n.* (tl) terraja, tarraja; (cm) existencias, inventario; materia prima; *v.* tener en existencia, almacenar

— **and dies**, terraja y dados

— **company**, (cm) compañía anónima

— **tank**, tanque de almacenamiento para petróleo crudo tratado

stockless anchor, (nt) ancla de patente

stoke, stoke: unidad estándard de viscosidad cinética en el sistema centímetro-gramo-segundo

stone, piedra

stop, *n.* (mc) tope, limitador, parador; (rr) parada; (door)

Glossary of the Petroleum Industry

tope; *v.* parar, detener; pararse,
detenerse; tapar, obstruir
— **check value,** válvula de cierre (o
de retención)
— **watch,** reloj de segundos muertos,
cronómetro
stopcock, llave de paso (o de cierre),
(Me) macho
stopper, tapón, tapadero
stopple, tapón
storage, almacenamiento,
almacenaje; (dp) memoria,
almacenamiento
— **battery,** (el) batería de
acumuladores; acumulador
— **bin,** depósito de
almacenamiento, arcón, tolva
— **gas,** gas que se almacena en un
yacimiento
storeroom, almacén, bodega,
depósito (q.v. **warehouse**)
storm, (land) tormenta, (mar)
temporal
— **choke,** válvula de seguridad de
tubería de producción
stove oil, combustible para estufas
(o para cocinas)
stove piping, soldadura de tubería
junta a junta, soldadura a estilo
tubo de estufa
straddle packer, doble empaque
straddle spread, (gf) tendido
cabalgado (o bilateral) (q.v.
split spread)
straddling, a horcajadas
straight, recto, derecho, en línea
— **chain hydrocarbon,** (qm)
hidrocarburo de enlace (o de
cadena recta)
— **countershaft,** contraeje recto
— **run distillate,** destilado de
destilación a presión
atmosférica, destilado íntegro
— **shank drill,** (tl) barrena (o
broca) de espiga cilíndrica

— **shank twist drill,** barrena
espiral de espiga cilíndrica
— **taper rotary collar,** collar
terraja fusiforme
straight-run gasoline, gasolina
destilada a presión atmosférica,
gasolina íntegra
straightener, enderezadora,
endererezador
strain, *n.* esfuerzo interno, reacción
al (o efecto del) esfuerzo
aplicado; (g) deformación; *v.*
deformar
— **gage,** medidor de deformación
strainer, colador, filtro
— **body,** caja del colador
— **screen,** hoja del colador
strange, (g) alóctono (q.v.
allochthonous)
strap, *n.* correa; (steel) barra chata,
solera, llanta; guarnición; *v.* (tk)
aforar, medir y registrar
— **hinge,** bisagra de paletas
— **in,** (prf) medir tubería conforme
se inserta
strata, estratos, lechos, capas
stratification, estratificación
stratify, estratificar
stratigraphic
— **column,** columna estratigráfica
— **correlation,** correlación
estratigráfica
— **interval,** intervalo estratigráfico
— **sequence,** orden estratigráfico
— **test,** perforación para prueba
estratigráfica
— **trap,** trampa estratigráfica
stratigraphy, estratigrafía
stratum, estrato, lecho, capa
stray sand, (g) formación de arena
extraviada
streak, (mn) filón, veta, (Ar)
cinteada
stream, arroyo, corriente de agua,
río
— **bed,** lecho de un arroyo

215

— **day,** (rf) día en activo, día de
operación
streamer, (mar gf) cable hidrófono
(o marino)
stream-line lubricator, lubricador
de tubería de vapor
streamlined, aerodinámico,
perfilado, fuselado, (Me)
correntilíneo, (Ur)
hidrodinámico, de línea
corriente
street elbow, street L, codo roscado
macho y hembra
strength, fuerza; resistencia; solidez
stress, *n.* esfuerzo, fatiga, tensión,
stress; *v.* someter a esfuerzo,
fatigar
— **concentration points,** puntos de
concentración del esfuerzo
— **relief heat treatment,**
tratamiento térmico para
reducir los esfuerzos
stretcher jack, estirador de correas
striae, franjas; (g) estrías
striated pebbles, guijarros estriados,
(Ar) rocalla, derrubio estriado
striation, estriación
striding level, nivel de a caballo
strike, *n.* (g) rumbo del estrato; *v.*
golpear
— **fault,** falla paralela al rumbo del
estrato, falla longitudinal
— **ridge,** filo de montañas paralelo
al rumbo del estrato
strike-slip, (g) rumbo
desplazamiento
— **fault,** falla de rumbo (o de
rumbo-desplazamiento) (q.v.
transcurrent fault)
— **diagonal fault,** falla diagonal de
rumbo
— **dip fault,** falla transversal de
rumbo
— **strike fault,** falla longitudinal de
rumbo

string of casing, sarta de tubería de
revestimiento
string of tools, juego de
herramientas para perforación
stringer, (cn) larguero, durmiente
longitudinal; (cm) agente,
contacto
— **bead,** soldadura de un solo
cordón (q.v. **bead**)
stringing, (p) repartir la tubería a
lo largo del trayecto
strip, *n.* franja, faja, tira, cinta;
(mu) tira; *v.* (ma) desguarnecer;
(mold) desencofrar, desmoldar,
quitar formas; (thread)
estropear; descortezar; (rf)
estabilizar la destilación, (Me)
agotar; (well) extraer la tubería
y varillas de succión; enjugar
tubería (de perforación)
stripped gasoline, gasolina
estabilizada
stripped oil, petróleo despojado de
fracciones livianas (q.v.
denuded oil)
stripper, (pr) enjugador de tubería
vástago (o cable) (q.v. **stripper
tower**)
— **tower,** (rf) torre rectificadora,
rectificador, (Me) despojadora,
estabilizador
— **well,** pozo casi agotado, pozo
mermado
stripping, (rf) destilación
estabilizadora; (pr) extracción
de la tubería junto con las
varillas de succión
— **in,** introducción de tubería a
presión
— **out,** sacar tubería a presión
— **still,** alambique de
despojamiento, alambique
despojador
— **vapor,** (rf) vapor despetrolizante
stroke, (piston) carrera, recorrido,
(Ve) juego, embolada; golpe

Glossary of the Petroleum Industry

— **counter,** cuentamboladas
— **(s) per minute,** emboladas por minuto
strong, resistente, fuerte
strong-motion seismograph, sismógrafo para movimientos fuertes
strontianite, estroncionita
structural
— **drilling,** (g) perforación de estudio estructural, perforación de correlación (q.v. **core drilling**)
— **geology,** geología estructural
— **high,** (g) estructura alta, alto estructural
— **mast,** mástil estructural, mástil con miembros angulares (q.v. **jacknife mast**)
— **steel,** acero estructural (o de construcción), (Ur) perfiles de acero
— **trap,** (g) trampa estructural
structure, (g) estructura; contextura
— **contour,** curvas de nivel de la estructura
strut, n. puntal, apoyadero, codal, jabalcón; (mn) estemple, (Ar) machón; v. apuntalar, acodar, acodalar
Stubb's wire gage, calibrador Stubb para alambres
stuck, pegado, adherido
stud, (mc) perno, husillo; (chain) travesaño; (carp) pie derecho, montante
— **bolt,** perno prisionero, tornillo opresor, (Ar) espárrago; (chain) travesaño
stud-link chain, cadena de eslabón con travesaños
stuffing box, prensaestopas, caja de estopas, cabeza de empaque
stuffing-box gland, casquillo del prensaestopas

style, estilo
stylus, punzón
styrene, feniletileno, estirina
sub, unión substituta, sub, unión en f orma de niple con extremos de diferentes tamaños o diseños de rosca; (perc) conexión de barra; (bm rods) niple de varilla
subaerial, al aire, depósitos f ormados en contacto con el aire
subangular grains, granos semiangulares
subaqueous, bajo el agua
subcapillary, subcapilar
subcooling condenser, condensador de baja temperatura
subduction, subducción
sublimation, sublimación
submarine, n. a. submarino (q.v. **subsea**)
submerged condenser, condensador sumergido
submergence, sumersión
submersible
— **barge,** barcaza parcialmente sumergible
— **drilling rig,** equipo sumergible de perforación
— **electrical pump,** bomba eléctrica sumergible
— **pump,** bomba de fondo
submersion, immersión
subnipple, q.v. **sub**
subsea, submarino, bajo el nivel del mar
— **BOP,** preventor marino
— **completion,** terminación submarina
— **elevation,** altura bajo el nivel del mar
— **production system,** sistema submarino de producción
— **tree,** árbol de navidad submarino
subsequent, subsecuente
— **stream,** arroyo subsecuente
— **valley,** valle subsecuente

English - Spanish

subset, (dp) modulador-
demodulador, modem
subside, v. hundirse; bajar el nivel
de un líquido;. subsidence, n.
hundimiento; descenso de un
fluido
subsill, subsolera, durmiente
inferior
subsoil, subsuelo
substitute natural gas, gas natural
sintético (q.v. synthetic natural
gas)
substratum, basamento, capa
inferior
substructure, subestructura
subsurface, n. subsuelo; a. del
subsuelo, subsuperficial, bajo
tierra
— map, mapa del subsuelo
— safety valve, válvula de
seguridad enterrada, válvula de
tormenta (q.v. tubing safety
valve)
— smapling, muestreo de fondo
subzero, bajo cero
sucker rod, varilla de bombeo (o de
succión)
— coupling, acoplamiento de
varilla de bombeo
— elevator, elevadores de varillas
de bombeo
— guide, guía de varillas de bombeo
— hanger, suspensor (o colgadero)
de varillas de succión, (Ve)
mochila
— hook, gancho para las varillas de
ucción, (Ve) gallito
— joint socket, enchufe que agarra
la varilla de bombeo por la
unión
— line swivel weight, peso para
bajar el cable de las varillas de
succión al piso de la torre
— pumping, bombeo mecánico
— socket, enchufe para varilla de
bombeo

— stripper, empaquetadura
limpiadora de varillas de
bombeo (q.v. oil saver)
— sub, varilla de bombeo substituta,
varilla corta machihembrada
— wrench, llave para varilla de
bombeo
sucre, sucre: moneda de Ecuador
suction, aspiración, succión
— end of pump, extremo de
aspiración
— hoist, elevador de manga de
succión
— lift, altura de aspiración
— line, línea de succión (o de
descarga)
— pipe, tubo de succión, aspirador
— pit, foso de succión
— pump, bomba aspirante bomba
de aspiración
— valve, válvula e aspiración (o de
succión)
suitcase sand, arena improductiva
suite, serie, colección, juego
sulfate, sulfato
— reducing bacteria, bacterias
reductoras de sulfatos
sulfide, sulfuro
sulphate, sulfato
sulphonation, sulfonación
sulphonic acid, ácido sulfónico
sulphur, azufre
— dioxide, dióxido de azufre,
anhídrido sulfuroso
— ore, pirita
— plant, planta de azufre
— test, determinación (o prueba)
de azufre
sulphuration, sulfuración
sulphuric, sulfúrico
— acid, ácido sulfúrico
— acid alkylation process,
alquilación con ácido sulfúrico
— acid contact plant, (rf)
instalación para refinar por
contacto con ácido sulfúrico

218

sulphurous, sulfuroso

summit of a curve, vértice de una curva

sump, sumidero, resumidero, poceta, pozo de recogida; (ma) colector de aceite

— **hole,** foso para lodo, presa de lodo

sun cracks, grietas producidas por el sol

sunken block, (g) fosa tectónica (q.v. **downthrown**)

superatmospheric conditions, condiciones superatmosféricas

superatmospheric pressure, presión superatmosférica

supercapillary, supercapilar

supercharger, superalimentador; supercompressor

supercharging pipe, tubo de sobrealimentación

supercomputer, superordenador, ordenador de gran potencia

superficial, superficial

superfractionation, superfraccionamiento

superfractionator, superfraccionador

superheat, *n.* recalentamiento, supercalor; *v.* sobrecalentar, recalentar

superheated steam, vapor recalentado

supernatant liquid, (qm) líquido obrenadante

superposed stream, arroyo superpuesto

superposition, superposición, yuxtaposición

— **of strata,** (g) superposición de estratos

supersaturated, sobresaturado

supersaturation, sobresaturación

supervised flame, llama supervisada (o vigilada)

supply, *n.* suministro, abastecimiento, abasto; *v.* abastecer, suministrar

support, *n.* soporte, descanso, apoyo, sostén; *v.* apoyar, sostener, soportar

supratenuous folds, (g) pliegues supratenuados (*op.* pliegues similares)

surf, mar de fondo (o de leva), resaca

surface, superficie

— **casing,** primera tubería de revestimiento (q.v. **drive pipe, conductor pipe**)

— **condenser,** condensador de superficie

— **controlled intermitter,** válvula intermitente de control

— **correction,** corrección superficial

— **gauge,** marcador paralelo

— **hole,** hoyo inicial de un pozo

— **moraine,** (g) morena superior

— **of unconformity,** superficie de estructura discordante

— **pipe,** (prf) tubería de revestimiento del hoyo inicial de un pozo, primera tubería de revestimiento

— **tension,** tensión superficial

— **waste,** pérdidas de superficie (debido a fugas, filtraciones, etc.)

— **waves,** (gf) ondas superficiales (q.v. **groundroll**)

surfactant, surfactante

surge, oleada, oleaje, golpe de mar

— **effect,** represionamiento

— **tank,** tanque de compensación, tanque iqualador (q.v. **balance tank, floating tank**)

surplus, (cm) superávit, excedente

survey, *n.* estudio, examen; (tp) levantamiento, planimetría, apeo, (Ar) relevamiento; *v.*

estudiar, examinar; levantar un plano

surveying, levantamiento de planos, agrimensura

surveyor, (oc) topógrafo, agrimensor

survival capsule, (nt) cápsula salvavidas

SUS (Saybolt universal second), segundo Saybolt universal

susceptibility, susceptibilidad

suspended impurities, impurezas en suspensión

suspended solids, sólidos en suspensión

suspender, cabeza de tubería de revestimento

suspension, suspensión

sussexite, susexita

suture, (g) sutura, (Ar) línea lobal

SW (salt water), agua salada

swab, *n.* limpiatubos, escobillón; pistón de achique, émbolo achicador, (Me) sonda, (Ve) chupador, lampazo; achicador para excitación de pozos; *v.* excitar, activar, limpiar, (Ve) suavear

— **rubber,** goma para limpiatubos

— **units,** unidades de achique de pozos

swabbing, limpieza con escobillón; limpiar un pozo; achique de excitación, activar, limpiar, (Ve) suavear

swage, enderezador

swaged nipple, manguito de reducción, niple de combinación

swath, anchura de corte; (gf) anchura de barrido

SWATH (small waterplane area twin hull), tipo de plataforma semisumergible

sway, *n.*(nt) ladeo, cimbreo; *v.* ladearse, cimbrearse

sweat residue, residuo de resudación

sweating oven, horno de resudación

sweating pan, bandejas de resudación

sweating surface, superficie de resudación

swedge, manguito de reducción, niple cuello de botella (q.v. **swaged niple**)

swedged pin, conexión macho cónica sin filetes, pasador cónico

sweep-gas, gas de barrido, gas de chimenea que se inyecta para forzar la salida de vapores indeseables

sweep saw, sierra de contornear

sweet crude, petróleo crudo dulce

sweeten, desulfurar (o desazufrar, endulzar) el petróleo, destufar

sweetened gasoline, gasolina tratada

sweetening still, alambique desulfurador (o destufador)

swell, *n.* (g) umbral continental, suave elevación de la superficie terrestre; (nt) oleada, marejada; *v.* hincharse, engrosarse

swelling, (g) intumescencia (q.v. **intumescence**)

swimmer propulsion unit, equipo de motobuceo

swimmer vehicle, sumergible inundado

swing, sostén oscilante

— **check valve,** válvula de retención a bisagra, válvula de charnela

— **connection,** conexión flexible

— **lever,** (perc) palanca articulada

— **line,** oleoducto móvil de servicio

— **pipe,** tubo giratorio

— **plant,** planta de producción alternativa

— **post,** sostén guía para varillas de tracción

swingline, extensión de la línea de succión

swirl, remolino

switch, (el) conmutador, interruptor, selector, (Co) suiche, (Cu) chucho; (rr) cambiavía, desvío; (v) desviar, cambiar

switchgear, (el) mecanismo de control, despositivo de distribución

swivel, (prf) unión giratoria, (Ar) cabeza giratoria

— **connector grip,** (ca) mordaza

— **joint,** junta giratoria

— **link,** eslabón giratorio

— **meter,** medidor giratorio

— **rope socket,** portacable giratorio

— **socket,** enchufe giratorio

— **wrench,** llave forma S, llave de doble curva, (Ve) llave de boca

SWL (safe working load), carga de trabajo segura

syderite, siderita

syenite, (g) sienita

symmetric, symmetrical, simétrico

— **anticline,** anticlinal simétrico

— **fold,** pligue recto; pliegue simétrico

sympathetic vibration, vibración simpática

synchronism, sincronismo, simultaneidad

synchronization, sincronización

synchronous, sincrónico

synclinal, *a.* sinclinal; **syncline,** *n.* sinclinal (*op.* anticline)

synclinorium, sinclinal compuesto, sinclinorio

syngenetic, (g) singenético

synthesis gas, gas de síntesis

synthetic, sintético

— **catalyst,** catalizador sintético

— **rubber,** caucho sintético

system, sistema; (g) q.v. **period,** e.g. Tertiary)

T

T, q.v. **tera; tesla**

T, (tu) unión en T

T beam, (cn) viga en T

T flip-flop, (dp) circuito biestable T

T iron, perfil (o hierro) en T

T spread, (gf) tendido (o despliegue) en T

table, mesa; cuadro, tabla; (mc) banco

— **mountain,** (tp) mesa, meseta (q.v. **mesa**)

— **ring gear,** (prf) corona dentada de la mesa, engranaje anular de la mesa

tabs, asas, orejas

tabular, *a.* tabular; **tabulate,** *v.* tabular

tachometer, tacómetro, indicador de velocidad

tack, tachuela

— **welding,** soldadura a puntos (o punteada)

tackle, aparejo de poleas, polipasto

tacky, pegajoso

tag, identificar, etiquetar; (prf) tocar un objeto en el fondo del pozo con la sarta

— **line,** cable de izar

tail, cola

— **bearing,** cojinete del contravástago, (Ve) cojinete de cola

— **chain,** (prf) cadena de izar

— **pipe,** (prf) tubo de fondo, apéndice de la tubería de producción, (Me) cola, escape

— **post,** (ca) poste de ancla; (perc) poste posterior de apoyo

— **rod,** contravástago

tailing-in, (perc) remate de la perforación; (rotary prf) arrimo a la torre, introducción en la

221

torre de la tubería o varillas de succión; *v.* rematar; arrimar

tailings, desechos, deslave, colas, relaves, (Me) residuo

take ground, (nt) varar

take-off post, poste de transmisión de movimiento del balancín

talc, talco

tall, alto

— **oil,** aceite de pino

tally register, cuentapasos

talus, (g) talud, (Ar) talud detrítico, rocalla

— **fan,** abanico (o cono) de deyección (q.v. **alluvial fan**)

TAME, q.v. **terciary amyl methyl ether**

tamp, apisonar; compactar el taco sobre la carga de explosivo

tamper-proof, a prueba de entremetido (o sabotaje)

tandem trailer, remolque en tándem, (Ar) acoplado en tándem

tandem survey, (electromag) levantamiento con separación fija desplazable, levantamiento en tándem

tang, espiga, pieza de extensión

tangent galvanometer, brújula de tangentes

tangent screw, tornillo tangente de alidada

tangential, tangencial

— **compression,** compresión tangencial

— **force,** fuerza tangencial

tank, tanque, depósito, (Co) aljibe; (rr) ténder

— **barge,** lanchón (o barcaza, chalán) tanque

— **battery,** batería de tanques

— **bolt,** perno de tanque

— **bottoms,** sedimentos

— **cap,** tapa de depósito

— **car,** vagón tanque

— **farm,** patio de tanques

— **fittings,** accesorios (o piezas) para tanques

— **flume,** canal (o saetín) de tanque

— **gage,** indicador de nivel del tanque

— **stairway,** escalera de tanque

— **station,** patio de tanques

— **truck,** camión tanque

— **type agitator,** agitador tipo tanque

— **vent,** respiradero de tanques

tanker, buque tanque

tantalite, tantalita

tap, *n.* (tl) macho de tarraja, machuelo, toma; (tu) grifo; (el) derivación, toma de corriente; *v.* roscar a macho, atarrajar con rosca interior; taladrar

— **and dies,** terraja y dados, terraja y hembras de roscar

— **drill,** broca para macho

— **wrapping,** (tu) revestimiento plástico

tape, *n.* cinta (magnética, métrica, etc.); (el) cinta de aislar; *v.* medir (o forrar, envolver, etc.) con cinta

— **deck,** unidad de cinta, bobinadora de cinta magnética

— **gage,** escala de cinta

— **header,** cabecera de cinta

— **reader,** lector de registros gráficos

taper, *n.* ahusado, ahusamiento, despezo; *v.* ahusar, despezar

— **shank twist drill,** mecha espiral de espiga cónica

— **tap,** machuelo arrancasondas (o cónico), (Ve) pescador de rosca

tapered, ahusado

— **bearing,** cojinete de rodillos cónicos

— **rotary tap,** (fishing tl) macho rotatorio fusiforme

— **string,** sarta telescopiada

Glossary of the Petroleum Industry

— **tubing,** tubería de extremidad
cónica
tapper, herramienta eléctrica para
cortar roscas hembras
— **tap,** macho para roscar tuercas
tappet, levantaválvulas,
alzaválvulas
tapping machine, máquina
taladradora de tubería bajo
presión
tar, *n.* brea, alquitrán; *v.* embrear,
alquitranar (q.v. **pitch**)
— **sand,** arena impregnada de brea
tariff, arancel, tarifa, derecho de
aduanas
tarn, (g) lago de circo
taut line, cable teso
tax, impuesto, contribución,
gravamen
taxites, (g) taxitas
TBP, q.v. **true boiling point**
TC (toxic concentration),
concentración tóxica; q.v. **total
carbon**
**TCC (Thermofor catalytic
cracking),** crácking catalítico
Thermofor (q.v. **cracking**)
TCE, q.v. **trichloroethtlene**
**TCR (Thermofor catalytic
reforming),** reformación
catalítica Thermofor
TD, q.v. **total depth**
TDM, q.v. **time division
multiplexing**
tear faults, fallas por
desgarramiento
technical hydrocarbon,
hidrocarburos puros (o no
contaminados)
technician, (oc) técnico
tectonic, tectónico
— **earthquake,** sismo de
dislocación, temblor tectónico
— **lake,** lago de fractura
tectonics, (g) fenómenos tectónicos
tektites, (g) tectitas

TEL (tetraethyl lead), plomo
tetraetilo
teleclinometer, teleclinómetro
telegage, telegauge, teleindicador
telemeter, telémetro
telemetering, medición a distancia
teleprocessing network, (dp) red de
teleproceso
telescope, *n.* telescopio, catalejo; *v.*
enchufar, telescopiar
telescopic alidade, alidada
telescópica
telescopic joint, junta (o unión)
telescópica
telescoping derrick, torre
plegadiza, torre de extensión,
(Me) mástil telescopiable
telescoping mast, mástil de
extensión, mástil telescópico (o
plegadizo)
teleseismic records, sismogramas
de temblores lejanos
telltale, delator de nivel
telluric, telúrico
— **current,** (el) corriente telúrica
— **water,** agua telúrica
tellurium, telurio
tellurometer, telurómetro
temper, *n.* temple; *v.* (steel)
templar; (mortar) ablandar
— **color,** color de recocido
— **screw,** tornillo alimentador (o
regulador) (q.v. **feeding screw**)
temper-screw elevator rope, cable
elevador del tornillo
alimentador
temperature, temperatura
— **compensation,** compensación
termostática
— **controller,** regulador de
temperatura
— **correction,** corrección de
temperatura
— **density,** densidad-temperatura
— **drop,** bajada (o descenso) de
temperatura

— **gradient,** gradiente de
temperatura, gradiente térmico
(o geotérmico)
— **indicator,** termómetro, (Me)
medidor de temperatura
— **relief valve,** válvula de alivio de
temperatura
— **rise,** aumento de temperatura
tempered, recocido, templado
Tempilstick, lápiz termométrico
template, plantilla, gálibo, patrón,
(Co) cercha; (gf) tendido (o
patrón) de emisión-recepción;
(dp) modelo, patrón, plantilla,
pauta, molde
temporary guide base, base guía
provisional
tender, lote; (nt) falúa, bote de
servicio, (Me) tender; (cm)
convocatoria (o llamada) a
licitación
tensile
— **axial loading,** carga tensil sobre
el eje, carga tensil axial
— **strain,** esfuerzo de tensión
— **strength,** resistencia a la tensión,
resistencia tensora
tensimeter, manómetro
tensiometer, tensiómetro
tension, tensión; tracción
— **block,** motón de tensión
— **failure,** rotura causada por la
tensión
— **leg platform,** plataforma de
cables en tensión
— **pulley,** polea tensora (o de
gravedad)
— **riser,** (mar) montante (o tubo
subiente) en tensión
— **stress,** esfuerzo de tensión
— **wrench,** llave indicadora de
tensión
tent, tienda de campaña, carpa de
lona
tephrite, tefrita

tera (T), tera, *pref.* SI = 10^{12}; sistema
binario = 2^{40}
tertiary recovery, recuperación
terciaria
terephthalic acid, ácido tereftálico
term, término
terminal, *n.* (dp) terminal; (rr)
estación terminal; (el) borne,
borne de conexión; *a.* terminal,
final
— **bond,** enlace final
— **moraine,** (g) morena frontal,
morena terminal
— **node,** (dp) nodo de hoja, nodo
terminal
terms, condiciones
ternary system, (mt) sistema
ternario
terrace, (g) terraza, terraplén
terrain, terreno, topografía
— **correction,** corrección
topográfica, corrección por
terreno
terreplein, (g) terraplén
terrestrial magnetism,
magnetismo terrestre
tert-butylbenzene, butilbenceno
terciario
tertiary, terciario; (g) era terciaria
— **amyl methyl ether,** éter amil
metilo terciario
— **carbon,** (qm) carbono terciario
— **carbon atom,** átomo de carbono
terciario
— **hydrocarbon,** (qm)
hidrocarburo terciario
teschenite, teschenita
teschermacherite, teschemacherita
tesla (T), tesla: unidad de inducción
magnética
test, *n.* prueba, ensayo; *v.* probar,
ensayar
— **and set,** prueba y ajuste
— **coverage,** alcance (o cobertura)
de prueba

— **run,** pase (o ejecución, operación) de prueba
— **tube,** probeta, tubo de ensayo
tester, probador, ensayador
testing production, (prf) hacer ensayos (o pruebas) de producción
testing pump, bomba de prueba
tetracosane, tetracosano
tetracyclic, tetracíclico
tetradecane, tetradecano
tetradecene, tetradeceno
tetra-ethyl lead, plomo tetraetilo
tetragonal, tetrágono, tetragonal
tetrahedral, tetraédrico
tetrahedrite, (mn) tetraedrita, mineral de plata y cobre
tetralin, tetralín
tetramer, tetrámero
tetramethyl, *pref.* tetrametil-
— **lead,** tetrametilo de plomo
tetramethylhexadecane, tetrametilhexadecano (q.v. **crocetane)**
tetravalence, *n.* tetravalencia; **tetravalent,** *a.* tetravalente
textural variation, variación textural
texture, (g) contextura, textura
TFL, q.v. **through flow line**
thaw, deshielo
theodolite, teodolito
therm, termia: unidad de valor calorífico equivalente a 1.000 calorías ó 100.000 Btu
thermal, térmico, termal
— **breakdown,** descomposición térmica
— **conductivity,** conductividad térmica
— **cracking,** craqueo térmico, disociación térmica (q.v. **cracking, reforming)**
— **diffusion,** difusión térmica
— **efficiency,** eficiencia térmica, rendimiento térmico

— **insulation,** aislamiento térmico
— **metamorphism,** metamorfismo térmico
— **polymerization,** polimerización térmica
— **reforming,** reformación térmica
— **unit,** unidad térmica
thermistor, resistencia térmica
thermit welding, soldadura de termita
thermocatalytic cracking, cracking (o craqueo) termocatalítico, disociación termocatalítica
thermocline, termoclinal
thermocouple, par térmico, pila termoeléctrica, (Ar) termocupla
thermodynamic instability, inestabilidad termodinámica
thermodynamics, *n.* termodinámica
thermometer, termómetro
— **clamp,** sostén del termómetro
thermophone, termófono
thermoregulator, termoregulador
thermosetting, fraguado térmico
thermostat, termóstato
thermostatic control, control termostático
thermostatic stream trap, interceptor termostático de agua
thermosyphon, termosifón
thick, grueso, espeso
thicken, *v.* espesar, condensar; **thickener,** *n.* espesador
thickening, espesamiento
thickness, (g) espesor (o potencia) de un estrato
— **gage,** lengüeta calibradora, calibre de espesor
thief, muestreador, ladrón
— **formation,** formación ladrona (que absorbe el fluido de perforación)

— **hatch,** escotilla (o boca) de aforo, portezuela del muestreador
— **sand,** arena de escape, arena estéril por la cual se fuga el petróleo, (Ve) arena ladrona
thiefing, muestrear con ladrón
thin, *a.* delgado; (fl) diluído, ligero, ralo; *v.* adelgazar; desleír
— **out,** *n.* (g). acuñamiento; *v.* acuñarse, adelgazarse (q.v. **wedge out**)
thinning, adelgazamiento
thinolite, tinolita
thiol, tiol
thionizer, tionizador
thiophane, tiofano
thiophene, tiofeno
thiosulphate solution, tiosulfato
thistle tube, (la) tubo embudado (o de seguridad)
thixotropy, tixotropía
thread, *n.* (mc) rosca, filete; cuerda, hilo; *v.* roscar, enroscar, tarrajar, atarrajar, filetear
— **cleaner,** limpiador de rosca
— **crest,** cresta de filete
— **filler,** relleno de rosca
— **gage,** calibrador de filetes de tornillo
— **pitch,** paso de rosca
— **protector,** (tu) guardarrosca
— **root,** fondo de rosca
threaded, roscado, fileteado
— **coupling,** acoplamiento roscado
— **joint,** unión de rosca, acoplamiento
— **packing retainer ring,** anillo fiador roscado de la empaquetadura
threader, terraja
threading, ensartamiento, enroscado
— **machine,** máquina de roscar, terraja mecánica

three-point suspension, suspensión en tres puntos
three-stroking, (tu) desenrosque a seis manos
three-way valve, válvula de tres pasos
thribble board, (prf) plataforma astillero para tramos de tres tubos (q.v. **finger board, fourble board**)
throttle, *n.* (a) válvula de estrangulación; *v.* estangular, obturar
— **valve,** estrangulador, válvula de estrangulación
through flow line, a través de la tubería de producción
throughput, rendimiento total (o específico), capacidad de tratamiento (o de producción), caudal; volumen de materia prima tratada, productividad
throw, *n.* (g) desplazamiento vertical de una falla, (Ar) salto vertical, rechazo vertical; *v.* lanzar, rechazar
thru, q.v. **through**
thrust, empuje; embate; (g) corrimiento
— **ball bearing,** cojinete de bolas de empuje, (Ar) cojinete de empuje a bolillas
— **bearing,** cojinete de empuje
— **fault,** falla de escurrimiento (o de corrimiento)
— **roller bearing,** cojinete de empuje a rodillos
— **washer,** arandela de empuje
thruster, impulsor, propulsor
thumbscrew, tornillo de mano (o de orejas)
thumper, (gf) dispositivo (de antigua marca registrada) para dejar caer una pesa (como fuente sísmica)
Thuringian, turingiense

tidal anomaly, anomalía de marea
tide, marea
tideland, marisma
tie, *n.* ligadura, atadura, enlace; (gf) liga, unión (de puntos previamente observados); (rr) traviesa, durmiente, travesaño; *v.* atar, amarrar, afianzar, ligar
— **band,** banda de amarre
— **rod,** tirante (q.v. **truss rod**)
— **rod clamps,** abrazaderas de tirante
tiedown flange, brida con ganchos (o torniquetes) de anclaje
tight, (mc) apretado, ajustado; (ca) tieso, teso, atesado; (hd) estanco, hermético
— **formation,** formación compacta
— **well,** pozo exploratorio secreto
tightness, tensión, estrechez
tile, (roof) teja; (floor) baldosa, loseta, baldosín; azulejo, (Ar) mosaico, (Me) solera (cn) bloque hueco, (Ve) losa celular
— **baffle,** tabique de baldosa para desviación
till, (g) depósito de ventisquero
tillite, (g) tilita (q.v. **boulder clay**)
tilt, *n.* inclinación; declive; *v.* bascular, inclinarse, ladearse; (mu) forjar con martinete de báscula; (g) inclinarse
tilted iron, hierro forjado
tilting, (g) inclinación
— **mixer,** (cement) hormigonera volcadora
timber, *n.* madera; tronco; madero, cuartón; *v.* entibar, ademar; enmaderar
time, tiempo
— **bomb,** bomba de cronómetro, bomba graduada a tiempo
— **break,** (gf) instante de tiro (o de explosión, de detonación), origen del tiempo

— **constant,** (gf) constante de tiempo
— **datum,** origen del tiempo
— **delay,** (gf) retraso
— **division multiplexing,** (dp) multiplexión de división de tiempo
— **domain,** (gf) dominio temporal
— **lead,** defasamiento (q.v. **lead**)
— **line,** línea de tiempo
— **of contact,** período de contacto
— **of transmission of earth waves,** tiempo de propagación de las ondas sísmicas
— **scale,** escala de tiempo
— **series,** serie cronológica
— **slicing,** división (o segmentación) del tiempo
— **tie,** (gf) liga de tiempo (q.v. **tie**)
— **variant,** (gf) variante de tiempo
time-depth chart, gráfica de tiempo y profundidad
time-distance curve, curva de tiempo y distancia
timeout, compás de espera, intervalo
timer, sincronizador; cronómetro, registrador de tiempo
timing, sincronización
— **gear,** engranaje de distribución del encendido, engranaje regulador del encendido
— **line shutter,** (gf) obturador cronográfico
tin, estaño
— **plate,** hojalata
tinguaite, (g) tinguaita
tinting strength, capacidad colorante
tip, *n.* punta, boquilla; *v.* volcar, bascular; volcarse; ladearse; (mc) revestir (o chapear) la punta de una barra, etc., con metal más duro
tire, (rubber) neumático, goma, llanta, (Ar, Ur) cubierta, (Ve)

caucho; (iron) llanta, cerco, calce
— **carrier,** portaneumático
— **cushion,** almohadillado
— **gauge,** indicador de presión, manómetro de neumáticos
— **holder,** portaneumáticos
— **tube,** cámara, tubo interior
titanite, titanita
titer test, titración, titulación
title, título de propiedad
titration, análisis volumétrico, análisis por titulación
TOC q.v. **total oil content**
to datum correction, corrección al nivel de referencia
toe, (ma) gorrón; (sd) intersección soldada con metal de base; (tp) pie, base; punta
toggle, fiador atravesado
— **joint,** junta de codillo, unión acodillada
tolane, tolano (q.v. **diphenylacetylene)**
tolerance, tolerancia
toluene, tolueno (q.v. **methylbenzene)**
toluenesulphonic acid, ácido toluensulfónico
toluol, tolueno crudo (o sin refinar)
tombolo, (g) tómbolo
ton, tonelada
tong die, dado de tenazas
tong-line, cable de las tenazas (o llaves)
— **pulley,** polea para el cable de las tenazas
tong-crushed pipe, tubo mutilado por tenazas (o llaves)
tongs, (tl) alicates, tenazas; (prf) llaves, tenazas; (la) tenacillas, pinzas
tongue-and-groove joint, junta (o ensambladura) machihembrada
tongue-and-groove-joint union, unión de espiga y caja

tonnage, capacidad, tonelaje
tool, *n.* herramienta, utensilio, útil de trabajo; *v.* trabajar; labrar
— **crane,** aparejo (o grúa) para herramientas
— **extractor,** extractor de herramientas
— **gage,** calibrador para herramientas
— **guide,** guía de herramientas
— **joint,** rosca de unión de tubería vástago
— **pusher,** (oc) jefe de cuadrilla de perforadores, perforador en jefe
— **steel,** acero de herramientas
— **tightener,** apretador de herramientas
— **wrench,** llave de herramientas
— **wrench liner,** suplemento para llave de herramientas
toolbox, (mc) (dp) caja de herramientas
toolkit, juego (o estuche) de herramientas
toothed bar, barra dentada
top, *n.* parte superior, parte de arriba; (mountain) cima, cumbre; (cn) cúspide, ápice; cabeza, remate, coronilla, superficie; (tree) copa; *v.* (rf) descabezar, someter el crudo a destilación primaria profunda
— **a formation,** *v.* (g) encontrar un estrato, topar una formación
— **and bottom guided valve,** válvula con guías de tope y fondo
— **dead center,** punto muerto superior
— **kill,** (prf) matar el pozo desde arriba
— **steam,** vapor de cima
— **water,** agua superyacente
top-down development, desarrollo de lo más básico a lo menos

básico, desarrollo de arriba a
abajo
tops, petróleo descabezado,
destilados sin refinar que se
obtienen en la destilación
primaria
topaz, topacio
topographic, topográfico
— **anomaly,** anomalía topográfica
— **correction,** corrección
topográfica
— **expression,** expresión
topográfica
— **loading effect**, efecto de
topografía accidentada
topography, topografía
topology, topología
topotype, (paleo) topotipo
topped crude, petróleo reducido,
(Ur) petróleo descabezado
topper, destiladora atmosférica
topping, (rf) destilación primaria
profunda, destilación inicial,
(Me) descabezamiento (q.v.
skimming)
topsets, depósitos sedimentarios
superiores
topsoil, tierra vegetal (o mantillosa,
negra), (Me) tierra franca, (Ur)
tierra húmica
torbonite, turbonital (q.v. **oil shale**)
torch, soplete; antorcha
torpedo, carga explosiva; torpedo
— **reel,** carrete para el alambre del
torpedo
torpedoing, torpedeo, dinamitación
torque, momento torsional (o de
torsión), par motor
— **converter,** convertidor de
torsión
— **gage,** indicador de torsión
— **indicator,** indicador de torsión
— **wrench,** llave de torsión
torsion, torsión
— **angle,** ángulo de torsión
— **balance,** balanza de torsión

— **fiber,** fibra de torsión
— **moment,** momento de torsión
Tortonian, tortoniense
total, total
— **amount,** monto (o suma) total
— **carbon,** carbono total
— **correction,** corrección total
— **depth (TD),** profundidad total
— **maximum daily load**, carga
diaria máxima total
— **oil content**, contenido de
petróleo total
— **oxygen demand (TOD),**
demanda total de oxígeno
— **petroleum hydrocarbons
(TPH),** hidrocarburos de
petróleo totales
— **reflection,** reflexión total
— **solids (TS)**, total de sólidos
— **suspended particulates (TSS),**
particulados suspendidos totales
— **trihalomethanes (TTHMs),**
trihalomethanos totales
totally enclosed treating facility,
(ec) instalación de tratamiento
totalmente cerrada
tourmaline, (g) turmalina
tow, remolcar
— **boat,** remolcador (q.v. **tug boat**)
— **ring,** aro (o argolla) de remolque
— **tractor,** tractor remolcador
tower, torre
— **bottoms,** residuos de fondo de la
torre
— **derrick**, grúa de torre
— **drill**, perforadora de torre
— **still**, alambique de torre
towing winch, cabria remolcadora,
cabrestante para remolcar,
malacate de arrastrar
towline, cable de remolque
toxic, tóxico
toxin, toxina
TPH, q.v. **total petroleum
hydrocarbons**

trace, *n.* trazo; rastro, huella; (gf) línea de registro, traza sísmica; *v.* trazar; (top) comprobar el tránsito
— **analysis,** análisis de trazas
— **gather,** (gf) muestreo de trazas (q.v. **gather**)
— **program,** (dp) programa de rastreo (o de seguimiento)
tracer, rastreador; trazador
trachydolerite, dolerita traquítica
trachylyte, traquilita
trachyte, traquita
track, vía, línea, carrilera; senda; (magn tape) pista; (tractor) oruga, banda de rodamiento; riel
track-type trailer, remolque tipo oruga
traction, (mc) tracción; (r) arrastre
tractor, tractor
— **oil,** tractorina, combustóleo de tractores, tractóleo
trade, comercio, negocios, intercambio
— **winds,** vientos alisios
trademark, marca registrada (o de fábrica)
traffic, tránsito, tráfico, circulación de vehículos
trail, brecha, vereda, senda
trailer, carro de remolque, remolque, (Ar) acoplado
train, tren, serie de eventos repetitivos y sucesivos
trajectory, trayectoria
transceiver, transmisor-receptor
transcurrent fault, falla de rumbo (q.v. **strike-slip fault**)
transducer, transductor
transfer rate, velocidad de transferencia
transform, transformation, (mt) transformación
transformer, transformador
— **oil,** aceite para transformadores
transgression, (g) transgresión

transgressive overlap, capa superpuesta por el proceso de transgresión
transient, momentáneo, transitorio, temporal, pasajero
transistor chip, microplaqueta (o chip) de transistor
transit, (in) tránsito, teodolito
transition zone, (gf) zona de transición
translucent, translúcido
transmission, transmisión, cambio de velocidades
— **case,** caja de la transmisión (o de velocidades)
— **chain,** cadena de transmisión (o de mando)
— **coefficient,** (gf) coeficiente de transmisión
— **countershaft,** contraeje de velocidades
— **coupling,** empalme de transmisión
— **load,** demanda de transmisión
— **rope,** cable de transmisión
— **shaft,** eje de transmisión, eje motor
transmit, transmitir
transom, traviesa, travesaño
transparent, transparente
transponder, transponder
transport, (dp) mecanismo de transporte (o arrastre)
transportation, transporte, acarreo, transportación, conducción
transpressional basin, cuenca transtensiva
transverse, transversal, transverso
— **fault,** falla transversal
— **secondary waves,** ondas transversales secundarias (q.v. **shear secondary waves**)
— **section,** sección transversal
— **valley,** valle transversal

Glossary of the Petroleum Industry

— **wave,** onda transversal (o de cizallamiento) (q.v. **shear wave**)

trap, *n.* (tu) trampa, sifón; (petrol) interceptor, separador; (vapor) colector (o separador) de agua; (gas) colector de condensado; (g) trampa; (dp) desvío, salto no programado; *v.* atrapar

— **rock,** dolerita; roca trapeana

trass, (g) trass

travel, *n.* viaje, recorrido; *v.* viajar

— **indicator scale,** (va) escala de indicador de posición

— **point,** aguja de indicador

— **sub,** sub amortiguador

traveler block, motón corredizo (o viajero)

traveling

— **barrel pump,** bomba de cilindro corredizo (o móvil, viajero)

— **block,** polea viajera (o móvil)

— **crane,** grúa viajera, puente grúa

— **full-barrel rod pump,** bomba de varillas con cilindro enterizo móvil

— **liner-barrel rod pump,** bomba de varillas con cilindro interior móvil

— **valve,** válvula viajera, (Ve) válvula de arriba

— **cup,** taza (o copa) de válvula viajera

traveltime, (gf) tiempo de propagación

— **curves,** curvas dromocrónicas, curvas de tiempo y distancia

traverse, *n.* (mc) carrera, juego; (gf) perfil, sección; (tp) trazado, rodeo; *v.* atravesar; trazar; (mc) trasladar

— **board,** (tp) plancheta con alidada de mirilla

— **fault,** falla cruzada

— **survey,** trazado de un poligonal

traversing, trazar un poligonal

travertine, (g) travertino, toba calcárea

tread, *n.* escalón, peldaño; (pulley) rodamiento; (wheel) cara, llanta, rodadura; (a) anchura de vía, trocha, huella

treat, (qm) tratar

treating plant, planta de tratamiento

treblet, mandril, punzón

trellis drainage, drenaje acostillado

tremolite, tremolita

tremor, temblor de tierra

trench, (g) fosa; zanja, foso, trinchera; canal, cuneta (q.v. **ditch**)

— **slope,** talud de trinchera

trenching machine, cavazanjas

trend, *n.* dirección, curso, giro, tendencia; (g) rumbo general *v.* dirigirse, tender, inclinarse

trending east-west, etc., dirigido de este a oeste, etc.

trestle, viaducto de caballetes

triacontane, triacontano (q.v. **myricyl**)

triacontene, triaconteno

trial and error, tanteos, aproximaciones sucesivas; a fuerza de ensayo, por experiencia

trial run, pasada de prueba (o de comprobación)

triangle, triángulo

triangular, triangular

— **coordinate,** coordenada triangular (o trilineal)

— **spacing pattern,** espaciado de pozos en forma triangular

triangulation, triangulación

— **net,** red de triángulos

Triassic, triásico

triaxial, triaxial

tributary, (g) tributario

trichlorethylene, tricloroetileno

231

English - Spanish

trichloroacetic acid, ácido
  tricloroacético
triclinic, triclínico
tricone bit, barrena de tres conos
tricosane, tricosano
tricosadiyne, tricosadiino
tricyclic, tricíclico
tridecadiyne, tridecadiino
trigger, *n.* gatillo, disparador; *v.*
  activar
trigonometric, trigonométrico
trim, *n.* (carp) contramarcos; (lock)
  guarnición; (nt) desnivel de proa
  a popa; *v.* desbastar; montar
  contramarcos; (nt) adrizar
trimethyl, *pref.* trimetil-
trimethylbenzene, trimetilbenceno
trip, (prf) viaje de ida y vuelta de la
  tubería
— **finger,** trinquete
— **in,** meter en el pozo
— **out,** sacar del pozo
— **spear,** arpón de disparo
triplex, triple
— **pump,** bomba triple, bomba de
  tres cilindros
tripod, trípode
— **pendulum,** péndulo de trípode
tripping out, sacada de la tubería
triptane, triptano
tritetracontane, tritetracontano
tritriacontane, tritriacontano
trouble shooting, localización de
  errores (o de averías)
trough, (g) fosa marginal, (Ar)
  cubeta sedimentaria; (gf) valle
  (*op.* peak)*;* (q.v. **sedimentary
  basin**)
— **line,** (syncl) charnela sinclinal
troughing, artesonado
trowel, paleta, llana, (Me) plana,
  (Cu) cuchara
troy weight, peso de joyería: unidad
  es la libra de 12 onzas
truck, *n.* camión; (mc) carro,
  carretilla, juego de ruedas;

(tractor) bastidor de las orugas;
  v. transportar por camión
true, verdadero, real; (tp) en línea
  recta
— **amplitude recovery,** (gf)
  recuperación de amplitud
  verdadera
— **boiling point,** punto verdadero
  de ebullición
— **course,** rumbo verdadero
— **density,** densidad verdadera (q.v.
  optical density)
— **equilibrium,** equilibrio
  verdadero
— **ground motion,** movimiento
  verdadero de la tierra (o del
  terreno)
— **north,** norte verdadero (o
  geográfico)
— **up,** *v.* rectificar, alinear,
  enderezar
— **velocity,** velocidad verdadera
— **vertical depth (TVD),**
  profundidad vertical verdadera
truncated anticline, anticlinal
  truncado
truncated mountain, montaña
  truncada
truncation, (g) (mt) (dp)
  truncamiento
— **effect,** effecto de truncado
— **error,** (dp) error de
  truncamiento (q.v. **roundoff
  error**)
trunk pipeline, oleoducto troncal;
  gasoducto troncal
trunnion, muñón, gorrón
— **bracer,** abrazadera de muñones
— **mounted,** montado en gorrones
truss, *n.* armadura, (Ar) reticulado,
  caballete; *v.* armar, atirantar
— **rod,** tirante (q.v. **tie rod**)
try cock, grifo de prueba
TS, q.v. **total solids**
TSS, q.v. **total suspended solids**
tsunami, tsunami

TTHMs, q.v. **total trihalomethanes**

tube, tubo; (a) tubo interior, cámara

— **beader,** bordeador de tubos, mandril de bordear tubos

— **bundle,** haz de tubos

— **cleaner,** limpiatubos

— **expander,** abocinador (o ensanchador) de tubos, expandidor de tubos

— **hanger,** suspensor de tubos

— **header,** cabeza de tubos, cabezal de tubos

— **heater,** calentador de tubos

— **sheet,** placa portatubos, placa de tubos

— **still,** alambique de tubos (q.v. **pipe still**)

— **support,** soporte para tubos

tube-and-tank process, refinación a tubo y tanque

tubescope, tuboscopio

tubing, tubería de producción, tubo productor, entubamiento, (Ve) tubería de disparo

— **anchor,** ancla del tubo de producción

— **and sucker rod line,** cable para tubería de producción y varillas de bombeo

— **bleeder,** válvula de purga para la tubería de producción

— **block,** aparejo para el entubado

— **board,** plataforma-astillero para el entubamiento

— **catcher,** agarrador de tubo de producción

— **clamps,** abrazaderas de tubería

— **disc,** disco de la tubería de producción

— **elevators,** elevadores de tubo de producción

— **hangers,** colgaderos (o suspensores) del tubo de producción

— **head,** cabeza de tubería de producción

— **hooks,** ganchos de maniobra para tubería de produción

— **oil saver,** economizador de petróleo para tubería

— **packer,** obturador de la tubería de producción

— **plug,** tapón para entubado

— **pressure,** presión en la tubería de producción

— **pump,** bomba introducida con la tubería de producción

— **ring,** anillo de tubería de producción

— **rotator,** volteador de la tubería de producción

— **socket,** enchufe pescatubo

— **spear,** arpón pescatubo

— **spider,** araña (o estrella) para tubería de producción, cubo de garras (o de cuñas dentadas)

— **strings,** sartas de producción

— **stripper,** empaquetadura limpiadora de tubería de producción

— **sub,** unión substituta para tubería de producción

— **swab,** limpiatubos (o escobillón) para tubería de producción

— **tail piece,** apoyo inferior del entubamiento

— **tongs,** tenaza (o llave) para tubería de producción

tubular, tubular

— **jointing,** (g) disyunción tubular

tuff, toba

tug pulley, polea lateral de la rueda motora; polea de remolque (o arrastre)

tugboat, lancha remolcadora (q.v. **tow boat**)

tugger line, cable de labor

tumbler, seguro, fiador, retén

tune, sintonizar, afinar

tungsten, tungsteno

— **steel,** acero tungsteno
— **wire,** alambre de tungsteno, alambre de wolfram
tuning fork, (la) diapasón
tunnel, túnel, socavón
turbidity, turbieza
turbine, turbina
— **mixer,** mezcladora de turbina
— **pump,** bomba de turbina
turbine-driven generator, generador a turbina
turboaerator, turboaereador
turboblower, turbosoplador
turbocompressor, turbocompresor
turboexpander, turboexpansora
turbogenerator, turbogenerador
turbogrid plate, bandeja de turborejilla
turbulence, turbulencia
turbulent flow, flujo turbulento
turf, (g) turba (q.v. **peat**)
turkey shoot, (gf) tiro de comparación
turn, *n.* vuelta, revolución, giro; (r) recodo; *v.* girar, revolver, hacer girar
turnaround, paro de revisión; tiempo de respuesta (o de inversión, de vuelta); (dp) tiempo de computación; (nt) tiempo de viraje
turnbuckle, torniquete, tensor
turning
— **arbor,** árbol de ballesta en un torno
— **joint,** charnela
— **point,** punto de cambio
— **radius,** radio de viraje
turnkey contract, (cm) contrato llave en mano
turnover of inventories, (cm) rotación de inventarios
turntable, placa (o mesa) giratoria
turpentine, trementina, aguarrás
— **oil,** aceite de aguarrás
turret, torrecilla, torre

turret-moored, amarrado a torre
TVD, q.v. **true vertical depth**
twin, gemelo
— **crank,** manivelas gemelas
— **pitman,** bielas gemelas
twinning, procedimiento para formar cristales gemelos
twist, torsión, torcedura
twistoff, rotura por torsión
— **failure,** rotura por torsión
two-dimensional, bidimensional, de dos dimensiones
two-pen gage, indicador de dos plumas
two-point seismograph, sismógrafo de dos componentes
two-position differential gap action, acción por intervalo diferencial de dos posiciones
two-stage pressure reducer, reductor de presión en dos etapas
two-step thread, (tu) rosca en dos series
two-stroking, (tu) desenrosque a cuatro manos
two-way branch clevis, conexión en Y
two-way radio communication, comunicación radiotelefónica en dos direcciones
two-way rasp, (fishing tl) raspa de dos caras
tying in, empate de secciones a la tubería principal
type, tipo
typical, característico
typomorphic minerals, minerales tipomorfos

U

U, q.v. **uranium**

Glossary of the Petroleum Industry

U bend, conexión en U (q.v. return bend)

U bolt, perno U, grampa U

U groove weld, soldadura de chaflán en U

U iron, pieza de hierro en U, hierro U

U shaped, en forma de U

U tube gage, indicador de tubo en U, manómetro en U

UHF (ultrahigh frequency), frecuencia ultraelevada (o extra-alta)

ULCC (ultra-large crude carrier), (nt) tanquero ultragrande

ultimate, último, final

— production, producción final

— recovery, producción final

— stress, esfuerzo de rotura

ultrafining, ultrafining

ultraforming, ultraforming

ultramicrometer, ultramicrómetro

unbedded deposits, (g) depósitos a trochemoche, depósitos mezclados sin formar estratos definidos

unconformity, (g) discordancia

unconsolidated, (g) no consolidado

unconverted olefins, olefinas no convertidas

undampened, no amortiguado

undecadiene, undecadieno

undecadiyne, undecadiino

undecane, undecano

undecene, undeceno

underbalanced, con insuficiente contrapeso

— drilling, perforación bajoequilibrada (con presión del pozo inferior a la de la formación)

underclay, capa de arcilla debajo de una capa de carbón

undercut, socavar

underflow, (dp) desbordamiento de la capacidad mínima, subdesbordamiento

underground storage, almacenaje subterráneo

underlie, subyacer

underline, subrayar

underlying, subyacente

undermine, socavar

undermining, (g) socavamiento

underpull jack, caballete de mando por debajo

underreamer, ensanchador (o escariador) de fondo (por debajo de la tubería de revestimiento)

undersaturation, saturación insuficiente

undersigned, (cm) firmante, infrascrito

underslung, colgante

underthrust, (g) bajoescurrimiento

— fault, (falla de) bajoescurrimiento

underwater, sumergido

underwriter, (insur) asegurador

undirectional flow, flujo no dirigido

undurated, (g) suelto, no consolidado

ungear, desengranar, desembragar, desconectar

uniaxial, uniaxial

unicellular organism, organismo unicelular

unifining, unifining

uniform, uniforme, homogéneo, constante; parejo

uniformity, uniformidad

union, unión, junta, empalme

unisol, unisol

unissued stock, (cm) acciones disponibles

unit, n. unidad, conjunto, grupo; a. unitario

— matrix, (dp) matriz de unidad (o de identidad)

unitization, (mc) unificación, combinación de varios motores (o funcionamientos); (pr) consolidación de varios campos petroleros

unitize, *v.* (mc) unificar, combinar en uno; (pr) consolidar el desarrollo de varios campos petroleros

universal chuck, mandril universal

universal joint, unión universal, junta universal, cardán

— **crude transfer,** junta universal de trasiego de crudo

unkink, desensortijar

unleaded sample, muestra de gasolina sin tetraetilo de plomo

unlevelled land, terreno desnivelado (o desigual)

unlimited liability, (cm) responsabilidad ilimitada

unloading, descarga; (nt) alijo

unmanned submarine, submarino no tripulado

unoriented, desorientado

unsaturated hydrocarbons, hidrocarburos no saturados

unsaturates, substancias no saturadas

unstable, inestable

unthrown, (g) levantado

UOP alkylation, alcohilación UOP

UPC (Universal Product Code) Código Universal de Productos

update, actualizar, poner al día

updip, buzamiento arriba

updraft convection section, sección de convección de tiro hacia arriba

upgrade, *n.* mejora del rendimiento (o servicio, etc.); *v.* mejorar, elevar de grado (o calidad, etc.)

uphill, cuesta arriba

uphole, a boca de pozo, pozo arriba

— **time,** (gf) tiempo vertical, tiempo de pozo

upkeep, conservación, mantenimiento

upland moon, (g) turbera emergida, turbera en forma de domo

uplift, (g) levantamiento, ascenso

upper, superior

— **bridging plug,** (prf) tapón puente superior

upright fold, pliegue parado (o normal) (q.v. **normal fold**)

upset

— **tubing,** q.v. **external upset ends**

— **wrinkles,** (tu) arrugas de doblez, arrugas en el interior de la curva al doblar un tubo

— **full strength joint,** acoplamiento semirás de recalcado exterior

upstream, corriente arriba

upstroke, carrera ascendente

upstructure, en la parte alta de la estructura geológica; estructura arriba

upthrown, (g) levantado

uptime, tiempo productivo (o activo)

upward compatibility, compatibilidad ascendente

uraninite, (mn) uraninita (radio y uranio)

urea dewaxing, desparafinación con urea

uric acid, ácido úrico

USC (unified soil classification; United States code), clasificación unificada del suelo; código de los Estados Unidos

useful load, carga útil

user friendly, fácil de utilizar, cómodo (o "amigable") para el usuario

utility guide frame, bastidor de servicio (o de entrada)

236

energía eléctrica, agua, combustible, etc.)

utilized capacity, capacidad aprovechada

UTM (Universal Transverse Mercator projection)

UV (ultraviolet), ultravioleta

V

V, q.v. **vanadium; volt**

V belt, correa trapezoidal, correa en V

— **drive,** transmisión por correa en V

V-belt sheave, roldana para correa trapezoidal

V-port plug, (va) vástago de orificio en V

V-shaped, en forma de V

vacuum, *n.* vacío; *a.* al vacío, en vacío, vacuo

— **control,** control al vacío

— **distillation,** destilación al vacío

— **distilling unit,** unidad de destilación al vacío

— **filter,** filtro de vacío

— **gage,** vacuómetro, indicador de vacío

— **indicating gage,** vacuómetro, indicador de vacío

— **pump,** bomba de vacío

— **relief valve,** ventosa al vacío, válvula reguladora de vacío

— **still,** alambique al vacío

— **trap,** interceptor al vacío

— **tube,** tubo al vacío

— **vapor heat exchanger**, intercambiador de calor con vapor

vadose water, agua meteórica, agua de gravedad

valence, valencia

valid, válido

validity check, (dp) verificación de validez (o de racionalidad)

valley, valle; (gf) q.v. **trough**

valuation, valía, tasa, avalúo

value, valor

valve, válvula

— **actuation,** mando de las válvulas

— **arrangement,** disposición de las válvulas

— **box,** caja (o registro) de válvula

— **cage,** cámara (o jaula) de válvula

— **chamber,** cámara de válvula

— **clearance,** espacio libre de una válvula, luz de la válvula

— **cock,** grifo de válvula

— **control,** mando (o control) de las válvulas

— **cooling,** enfriamiento de las válvulas

— **cup,** copa de válvula

— **face,** cara de una válvula

— **grinder,** rectificadora (o esmeriladora, refrentador) de válvulas

— **groove,** ranura de válvula

— **guide,** guía de válvula

— **head,** cabeza de válvula

— **in head,** válvula a la culata

— **inserts,** asientos cambiables (o insertados) de válvula

— **jacket,** camisa de válvula

— **lifter,** levantaválvula

— **plug,** macho de válvula

— **push rod,** barra (o varilla) de empuje de válvula

— **rod,** varilla de válvula

— **rod sub,** unión substituta para vástago de válvulas

— **seat,** asiento de válvula, (Ve) silla

— **seat puller,** extractor de asientos de válvula

— **spear,** arpón pescaválvulas

— **spring,** resorte de válvula

— **spring cover,** tapa (o cubierta) de resorte de válvula

— **spring seat,** asiento de resorte de válvula
— **stem,** vástago de válvula
— **stem adjuster,** ajustador de vástago de válvula
— **stem bushing,** buje de vástago de válvula
— **tappet,** botador de válvula, levantaválvula
— **tappet clearance,** luz del levantaválvula
— **timing,** regulación de las válvulas, sincronización de las válvulas
— **travel,** carrera (o recorrido) de una válvula
valve-grinding compound, pasta para pulir (o esmerilar) válvulas
valve-in-head, válvula en la culata
vanadium (V), vanadio
vane pump, bomba de aleta (o aletas)
vapor, vapor
— **baffle,** desviador de vapor
— **barrier,** barrera de vapor
— **lock,** falla causada por la formación de burbujas en un motor, traba de vapor
— **phase hydrodesulfurization,** hidrodesulfuración en fase de vapores
— **pressure,** presión de vapor (Ar) tensión de vapor
— **recovery plant,** planta para recuperación de vapor
— **temperature,** temperatura del vapor
— **tight,** hermético (o estanco) al vapor
vapor-phase
— **cracking,** crácking por el método de fase de vapor
— **process,** método de fase de vapor
— **refining,** refinación por el método de fase de vapor

— **treating process,** tratamiento por el método de fase de vapor
vaporimeter, vaporímetro
vaporization temperature, emperatura de vaporización
vaporizer, vaporizador
vaporizing point, punto de vaporización
vara, vara: antigua unidad española de longitud equivalente a unos 85 centímetros
variator, (in) variador
variegated, abigarrado
varnish, barniz
— **remover,** disolvente de barniz
varve, varve, capa de cieno
vaseline, vaselina
VDL (variable density log), registro de densidad variable
vegetation, vegetación
vein, (g) filón, veta; mena (q.v. **dike**)
— **accompaniments,** (g) séquito de filón, esquizolitos
velocity, velocidad
— **bed,** (gf) capa de velocidad
— **curve,** curva de la velocidad
— **distribution,** (gf) distribución de velocidades
— **head,** altura de velocidad de un fluido, carga de velocidad, altura dinámica
— **inversion,** inversión de velocidad
— **layer,** (gf) capa de velocidad
vent, respiradero, orificio de escape, ventosa
— **cock,** llave de respiración (o de ceba)
— **riser,** tubo ascendente del respiradero
— **valve,** válvula de respiradero
ventifact, gliptolita
ventilation, ventilación
Venturi meter, venturímetro, medidor (o contador) venturi
Venturi tube, tubo venturi

Venturi meter, venturímetro, medidor (o contador) venturi

Venturi tube, tubo venturi

venylacetylene, venilacetileno. (q.v. butenyne)

vermiculite, vermiculita

vernier, nonio, vernier

— caliper, calibre de nonio

vertebrate, vertebrado

vertical, vertical

— component magnetic field, (gf) campo magnético de componente vertical

— fault, falla vertical

— gravimeter, gravímetro vertical

— interval, intervalo vertical

— magnetic anomaly, anomalía magnética vertical

— magnetic intensity, intensidad magnética vertical

— projection, proyección vertical

— scale exaggerated, escala vertical exagerada

— section, sección vertical

— stack, apilamiento vertical

— vertical seismic profiling (VSP), perfilaje sísmico vertical

— time, (gf) tiempo vertical

— travel, dromocrónica vertical

vertically loaded anchor, ancla de leva vertical

vesicle, vesículas

vesicular, vesicular

vessel, vasija, recipiente; (nt) barco, buque, embarcación; (rf) recipiente (tanques, cilindros, cámaras, etc.)

vesuvianite, vesuvianita

VGC, q.v. viscosity gravity constant

VI, q.v. viscosity index

vibrating mud screen, colador vibratorio, colador trepidante para el lodo

vibration, vibración, oscilación

— dampener, amortiguador de vibraciones

— insulation, aislamiento de vibraciones

vibroseis, (gf) vibroseis (antigua marca de Conoco), camión vibrador, vibrador hidráulico

village, pueblo

vinyl acetylene, vinilacetileno

vinyl chloride, cloruro de vinilo

vinylation, vinilación

vinylbenzene, vinilbenceno

virgation, (gf) virgación

virgin stock, aceite virgen

visbreaker, viscoreductora, reductora de viscosidad

visbreaking, viscorreducción

viscosimeter, viscosímetro

viscosity, viscosidad

— breaker, separador de viscosidades

— curve, curva de viscosidad

— gravity constant, índice de viscosidad-gravedad

— index, índice de viscosidad

— meter, viscosímetro

— yield, rendimiento de viscosidad

viscous, viscoso

— flow, flujo viscoso

— neutral oil, aceite neutro viscoso

— oil, aceite viscoso

vise, prensa de tornillo, tornillo de banco, cárcel, (Ur) morsa, (Ar) sargento

— grips, mordazas de una morsa

visibility, visibilidad

vitric tuff, toba de cenizas

vitrified clay, barro vitrificado

vitrified glazed clay pipe, tubería de barro vitrificado

VLCC (very large crude carrier), (nt) tanquero gigante: mayor que los convencionales pero menor que los ULCC. (q.v. ULCC)

volatile, volátil
— **oil,** aceite volátil (q.v. **essential oil)**
— **organic compounds,** compuestos orgánicos volátiles
volcanic, volcánico
— **ash,** ceniza volcánica
— **bomb,** bomba volcánica
— **breccia,** brecha volcánica
— **eruption,** erupción volcánica
— **glass,** vidrio volcánico (q.v. **obsidian)**
— **neck,** cuello volcánico
— **rock,** roca volcánica
— **sand,** arena volcánica
volcanism, volcanismo
volcano, volcán
volt (V), voltio: símbolo SI de potencial eléctrico
voltage, voltaje
— **curve,** curva de tensión eléctrica (o de voltaje)
— **regulator,** regulador de voltaje
volt-ampere (va), voltamperio
voltmeter, voltímetro
volume, volumen
— **control,** control de volumen
— **control circuit,** circuito de control de volumen
— **tank, (gas p)** tanque compensador
volumetric, volumétrico
— **efficiency,** eficiencia volumétrica
vortex, vórtice
voucher, comprobante
VSP, q.v. **vertical seismic profiling**
vug, caverna, cavidad en una roca
vugular porosity, porosidad de disolución
vulcanism, plutonismo, vulcanismo
vulcanization, vulcanización
vulcanize, vulcanizar

W, q.v. **watt; wolfram**
wabble, bambolear, balancear, oscilar (q.v. **wobble)**
— **failure,** (prf) falla por bamboleo
wad, taco, grafito
wagon, vagón, carro, carretilla
— **tongue,** lanza para remolque
walk, n. pasillo
— **a bed,** v. (g) recorrer el afloramiento de un estrato para cartografiarlo
— **through,** (dp) revisión
walking
— **beam,** balancín
— **beam pump,** bomba de balancín
— **crane,** grúa móvil (o rodante)
walkway, pasarela, balconcillo elevado
wall, pared; muralla
— **core,** núcleo lateral, (Ar) testigo de pared
— **hook,** gancho centrador de barrena
— **packer,** obturador de pared (para sellar las paredes del estrato)
— **sampler,** cogemuestras de las paredes del estrato
— **scraper,** escariador de las paredes de un pozo
— **thickness,** (tu) espesor
walnut, nogal
warehouse, almacén, bodega, depósito (q.v. **storeroom)**
warp, n. comba, torcimiento; **warped,** v. torcido, combado
warping, combado, doblegado
wash, lavado
— **pipe,** (fishing tl) tubo de lavado
— **tower,** torre depuradora
washer, (mc) arandela; (sand) lavadora, (Ve) guasa

Glossary of the Petroleum Industry

washing, (g) lavaje, remoción (q.v.
   denudation)
washout, derrumbe,
   derrumbamiento, socavamiento,
   arrastre
washover string, (fishing tl) sarta
   de lavado
waste, estopa; desperdicio
— disposal, destrucción de
   desperdicios (o de desechos, de
   basura)
— gas, (rf) gas de desecho (o de
   desperdicio)
— heat, calor perdido
— heat boiler, caldera de calor
   perdido
— lubrication, lubricación con
   hilacha
— water, agua de desperdicio
wasteload allocation, (ec)
   asignación de carga de
   desperdicios
watch, reloj de bolsillo; vigilancia,
   cuidado, observación
water, agua
— blender, (rf) mezcladora de agua
— casing, tubería de revestimiento
   intermedia (q.v. intermediate
   casing)
— conditioning unit, planta para
   acondicionamiento de aguas
— coning, conificación del agua
— cooler, enfriador de agua
— cooling, enfriamiento por agua
— cushion, columna de agua
   amortiguadora
— density, densidad del agua
— depth, tirante, profundidad del
   agua
— disposal, (pr) eliminación del
   agua salada
— drive, empuje hidrostático (o
   hidráulico)
— encroachment, intrusión de las
   aguas marginales
— flooding, inyección de agua

— gage, indicador de nivel de agua
— gage cock, grifo indicador de
   nivel de agua, grifo de
   confrontación (o de
   manómetro)
— gage illuminator, iluminador de
   indicador de nivel de agua
— gap, (g) valle de drenaje, (Ar)
   quebrada
— hammer, ariete hidráulico
— immersion test, prueba de
   inmersión en agua
— jacket, camisa de agua
— knockout, separación del agua
   del petróleo; separador
— leaching, percolación de agua
— leg, (cl) placa de agua, hervidero;
   (pr) asentador preliminar
— level, nivel de agua
— line, (nt) línea de agua
— meter, contador (o medidor) de
   agua
— of compaction, agua de
   expulsión
— pipe, tubo de agua, caño (o tubo,
   cañería) de agua
— plane, (g) capa (o napa) de agua
   subterránea
— pump, bomba de agua
— scrubber, depurador por agua
— seal, (bm) cierre hidráulico,
   cierre de agua
— shed, hoya hidrográfica
— shut off test, prueba de la
   aislación del agua
— softener, generador de agua
   dulce, suavizador (o
   ablandador) de agua
— soluble oil, aceite soluble en
   agua
— string, (prf) tubería de
   revestimiento final, (Ar)
   columna aisladora (q.v. oil
   string)

— **table,** (derrick) marco base del
portapoleas de corona; (cn)
botaguas, retallo
de derrame; (g) napa freática,
lámina acuífera, (Cu) tabla de
agua, (Ve) mesa de agua
— **table beam,** viga lateral del
marco base del portapoleas de
corona
— **vapor,** vapor de agua
— **wash tower,** torre de lavado con
agua
— **well,** pozo de agua
water-based mud, lodo a base de
agua
water-cooled engine, motor
enfriado por agua
water-jacketed coil heater,
serpentín calentador con camisa
de agua
water-level gage, indicador de nivel
de agua (q.v. **water gage cock**)
water-treating chemical,
substancia química para
regenerar el agua
water-tube boiler, caldera de tubos
watercourse, conducto de la
barrena (para el fluido de
perforación)
watered out, invadido por agua
waterfall, salto, cascada, catarata,
caída de agua
waterflood, inyección de agua
watermelon, (bm) peso sobre la
unión giratoria del cable de las
varillas de succión
waterproof, impermeable (q.v.
impervious)
watershed, (g) divisoria de aguas
watertight, impermeable
watt (W), vatio, (Me) watt: unidad
SI de fuerza, igual a un joule por
segundo
— **meter,** vatímetro
wave, (gf) (radio) onda; (mar) ola

— **breaking perforations,** orificios
rompeolas (en plataformas de
concreto)
— **mark,** impresión de ola
— **period,** periodo de ola
— **train,** tren (o grupo) de ondas
wave-built terrace, (g) terraza de
sedimentos marinos (aportados
por las olas)
wave-cut terrace, terraza cortada
por la acción de las olas
waveform, (gf) forma de onda
wavefront, frente de ondas
wavelength, longitud de onda
wavelet, (gf) ondícula
wax, cera; parafina
— **chiller,** congelador de parafina
— **crystallization modifier,**
modificador de la cristalización
de parafina
— **distillate,** destilado parafínico
— **filter,** filtro desparafinador
— **fractionation,** fraccionamiento
de parafina
— **molding,** moldeo de parafina
— **oil,** aceite parafínico
— **plant,** fábrica (o planta) de
parafina
— **sweater,** cámara de resudación
de parafina
— **sweating,** (rf) resudamiento de la
parafina
wax-free oil, aceite sin parafina
wax-sweating stove, estufa para
resudamiento de parafina
way, sendero, camino, vía; modo de
obrar
weak acid, ácido débil
wear and tear, desgaste, deterioro
wear sleeve, (tu) protector
wear sub, sub sacrificable
wearing surface, superficie de
desgaste
weather, (atmos) tiempo

Glossary of the Petroleum Industry

weathered crude petroleum, petróleo crudo oreado (o intemperizado)

weathered layer, (gf) capa superficial, horizonte de baja velocidad sísmica

weathering, (g) denudación, erosión, meteorización de las rocas; (gf) intemperismo (q.v. **low velocity layer**)

— **belt,** (g) zona de desgaste (o disolución)

— **correction,** (gf) corrección para tomar en cuenta la denudación de la capa superficial

— **process,** (gas) método de tratamiento al aire libre, evaporación al aire libre (de ciertas substancias de la gasolina derivada de gas natural)

weatherometer, oreómetro

weatherproof, a prueba de intemperie

weaving, (sd) soldadura de tejido (o de vaivén)

weber (wb), weber: medida SI del flujo magnético

wedge, *n.* (mc) (g) cuña, calce; *v.* calzar, acuñar

— **bolt,** perno cabeza de cuña

— **edge,** estrato cuña

— **fault,** falla cuneiforme (o de cuña), falla en clave de arco (q.v. **keystone fault**)

— **out,** *n.* (g) acuñamiento, adelgazamiento; *v.* acuñarse, adelgazarse

— **point crowbar,** barra de punta cuneiforme

wedging, (g) encuñamiento, acuñamiento

weep hole, lloradero

weight, peso; pesa

— **drop,** (gf) caída de una pesa (como fuente sísmica) (q.v. **thumper**)

weighted array, (gf) arreglo pesado

weighted least squares, cuadrados mínimos (o mínimos cuadrados) ponderados

weighting materials, materiales densificantes

weights, pesas

— **for analytical balance,** pesas de balanza de precisión

weir, vertedero, rebosadero, presa

weld, *n.* soldadura; *v.* soldar

— **leak clamps,** abrazaderas para cerrar fugas en soldaduras

welded joint, junta (o unión) soldada

welder, (oc) soldador; (ma) soldadora

welding, soldadura

— **clamp,** abrazadera de soldar

— **electrode,** electrodo para soldar

— **electrode holder,** portaelectrodo

— **ell,** L para soldar, L soldable

— **fittings,** conexiones de soldar

— **flange** brida para conexión a soldadura

— **ground,** tierra de la soldadura

— **hose,** manguera de soldar

— **leads,** cables conductores

— **neck flange,** brida de cuello

— **rod,** varilla para soldar

— **saddle,** silla para soldadura

— **slip on flange,** brida corrediza

— **tee,** T para soldar

— **torch,** antorcha (o soplete) de soldar

— **wire,** alambre de soldadura

weldment, pieza soldada

well, pozo

— **assorted conglomerate,** (g) conglomerado bien surtido

— **casing,** tubería de revestimiento

— **density,** densidad de pozos, número de pozos por hectárea

— **log,** registro (o informe) diario de perforación; perfil (o corte) geológico de pozo

— **screen,** tubo de revestimiento perforado
— **servicer,** equipo de limpieza de pozos
— **shooting,** (g) detonaciones sismográficas realizadas en pozos profundos; (pr) voladura en el fondo del pozo para crear hendiduras
wellbore, hoyo, agujero
wellhead, cabezal de pozo
— **connector,** conector (o empalmador) del cabezal del pozo
— **housing,** armazón (o funda) del cabezal
— **price,** precio a bocapozo
well-measuring meter, indicador de metraje adjunto al carretel de la cuerda de medición
well-measuring reel, carrete para la cuerda de medición de profundidad
welt, (cn) ribete; (carp) refuerzo, costurón
west, oeste
— **east,** de oeste a este (O a E)
— **by north,** oeste cuarta al norte (O 1/4 al N)
— **by south,** oeste cuarta al sudoeste (O 1/4 SO)
— **northwest,** oesnoreste (ONO)
— **of north,** oeste del norte (O del N)
— **southwest,** oessudoeste (OSO)
wet, *n.* mojado, húmedo, impregnado; *v.* mojar, humedecer
— **bulb temperature,** temperatura de ampolleta mojada
— **Christmas tree,** árbol de navidad (submarino) mojado (sin cámara impermeable)
— **gas,** gas húmedo
— **natural gas,** gas natural húmedo
— **oil,** petroleo húmedo

— **sleeve,** camisa en contacto con el agua
— **submersible,** sumergible inundado
wetting, *a.* humectante
Weymouth formula, fórmula Weymouth para calcular el flujo de gas en tubería de gran diámetro
wheel, rueda
— **alignment,** alineación (o alineamiento) de las ruedas
— **spider,** maza y rayos de una rueda
wheelbarrow, carretilla
wheeled, rodado, con ruedas
— **rod guide coupling,** uniones rodadas de guía para varillas
whipstock, (prf) desviador, guiabarrena, (Ar) guiasondas
— **orientation,** orientación del desviador (o guiasondas)
whirler cementing collar, collar de remolino para cementar
whirler shoe, zapata de remolino
whistle valve, válvula del pito
white, blanco
— **lead,** albayalde
— **metal,** metal blanco
— **noise,** (gf) ruido blanco, energía errática
— **oil,** aceite blanco, aceite altamente refinado
— **spirits,** espíritu de petróleo (q.v. **petroleum spirits**)
whiten, (gf) uniformización de amplitud
wholesale, al por mayor
WHSV, peso/hora/velocidad espacial
wick, mecha, pabilo
— **feed lubrication,** lubricación por mecha
wicker, (ca) alambres rotos que se proyectan hacia fuera; (fishing tl) garras roscadas

— **thread,** rosca dividida

widespacing, espaciar los pozos ampliamente

wild gasoline, gasolina no estabilizada

wild well, pozo fuera de control

wildcat, pozo exploratorio, perforación de ensayo, pozo de cateo

wimble, berbiquí; barrena

winch, malacate, cabrestante, montacargas, huinche, guinche

wind, viento

— **gap,** ventisquero

— **gust,** ráfaga, racha de viento

— **load capacity,** (derrick) resistencia al viento

winding, arrollamiento, devanado

wind-made crossbedding, estratificación entrecruzada eólica

windlass, torno, malacate, montacarga, cabria, (Ar) guinche de mano

window, ventana, ventanilla; (g) peladura, abertura ocasionada por la erosión y por la cual aflora el estrato subyacente

windshield, parabrisas

windward, barlovento

wing, ala, aleta; (cn) alero

— **connection,** conexión de orejas

— **nut,** tuerca de aletas, tuerca mariposa

— **union,** una de las ramas del árbol de conexiones

wing-screw, tornillo de mariposa

wiper, limpiador, limpiaparabrisas, desempañador; (mc) álabe, leva

— **ring,** anillo enjugador

wire, *n.* alambre, cable de acero delgado; *v.* alambrar

— **brush,** cepillo de alambre

— **cable,** cable de alambre

— **cable clip,** grapas para cable de acero

— **cloth,** tela metálica

— **conduit,** conducto de cable

— **gage,** calibrador de alambre

wire-line, cable de alambre; (prf) cable de las poleas, cable de acero

— **clamp,** abrazadera para línea y cable de perforación

— **core catcher,** sacanúcleos a cable

— **core drill,** barrena sacatestigos a cuerda de alambre

— **cutter,** cortacables

— **depth measurer,** medidor de profundidad con cable de alambre

— **formation tester,** probador de formación de cable

— **guide,** guía del cable de las poleas

— **hager,** colgadero (o sujetador) de cable de acero

— **pump,** bomba de cable de acero

— **socket,** enchufe del cable de acero (o de las poleas)

wire rope, cable de alambre (o de acero)

— **center,** núcleo de cable

— **clip,** grampa para cable

— **cutter,** cortacables

— **grab,** abrazadera para cable de acero

— **kink,** torcedura, nudo

— **knife,** cortacables

— **thimble,** ojal para cable de acero, guardacabos

— **windlass,** grúa (o guinche) de mano para cable de acero

wireless indicator, indicador inalámbrico

wiring, instalación eléctrica

Wisconsian, wisconsiense

withstand, resistir, soportar

WOA (water, oil and gas), (va) presión de agua, petróleo o gas

wobble, tambaleo, bamboleo

wolfram (W), volframio, tungsteno

wolframite, volframita, wolframita

woolastonite, wollastonita
wood screw, tornillo para madera
wooden, de madera
WOR (water-oil ratio), relación agua-petróleo
workload, carga de trabajo
working
— **barrel,** (bm) cilindro del émbolo (q.v. **pump barrel, sucker-rod pump**)
— **parts,** piezas móviles
— **pressure,** presión efectiva
workmanship, mano de obra, ejecución, hechura, confección
workover, (pr) rehabilitación de un pozo, reperforación, limpieza de pozo, reacondicionamiento
— **rig,** equipo de reparación y terminación de pozos
workshop, taller
worm (write once, read many times), (dp) grabable una vez, legible muchas veces
worm gear, engranaje de tornillo sin fin
worm wheel gear, engranaje de rueda helicoidal
WOT (weight on bit), peso sobre la barrena
woven brake lining, forro tejido para frenos
wrap-around, *a.* tipo envoltura
wrapping machine, máquina de envolver tubería
wrecking bar, barra sacaclavos
wrench, llave, llave de tuerca, llave inglesa
wrinkle bend, dobladura con arrugas
wrist, (mc) muñón
— **pin,** pasador de articulación, gorrón de pie de biela
wrist-pin bearing, cojinete del pasador de articulación, (Ve) cojinete de brazo

wrist-pin puller, extractor de pasadores de articulación
wrought iron, hierro forjado (o fraguado), hierro dulce
wt, q.v. **weight**
WT, q.v. **wall thickness**
wurtzilite, wurzilita; betún

X

X bracing, diagonales cruzadas, aspas, contravientos, crucetas
X-ray, rayos X
— **fluorescence,** fluorescencia de los rayos X
xenolith, xenolita
xenomorphic, (g) xenomorfo, alotriomorfo (q.v. **allotriomorphic**)
xerophytic, xerofítica
Xmas tree, árbol de navidad (q.v. **Christmas tree**)
xylene, xileno

Y

Y, bifurcación
Y branch, ramal Y (o de 45°)
Y connection, (el) conexión de estrella, conexión en Y
yard, yarda: 0,914399 metros; (rr) patio; (nt) embarcadero, muelle
yardstick, criterio, patrón, modelo
yaw, (nt) guiñada
year-to-date, lo que va de año
yield, producción, rendimiento
— **point,** punto cedente, límite elástico aparente; punto de deformación
— **strength,** fuerza de rotura

yoke, (mc) horqueta, horquilla,
araña; (el) culata; yugo
young, (g) reciente; joven
Young's modulus, módulo de
Young

Z

z transform, (gf) transformada z
zenith, cenit
— **distance,** distancia cenital
zeolite, zeloita, ceolita
zero, cero
— **aniline equivalent,** equivalente
anilínico cero
— **gas governor,** regulador de gas
— **matrix,** (dp) matriz cero (o
nula)
— **potential,** tensión nula,
potencial cero
— **pour,** fluidez cero
— **shift,** (gf) sin variación
— **suppression,** supresión (o
eliminación) de ceros no
significativos
zinc, zinc
— **chloride,** cloruro de zinc
zircon, circón
zoisite, zoicita
zone, zona
— **of aeration,** zona de aereación,
zone del agua en suspensión
— **of saturation,** zona de
saturación
— **of suspended water,** zona del
agua en suspensión; zona de
aereación
zymothermic, zimotérmico

247

Notes / Notas

Notes / Notas

Español - Inglés

Español-Inglés

Prefacio

Esta obra, fue originalmente compilada en 1947 por la Redacción de Petróleo Interamericano (luego *Petróleo Internacional*) y editada por PennWell Publishing Co., que actualmente publica *Oil & Gas Journal Revista Latinoamericana.*

La tercera edición del Glosario revisa y amplía la versión previa en más de un 20 porciento. Se incluyen nuevos términos técnicos y generales de uso en las industrias del petróleo y del gas, así como palabras de ramos estrechamente vinculados, como informática, electricidad, navegación, geología y geofísica, construcción, soldadura, comercio y otros. Para esta tercera edición el previo contenido ha sido revisado y reorganizado, y la nueva terminología compilada e insertada por María-Dolores Proubasta, ex-jefe de redacción de *Petróleo Internacional* y coordinadora de traducciones para *Revista Latinoamericana.*

A

abanico, fan
— aluvial, alluvial fan
— aluvioso, alluvial fan
— de deyección, (g) talus fan,
alluvial fan
— espantainsectos, bug blower
— fandeltaico, fan delta
abastecimiento, supply
— de la demanda interior,
domestic supply
abasto, supply
abertura, aperture, opening; cleft,
crevice, fissure; hemlock
— de la boca de una llave inglesa,
span of wrench jaw
— de chispa, spark gap
abierto, open
abigarrado, mottled, motley,
variegated
abiosis, (g) abiosis: absence of
organic life
abiótico, abiotic
abisal, abyssal
abismo, (g) steep face, abyss; abysm
ablación, ablation
ablandador de agua, water softener
abocardar, to counterbore
abocardo, (tl) countersink
— de fondo plano, counterbore
abocinador de tubos, tube expander
abordar, board (a ship)
abrasión, abrasion
abrasivo, abrasive
abrazadera, clamp, clip; clevis;
cleat; clasp, buckle, capuchine
— contra fugas, leak clamp
— de anclaje, anchor clamp
— de la barra de suspensión, rod
hanger clamp
— de caldera, belly brace
— de codos, angled hoop

— de combinación para varillas de
tracción, combination pullrod
clamp
— de correa, belt clamp
— de eje, axle clamp
— de empaquetadura, packing
clamps
— de golpeo, drive clamp
— de muñones, trunnion bracer
— de puntal, prop clasp, (o strap)
— de rebote, rebound clip
— de silla, saddle clamp
— de soldar, welding clamp
— de tirante, tie-rod clamp
— de tornillo, adjusting clasp
— de tubería de revestimiento,
casing clamp
— de unión, coupling clamp
— de unión para tubería, pipe-
joint clamp
— del vástago pulido, (bm)
polished-rod clamps
— giratoria, revolving or swivel
clamp
— graduable, adjusting clamp
— interior de alineamiento, (p)
inside line-up clamp
— limpiadora de lodo, mud wiper,
mud saver
— para cable de acero, wire-rope
grab
— para cable de perforación, wire-
line clamp
— para cerrar fugas en
soldaduras, weld leak clamps
— para reparar tuberías, repair
clamps
— para silla, (mc) saddle clamp
— para tubo, pipe clamp
— para varillas de tracción, pull-
rod clamps
abretubos, swedge
— acanalado, fluted swedge
— de rodillos, roller swedge
abreviatura, abbreviation

251

Español - Inglés

abrir y cerrar el pozo intermitentemente para aumentar la presión, to rock (o activate)a well

abscisa, abscissa

absoluto, absolute

absorbechoque, shock absorber

absorbedor, absorber

absorbente, absorbent, sorbent

absorber, to absorb

absorción, (hd) (el) (qm) absorption

— preferencial, prefential absorption

acabamiento de un pozo, (prf) well completion

acanalado, fluted

acanalamiento, (g) grooving

acantilado, n. cliff; a. steep

acarreador, carrier

acarreo, hauling, haul, cartage, transportation

— de glaciar, (g) glacial drift

acceso, access

— alazar, (dp) random access

accesorios, fittings, accessories, appurtenances

— de alumbrado o iluminación, lighting fixtures

— de inserción, (mc) inserts

— de taller, ship equipment

— embridados, flanged fittings

— para calderas, boiler fittings

— para engrase alemite, alemite fittings

— para tanques, tank fittings

— para tubería, pipe fittings

accidente, accident

acción, action

— de desazufrar el petróleo, (rf) weetening

— de la gravedad, gravitational attraction

— de palance, leverage

— de repartir la tubería a lo largo del trayecto, (p) stringing

— elástica retardada, (gf) lagelastic action

— galvánica, galvanic action

— gravitativa, gravitational attraction

— thermal retardada, (gf) lagthermal action

accionado manualmente, hand-actuated

accionado por pedal, foot-actuated (o operated)

accionado por reloj, clock-driven

accionamiento eléctrico, electric drive

accionar, drive, actuate, operate

acciones, (cm) shares, stock

— amortizables, redeemable shares

— de capital, capital stock

— disponibles, unissued stock

— votantes, common stock

aceite, oil (q.v. petróleo)

— aislante, insulating oil

— azul, blue oil

— blanco, white oil

— bruto, raw oil

— condensado, drip oil

— craso o graso, fatty oil

— de absorción de bajo peso molecular, low molecular weight absorption oil

— de aguarrás, turpentine oil

— de aviación, aviation oil

— de cárter, crankcase oil

— de castor, castor oil

— de creosota, dead oil

— de enjuagar, oil flushing

— de estreno, break in oil

— de flotación, flotation oil

— de lámpara, burning oil

— de lutita, shale oil

— de parafina, foots oil

— de pata, foots oil

— de pie de vaca, neatsfoot oil

— de transmisión de calor, heat transfer oil

— diluíble en agua, soluble oil

— **empireumático,** empyreumatic oil
— **emulsificado,** emulsified oil, cut oil
— **enjuto,** (rf) lean oil
— **enriquecido,** (rf) fat oil
— **esencial,** essential oil
— **fluidificante,** flux oil
— **magro,** (rf) lean oil
— **medicinal,** medicinal oil
— **mezclado,** compounded oil
— **mineral,** mineral oil
— **mineral de foca,** mineral seal oil
— **muerto,** dead oil
— **negro,** black oil
— **neutro,** neutral (o pale, red oil)
— **para alumbrado,** illuminating oil
— **para ba–ar piezas recién fresadas,** slushing oil
— **para caminos,** road oil
— **para cilindros,** cylinder oil
— **para corte,** cutting oil
— **para chumaceras de vagones,** railroad oil
— **para fresar,** cutting oil
— **para husillos,** spindle oil
— **para limpiar,** cleansing oil
— **para lubricar martillos y taladros neumáticos,** air drill oil
— **para motor,** motor oil
— **para pulir,** buffing oil
— **para se–ales,** mineral seal oil
— **para temple,** quenching oil, heat treating oil
— **para transformadores,** transformer oil
— **para válvulas y cilindros de locomotora,** railway valve oil
— **parafínico,** wax oil, paraffin oil
— **penetrante,** penetrating oil
— **pobre,** (rf) lean oil
— **recuperado,** reclaimed oil
— **residual,** residual oil
— **sin parafina,** wax-free oil

— **soluble en agua,** water soluble oil
— **virgen,** virgin stock
— **viscoso,** viscous oil
— **volátil,** volatile oil, essential oil
aceitera, oil can
— **de goteo,** drill oiler
aceitoso, oily
aceleración, acceleration
— **centrífuga,** centrifugal acceleration
acelerador, accelerator
— **de pedal,** foot throttle
— **die pie,** foot accelerator
acelerante, accelerating
acelerar, to accelerate
acenaftileno, acenaphythylene
aceptación, (cm) acceptance
— **comercial,** trade acceptance
— **de pedido,** order acceptance
acero, steel
— **acanalado,** channel steel
— **ácido,** acid steel
— **al carbono,** carbon steel
— **al cobre,** copper-bearing steel
— **al crisol,** crucible steel
— **al cromo,** chromium steel
— **al molíbdeno,** molybdenum steel
— **austenítico,** austenitic steel
— **de aleación,** alloy steel
— **de arado,** plow steel
— **de construcción,** structural steel
— **de herramientas,** tool steel
— **de horno eléctrico,** electric steel
— **de proceso básico,** basic steel
— **de resortes,** spring steel
— **dulce,** mild steel, soft steel
— **estructural,** structural steel
— **extraduro,** extra hard steel
— **forjado,** forge steel
— **inoxidable,** stainless steel
— **para ballestas,** spring steel
— **prensado,** pressed steel
— **recocido,** annealed steel
— **resistente a la corrosión,** corrosion-resisting steel

253

— **resistente al calor,** heat-resisting
  steel
— **tungsteno,** tungsten steel
aceroníquel, nickel steel
acetato, acetate
— **butílico,** butyl acetate
acético, acetic
acetileno, acetylene
acetona, acetone
acíclico, acyclic
acicular, acicular
acidez, acidity
acidificar, acidify
ácido, acid
— **acético,** acetic acid
— **acrílico,** acrylic acid
— **adípico,** adipic acid
— **ascórbico,** ascorbic acid
— **barbitúrico,** barbituric acid
— **benzoico,** benzoic acid
— **benzolsulfínico,** benzolsulphinic
  acid
— **bórico,** boric acid
— **butírico,** butyric acid
— **caprílico,** caprylic acid
— **carbólico,** carbolic acid
— **carbónico,** carbon dioxide
— **ciánico,** cyanic acid
— **clorhídrico,** hydrochloric acid
— **crómico,** chromic acid
— **crotónico,** crotonic acid
— **de contacto,** contacting acid
— **esteárico,** stearic acid
— **fluorhídrico anhidro,**
  anhydrous hydrofluoric acid,
  anhydrous hydrogen fluoride
— **fórmico,** formic acid
— **fosfórico,** phosphoric acid
— **ftálico,** phtalic acid
— **fumárico,** fumaric acid
— **gálico,** gallic acid
— **glicérico,** glyceric acid
— **glioxílico,** glyoxylic acid
— **haloideo,** haloid acid
— **hidroclórico,** hydrochloric acid
— **isobutírico,** isobutyric acid

— **láctico,** lactic acid
— **láurico,** lauric acid
— **lebulínico,** lebulinic acid
— **libre,** free acid
— **maléico,** maleic acid
— **málico,** malic acid
— **mesotartárico,** mesotartaric
  acid
— **muriático,** muriatic acid
— **nafténico,** naphthenic acid
— **nítrico,** aqua fortis, nitric acid
— **Norhdausen,** oleum
— **oléico,** oleic acid
— **oxálico,** oxalic acid
— **palmítico,** palmitic acid
— **priofurfúrico,** fuming acid
— **regenerado,** recovered acid
— **salicílico,** salicylic acid
— **silícico,** silicic acid
— **succínico,** succinic acid
— **sucio (o lodoso),** sludge acid
— **sulfanílico,** sulphanilic acid
— **sulfónico,** sulphonic acid
— **sulfúrico,** sulphuric acid
— **sulfúrico humeante,** oleum
— **tartárico,** tartaric acid
— **tereftálico,** terephtalic acid
— **toluensulfónico,**
  toluenesulphonic acid
— **tricloracético,** trichloracetic
  acid
— **úrico,** uric acid
acidulación, acidizing
acidular, acidulate
aclínico, aclinic
acmita, acmite
acolchadura, (ca) lay
acombado, bent, warped, bellied
acondicionador de lodo, mud
  conditioner
acoplado, *n.* joined trailer;
acoplador, coupler, coupling
— **de tubo (o manguera) de aire,**
  air coupling
— **hidráulico,** hydraulic coupling

— (o **ajustador**) **para bombeo,**
pumping adjuster

acoplamiento, coupling, splice,
joint, connection; clutch

— **API,** API joint

— **a ras,** flush joint

— **a rascon manguito,** coupling
flush joint

— **atornillado,** screw coupling

— **con collar a soldadura,** collar
weld joint

— **con collar a tope,** butt welded
joint

— **cónico,** conical seal joint

— **de inserción a soldadura,** insert
weld joint

— **de manguera,** hose coupling

— **de rosca,** threaded joint

— **de rosca larga con manguito,**
long threads and coupling joints

— **de varillas,** pull-rod coupling

— **de varilla de bombeo,** sucker-rod
coupling

— **directo,** (mc) direct drive

— **empernado,** bolted coupling

— **en bucles,** loop connection

— **estrafuerte de recalcado
exterior,** upset full strength joint

— **mútuo,** (dp) interface

— **para el cilindro de la bomba,**
working-barrel coupling

— **roscado,** threaded coupling

— **semirás con manguito,** semi-
flush joint coupling

— **semirás de recalcado exterior,**
upset semi-flush joint

acorazado, ironclad, steel clad

acortarse, shrink

acotación paralela, parallel
contouring

acotamiento, (rd) shoulder; setting
boundary monuments;
dimensioning

acre, acre: 40.46 areas, 4,046.88 m²;
a. sour

acreedor, (cm) creditor

acrepié, acre-foot

actinolita, (g) actinolite

activación, (cataliz) activation

activar el pozo, rock (o activate) a
well

activador de gas, gas actifier

activación de la arcilla, (rf) clay
activation

activo, *n.* (cm) assets; *a.* active

— **circulante,** (cm) liquid assets

actualizar, update

acuagel, aquagel

acueducto, aqueduct

acuerdo, (cm) agreement,
resolution, decree

acuiclusa, (g) aquiclude

acuífero, (g) aquifer

acuifuga, (g) aquifuge

acumulación, accumulation;
gathering; (cm) accrual

— **aluvial,** alluviation, alluvial
accumulation

acumulador, (el) storage battery,
storage cell; accumulator

acumular, accumulate

acuñamiento, *n.* (g) wedge out;
wedging; *v.* **acuñarse,** thin (o
wedge) out

acuñarse, (g) thin out, wedge out

acuoso, aqueous

acústico, acoustic

achicador, bailer

— **de arena,** sand bailer, sand pump

— **de dardo,** dart bailer

— **de lodo,** mud socket

— **hidrostático,** hydrostatic bailer

— **seccionado con uniones
enrasadas,** flush-joint sectional
bailer

achicar, bail, drain, scoop

achique, (prf) bailing

— **de excitación,** (oil well)
swabbing

adaptador, (mc) adapter; (p)
transition piece, fitting

— **para bomba,** pump adapter

— **para el colocador de tubería revestidora de fondo,** liner-setter adapter

— **para tubería de revestimiento,** casing adapter

adelanto, progress, advance; (cm) advance payment

— **en cuenta corriente,** overdraft

adelfotipo, (paleo) adelfotype

adelgazamiento, thinning

adelgazamiento del estrato, pinching of strata

adelgazarse, (g) thin out

adelgazarse discordantemente, (g) pinch out

adelgazador del lodo, mud thinner

adherido, stuck

adherir, adhere

adhesión, adhesion, bond; freezing

adiabático, adiabatic

adición por sedimentación, (g) aggradation

aditamentos, fittings

aditivo, additive

— **gelatinizador,** gelling agent

administración, administration, management

— **unificada,** unit operation

administrador, manager

admisión, admission

admisor de aire, air inlet

adsorber, adsorb

adsorción, adsorption

aduana, customs

adularia, adularia

ad valorem, ad valorem

aerador, aerator

aereador, aerator

aerear, aerate

aéreo, aerial; (radio) aerial

aerificar, aerify

aerodinámico, streamlined

aerofotografía, aerial photograph, aerial photography

aerofotogrametría, aerial mapping

aerogasolina, aviation gasoline

aerolito, (g) aerolite

aerómetro, aerometer, hydrometer

aerosfera, aerosphere

afanítico, aphanitic

afiladora, grinder, sharpener, grindstone, whetstone

— **de bolas,** ball grinder

aflojar, loosen, slack; release

afloramiento, (g) exposure, outcrop

aflorar, crop out

afluencia, influx, abundance

afluente, *a.* affluent, copious, abundant; *n.* tributary, affluent

aforador, gager; appraiser, (mc) stream gage

— **de aduana,** customs inspector

aforar, gage, measure; appraise

agarradera, handle grip; clamp; grouser

— **del vástago pulido,** polished-rod grip

agarrador del revestidor auxiliar, (prf) liner catcher

agarrador de tubo de producción, tubing catcher

agarrar, grip

agarratubo de fondo, (prf) liner catcher

agarre, (mc) (revet) grip

ágata, agate

— **musgosa,** moss agate

agente, agent

— **aduanal,** customs agent

— **catalítico,** catalytic medium

— **de fletes,** (cm) forwarding agent

— **de tierras,** landman

— **dispersador,** (qm) dispersing agent

— **expedidor,** forwarding agent

— **floculador,** flocculating agent

— **mezclante,** (rf) blending agent

— **refinador,** refining agent

— **vendedor,** salesman

agitación, agitation

agitador, agitator, stirrer

256

— **con una sola paleta,** single paddle stirrer
— **tipo de hélice,** propeller type agitator
— **tipo tanque,** tank-type agitator
agitar, agitate
aglomerado, agglomerate
aglomerante, (rd) binder; (qm) matrix
agnostozoico, Agnotozoic, Algonkian, Proterozoic
agolpamiento, (g) impounding
agotador, exhauster
agotamiento, (well) depletion
agotar, (rf) strip, stabilize oil being refined; drain off; exhaust
agradación, (g) aggradation
agrandamiento, enlargement
a granel, (cm) in bulk
agregado, (g) aggregate
— **cristalino,** (g) crystalline aggregate
agrimensor, surveyor
agrimensure, surveying
agrio, sour
agrupar, assemble, group, bank
agua, water
— **amoniacal,** aqua ammonia
— **artesiana,** artesian water
— **blanda** (o **suave**), soft water
— **connata,** connate water
— **de cal,** lime water
— **de expulsión,** water of compaction
— **de fondo,** bottom water
— **de gravedad,** meteoric water, vadose water
— **densa,** heavy water
— **destilada,** distilled water
— **dulce,** fresh water
— **freática,** surface water
— **innata,** connate water
— **intermedia,** intermediate water
— **intersticial,** connate water
— **meteórica,** meteoric water, vadose water

— **neutralizada,** neutralized water
— **pelicular,** pellicular water
— **potable,** drinkable water, potable water
— **regia,** aqua regia
— **rejuvenecida,** rejuvenated water
— **salada,** salt water, brine
— **salobre,** brackish water
— **singenética,** connate water
— **subterránea,** ground water
— **subterránea endicada,** perched ground water
— **subterránea fija,** fixed ground water
— **superficial,** surface water
— **superyacente,** top water
— **telúrica,** telluric water
— **marginal,** edge water
aguantar, resist, hold firm, support, back up
aguilón, boom; gib
aguijón, stinger
aguja, needle; (in) hand; (cn) shore, spreader; (hd) needle beam; (carp) brad, finishing nail; (mn) small branch vein
— **azimutal,** azimuthal compass
— **de calibración,** metering pin
— **de medición,** metering pin
— **de rebote,** bouncing pin
— **indicadora,** (mc) bouncing pin
— **magnética,** magnetic needle
agujero, hole
— **de hombre,** manhole
— **desviado,** (prf) deflected hole
ahorquillado, forked
ahusado, tapered
ahusamiento, tapering
ahusar, taper
aire, air
— **arrastrado,** entrained air
— **atmosférico,** free air
— **comprimido,** compressed air
— **de admisión,** intake air
— **puro,** fresh air
— **viciado,** bad air

aislador, electric insulator, insulator
— **de carrete,** (el) insulator spool
— **de las placas del acumulador,** plate separator
aislamiento, insulation, insulator, isolation
— **contra el calor,** heat insulation
— **de asbesto,** asbestos insulation
— **de vibraciones,** vibration insulation
— **térmico,** thermal insulation
aislar, isolate; insulate
ajustable, adjustable
ajustadera, marlinespike
ajustado, tight; adjusted; fitted; adapted
ajustador, adjuster; (mc) (carp) adjuster, adjusting tool; machinist fitter
— **del freno,** brake adjuster
— **de vástago de válvula,** valve stem adjuster
— **o acoplador para bombeo,** pumping adjuster
ajustar, adjust, fit, make true, balance; regulate
ajuste, adjustment; (in) calibration
— **de cabos de cable,** splice
— **de instrumentos,** instrument calibration
— **del freno,** brake adjustment
ala, (g) limb; (in) limbo; (bldg) wing; leaf of a hinge
alabastro, alabaster
álabe, (mc) wiper
— **director,** (tr) gate
— **giratorio,** (tr) gate
a la intemperie, exposure
alambique, still, alembic
— **acorazado,** shell still
— **al vacío,** vacuum still
— **de asfalto,** asphalt still
— **de coque,** coke still
— **de coraza,** shell still
— **de cráqueo** cracking still

— **de despojamiento,** (rf) stripping still
— **de petróleo,** petroleum still
— **de presión,** pressure still
— **de torre,** tower still
— **de tubos,** tube (o pipe) still
— **para destilación primaria,** reducing still
— **para redestilación,** (rf) rerun still
— **despojador,** (rf) stripping still
— **destufador,** sweetening still
— **desulfurador,** sweetening still
alambiquero, stillman
alambre, wire
— **de cierre,** (el) jumper
— **de disparo,** shooting cable; (gf) shot line
— **de soldadura,** welding wire
— **de tungsteno,** tungsten wire
— **de wolfram,** tungsten wire
— **disparador,** (gf) shot line
— **eléctrico,** electric wire
— **para imanes,** magnet wire
— **estadimétricos,** stadia hairs
— **rotos que se proyectan hacia afuera,** (ca) wicker
alanita, allanite
alargado, oblong
alargadores, (qm) extenders
alarma, alarm
álave, bucket of a water wheel
albayalde, white lead
— **rojo,** red lead
albertita, albertite, asphalt rock
albiense, albian
albita, albite
alcadieno, alkadiene
alcadiino, alkadiyne
álcali, alkali
— **cáustico,** caustic alkali
alcalímetro, alkalimeter
alcalinidad, alkalinity
alcalino, alkaline
alcalino-cal, calc-alkali
alcance, reach; range

alcano, alkane
alcohilación, alkylation (q.v.
   alquilación)
alcohol, alcohol
— amílico, amyl
— dibromopropilo, dibromopropyl
   alcohol
— etílico, ethyl alcohol, grain
   alcohol
— metílico, methyl alcohol
— neutro, neutral alcohol
— propílico, propyl alcohol
al contado, (cm) paid in cash
alcotana, pick
aldaba de gozne para candado,
   hasp, safety hinge
aldehído, aldehyde
al detalle, (cm) retail
aleación, n. alloy, alligation
— de hierro colado, cast iron alloy
— de plata y aluminio, aluminum-
   silver alloy
— de plation e iridio, platinum-
   iridium alloy
— dura para chapear o refrentar,
   hard-facing alloy, hard-
   surfacing alloy
— ferrosa, ferrous alloy
— metálica, metal alloy
— no ferrosa, nonferrous alloy
alero, (bldg) wing
aleta, wing; (mc) lug, fin, gill; (tr)
   vane, wicket; (hinge) leaf
— amortiguadora, damping vane
— desviadoras, deflecting blades
alfa, alpha
alfametilnaftalina, alpha
   methylnaphthalene
algas, algae
algonkiano, Algonkian
aliáceo, alliaceous
alicates, pliers, pincers, tongs
— de electricista, electrician's
   pliers
— de expansión, slip joint pliers
alidada, alidade

— de pínula (o mira abierta), open
   sight alidade
— telescópica, telescopic alidade
alifático, aliphatic
aligerar, lighten
alilacetileno, allylacetylene,
   pentenyne
alimentación, (el) (cl) feed
— automática, automatic feeding
— de combustible, fuel feed
— por gravedad, gravity feed
alimentador, feeder
— de aceite, oil feeder
— de substancias químicas,
   chemical feeder
alineación, alignment
— automática, self-centering
— (o alineamiento) de ruedas,
   wheel alignment
alineador del vástago pulido,
   polished-rod liner
alineamiento, alignment
alinear, line, line up, align
alivio, (pressure) relief
alizarina, alizarin
aljibe, tank
almacén, storeroom, warehouse,
   store, storage house, depot,
— de ventas a granel, bulk station
almacenaje, (cm) storage charge
— subterráneo, underground
   storage
almacenamiento, storage
— del petróleo, oil storage
almacenar, store, stock
alma de cáñamo, hemp center
almádena, sledge hammer
almandita, almandite
almarjal, (g) marsh
almártage, litharge
almohadilla, friction block
— de un neumático, tire cushion
almohadón, squab, cushion
alocromático, (g) allochromatic
alóctono, (g) strange, allochthonous
alotígeno, (g) allothegenic

alotriomorfo, allotriomorphic,
xenomorphic
alotrópico, allotrope
alpinense, Alpine
alpino, Alpine
al por mayor, (cm) in bulk,
wholesale
al por menor, (cm) retail
alqueno, alkene
alquilación, (rf) alkylation
— catalítica, catalytic alkylation
— con ácido sulfúrico, sulphuric
acid alkylation process
alquilato, alkylate
alquilbenceno, alkylbenzene,
phenylpropene
alquileno, alkylene
alquiler, *n.* rent
alquilo, alkyl
alquimia, alchemy
alquitrán, tar, pitch
— de hulla, coal tar
— de petróleo, oil tar
alta frecuencia, (el) high frequency
altar de hornalla, bridge wall, fire
bridge
altazimut, altazimuth
alteración, alteration
alterno, alternating
altímetro, altimeter
altiplanicie, (g) plateau
altiplano, (g) plateau
altitud, altitude, elevation, height
alto, high
— horno, blast furnace
al tresbolillo, staggered
altura, height, altitude, elevation
— bajo el nivel del mar, subsea
elevation
— de aspiración, (bm) lift
— debida a la velocidad de un
fluido, (fl) velocity head
— hidrostática, hydrostatic head
— interior, interior height
— negativa, negative elevation
— positiva, positive elevation

alumbrado, *n.* light, lighting; *a.*
lighted; treated with alum
alumbrar, light; treat with alum;
(ground water) emerger
alumbre, alum
alúmina, alumina
aluminio, aluminum, aluminium
alundo, alundum
alunita, alunite, alum stone
aluvial, alluvial
aluvión, alluvium
al vacío, a. vacuum
álveo, river bed, channel
alza, *n.* lift, rise; shim; (hd)
flashboard
alzaprima, bar, crowbar, lever
pinch bar
alzatubos, pipe jack
alzaválvulas, tappet
amago de reventón, (prf) kick
amainar, (nt) abate
amalgama, amalgam
amargo, bitter
amarre, anchorage, mooring; splice,
tie, lashing;
amatista, amethyst
ámbar, amber
amianto, amianthus, asbestos, earth
flax
amigdaloide, (g) amygdaloidal
amilacetileno, amylacetylene,
heptyne
amilbenceno, amylbenzene,
phenylpentane
amileno, amylene, pentene
amilo, amyl
amina, amine
amoladora, grinding machine,
grinder
— de barrenas, bit dresser
— de bolas, ball grinder
— neumática, pneumatic grinder
— portátil, portable grinder
amolar, grind, sharpen
amoníaco, ammonia
— anhidro, anhydrous ammonia

Glossary of the Petroleum Industry

— **seco,** anhydrous ammonia
amonio, ammonium
amonita, ammonite
amontonar, stack
amorfo, amorphous
amortiguador, (mc) shock
  absorber; dash pot; damper;
  softener; (a) snubber
— **de ruido,** sound damper
— **de vibraciones,** vibration
  dampener, pulsation dampener
— **de vibraciones para indicador,**
  gage pulsation dampener
amortiguamiento, (mc)
  absorption; (sound) deadening
— **crítico,** critical damping
— **electromagnético,**
  electromagnetic damping
amortiguar, damp, dampen
amortización, (cm) amortization
amortizar, amortize
a motor, engine driven
amperaje, (el) amperage
amperímetro, ammeter
amperio, ampere
— **vuelta,** ampere turn
amperio-hora, ampere hour
ampliar, amplify, enlarge, extend
amplificación, magnification;
  amplification
— **dinámica,** dynamic
  magnification
amplificador, amplifier
amplificar, amplify
amplitud, amplitude
ampolla, (lamp) bulb; decanter
— **de decantación,** (la) decanter
anaclinal, anaclinal
anaeróbico, anaerobic
analcita, analcite
análisis, analysis
— **de finos,** roller analysis
— **del gas del suelo,** soil gas
  analysis
— **de mineral,** ore assaying

— **de muestras o testigos,** (g) core
  analysis
— **de tierras,** soil analysis
— **por titulación,** titration
— **fraccionario,** fractional analysis
— **volumétrico,** titration
analista, analyst
analítico, analytical
analógico, analog
anamorfismo, (g) anamorphism
anamorfosis, anamorphosis
anaquel, shelf
anatasa, anatase
ancla, (nt) (mc) (str) anchor
— **de bomba,** bottom hold-down
— **de contraviento,** guy-line anchor
— **de patente,** (nt) stockless anchor
— **de pilotes hincados,** anchor
  piles, drilled-in anchor
— **del tubo de producción,** tubing
  anchor
— **de tubería,** (p) river clamp
— **flotante (o de capa),** drag
  anchor, floating anchor
— **para cable contraviento,** guy
  line anchor
— **para varilla,** rod anchor
anclaje, mooring
ancho, breadth, width
— **de vía,** (rr) gage, gauge
andalusita, andalusite
andarivel, aerial tramway, ferry
  cable
andesina, andesine
andesita, andesite
andradita, andradite
anemómetro, anemometer
anfíbol, (g) hornblende; amphibole
anfibolita, amphibolite
anfiteatro morénico, moraine belt
anglisita, anglisite
angosto, narrow
angostura, (tp) gap, defile
angstrom, Angstrom
angular, angular
ángulo, angle

— **agudo,** acute angle
— **(o conicidad) de asiento de válvula,** angle seat
— **crítico,** critical angle
— **crítico de incidencia,** critical angle of incidence
— **de asiento de válvula,** angle of seat
— **de buzamiento,** (g) angle of dip
— **de deriva,** drift angle
— **de desfasamiento,** phase angle
— **de deslizamiento,** (g) angle of slide
— **de elevación,** angle of elevation
— **de emergencia,** (g) angle of emergence
— **de emplame,** joint angle
— **de hierro,** angle iron
— **de inclinación,** (g) angle of dip
— **de incidencia,** (g) angle of incidence
— **de oscurecimiento,** (gf) extinction angle
— **de polarización,** angle of polarization
— **de reflexión,** angle of reflexion
— **de refracción,** angle of refraction
— **de reposo,** angle of repose
— **de retraso de fase,** phase angle
— **de rumbo,** (g) angle of strike
— **de talud natural,** angle of repose
— **de torsión,** torsion angle
— **de la visual,** angle of sight
— **direccional,** (g) angle of strike
— **libre,** releasing angle
— **óptico,** optic angle
— **recto,** right angle
angulosidad, angularity
anhídrido, anhydride
— **acético,** acetic anhydride
— **ftálico,** phthalic anhydride
— **sulfuroso,** liquid sulphur dioxide
anhidrita, anhydrite
anhidro, anhydrous

anilina, aniline
anillo, ring, hook, collar, rim
— **de estopas,** junk ring
— **de excéntrica,** eccentric strap
— **de expansión,** expansion ring
— **de guarnición,** ring gasket
— **de pistón,** piston ring
— **de presión,** snap ring
— **de refuerzo de una rueda dentada,** shroud
— **de retén,** junk ring
— **de retenida,** (mc) guy ring
— **de rosca partida,** split lock ring
— **de soporte (o de sostén),** support ring
— **de suspensión,** casing spider bolt
— **de tubería de producción,** tubing ring
— **empaquetador,** packing ring
— **enjugador,** wiper ring
— **fiador de la empaquetadura,** packing retainer ring
— **fiador roscado de la empaquetadura,** threaded packing retainer
— **guía,** guiding ring
— **portabolas,** (ma) cage
— **protector,** grommet
— **protector para conexiones soldadas,** chill ring
— **sellador del casquete,** bonnet seal ring
— **y cuña de suspensión,** spider and slips
— **raschig,** raschig rings
anión, anion
anisométrico, anisometric
anisotrópico, anisotropic
anisótropo, anisotrope
ankerita, ankerite
ánodo, anode
— **de sacrificio,** sacrificial anode
anomalía, anomaly
— **combinada de aire libre y Bouguer,** free air and Bouguer anomaly

— **de aire libre,** free air anomaly
— **de Bouguer,** Bouguer anomaly
— **de intensidad,** (gf) intensity anomaly
— **de latitud,** latitude anomaly
— **de marea,** tidal anomaly
— **gravimétrica,** gravity anomaly
— **isostática,** isostatic anomaly
— **local,** local anomaly
— **magnética,** magnetic anomaly
— **magnética horizontal,** (gf) horizontal magnetic anomaly
— **magnética negativa,** magnetic low
— **magnética positiva,** magnetic high
— **magnética vertical,** (gf) vertical magnetic anomaly
— **negativa,** minimum gravity
— **regional,** (g) regional anomaly
— **residual,** residual anomaly
— **topográfica,** topographic anomaly
anormal, abnormal
anorogenética, (g) nonorogenic
anortita, anorthite
anotación de errores, (dp) logging
anotaciones cronólogicas de la perforación, logging
antena, aerial
antepaís, (g) foreland
antepozo, (oil well) basement, (prf) cellar
anteproyecto, preplanning
anticlinal, *n.* anticline; *a.* anticlinal
— **abierto,** (g) nose
— **asimétrico,** asymmetric anticline
— **compuesto,** anticlinorium
— **fallado,** faulted anticline
— **fracturado,** breached anticline
— **regional,** geoanticline
— **simétrico,** symmetrical anticline
— **terraza,** arrested anticline
anticlinorio, anticlinorium
anticohesor, anticoherer
anticongelante, antifreeze

— **de tipo glicol,** glycol type antifreeze
antiespumante, antifoam agent
antimonio, antimony
antimonita, stibnite
antiparras, goggles
antofilita, anthophyllite
antorcha, torch
— **de oxiacetileno,** oxyacetylene torch
— **para soldar,** welding torch
antraceno, anthracene
antracita, anthracite
antracítico, anthracitous
antraconita, anthraconite
anual, annual
anualidad, annuity
anular, *a.* annular; *v.* cancel, annul
anuncio, (cm) advertising; announcement; advertisement; notice
anverso, obverse
añadir tramos suplementarios, (p) loop
año fiscal, fiscal year
apagado al aire, air-slacked
apagar, extinguish, quench, blow out
aparato, apparatus, appliance, device
— **contra incendios,** fire fighting apparatus
— **de cementación a varios niveles,** multiple stage cementing tool
— **para prueba de detonación,** (gasol) knock-testing apparatus, CFR fuel-testing unit
— **perforador,** perforator, perforating gun
aparejo, (mc) purchase; block and fall; chain block; tackle, rigging
— **a engranaje,** geared hoist
— **de cadenas,** chain hoisting block
— **de perforación,** rig
— **de poleas,** tackle

— **para el entubado,** tubing block
— **para herramientas,** tool crane
apéndice del revestidor de fondo,
n. (prf) tail pipe
apeo, a survey; timbering, shoring;
cutting of trees
apero, *n.* outfit, tools, equipment
ápice, apex
apisonar, tamp
apizarrado, (g) slaty
aplanadora, (cn) roller, grader,
beetle, dresser
aplastamiento, (p) eggshelling;
flattening of the pipe by
excessive pressure on the
wrenches
a pleno flujo, open flow
aplita, aplitic rock
apoderado, (cm) holder of a power
of attorney, trustee
apófisis, (g) apophysis
apoyo, support, bearing, cradle
— **de expansión,** expansion bearing
— **inferior del entubamiento,**
tubing tail piece
— **del motor,** engine supports
apretado, (mc) tight
apretador, tightener
— **de herramientas,** tool tightener
— **de herramientas tipo palanca y
cadena,** bar-and-chain tool
tightener
apretadora para tubo flexible,
pinchcock
a prueba de, -proof
— **ácido,** acidproof
— **aire,** air proof
— **explosión,** explosion proof
— **fuego,** fireproof
— **fugas,** leak proof
— **intemperie,** weatherproof
— **polvo,** dustproof
aptiense, Aptian
apuntalar, shore, brace, prop
aragonita, aragonite
arancel, tariff

arandela, washer, gasket; burr;
collar plate; rivet plate
— **acopada,** cup washer
— **de cuero,** leather washer
— **de empuje,** bronze thrust washer
— **de fieltro,** felt washer
— **de presión,** lock washer; spring
washer
— **de resorte,** spring washer
— **de seguridad,** lock washer
— **plana,** flat washer
— **suplementaria,** filler washer
araña, spider
— **centradora de la tubería de
revestimiento,** casing landing
spider
— **para tubería de producción,**
tubing spider
— **partida,** split spider
— **portamontantes,** (mar) marine
riser handling spider
árbol, (mc) axle, shaft; arbor;
spindle; drill; (nt) mast; (ma)
upright post
— **de ballesta en un torno,** turning
arbor
— **de cambio de marcha,** (mc)
reversing shaft
— **de cambio de velocidades,** (mc)
shifting shaft
— **de conexiones,** (pr) Christmas
tree
— **de conexiones de dos ramas,**
(pr) double wing Christmas tree
— **de eje,** axle shaft
— **de mando,** propeller shaft
— **de Navidad,** (pr) Christmas tree
— **dentado,** notched beam
— **giratorio,** revolving beam
— **motor,** crankshaft
arborescente, arborescent
arcadiense, Arcadian
arcaico, Archean
arcifinio, arcifinial
arcilita, claystone
arcilla, clay

— **activada,** activated clay, activated shale
— **arenosa,** sandy clay
— **blanqueadora,** bleaching earth
— **de alfarero,** brick clay
— **de filtro,** filter clay
— **decolorante,** Fullerís earth
— **esquistosa bituminosa,** bituminous shale
— **ferruginosa,** clay-ironstone
— **infusible,** fire clay
— **nativa,** (g) native clay
— **neutralizador,** neutralizing clay
— **pirito-bituminosa,** alum earth
— **regenerada,** (rf) restored clay
— **restaurada,** (rf) restored clay
— **sapropel,** sapropel clay
arcilloso, argillaceous, argillous
arco, (el) (sd) (g) arc; arch;
— **Beaman,** Beaman stadia arc
— **fallado,** (g) faulted arch
— **natural,** natural arch
— **taquimétrico,** stadia arc
arcón, bin, bunker; caisson
arcosa, arkose
arder, burn
área, area
— **de fracturación,** (g) fracture zone
— **de inundación,** flood plain
— **perturbada,** (g) disturbed area
areal, areal
arena, sand
— **cuarzosa,** quartz sand
— **de escape,** thief sand
— **gasífera,** gas sand
— **impregnada de brea,** tar sand
— **ladrona,** thief sand
— **movediza,** quicksand, drift sand
— **negra,** black sand
— **petrolífera,** oil sand
— **productiva,** pay sand
— **seca,** dry sand
— **suelta,** (well) float sand
arenáceo, arenaceous

arenal, sand bank (o sand bar, pit, deposit)
arenilla, fine sand, grit
arenisca, sandstone
— **arcillosa,** argillaceous sandstone
— **asfáltica,** asphaltic sandstone
— **bituminosa,** bituminous sandstone
— **coralina** (o **coralígena**), coral sandstone
— **gruesa,** coarse sandstone
arenoso, gritty; sandy, arenaceous
argamasa, mortar
argentita, (g) argentite
argilita, argillite
argilolita, claystone
argirosa, (g) argentite
argolla, ring, staple, shackle
— **de remolque,** tow ring
argón, argon
árido, arid
ariete, aries; ram; water hammer
— **cortador,** shear ram
— **empaquetador,** packing ram
— **hidráulico,** water hammer, hydraulic ram
— **moldeador de barrenas,** bit ram
arista ensanchadora, reaming edge
aritmética, arithmetic
— **de coma flotante,** floating point arithmetic
— **de punto flotante,** floating point arithmetic
arkansiense, Arkansan
armadura, *n.* framework; (magnet) armature; erection, assembly; concrete forms, (cn) mounting
— **de un imán artificial,** keeper
armar, assemble, erect, frame, reinforce; truss
armazón, framework, frame, skeleton, chassis; concrete reinforcement
— **A,** A-frame
— **de polines,** skid frame

armella, staple; eyebolt
— **del vástago pulido,** (bm) polished-rod eye
aro, hook, ring; (a) tire rim
— **de acero,** steel ring
— **de compresión,** piston ring
— **de empaque de la parte posterior de un ariete,** ram-rear steel ring
— **de émblo,** piston ring
— **de remolque,** tow ring
— **de resorte,** snap ring
— **de rodillos,** bearing cage
— **de dos mitades,** (mc) split ring
— **divisorio,** (cracking tower) partition ring
— **partido,** (mc) split ring
aromático, aromatic
arpón, spear
— **de disparo,** trip spear
— **de pesca para percusoras,** jardown spears
— **pescador desprendible y de dirculación,** (fishing tl) releasing and circulating spear
— **pescatubos,** (fishing tl) bulldog; casing spear, tubing spear
— **pescatubos hueco,** hollow casing spear
— **pescaválvulas,** valve spear
arqueano, Archean
arqueozoico, Archeozoic
arrabio, chilled casting
arrancador, (el) startingbox; starting compensator; (a) starter, self-starter; grubber, ripper,
arrancar, start, pull, draw, root out
arrancasondas, drill extractor
arranque automático, self starter
arrancarraíces, rooter
arrastrar, haul, move, pull, draw, drag; (hd) scour, wash out; (r) carry in suspension; (hd) (qm) entrain

arrastre, dragging; hauling; washout; drag mill; (qm) (hd) entrainment
— **de émbolo,** (mc) piston drag
arrecife, reef
— **coralígeno,** coral reef
— **costero,** fringing reef, shore reef
— **de barra,** (g) barrier reef
arreglo, arrangement
— **disperso,** (gf) split setup
arrendador, (cm) lessor
arrendar, lease, let, rent
arrendatario, (cm) lease holder, lessee
arrestador de chispas, spark arrester
arrestallamas, engine arrester, flame arrester
arriba, overhead, above, on high; upstairs
arrimo de tubería a la torre, (prf) tailing-in
arrollado del estator, stator winding
arrollamiento, winding
arroyo, stream, brook, creek
— **consecuente,** consequent stream
— **obsecuente,** obsequent stream
— **subglaciario,** glacial stream
— **subsecuente,** subsequent stream
— **superpuesto,** superposed stream
— **resecuente,** desiccant stream
arroyuelo, creek
arrugamiento, crenulation; corrugation, wrinkling, crumpling; minute folding
arrugas de doblez, (p) upset wrinkles
arrumar (tubería), rack (pipe)
arsénico, arsenic
arsenopirita, arsenophyrite
artefacto, appliance, fixture
artesa, (g) basin; tray; trough
— **para el lodo,** mud box, mud crib
artesiano, artesian
artesonado, (g) troughing

articulación, joint, hinge,
articulation, knee joint
— **de rótula,** ball-joint union
— **esférica,** socket joint; ball joint,
ball and socket joint
asa, handle, haft; tab, bail
asas del elevador, elevator bails
asbesto, earth flax, asbestos
ascenso, uplift
asegurador, underwriter; fastener,
anchor; insurer
asegurador de correa, belt fastener
asentador preliminar, (pr) water
leg
asentamiento, settling; settlement
— **de la parafina,** (rf) cold settling
asentamiento por gravedad,
gravity settling
asentarse, settle; bed
asfalteno, asphaltent
asfáltico, asphaltic
asfaltina, asphaltent
asfaltita, asphaltite
asfalto, asphalt
— **de fraguado lento,** slow-curving
asphalt
— **de penetración,** penetration
asphalt
— **diluído,** cutback asphalt
— **emulsionado,** emulsified asphalt
asfixiar, asphyxiate
asiderita, (g) asiderite
asiento, seat; (va) seat
— **corredizo,** sliding seat
— **de cu–as,** slip seat
— **de la bomba,** pump seat
— **del resorte,** (va) spring seat
— **de resorte de válvula,** valve
spring seat
— **de válvula,** valve seat
— **de válvula insertado,** valve
insert
— **para chaveta,** (mc) keyseat
asimétrico, asymmetric,
asymmetrical
asimilación, assimilation

asimilar, assimilate
asísmico, aseismic
asomo, (g) outcrop
asperón, coarse sandstone
aspiración, draft, suction
— **del émbolo,** plunger lift
aspirador, exhauster, aspirator
asquístico, (g) aschistic
asquisto, aschistic rock
asta, mast
astático, astatic
astatización, (gf) astatization,
astatizing
astatizar, (gf) astatize
astilla de piedra, (g) spall
astillarse, spall, splinter
astillero, dockyard
astronómico, astronomical
atacar, (blasting) tamp, ram, stem
atacarga, load binder
atador de carga, load binder
atadura, *n.* tie
ataguía, (hd) cofferdam; (mc)
guides
atajo, dike; cofferdam; cutoff wall
atar, fasten
atascar, (ma) stall; stop up; obstruct
atasco por gas, (bm) gas lock
aterrajador de tubos, pipe threader
atezador de correa, belt stretcher
atizador, poker
atómico, atomic
atomizador de pintura, paint gun
atomizar, atomize, pulverize
atmósfera, atmosphere;
— **absoluta,** absolute atmosphere
atmosférico, atmospheric
atol, atoll
atomización, atomization
atomizador, atomizer
atomizar, atomize
átomo, atom
— **de carbono terciario,** (qm)
tertiary carbon atom
atornillar, screw; bolt
atracción, attraction

— **de la gravedad,** gravitational attraction

— **magnética,** magnetic attraction

atrapador de mandíbulas, alligator grab

atrapadora de agua, steam scrubber (o trap)

atrapadora de arena, sand hog

atrapanúcleos, (prf t) core catcher

atrapatestigos, (prf t) core catcher

atraque, mooring

atraso de la chispa (o del encendido), (mo) spark delay

a través, across

audífono, earphone

audiofrecuencia, audiofrequency

auditor, (cm) comptroller, auditor

auganita, (g) auganite

augita, (g) augite

aumentador de presión, pressure booster

aumentar, magnify, increase, augment

aureola, (g) aureole, contact zone

auricular, earphone

austenite, (g) austenite

autígeno, (g) authigene, authigenic, authigenous

autocatalítico, autocatalytic

autoclástico, autoclastic

autoclave, autoclave

autóctono, autochthonous, indigenous

autoelevadizo, *a.* self-elevating

automático, automatic, self-acting

autometamorfismo, autometamorphism

automultiplicación de fuerza, self-energizing

autopotencial, self-potential

autotrabante, *a.* self-locking

autuniense, Autunian

auxiliar, *a.* auxiliary; help, assist

avalar, endorse

avalancha, avalanche, flood; slump

avaluar, evaluate

avalúo, appraisal, valuation

avance, (p nl) roading; (mc) feed, advance; (rr) (el) lead, pitch

— **de la chispa,** (mo) spark advance

— **del escape,** exhaust lead

— **de fase,** phase displacement, phase difference, phase lead

— **del encendido,** early spark

avanzada de onda, (gf) front wave

avanzar, advance

avellanado, countersunk

avellanador, (tl) countersink

avellanar, countersink

avenamiento radial, radial drainage

avería, average; damage

aviación, aviation

avión, airplane

aviso, advertisement; notice, announcement; warning

avoirdupois, avoirdupois

axinita, axinite

azada, spade, hoe

azadón, large spade

azimut, azimuth

— **de epicentro,** azimuth (o bearing) of epicenter

azogue, quicksilver

azoico, azoic

azuela, adze, blocker

azufre, sulphur, sulfur

— **fundido,** brimstone

— **elemental,** elemental sulfur

— **puro,** elemental sulphur

— **vivo,** brimstone

azulado, blueish

azurita, azurite, blue malachite

B

babbitt, bearing material

babor, (nt) port

bacteria, bacteria

bahía, bay
bajo, low
bajada pluvial, downspout, leader
bajamar, (mar) low-water mark;
    low (o ebb) tide
bajante, low water, leader,
    downspout; (tu) riser, standpipe
bajar el nivel de un líquido, subside
bajío, sand bar, shoal; lowland;
    barrier beach
bajo, sand bar, shoal; (mn)
    footwatt; *a.* low
— cero, subzero
— el agua, subaqueous
— el nivel del mar, subsea
bajocciense, Bajoccian
bajoescurrimiento, (g) underthrust
    fault
bakelita, bakelite
balance, (cm) balance
— de caldeo, heat balance
— de energía, energy balance
balancear, wobble; (mc) balance
balanceo, (nt) sway
balancín, working (o balance
    walking) beam; rocker arm;
    pump jack
— de la brújula, gimbal
— de perforadora inicial, spudding
    beam
— de válvulas, (mc) rocker arm
— tiracable para la barrena
inicial, spudder arm
balanza, scale, balance
— analítica, analytical balance
— de contrapeso, beam balance
— de precisión, analytical balance
— de torsión, torsion balance
— magnética, magnetic balance,
    magnetometer
balconcillo astillero, monkey
    board, fourble board, thribble
    board
balconcillo elevado, walkway
balde, bucket, pail
baldosa, (floor) tile

balinera, roller bearing
baliza, buoy; (tp) pole; marker;
    beacon
balón Engler, (la) Engler flask
bálsamo, balsam
— del Canadá, Canada balsam
bambolear, wobble
banco, (cm) bank; (g) stratum; (r)
    sand bar; (carp) bench; (tp)
    level ground
— coralígeno, coral reef
— de arena, sand bank, sand bar,
    shoal
— de cota fija, bench mark
— de descanso, (derrick) lazy
    bench
— submarino, ocean bar
banda, belt, band
— de amarre, tie band
— de freno, brake band
— de metal duro, hardbanding
bandeja, tray
— de aceite, oil pan (o sump)
— de burbujeo, (rf) bubble deck,
    bubble plate
— de inmersión para probetas, test
    tube and immersion tray
— de resudación, sweating pan
— de turborejilla, turbogrid plate
— tamizadora, sieve plate
banquina, shoulder
banquisa, pack ice
baño, bath; bathtub; bathroom;
    (paint, etc.) coating
— antiácido, acid washing
— congelador, freezing bath
— de aceite, oil bath
baranda, railing, guard rail
barcana, (g) barchan
barcaza, barge
— insumergible, floating barge
— parcialmente sumergible,
    submersible barge
— tiendetubos, pipelaying barge
barco, ship
bario, barium

barisfera, barysphere
barita, baryta
baritina, barite
barniz, varnish
— aislador, electric varnish
barlovento, (nt) windward
barométrico, barometric
barómetro, barometer
— aneroide, aneroid barometer
barógrafo, barograph
barra, bar, rod; sand bar
— abreválvulas, (p) sticker
— chata, (steel) strap
— de apoyo, bearing bar
— de cambio de velocidades, gearshift rail
— de dirección, drag link
— de fijación, (mc) locking bar
— de lastre, (prf) sinker bar
— de perforación, drillpipe
— de peso, (prf) sinker bar
— de punta cuneiforne, wedge point crowbar
— de sección cuadrada, (prf) polished rod
— de sondeo, drillpipe
— de suspensión, (bm jack) hanger, beam hanger, rod hanger
— de tiro, drawbar
— dentada, toothed bar
— equilibradora, equalizer arm
— igualadora, equalizer arm
— lisa, (bm) polished rod
— llave, (p) sticker
— maestra, (prf) drill collar
— (o varilla) de empuje de válvula, valve pushrod
— para desconección, (prf) breakout post
— portavarillas, carrier bar
— punta de escoplo, pinch-point crowbar
— sacaclavos, wrecking bar
— portatubos, carrying bars

barranco, (tp) gap; cliff; bluff; gorge, ravine
barrena, auger, bit, drill
— adamantina, adamantine drill
— afilada a máquina, machine-dressed bit
— cola de pescado, fish-tail bit
— corriente, (tl) jobbersí drill
— corta de mano, (tl) jumper
— de arrastre, drag bit
— de cesto, basket bit
— de circulación de agua, jetting bit
— de cuatro alas, four-wing rotary bit
— de cuatro fresas, four-wing rotary bit
— de cruz, star bit
— de diamante, adamantine drill
— de discos, disc bit
— de espiga cilíndrica, (tl) straight-shank drill
— de expansión, expansive bit
— de extensión, extension bit
— de fricción, drag bit
— de mano, (tl) hand drill
— de paleta, Mother Hubbard bit
— de pecho, breast auger
— de perforación lateral, lateral formation drill
— de punta de diamante, diamond-point rotary bit, diamond drill
— de rodillos, roller bit
— espiral, auger bit
— espiral de espiga cilíndrica, straight-shank twist drill
— excéntrica, eccentric bit
— giratoria de disco, rotary disk bit
— para centrar, (tl) center drill
— para eclisar rieles, (tl) bonding drill
— para hoyos de poste, post-hole auger
— para macho, (tl) tap drill

— **para perforación de disparo,** shot hole drill

— **para perforaciones de voladura,** blast hole drill

— **para perforadora rotatoria,** rotary bit, rotary drill

— **para roca,** rotary rock bit

— **para taladro de chicharra,** ratchet drill

— **para taladro de trinquete,** ratchet drill

— **percutente,** cable drilling bit

— **piloto,** pilot bit

— **principiadora,** spudder

— **rotatoria (o giratoria),** rotary bit, rotary drill

— **sacamuestras,** annular borer, core drill; core bit,

— **sacanúcleos,** core drill

— **sacanúcleos a cable,** wire-line core drill

— **sacatestigos,** core drill

— **taponada,** plugged bit

— **tipo escoplo para perforación inicial,** spudding bit

— **trituradora,** drill-out bit

barreno de fondo de pozo, (prf) rathole

barrera, barrier

barreta, pinching bar

barrido de gases de combustión, scavenging

barril, barrel,

barro, mud, clay, silt; sludge; adobe; mud, slush; loam

— **con silicato de sodio,** sodium-silicate mud

— **de perforación,** drilling mud

— **vitrificado,** vitrified clay

basal, basal

basálitco, basaltic

basalto, basalt

— **analcítico,** analcite basalt

— **prismático,** (g) columnar basalt

basamento, (g) basement, basal complex; substratum

basanita, basanite

base, basis; base; rail flange

— **de acero,** steel base

— **de electrodo,** electrode basis

— **de la soldadura,** (sd) root of weld

— **de triangulación,** base (o triangulation) line

— **para instalar un motor,** motor mounting

— **vidriosa del pórfido,** (g) groundmass, matrix

básico, basic

basitas, basic rocks

bastidor, frame, bedframe

— **de corredera,** skid frame

— **de motor,** engine frame

— **de servicio (o de entrada),** utility guide frame

— **tipo cajón,** box frame

batea, trough, launder; tray, mortar tub; paved ditch;

— **de aceite,** oil pan (o sump)

batería, battery

— **de acumuladores,** (el) storage (o accumulator) battery

— **de pilas secas,** dry-cell battery

— **de tanques,** tank battery

— **de tubos de convección,** convection bank

— **seca,** dry-cell battery

batial, bathyal

batolito, (g) batholith

bauxita, bauxite

benceno, benzene

bencilacetileno, benzylacetylene

bencina, benzine

bentonita, bentonite

benzol, benzol, benzole

berbiquí, wimble; carpenter's brace; crankshaft

— **de herrero,** breast drill

— **y barrena,** brace and bit

berilio, beryl

betún, wurtzilite; bitumen, pitch

biaxial, biaxial

271

bicrabonato, bicarbonate, soda
biciclohexano, bicyclohexane
bicloruro, bichloride
— **de etileno,** ethylene dichloride
bicromato, bichromate
bidireccional alternativo,
  (communications) half-duplex
bidón, (la) beaker
biela, (mc) connecting rod, pitman
bielas gemelas, twin pitman
bienes, assets
— **de capital,** capital assets
— **inmuebles,** real estate
— **nacionales,** property of the state
— **raíces,** real estate
bifurcación, (g) forking; branch
bigornia, anvil
binario, binary (dp)
— **en columna,** column binary
— **en fila,** row binary
binocular, binocular
biolita, (g) biolith
biósfera, biosphere
biotita, (g) biotite
bióxido de carbono, carbon dioxide
biozónido, diozonide
bipolo, dipole
birrefringencia, (gf) birefringence
bisagra, hinge, butt hinge
— **al tope,** butt hinge
— **de paletas,** strap hinge
— **en T,** tee hinge
bisel, bevel
biselar, bevel
bisectriz, bisector, bisectrix
— **aguda,** acute bisectrix
— **obtusa,** obtuse bisectrix
bismuto, bismuth
bisulfuro, disulfide
bitumen, bitumen
bituminoso, bituminous
bivalente, bivalent
blanco, (mc) gear blank; target;
  (cm) blank
— **para registros,** recording chart
blando, soft

blanqueo, bleaching
blastoporfirítico, blastoporphyritic
blindado, shielded; armored,
  ironclad
bloque, block
— **cojinete,** pillow-block bearing
— **de cilindros,** cylinder block
— **de corona,** (prf) crown block
— **de desenganche,** knock-off block
— **de impresión,** impression block
— **de motor,** engine block
— **hueco,** (cn) tile for interior of
  walls.
— **magnético,** magnetic block
bobina, (el) coil
— **de chispa,** spark coil
— **del inductor,** field coil
boca, mouth
— **de inspección,** manhole
— **inferior de llave,** wrench jaw
— **para tomar muestras,** thief
  hatch
bocina, horn
bodega, warehouse, storehouse; (nt)
  hold; cellar; storeroom
bodeguero, warehouse man
bola, ball
— **y asiento,** (va) ball and seat
bolitas de cojinete, bearing balls
bolsa, sack, bag; pocket; (cm) stock
  exchange; (mn) pocket of rich
  ore
bolsón, bolson
bomba, pump; bomb; squib
— **a chorro,** ejector pump
— **a motor,** power pump
— **a motor para el lodo,** power
  driven mud pump
— **acelerante,** accelerator pump
— **alimentadora de agua,**
  feedwater pump
— **alternativa,** reciprocating pump
— **alternativa doble,** reciprocating
  duplex pump
— **aspiradora,** exhausting pump

Glossary of the Petroleum Industry

— **aspirante,** lifter (o suction)
pump

— **auxiliar,** donkey (o auxiliary)
pump

— **centrífuga,** centrifugal pump

— **centrífuga de una etapa,** single-
stage centrifugal pump

— **común,** common pump

— **con engranajes reductores de la
velocidad del motor,** gear-
reduction pumping unit

— **con recubrimiento del cilindro
de bombeo,** liner pump

— **de acción directa,** direct-acting
pump

— **de acción simple,** single-acting
pump

— **del aceite,** oil pump

— **de aceleración,** accelerating
pump

— **de aire,** air pump, air pressure
pump

— **de agua,** water pump

— **de aletas,** vane pump

— **de arena,** sand pump

— **de aspiración,** suction pump

— **de balancín,** walking beam pump

— **de cable de acero,** wire-line
pump

— **de cadena,** chain pump

— **de caja doble,** double case pump

— **de cilindro corredizo,** traveling
barrel

— **de cilindro enterizo,
introducida con el tubo de
producción,** full-barrel tubing
pump

— **de cilindro fijo,** stationary barrel
pump

— **de cilindro interior,** liner-barrel
pump

— **de cilindro interior seccionado,**
sectional liner-barrel pump

— **de cilindro móvil,** traveling
barrel pump

— **de circulación,** circulating pump

— **de cronómetro,** time bomb

— **de cubo,** bucket pump

— **de doble acción,** double-acting
pump

— **de doble efecto,** duplex pump

— **de émbolo,** piston pump

— **de émbolo,** buzo, plunger pump

— **de engrase,** grease pump

— **de inflar neumáticos,** tire pump

— **de inserción,** insert pump

— **de inyección del combustible,**
fuel injector pump

— **de inyección de lodo,** slush pump

— **del lodo,** mud pump

— **de lubricación,** lubricating pump

— **de madre de barril,** liner-barrel
pump

— **de mano,** hand pump

— **de pozo petrolífero,** oil well
pump

— **de presión de vapor Reid, tipo
de inmersión,** Reid vapor
pressure bomb, immersion
type

— **de producción por la tubería de
revestimiento,** casing pump
de profundidad, deep well
pump

— **de prueba,** testing pump

— **de temperatura de fondo,**
bottom hole temperature bomb

— **de tornillo,** screw pump

— **de tres cilindros,** triplex pump

— **de turbina,** turbine pump

— **de vacío,** vacuum pump

— **de varillas,** rod pump

— **de varillas con cilindro
enterizo,** stationary full-barrel
rod pump

— **de varillas con cilindro enterizo
móvil,** traveling full-barrel rod
pump

— **de varillas con cilindro interior
móvil,** traveling liner-barrel rod
pump

— **dosificadora,** proportioning
  pump
— **eléctrica,** electric pump
— **eléctrica sumergible,**
  submersible electrical pump
— **graduada a tiempo,** time bomb
— **introducida en la tubería de
  producción,** tubing pump
— **inyectora de chorro de vapor,**
  steam-jet pump
— **mecánica,** power pump
— **medidora de presión de fondo,**
  bottom pressure bomb
— **montada en cojinetes,** bearing
  pump
— **para agua de alimentación,**
  feed-water pump
— **para barro de circulación,** slush
  pump
— **para chorro de agua,** jet pump
— **para gas,** gas pump
— **para pozos profundos,** deep-well
  pump
— **para la solución eliminadora de
  suciedad,** foul solution pump
— **portátil,** portable pump
— **recíproca,** reciprocating pump
— **recogedora,** pickup pump
— **Reid para medir la presión del
  vapor,** Reid vapor pressure
  pump
— **reforzadora,** booster pump
— **reguladora,** metering pump
— **rotatoria,** rotary pump
— **triple,** triplex pump
— **volcánica,** volcanic bomb
bombeador, pumper
bombeo, pumping
— **hidráulico,** hydraulic pumping
— **neumático,** gas lift
bombero, firefighter
bombilla eléctrica, electric bulb
bonete alado, finned bonnet
bonificación sobre fletes, (cm)
  freight allowances
bono, (cm) bond; bonus

boquilla, manhole
— **con válvula piloto,** pilot nozzle
— **de engrase,** lubricant fitting
— **del carburador,** carburetor
  nozzle
— **del quemador de la llama de
  prueba,** test flame burner tip
— **de regar,** spray nozzle
— **de velocidad sin carga,** idling
  nozzle
— **embridada,** flanged nozzle
— **mezcladora,** mixing nozzle
— **para barrenas,** drill sleeve
— **para la extracción de productos
  líquidos,** nozzle for liquid
  product removal
— **roscada,** threaded nozzle
boracita, boracite
bórax, borax
borde, border; edge; dike; levee
— **continental,** continental fringe
— **de la soldadura,** toe of weld
bordeador de tubos, tube beader
boreador de tubos de caldera, flue
  beader
borne de conexión, (el) terminal
bornita, bornite
boro, borium, boron
bostonita, bostonite
botador de válvula, valve tappet
botalón, derrick boom
botar, (nt) launch
bote, boat
botella, bottle
botiquín de primera cura,
  emergency kit
botón, button
— **colador,** (prf) button screen
— **de contacto,** push button
— **de control para el obturador y
  la llama de prueba,** (la) shutter
  and test flame control knob
— **de presión,** push button
bóveda del hogar, furnace arch
boya, buoy

braza, (nt) fathom: equals 1.67m
brazo, arm; leg of an angle; (r) branch of a stream
— **de carga,** loading arm
— **de gobierno,** (mc) control arm
— **de palanca,** lever arm
— **de sostén,** holdover post
— **muerto,** (g) oxbow lake
— **oscilante,** (mc) rocker
— **trabador,** locking arm
— **volado,** cantilever arm
brea, pitch, brea
— **mineral,** maltha
breccia, breccia
brecha, trail; breach; opening; crevasse; (g) breccia
— **volcánica,** volcanic breccia
brida, lifter
— **ciega,** blind flange
— **ciegatubos,** figure-eight blank
— **con ganchos** (o torniquetes) **de anclaje,** tiedown flange
— **corrediza,** (sd) welding slip on flange
— **de camisa,** slip-on flange
— **de cojinete,** bearing flange
— **de collar,** collar flange
— **de cuello,** (sd) welding neck flange
— **de hierro fundido,** cast flange
— **de la cámara de encauzamiento,** (heat exchanger) channel flange
— **de metal maleable,** malleable flange
— **de obturación,** blank flange
— (o **reborde**) **de orificio,** orifice flange
— **para conexión a soldadura,** welding flange
— **sostenedora de la tubería de revestimiento durante su inserción,** casing-landing flange
bridas gemelas, companion flange
— **con ganchos de anclaje,** tiedown companion flange

brigada, gang, party, squad
brightstock, brightstock
brillo, luster
briqueta, (carbon) briquet
broca, bit
brocha, brush
broche, fastener
— **para correa,** belt clamp
bromar, brominate
bromación, bromination
bromo, bromine
bromofenol, bromopohenol
bromoforma, bromoform
bronce, bronze
— **de aluminio,** aluminum bronze
— **fosforado,** phosphor bronze
— **tobin,** Tobin bronze
broncita, bronzite
brookite, brookite
brotadero, seepage
brotar, emerge; crop out
brucita, brucite
brújula, compass
— **Brunton,** Brunton compass
— **de inclinación,** (in) dip needle
— **de tangentes,** tangent galvanometer
bucle de realimentación, (dp) feedback loop
buje, bushing sleeve
— **al ras,** flush bushing
— **de cojinete,** bearing bushing
— **de eje,** axle bushing
— **de pasador de émbolo,** piston pin bushing
— **de reducción para grapa de anillos,** casing bushing
— **de resalto,** shoulder bushing
— **de transmisión,** drive bushing
— **de vástago de válvula,** valve stem bushing
— **maestro,** master bushing
— **principal,** master bushing
— **del pasador,** pin bushings
bujía, spark plug
bulón, bolt

bulto, (cm) package, parcel
buque, ship
— **amarrado a torre,** turret-
  moored
buque de perforación, drillship
burbuja, bubble
burel, marlinespike, fid
bureta, burette
butano, butane
— **normal,** n-butane
butadieno, butadiene
butano-n, n-butane
buteno, butene, butylene
butenino, butenyne
butilacetileno, butylacetylene,
  hexyne
butilbenceno, butylbenzene
— **secundario,** sec-butylbenzene
— **terciario,** tert-butylbenzene
butileno, butylene, butene
— **isomérico,** isomeric butylene
buzamiento, (g) dip, inclination,
  head
— **aparente,** apparent dip
— **arriba,** updip
— **de falla,** fault dip
— **empinado,** steep dip
— **inicial,** initial dip
— **invertido,** overturned dip
— **regional,** (g) regional dip
buzo, diver

C

caballete, (mc) saddle; trestle bent,
  A-frame; truss; sawhorse; ridge
  of a roof; (va) yoke (carp) horse
— **de mando por debajo,** underpull
  jack
— **de bombeo,** pumping jack
— **portapoleas,** (prf) crown block
caballos de fuerza, horsepower,
— **al freno,** brake horsepower
— **de caldera,** boiler horsepower

— **efectiva,** actual (o effective)
  horsepower
— **en la barra de tiro,** drawbar
  horsepower
cabeza, (fl) (tl) head; (girder)
  flange. (q.v. **cabezal**)
— **de barrena,** cutter head
— **de circulación,** (prf) circulating
  head
— **de descarga,** flowhead
— **de émbolo,** piston head
— **de empaque,** stuffing box
— **de la torre de perforación,** mast
  head
— **de sacanúcleos** (o **sacatestigos**),
  core head
— **de seguridad,** safety head, relief
  head
— **de tope,** landing head
— **de tubería de producción,**
  tubing head
— **de tubería de revestimiento,**
  casing head
— **de tubos,** tube header
— **de un pliegue terraplenado** (o
  monoclinal), head
— **de válvula,** valve head
— **flotante,** (heat exchanger)
  floating head
— **giratoria,** (prf) swivel
cabezadas, (pr) by heads
cabezal, cap header, lintel; bridle;
  header brick. (q.v. **cabeza**)
— **amortiguador de enganche,**
  latch bumper head
— **con prensaestopa,** bradenhead
— **de balancín,** (bm) beam head;
  horsehead
— **de cementación,** cementing
  head
— **de perforar,** boring head; drilling
  head
— **de pozo,** wellhead
— **de seguridad para tubería de
  revestimiento,** control casing
  head

Glossary of the Petroleum Industry

— de tubería de revestimiento, casing head
— de tubos, tube header
— en U, header box, return bend
— obturador, packing head, packoff head
— obturador de control, controlhead packer
— para inyección de ácido, acid treating head
cabilla, spoke
cabina, cab; elevator car
cable, cable, rope, line; (el) cable;
— acorazado, armored cable
— blindado, armored cable
— contraviento, guy line
— de acero, wire-line, wire-rope
— de acero delgado, wire, thin wire cable
— de acero desnudo, bright rope
— de alambre, wire line, wire cable, wire rope
— de arrastre, dragline
— de la barrena, drilling line
— de cabrestante auxiliar, catline
— de colchado (o trenzado) a la derecha, right-lay cable
— de cuchareo, (prf) sand line
— de draga, aerial spud
— de empalme, jumper head
— de enroscar y desenroscar tubería, spinning line
— de las llaves, (prf) jerk line
— de Manila, Manila cable
— de medición de profundidad, (prf) measuring line
— de freno, brake cable
— del malacate, bull rope
— de las poleas, (prf) wire-line
— de retenida, guy line
— del torno de herramientas, bull rope (o wheel)
— de torpedo, torpedo line
— de la tubería de revestimiento, casing line
— eléctrico, electric cable

— elevador del tornillo alimentador, temper-screw elevator rope
— flexible de emplame, jumper
— muerto, (block) dead line
— para perforación rotatoria, rotary drilling line
— para tubería de producción y varillas de bombeo, tubing and sucker rod
— para tubería de revestimiento, casing line
— sin fin, endless line
— tensor, guy line
— teso, taut line
— conductor, welding lead
cablecarril, cableway, aerial tramway
cabo, (geog) cap; rope strand; end
— de Manila, Manila cable
cabotaje, coastwire shipping
cabrestante, winch, capstan, crab; A frame, breast derrick, house derrick
— auxiliar de servicio en una torre de perforación, handy hoist
cabria, winch, capstan, crab, windlass; crane; derrick, A frame, rig; gin; breast derrick
— transportadora de troncos, logging arch
cabriada, (pile hammer) leads
carcaraña, pitting
cadena, chain; (g) range,
— de amarre, binding chain
— de doblar, bending chain
— de eje del torno auxiliar, line shaft drive chain
— de eslabones afianzados, (o con travesaño), stud link chain
— de hidrocarburos, carbon chain
— de mando, drive chain
— de rodillos, roller chain
— de rodillos de ancho doble, double-width roller chain

277

— **de rodillos de ancho cuádruple,** quadruple-width roller chain

— **de rodillos de ancho sencillo,** single-width roller chain

— **de rodillos de ancho triple,** triple-width roller chain

— **de transmisión,** transmission chains

— **intermediaria de transmisión,** intermediate rotary chain

— **para engranaje,** sprocket chain

— **primaria de transmisión del tambor,** drum drive chain

— **silenciosa,** silent chain

— **sin fin,** endless chain

— **transmisora de la mesa rotatoria,** rotary chain

— **de neumático,** tire chains

caída, fall

— **de agua,** waterfall

— **de presión,** pressure drop

— **de temperatura,** temperature drop

— **libre,** free fall

caimán, Stillson wrench; relief man; ore chute

caja, box, case; car body; (carp) mortise, recess; (ma) housing, casing; (el) outlet box, junction box; (cm) cash; safe, cashbox; cashier's office

— **colectora,** drip box

— **de acumulador,** battery box

— **de cambio de velocidades,** gear shifter housinig

— **del catalizador,** catalyst case

— **de cigüeñal,** crankcase

— **de chumacera,** pillow block, bearing

— **de cojinete de la cruceta,** crossbearing box

— **de colador,** strainer body

— **del diafragma,** diaphragm case

— **de eje,** axle housing

— **de eje trasero,** real axle housing

— **de embrague,** clutch housing (o case)

— **de engranajes,** gear case

— **de engranajes de cambio,** speed-reduction unit, gear box

— **de estopas,** stuffing box

— **del freno,** brake box

— **de grasa,** (o engrasadora), grease box

— **de herramientas,** tool box

— **de humos,** smokebox, breeching

— **de inspección,** look box

— **de prensaestopa,** packing gland

— **de recocer,** annealing box

— **de la transmisión,** transmission case

— **esférica,** ball housing

— **principal,** main case

— **refrigerante,** condenser jacket

cajera del eje, pillow block

cajero, cashier

cajón, (g) gorge, canyon; (ma) packing case; caisson; bin; skip, scalepan; car body drawer

— **del lodo,** mud box (o crib)

cal, lime

cala, (nt) hold

calafateadura, calking, caulking

calafatear, caulk, calk

calafateo, calking, caulking

calamina, calamine

calamita, (g) lodestone

calaverita, calaverite

calcáreo, calcareous

calcedonia, chalcedony

cálico, calcic

calcinar, calcine

calcio, calcium

calcita, calcite

— **bituminosa,** anthraconite

calco, (g) cast

calcopirita, chalcopyrite

calcosita, chalcocite

cálculo, calculation, computation, estimate

calda, heating, (steel) a heat

— **a martillo hidráulico,** (sd)
hammer roll, forge welding,
blacksmith roll
— **de herrero,** (sd) hammer roll,
forge welding, blacksmith roll
caldear, heat; weld; (sd) hammer
roll, forge welding
caldera, (vlc) caldera; (ma) boiler
— **de calor de desecho,** waste-heat
boiler
— **de campo petrolero,** oil-field
boiler
— **de grasa,** grease kettle
— **de tubos,** water-tube boiler
— **de vapor,** steam boiler
caldero de colada, melting ladle
caledoniense, Caledonian
calentador, heater
— **alimentador de agua para
calderas,** boiler feed-water heater
— **con calefacción a ambos
extremos,** double end heater
— **con fuego por un solo lado,**
single-end heater
— **de agua a fuego directo,** direct-
fire water heater
— **de aire de fuego directo,** direct-
fire air heater
— **de la carga** con gas (o con vapor
de escape), exhaust feed heater
— **del gas,** gas heater
— **de tubos,** tube heater
— **mediante vapor de sangría,** (rf)
blowdown heat exchanger
calentamiento, heating
— **por ácido,** (rf) acid heat
caleta, cove, small bay, inlet
calibración, calibration
— **de instrumentos,** instrument
calibration
— **de medidores,** meter calibration
calibrador, gage, calipers; shifting
gage; (rr) clearance template;
sizer
— **de alambre,** wire gage
— **de barrenas,** bit gage, drill gauge

— **de espigas,** pin template
— **de exteriores,** outside calipers
— **de filetes de tornillo,** thread
gauge
— **de interiores,** inside calipers
— **de macho,** plug gage
— **de mechas,** drill gage
— **de paso de rosca,** screw pitch
gage
— **de trépanos,** drill gage
— **para herramientas,** tool gage
— **para planchas,** plate gage
calibrar, calibrate, gage caliper
calibre, gage, caliber, bore; (in)
gage, jig, calipers
— **a rosca,** screw gage
— **de espesor,** thickness gage
— **de nonio,** vernier caliper
— **deslizable,** slide gage
— **normal,** end measuring rod
calibrescopio, borescope
caliche, (mn) caliche
calidad, quality
caliente, warm; hot
caliza, limestone
— **asfáltica,** asphaltic limestone
— **bituminosa,** bituminous
limestone
— **cavernosa,** cavernous limestone
— **coralina,** coral limestone
— **cristalina,** crystalline limestone
— **dolomítica cristalina,**
crystalline dolomitic limestone
calizo, limy, calcareous
calor, heat
— **al rojo oscuro,** black-red heat
— **de combustión,** combustion
heat, heating valve
— **de fusión,** fusion heat
— **de proceso,** exhaust heat
— **específico,** specific heat
— **latente,** latent heat
— **perdido,** waste heat
— **rojo,** red heat
— **sensible,** sensible heat
caloría, calorie

calorímetro, heat prover, calorimeter

calzo (calza, calce), wedge, chock; shim; (ma) shoe; foot block; friction block

cama de eje, lifter

cama de roca, (g) shelf

camada, layer

cámara, *a.* tire tube, inner tube chamber; room; camera

— **colectora de horno,** plenum chamber

— **de aceite,** (mc) oil reservoir

— **de aire,** air vessel, air chamber

— **de alta presión,** high pressure chamber

— **de amortiguamiento,** cushing chamber

— **de baja presión,** low pressure chamber

— **de la arcilla,** (rf) clay chamber

— **de catalización,** catalyst chamber

— **de combustión,** combustion chamber

— **de comercio,** (cm) chamber of commerce

— **de destilación oir expansión instantánea,** (rf) flash chamber(o drum, tower)

— **de emanación,** emanation chamber

— **de escape,** exhaust chamber

— **de expansión para deshidratar el gas,** knockout chamber

— **de fusión,** (rf) muffle; combustion chamber

— **del freno,** brake chamber

— **de reacción,** (rf) soaker, reaction (o soaking chamber)

— **de resudación de parafina,** wax sweater

— **de separación primaria,** primary separating chamber

— **de separación secundaria,** secondary separation chamber

— **de válvula,** valve cage (o chamber)

— **de válvula fija,** standing valve cage

— **fotográfica,** camera

— **lúcida,** camera lucida

cambiador, (el) switch; (rf) exchanger

— **de calor,** (rf) heat exchanger

— **intermedio de temperatura,** intercooler

— **de líquido a líquido,** liquid-to-liquid exchanger

cambio, (cm) exchange; change

— **de facies,** (g) change of facies

— **de fase,** phase shift

— **de velocidades,** gear shifting

— **diurno,** diurnal change

— **secular,** (gf) secular change

cámbrico, Cambrian

camino, road

camión, motor truck

— **de instrumentos registradores,** (gf) recording truck

— **de plataforma,** flat truck

— **tanque,** tank truck

— **volcador,** tilting truck

camionero, truck driver

camisa, (mc) sleeve, bushing; drill chuck; jacket, lagging

— **de agua,** cylinder water packet, water jacket

— **de caldera,** boiler jacket

— **de cilindros,** cylinder sleeve, cylinder liner

— **de eje,** axle bushing

— **de válvula,** valve jacket

— **en contacto con el agua,** wet sleeve

campana, bell

— **corrugada para pesca,** (fishing tl) corrugated socket

— **de aire,** air receiver, tank for compressed air

— **de burbujeo,** babble cap

— **de pesca,** (prf) fishing socket

— **de pesca circular con aletas,** full-circle socket slip

— **de pesca combinada,** combination socket

— **de pesca con aletas,** slip socket

— **de pesca con cuñas,** slip socket

— **de pesca con cuñas circulares,** full-circle socket slip

— **de pesca,** sencilla, con aletas, regular socket slip

campo, field; mining camp

— **de gas,** gas field

— **de gravedad,** (gf) gravitational field

— **eléctrico,** electric field

— **electroestático,** electrostatic

— **electromagnético,** electromagnetic field

— **geomagnético,** (gf) geomagnetic field

— **magnético,** magnetic field

— **magnético de componente vertical,** (gf) vertical component magnetic field

— **magnético terrestre,** earth's magnetic field

— **petrolero,** oil field

— **petrolífero,** (g) oil field

canal, canal, channel, gullet; chute, flume, race

— **de erupción,** (g) chimney, pipe

— **de inyección,** (prf) mud trough

— **del lodo,** (prf) mud trough

— **de rango vocal,** (dp) voice-grade channel

— **de tanque,** tank flume

cancaneo, (gasoline) knocking

canchal, (g) bouldery ground

candado, padlock

canfano, camphane, trimethylbicycloheptane

canfeno, camphene, methylenedimethylbicycloheptane

cangrejo pescatubos, casing spear, bulldog spear

cantalita, pitchstone, cantalite

canteador, edger

cantera, (g) quarry

cantidad, quantity; amount

cantilever, cantilever

canto, edge; thickness of a board; ashlard stone; boulder pebble

— **de la polea de remolque,** band tug rim

— **rodado,** boulder

— **rodado mediano,** cobble

cantonera, angle iron

cañada, (g) dell

cañadón, canyon

cañería, pipe, piping, conduit (q.v. **tubería**)

— **aisladora,** casing

— **de entubación,** casing

— **de lubricación,** oil line

— **reforzada,** extra strong pipe

caño, pipe, conduit; gutter; roof leader; small stream (q.v. **tubería**)

— **de agua,** water pipe

— **del combustible,** fuel pipe

— **de descarga,** down pipe, dischage pipe

— **de perforación,** drill pipe

— **filtro,** (prf) perforated liner

— **para vástago de perforación,** drill pipe

— **punzonado,** perforated pipe

caño-soporte de manguera, standpipe

cañón, gun; gorge, canyon; barrel of an arch; perforating gun; cannon

— **perforador,** perforator, perforating gun

capa, (g) stratum, layer; ply; (painting) coat (mn) seam, vein;

— **acuífera,** aquifer

— **basáltica,** basaltic layer

— **continental,** continental layer

— **de acumulación interglacial,** forest bed

— **de agua subterránea,** water
plane
— **de arcilla debajo de una capa de
carbón,** underclay
— **de arcilla roja,** red bed
— **de comparación,** key bed, key
horizon
— **de desgaste,** (rd) blanket
— **de refuerzo,** (mc) facing
— **de velocidad,** (gf) velocity layer
— **freática,** aquifer
— **frontal deltáica,** foreset bed
— **gasífera,** gas cap
— **inferior,** substratum
— **interfacial,** interfacial film
— **intrusiva,** sill
— **invertida,** overturned bed
— **mineralífera,** ore bed
— **perservativa de asfalto,** asphalt
coating
— **refractaria,** ganister lining
— **superficial,** (gf) weathered layer
— **superpuesta,** superimposed layer
— **superpuestas por el proceso de
transgresión,** (g) transgressive
overlap
— **de contactos paralelos,** (g)
conformable beds
— **perturbadas,** (g) disturbed beds
— **plegadas,** folded strata
capacidad, capacity
— **aprovechada,** utilized capacity
— **calculada,** (mc) design capacity
— **colorante,** tinting strength
— **de calcinación,** char value
— **de carga,** rate of charge
— **estimada,** rated capacity
— **nominal,** rated capacity
— **normal,** rating
caparazón, shell
capilar, capillary
capilaridad, capillarity, capillary
action
capillo de prensaestopas, packing
gland
capó, (a), hood

cápsula, capsule; (expl) cap,
exploder
captación, (g) capture; (hd)
impounding, catchment;
diversion; (gf) detection of
waves by recording instrument
captación en abanico, (gf) arc
shooting
cara, face; (sheet) side
— **de la soldadura,** face of weld
— **de una válvula,** valve of face
— **triturante de la barrena,**
crushing face of the bit
característica, property,
characteristic
característica de detonación,
(gasol) detonation
characteristic, octane number
carámbano, icicle
carbeno, carbene
carbón, coal; charcoal; carbon
— **amorfo,** amorphous carbon
— **animal,** bone coal
— **antracita,** anthracite coal
— **argiláceo,** bone coal
— **bituminoso,** bituminous coal
— **de ampelita,** cannel coal
— **de bujía,** cannel coal
— **de madera,** charcoal
— **de piedra,** hard coal
— **en polvo,** blacking
— **estable,** fixed carbon
— **libre,** free carbon
— **menudo,** (coal) slack
carbonato, carbonate
— **de amonio,** ammonium
carbonate
— **de sodio calcinado,** soda ash
— **sódico,** sodium carbonate
carbonífero, carboniferous; coal-
bearing
— **inferior,** Mississippian, lower
carboniferous
carbonilo sulfúrico , carbonyl
sulfide

carbonización, carbon formation, carbonization
carbono terciario, tertiary carbon
carbonoso, carbonaceous
carborundo, carbide of silicon, carborundum
carburador, carburetor
— **de corriente descendente,** down-draft carburetor
carburar, carburate
carburo, carbure, carbide
— **aromático,** aromatic hydrocarbon
— **de níquel,** nickel carbide
carcavas, (g) gully; ditch, gutter
cárcel, clamp, cramp; vise
cardán, universal joint
carga, load, loading; (el) (rf) (cl) charge; (hd) head; freight; cargo, lading; (rf) (gas) feedstock
— **accidental,** live load
— **de calor,** heat load
— **de gasolina,** gasoline charge
— **de reciclo,** (rf) recycle stock
— **de repaso,** (rf) recycle stock
— **de trabajo,** work load
— **de velocidad,** velocity head
— **excéntrica,** eccentric load
— **excesiva,** overcharge
— **explosiva,** torpedo, explosive charge
— **máxima,** peak load
— **muerta,** dead load
— **útil,** useful load
— **virgen,** (rf) fresh feed
— **viva,** live load
cargamento, cargo
cargar, load
— **en cuenta,** (cm) charge
carnalita, carnallite
carpa, tent, canvas house
carpeta de asfalto, (rd) blanket
carrera, strongback, water, stringer, ranger; girder; (carp) wall plate; purlin; girt; highway; avenue; (ma) stroke, throw, travel

— **ascendente,** upstroke
— **de admisión,** (bm) admission stroke; (plunger) intake stroke
— **de clasificación,** rated travel
— **de compresión,** compression stroke
— **del émbolo,** piston stroke
— **de escape,** exhaust stroke
— **de expansión,** expansion stroke
— **de impulsión,** power stroke
— **de retroceso del émbolo,** back stroke
— **motriz,** power stroke
— **(o recorrido) de una válvula,** valve travel
carreta de pantano, marsh buggy
carrete, reel, coil; spool; (el) coil
— **del cable de la cuchara,** (prf) sand reel
— **de cuchareo,** (prf) sand reel
— **para el alambre del torpedo,** torpedo reel
— **para la cuerda de medición de profundidad,** well-measuring reel
carretel, reel, spool
— **a motor,** power-driven reel
— **manual,** hand-powered reel
carretera, highway; road
carretilla, wheelbarrow; hand truck; small car
— **de rodillos,** dolly
— **para tuberías,** casing wagon
carro, car; wagon, truck, car; automobile
— **de mano,** hand cart
— **de plataforma,** (rr) flat car
— **de remolque,** trailer
— **tanque,** tank car
carta, chart, map; letter, document
— **circular,** (cm) circular letter
— **de crédito,** letter of credit
— **de crédito permanente,** revolving letter of credit
— **de puntos,** dot chart
— **de registro,** recording chart

283

— **dinamométrica,** dynamometric
card
cartabón, (carp) square; gage
cartel, billboard
cárter, crankcase
cartografía, mapping, cartography
— **aérea,** airplane mapping
cartográfico, cartographic
cartucho de nitroglicerina, squib
cartucho de voladura, blasting
cartridge
casa, house, building
— **de máquinas,** engine house
— **de motores,** power house
— **en secciones,** sectional house
— **portátil,** portable house
cascada, waterfall
cascajo, gravel; quarry waste; grit;
cobbles
cáscara, (prf) mud cake
casco, (mc) shell; casing; cask; (nt)
hull; (p) shell; hard hat, helmet
— **anticorrosión,** corrosion cap
— **de encastre,** socket bowl
— **de radiador,** radiator shell
caseta, (prf) doghouse
— **de los contadores,** meter house
— **del perforador,** doghouse
casilla, post-office box; shed, small
building
— **de la correa,** belt house
casillero, (tu) rack
casiterita, cassiterite
caso fortuito, act of God,
contingency
casquete, cap, shell,
— **de burbujeo,** (rf) bubble cap
— **de gas,** gas cap
— **de hincar,** (pile) drive cap
— **de la válvula,** valve bonnet
casquillo, (ca) basket; gland;
ferrule; sleeve, bushing; socket;
(mn) blasting cap; pipe cap
— **de electrodo,** electrode tip,
electrode point
— **del empaque,** packing follower

— **del presaestopas,** (ma) gland,
stuffing-box gland
— **de protección,** driving cap
— **roscado,** cap nut
cataclástico, (g) cataclastic
catalina, sprocket; flying wheel
catálisis, catalysis
catalítico, catalytic
catalizador, catalyst
— **de gel de óxido de cromo,**
chromic oxide gel catalyst
— **de lecho fijo,** fixed-bed catalyst
— **de óxido metálico,** metal oxide
catalyst
— **del tipo de óxido metálico,** (rf)
metallic oxide-type catalyst
— **rgenerado,** regenerated catalyst
— **sintético,** synthetic catalyst
— **sólido,** solid catalyst
— **usado,** spent catalyst
catálogo, catalog
— **de piezas,** parts catalog
catamorfismo, (g) catamorphism
catarata, waterfall
catazona, (g) katazone
cateo, prospecting, exploration;
sampling
catión, cation
catódico, cathodic
cátodo, cathode
cauce, (r) riverbed, channel
caucho, rubber
— **sintético,** synthetic rubber
cáustico, caustic
cautín, soldering iron
cavar, dig, excavate
cavas, (g) rills
cavazanjas, trenching machine
caverna, cavern
cavernoso, spelaean, cavernous
cavidad, (sd) cavity; blow hole, gas
pocket;
cazo de fundir, smelting pot
cebador, (bm) priming cap; *a.* choke
— **adjustable,** (mo) adjustable
choke

celda, cell; bin
— fotoeléctrica, photoelectric cell
célula, cell, cubicle
celulosa, cellulose
cementación, lutation;
cementation, cementing
— bajo presión, squeeze cementing
— forzada, squeeze cementing
— por la boca de fondo de la
tubería, full-hole cementing
cementita, cementite
cemento, cement
— a inyección forzada, squeezed
cement
— armado, reinforced concrete
— de alúmina de fraguado rápido,
Lumnite
— portland, portland cement
— refractario, refractory cement
cenegal, bog, swamp
cenicero, ash pit
ceniza, ash, cinders
— de soda, soda ash
— volcánica, volcanic ash
cenomaniense, Cenomanian
cenozoico, Cenozoic
centígrado, centigrade
centígramo, centigram
centilitro, centiliter
centímetro, centimeter
— cuadrado, square centimeter
centímetro-gramo-segundo,
centimeter-gram-second
centinela, watch, watchman, guard
centipoise, centipoise
centistoke, centistoke
centrador, centralizer
— de la tubería de revestimiento,
casing centralizer
central, *a.* central; *n.* plant, station;
powerhouse; telephone exchange
— de bombeo de engranaje de
fuerza mecánica, central geared
power
— de energía, power house

centralización automática, self-
centering
centrar, (tu) stab; center; align
centrífugo, centrifugal, *n.*
centrifuge
centro, center
— de gravedad, center of gravity
cepillar, plane; brush; polish
cepillo, brush; paint brush
— de alambre, wire brush
cepo, waler, ranger, ribbon, string-
piece; shell of a tackle block,
stock of an anvil; stock of an
anchor
cera, wax
— amorfa, amorphous wax
— de parafina, paraffin wax
cercha, rib of an arch center; truss;
template; screen
ceresina, ceresin
— de petróleo, petroleum ceresin
cero, zero
— absoluto, absolute zero
— a la izquierda, leading zero
— normal, datum
— o punto nulo, null point
cerrado, closed, shut, (curve) sharp;
a. shutdown; shut in
cerradura, lock
— de resorte, snap lock
cerrar, close, fasten, lock seal
cerrojo, bolt, latch
— de la trampa del respatubos,
(p) scraper trap closure
— (o seguro) de la caja de la
transmisión, transmission lock
cerro sepultado, buried hill
certificación, certification
certificado de origen, certificate of
origin
cerficicado de seguro, certificate of
insurance
cerusita, cerusite
cesio, Caesium
cesto, basket
— de pesca, (prf) fishing basket

— **de pesca para despojos,** (prf) junk basket

— **de barrena,** bit basket

— **de cementación,** cementing basket

cetano, cetane, hexadecane

cianita, cyanite, kyanite

ciclo, (el) (mc) (qm) cycle

— **de cuatro tiempos,** four-stroke cycle

— **de erosión,** cycle of erosion

— **de funcionamiento,** operating cycle

— **de perforación,** drilling cycle

cicloalcano, cycloalkane

ciclobutano, cyclobutane (q.v. **tetrametileno**)

ciclobuteno, cyclobutene

cicloheptano, cycloheptane

ciclohepteno, cycloheptene

ciclohexano, cyclohexane (q.v. **hexametileno**)

ciclohexeno, cyclohexane (q.v. **tetrahidrobenceno**)

ciclón, tornado, cyclone

cicloocteno, cyclooctene

ciclopentano, cyclopentane (q.v. **pentametileno**)

ciclopenteno, cyclopentene

ciclopropano, cyclopropane

ciclopropeno, cyclopropene

ciclotización, (rf) cyclization

ciego, blind

cielo de hogar, (cl) crown sheet

cieno, sludge, mud, silt

— **endurecido,** mudstone

cierre, *n.* shutdown; shut in; closure, sealing, locking

— **anticlinal,** anticlinal closure

— **de aceite,** oil seal

— **de agua,** water seal

— **de la curva de nivel,** (g) closure

— **hidráulico,** (bm) water seal

cigüeña, crank; sweep; winch, windlass, capstan;

cigüeñal, crankshaft

— **hueco,** hollow crankshaft

cilindrada, (mc) piston displacement, cylinder capacity

— **de émbolo,** piston displacement

cilindro, cylinder; roller, roll

— **de bomba,** pump barrel

— **del émbolo de una bomba,** working barrel

— **del freno,** brake cylinder

— **exterior,** (ma) outer barrel

— **insertado,** (ma) insert barrel

— **interior,** (bm) liner-barrel

— **maestro,** master cylinder

— **maestro del freno,** brake master cylinder

— **móvil de bomba,** working barrel

— **para coquificación,** oil-coking drum

— **principal,** master cylinder

— **fundidos en bloque,** block cast cylinder

cima, crest, summit, peak, top

cimbra, (prf) jar

cimiento, foundation

— **de la torre,** derrick foundation

— **sedimentario,** (g) bottomsets

cinabrio, cinnabar

cincel, chisel, cutter, graver

— **de calafatear,** calking chisel

— **de recalcar,** calking chisel

— **desvastador,** drove chisel, bolster; burr

— **o formón dentado,** ripping chisel

cinética, *n.* kinetics

cinta, belt; tape; strip; waler; ribbon; girt

— **aisladora,** electric tape

— **de control del carro,** (dp) carriage control tape

— **de freno,** brake band

— **de medición,** (tk) gauging tape

— **métrica,** measuring tape

— **semiperforada,** (dp) chadless tape

— **estratigráficas de arena,** (g) shoestring sand

cinteada, (g) streak

cinturón, belt
— de seguridad, safety belt
— morénico, (g) moraine belt
— salvavidas, safety belt
cinc, zinc
ciprita, cyprite
circo, (g) cirque
— glaciárico, corrie, corry
— glaciario, glacial circus
circón, zircon
circuito, circuit
— a tierra, (el) grounded circuit
— de control de volumen, volume
    control circuit
— de entrada, input circuit
— de filtros, (gf) circuit channel
— de mezcla, mixing circuit
— de resonancia, resonant circuit
— de salida, output circuit
— eléctrico, electric circuit
— en puente, bridge circuit
— posterior, downstream
— sismográfico, filter circuit
circulación, circulation
— del reactivo, reagent circulation
— inversa, reverse circulation
— normal, normal circulation
circular, *a.* circular; *n.* circular; *v.*
    circulate
circunferencia, circumference
cisco, coal dust, culm, slack
cisterna, cistern
cizallas, bench shears
cizallamiento, *n.* shearing; shearing
    stress
clarificador, clarifier
— centrífugo, centrifugal clarifier
clarificar, clarify
claro, (color) light; clear
clarolina, claroline
clasificadora, (dp) sorter
cláusula, clause
clave, code; key, keystone,
    (concrete) bounding key;
clavija, linch pin; pin, peg, dowel,
    drift-bolt; plug, pintle

— de eje, axle pin
— hendida, cotter pin
clavo, nail
— largo, spike
cliente, customer, client
clima, climate
climático, climatic
clinógrafo, clinograph
clinómetro, clinometer
clivaje, (mn) slaty cleavage
— de flujo, (g) flood cleavage
— de fractura, (g) fracture
    cleavage
cloaca, sewer
clorex, chlorex
clorinación, chlorination
clorita, chlorite
cloritoide, chloritoid
cloro, chlorine
cloroacetona, chloracetone
cloroanilina, chloroaniline
cloroformo, chloroform
cloruro, chloride
— de aluminio anhidro, anhydrous
    aluminum chloride
— de calcio, calcium chloride
— de calcio anhidro, anhydrous
    calcium chloride
— de hidrógeno anhidro,
    anhydrous hydrogen fluoride
— de polivinilo, polyvinyl chloride,
    PVC
— de vinilo, vinyl chloride
— de zinc, zinc chloride
coagulación, coagulation
coagulador, coagulator
cobaltita, cobaltite
cobalto, cobalt
cobijadura, (g) overthrust
coblentziense, Coblentzian
cobre, copper
— bruto, anode copper
— desoxidado, deoxidized copper
cobro contra entrega, (cm) cash on
    delivery
cobros, (cm) collections

cochada, coction; batch of oil put through a refinery
cochura, (rf) batch; coction; boiling
cocodrilo, rope grab
codímero, codimer
codo, (p) elbow, bend; crank; knee
— **compensador,** expansion bend
— **(o curva) de tubería,** pipe bend
— **de árbol cigüeñal,** crank throw
— **de 1800,** return bend
— **de hierro,** gusset
— **de palanca,** (mc) quadrant; crank
— **de soporte de 900,** 900 base elbow
— **escariador,** kickoff joint
— **macho y hembra roscado,** street elbow, street ell
coeficiente, coefficient; module
— **de dilatación lineal,** coefficient of linear expansion
— **de elasticidad,** coefficient of elasticity
— **de expansión,** coefficient of expansion
— **elástico,** elastic coefficient
coexistente, coexistent; (g) concurrent
cogedero, grip, handle; bail
cogemuestras de las paredes del estrato, wall sampler
cohesión, cohesion
cohete, squib; rocket
cojín, squab; cushion, pad; pillow block, bearing
cojinete, bearing, pillow block, journal box; bushing; (threads) die
— **a bolillas,** ball bearing
— **a bolilla de auto-alineación,** self-aligning ball bearing
— **bipartido,** split bearing
— **central,** center bearing
— **con buje de bronce,** bronze-bushed bearing
— **de agujas,** needle bearing
— **de antifricción,** antifriction bearing
— **de biela,** connecting rod bearing, pitman bearing
— **de bolas,** ball bearing
— **de bolas de alineación automática,** self-aligning ball bearing
— **de bolas radial,** radial ball bearings
— **de bolas radio-axial,** radial-thrust ball bearing
— **de brazo,** wrist-pin bearing
— **de bronce,** brass bearing
— **de cola,** tail bearing
— **de doble hilera,** double row bearing
— **de empuje,** thrust bearing
— **de empuje a rodillos,** thrust roller bearing
— **de empuje de bolillas,** thrust ball bearing
— **del gorrón del pie de biela,** wrist-pin bearing
— **de guía,** pilot bearing
— **de latón,** brass bearing
— **del pasador de articulación,** wrist-pin bearing
— **de poleas de corona,** crown-block bearing
— **de rodillos,** roller bearing
— **de rodillos cónicos,** tapered bearing
— **de rodillos de alineación automática,** self-aligning roller bearing
— **del árbol de levas,** camshaft bearing
— **del contravástago,** tail bearing
— **del eje del piñón,** pinion shaft bearing
— **del pasador de la cruceta,** crosshead pin bearing
— **en dos mitades,** split bearing
— **principal,** main bearing

— **principal de la mesa rotatoria,** table main bearing
— **principal delantero,** front main bearing
— **principal trasero,** main rear bearing
— **reforzado con metal blanco,** babbitted bearing
cok, coke
colación-filtración, percolation filtration
cola de ratón, (prf) taper tap
colada, (mu) a melt; (concrete) a pour (o lift) batch
— **de lava,** lava stream
— **hormigonada,** (cn) lift
colado en moldes de arena, sand casting
colador, strainer
— **de fondo,** (prf) perforated liner
— **de lodo,** (prf) mud screen, mud shaker
— **sacudidor del lodo,** shaker, mud shaker, mud screen
— **vibratorio,** shale shaker, vibrating mud screen
— **trepidante para el lodo,** vibrating mud screen
colas, (mn) tailings
colchado, colchadura *n.* (ca) lay
— **a la derecha,** right lay
— **a la izquierda,** left lay
colchón, cushion, mattress
colector, collector; catch basin, trap; (el) commutator, collector
— **de aceite,** oil pan, oil sump
— **de aire,** air trap
— **de agua,** steam trap
— **de barro,** mud trap
— **de condensación,** drip pocket, drill well; gas trap
— **de emanaciones o gases,** fume hood
— **de gas,** gas trap, gas stack
— **de lodo,** (rotary table) mud ring
— **de solución,** solution sump

— **del condensado,** drip accumulator
colgadero, hanger; beam hanger
— **del émbolo buzo,** plunger hanger
— **(o suspensor) de varillas de bombeo,** sucker-rod hanger
— **para varillas asido a la cabeza del balancín,** mule-head hanger
— **(o suspensores) del tubo de producción,** tubing hanger
colgador de dos tirantes para tubería, double-strap hanger
colgador de tubería para emergencias, emergency drillpipe hang off tool
colgante, (cn) hanging tie; underslung
colimación, collimation
colimador, collimator
colina, (g) hillock
collar, (mc) collar, collet
— **de cementación,** cementing collar
— **de flotación,** (prf) floating collar
— **de flotación para cementar,** cement float collar
— **de perforación,** drill collar
— **giratorio para cementar,** whirler cementing collar
— **obstructor,** baffle collar
— **para circulación de lodo,** mud collar
— **para fugas en tuberías,** collar leak clamp
collar-terraja fusiforme, straight taper rotary drill collar
collarín de dados, die collar
colocación de la tubería de revestimiento, casing setting
colocar, place, locate, set; invest
coloide, colloid, colloidal
color, color, colour
— **de recocido,** annealing color
columbita, columbite
columna, column; (rf) tower, column

— **aisladora,** oil string; water string
— **conductora,** surface pipe
— **de agua amortiguadora,** water cushion
— **de flúido,** fluid column
— **de lavado cáustico,** (rf) caustic wash tower
— **estratigráfica,** (g) columnar section
— **geológica,** (map) geologic column, geologic section
— **reguladora,** (hd) standpipe
columnar, (g) columnar
columpio graduador de carrera, pendulum stroke multiplier
columpio multiplicador del largo de la carrera, pendulum stroke multiplier
comancheano, Comanchean
comba, warp, bulge, camber; (rd) crown; maul, sledge
— **inferior de un monoclinal,** foot of monocline
— **superior de un monoclinal o terraplén,** head of terrace
combado, warped
combarse, bend
combinación, combination
combustible, fuel
— **antidetonante,** antiknock fuel
— **de norma,** reference fuel
— **de reacción,** rocket fuel
— **de cocina,** stove oil
— **de motores,** motor fuel
— **primario de referencia,** primary reference fuel
combustión, combustion
— **espontánea,** spontaneous combustion
— **interna,** internal combustion
combustóleo, fuel oil
— **de calefacción,** furnace oil
— **de tractores,** tractor oil
— **de barcos,** bunker fuel
comercial, commercial

comercio, trade, commerce, business
comisión, (cm) commission; (cm) brokerage; mandate; party, commission
comisura estratigráfica, bedding plane
compactación, compaction
— **differencial,** (g) differential compaction
— **por gravedad,** (g) gravitational compaction
compañía, company
— **afiliada,** (cm) branch office
— **anónima,** stock company
— **dominatriz,** holding company
— **en comandita,** limited partnership
— **matriz,** holding (o parent) company
comparación, comparison
compás, compass, dividers, calipers
— **de puntas secas,** dividers
— **interior,** inside calipers
compensación, compensation
— **automática,** self-equalizing
— **isostática,** isostatic compensation
— **termostática,** temperature compensation
compensador del movimiento de la sarta, drill-string compensator
compensador de vibraciones, (gf) harmonic balancer
competencia, competition
competente, competent
competidor, competitor
complejo, *a.* complex, intricate; *n.* (g) complex
— **basal,** basal complex, basement
— **de falla,** fault complex
— **petróleo-gas,** (g) oil and gas complex
componente, component

— **horizontal del campo
magnético,** (gf) horizontal
component magnetic field
— **lógico,** (dp) software
comportamiento, behavior
composición, composition
compoundaje, (mo) (el)
compounding
compra, *n.* purchase
comprador, purchaser
compresibilidad, compressibility
compresión, compression
— **tangencial,** tangential
compression
compresor, compressor
— **accionado por correas,** belt-
driven compressor
— **alternativo,** reciprocating
compressor
— **a motor,** engine-driven
compressor
— **centrífugo,** centrifugal
compressor
— **con motor a expansión de gas,**
expander driven compressor
— **de aire,** air compressor
— **de amoníaco,** ammonia
compressor
— **de tipo angular,** angle-type
compressor
— **multietapa,** multistage
compressor
— **portátil,** portable compressor
— **sencillo,** single-stage compressor
comprobar, check, verify, prove
— **el tránsito,** (gf) trace
compuerta, (hd) gate
— **de cierre total,** ram gate
— **de tiro,** furnace damper
compuesto, *n.* (qm) preparation,
compound; (mc) compound;
composed; repaired
— **aromático,** aromatic compound
— **cristalino,** crystalline compound
— **para lubricar engranajes,** gear
compound

— **para preservar cables de acero,**
cable-coating compound
computación gráfica, graphical
computation
cómputo, computation
— **de orificio,** orifice computation
comunicación, communication
— **radiotelefónica en dos
direcciones,** two-way radio
communication
cóncavo, concave
concentración, concentration
concentrado, *n.* (qm) concentrate;
a. concentrated
concéntrico, concentric
concesión, (land) lease, concession
concesionario, grantee; licensee
concordancia, conformity
concordante, (g) conformable,
concordant
concreción, concretion
concreto, concrete
— **asfáltico,** asphaltic concrete
— **reforzado,** reinforced concrete
concurrente, (g) concurrent
concha, shell; casing; boiler scale;
mill scale
— **de cojinete,** bearing shell;
bearing cup
condensado, distillate
condensación, condensation
— **equilibrada,** equilibrium
condensation
— **retrógrada,** retrograde
condensation
condensado, condensate
condensador, condenser
— **a chorro,** ejector pump
— **albrecht,** albrecht condenser
— **atmosférico,** atmospheric
condenser
— **barométrico,** barometric
condenser
— **de aire,** air condenser
— **de baja temperatura,** subcooling
condenser

— **de caja,** box condenser
— **de chorro,** jet condenser
— **de superficie,** surface condenser
— **de vapor,** steam condenser
— **eléctrico,** electric condenser
— **sumergido,** submerged
   condenser
condensar, condense, thicken
condiciones, terms; conditions
condrodita, chondrodite
conducción, transportation;
   conduction; cartage; (a) driving
— **electrolítica,** electrolytic
   conduction
— **electrónica,** electronic
   conduction
conductibilidad, conductivity
conductibilidad térmica, thermal
   conductivity
conductividad, electric
   conductivity
conducto, conduit; aqueduct; flume;
   duct; flue; chute
— **de cable,** wire conduit
— **de ventilación,** fume duct
— **en forma de hoja de trébol,**
   clover leaf duct
— **portacables,** electric conduit
conductor, (el) conductor; (a)
   driver; conveyor; (sd) lead
— **del lodo,** mud conveyor, mud
   line
conectar, (mc) (el) connect
— **tubos roscados,** (tu) stabbing
conector de salida, (dp)
   outconnector
conexión, hookup; connection, joint
— **a presión,** hot tap
— **articulada,** knee joint
— **de barra,** sub
— **de brida,** flange connection
— **de estrella,** Y connection
— **de fácil desenganche,** knock-off
   joint, hook-off joint
— **de manguera,** hose coupling
— **de orejas,** wing connection

— **de una de las ramas del árbol
   de conexiones,** wing union
— **embridada,** flange connection
— **en circuito,** (el) loop
— **en U,** return bend, U bend
— **en Y,** Y connection; two-way
   branch clevis
— **flexible,** swing connection
— **giratoria para tubería de
   revestimiento,** casing swivel
— **macho cónica, sin filetes,**
   swedged pin
— **sin rosca y a fricción,** ground-in
   joint, ground-joint
— **de rosca,** screw connection
— **de soldar,** welding fitting
— **macho y hembra,** (p) box and
   pin
— **para tubería,** pipe fitting
— **para tubo acanalado,** grooved
   pipe fitting
confirmación, *n.* confirmation
confirmar, confirm
congelador, freezing
— **de parafina,** wax chiller
congelar, freeze
conglomeración, conglomeration
conglomerado, (g) conglomerate;
— **basal,** (g) basal conglomerate
— **bien surtido,** well-assorted
   conglomerate
— **cruzado,** cross-bedded
   conglomerate
— **de canto,** edgewise conglomerate
— **de canto rodados,** boulder
   conglomerate
— **de gránulos,** granule
   conglomerate
— **de peñas,** cobble conglomerate
— **estratificado,** bedded
   conglomerate
— **guijarroso,** pebble conglomerate
cónico, conical
conificación del agua, water coning
conjunto, (mc) assembly, unit; set

— **de bloque de cilindros,** cylinder
block assembly
— **de datos, data set**
— **de embrague,** clutch assembly
— **de estratos,** (g) sedimentary
complex
— **de estratos superpuestos,** (g)
overthrust mass
— **de freno,** brake assembly
— **de manivela y contrapeso,**
crank and counterbalance
assembly
— **de motor y generador,** engine
generator set
— **magnético,** magnetic system
conmutación de circuitos, (dp) line
switching
conmutador, (el) commutator,
switch
— **de aceite,** oil switch
— **de alteración,** (dp) alteration
switch
cono, cone
— **aluvial,** (g) apron
— **de barrena,** bit cone, bit cutters
— **de deyección,** (g) talus fan,
alluvial fan
— **de embrague,** clutch cone
— **de erupción,** (vlc) eruption cone
— **de explosión,** explosion cone
— **de fricción,** friction cone
— **radiante,** radiating cone
conocimiento de embarque, (cm)
bill of lading
conservación, upkeep;
maintenance; conservation
— **de la presión,** pressure
maintenance
consignación, (cm) consignment
consignador, consignor
consignatario, (cm) consignee
consistencia, consistency
consola colgante, shaft hanger
consolidación, (g) differential
compaction, (pr) unitization
consolidado, consolidated

constantano, constantan
constante, constant
— **de conversión,** conversion
constant
— **de la densidad de la viscosidad,**
viscosity gravity constant,VGC
— **de gravitación,** (gf)
gravitational constant
— **de instrumento,** (gf) instrument
constant
— **dieléctrica,** dielectric constant
— **elástica,** elastic constant
construcción, construction
— **enteramente soldada,** all welded
construction
constructor, constructor, maker,
builder
construir, build, construct, erect
consumidor, consumer
contabilidad de costos, (cm) cost
accounting
contacto, contact
— **con la arcilla,** (rf) clay
contacting
— **gas-petróleo,** gas-oil contact
— **externo,** external contact
— **petróleo-agua,** oil-water contact
contactor, (el) contactor
contactor de chorro, jet contactor
contador, (el) (gas) (water) meter
— **de desplazamiento de gas,** gas
displacement meter
— **de desplazamiento positivo,**
positive displacement meter
— **de flujo,** meter flow
— **de intervalos,** (dp) interval
timer
— **de orificio,** orifice meter
— **de petróleo,** oil meter
— **integrador,** integrating meter
— **integrador tipo orificio,**
integrating orifice meter
— **rotativo,** rotameter
— **tipo de desplazamiento,**
displacement meter

contaminación, pollution, contamination
contaminar, to contaminate
contemporáneo, contemporaneous
contener, contain, hold; comprise, include, check, curb, restrain, stop
contenido, content
— **olefínico,** olefinic content
contextura, structure; (g) texture
continental, continental
continuo, continuous
contorsión, contorsion; (g) fold
contrabalancín, balance bob
contrabando, contraband
contracción, shrinking; contraction
contraclavija, gib
contracorriente, opposed flow, countercurrent; counterflow
contracurva, inflected curve
contraeje, countershaft
— **de embrague,** clutch countershaft
— **de la transmisión,** transmission countershaft
— **recto,** straight countershaft
contraexplosión, (mo) back firing
contraerse, shrink, contract
contrafuerte, (tp) abutment; (g) spur; counterfort, buttress
— **facetado,** faceted spur
— **labrado en facetas,** faceted spur
contragolpe, lash-back
contrapeldaño, (stairs) riser
contrapesar, balance
contrapeso, balance weight, counterweight
— **antivibratorio,** (gf) harmonic balancer
— **de balancín,** beam-type counterbalance
— **de cola del balancín,** tailboard counterbalance
— **del cigüeñal,** crank disk
— **graduable del balancín,** adjustable beam weight

— **para varillas de tracción,** rodline counterbalance
— **rotatorio,** (bm) rotary counterbalance
— **saltón,** grasshopper counterbalance
contrapresión, back pressure
contrario a las agujas del reloj, counterclockwise
contrario al order cronométrico, counterclockwise
contrarremachador, dolly
contraseña, password
contratiro, downdraft, backdraft
contratista, contractor
contrato, contract
— **de perforación,** drilling contract
contra todo riesgo, (cm) against all risks
contratuerca, lock (o jam, check) nut
contravástago, tail-rod
contraviento, guy; wind bracing; outrigger
contribución, (cm) tax; contribution
— **predial,** property tax
control, control
— **a motor,** motive control
— **al vacío,** vacuum control
— **de la amplitud,** amplitude control
— **de diafragma,** diaphragm control
— **de encendido y apagado,** on-off control
— **de la perforación,** drilling control
— **del freno,** brake control
— **de nivel de líquidos,** liquid-level control
— **de la presión sobre la barrena rotatoria,** rotary-feed control
— **de paridad par,** (dp) evenparity check

— **de paridad par-impar,** (dp) odd-even check
— **de tiro,** draft control
— **de las válvulas,** valve control
— **de volumen,** volume control
— **primario,** primary control
— **termostático,** thermostatic control
convección, convection
convenio, (cm) agreement
convergencia, convergence
conversión, conversion
— **de la carga por cada recorrido a través de la torre de reformación,** (rf) conversion per pass
— **del carbón amorfo en grafita,** graphitization
convertible, convertible
convertidor, converter
convexo, convex; bellied
coordenada, (math) coordinate
— **triangular,** triangular coordinate
— **trilineal,** triangular coordinate
copa, cup, (la) beaker
— **de asiento,** seating cup
— **de cuero sintético,** (bm) composition cup
— **de válvula,** valve cup
— **de válvula viajera,** traveling valve cup
— **porosa para la extracción de substancias en solución,** extraction thimble
copia, copy
— **azul,** blueprint
— **heliográfica,** blueprint
copilla aceitera, oil cup
copilla grasera, grease cup
copolimerización, copolymerization
cobre, copper
— **catalizador de,** copper catalyst
— **cojinetes de,** copper bearings
coprolitos, (g) coprolites

coque, coke
coquificación, coking
— **de petróleo,** petroleum coke
— **retardada,** delayed coking
coquina, coquina
coral, coral
coralino, *a.* coral-like
coraza, armor, shell, protective covering
— **del autoclave,** autoclave shell
corazón de cáñamo, hemp center
corazonar, (prf) core
corcho, cork
cordaje, cordage
cordierita, cordierite
cordillera, cordillera
cordón, cord, strand of rope; cord, flange; (sd) bead; (tu) spigot end
— **de acabado,** (w) finishing bead
— **de obturación,** seal weld, bead weld
— **estratigráfico,** (g) shoestring sand
coriáceo, leathery
corindón, corundum, corindon
cornisa, cornice
— **de la torre,** derrick cornice
corona, annual space; ring gear; (el) corona; (dam) crest; (a) rim; tubular drill bit; halo
— **cortante,** (prf) boring head
— **dentada,** ring gear, sprocket
— **dentada de la mesa rotatoria,** table ring gear
corrasión, (g) corration
correa, belt, strap; purlin, girt
— **articulada,** link belt
— **(o banda) para roldanas de acanalado múltiple en V,** multiple V-belt
— **de balata,** balata belt
— **de caucho con borde en rústico,** raw-edge rubber-covered belt
— **de caucho con borde plegado,** folded-edge rubber-covered belt

— **de lona pespuntada,** canvas-stitched belt
— **en V,** V-belt
— **plana sin fin,** endless flat belt
— **sin fin,** endless belt
— **trapezoidal,** V-belt
correaje, belting
corrección, correction
— **al nivel de referencia,** datum correction
— **barométrica,** barometric correction
— **cartográfica,** cartographic correction
— **combinada de Bouguer y aire libre,** Bouguer and free air correction
— **de aire libre,** free air correction: gravimetric anomaly corresponding to changes in altitude
— **de alturas,** (gf) elevation correction
— **de base,** magnetometer correction; (gravim) base correction
— **de curvatura,** correction for curvature
— **de deriva del gravímetro,** drift correction
— **de fase,** phase correction
— **de latitud,** latitude correction
— **de longitud,** longitude correction
— **de temperatura,** temperature correction
— **isostática,** isostatic correction
— **para compensar la angulosidad,** (g) angularity correction
— **para tomar en cuenta la denudación de la capa superficial,** weathering correction
— **por flotabilidad,** buoyancy correction

— **por la profundidad de la explosión,** shot hole correction
— **superficial,** surface correction
— **topográfica,** topographic correction
correcto, accurate, correct
corredera, track, slide; skid; slide valve; (gf) target; (in) cursor, slide; door hanger; (naut) log line; coulisse
— **de cambio de velocidades,** gearshift rail
— **para el cable de perforadora inicial,** spudding shoe
corredor, (cm) jobber, broker
correlación, correlation
— **continua,** continuous correlation
— **discontinua,** (gf) spot correlation
— **estratigráfica,** stratigraphic correlation
correlacionar, correlate
correntada, (g) current
correntilíneo, streamlined
correo, *n.* mail, post, post office
— **aéreo,** air mail
corriente, *n.* current, course, tendency; *a.* current, running, flowing; present (month), instant; plain; common; standard; regular; general
— **abajo,** downstream
— **alterna,** (el) alternating current, AC
— **arriba,** upstream
— **continua,** (el) direct current, DC
— **de gases y productos de evaporación,** overhead gas stream, overhead products
— **de lava,** lava flow, lava stream
— **eléctrica,** electric current
— **laminar,** (g) laminar flow
— **local,** (gf) local current

— **marina,** sea current
— **pulsatoria,** (el) pulsating current
— **radial,** radila flow
— **telúrica,** (el) telluric current
— **natural,** (gf) earth currents
— **parásitas,** eddy currents
— **terrestres,** (gf) earth currents
corrimiento, (g) thrust, overthrust
— **horizontal,** (g) horizontal thrust
corroer, corrode
corrosión, corrosion
— **causada por ácidos,** acid
  corrosion
— **en forma de empeine,** ringworm
  corrosion
corrosivo, corrosive
corrugado, corrugated
cortacables, rope chopper; wire-line
  cutter
cortacircuito, electric fuse, electric
  switch
— **de solenoide,** solenoid switch
cortadora, cutter, cutting machine
— **de cables,** wire-line cutter
— **de correa,** belt cutter
— **de tubos de vidrio,** glass tube
  cutter
— **manual,** hand cutter
— **rotatoria de metales,** milling
  cutter
cortadura con soplete, flame
  cutting
cortafrío, cold chisel
— **con punta rómbica,** diamond
  point chisel
— **ranurador,** cape chisel
cortaplumas, pocketknife
cortatubos, casing cutter, pipe
  cutter
— **hidráulico,** hydraulic pipe cutter
— **biselador,** pipe-beveling cutter
— **por el exterior,** external drillpipe cutter
corte, (map) cross section; (rf) cut,
  petroleum fraction; cutting edge;
  shearing stress; section; (sd) kerf

— **con arco metálico,** (sd) metallic
  arc cutting
— **con gas,** (sd) gas cutting
— **del medio,** heart cut
— **final,** (rf) end
— **geológico de pozo,** well log
— **lateral,** side-cut stream
— **liviano final,** (rf) light end
— **para lubricante,** lube cut
— **pesado final,** (rf) heavy end
— **transversal,** cross section
— **cerrados,** (rf) narrow cuts
— **estrechos,** (rf) narrow cuts
corteza terrestre, earth's crust
cortina arrolladiza, roll up curtain
corto, short
cosmogenético, cosmogenetic
costa, coast
— **arcantilada,** steep coast
costa-playa, low coast
costado, side; side piece
costo, cost
— **seguro y flete,** cost, insurance
  and freight
costra, crust; scale; (prf) mud cake
— **de lodo,** mud cake, filter cake
— **porosa,** porous crust
costura, (tu) seam
costura de la correa, belt lacing
cota, (tp) number indicating the
  elevation of a point above
  datum
cotana, mortise
cotipo, (paleo) cotype
cotización, (cm) quotation
covelita, covellite
crácking, cracking
— **catalítico,** catalytic cracking
— **catalítico fluido de un solo
  paso,** single-stage fluid catalytic
  cracking
— **con vapor,** steam cracking
— **en fase mixta,** mixed-phase
  cracking
— **por el método de fase de vapor,**
  vapor-phase cracking

— **térmico,** thermal cracking. (q.v.
   disociación térmica)
— **termocatalítico,**
   thermocatalytic cracking. (q.v.
   disociación termocatalítica)
   craquear, (rf) cracking
   (q.v.**desintegrar, crácking)**
   craqueo, (rf) cracking (q.v.
   desintegración)
— **catalítico,** catalytic cracking.
craso, fatty
cráter, crater
— **de explosión,** explosion crater
— **parasitario,** (g) parasitic crater
crédito, (cm) credit
creciente, *n.* flood; tide;
cremallera, rack, rack rail, cograil;
   gear rack
creosol, creosol
cresta, crest
— **de un anticlinal,** anticlinal crest
   (o ridge)
crestón, (tp) crest; (g) outcrop
creta, chalk
cretáceo, Cretaceous,
criadero, (oil) pool; (mn) seam,
   vein, deposit
criba del lodo, (prf) mud screen
cric (o gato) de cremallera, rack
   jack
criolita, cryolite
criptocristalino, cryptocrystalline
criseno, chrysene
crisol, melting pot, smelting pot,
   crucible
— **de horno,** hearth
— **de porcelana,** porcelain crucible
— **para acero,** skillet
crisotilo, (g) chrysotile
cristal, crystal
— **de seguridad,** safety glass
— **inastillable,** safety glass
— **mineral,** mineral crystal
— **de cuarzo,** quartz crystal
cristalino, crystalline
cristalización, crystallization

cristalizar, crystallize
cristaloblástesis, crystalloblastosis
cristaloblástico, crystalloblastic
cristalografía, crystallography
cristográfico, crystographic
crocetano, crocetane.
crocita, crocoite
cromado, chrome plated
cromel, chromel
cromita, chromite
cromo, chromium, chrome
cromoforo, chromophore
cromómetro, chromometer
cronógrafo, chronograph
cronolito, chronolite
cronómetro, chronometer
croquis, diagram
cruce de río, river crossing
cruceta, (wheel) spider; crossarm;
   crosshead; crosspiece
— **para tubería de revestimiento y
   de producción,** casing and
   tubing (landing) spider
crudo, *n.*(petrol) crude; *a.* raw (q.v.
   petróleo)
cruz, cross; (pr) Christmas tree
cuadrante, quadrant; dial of an
   instrument
cuadrilla, (g)party,crew; gang,squad
cuadrado, *a.* square; square
cuadro, *n.* square; table of figures,
   tabulation; timber frame
— **de medición,** gage table
— **esquemático del flujo,**
   schematic flow sheet
— **de maniobras,** draw works
cualidad, quality
cuantitativo, quantitative
cuarcífero, quartziferous
cuarcita, (g) quartzite
cuarteadura, crack, split
cuartear, *v.* quarter
cuarto, quarter, fourth
— **de galón,** quart
cuarto nordeste, north by east
cuarzo, quartz

Glossary of the Petroleum Industry

— **ahumado,** smoky quartz
— **diorítico,** diorite quartz
— **fundido,** fused quartz
— **monzonítico,** monzonite quartz
— **rosado,** rose quartz
cuarzoso, quartzose
cuaternario, Quaternary
cubeta, (g) bucket, pail, tub, keg; basin
— **de cojinete,** bearing cup
— **sedimentaria,** (g) trough, sedimentary basin
cubicación directa, innage
cubicación indirecta, outage
cúbico, cubic
cubierta, cover, covering, lid; roof, roof covering (nt) deck; (mc) casing, hood; (excavation) overburden; face slab
— **de seguridad,** safety cover
— **de ventilador,** fan shroud
— (o **tapa**) **de resorte de válvula,** valve spring cover
cubierto (o **revestido**) **de acero,** steel clad
cubilete, (la) beaker
— **de vertedero,** beaker with lip and spout
cubo, (wheel) hub; pail; bucket; cube
— **de cuñas dentadas,** tubing spider
— **de garras,** (prf) spider
— **de mordaza,** clamp hub
cubreneumáticos, tire cover
cuchara, trowel; (prf) bailer
— **estriadora,** (foundry) flute
— **limpiapozos,** cleanout bailer
— **vertedora de cemento,** (prf) cement dump bailer
cuchareo, (prf) bailing
cucharín de arrastre, (rd) scraper
cucharín de colada, melting ladle
cucharón de fundición, ladle
cuchilla, (g) hogback
— **dentada,** sawtooth ridge
— **irreversible,** nonreversible blade
cuello, neck; (p) collar

— **de boquilla,** nozzle neck
— **de eje,** shaft collar
— **de perforación,** drill collar
— **de pozo de visita,** manhole neck
— **de la soldadura en ángulo,** throat of fillet weld
— **de tobera,** nozzle neck
— **de tubería vástago,** (prf) drill collar
— **volcánico,** volcanic neck
cuenca, (g) basin; (hd) drainage area, watershed
— **cerrada,** (g) closed basin
— **compresiva,** compressive basin
— **de desgarramiento,** pull-apart basin
— **de falla,** fault through, graben fault
— **de represa,** barrier basin
— **marítima,** ocean basin
— **sedimentaria,** sedimentary basin, trough
— **talud-fosa, trench**
— **transtensiva,** transpressional basin
cuenta, (cm) account, bill, invoice
— **abierta,** open account
— **corriente,** current account
cuentaemboladas, stroke counter
cuentagotas de engrase visible, sight-feed lubricator
cuentapasos, tally register; pace counter; odometer
cuentavueltas, revolution counter
cuerda, cord, line, rope; cord of wood; (girder) flange; screw thread; beam, joint
— **de áloe,** aloes rope
cuero, leather
— **de bomba,** cup
— **de émbolo,** (bm) leather cup
cuerpo, body
— **del prensaestopas,** stuffing box body
— **de pasador,** pin shank
— **efusivo,** (g) extrusive body

— **elíptico,** elliptic body
— **ígneo,** igneous body
cuerpos extraños incluídos, (g)
enclosed bodies
cuesta, grade, slope, hill; (g) cuesta
— **arriba,** uphill
cueva, cave
culata, butt; haunch; yoke;
(cylinder) head
culombio, coulomb
cumeno, cumene (q.v.
isopropilbenceno)
cumulativo, cumulative
cumulitos, cumulites
cumulofírico, cumulophyric
cuneta de desagüe, ditch, trench
cuña, wedge, chock; key, gib; gad;
paving stone; frog of a plane;
(prf) slip
— **de corredera,** feather key
— **de cuarzo,** quartz wedge
— **delgada,** shim
— **para excéntrica,** eccentric key
— **para tubería de revestimiento,**
casing slip
cuota, quota
cúpula, dome, cupola
— **gasífera,** gas cap
— **salina,** (g) salt dome
— **salina profunda,** (g) deep-seated
salt dome
curso, stroke, throw, course, travel
curva, a curve, bend
— **compensada,** smoothed curve
— **de amplitud,** amplitude curve
— **de contacto,** contact curve
— **de declinación,** decline curve
— **de destilación,** distillation curve,
true-boiling-point curve
— **de dilatación,** (p) expansion
bend (o loop)
— **de elevación,** elevation curve
— **de equilibrio termodinámico,**
equilibrium curve
— **de escape,** exhaust curve
— **de expansión,** expansion curve

— **de gravedad,** gravity curve
— **de nivel,** contour
— **de nivel cerrada,** closed contour
— **de nivel de la estructura,** (g)
structure contour
— **de nivel de referencia,** contour
datum, datum plane
— **de nivel isoclinal,** isoclinal
curve
— **de potencia,** power curve
— **de porcentaje medio,** mid-
percent curve
— **de producción,** production curve
— **de punto de flexión,** curve of
flexure point
— **de rendimiento,** efficiency curve
— **de retorno,** return bend
— **de selector de frecuencia,** (gf)
filter curve
— **de solubilidad,** solubility curve
— **de tensión eléctrica,** voltage
curve
— **de la velocidad,** velocity curve
— **de viscosidad,** viscosity curve
— **dromocrónica,** (gf) distance-
time curve
— **elipsoidal,** ellipsoidal curve
— **gravimétrica,** gravity curve
— **isoclinal** (o **isoclínia**), isoclinal
curve
— **isogama,** gravity contour
— **plana,** flat curve
curvas de nivel equidistantes,
equispaced contouring
curvatubos, pipe bender
curvatura de la cara de la polea,
crowning of pulley
curvo, curve; aduncous
cúspide, cusp, crest, apex, vortex

CH

chaflán, bevel, chanfer, bearding
chaflanar, *v.* bevel

chalán, barge
— de perforación, drilling barge
champlainiense, Champlainic
chamuscar, flame priming
chango, (prf) derrickman
chapa, sheet, plate; veneering
— de metal, sheet metal
— metálica, sheet metal
— (o placa) de indentificación,
     nameplate
— protectora, (mc) apron
chapaleta, flapper
chaparrón, cloudburst, downpour
chapear la punta de una barra, tip
charca, pond
charnela, hinge, knuckle,
     articulated joint, turning point
— anticlinal, (g) crest line of an
     anticline (o trough line)
charpar, v. (carp) scarf
chasis, chassis
chaveta, cotter, key, gib, wedging
     piece
— con cabeza, gib-head key
— de pasadores, pin key
— de tracción, draw-key
— hendida, (ma) split pin, cotter
     pin
chicana, baffle
chicharra eléctrica, electric buzzer
chimenea, chimney, stack;
     fireplace; shaft; (vlc) chimney;
     smoke stack
— enteriza, integral stack
chirrido, squeak
chispa, spark
— avanzada, early spark
— retardada, late spark
chispero, engine arrester, flame
     arrester spark arrester
choque, shock, impact, collision;
     crash
chorro de arena, sand blasting
chubasco, shower
chumacera, journal bearing, pillow
     block, journal box; rowlock

— del malacate de herramientas,
     bull-wheel bearing
— del malacate de la tubería de
     producción, calf-wheel bearing
— posterior del poste de la rueda
     motora, back-jack post box
chupador, (oil well) swab

D

dado, die; capstone; jackbit
— de tenazas, tong die
— para terraja de tubos, pipe dies
dados de terraja, bolt dies
— para filetes de pernos, bolt dies
— y machos de terraja, pipe and
     bolt dies and taps
dacita, dacite
daniense, Danian
dardo, dart
— obturador que se inserta en el
     pozo por medio del fluido
     inyectado a bomba,
     pump-down dart plug
dato, datum
datos, data
datolita, datolite
decadieno, decadiene
decadiino, decadiyne
decalador de fase, phase shifter
decalina, decalin (q.v.
     biciclodecano)
decano, (qm) decane
deceno, decene
decino, decyne
decilacetileno, decylacetylene. (q.v.
     dodecino)
declinación magnética, magnetic
     declination
declive glaciario, glacial tilt
— de un río, fall of a river
decremento, decrement
de doble efecto, double-acting

de enfoque exterior, exterior focusing
defectos de fábrica, mill defects
deflación, (g) deflation. (q.v. denudación eólica)
deflegmador, separator
deformación, deformation; strain; distortion
— **elástica,** elastic deformation
— **mecánica,** mechanical strain
de funcionamiento neumático, air-operated
degradación, *n.* (qm) (g) degradation; **degradar,** *v.* degrade
delgado, thin; light
delinear, design, draw
del medio, median
delta, delta
— **lobulado,** (g) lobate
deltaico, deltaic
demanda, (cm) demand
— **del comercio interior,** domestic demand
demulsificación, demulsification
dendrítico, dendritic
densidad, density
— **crítica,** critical density
— **del agua,** water density
— **del aire,** air density
— **de pozos,** well density
— **eléctrica,** electric gravity
— **específica,** specific gravity
— **óptica,** optical (o true) density
— **temperatura,** temperature density
— **verdadera,** true (o optical) density
densificantes, weighting materials
densímetro, densimeter
denso, dense, heavy
denudación, (g) weathering
— **eólica,** (g) deflation. (q.v. deflación)
de oeste a este (O a E), west-east (W E)

departamento, department
— **de compras,** (cm) purchasing department
— **de ventas,** sales department
depleción, depletion
deposición, (g) deposition
— **uniforme (de regiones áridas),** aggradation
depositado, *a.* (g) depositional; deposited
depositario, *n.* depositary, trustee, receiver; consignee; *a.* related to a depository
depósito, deposit; storehouse, warehouse; store; bin; tank; reservoir; sediment, precipitate; (g) deposition
— **a la intemperie,** atmospheric reservoir
— **aluvial,** alluvial deposit
— **auxiliar de combustible,** emergency fuel tank
— **de almacenamiento,** storage bin
— **de gasolina,** gasoline storage
— **de grasa,** grease reservoir
— **de residuos,** residual deposit
— **de sedimentos orgánicos,** organic deposits
— **de sedimentos marinos,** marine deposits
— **de ventisquero,** (g) till
— **estuarino,** estuarine deposit
— **fluvial,** fluviatile deposit
— **lacustre,** lacustrine deposit
— **mineral,** (mn) mineral deposit
— **regulador,** (hd) standpipe
depositos
— **a trochemoche,** (g) unbedded deposits
— **continentales,** continental deposits
— **eólicos,** eolian deposits
— **litorales,** littoral deposits
— **residuales,** residual deposits
— **sedimentarios superiores,** topsets

depresión, (tp) depression, hollow;
gap, pass; (hd) drawdown;
— del horizonte, dip of the horizon
— eólica, blowout
depurador, *n.* purifier; *a.* purifying
— centrífugo, centrifugal purifier
— de aceite, oil filter
— de aceite lubricante, oil
reclaimer
— de aire, air cleaner, air scrubber
— de gas, gas scrubber
depurar, (rf) scrub; purify; filter
— (o eliminar) fallos, (dp) debug
derecho, law, right; grant,
concession; *a.* right; straight
— a la vía, right-of-way
derechos de aduana, tariff, customs
duty
derechos industriales, (cm)
royalties
deriva, (gf) drift
derivación, (p) bypass; diversion;
service connection; overflow;
(el) shunt
derivado, (qm) derivative; branch
— intermedio, (rf) side-cut stream
— lateral, (rf) side-cut stream
derramamiento, *n.* (hd) runoff;
spill; *v.* derramar, spill
derramarse, overflow; run off
derretimiento, *n.* melting; derretir,
v. melt
derrubio estriado, straited pebbles
derrumbamiento, washout,
landslide; slip; cave-in
derrumbarse, cave in; fail;
collapse; (earth) slide
derrumbe, washout; fall, failure;
slip, landslide; cave-in
desaceleración, n. deceleration;
desacelerar, *v.* decelerate
desacoplar, uncouple; disconnect,
disengage
— de embrague, clutch release
desactivar, (dp) disable
desaereador, deaerator

desaguador de vapor, steam drain
desaguar, dewater; desiccate; drain
desagüe, drain, drainage, drain pipe;
gutter
desajuste, out of order, lack of
adjustment, disarrangement,
back lash
desalación eléctrica, electric
desalting
desarenador(-a), desander
— de lodo, drilling-fluid desander
— eléctrico, electric desander
desarmable, collapsible, detachable;
folding
desarmar, dismantle, disassemble;
dismount
desarraigador, (rd ma) rooter
desarrollo, development
desasfaltación, deasphalting
desazufrar (o desulfurar) sweeten
oil
desbarbadura, fettling
desbastador, (saw mill) trimmer;
dresser; hewer
desbordamiento de la capacidad
mínima, (dp) underflow
desbordarse, overflow
desbutanizador, (rf) debutanizer
desbutanizar, (rf) debutanize
descabezamiento, (rf) topping,
skimming
descamación, (g) peeling
descaptación, (rf) deoiling
descarbonización, decarbonizing
— del acero, softening (o
decarbonization) of steel
— por disolventes, solvent
decarbonizing
— por propano, propane
decarbonizing
descarga, (bm) discharge
— de agua rebosada, backwash
discharge water
— sismográfica para determinar
el buzamiento, dip shooting

descargar, unload, dump; (hd) discharge; (ma) exhaust; (el) discharge

descartar, discard

descenso, descent; lowering; fall; decline

— **de un fluido,** subsidence

descensor, cable slide

descoloramiento, discoloration, discoloring

descomponer, decompose

descomposición, decomposition

— **de fuerzas,** resolution of forces

— **del calor,** heat decomposition

— **primaria,** primary decomposition

— **térmica,** thermal breakdown (o decomposition)

desconcharse, scale off, spall; exfoliate

desconectador, electric circuit breaker

desconectador de barrena, bit breaker

desconectar, disconnect; (tu) break

descontinuid q.v. **discontinuidad**

descostrarse, spall, scale

descripción esquemática, schematic description

descubrimiento, discovery

descuento, (cm) discount, rebate

desecación, desiccation

desecador, desiccator

desecar, dewater; desiccate

desechar, scrap, discard; junk

desechos, tailings

desembarrancar, (nt) get afloat

desembragar, disengage, release a clutch

desengrasar, degrease

desenroscar, unscrew; untwist; (tu) disconnect, break

desenrosque, unscrewing; untwisting

— **a cuatro manos,** (tu) two-stroking

— **a seis manos,** (tu) three-stroking

desfasado, phase displacement (o difference)

desfasamiento, phase displacement (o difference)

desfiladero, (tp) gap, pass, defile

desflecar el extremo de una soga (o **cable**), *v.* mule-tail

desflemador, dephlegmator

desgarramiento, (g) tear fault

desgasificador, degasser

desgastado, eroded

desgastar, erode, wear, abrade

desgaste, erosion, abrasion, wear

— **de roscas,** ablation

— **excéntrico,** eccentric wear

— **por frotamiento,** attrition

deshidratación, dehydration

— **eléctrica,** electric dehydration

deshidratador, dehydrator

— **eléctrico,** electric dehydrator

— **mecánico para gas,** knockout chamber

deshidratar, dehydrate

deshidrogenación, dehydrogenation

— **catalítica,** catalytic dehydrogenation

deshielo, thaw

deshumedecer, dehumidify

desierto, desert

desimantar, demagnetize

desincrustante para calderas, boiler compound

desintegración, disintegration; (rf) cracking. (q.v. **crácking, craqueo**)

— **catalítica,** catalytic cracking.

desintegrar, disintegrate, (rf) crack

desisobutanizador, deisobutanizer

deslave, tailings; eroded material; erosion

desleimiento, dilution

desleír, (fl) thin; dilute

deslizamiento, (g) slip; (pulley) slip; (mo) slip

— **cortante,** shearing
— **de faldeo,** landslide
— **brillosos,** (g) slicken-sides
desliz horizontal, (g) shift
desmaganetizar, demagnetize
desmantelar, dismantle
desmontable, detachable,
　removable, collapsible
desmontar, (mc) dismount
desmoronadizo, *a.* crumbly
desmoronarse, *v.* crumble
desmulsificador, demulsifier
desmultiplicación,
　demultiplication
— **de engranajes,** gear reduction
— **doble,** double reduction
desnaftado, redistillation
desnaftadora, naphtha scrubber
desnatación, (rf) skimming
desnatado, (rf) skimming
desnatar, (rf) skim
desorientado, unoriented
desoxidar, deoxidize
despacho, office; shipping, shipment
— **de aduana,** customs clearance,
　customs office
desparafinación, (rf) dewaxing
— **al benzol-ketona,** benzol-ketone
　dewaxing
— **con urea,** urea dewaxing
desparafinar, dewax
despejo, (mc) clearance
despeñadero, (g) steep face, abyss
despentanizador, depentanizer
despentanizar, (rf) depentanize
desperdicio, waste
despetrolizador del catalizador,
　(rf) catalyst stripper
desplazamiento, (g) displacement;
　(gf) offset; (rr) relocation;
— **cíclico,** cyclic shift
— **de fase,** phase displacement (o
　difference)
— **lateral,** (g) lateral (o horizontal)
　offset
— **vertical de una falla,** (g) throw

despliegue, unfurling, unfolding;
　spreading out;
— **de detectores,** (gf) detector
　spread
— **en abanico,** (gf) fan shooting (o
　spread)
— **en cruz,** (gf) cross spread
desplome de montaña, landslide
despojadora, (rf) stripper tower
despojos, debris, rubbish, spoil
— **de plantas,** plant debris
— **piroclásticos,** pyroclastic debris
desprendimiento, landslide; slough;
　slip; loosening
despropanizador, (rf) depropanizer
desrecalentador, (rf) desuperheater
destemplar, *v.* (mu) anneal
destilacion, distillation
— **al vacío,** vacuum distillation
— **a vapor,** steam distillation (o
　stripping)
— **azeotrópica,** zaeotropic
　distillation
— **de norma ASTM,** ASTM
　distillation
— **estabilizadora,** (rf) stripping
— **fraccionada,** fractional
　distillation
— **inicial,** (rf) topping, skimming
— **por cochadas,** (rf) batch
　distillation
— **por expansión intstantánea,**
　(rf) flash distillation
— **primaria inicial,** (rf) skimming,
　topping
— **relámpago,** (rf) flash distillation
destilado, distillate
— **a presión,** pressure distillate
— **a presión atmosférica,** straight-
　run distillate (q.v. **destilado
　íntegro**)
— **a presión sin tratar,** (rf) raw
　pressure distillate
— **de crácking,** cracked distillate
　(q.v. **destilado reformado**)

— **de filtro prensa,** pressed (o paraffin) distillate

— **de parafina,** paraffin (o pressed) distillate

— **fraccionario,** fractional distillate

— **íntegro,** straight-run distillate (q.v. **destilado a presión atmósferica)**

— **parafínico,** wax distillate

— **para motores,** engine distillate

— **reformado,** cracked distillate (q.v. **destilado de crácking)**

destiladora, *n.* still

— **atmosférica,** topper

destilar, distill

destilería, refinery; distillery

destornillador, screwdriver

destrabador, (prf) bumper jar

destrucción, destruction

— **de desperdicios,** desechos o basura

destufar, sweeten

desulfurar (o **desazufrar) el petróleo,** sweeten oil or gasoline

— **por aire,** air sweetening

desulfuración, (rf) desulfurization

— **catalítica,** catalytic desulfurization

desviación, deviation, deflection; oblique direction; deviation from the meridian; variation of the magnetic needle

— **de la vertical,** plumb-line deviation, deviation from the vertical

— **del hoyo,** (prf) sidetracking; deviation of the hole

— **del hoyo con herramienta de unión articulada,** (prf) hole deflection with knuckle joint

— **de una falla,** (g) shift of a fault

desviador, deflector, baffle; diversion dam; (prf) whipstock; (frn) baffle

— **anular,** (frn) ring baffle

— **de admisión,** inlet deflector

— **de cabeza flotante,** floating head baffle

— **de canal,** channel baffle

— **de seguridad para el lodo,** safety mud baffle

— **de vapor,** vapor baffle

desviadores horizontales alternoescalonados, (cracking tower) side,to,side pans, offset horizontal baffles

desviar, deflect; divert; (rr) switch

desviarse, deviate, branch off

desvío, bypass; detour; spur; diversion; (p) loop; (hd) (frn) baffle; deviation;(rr) siding

— **suplementario,** (p) loop

desviómetro, drift meter

detallista, (cm) retail dealer

detector, detector

— **con amortiguamiento de aceite,** (gf) oil,damped detector

— **de amortiguamiento electromagnético,** electromagnetically damped detector

— **de gas,** gas detector

— **de huecos,** (p) holiday detector

— **de llama,** flame detector

— **mútiple,** multiple detector

— **piezoeléctrico,** piezoelectric detector

— **térmico,** hot,wire detector

detener, stop, detain, check, arrest; keep back; retain, reserve; tarry, stay, stop over, halt; pause

deterioro, wear and tear

determinación, determination

— **de azufre,** sulfur test

— **teórica,** (la) blank determination

detonaciones sismográficas en pozos, well shooting

detonator, (gf) shooting box; detonator; blaster

detonancia, (gasol) knocking

detrítico, detrital

detritos, detritus
devanado, winding
— del inductor, (el) field winding
devoniano, Devonian
diabasa, (g) diabase
diablo, (p) go,devil
diacetileno, diacetylene. (q.v.
  butadiino)
diaclasa, (g) diaclasse
— transversal, (g) end joint
diaesquisto, diaschistic
diaftoresis, (g) diaftoresis
diagénesis, (g) diagenesis
diagrama, diagram
— de circulación, (rf) flow diagram
  (o sheet, chart)
— de elaboración, (rf) flow sheet
— de flujo, flow chart
— estereográfico, block diagram
— por bloques, (dp) block diagram
dialileno, diallylene (q.v. hexeino)
diálisis, dialysis
diamagnético, (g) diamagnetic
diamante, diamond
diámetro, diameter
— exterior, outside diameter
— exterior constante, external
  flush
— interior, bore; inside diameter,
  ID
— interior de cilindro, cylinder
  bore
diapasón, (la) tuning fork
diario, journal, diary, log book;
  daily; daily newspaper
— del perforador, driller's log
diásporo, diaspore
diástema, diastem
diastrofismo, diastrophism
diatomea, diatom
diatómico, diatomic
diatomita, diatomite, diatomaceous
  earth, infusorial earth
diatrema, maar
diaxial, biaxial

dibencilo, dibenzyl. (q.v.
difeniletano)
dibujante, (oc) draftsman
dibujo, sketch, drawing
— mecánico de curvas de nivel,
  mechanical contouring
dibutil secundario, di-sec-butyl
dicíclico, dicyclic
dicroísmo, (g) dichroism
diente, tooth
— de engranaje, gear tooth
— de rueda, cog
— suplementario de una rueda
dentada, hunting cog
diesel, diesel
dietilbenceno, diethylbenzene
dietil carbinol, diethyl carbinol
dietildodecano, diethyldodecane
dietilhexano, diethylhexane
dietyloctano, diethyloctane
difenilacetileno, diphenylacetylene.
  (q.v. tolano)
difeniletano, diphenylethane (q.v.
dibencilo)
difeniletileno, diphenylethylene
difenilo, diphenyl. (q.v.
  fenilbenceno)
difenilsulfona, diphenyl sulphone
diferencia, difference
— de base, (gravim) base difference
— del ánodo, (sd) anode drop
— de potencial, difference in
  potential
diferencial, differential
— cónico, bevel differential
difracción, diffraction
difundir, diffuse
difusión, diffusion
dígito binario, binary digit, bit
diisoamilo, diisoamyl
diisobutilo, diisobutyl
diisopropilo, diisopropyl
dilatación, (g) dilation; expansion
dilución, dilution
diluente, dilutent
— del lodo, mud thinner

diluído, (fl) thin, diluted
dimensión, dimension
dímero, dimer
dimetil-, *pref.* dimethyl-
dina, dyne
dinágrafo, dynagraph
dinámica, *n.* dynamics; **dinámico,**
    a. dynamic
dinamita, dynamite
— **gelatinosa,** gelatin dynamite
dynamitación, (gf)(expl) shooting;
    dynamiting, blasting, torpedoing
— (o **torpedeamiento) de un pozo,**
    well shoot
dinamitar, blast
dínamo, dynamo
dinamómetro, dynamometer
— **de bombeo,** pumping
    dynamometer
diolefinas, diolefins
— **alifáticas,** aliphatic diolefins
— **grasas,** aliphatic diolefins
diópsido, diopside
diorita, (g) diorite
dióxido de sulfuro, sulfur dioxide
dipolo, dipole
— **magnético,** magnetic dipole
dipropildecadienino,
    dipropyldecadienyne
dipropildecano, dipropildecane
dipropiloctano, dipropiloctane
dique, mound; (g) dike; dock; dry
    dock
dirección, (a) steering; (cm)
    management; board of directors;
    address; direction; instruction
dirigido de este a oeste, etc.,
    trending east-west, etc.
disco, disc, disk
— **de embrague,** clutch disc
— **de fricción,** friction disc
— **de la tubería de producción,**
    tubing disc
— **de mando de embrague,** clutch
    driving disc
— **de manivela,** crank disc

— **de orificio,** orifice plate
discontinuidad, discontinuity
— **elástica,** (gf) elastic discontinuity
discordancia, (g) disconformity,
    unconformity; discordance
— **angular,** angular unconformity
— **local,** local unconformity
— **regional,** regional unconformity
discordant, dissonant; discordant;
    (g) unconformable
diseño, design; sketch
disgregar, disintegrate, separate
disipar, dissipate
dislocación, dislocation; (g) falla
— **circular,** fault-pit
— **periférica,** circular fault
— **rumbeante,** dip fault
disociación, dissociation, separation
— **térmica,** thermal crácking. (q.v.
    crácking térmico)
— **termocatalítica,**
    thermocatalytic cracking.
disolvente, (qm) remover; solvent
— **de barniz,** varnish remover
— **neutral,** neutral solvent
— **para parafina,** paraffin solvent
disolver, dissolve
disparador, tripper; discharger;
    release
disparadora, (gf) blasting machine
disparo, shot, discharge, explosion;
    trip
— **con los detectores dispuestos en
    línea recta,** (gf) refraction
    shooting
— **para el registro de ondas
    refractadas,** refraction shooting
dispersión, dispersion
disposición, arrangement;
    disposition; disposal
— **de las válvulas,** valve
    arrangement
— **discordante,** (g) unconformity
dispositivo, appliance, device,
    fixture, arrangement; layout
— **de distribución,** (el) switch-gear

— **de paro,** shutdown device
distancia, distance
— **de explosión,** shooting distance
— **del detector,** shot-detector
distance
— **epicentral,** epicentral distance
distribución, distribution; (gf)
spread
— **de velocidades,** (gf) velocity
distribution
distribuidor, (el) (cm) distributor;
(p) manifold
distributivo, distributary
disturbio, disturbance, outbreak
— **electroestático,** electrostatic
disturbance
disyunción, disjunction, separation;
(g) fracture
— **prismática,** columnar jointing
— **tubular,** tubular jointing
disyuntor, (el) circuit breaker;
disjunctor
diurno, diurnal
divergente, divergent
divinilacetileno, divinylacetylene.
(q.v. **hexadienino**)
divisoria de aguas, (g) watershed,
divide
divorcio de aguas, drainage divide
dobladura, bending
doble, double; duplex
— **cabeza del cierre capsular,**
return header (for bend
connection), return bend
doblez, a bend, a kink
— **en frío,** (mu) cold bend
— **en hoz,** sickle bend
— **pata de perro,** dogleg
docena , dozen
docosano, docosane
docoseno, docosene
documentos contra aceptación,
(cm) documents against
acceptance
dodecadieno, dodecadiene
dodecadiino, dodecadiyne

dodecano, dodecane
dodeceno, dodecene
dodecilbenceno, dodecylbenzene
dodecino, dodecyne (q.v.
decilacetileno)
dohexacontano, dohexacontane
doladera, butt howel; broadax
dolerita, (g) trap rock
— **traquítica,** trachydolerite
dolina, (g) dolin, sand gall, sand
pipe
dolomía, dolomia (q.v. **dolomita**)
dolomita, dolomite
domo, dome
— **exhumado,** exhumed dome
— **exógeno,** exogeneous dome
— **salino,** salt dome
— **salino achatado,** shallow salt
dome
— **salino penetrante,** piercement-
type salt dome
— **salino profundo,** deep-seated
salt dome
— **salino que no rompe a través de
los estratos superiores,**
nonpiercement,type salt
dome
— **salino que rompe a través de los
estratos superiores,**
piercement,type salt dome
dopentacontano, dopentacontane
dosificador, proportioner, dosing
apparatus; batcher
— **de alimentación,** flow
proportioner
dosificar, proportion a mixture
dotación lógica, (dp) software
dotetracontano, dotetracontane
dotriacontano, dotriacontane
draga, drag; dredge; dragline outfit
dragado, dredging
dragalina, dragline
dragar, dredge; (nt) drag
dren, drain
drenaje, drainage
— **acostillado,** trellis drainage

— **de combustible,** fuel drain
— **dendrítico,** dendritic drainage
— **vertical,** (gf) vertical travel
drusa, (g) druse
dúctil, ductile
ductilidad, ductility
duela, stave
duna, dune
dunita, dunnite
duoservo, duo servo
duplex, duplex
durmiente, groundsill, ground plate, solepiece, mudsill; (hd) gate sill; (rr) tie, crosstie
— **inferior,** subsill
— **longitudinal,** (derrick) stringer
duro, hard

E

ebonita, ebonite
ebullición, ebullition, boiling
ebullioscopia, ebullioscopy
ebullioscopio, ebullioscope
echado, (g) start
echar a andar, (mo) start
echar a andar en ralenti (o **en vacío**), idle
eclímetro, eclimeter
eclogita, eclogite
ecología, ecology
ecómetro, echometer
economizador, (mc) economizer
— **de combustible,** fuel economizer
— **de lodo,** mud economizer
— **de petróleo,** oil economizer
ecosonda, echosounder
ecuación, equation
edad, age
— **del hielo,** ice age
— **geológica,** geologic age
edafología, edaphology
edificio, building

— **de estructura de acero,** steel building
educción, eduction, discharge
efecto, effect
— **binauricular,** (gf) binaural effect
— **cortante,** shear action
— **de chimenea,** stack effect
— **del esfuerzo aplicado,** strain
— **superficial,** (el) skin effect
eficiencia, efficiency
— **del tiempo consumido por un ciclo,** cycle time efficiency
— **térmica,** thermal efficiency
— **volumétrica,** volumetric efficiency
efusion, effusion
eflorescencia, *n.* efflorescence;
eflorescente, *a.* efflorescence; *v.*
eflorescerse, effloresce
efluvio, effluvium
efluente, effluent
efusión, effusion; (g) extrusion
efusivo, effusive; (g) extrusive
eicosadieno, eicosadiene
eicosadiino, eicosadiyne
eicosano, eicosane
eicoseno, eicosene
eicosino, eicosyne
eje, axis; shaft, axle, sheave pin; core
— **accesorio,** accessory shaft
— **acodado,** dropped axle
— **anticlinal,** anticlinal axis
— **cardán,** propeller shaft
— **de cambio de velocidades,** shifter shaft
— **de contramarcha,** reversing countershaft
— **de embrague,** clutch shaft
— **de hélice,** (nt) propeller shaft
— **delantero,** front axle
— **de la rueda motora,** band wheel shaft
— **de la soldadura,** axis of a weld
— **del freno,** brake shaft

— **del malacate de herramientas,** bull wheel shaft

— **del malacate de las tuberías de producción,** calf wheel shaft

— **del piñón,** pinion shaft

— **del tambor auxiliar,** line shaft

— **de propulsión,** (a) propeller shaft

— **de transmisión,** transmission (o line) shaft

— **enteramente flotante,** full floating axle

— **flotante,** floating axle

— **maestro,** main shaft

— **motor,** drive (o transmission, main) shaft

— **muerto,** dead axle

— **óptico,** optic axis

— **oscilante,** rock shaft

— **partido,** split shaft

— **principal,** main shaft

— **principal de la transmisión,** transmission mainshaft

— **propulsor,** axle shaft

— **real (o imaginario),** real (o imaginary) axis

— **sísmico,** seismic axis

— **trasero,** rear axle

ejecución, workmanship; execution, performance

ejemplar, specimen

ejemplo, example

elaboración hasta el coque residual, (rf) rerunning to coke

elaborar, elaborate, process

elasticidad, elasticity; resilience, resiliency

elástico, elastic

— **igualador,** equalizing spring

elastómero, elastomer

elaterita, elaterite, anthraxolite

ele, (tu) ell

— **articulada,** ell swivel

electricidad, electricity

electricista, (oc) electrician

eléctrico, electric

electrodinámica, n. electrodynamics

electrodo, electrode

— **compuesto,** composite electrode

— **de alta tensión,** high tension electrode

— **de carbono,** carbon electrode

— **de energización,** energizing electrode

— **de expansión,** expanding electrode

— **de línea,** line electrode

— **de mercurio,** mercury electrode

— **de potencia,** power electrode

— **de punto,** point electrode

— **de vaso poroso,** porous pot electrode

— **desnudo,** bare electrode

— **despolarizante,** depolarizing electrode

— **explorador,** search electrode

— **explorador,** exploring electrode

— **impolarizable,** nonpolarizable electrode

— **no polarizado,** nonpolarized electrode

— **para soldar,** welding electrode

— **potencial,** potential electrode

— **primario,** primary electrode

— **revestido,** coated electrode

— **secundario,** secondary electrode

electroestático, electrostatic

electrofiltración, electrofiltration

electrogalvánico, electrogalvanic

electroimán, electromagnet

electrólisis, electrolysis

electrólitro, electrolyte, battery acid

electrolítico, electrolytic

electromagnético, electromagnetic

electrometalurgia, electrometallurgy

electrómetro, electrometer

electrón, electron

electronegativo, electronegative

electrónica, n. electronics

electrónico, electronic
electroosmosis, electroosmosis
electropirómetro, electropyrometer
electropositivo, electropositive
electroquímica, *n.* electrochemistry
electroquímico, electrochemical
electroscópico, electroscopic
electroscopio, electroscope
electrotécnica, electrotechnical
elemento, (qm) (el) (mt) (mc)
  element
— **filtrante,** filter medium
elevación, elevation
— **lateral,** side elevation
— **sobre el nivel del mar,** above
  sea-level elevation
elevador, elevator
— **a mordazas, para tubería de**
  revestimiento, slip-casing
  elevator
— **de araña,** (prf) lifting spider
— **de cierre central,** central-latch
  elevator
— **de cierre lateral,** side-door
  elevator
— **de manga de succión,** suction
  hoist
— **de niple,** (prf) lifting nipple
— **de potencial,** (el) booster
— **doble para vástago perforador,**
  kelly connection elevator
— **neumático,** air hoist
— **para barras de bombeo,** socket
  rod elevator
— **para tubería de perforación,**
  drillpipe elevator
— **para tubería de producción,**
  tubing elevator
— **para tubería de revestimiento,**
  casing elevator
— **para varillas de succión,** sucker-
  rod elevators
— **tipo cuña,** slip-type elevator
— **de tubo de producción,** tubing
  elevator

eliminación del agua salada, (pr)
  water (o salt-water) disposal
elipse, ellipse
— **de polarización,** polarization
  ellipse
elipsoidal, ellipsoidal
elipsoide, ellipsoid
— **de referencia,** reference ellipsoid
— **de revolución,** rotation ellipsoid
— **internacional,** international
  ellipsoid
elíptico, elliptic, elliptical
elongación, elongation
elutriación, elutriation
eluvial, eluvial
emanación, emanation
emanómetro, emanometer
embalaje, (cm) packing
embalse, (hd) reservoir, dam
embarcadero, loading platform;
  wharf; ferry; ferry slip
embarque, shipment
emblema, emblem, symbol
embobinador del cable, line spooler
embolita, embolite
émbolo, embolus; (bm) plunger
— **auxiliar de compresión,** (bm)
  displacer
— **buzo,** plunger
— **de bomba de desplazamiento,**
  displacement plunger
embotado, blunt
embragar, (mc) engage; throw in a
  clutch; sling
embrague, clutch
— **a mandíbulas,** jaw clutch
— **cónico de fricción,** friction cone
  clutch
— **corredizo,** sliding clutch
— **de aire,** air clutch.
— **de banca,** band clutch
— **de disco mútiple,** multiple-disc
  clutch
— **de disco seco,** dry-disc clutch
— **de fricción,** friction clutch

— **de fricción con expansión interna,** expanding friction clutch

— **de fricción de disco,** friction disc clutch

— **de fricción del tipo de tambor,** friction drum clutch

— **de fricción maestro,** master friction clutch

— **de mando de la mesa rotatoria,** rotary drive shaft

— **de marcha atrás,** reverse clutch

— **de mordaza,** jaw clutch

— **de platillo único,** single plate clutch

— **maestro,** master clutch

— **neumático,** air clutch

— **reversible,** reversible clutch

embudo, funnel; leader head; hopper

— **separador,** separating funnel

emergencia, emergency; (g) emergence;

emisor de chorro de vapor, steamjet blower

empacar, package, crate

empalmar, abut, join, couple, connect

empalme, (tu) connection, joining; (carp) eking, fay, scarf, joint, assemblage; (rr) junction

— **de alineación automática,** self-aligning coupling

— **de eje,** shaft coupling

— **de manguera,** hose coupling

— **de transmisión,** transmission coupling

— **de un cable,** splice

— **en bucles,** (el) loop

empaque, (prf) packing;

— **con láminas,** sheet packing

— **de anclaje para tubería de revestimiento,** casing anchor packer

— **laminado,** sheet packing

— **moldeado,** molded packing

empaquetadura, packing, gasket

— **anular,** ring gasket

— **a presión,** pressure packer

— **con coraza rellena de asbesto,** single-shell asbestos-filled gasket

— **con nervadura de asbesto,** asbestos-ribbed gasket

— **con nervadura interior de asbestos,** inner-lap asbestos-ribbed gasket

— **con nervio de asbesto y borde interno arrollado,** asbestos-ribbed gasket with inner lap

— **con sello de plomo,** lead-seal packer

— **contra grasa,** grease seal

— **corrugada doble,** duplex corrugated gasket

— **de asbesto,** asbestos packing

— **de corcho,** cork gasket

— **de cuero,** leather gasket (o cup)

— **de fibra,** fiber gasket (o packing)

— **de goma,** rubber gasket

— **del émbolo buzo,** plunger cap

— **del limpiavástago,** oil wiper packer

— **de lino,** flax packing

— **del lodo,** mud seal

— **del pistón de la bomba de lodo,** slush pump rod packing

— **de material plástico,** plastic packing

— **de plancha de metal corrugada,** corrugated metal gasket

— **elástica,** resilient packing

— **hidráulica,** hydraulic packing

— **limpiadora de tubería de producción,** tubing stripper

— **limpiadora de varillas de bombeo,** sucker-rod stripper, oil saver

— **metálica,** metallic packing (o gasket)

— **para el ancla del entubamiento,** anchor packing

— **semimetálica,** semimetallic gasket

empaquetar, (ma) pack; stuff

emparejar, grade, level off; even up a surface

emparrillado, grillage, grating, grate, grid

— **para pisos,** floor grating

empernar, bolt

empinado, steep

emplazamiento dinámico, (nav) dynamic positioning

empotrado, (g) embedded; (beam) fixed

empresa de transporte de servicio público, common carrier

empréstito, loan

empujadora niveladora, bulldozer

empujar, to push

empuje, thrust, push, pressure; (rivet) o (pin) bearing

— **hidrostático,** (pr) water drive

— **lateral,** (g) lateral thrust

— **longitudinal,** (g) end thrust

— **por gas en solución,** gas drive, gas solution drive

— **por gas libre,** (pr) gas cap drive

— **radial,** radial thrust

emulsión, emulsion

— **asfáltica de rotura lenta (o media, rápida),** emulsified slow (o medium quick) breaking asphalt

— **de aceite en agua,** oil-water emulsion

— **de petróleo,** oil emulsion

— **estable,** hard emulsion, stable emulsion

— **fresca,** fresh emulsion

emulsionador, emulsifier

emulsivo, emulsive

enargita, enargite

encajadora de la tubería de revestimiento, casing snubber

encaje de cojinete, bearing cage

encastrado, (g) embedded

encastre, groove; socket; insert

encausamiento de gases en las bandejas de burbujeo, channeling

encenderse, to ignite

encendido, (mo) ignition

— **anticipado,** preignition

— **atrasado (o retardado),** delayed (o retarded, late) ignition

— **por acumulador,** battery ignition

— **prematuro,** preignition

encerado, oil cloth

encerrado, enclosed

encogimiento, shrinkage

en corriente, (rf) on-stream

encorvadura, bending; curvature; aduncity

— **en ángulo recto,** right-angle bend

encostramiento, (prf mud) caking

encuelladero, (rig) finger (o fourble, thribble) board

enchaquetado, jacketed

enchavetamiento, (prf) keyseating

enchufacollar, collar socket

enchufacuello, collar socket

enchufar, telescope, nest; mesh; plug in

enchufe, bell end of a pipe; bell-and-spigot joint; (el) socket, plug; (ca) socket

— **ahorquillado,** (fishing tl) hair-pin socket

— **de campana,** (fishing tl) bell screw

— **de campana provisto de cuñas dentadas,** (fishing tl) bell socket

— **del cable de acero (o de las proleas),** wire-line socket

— **de empuje,** drive-down socket

— **de lodo,** mud crib (o box)

— **de mandril,** mandrel (o swivel) socket

— **de pesca,** overshot, fishing socket, bell screw

— **de pesca de fricción y corrugado,** corrugated friction socket
— **excéntrico de pesca,** eccentric releasing overshot
— **giratorio,** swivel socket
— **para tubería de revestimento,** casing socket
— **para varilla de bombeo,** sucker-rod socket
— **pescatubo,** tubing socket
— **que agarra la varilla de bombeo por la unión,** sucker-rod joint socket
— **rígido,** stiff-neck socket
— **sólido para cable,** stiff-neck socket
endentado de piezas por medio de machos (o dados), coaking
enderezadora, pipe straightener
enderezador de vástago, stem straightener
enderezar, align, straighten
endicamiento, (g) impounding
endogenético, endogenetic, endogenous
endógeno, endogenetic, endogenous
endomórfico, endomorphic
endomorfismo, endomorphism
endosar, *v.* (cm) endorse; **endoso,** *n.* endorsement
endotérmico, endothermic
endulzar el petróleo, sweeten (q.v. desulfurar)
endurecido, indurated
energía, energy, power, force
— **cinética,** kinetic energy
— **libre,** free energy
— **mecánica,** mechanical energy
— **neta en caballos,** effective (o actual) horsepower
— **química,** chemical energy
— **radiante,** radiant energy
— **térmica,** heat (o thermal) energy
en escalón, in echelon
en existencia, (cm) in stock

enfermedades laborales, occupational diseases
en forma de lúnula, crescentic
en forma de U, U-shaped
en forma de V, V-shaped
enfriador, cooler
— **de agua,** water cooler
— **de aire,** air cooler
— **de catalizador,** catalyst cooler
— **de gas,** gas cooler
— **de motor,** engine cooling unit
— **de serpentín en caja,** coil-in-box condenser (o cooler)
— **de tubos doble,** double pipe chiller
— **intermedio,** intercooler
enfriamiento, *n.* cooling
— **de las válvulas,** valve cooling
— **por agua,** water cooling
— **por aire,** air cooling
— **por evaporación,** evaporative cooling
enfriar, cool
en funcionamiento, on-stream
enganche, (mc) hitch
engargolar, groove; make a male-and-female joint
engomarse, *v.* (oil) gum
engranaje, gear
— **compensador,** equalizing gear
— **cónico,** bevel gear
— **cónico-helicoidal,** spiral-bevel gear
— **corredizo,** sliding gear
— **de alta velocidad,** high-speed gear
— **de arranque,** starting gear
— **de baja (o primera) velocidad,** low gear
— **de cambio de marcha,** speed change gear
— **de distribución del encendido,** timing gear
— **de espinas de arenque,** herringbone gear
— **de espuela,** spur gear

315

— **de mando de la bomba,** pump drive

— **de marcha atrás,** reverse gear

— **de piñón,** pinion gear

— **de piñón de mando,** drive pinion gear

— **de primera velocidad,** starting gear

— **de reducción,** reduction gear

— **de reducción en el eje trasero,** rear axle reduction

— **de rueda helicoidal,** worm wheel gear

— **de tornillo sin fin,** worm gear

— **doble helicoidal,** herringbone gear

— **en ángulo,** bevel gear

— **en bisel,** bevel gear

— **helicoidal,** helical gear, spiral gear

— **intermedio,** intermediate gear

— **inversor (o inversión) de marcha,** reversing gear

— **loco,** idler gear

— **principal,** main gear

— **recto (o de dientes rectos),** spur gear

— **regulador de encendido,** timing ring gear

— **reductor de velocidad,** speed reducing gear

— **secundario,** idler gear

engranarse, *v.* mesh

engrasador a presión, grease gun

engrasadora, grease box; grease gun; grease cup; oiler

engrosarse, swell

enjugador de tubería vástago (o cable), (pr) stripper, stripper tower

enlace, (rr) crossover; ladder track

— **final,** (rf) terminal bond

enlazar, (rf) loop; join; connect

en operación, (rf) onstream

enrejado, grillage, lattice

enroscar, thread; screw up

— **tubería,** makeup pipe

ensambladura machihembrada, tongue-and-groove joint

ensamblar, abut, join, couple, connect

— **a cola de milano,** dovetail

ensanchador, expander, enlarger, reamer

— **de agujeros,** (prf) hole enlarger

— **hueco,** (prf) hollow reamer

ensanchar, ream

ensanchatubos, pipe expander

ensayador, tester

— **de la formación por la tubería vástago,** drill stem tester

ensayo, test, assay

— **de emulsión,** emulsion test

— **de fuerza de tracción,** pull test

— **de reacción exotérmica por ácido,** acid heat test

ensenada, (g) embayment; cove, small bay

enstatita, enstatite

entalpía, entalpy

enterizo, self-contained; in one piece; solid, integral, single made

entrada, entrance; (hd) intake; (cm) cash receipts; (mc) the point of a reamer or similar tool; (mn) entry

— **de admisión de combustible,** (mo) fuel inlet

— **de alimentación,** feed inlet

en tránsito, (cm) in transit

entrega, *n.* delivery; **entregar,** *v.* deliver

entrelazado, interlocking

entropía, entropy

entubación, pipe setting; piping, tubing, well casing

en zigzag, staggered

eoceno, Eocene

eólico, aeolian, eolic

eolio, eolian, eolic

eozoico, Eozoic

epicentro, epicenter

epicontinental, (g) epicontinental;
neritic
epidota, epidote
epigenético, (g) epigenetic
epirogenia, epeirogeny
epirrocas, (g) epirocks
epizona, epirocks
época, epoch
— **interglaciales,** interglacial epoch
equilibrio, equilibrium, balance
— **del horno,** furnace equilibrium
— **dinámico,** dynamic equilibrium,
dynamic balance
— **entre sólido y líquido,** solid-
liquid equilibrium
— **inestable,** false equilibrium,
unstable equilibrium
— **verdadero,** true equilibrium
equipo, *n.* equipment
— **auxiliar,** ancillary equipment;
standby equipment
— **congelador por intercambio,**
chilling machine exchanger
— **de combinación,** (prf)
combination rig
— **de limpieza de pozos,** well
servicer
— **de perforación,** drilling
equipment, rigging
— **de perforacion con
motogeneradores,** motor
generator rig
— **de perforación para hoyos de
diámetro reducido,** slim-hole
rotary drilling rig
— **de perforación para pozos de
explosión,** shot-hole drilling rig
— **de perforación portátil,**
portable drilling rig
— **de producción,** production
equipment
— **de relevo,** standby equipment
— **de servicio,** service equipment
— **de servicio y reparaciones de
pozos petroleros,** (prf) pulling
unit

— **de tratamiento,** processing
equipment
— **físico,** (dp) hardware
— **iniciador de pozos,** spudder unit
— **motogenerador,** engine
generator set
— **motor frontal,** front-end power
unit
— **para boca de pozo,** wellhead
equipment
— **para cementación por etapas,**
stage cementing equipment
— **para perforaciones de diámetro
reducido,** slim-hole rig
— **para perforación inicial,**
spudding machine
— **para probar muestras de
formaciones,** (g) core-testing
equipment
— **para terminación de pozos,**
drilling-in unit
— **registrador del sismógrafo,**
seismograph recording unit
equivalente, equivalent
— **anilínico,** aniline equivalent
— **anilínico cero,** zero aniline
equivalent
— **anilínico negativo,** negative
aniline equivalent
— **anilínico positivo,** positive
aniline equivalent
— **directo de radiación,** direct
radiation equivalent
era, (g) era
ergio, erg
erosión, weathering
— **diferencial,** (g) differential
erosion
— **mecánica,** mechanical erosion
errático, erratic
error, error; inaccuracy
— **de cierre,** (map) error of closure
— **de redondeo,** (mt) rounding
error
— **de truncamiento,** (dp)
truncation error

Español - Inglés

— **probable de cierre,** (map) probable misclosure
erupción, (g) extrusion; eruption
eruptivo, eruptive, volcanic
escala, ladder; scale; gage; (mar) port of call
— **de cinta,** tape gage
— **de ebullición limitada,** (rf) narrow boiling range
— **de intensidades,** (gf) scale of intensities
— **de Reaumur,** Reaumur's scale
— **de tiempo,** time scale
— **natural,** natural scale
— **normal de gasolina,** normal gasoline range
— **vertical exagerada,** (gf) vertical scale exaggerated
escalera, stairway, ladder
— **de extensión,** extension ladder
— **de la torre,** derrick ladder
— **de tijeras,** step ladder
escalón, step, rung, stair tread; (g) step; (mn) stope
— **de fractura,** (g) fault scarp
escama, scale, flake
escamoso, flaky
escape, (bm) slip; leak; outlet; exhaust; (rr) siding
— **libre,** open exhaust
escapolita, scapolite
escaramujo, (mar) barnacle
escariador, reamer
— **de fondo,** bottom-hole scraper
— **hueco,** (prf) hollow reamer
— **piloto,** pilot reamer bit, pilot reamer hole enlarger
escariar, ream
escarificador, ripper
escarpa, (g) escarpment; scarp; bluff
— **de fractura,** fault scarp
escisión, (atom) splitting
escleroscopio, scleroscope
esclusa, sluice; air lock; navigation lock
escobilla, brush; (el) brush

escobillón, (p) swab; boiler flue cleaner; push broom
escofina, rasp
— **mediacaña,** half-round rasp
escoger, sort, choose
escollo de erosión, stack
escombros, debris
escoplo, chisel, socket chisel, framing chisel
escoria, scoria, clinker, slag
escotadura, indentation
escotilla, (elevator) shaft; hatchway, trap door
— **de aforo,** thief hatch, gage hatch
— **de perforación,** (mar prf) moonpool
escrepa de empuje, bulldozer
escrúpulo, pennyweight
escuadra, (carp) square
— **plegable,** bevel
escudo, shield; guard
— **continental,** (g) continental shield (o core) (q.v. **núcleo continental)**
esexita, essexite
esfera, sphere; dial of a gage
esférico, spherical
esferoide, spheroid
esferómetro, spherometer
esferulitas, spherulites
esfuerzo, stress; effort
— **cizallante,** shear (o shearing) stress
— **cortante,** shear (o shearing) stress
— **de flexión,** bending stress
— **de rotura,** ultimate stress
— **de tensión,** tensile strain, tension
— **de torsión,** torque
— **interno,** strain
— **mecánico,** mechanical stress
— **por compresión,** compression stress
— **restante,** (sd) residual stress
eslabón, link

318

Glossary of the Petroleum Industry

— **compensador,** offset link
— **de cambio rápido,** quick-change link
— **de elevador,** elevator link
— **de repuesto,** repair link
— **de rodillo,** roller link
— **extra,** offset link
— **giratorio,** swivel link
— **maestro,** master link
— **grillete,** end clevis
— **(o estribo) de elevador de tubería,** pipe elevator link
eslinga, sling
esmalte asfáltico, asphalt enamel
esmaltita, smaltite
esmeralda, emerald
esmeril, emery
esmeriladora, emery grinder, emery wheel
— **de bolas,** ball grinder, emery wheel to grind balls
— **de válvulas,** valve grinder
— **portátil,** portable grinder
espaciado, spacing
— **de pozos en forma triangular,** triangular spacing pattern
espaciador, spacer, separator, packing block
— **de electrodos,** electrode spacer
— **de empaquetadura del émbolo buzo,** cup spacer
— **del balancín,** (bm) beam spacer
— **de resorte,** spring spacer
espaciar, space
espacio, space
— **anular,** annulus
— **libre de una válvula,** valve clearance
— **libre (o luz) del émbolo,** piston clearance
esparcidor de aceite, oil slinger
espantainsectos, (rig) bug blower
espárrago, stud bolt
espátula, spatula
especies, species
especificación, specification

espécimen, specimen
espectro, spectrum
espectrométrico, spectrometric
espectrómetro, spectrometer
— **colectivo,** mass spectrometer
— **global,** mass spectrometer
espectroscopio, spectroscope
espejo, mirror
— **espejos de fricción,** (g) slickensides
espesamiento, thickening
espesar, thicken
espersartita, spessartite
espeso, thick, dense; curdy; heavy
espesor, thickness; (sheet) gage; (slab) depth
— **laminado,** laminated shim
— **(o potencia) de un estrato,** (g) thickness of a stratum
espiga, pin, shank, spike, dowling pin; ear, stem; fang; (tu) spigot
— **del gancho,** (prf) hook shank
— **(o cola) de una herramienta,** fang
— **roscada,** dowel screw
espinela, spinel
espiral, n. coil, spiral; a. spiral
espirífero, spirifer
espírtu de petróleo, white spirits
espita, cock, faucet, spigot
espodumen, spodumene
espongina, spongin
esporádico, occasional
espuma, foam, froth
— **apagadora,** fire foam, foamite
— **contra indendios,** foamite
esqueleto, (cn) frame, skeleton
esquema gráfico, graph
esquina, corner
esquisto, schist
— **aluminoso,** alum schist
— **cuarzoso,** shale-like schist
esquistosidad, schistosity
— **transversal,** (g) slaty cleavage
esquistoso, slaty
esquizolitos, vein accompaniments

319

essudeste, east southeast
estabilidad, stability
estabilizador, stabilizer
— de manómetro, pressure gage
  stabilizer
— preliminar, preliminary charge
  stabilizer, preflash tower
estabilizadora, (rf) stripper tower
estabilizar, stabilize
establecer, establish
estaca de sostén para varillas de
  tracción, pull-rod hold-up
estaca para contravientos, guy line
  stakes
estación, station; plant; (annual)
  season
— auxiliar de bombeo, booster
  pump station
— central de bombeo, central
  pumping station
— de base, (gf) base station
— de bombas, pump station
— de cierre, control station
— de control, control station
— de gravímetro, gravity station
— del péndulo, pendulum station
— de referencia, (gf) reference
  station
— de servicio, service station
— gravimétrica, gravity station
— recolectora, gathering station
— sismológica, seismological
  station
— terminal, terminal
estacionario, stationary
estadal, level rod: a measure of
  length about 3.3 meters; square
  measure about 11.2 meters^2
estadia, stadia
estadística, statistics
estado natural, natural state
estado virgen, natural state
estalactita, stalactite
estalagmita, stalagmite
estampa, dolly; swage; rivet set

estanco, watertight, airtight,
  weathertight
— al gas, gastight
— al vapor, vapor tight
estándar -d, standard (q.v. patrón,
  norma, modelo)
estandardización, n.
  standardization; v.
estandardizar, standardize
estaño, tin
estanque, reservoir, basin
etapa, stage
estática, static
estator, stator
estaurolita, staurolite
este, east
— cuarta al nordeste, east by north
— cuarta al sudeste, east by south
— del norte, east of north
— nordeste, east northeast
ester, ester
— de ácido hidrolizable,
  hydrolyzable acid esters
esterelita, esterellite
estereograma, block diagram
estéril, (well) dry, unproductive;
  (land) barren
estiaje, (r) low-water mark
estibnita, stibnite
estilbita, stillbite
estilo, style
estilolita, (g) stylolite
estipulación, stipulation
estirado en frío, (mu) cold drawn
estirador, stretcher
— de correa, belt stretcher,
  stretcher jack
estiramiento por presión, (g)
  extrusion
estirina, styrene
estopa, oakum, calking yarn;
— de plomo, lead wool
estopera, stuffing box
estrangulador, choke; flow nipple,
  bean, flow plug; chocker;
  throttle valve

Glossary of the Petroleum Industry

— **de fondo,** bottom choke
— **de tipo positivo,** positive type choke
— **graduable,** adjustable choke
— **limitador,** restrictor choke
estrangular, *v.* throttle; choke
estratificación, (g) bedding, stratification
— **cuneiforme,** lentil, lensing
— **entrecruzada,** wind-made crossbedding
— **regresiva,** repressive overlap
estratificado, bedded, stratified
estratigrafía, stratigraphy
estrato, (g) stratum, layer
— **arenoso,** sand bed
— **carbonífero,** coal bed
— **cuña,** wedge-edge
— **filtrante,** filering bed
— **guía,** key bed, guide formation
— **hendido,** joint bed
— **impermeable,** impervious bed
— **impermeable de basamento,** basement rock
— **impermeable de cobertura,** caprock
— **índice,** key bed (o horizon)
— **intruso de lutita,** shale rock
— **invertido,** (g) overturned strata
— **productivo,** reservoir rock
— **frontales,** (g) foreset bed
— **perturbados,** disturbed bed
estrecho, narrow
estrella para tubería de producción, tubing spider
estrella polar, Polaris
estría, (g) flute, stria; a groove, fluting
— **de lubricación,** oil groove
estriación, striation
estriado, fluted
estribación, counterfort; (tp) spur, foothills
estribo, stirrup; abutment; buttress; (cn) joist hanger
— **de la biela,** (ca tl) pitman stirrup

— **de soporte,** yoke structure
estribor, (nt) starboard
estroncianita, strontianite
estructura, (g) structure
— **abajo,** down structure
— **arriba,** upstructure
— **concéntrica,** concentric structure
— **de cono entre cono,** cone-in-cone structure
— **gneísica,** gneissic structure
— **magnética,** magnetic structure
— **microscópica,** microtexture
— **petrolífera,** oil-bearing structure
— **seudoporfirítica,** pseudoporphyritic
estuario, (g) estuary
estuche, box, case, kit
— **para la dinamita,** (prf) bumper housing
estudio, *n.* survey; study, consideration; designing, planning
— **aerotopográfico,** aerial survey
— **dinamométrico de un pozo,** dynamometric well survey
— **geoeléctrico,** geoelectric survey
— **geológico,** geological survey, geological study
— (o **investigación**) **gravimétrica,** gravity survey
— **por registros eléctricos,** electric logging
— **sismográfico,** seismograph survey
estufa, stove, heater
— **de resudamiento de parafina,** wax-sweating stove
etano, ethane
etanoato de etilo, ethyl acetate
etanol, ethanol
eteno, ethene
éter, ether
— **acético,** ethyl acetate
— **de petróleo,** petroleum ether
etil-, *pref.* ethyl-

321

etilacetileno, ethylacetylene
etilbenceno, ethylbenzene
etilciclohexano, ethylcyclohexane
etildiacetileno, ethyldiacetylene
etileno, ethylene
etilo, ethyl
— cloroacetato, ethyl cloracetate
etilpenteno, ethylpentene
etino, ethyne
eudiómetro, eudiometer
eutéctica, (mc) eutectic
evacuación, *n.* evacuation; *v.*
evacuar, evacuate
evaluación, evaluation, assay
evaporable, evaporable
evaporación, evaporation
— instant nea en equilibrio, flash
    equilibrium evaporation
evaporador, evaporator
— al vacío, vacuum evaporator
— de efecto mútiple, multiple-
    effect evaporator
evaporarse, evaporate
evaporita, evaporite
evaporómetro, evaporimeter,
    atmometer
evolución, evolution
exactitud, accuracy, precision
exacto, accurate, exact
examen, examination; survey
excavadora, excavator
— de arrastre, dragline
— mecánica, power shovel
excedente, excess; surplus
excentricidad, eccentricity
excéntrico, eccentric; offset
exceso de utilidades, (cm) excess
    profits
excitador, excitator, exciter
excitar, excite, stir up, rouse; (oil
    well) swab
excitatriz, exciter, excitator
excoriación, excoriation
excoriar, excoriate
excrecencia, excrescence
exención, exemption

exento de toda avería, (cm) free of
    all average
exfoliación, *n.* (g) exfoliation,
    foliation; exfoliarse, *v.* exfoliate
exhalación, exhalation
exhalar, exhale
existencia, (cm) in stock; existence;
    occurrence
exógeno, (g) exogeneous
exogenético, exogenetic
exomórfico, exomorphic
exomorfismo, exomorphism
exotérmico, exothermic
expandible, expansible, expandable
expandidor de tubos, tube
    expander
expansión, expansion
— adiabática, adiabatic expansion
— interna, internal expansion
— isotérmica, isothermal
    expansion
— politrópica, polytropic
    expansion
expansor, expander
expedición de sismólogos,
    seismograph party (o crew)
expirar, (cm) expire
exploración, (g) exploration
— por el método de
    radioactividad, radioactive
    prospecting
— sísmica, seismic exploration
explorador, explorer
— de barrido, scanner
— de punto móvil, (dp) flying spot
    scanner
explosímetro, explosimeter
explosión, explosion, (mn) blast
— amortiguada por aire, air shot
— atrasada o retardada, delayed
    explosion
— generadora de ondas, wave-
    generating explosion
explosivo, explosive
explosor eléctrico, electric blaster

explotar, operate, work; exploit, develop; explode
exponente, exponent
exportación, export
exportador, exporter
expresión topográfica, topographic expression
expreso, express
— **aéreo,** air express
expulsanúcleos, (prf) core pusher
expulsatestigos, (prf) core pusher
expulsión, expulsion
extender, (cm) renew; stretch; lay out, (note) extend; (document) draw
extensómetro, extensometer
exterior, exterior, external
externo, external, exterior
extinguidor (o extintor), extinguisher
— **a base de CO_2, CO_2** extinguisher
— **de fuego,** fire extinguisher
— **de incendios,** fire extinguisher
extracción, extraction
— **artificial por gas,** gas lift
— **de aire,** air extraction, (mc) airbleed
— **de crudo por la recirculación de gas,** rotation gas lift
— **de la tubería de un pozo junto con las varillas de succión,** stripping
— **por aire,** (pr) air lift
— **por dos disolventes,** double solvent extraction
— **por gas en varias etapas,** multistage gas-lift
extracto, extract
extractor, (tl) puller; gear puller
— **a contracorriente de etapas múltiples,** multistage counter-current extractor
— **de asientos de válvula,** valve seat puller
— **de bujes,** bushing extractor

— **de camisa de cilindro,** (tl) liner puller
— **de chavetas (o cuñas),** key puller
— **de estrangulador de fondo,** bottom hole choke extractor
— **de gorrones de pie de biela,** wrist-pin puller
— **de herramientas,** tool extractor
— **de muestras,** sampler
— **de neblina de aceite,** mist extractor
— **de niebla,** mist extractor
— **de núcleos (o testigos),** core extractor
— **de pasadores de articulación,** wrist-pin puller
— **de testigo,** core extractor
extrapolar, extrapolate
extremo, end; (rf) final fraction (o cut)
— **de aspiración (o succión)** (bm) suction end
— **de descarga** (bm), discharge end
— **expulsor de una bomba de lodo,** mud end of pump
— **móvil,** (heat exchanger) expansion end
— **roscado,** (p) screwed end
— **superior,** mast head
— **trasero,** rear end
extrusión, (g) extrusion
extrusivo, extrusive
exudar, exude
eyector, ejector, eductor
— **a vapor,** steam ejector
— **de dos etapas,** two-stage ejector
— **de vapor para eliminar gases,** steam-jet ejector
— **simple,** single ejector

F

fábrica, factory, mill, shop (q.v. **planta)**

fabricado a la orden, custom built
fabricante, manufacturer, maker
faceta, facet
facies, (g) facies
— **lacustre,** lacustrine (o limnetic) facies
— **marina,** marine facies
factor, factor
— **constante de equilibrio,** equilibrium constant
— **constante de gas,** gas constant
— **de compresión,** compression factor
— **de contracción,** contraction factor
— **de fricción,** friction factor
— **de potencia,** power factor
— **de seguridad,** safety factor
— **físico constante,** physical constant
factura, (cm) invoice, bill
— **consular,** consular invoice
— **pro forma,** pro forma invoice
faja, belt, strip
falla, (g) fault, fracture; (mc) failure, breakdown
— **axial,** longitudinal fault
— **compleja,** complex fault
— **compresional,** compression fault, buried fault
— **con ángulo abierto,** right fault
— **con ángulo cerrado,** low-angle fault
— **cruzada,** traverse fault
— **cuneiforme,** keystone (o wedge) fault
— **de ángulo menor,** low angle fault
— **de bajoescurrimiento,** underthrust fault
— **de bisagra,** hinge fault
— **de buzamiento,** dip-slip fault
— **de corrimiento,** thrust fault
— **de cuña,** wedge (o keystone) fault
— **de escurrimiento,** thrust fault

— **de pivote,** pivotal fault
— **de rumbo,** strike-slip (o transcurrent) fault
— **de sobreescurrimiento,** overthrust fault
— **del subsuelo,** buried fault
— **diagonal,** oblique (o diagonal) fault
— **diagonal de buzamiento,** dip-slip diagonal fault
— **diagonal rumbo,** strike-slip diagonal fault
— **diagonal oblicua,** oblique-slip oblique fault
— **en clave de arco,** (g) keystone fault
— **en espigación,** hinge fault
— **en pivote,** pivotal fault
— **epianticlinal,** epi-anticlinal fault
— **estratigráfica,** bedded fault
— **giratoria,** rotational fault, hinge fault
— **gran angular,** high-angle fault
— **inferida,** probable (o inferred) fault
— **inversa,** reversed fault
— **invertida,** reverse fault
— **longitudinal,** strike fault
— **longitudinal de buzamiento,** dip-slip strike fault
— **longitudinal de rumbo,** strike-slip strike fault
— **longitudinal oblicua,** oblique-slip strike fault
— **marginal,** marginal fault
— **múltiple,** multiple fault
— **normal,** normal fault
— **oblicua,** oblique-slip fault
— **paralela al buzamiento y rumbo del estrato,** bedding fault
— **paralela al rumbo del estrato,** strike fault
— **pivotal,** scissors fault, rotatorial fault

Glossary of the Petroleum Industry

— **por bamboleo,** (prf) wobble
failure
— **por gravedad,** gravity fault
— **por rotación,** rotational fault
— **probable,** inferred (o probable)
fault
— **ramificada,** branching fault
— **sobrepuesta,** overlap fault
— **transversal,** transverse fault
— **transversal de buzamiento,** dip-
slip dip fault
— **transversal de rumbo,** strike-
slip dip fault
— **transversal oblicua,** oblique-slip
dip fault
— **vertical,** vertical fault
fallas
— **al tresbolillo,** echelon (o
staggered) faults
— **conformes,** conformable beds (o
faults)
— **escalonadas,** in echelon (o
distributive, step) faults
— **marginales,** boundary faults
— **paralelas,** parallel faults
— **periféricas,** radial faults
— **por desgarramiento,** tear faults
— **radiales,** radial faults
falsa escuadra, bevel
falúa, (nt) tender
fanglomerado, (g) fanglomerate
fango, mud, muck, silt; sludge
— **mineral,** (mn) sludge
fangoso, oozy, muddy
farero, derrickman
faro, lighthouse; lamp; (prf) derrick
fase, phase, aspect; (el) phase
— **continua,** continuous phase
— **de la coda,** coda phase
— **final,** coda phase, final phase
fasómetro, phase meter
fatiga, (mu) fatigue
— **por corrosión,** corrosion fatigue
— **por mellas,** notch fatigue
fecha, date
feldespato, feldspar

feldespatoide, feldspathoid
felsita, (g) felsite
fenatreno, phenanthrene
fenestra, (g) inlier
fenil- *pref.* phenyl-
fenilacetileno, phenylacetylene
fenilbenceno, phenylbenzene (q.v.
difenilo)
fenilmetano, phenylmethane
fenocristales, phenocrysts
fenol, phenol
— **anhidro,** anhydrous phenol
fenolftaleína, phenolphtalein
fenómenos de contacto, (g)
contaction
fermentación, fermentation
ferrato, ferrate
ferretería, hardware
férrico, ferric
ferrito, -a, (qm) ferrite
ferrocarril, railroad
ferrogusita, fergusite
ferromagnesiano, mafic
ferromagnético, ferromagnetic
ferromagnetismo, ferromagnetism
ferroso, ferrous
fiador, fastener, retainer; catch
— **atravesado,** toggle
— **de embrague,** clutch dog
— **del freno,** brake dog
fianza, (cm) bond; bail,
guarantee, security, surety
fibra, fiber
— **de torsión,** torsion fiber
fichero de datos, data file
fieltro, felt
fijo, stationary, fixed
fila, queue, line
filástica de plomo, lead wool
filete, (tu) (screw) thread; fillet
— **acme,** acme thread
— **de tubo,** pipe thread
fileteado, threaded
filita, (g) phyllite
filo, cutting edge; (tp) ridge

325

— **de montañas paralelo al rumbo del estrato,** strike ridge
filogenia, (g) phylogeny
filón, (mn) streak, vein, seam, lode
— **intrusivo,** (g) igneous rock
— **metalífero,** (mn) ore vein
filtración, filtration; seepage, creep, percolation
filtración a través de arcilla, (rf) clay filtration
filtración de petróleo, oil seep
filtrado, *n.* filtrate; **filtrar,** *v.* filter, percolate
filtro, (tu) perforated pipe; filter
— **al vacío,** vacuum filter
— **de aire,** air cleaner, air filter
— **de arena a presión,** press-type sand filter
— **de aceite,** oil filter
— **del combustóleo,** fuel filter (o strainer)
— **de entrada,** input filter
— **de hojas,** leaf-type filter
— **de pedregullo,** sand screen
— **de salida,** output filter
— **desparafinador,** wax filter
— **intermedio,** interstage filter
— **percolador,** percolating filter
— **prensa,** filter press
finalización de un pozo, well completion
finos, fines; fine dust
finura, fineness; grain
fiord, fjord
firmante, undersigned
física, *n.* physics
fisiografía, *n.* physiography;
fisiográfico, *a.* physiographic
fisura, fissure, seam
— **de falla,** fault fissure
flanco, side, slope of a wall, limb; flank
— **de anticlinal,** limb of anticline
— **del pliegue,** limb of fold
flecha, arrow; (mc) shaft, axle; (wagon) pole; deflection sag

— **de eje,** axle shaft
fleje, band, iron strap, hoop
— **de fondo,** (tk) apron ring
flete, freight
— **férreo,** railroad freight
— **fluvial,** river freight
— **marítimo,** (cm) ocean freight
flexible, flexible
flexión, bending, flexure; (g) fold
floculación, flocculation
floculento, flocculent
flogopita, phlogopite
floridina, floridin
flotabilidad, buoyancy
flotador del carburador, carburetor float
flotante, floating
fluctuación, fluctuation
fluctuar, fluctuate
fluencia elástica, elastic flow
fluidez, fluidity
— **cero,** zero pour
— **estable,** pour stability
fluido, *n. a.* fluid; (g) fluidal; fluxional
— **perfecto,** perfect fluid
flujo, flow, flux; (mu) creep; (mar) ebb
— **de barro,** fango (o lodo), mud flow
— **de fractura,** frac fluid
— **de lava,** lava flow
— **isotermo,** isothermal flow
— **plástico,** (g) plastic flow
— **turbulento,** turbulent flow
— **viscoso,** viscous flow
fluorescencia, fluorescence
— **del petróleo,** bloom (o cast) of oil
fluorina, fluorine
fluorita, fluorite
flus, flue
fluvial, fluvial
fluvioglacial, fluvioglacial
fluviomarino, fluviomarine
fluxion, (mt) fluxion, differential

focal, focal
foco, focus
— **eléctrico,** floodlight
fogueo, firing
fomento, development (q.v.
  desarrollo)
fondo, (gf) trough (or valley) of
  observed reflection; bottom, far
  end, base, bed; fund; depth
— **de rosca,** thread root
— **falso,** false bottom
— **y primer anillo,** (tk) apron ring
fonalita, phonolite
foraminífero, *a.* foraminiferal
forja, forge
forjado bruto, (mu) blackwork
forjadura, forging
— **a martinete,** drop forging
formación, (g) formation
— **aflorante,** outcropping
  formation
— **compacta,** tight formation
— **de arena extraviada,** (g) stray
  sand
formaldeído, formaldehyde
formón, wood (o socket) chisel
fórmula, formula
— **empírica,** empirical formula
formulario, (cm) blank form
forrado, lined
forro, (well) casing; (cylinder) liner;
  lining, lagging, sheathing;
  bushing
— **aislante en secciones,** sectional
  insulation
— **de caldera,** boiler jacket
— **de cilindros,** cylinder sleeve (o
  liner)
— **de embrague,** clutch lining
— **de freno,** brake lining
— **de tela de vidrio para tubería,**
  glass mat
— **tejido para frenos,** woven brake
  lining
fosa, grave; pit; drain; (mu) sow

— **causada por un hundimiento,**
  (g) sink hole
— **de hundimiento en forma de
  embudo,** (g) sink funnel
— **de peñascos,** (g) boulder graben
— **marginal,** (g) trough,
  sedimentary basin
— **tectónica,** fault trough, graben
  fault, downthrown (o sunken)
  block
fosfato, phosphate
fosforita, phosphorite
fósforo, phosphorous
fósil, fossil
— **indicador,** index fossil
fosilífero, fossiliferous
foso, ditch, trench, pit
— **de acondicionamiento,**
  conditioning pit
— **de desperdicios,** shale pit
— **del lodo de perforación,** slush pit
— **de mezclar,** mixing pit
— **de ripio,** shale pit
— **de succión,** suction pit
— **para lodo,** sump hole
— **para trampa de raspatubos,** (p)
  scraper trap pit
fotoeléctrico, photoelectric
fotografía, photograph,
  photography
— **aérea,** aerial photograph
fotómetro, photometer
fracción, (rf) fraction
— **de alta ebullición,** boiling
  fraction
— **derivada del petróleo,** cut,
  fraction
— **final,** end
— **liviana de petróleo,** light
  fraction
— **pesada,** heavy fraction
— **volátil,** light end
fraccionación, (rf) fractionation,
  cracking; rectification

fraccionadora, (rf) fractionating
column (o tower), stabilizing
column, fractionator
fraccionamiento, fractionation
fractura, (g) fracture, rupture,
breaking
— **concoidea,** conchoidal fracture
— **curvilínea,** conchoidal fracture
— **escalonada,** step faults
— **de extensión,** extension fracture
fracturado, fractured
fracturar, *v.* fracture, break
frágil, fragile, brittle
fragmentación, fragmentation
fragmento, *n.* fragment,
fragua, forge; blacksmith shop
— **para barrenas,** bit forge
fraguado, forging; (cement) setting
— **térmico,** thermosetting
franco a bordo (FAB), free on
board (FOB)
franco al costado del buque (FAS),
free alongside ship (FAS)
franco de comisión, (cm) free of
brokerage
franja, a strip, a band; zone; (g)
striae
— **capilar,** capillary fringe
franklinita, franklinite
franquear, *v.* span, clear
frasco, flask
frecuencia, frequency
— **de oscilación,** frequency of
oscillation
— **intermedia,** intermediate
frequency
frenaje, braking
frenita, phrenite
freno, brake
— **automático,** automatic brake
— **de alta torsión,** high-torque
brake
— **de banda,** band brake
— **del cabrestante de la cuchara,**
back brake
— **de cinta,** band brake

— **de doble efecto,** double-acting
brake
— **de embrague,** clutch brake
— **de emergencia,** emergency brake
— **de expansión,** expansion brake,
expanding brake
— **de mano,** hand brake
— **dinamométrico,** dynamometric
brake
— **duoservo,** duo servo brake
— **(s) en cuatro ruedas,** four-wheel
brakes
— **hidroautomático,** hydromatic
brake
— **neumático,** air brake
frente, front
— **a un glacial,** englacial
— **de onda,** (gf) wave front
— **de llama,** flame front
— **de pliegue,** (g) brow, crown
fresa, bit, milling tool, counter-
sinking bit, milling cutter
— **de barrena,** bit cutter
— **de cuchillas extensibles para
tubería de revestimiento,**
expanding casing mill
— **de fondo plano,** flat-bottom
rotary milling tool
— **de punta redonda,** round-nose
rotary milling tool
— **rectificadora,** gauge cutter
fresadora, milling machine (o tool)
— **para formaciones duras,** hard
formations cutter head
friable, friable
friabilidad, embrittlement
fricción, friction
frío, cold
fritamiento, fritura (g) chilling
effect
frontal, frontal
frontón, (mn) pediment
ftalato dibutílico, dibutyl phthalate
fuego, fire
— **expontáneo,** breathing fire
fuelle, bellows, blower

— **de fragua,** forge flower
fuente, fountain, spring, water well
— **artesiana,** artesian well
— **termal,** hot spring
fuerte, strong; (grade) heavy; (curve) sharp
fuerza, strength, force, power
— **centrífuga,** centrifugal force
— **compensadora** (o **estabilizadora),** (gf) restoring force
— **compresora,** compressive strength
— **de adherencia,** soil stress
— **de arrastre con cable,** line pull
— **de astatización,** astatizing force
— **de estatización,** estatizing force
— **de flotación,** buoyant power
— **de labilización,** labilizing force
— **de rotura,** yield strength
— **dieléctrica,** dielectric strength, disruptive strength
— **electromotriz,** electromotive force
— **magnética,** magnetic force
— **motriz,** (mc) power
— **tangencial,** tangential force
— **total del magnetómetro,** magnetometer force
fuga, leak
fulcro, growler, fulcrum
fulgurita, (g) fulgurite
fulmicotón, gun cotton
fulminante, blasting cap
— **de dinamita,** dynamite cap
— **eléctrico,** electric blasting cap
fuloniense, Fullonian
fumarola, (vlc) fumarole
función sencilla, single duty
funcionamiento, (mc) operation; functioning, performance, running
fundamento, foundation
fundente, welding compound, flux
fundición, smelting works; foundry; casting

— **en bloque,** block casting
— **endurecida,** chilled casting
fundir, *v.* cast; melt, smelt; (fuse) blow out
furfural, furfural
furgonada, carload, truckload
fuselado, streamlined
fusible, *n.* fuse; *a.* fusible; (mu) liquefiable
— **de cinta,** (el) link fuse
— **eléctrico,** electric fuse
fusil, gun
fusión, fusion; melting
fuste, column shaft; (r) shank; (bit) stem
— **de pasador,** pin shank

G

gabarra, barge
— **de perforación,** drilling barge
gabro, (g) gabbro
gafas protectoras, goggles
gal, gal: unity of gravimetric acceleration
galactita, Fuller's earth
galena, galena
gálibo, template, jig; straightedge; clearance diagram
gálibo de polea, crowning of pulley
gallito, sucker-rod hook
galón, gallon
galones por cada mil pies cúbicos, gallons per thousand feet
galones por minuto, gallons per minute
galvanizado, galvanized
galvanómetro, galvanometer
gamma, gamma
ganancia, (cm) gain, profit
gancho, hook; gab
— **centrador de barrena,** wall hook
— **de aparejo para tubería de revestimiento,** casing hook

— **de pared,** wall hook
— **de maniobra para tubería de producción,** tubing hook
— **de perforación para rotatoria,** rotary drilling hook
— **de pesca,** (prf) fishing grab
— **de seguridad,** pintle hook, safety hook
— **de tornillo,** screw hook
— **de varillas de succión,** sucker-rod
— **para el cable de las llaves (o tenazas),** tong-line hanger
— **para centrar la barrena en el hoyo,** wall hook
— **para entubamiento,** tubing hook
— **portabarrenas,** bit hook
ganga, (mn) matrix, gangue
garantía, *n.* guaranty
garantizar, *v.* guarantee; vouch for
garfio, hook
— **del freno del malacate de las herramientas,** (prf) brake staple for bull wheel
— **del freno del malacate de tuberías,** (prf) brake staple for calf wheel
garganta, (tp) gap; (mc) groove, channel; (saw) gullet
gárgol, (carp) gain, groove, notch
garlancha, spade
garnierita, garnierite
garra, (mc) grip, clutch, catch, claw; (ca) roddle (q.v. **mordaza**)
— **de correa,** belt clamp, belt grip
— **para tubería**
— **roscada,** (fishing tl) wicker
garrucha, sheave, pulley
—**de la cuchara,** sand-sheave pulley
—**de engranaje,** geared hoist
gas, gas
— **absorbido,** occluded gas
— **acetileno,** acetylene gas
— **azul,** blau (o blue) gas
— **combustible,** fuel gas

— **en botellas,** bottled gas, LPG
— **de absorción,** absorption gas
— **de aire,** aerogene (o producer, air) gas
— **de alambique de crácking,** cracking still gas
— **de aspirador,** exhauster gas
— **de barrido,** sweep-gas
— **de carbón,** coal gas
— **de chimenea,** flue gas
— **de desecho,** waste gas
— **de perdicio,** waste gas
— **de expulsión,** purge gas
— **de pantano,** marsh gas
— **de síntesis,** synthesis gas
— **del escape,** exhaust gas
— **extráneo,** extraneous gas
— **grisú,** fire damp
— **húmedo,** wet gas, casing head gas
— **inerte,** inert gas
— **innato al estrato,** formation gas
— **inofensivo,** innocuous gas
— **libre,** free gas
— **licuado de petróleo (GLP) ,** liquefied petroleum gas, LPG
— **licuado de refinería,** liquefied refinery gas, LPG
— **natural,** natural gas
— **natural húmedo,** wet natural gas
— **natural seco,** dry natural gas
— **ocluido,** occluded gas
— **pobre,** aerogene (o producer) gas
— **portador,** carrier gas
— **residual,** residue gas
— **seco,** dry gas
gasa, gauze
gaseoso, gaseous
gasificar, gasify, aerify
gasoducto, gas pipeline
— **troncal,** trunk pipeline for gas
gasógeno, gas generator
— **de acetileno,** acetylene generator
gasóleo, gas oil
gasolina, gasoline
— **bruta,** raw gasoline

— **cruda,** raw gasoline
— **de alta gravedad,** light gasoline
— **de aviación,** aviation gasoline (o fuel), avgas
— **de crácking,** cracked gasoline (q.v. **gasolina reformada)**
— **de destilación a temperatura límite,** end-point gasoline
— **destilada a presión atmosférica,** straight-run gasoline
— **estabilizada,** stripped gasoline
— **íntegra,** straight-run gasoline
— **natural,** (rf) cashinghead (o natural) gasoline
— **no estabilizada,** wild gasoline
— **polímera,** polymer gasoline
— **reformada,** cracked gasoline
— **tratada,** (rf) sweetened gasoline
gasómetro, gas holder, gasometer
gasto no medido (o **gasto no registrado),** slippage
gastos, (cm) expenses, expenditures
— **de explotación,** revenue expenditures
— **de iniciación de operación,** startup expenses
— **fijos,** overhead
gastrolito, gastrolith
gatillo, trigger
gato, jack
— **de bombeo,** pumping jack
— **de cremallera y circular,** rock and circle jack
— **de cremallera y palanca,** rack and lever jack
— **de palanca,** lever jack
— **de tornillo,** screw jack
— **de trinquete,** ratchet-type lifting jack
— **hidráulico,** hydraulic jack
— **mecánico,** lifting jack
— **(o cric) de cremallera,** rack jack
— **para tubería,** pipe jack
— **para tubería de revestimiento,** casing jack
— **rodante,** (a) dolly

gaussio, gauss, gauss
geiser, geyser
gieserita, geyserite
gel, (prf) gel
gelatinoso, gelatinous
gemelo, *n.* shackle *a.* twin, duplex; double
generador, generator
— **a turbina,** turbine-driven generator
— **de acetileno,** acetylene generator
— **de agua dulce,** water softener
— **de energía eléctrica,** electric generator
— **de vapor de tipo intercambiador,** exchanger-type steam generator
género, genus
genotipo, (paleo) genotype
géoda, (g) geode
geodesia, geodesy
geodético, geodetic
geofísica, geophysics
geófono, geophone, doodlebug, detector
— **detector,** seismometer, seismograph
geogenia, geogeny
geognosia, geognosy
geográfico, geographic
geoidal, geoid
geoide, geoid; (g) geoide
geología, geology
— **estructural,** structural geology
— **superficial,** areal geology
geológico, geologic, geological
geometría, *n.* geometry;
geométrico, *a.* geometric
geomorfología, morphological geology, geomorphology
geoquímica, *n.* geochemistry
georgiense, Georgian
geosinclinal, geosyncline
geotérmico, geothermal, geothermic
gerente, manager

331

gestion de datos, data management
giba, (g) hump
gibsita, gibbsite
gilsonita, gilsonite
girador, revolving
— **de junta kelly,** kelly spinner
girar, spin
— **sobre un punto** (eje), slue
giro, (cm) draft; revolving, sluing; (ma) revolution
— **la vista,** sight draft
— **bancario,** bank draft
— **postal,** money order
giroscopio, gyroscope
glaciación, (g) glaciation
glacial, *a.* glacial
glaciar, glacier
— **alpino,** Alpine glacier
— **colgante,** hanging glacier
glauconita, glauconite
gleba, (g) horst, heaved block
— **tectónica,** (g) fault block
glicol, glycol
— **dietileno,** diethylene glycol
gliptolita, ventifact
gliptolitos, glyptoliths
globulitos, globulites
glóbulo, globule
glomeroporfirítico, glomeroporphyritic
gneiss, gneiss
gobernador, (rf) governor; (mc) control, governor, regulator, controller
gobierno, government; (mc) control
— **de la amplitud,** amplitude control
— **del freno,** brake control
golfo, gulf
gollete, gullet; neck, spout
—**de botella,** bottleneck
golpe, blow, shock, stroke; throw
— **de retroceso del émbolo,** back stroke
— **seco,** dead blow
goma, rubber; a rubber tire; gum

— **laca,** shellac
— **sintética,** artificial rubber, synthetic rubber
gomosidad, *n.* gummy quality; *a.*
gomoso, gummy
góndola, athey wagon, (rr) gondola car
goniómetro, goniometer; angle meter
gorrón, (ma) toe
— **de manivela,** crankpin
gorronera, journal box (o bearing)
gota, drop
goteras calcáreas, (g) sinter deposits
gotero, pipette
grabar, emboss, engrave, carve
grabenfosa tectónica, graben fault
gradiente, gradient
— **de la gravedad,** gravity gradient
— **de temperatura,** temperature (o geothermal) gradient
— **geotérmico,** temperature gradient
— **gravimétrica,** gravity gradient
— **lateral de la velocidad,** horizontal (o lateral) velocity gradient
— **local,** (gf) local gradient
— **magnético,** magnetic gradient
— **real,** actual gradient
— **recíproco,** reciprocal gradient
— **recíproco de temperatura,** geothermal gradient
— **regional,** (g) regional gradient
— **térmico,** thermal gradient, temperature gradient
gradiómetro, gradiometer
grado, (ma) stage; (mt) degree; grade, class, rate
— **de octano,** octane rating
graduación, gradation
— **cetánica,** cetane rating
— **del magnetómetro,** magnetometer scale division
gradual, gradational

332

graduar, grade; classify; graduate;
(mc) index, gage
gráfica, diagram, graph; graphics
— **de presión-volumen,** P-V
diagram
— **de tiempo y distancia,** time-
distance graph
— **representativa de la tierra sin
las capas superiores,** curve for
the stripped earth
graficado, plotting
gráfico, graphic
grafito, wad, graphite
grahamita, grahamite, asphalt
gramil, (carp) marking gage; router;
shifting gage
gramo, gram
grampa, clamp, clip, cramp; staple
— **cabeza,** blowout preventer (q.v.
preventor de reventones)
— **contrafugas,** lead clamp
— **de electrodo,** electrode clamp
— **para cables,** wire-rope clip
— **U,** U bolt
granate, garnet
granítico, granitic
granito, granite
— **con predominio de aluminio,**
quartzite granite
grano, (wt) (lumber) grain
— **clástico,** clastic grain
— **de arena,** sand grain
— **fino,** fine grained
— **de cuarzo,** quartz grain
— **semiangulares,** subangular grain
granoblástico, granoblastic
granodiorita, granodiorite
granofírico, granophyric
grano-mol, grain-mole
granulación, granulation
granular, granular
granulita, granulite
gránulo, granule
granuloso, granulose
grapa, clip, clamp, cramp; staple
— **angular,** corner clamp

— **tapafugas para cañería,**
emergency pipe clamp
— **para cable de acero,** wire-cable
clip
grasa, grease
— **con base de cal,** lime-base grease
— **de engranajes,** gear compound
— **de grafito,** graphite grease
— **para ejes,** axle grease
grasera, grease cup, grease nipple,
lubricator fitting
— **de copa,** grease cup
— **tipo botón,** button-head fitting
gratis, free of charge
grauvaca, graywacke
grava, gravel
— **de cantos rodados grandes,**
boulder gravel
— **de cantos rodados medianos,**
cobble gravel
guijarrosa, pebble gravel
guijosa, grit, granule gravel
gruesa, coarse gravel
gravamen, tax; encumbrance, lien
gravedad, gravity
— **aparente,** apparent gravity
— **absoluta,** absolute gravity
— **de la base,** (gravim) base gravity
— **específica,** specific gravity
— **normal,** normal gravity
— **terrestre,** earth's gravity
gravilla, granule gravel, grit
— **de desierto,** lag gravel
gravímetro, gravimeter, gravity
meter
— **dinámico,** dynamic gravimeter
— **vertical,** vertical gravimeter
gravitación, gravitation
gravitativo, gravitative
graywacke, graywacke
greda, marl
gres, greisen
grieta, crack, seam; chink; (g) joint
crevice
— **de glaciar,** crevasse, diaclase
— **de aire,** air cock

— **de cinco pasos**, five-way cock
— **de cinco vías,** five-way cock
— **de confrontación**, water gage cock
— **de desagüe,** drawoff valve
— **de drenaje**, drain cock
— **de manómetro,** water (o boiler) gage cock
— **de prueba**, try cock
— **de purga,** purging cock
— **de la válvula**, valve cock
— **indicador de nivel de agua,** water gage cock
grietas producidas por el sol, sun cracks
grifo, faucet, cock, bibb; tap; spigot
grillete, shackle; socket; clevis
grosularita, grossularite
grúa, crane; derrick; hoist, tow truck
— **con montaje en patín,** skid hoist
— **de brazo,** jib crane
— **de cadena,** chain hoist
— **móvil,** walking crane
— **para herramientas,** tool crane
— **rodante,** walking crane
— **viajera,** traveling crane
grueso, *n.* density, thickness, *a.* thick, bulky, corpulent; coarse, dense; heavy
grupo, group, (mc) unit
— **de falla,** fault bundle
— **de ondas,** (gf) wave train
— **electrógeno diesel,** diesel electric unit
— **motobomba,** power pumping unit
guardabarro, (a) fender
guardacabos, wire-rope thimble
guardacuerpo, safety railing
guardaderrumbes, cave packer
guardafango, dashboard
guardamesa, table guard
guardarrosca, thread protector
guardavolante, flywheel guard
guardia, guard; protection

guarnición, packing; (mc) insert; (carp) trim
— **de cojinete,** bearing insert (o sleeve)
— **de culata de cilindros,** cylinder head gasket
guasa, (va) ball and seat, washer
gubia, gouge, inside tool
guía, *n.* (mc) guide; (g) branch vein; (mn) leader; (rr) waybill; slide bar; pilot, *a.* thick, bulky, corpulent; coarse, dense; heavy
— **de cruceta**, crosshead guides
— **de herramientas,** tool guide
— **de válvula,** valve guide
— **de las varillas de bombeo,** sucker-rod guide
— **de zapata,** guide shoe
— **del cable de las poleas,** wire-line guide
— **del enchufe de pesca**, overshot guide
— **para plomada de vástago de barrena,** auger sinker-bar guide
— **que distribuye uniformemente el cable al arrollarse éste en el tambor,** spooler
— **separadora del cable,** (draw works) divider drum
— **del martinete**, lead
guía barrena, (prf) whipstock
guiador, guiding ring; guide
guiasondas, whipstock
guija, granule
guillotina, shear
guinche, hoisting engine, winch, windlass; crane
— **a engranaje,** geared hoist
— **de mano,** windlass
guiñada, (nt) yaw
gunita, gunite
gusanillo, gimlet, twist drill
— **de rosca**, thread fillet

H

hacer girar, *v.* spin
hacer perforaciones sismográficas
    para efectuar la correlación
    geológica, (g) correlation
    shooting
hacha, axe
— de dos filos, double-bit axe
hachuela, blockaxe
hachuras, hachures, hatching
hacia el afloramiento, a-cropping
hacienda nacional, national
    treasury
hacinar, *v.* stack
halita, halite
halo, halo
halógeno, halogen
haluro, halide
— metálico, metal halide
harina fósil, diatomaceous earth
haz, bundle; fagot
— (o despliegue) de geófonos,
    geophone spread
— de tubería en pie, (prf rig) stand
    of pipe, pipe setback
— de tubos, tube bundle
heces, sludge
hactárea, hectare
hectárea-metro, hectare-meter
hedenburguita, hedenbergite
helero, glacier
hélice, helix, propeller
hélico, helical
helicoidal, helical
helio, helium
heliografía, blueprint, sun print
helvetiense, Helvetian
hematita, hematite
hemera, (g) hemera
hemimetileno, hemimethylene.
    (q.v. trimetilbenceno)
hemipelágico, (g) hemipelagic
hendible, fissile

hendidura, (g) rift; split, crack,
    crevice; (mn) cleat; cleavage
heneicosano, heneicosane
heneicoseno, heneicosene
henheptacontano,
    henheptacontane
hentetracontano, hentetracontane
hentriacontano, hentriacontane
heptadecano, heptadecane
heptadeceno, heptadecene
heptahexacontano,
    heptahexacontane
heptano, heptane
hepteno, heptene
heptatriacontano,
    heptatriacontane
hermético, hermetical, airtight,
    airproof
— al aceite, oiltight
— al gas, gastight
— al vapor, vapor tight
herraje, ironwork, hardware
— de aparejo, rig irons
— de cabria, rig irons
— de perforadora, rig irons
— para torre de perforación, (prf)
    standard rig irons
herramienta, tool
— alisadora de rebordes, (tu)
    shoulder-dressing tool
— alisadora del reborde de
    uniones de tubería vástago,
    tool-joint shoulder-dressing
    tool
— con ranura de enchufe en
    forma de J, J tool
— de ajuste, setter, setting tool
— de empacar el prensaestopas,
    packing tool
— de empalmar, splicing tool
— de fresar, milling tool
— de inserción y ajuste, setting
    tool
— de mano, hand tool

Español - Inglés

— **de orientación direccional,** (prf)
directional orientation tool
DOT
— **de pesca,** (prf) fishing tool
— **de rescate,** pickup tool
— **desviadora,** sidetracking tool
— **eléctrica para cortar roscas
hembras,** tapper
— **mecánica,** mechine tool
— **para colocar tubería
revestidora de fondo,** liner-
setting tool
— **para desviar,** sidetracing tool
— **para insertar accesorios en
pozos,** setting tool
— **para recoger fragmentos
pequeños de hierro
del fondo del pozo,** mousetrap
— **rotatoria de pesca,** rotary fishing
tool
— **viajera de rosca de paso
izquierdo,** left-hand-thread
running tool
herramientas
— **a prueba de chispa,**
nonsparking tools
— **de cable,** (prf) cable tools
— **para perforación a percusión,**
cable drilling tools
herrero, (oc)blacksmith
herrumbre, rust
hervidero, waterleg
hervidor, boiler, bootleg, waterleg;
small boiler
heterogéneo, heterogeneous
hexacontano, hexacontane
hexacosano, hexacosane
hexadecano, hexadecane
hexadeceno, hexadecene
hexaetilbenceno, hexaethylbenzene
hexágono, hexagon
hexahexacontano,
hexahexacontane
hexametilbenceno,
hexamethylbenzene

hexametileno, hexamethylene. (q.v.
ciclohexano)
hexametiletano,
hexamethylethane.
hexano, hexane
— **normal,** n-hexane
hexatriacontano, hexatriacontane
hexeno, hexene
hexildocosano, hexyldocosane
hexileicosano, hexyleicosane
hexino, (q.v. butilacetileno)
hialopilítico, hyalopilitic
hiato, hiatus
hidatógeno, (g) hydatogenic
hidratación, hydration
hidrator, hydrator
hidrato, hydrate
— **de amonio,** aqua ammonia
hidráulica, n. hydraulics
hidráulico, a. hydraulic
hidrindano, hydrindane. (q.v.
biciclononano)
hidrindeno, hydrindene
hidrocarburo, hydrocarbon
— **anular,** cyclic (o ring)
hydrocarbon
— **clorinado,** chlorinated
hydrocarbon
— **de cadena ramificada,** (qm)
branched-chain hydrocarbon
— **de cadena recta,** straight-chain
hydrocarbon
— **de doble enlace,** double-bonded
hydrocarbon
— **de enlace,** (qm) straight-chain
hydrocarbon
— **de enlace de cadena lateral,**
(qm) side-chain hydrocarbon
— **de etileno,** ethylene hydrocarbon
— **gaseoso,** gaseous hydrocarbon
— **no contaminado,** technical
hydrocarbon
— **no saturado,** unsaturated
hydrocarbon
— **olefínico,** olefin hydrocarbon
— **pesado,** (rf) heavy hydrocarbon

— **puro,** technical hydrocarbon
— **terciario,** (qm) tertiary
 hydrocarbon
hidrocarburos
— **cicloolefínicos,** cyclo-olefins
— **cicloparafínicos,** cycloparaffins
— **diolefínicos,** diolefin
 hydrocarbons
— **nafténicos,** naphythenic
 hydrocarbons
hidrodesintegración,
 hydrocracking
hidrodesulfuración,
 hydrodesulfurization
— **en fase de vapores,** vapor-phase
 hydrodesulfurization
hidrodinámica, *n.* hydrodynamics
hidrodinámico, a. hydrodynamic;
 streamlined
hidrófilo, hydrophylic
hidroformación, hydroforming
hidrogenación, hydrogenation
hidrógeno, hydrogen
— **atómico,** atomic hydrogen
hidrografía, hydrography
hidrólisis, hydrolysis
hidrómetro, gasoline tester; stream
 gage
hidrósfera, hydrosphere
hidrosilicato, hydrosilicate
hidrostático, hydrostatic
hidrotérmico, hydrothermal
hidróxido, hydroxide
— **de potasio,** potassium hydroxide
hielo, ice
— **seco,** dry ice
hierro, iron
— **angular,** angle iron
— **angular de refuerzo,** gusset
— **carbonilo,** iron carbonyl
— **cementado,** iron-case hardened
— **colado,** cast iron
— **de canal,** channel iron
— **de fundición gris,** gray iron
— **de soldar,** soldering iron
— **dulce,** wrought (o ingot) iron

— **dulce Armco,** Armco iron
— **en lingotes,** pig iron
— **en T,** T-iron
— **en U,** channel iron
— **forjado,** wrought iron
— **fundido,** cast iron
— **gris,** gray iron
— **gris de fundición,** gray iron
— **magnético,** magnetite
— **maleable,** malleable (o ductile)
 iron
— **para remaches,** rivet steel
— **quebradizo al rojo,** red short
 iron
— **templado,** chilled iron
— **viejo,** scrap iron
hierroníquel, nickel iron
higrómetro, hygrometer
hilos de estadía, stadia cross wires,
 stadia hairs
hincharse, swell
hiperesteno, hypersthene
hiperstenita, hypersthenite
hipocentro, hypocenter
hipoclorito, hypochlorite
hipocristalino, hypocrystalline
hipofosforoso, hypophosphorous
hipótesis, hypothesis
hipsómetro, hypsometer
histéresis, hysteresis
histograma, histogram
— **radioactivo de un pozo,**
 radioactive well logging
hito, survey monument; guidepost
hoja, leaf; sheet; ply; blade; light;
 window sash
— **cortante,** knife edge
— **del colador,** strainer screen
— **de filtro,** filter leaf, filter screen
— **de palastro,** iron sheet
— **delgada de metal,** foil
— **niveladora de empuje,** (rd ma)
 bulldozer
— **(o cuchilla) magnética,**
 magnetometer, magnetic blade
hojalata, tin plate

hogar, firing chamber, fire box, furnace
— de forja, hearth
hollín, lampblack, soot
holoceno, Holocene
holocristalino, holocrystalline
holohialino, holohyaline
holoeucrático, holoeucratic
holotipo, (paleo) holotype
hombrillo, (rd) shoulder
hombro, (sd) shoulder
homoclinal, homocline
homogeneidad, homogeneity
homogéneo, uniform, homogeneous
hondonada, (tp) basin, low land, saddle, depression, gap
honorarios, (cm) fee
horas extras, overtime
horario, schedule
horizontal, horizontal
horizonte, horizon; (g) stratum
— acústico, acoustic horizon
— de baja velocidad sísmica, (gf) weathered layer
— de correlación, correlation horizon
— de refracción, (gf) refraction horizon
— geológico, geologic horizon
— guía, datum horizon, guide formation
— imaginario, phantom horizon
— llave, (g) key horizon (o bed)
— petrolífero, (prf) oil zone
hormigón, (cn) concrete
— armado, reinforced concrete
hornblenda, (g) hornblende
hornear, v. bake
hornfelsa, (g) hornfels
hornilla, (cl) duck nest; brick kiln; furnace fire pot
hornillo de soldar, fire pot
horno, oven
— cuadrado para carburación, carburizing box
— de aire, air furnace

— de calcinación, calcining furnace
— de crisol, crucible furnace
— de descostrar, scaling furnace
— de fundición, blast furnace
— de gas, gas furnace
— de recocer, annealing box (o furnace)
— de refinería, refinery heater furnace
— de resudación, sweating oven
— de reverbero, reverberatory (o draught) furnace
— de secar, dry oven, kiln
— eléctrico, electric furnace
— para planta de reformación térmica, cracker furnace
— para recocer, annealing furnace, annealing box
— para tratamiento térmico, heat-treating furnace
— secador de aire, air oven
— Siemens-Martin, open-hearth furnace
hornsteno, hornstone
horquilla, fork
— de desacople de embrague, clutch release fork
— de cambio de velocidades, gearshift (o shifter) fork
horst, horst fault
horsteno, chert, hornstone
hoya, (g) basin; drainage area, watershed
— de falla, fault trough, graben fault
— glacial, kettle hole
— hidrográfica, watershed
hoyo, pit
— abajo, (prf) downhole
— del soldador, bell hole
— inicial de un pozo, surface hole
— (o pozo) de la explosión, (gf) shot hole
hueco, n. void, hollow, cavity; hole, well; a. hollow

— **del descanso,** (prf) rathole
huella, stair, tread, run; (rd) trail, track, rut; width of tread of a vehicle
— **de derrumbe,** (g) land scar
— **de riachuelos,** rill mark
huérfano, (g) huerfano
hueso, bone
hule, oilcloth, oilskin; rubber
hulla, coal
humectante, *a.* wetting
humedad, moisture, humidity
— **absoluta,** absolute humidity
— **relativa,** relative humidity
humedecer, humidify
húmedo, humid, wet, moist, damp
humero, (frn) flue; breaching; smoke jack
— **interno,** internal flue
húmico, humic
humo, smoke
humus, (g) humus
hundimiento, subsidence
— **de un eje de pliegue,** (g) pitch
hundir, sink
hundirse, subside
huracán, tornado, hurricane
huroniense, Huronian

I

iceberg, iceberg
identificación, identification
ígneo, igneous
ignífugo, fireproof
igualador del freno, brake equalizer
igualamiento automático, self-equalizing
illinoisiense, Illinoisan
ilmenita, ilmenite
iluminación, light, lighting, illumination
iluminador, illuminator

imagen, image
imán, magnet
imantar, magnetize
imbibición, imbibition
imbricación, *n.*(g) imbrication; *a.*
imbricado, imbricated
impacto, impact
impedancia, impedance
impermeable, waterproof, impervious; watertight
ímpetu, impetus, impulse
ímpetus previos, (gf) forerunners
impiderreventones, (prf) blowout preventer
— **de ariete,** ram-type blowout preventer
— **tipo de diafragma,** diaphragm-type blowout preventer
— **tipo de inserción,** insert-type blowout preventer
importación, imports, importation
impregnaciones de petróleo, show of oil
impregnado, impregnated, saturated
impregnar, *v.* impregnate
impresión de ola, (mar) wave mark
impresión azul, blueprint
impresora, printer
— **al vuelo,** (dp) hit-on-the-fly printer
— **por líneas,** (dp) line printer
imprimador, (paint) primer
impronta, (g) mold, cast
impsonita, impsonite
impuesto, tax
— **de explotación,** exploitation tax
— **de timbre,** seal tax
impulsión por cuatro ruedas, four-wheel drive
impulso, impulse
— **elástico,** elastic impulse
— **eléctrico,** electric drive
impulsor, impeller, actuator
impurezas, impurities

— **en suspensión,** suspended
impurities
inalámbrico, *a.* wireless
incandescente, incandescent
incidencia, (gf) incidence
— **normal,** normal incidence
— **oblicua,** oblique incidence
incineración, incineration
inclinación, (g) dip, rake,
inclination, tilting
— **de anticlinal,** plumb-line
deviation of an anticline, pitch
(o plunge) of anticline
— **magnética,** magnetic
inclination, magnetic dip
— **principal,** primary dip
— **y convergencia,** pitch and gather
inclinómetro, dipmeter
inclusión, (g) inclusion
inconveniente, inconvenient,
troublesome, trouble, difficulty
incrustación, (cl) scale,
incrustation; sinter
— **de sílice,** siliceous sinter
incrustaciones, incrustations
indeno, indene
indicador, indicator, gage
— **de azul de bromofenol,**
bromophenol blue indicator
— **de cero,** null instrument
— **de desviación,** drift indicator
— **de diafragma,** diaphragm gage
— **de dos plumas,** two-pen gage
— **de fuerza de torsión,** torque gage
(o indicator)
— **de gas,** gas indicator, gas meter
— **de golpeteo,** (mc) bouncing pin
— **de metraje adjunto al carretel
de la cuerda de medición,** (prf)
well-measuring
meter
— **del nivel de aceite,** oil gage
— **del nivel de aceite tipo
bayoneta,** bayonet gage
— **del nivel de aceite lubricante,**
oil-level indicator

— **del nivel de agua,** water-level
gage, water gage cock
— **del nivel de combustible,** fuel
gage
— **del nivel de líquidos,** liquid-level
gage
— **del nivel de tanques,** tank gage
— **de peso,** weight indicator
— **del peso del lodo,** mud weight
indicator
— **de pH,** pH indicator
— **de la presión del aceite,** oil gage
— **de la presión del lodo,** mud-
pressure indicator
— **de la presión en la bomba para
lodo,** mud-pump pressure gage
— **de presión de neumáticos,** tire
gage
— **de presión del vapor,** steam-
pressure gage
— **de tubo en U,** U-tube gage
— **de vacío,** vacuum gage
— **de velocidad,** tachometer, speed
indicator
— **térmico,** temperature indicator
índice, index
— **de acidez,** acid number
— **de base,** (qm) base number
— **de dureza según la escala
Brinell,** Brinell hardness
number
— **de mezcla,** mixing index
— **de productividad,** productivity
index
— **octano,** octane index
— **de refracción,** (gf) refraction
index
— **de viscosidad,** viscosity index
— **de viscosidad-gravedad,**
viscosity gravity constant
indicios de petróleo, show of oil
inducción, induction
— **eléctrica,** electric induction
— **magnética,** magnetic induction
inducido, (el) armature
— **de jaula,** squirrel cage

inductancia, inductance
inductor terrestre, (gf) earth
   inductor
inercia, inertia
inestabilidad termodinámica,
   thermodynamic instability
inestable, unstable
inexactitud, inaccuracy
inflador de neumáticos, tire pump
inflamable, inflammable
inflexión, inflection
informe, report
— de estado de cuentas, (cm)
   financial statement
— de perforación, driller's log
— geológico, geologic report
— gráfico, (gf) graphic log
infrascrito, undersigned
infusible, apyrous
ingeniería, engineering
ingeniería de yacimientos,
   reservoir engineering
ingenio, (ma) device
ingrediente, ingredient
ingresión, ingression
inhibidor, inhibitor
— de ácido, acid inhibitor
inhomogeneidad, inhomogeneity
iniciador, starter
iniciar, start, begin, commence
— la perforación de un pozo, spud
— el flujo en un pozo por medio
   de gas (o aire comprimido),
   (pr) kick off
inmersión, immersion
inmiscible, immiscible
inorgánico, inorganic
insertador de tubería, (prf)
   snubber
insertador de tubería contra
   presión, (prf) snubber
insolación, insolation
insoluble, insoluble
insondable, abyssal; fathomless
inspector de aduana, customs
   inspector

instalación, (mc) installation,
   assembly, plant
— eléctrica, wiring
— para refinar por contacto con
   ácido sulfúrico, sulfuric acid
   contact plant
— por telemando, remote
   installation
instalar, install, erect, place
— una cabria, rip up, rigging
— un equipo de perforación, rig
   up, rigging
instante de la explosión, (gf) shot
   break (o instant)
instrumento, instrument
— magnético, magnetic
   instrument
insuflador, bellows, blower
— centrífugo, centrifugal blower
— de chimenea, stack blower
integración, integration
integrador múltiple, multiple
   integrator
intensidad, intensity
— de campo, (gf) field strength
— magnética, magnetic intensity
— magnética horizontal, (gf)
   horizontal magnetic intensity
— magnética vertical, vertical
   magnetic intensity
intercalación, intercalation
intercalado, intercalated
intercambiable, interchangeable
intercambiador de calor con
   vapor, vacuum vapor heat
   exchanger
intercambiador de líquido a
   líquido, liquid-to-liquid
   exchanger
intercambio, trade; exchange
— de calor, (rf) heat exchange
interceptor, (oil) trap
— al vacío, vacuum trap
— de agua, steam scrubber, steam
   trap

— **de cubo invertido,** inverted
bucket trap
— **termostático de agua,**
thermostatic steam trap
interestratificación,
interstratification
interestratificado, interbedded
interferencia, interference
— **electromagnética,**
electromagnetic interference
interferómetro, interferometer
interformacional, interformational
intergranular, intergranular
interlaminado, interlaminated
interno, internal
interpolación, interpolation; (dp)
interleave
interpretación, interpretation
— **de Reynold,** Reynold's criterion
interrupción, interruption; (el)
break
— **de la sedimentación,** breaking
sedimentation
interruptor, electric switch;
interrupter
— **automático,** electric circuit
breaker
— **de botón,** push-button switch
— **de corto circuito,** (el) shorting
switch
— **de cuchillo,** knife switch
— **de retroceso,** reversing switch
— **de solenoide,** solenoid switch
— **(o conmutador) de mercurio,**
mercury switch
— **por cortocircuito del**
encendido, ignition shorting
switch
intersección, intersection
— **soldada con metal de base,** (ma)
toe
intersticial, interstitial
intersticio, interstice
intervalo, interval
— **entre curvas,** (tp) contour
interval

— **entre las ondas,** (gf) *S-P* interval
— **vertical,** (gf) vertical interval
interyacente de lutita, shale break
intraformacional,
intraformational
intromisión, influx
intrusión, (g) encroachment,
intrusion
— **de aguas,** water encroachment
intrusivo, intrusive
intumescencia, (g) swelling,
intumescence
inundación, *n.* overflow, flood
— **de avenida,** sheetflood
invar, invar
investigación, research
— **sismográfica,** seismographic
survey
inversion, reversal; (cm)
investment
— **del gas,** gas reversion
— **estratigráfica,** stratigraphic
interval
inyección, injection, grouting;
drilling mud
— **de aire,** (pr) air flooding (o
injection)
— **de agua,** waterflooding
— **de cemento en la formación**
geológica, squeeze job
— **de gas,** (pr) air flooding; gas
injection
— **directa,** direct injection
— **sin aire,** solid injection
— **sólida,** solid injection
inyector, injector
— **de ácido,** acid (jet) gun
— **de agua de caldera,** feed-water
injector
— **de casquete,** cap jet
— **del combustible,** fuel injector
— **de lodo,** mud gun
— **mezclador de lodo,** mud-mixing
gun
— **para calderas,** boiler injector

iones intercambiables, exchange
ions
ionización, ionization
irradiación, radiation
irrevocable, (cm) irrevocable
isla, island
isobaras, isobar lines
isóbatas, isobath lines
isobutano, isobutane (q.v.
metilpropano)
isobuteno, isobutene (q.v.
metilpropeno)
isobutileno, isobutylene
isocarbónica, *n.* isocarb
isoclinal, isoclinal
isocora, isochore
isócrona, isochrone
isocronismo, isochronism
isodina, isomagnetic line
isodinámico, isodynamic
isododecano, isododecane
isógala, isogal
isógama, isogam
isogeoterma, isogeotherm
isogiros, isogyres
isogona, isógono, isogonic contour
isogónica, isogonic
isograma, isogram
isoheptano, isoheptane. (q.v.
metilhexano)
isohexano, isohexane. (q.v.
metilpentano)
isohieto, *n.* (g) isohyet, *a.* isohyetal
isoipsas, contour lines
isomérico, isomeric
isomerización, (qm) isomerization
isómero, isomer
isométrico, isometric
isomórfico, isomorphic
isomorfismo, isomorphism
isononano, isononane. (q.v.
metiloctano)
isooctano, isooctane
isoocteno, isooctene
isopaco, isopachous
isoparafina, isoparaffin

isopático, isopachous
isopentano, isopentane (q.v.
metilbutano)
isopluvial, (g) isohyetal, isopluvial
isopreno, isoprene
isopropanol, isopropanol
isopropilbenceno,
isopropylbenzene. (q.v. **cumeno)**
isostasia, (g) isostasy
isoterma, isotherm
isotérmico, isothermic
isotermo, *a.* isothermal
isótopo, isotope
isotriacontano, isotriacontane. (q.v.
melisano)
isótropo, (g) isotropic
ístmico, isthmian
istmo, isthmus, land bridge
itinerario, itinerary, schedule

J

jabalcón, prop
jabón de aluminio, oil pulp
jade, jade
jalón, milepost, milestone; rod, pole,
range pole
— **de mira,** level rod
jaspe, jasper
jasperoide, jasperoid
jaspilita, jaspilite
jaula, (shaft) cage; cattle car; crib
— **de la bola de la válvula de una
bomba,** pump cage
— **de válvula,** valve cage
— **portabolas de cojinete,**
ballbearing cage
jefe, boss; foreman; chief, head man
jornada, working day; stage,
journey, travel, trip
jornal, wage
juego, *n.* set; (ma) throw; play,
clearance; backlash
— **de ejes,** shafting

— **de herramientas para perforación,** string of tools
— **de llaves de cubo,** joint wrench set
— **de plantillas para rosca,** screw pitch gage
— **de válvulas de cabezal de pozo,** (pr) Christmas tree
— **logitudinal,** end play
junta, connection, joint, splice; gasket; (cm) board, council, commission
— **abocinada,** flared joint
— **a ras,** flush joint
— **a tope,** (sd) butt joint
— **biselada,** (carp) scarf joint
— **charpada,** scarf joint
— **compuesta,** (sd) composite joint
— **con abrazadera (o manguito) de expansión,** sleeve expansion joint
— **de bisagra,** hinged joint
— **de bola,** ball union
— **de canto,** (sd) edge joint
— **de cardán,** cardan (o universal joint)
— **de codillo,** toggle joint
— **de dilatación,** expansion joint
— **de doble bisel,** saddle joint
— **de enchufe acampanado,** slip-joint casing
— **de inserción para tubería de revestimiento,** inserted-joint casing
— **de seguridad,** safety joint
— **de solapa,** (sd) lap joint
— **de tubería vástago de diámetro igual al del hoyo,** full-hole tool joint
— **esférica,** ball joint union
— **esquinada,** (sd) corner joint
— **flexible,** slip joint, flex joint
— **giratoria,** swivel joint
— **kelly,** kelly joint
— **lisa,** flush joint

— **machihembrada,** groove-joint union, tongue and groove joint
— **mayor,** master joint
— **perkins,** Perkins joint
— **principal,** master joint
— **remachada,** riveted joint
— **soldada,** soldered joint (o welded) joint
— **soldada en ángulo,** fillet-welded joint
— **universal,** universal joint, gimbal joint, cardan joint
jurásico, Jurassic

K

kansaniense, Kansan
kaolín, kaolinite
kaolinita, kaolinite
karst, karst topography
kerógeno, kerogen
kerosina, kerosene, coal oil
ketona, ketone
kilolitro, kiloliter
kilogramo, kilogram: 1 kg = 2.2 pound
kilográmetro, kilogrammeter
kilómetro, kilometer: 1 km = 0.62 mile
kilovatio, kilowatt
— **horas,** kilowatt hours: 1 kwh = 3,412.14 Btu
kimeridgiense, Kimeridgian

L

labio, lip
— **de falla,** (g) fault limb
labradorita, labradorite
laca, lac, gum lac, lacquer
— **aromática,** aromatic lacquer

lacolito, (g) laccolith
lacustre, lacustrine
ladera, foothills
lado, side
— **de la soldadura en ángulo,** (sd)
  leg of fillet weld
ladrillo, brick
— **aislante,** insulating brick
— **angular,** arch brick
— **cuadriculado,** checkered brick
— **jaquelado,** checkered brick
— **para tabiques interceptores,**
  baffle tile
— **refractario,** insulating brick
ladrón de aceite, oil thief
lago, lake
— **de circo,** tarn
— **de fractura,** tectonic lake
— **endicado,** barrier lake
— **salado,** salt lake
laguna, lagoon
laja, flagstone, slab; layer; stratum
  of rock, spall; ledge
lámina, (mu) sheet; (g) lamina
— **acuífera,** water table
— **corrugada de metal,** corrugated
  sheet metal
— **de acero,** steel sheet
— **de calzar,** shims
— **de hierro,** iron sheet
— **de plomo,** sheet lead
laminación, lamination
— **de acero,** hot roll
laminado, lamella; laminated; platy
— **en frío,** (mu) cold rolling
laminar, laminate
laminilla, (rust) scale
lámpara, lamp, bulb
— **de soldar,** blowtorch
— **eléctrica de extensión,** electric
  drop light
— **proyectante,** floodlight
lancha, boat
— **remolcadora,** tug boat, tow boat
lanchón, barge
lanchón-tanque, tank-barge

lanza para remolque, wagon
  tongue
lanzar, *v.* throw, dart, hurl, fling;
  launch; throw up
lapa, (mar) barnacle
lapilli, (g) lapilli
lápiz, pencil
— **termométrico,** Tempilstick
largo, long
— **plazo,** (cm) long term
larguero, stringer, girt, purlin;
  waler, ranger, strongback; sill;
  skid; pile cap
— **acanalado,** side channel
— **de asiento del motor,** engine
  pony sill
— **del torno de herramientas,** bull
  wheel girt
— **subauxiliar,** (rig) sand-reel tail
  sill
lasca, a spall
lastrabarrenas, drill collar
lastre, ballast
lastre de tubería, (p) river clamp
lata, can
laterita, (g) laterite
laterización, (gf) laterization
latita, (g) latite
latitud, latitude
latón, brass
laurentiense, Laurentian
lava, lava
— **cordada,** pillow-lava
— **elipsoidal,** pillow-lava
— **de gas,** gas scrubber
lavaduras de falda, slope wash
lavaje, (g) denudation; washing
lavar, *v.* wash
lazo, *n.* loop, tie
lecho, river bed, stratum; (mn) floor
— **de un arroyo,** stream bed
— **de creciente,** flood plain
— **mayor,** flood plain
lectotipo, (paleo) lectotype
letra de cambio, (cm) bill of
  exchange

lectura, reading
— **dispersa,** (dp) scatter read
— **frontal,** (tp) foresight
— **gravimétrica,** gravity reading
lencitita, lencitite (q.v. **nefelenita**)
lengua de tierra (o arena) unida a la costa, (g) spit
lengüeta calibradora, thickness gauge
lente, (in) (g) lens;
— **objetivo,** objective lens
lenticular, lenticular
leñoso, ligneous
lepidolito, lepidolite
lesnordeste, east northeast
letal, lethal
leucita, leucite
leucitófiro, leucitophyre
leucocrático, leucocratic
leva, pawl, dog, catch; cam; (mc) wiper
— **de admisión,** inlet (o admission) cam
— **de eje,** lifter
— **de eje giratorio,** lifter cog
— **(o cama) de un eje (o árbol),** lifter
levantado, (g) up-thrown
levantamiento, (g) uplift, upheaval, lifting, emergence; (tp) land surveying;
— **a plancheta,** plane table surveying
— **con método eléctrico,** electric survey
— **de planos,** mapping, surveying
— **geofísico,** geophysical mapping
— **topográfico,** plane table surveying
— **trigonométrico,** trigonometrical survey
levantar, *v.* raise, lift
levantaválvulas, tappet, push rod, valve lifter
levante, lift; raising, hoisting; east
levigación, elutriation

levigador, elutriation apparatus
ley de distribución, (gf) distribution law
lezna, awl
— **de marcar,** scratch awl
LGN (líquidos del gas natural), NGL (natural gas liquids)
libra, pound
libra-pié, foot-pound
libre, free
licencia, license
licuable, (gas) liquefiable
licuación, liquefaction
licuefacción, liquefaction
lidita, chert, hornstone
liga, league, coalition; (mu) alloy, allegation
ligador, (rd) binder
ligadura, *n.* tie, lashing; rail bond
ligazón, bond; tie, fastening
ligero, (veloc) fast; (wt) light
lignito, (g) lignite
lima, file; hip (or valley) of a roof
— **ahusada,** tapered file
— **cilíndrica,** gullet
— **cuadrada,** square file
— **media caña,** half-round file
— **plana,** flat file
— **plana diagonal,** mill file
— **rabo de rata,** rat-tail file
— **redonda,** round file
— **triangular,** cant file, three square file
limitador, (hd) spillway; (el) limiter; (a) fuel (or speed) regulator (mc) a stop
límite, boundary, limit
— **de ebullición,** boiling range
— **de resistencia,** endurance limit
— **elástico,** elastic limit
límnico, (g) limnic
limnología, limnology
limo, ooze, mud, silt
— **de derrubios,** (g) boulder clay, tillite
limolita, siltstone

limonita, (g) limonite, bog iron ore
limonitizado, (g) limonitic
limoso, muddy, oozy, silty
limpiador, wiper, cleaner
— **del cable,** (prf) line wiper
— **de rosca,** thread cleaner
— **de tubos de caldera,** flue cleaner, boiler tube cleaner
limpiadora, (mn) sluice
limpiaparabrisas, wiper
limpiar, *v.* clean
— **con taco** (o **diablo),** (p) pigging
— **un pozo,** swabbing, cleaning of a well
limpiatubos, tube cleaner, pipe wiper, swab, casing swab, (cl) scraper, go-devil
— (o **escobillón) para tubería de producción,** tubing swab
limpieza, stripping, clearing, cleaning
— **con chorro de agua,** flushing
— **con escobillón,** (well) swabbing
— **de foso,** cleanout
— **en seco,** dry cleaning
lindero, boundary, limit
línea, line, track
— **adiabática,** adiabatic line
— **agónica,** agonic line
— **axial,** axial line
— **costanera,** shoreline
— **costera,** coastline
— **de base,** base line
— **de centro,** (rotary table) center line
— **de energía eléctrica,** power line
— **del gas combustible,** gas-fuel line
— **de mira,** (tp) line of sight
— **de montaje,** assembly line
— **de oleaje,** swash line
— **de plomada,** plumb line
— **de registro,** (gf) trace
— **de retardo sónico,** (dp) sonic delay line
— **de tiempo,** (gf) time line

— **divisoria de aguas,** drainage divide
— **isobata,** (surv) isobath line
— **isodinámica,** isodynamic line
— **isogeotérmica,** isogeotherm line
— **isopaca,** isopachous line
— **isosista,** isoseismic line
— **isoterma,** isotherm line
— **lobal,** (g) suture
— **magnética,** magnetic line
— **que sigue una falla,** fault line
líneas
— **de estrangular y matar,** choke and kill line
— **de flujo,** flow line
— **guía,** guideline
— **de igual anomalía magnética,** magnetic iso-anomaly line
— **isócronas,** isotime line
— **isogamas,** magnetic isoanomaly line
— **isosímicas,** isoseismal line
— **isosistas,** isoseismal line
lineal, linear
lingada, joint of pipe
lingote, ingot
lino, flax
linterna, lantern
— **eléctrica,** electric lantern
liparita, liparite**liquidación,** (cm) liquidation
liquidar, *v.* (cm) liquidate; liquefy;
líquido, *n. a.* liquid
— **del freno,** brake fluid
— **enfriador** (o **refrigerante),** coolant
— **higroscópico,** hygroscopic liquid
— **no corrosivo,** noncorroding liquid
— **obturador,** sealing liquid
— **sobrenadante,** (qm) supernatant liquid
lista de embalaje, (cm) packing list
lista de precios, (cm) price list
litargirio, litharge
lítico, lithic

litificación, lithification
litificado, lithified
litoclasa, lithoclase
litofisuras, lithophysae
litogénesis, lithogenesis
litología, lithology
litológico, lithologic
litoral, coast, shore; (g) littoral
litosfera, lithosphere
litosiderita, (g) lithosiderite
litro, liter
liviano, *a.* light
lixiviación, *n.* (g) lixiviation,
  leaching; lixiviar, *v.* leach
lóbulo, (g) lobe
localización, location
— de errores (o averías), trouble-
  shooting
lodo, (prf) slush, mud
— a base de agua, water-base mud
— a base de petróleo, oil-base mud
— coloidal, colloidal mud
— con base de petróleo, oil-base
  mud
— de circulación, mud-laden fluid
— de emulsión de petróleo, oil
  emulsion mud
— de perforación, drilling mud
— parafínico, paraffin dirt
loes, loess
logaritmo, logarithm
lomo, (mc) boss; (g) hogback, ridge;
  (rd) shoulder; back of a saw
— de machihembrado, guide rib
— de montaña, ridge
— de perro, (g) hogback
lona, canvas
longitud, longitude
— de onda, (gf) wave length
— de tubería tendida, lain length
— focal, focal length
longitudinal, longitudinal
losa celular, (cn) tile for interior of
  walls
lote, lot; (rf) batch; a land measure:
  of 100 hectares or more,

depending on country; share,
  part
L para soldar, welding ell
L soldable, welding ell
lubricación, lubrication
— automática, self-lubricating,
  self-oiling
— a presión, pressure lubrication,
  force-feed lubrication
— con hilacha, waste lubrication
— por alimentación forzada,
  force-feed lubrication
— por salpique, splash lubrication
lubricador, oil feeder, lubricator
— de alimentación forzada, force-
  feed lubricator
— de gota visible, sight-feed
  lubricator
— del cilindro superior del motor,
  engine upper cylinder lubricator
— de lodo, mud lubricator
— de tubería de vapor, stream-line
  lubricator
— transparente, sight-feed
  lubricator
— visible, sight-feed lubricator
lubricante, lubricant
— consistente, grease
— consistente a la cal, lime-base
  grease
— para chasis, chassis lube
— para máquinas frigoríficas,
  ammonia oil
— para el mecanismo de
  transmisión, transmission
  lubricant
lubricantes terminados, finished
  lube oils
lucha por las divisorias, fight
  among streams, stream piracy
ludiense, Ludian
ludimiento, gall
lupia de acero, steel pig
lustre, luster
luteciense, Lutetian
lutita, shale

— **aluminosa,** alum shale
— **bituminosa,** bituminous shale, oil shale
— **carbonífera,** black stone, black shale
— **diatomácea,** diatomaceous shale
— **floja,** clay shale
— **intrusa,** shale break
lutítico, shaly
lutolita, mudstone
luz, light; (mc) clearance
— **de detección,** (dp) sense light
— **de la válvula,** valve clearance
— **del émbolo (o espacio libre),** piston clearance
— **del levantaválvula,** valve tappet clearance
— **entre dientes de engranajes,** lash-back
— **(o distancia libre) en los dientes de un engranaje,** gear clearance

LL

llama, flame
— **de oxidación,** oxidizing flame
— **de retorno,** return flame
— **interior,** flashback
— **oxiacetiléncia,** oxyacetylene torch
— **vigilada,** supervised flame
llana, plasterer's trowel
— **de madera,** wood float
llanta, iron tire, tire rim; tread; rubber tire
— **acanalada,** drop center rim
— **acanalada del malacate de las tuberías de producción,** calf-wheel rim
— **del malacate de las tuberías de producción,** calf wheel cant
llanura, flatland
— **costanera,** coastal plain
— **de lodo,** mud flat

— **troncal,** peneplain
llave, (mc) key, wedge; valve, cock, bib, faucet; (cm) header; keystone; (el) key, switch; (p) wrench; (prf tl) tongs
— **acodada,** bent wrench
— **cerrada,** box wrench
— **ciega,** blank key
— **con mango en ángulo,** bent wrench
— **de aguante,** buck up tongs
— **de boca,** end wrench
— **de boca sencilla,** end wrench
— **de boca tubular,** joint wrench
— **de broches,** ratchet wrench
— **de cadena,** boll-weevil (o chain) tong
— **de cadena para tubería,** pipe-fitting tongs
— **de cadena para tuberías de revestimiento y perforación,** casing and drillpipe tongs
— **de ceba,** vent cock
— **de cierre,** stopcock
— **de contrafuerza,** backup tong
— **de copa,** socket wrench
— **de desenrosque,** lead tongs
— **de doble curva,** S wrench
— **de fuerza de torsión limitada,** torque-limiting wrench
— **de gancho,** hook wrench
— **de grifos,** box wrench
— **de herramientas,** tool wrench
— **de herramientas enteriza de disco con cremallera,** built-in tool wrench
— **de horquilla,** fork wrench, pin wrench
— **de montaje,** makeup wrench
— **de mordaza,** alligator wrench
— **de muletilla,** socket wrench
— **de paso,** stopcock
— **de purga,** purging cock, petcock
— **de respiración,** vent cock
— **de roquete,** ratchet wrench
— **de trinquete,** ratchet wrench

— **de tubos,** pipe (o joint) wrench
— **de tuerca,** wrench
— **de varilla de succión,** snap-on
  wrench
— **dentada,** alligator wrench
— **en S,** S wrench
— **espitera,** cock wrench
— **inglesa,** monkey spanner
  (wrench), shifting wrench
— **inglesa regulable** (o **graduable),**
  adjustable wrench
— **para espita,** cock wrench
— **para tornillo de ajuste,** set screw
  wrench
— **para tornillo de presión,** set
  screw wrench
— **para tuercas circulares,** hook
  wrench
— **para tubería de revestimiento,**
  casing tongs
— **para varilla de bombeo,** sucker-
  rod wrench
— **reversible de trinquete,**
  reversible ratchet wrench
— **semifija,** adjustable wrench
— **tenedor,** fork (o pin) wrench
— **tubular,** socket wrench
llegada, arrival
lloradero, weep hole; seepage
lluvia, rain

M

maar, (g) maar
macádam, macadam
— **asfáltico,** asphaltic macadam
macho, *n.* dowel; pintle; mandrel,
  shaft, journal, spindle; gudgeon;
  sheave pin; sledge hammer; pier,
  buttress; *a.* (mc) male
— **de pesca,** (prf) fishing tap
— **de terraja plegable,** collapsible
  tap
— **de válvula,** valve plug

— **fusiforme con tres escalones,**
  three-step rotary taper tap
— **para roscar tuercas,** taper tap
— **rotatorio,** (fishing tl) rotary tap
machuelo arrancabarrena, screw
  grab
machuelo arrancasondas, tapered
  tap, screw grab
machuelo cónico, tapered tap
macizo, *n.* bulk; mass; (g) main
  mountain range; *a.* massive,
  solid, heavy
— **de anclaje,** deadman
— **intrusivo,** (g) boss
macroclástico, (g) macroclastic
macroscópico, macroscopic
macrosísmico, (g) macroseismic
madera, wood, lumber
— **dura,** hardwood
— **laminada,** plywood
madurez, maturity
magdaleniense, Magdalenian
magma, magma
— **básico,** basic magma
magmático, magmatic
magnesio, magnesium
magnesita, magnesite
magnético, magnetic
magnetismo, magnetism
— **inducido,** induced magnetism
— **terrestre,** terrestrial magnetism,
  (gf) earth magnetism
magnetita, (g) magnetite, lodestone
magnetizar, magnetize
magneto, magneto
magnetófono, magnetophone
magnetómetro, field balance,
  magnetometer, magnetic
  balance, magnetic variometer
magnitud, magnitude
malacate, hoisting engine, winch,
  hoist, grab
— **de herramientas,** bull wheel
— **de las tuberías de producción,**
  calf wheel
malaquita, malachite, chrysocolla

maleable, malleable, ductile
malecón, mound, sea wall
malla, *n.* mesh
manadero de petróleo, seepage
manak, manak
manantial, spring
— **de falla,** fissure spring
— **termal,** hot spring
mancha, stain
manchita, speck
mandado por correa, belt driven
mandato, (dp) command
mandil, (mc) apron
mando, drive, control, operation
— **de cadena,** chain drive
— **de las válvulas,** valve actuation
   (o control)
— **de ventilador,** fan drive
— **directo,** (mc) direct drive
— **hidráulico,** hydraulic drive (o
   transmission)
— (o **impulsión) por transmisión,**
   transmission drive
— **por correa,** belt drive
— **rotatorio,** (prf) rotary drive
mandril, mandrel, (lathe) chuck;
   spindle, drift pin; boring tool;
   treblet
— **de bordear tubos,** tube beader
— **de expansión,** tube expander
— **para enchufe de cable giratorio,**
   mandrel for swivel rope socket
— **para portacable giratorio,**
   mandrel for swivel rope socket
— **para revestir cilindros,** relining
   mandrel
— **para tubería de revestimiento,**
   casing swedge (o mandrel)
— **trasero expulsor,** ejector tailgate
— **universal,** universal chuck
manecilla, (in) hand
manga, (nt) breadth
manganeso, manganese
mango, handle, grip, shank, haft
— **de barrena,** auger handle
manguera, hose

— **de aire,** air hose
— **de bombero,** fire hose
— **de cementación,** cementing hose
— **de inyección,** mud hose
— **de lodo,** mud hose
— **de soldar,** welding hose
— **para perforadora rotatoria,**
   rotary drilling hose
— **para vapor,** steam hose
manguito, (tu) nipple, boot,
   coupling, sleeve; bushing; small
   handle; chuck, thimble
— **de inserción para reducir el
   flujo,** flow beam
— **de reducción,** swedge, swedged
   nipple; swaged nipple
— **reductor,** reducing nipple
— **tarraja,** dye nipple
manivela, crank; handle
— **de arranque,** starting crank
— **de bombeo,** pumping crank
— **de contrapeso,** counterbalance
   crank
manivelas gemelas, twin cranks
mano, hand
— **de almirez,** (la) pestle
— **de obra,** workmanship
— **de pintura,** coating, coat
— **de pintura protectora,**
   protective coating
manómetro, manometer, gage
— **de diafragma,** diaphragm gage
— **de neumáticos,** tire gage
— **de reflejo,** reflex gage
— **diferencial,** differential gage
— **en U,** U-tube gage
— **indicador,** indicating meter
— **para la presión controlada,**
   controlled pressure gage
— **para tubo de producción,** tubing
   gage
— **registrador,** recording gage
mantenimiento, upkeep,
   maintenance
manto, (g) overthrust mass; mantle
   rock; stratum; nappe

Español - Inglés

— **de arena,** sand blanket
— **de sobreescurrimiento,** (g) overthrust
— **efusivo,** extrusive sheet
— **glacial,** ice cap
— **sobreescurrido,** nappe, overthrust mass
manual, hand book
manufacturero, manufacturer (q.v. fabricante)
manutención, maintenance
mapa, map
— **acotado,** contour map
— **de referencia,** base map
— **del subsuelo,** subsurface map
— **geognóstico,** geognostic map
— **isogónico,** isogonic map (o chart)
— **isopaco,** isopachous map
— **topográfico,** relief block
máquina, machine, engine
— **biseladora,** beveling machine
— **compound,** compound engine
— **cortadora de tubería,** pipe-cutting machine
— **de barnizar tubería,** dope machine
— **de chaflanar,** chamfering machine
— **de enroscar,** pipe and bolt machine
— **de envolver tubería,** wrapping machine
— **de expansión,** expansion engine
— **de ladrillos,** brick machine
— **de limpiar tubos,** pipe-cleaning machine
— **de roscar,** threading machine
— **de roscar pernos,** bolt threading machine
— **de servicio y reparaciones,** (prf) servicing (o pulling) unit
— **de tracción,** pulling machine
— **de vapor,** steam engine
— **de vapor a expansión,** expansion engine

— **dobladora,** bending machine
— **enfriadora,** chilling machine
— **esmeriladora,** refacer
— **para empalmes a la fuerza,** (tu) bucking-on machine
— **para enderezar tubos,** pipe straightener
— **rebordeadora,** flanging machine, flanger
— **taladradora de tubería bajo presión,** tapping machine
mar, sea
— **antiguo,** relic sea
— **de fondo,** surf
— **de leva,** surf
— **del schelf,** epicontinental sea
— **epicontinental,** epicontinental sea
marca, *n.* mark, brand
— **de fábrica,** trademark, brand
— **(o ranura) labrada por las cuñas de agarre,** slip mark
— **y modelo,** make and model
marcado con líneas, lined
marcador, (hd) (in) gage, gauge
— **paralelo,** surface gage
marcasita, marcasite
marcha atrás, reverse
marco, frame; yoke;
— **base del portapoleas de corona,** (derrick) water table
marea, tide
— **menguante,** ebb tide
marga, marl; loam
margen de seguridad, margin of safety
marino, marine
mariposa, (va) butterfly; wing nut; (a) throttle
— **del carburador,** carburetor throttle
marisma, salt lake
marjal, (g) marsh
marmita, small boiler, small furnace, tar kettle, pot, autoclave

352

— **de gigante,** pothole
— **de grasa,** grease kettle
— **de mezclar,** compounding kettle
mármol, marble
martillo, hammer
— **de bola,** ball-peen hammer
— **de carpintero,** nail hammer
— **de forja,** blacksmith hammer
— **descostrador,** pitting hammer
— **grande de madera,** maul
— **neumático,** air hammer
martinete, drop happer, drop press,
    pile driver
— **a vapor,** steam hammer
masa, mass, bulk; (el) ground
— **inerte,** steady mass
máscara antigás, gas mask
máscara contra el polvo,
    respirator, dust mask
masilla, mastic
mástil, mast
— **de extensión,** telescoping mast
— **en A,** A-frame
— **(o torre) de extensiones**
    enchufadas, telescoping mast
— **plegadizo,** telescoping mast
— **portátil,** portable mast
mástique, mastic
— **asfáltico,** asphaltic mastic
matar un pozo, kill a well
materia, matter
— **extraña,** foreign material
— **prima,** (rf) charge stock; raw
    material
— **saponificable,** saponifiable
    matter
materias en fusión, molten matter
material, material
— **aislante,** insulation material
— **de base,** (rf) base stock
— **de carga,** (rf) charge stock
— **detrítico,** detrital material
— **para láminas de calzar,** shim
    stock
matraz de boca angosta, narrow
    mouth flask

matriz, *n.* die, mold, form; matrix;
    a. main, principal; (mc) female
— **de estampa,** stamping die
máximo, maximum
— **de gravedad,** gravity maximum
— **gravimétrico,** maximum gravity
— **magnético,** magnetic (o
    magnetic high)
maxwell, maxwell
mayorista, wholesale dealer
maza, drop (o pile) hammer; stamp;
    mallet
— **de vapor,** steam hammer
— **y rayos de una rueda,** wheel
    spider
mazo, maul, sledge, beetle, mallet;
    hammer
meandros, meander
mecánica, *n.* mechanics; *a.*
    mechanical
mecánico, *n.* (oc) mechanic
mecanismo, mechanism
— **de arranque,** starter
— **de control,** (el) switchgear
mecha, bit; wick
— **espiral de espiga cónica,** (tl)
    taper shank twist drill
— **racha,** roller bit
mechero, burner
— **de acetileno,** acetylene burner
media suela, (tu) half sole
mediacaña guiadora, (fishing tl)
    half skirt
mediacaña escariadora, side rasp
mediano, median, medium
medición a distancia, telemetering
medida, measure, measurement;
    rule, measuring tape
— **con hilo de alambre,** steel line
    measurement
medidor, meter, gage; batcher; sizer
— **de agua,** water meter
— **de caudal,** fluid (o flow) meter
— **de formación,** strain gauge
— **de desplazamiento de aire,** air
    displacement meter

— **de evaporación,** evaporation
gauge
— **de gas,** gas indicator (o meter)
— **de neumáticos,** tire gauge
— **de orificio,** orifice meter
— **de pH,** pH meter, petrology
meter
— **de petróleo,** oil meter
— **de profundidad con cable de
alambre,** wire-line depth
measurer
— **eléctrico,** electric meter
— **venturi,** Venturi meter
medio, *n.* middle, mean; medium *a.*
half, mean
— **ambiente,** environment
— **cojinete,** (mc) half bearing
medir, *v.* measure
— **a pasos,** pacing
— **tubería a medida que se extrae,**
(prf) measure out
— **tubería a medida que se inserta,**
(prf) measure in
mediterráneo, Mediterranean
megohmio, megohm
meláfero, (g) melaphyre
melanocrático, melanocratic
melisano, melissane (q.v.
isotriacontano)
melita, mellite
memoria, memory; (dp) storage
— **de acceso en paralelo,** parallel
storage
— **de núcleos magnéticos,** core
storage
— **imborrable,** noneraseable
storage
— **intermedia,** buffer
— **intermedia periférica,**
peripheral buffer
mena, ore vein
mena ferruginosa, lodestone
mene, seepage
menisco, meniscus
ménsula, bracket, corbel; column
cap; haunch

— **de garrucha,** sheave bracket
mentol, menthol
mercancía de contrabando,
smuggled goods
mercado, market
— **de exportación,** export market
mercaptano, mercaptan
mercaptida, mercaptide
mercurio, mercury, quicksilver
— **dibutílico normal,** di-n-butyl
mercury
— **dibutílico secundario,** di-sec-
butyl mercury
— **dimetilo,** dimethyl mercury
meridiano, meridian
— **magnético,** magnetic meridian
merma, shrinkage
mesa, table; (g) mesa; plateau,
tableland; stair landing; wall
plate
— **de ensayos,** test bench
— **giratoria,** turntable
— **glaciárica,** glacier table
— **rotatoria,** (prf) rotary table
meseta, mesa, plateau, tableland;
stair landing
mesitileno, mesitylene (q.v.
trimetilbenceno)
mesorrocas, mesorocks
mesotérmico, mesothermal
mesozoico, Mesozoic
mesozona, (g) mesorocks, mesozone
metacristal, metacryst
metafosfórico, metaphosphoric
metafosforoso, metaphosphorous
metal, metal
— **alcalino,** alkali metal
— **almirantazgo,** admiralty metal
— **antifricción,** antifriction metal
— **blanco,** bearing metal (o white)
babbitt
— **corrugado,** corrugated metal
— **de antifricción,** antifriction
metal, babbitt
— **de campana,** bell metal
— **de cojinetes,** box metal

— **estirado por presión,** extruded
metal
— **everdur,** everdur
— **laminado,** sheet metal
— **monel,** monel metal
metálico, metallic
metalúrgico, metallurgic
metamorfismo, metamorphism
— **cáustico,** caustic metamorphism
— **de carga y descarga,** general (o
load) metamorphism
— **de contacto,** contact
metamorphism
— **de dislocación,** dynamic
metamorphism
— **dinámico,** dynamic
metamorphism
— **dinámico-estático,** dynamic-
static metamorphism
— **estático,** static metamorphism
— **general,** general metamorphism
— **hidrotérmico,** hydrothermal
metamorphism
— **local,** contact metamorphism
— **plástico,** flowage
— **regional,** regional (o dynamic-
static) metamorphism
— **térmico,** thermal metamorphism
metano, methane, marsh gas
metanol, methanol
metasedimentario,
metasedimentary
metasomatismo, (g) metasomatism
metasomatosis, (g) metasomatosis,
metasomatism
metatipo, (paleo) metatype
metaxita, metaxite
meteorito, meteorite
meteorización de las rocas,
weathering
meteorización diferencial, (g)
differential weathering
metilacetileno, methylacetylene
(q.v. **propano**)
metilbenceno, methylbenzene (q.v.
tolueno)

metilciclobutano,
methylcyclobutane
metilbutano, methylbutane (q.v.
isopentano)
metilciclobuteno,
methylcyclobutene
metilcicloheptano,
methylcycloheptane
metilciclohexano,
methylcyclohexane
metilciclopentano,
methylcyclopentane
metileno, methylane (q.v. **nafteno**)
metiletilketona, methyl-ethyl-
ketone, MEK
metilhepteno, methylheptene
metilhexeno, methylhexene
metilnaftaleno,
methylnaphthalene
metilo, methyl
metilpropeno, methylpropene (q.v.
isobuteno)
metilundeceno, methylundecene
método, method, process
— **coquificante,** (rf) coking process
— **de abanico,** (gf) fan shooting, fan
spread
— **de absorción,** absorption method
— **de alta (o baja) frecuencia,** (el)
inductive method
— **del cero,** null method
— **de coincidencia,** coincidence
method
— **de conducción,** conduction (o
conductive) method
— **de contacto del equilibrio,**
equilibrium contacting method
— **de contacto múltiple,** multiple
contact method
— **de disponer los disparos,** (gf)
shooting system
— **de fase de vapor,** vapor-phase
process
— **de fase líquida,** liquid-phase
process

— **de inducción,** (el) inductive method

— **de inducción de alta (o baja) frecuencia,** high (or low) frequency method

— **de refracción,** (gf) refraction method

— **de resistividad,** resistivity method

— **de tratamiento al aire libre,** weathering process

— **eléctrico,** electric method

— **electromagnético,** electromagnetic method

— **electroquímico,** electrochemical method

— **Reid para determinar la presión de vapor (de productos volátiles),** Reid vapor pressure test

metro, meter; (water, gas, oil) meter; measuring tape

— **de bolsillo,** folding rule

mezcla, mixture, blend

— **aguada,** slurry

— **crasa,** rich mixture

— **de barro aguado ya usado,** spent clay slurry

— **de chorreaduras de condensados,** (rf) double blending

— **de cobre y plomo,** high-lead

— **de contacto,** (p) slop

— **de detonancia máxima,** maximum knock mixture

— **del metal de aporte con el metal de base fundido,** (sd) puddling

— **delgada,** lean mixture

mezclable, miscible

mezclado, blended

mezcladora, mixer

— **de agua,** (rf) water blender

— **de cemento,** cement mixer, cementing unit

— **de cemento montada en camión,** cementing truck

— **de hormigón,** concrete mixer

— **de lodo,** mud mixer

— **de paletas,** paddle mixer

— **de turbina,** turbine mixer

— **hidráulica,** hydraulic mixer

mezclar, *v.* temper, blend, mix

— **al vapor,** steam mixing

miarolítico, miarolitic

miascita, miascite

mica, mica

micáceo, micaceous

micasita, micaschist

microclástico, microclastic

microclino, microcline

microcristalino, microcrystalline

microestructura, microstructure

micrófono, microphone

micrófono para explosión, (gf) blastophone

microfósiles, microfossils

microfotografía, microphotograph

micrográfico, micrographic

microgranítico, microgranitic

microlitos, microlites

micrómetro, micrometer

micromicosegundo, picosecond

micropaleontología, micropaleontology

micropegmatítico, micropegmatitic

microplaquetas de transistor, (dp) transistor chips

microprogramación, microprogramming

microscopio, microscope

— **binocular,** binocular microscope

— **de polarización,** polarizing microscope

— **monocular,** monocular microscope

microsismo, microseism

microsísmico, microseismic

miembro, member

migajón, (g) loam

migmatitas, (g) migmatites

migración, migration
migración de petróleo, oil migration
miliamperímetro, milliammeter
miligal, milligal
miligramo, milligram
mililitro, milliliter
milímetro, millimeter
milivoltio, millivolt
milla, mile,
millaje, mileage
milonitas, (g) mylonites
milonítico, mylonitic
milonitización, mylonitization
mimetismo, mimetism
mina, mine
mineral, ore, mineral
— de hierro, iron ore, iron stone
— ferromagnesiano, ferro-magnesium mineral
— filoniano, gangue mineral
minerales
— de contacto, contact minerals
— neumatolíticos, pneumatolytic minerals
— secundarios, accessory minerals
— tipomorfos, typomorphic minerals
mineralización, mineralization
mineralizar, mineralize
mineralogía, mineralogy
minimo, minimum
— de gravedad, gravity minimum
— gravimétrico, minimum gravity
— magnético, magnetic minimum (o low)
minio, red lead
minorista, (cm) retail dealer
minuto, minute
mioceno, Miocene
mira, level rod; (rod) target; a sight; stream gage
— de corredera, (tp) level rod
— taquimétrica, stadia rod
miradero, fenster

miricilo, myricyl. (q.v. triacontano)
mirilla, peephole
miscible, miscible
misisipiense, Mississippian
misuriense, Missourian
misurita, missourite
mixtura, mixture, admixture
— congeladora, freezing mixture
mnemotécnico, mnemonic
mobilidad, mobility
mochila, tool bag; sucker rod hanger
modelo, model; mold; pattern; standard; blank form
moderador, (nuclear phys) moderator
modificador de la cristalización de parafina, wax crystallization modifier
modulador-demodulador, (dp) subset
módulo, modulus; (mc) module; (hd) module
— de elasticidad, modulus of elasticity
— de rotura, modulus of rupture
— de volumen, bulk modulus
— de Young, Young's modulus
mofeta, (vlc) mofette
moho, mold, rust
mohoso, rusty
mojado, wet
mojón, monument, landmark; milestone; hub, transit point
mol, mol
molal, molal
molasa, (g) molasse
molde, (g) mold, (foundry) cast
moldear, *v.* cast, mold
moldeo, molding
moldura, molding
molécula, molecule
molécula-gramo, mol, mole, gram, molecule
molecular, molecular

moledora, grinder
molibdenita, molybdenite
molibdeno, molydbenum
molinete, carb; current meter;
  turnstile; winch head
molino, mill
— **glaciárico, glaciario,** ice mill,
  pothole
molusco, mollusc
momentáneo, transient
momento, moment, momentum
— **de inercia,** moment of inertia
— **de torsión,** torsion moment
— **magnético,** magnetic moment
— o **(impulso) de rotación,** torque
monadnock, (g) monadnock
monoboya, single buoy
— **de carga para mar abierta,**
  (ELSBM) exposed location
  single-buoy mooring
— **de carga y descarga,** single-buoy
  mooring (SBM), single-point
  mooring (SPM)
monocilíndrico, single cylinder
monoclinal, monoclinal, monocline
— **fallado,** faulted monocline
monoclínico, monoclinic
monocromático, monochromatic
monoetanolamina, MEA
monopodio, single leg
monovalencia, *n.* monovalence; *a.*
monovalente, monovalent
montacargas, elevator, windlass
— **de cadenas,** chain hoist
— **tipo palanca con trinquete,**
  ratchet lever hoist
montado sobre orugas, crawler-
  mounted
montaje, (mc) assembly,
  installation
montante, upright, post, stud; jamb,
  guide; stiffener of a girder; side
  piece; sash bar; transom; riser
— **en tensión,** tension riser
— **marino,** marine riser
— **multipozo,** multibore riser

montaña, mountain
— **de cobijadura,** overthrust
  mountain
— **de dislocación,** (g) dislocation
  mountain
— **sobreescurrida,** overthrust
  mountain
— **truncada,** truncated mountain
montar, *v.* assemble, erect, mount,
  set
monte, mount
— **aislado,** island mountain (o
  mount)
— **testigo,** monadnock
montículo de erosión, island
  mountain (o island) mount
monto, total amount
montón, *n.* stack, pile
montura, saddle; mounting, setting,
  erection, assembly
— **de motor,** engine setting
monzonita, monzonite
monzonítico, monzonitic
mordaza, clamp, jaw grip (q.v.
  garra)
— **ara tubería,** pipe grip
— **de una morsa,** vise grips
morena, (g) moraine
— **central,** medial moraine
— **de fondo,** basal moraine
— **frontal,** frontal (o terminal)
  moraine
— **lateral,** lateral moraine
— **superior,** surface moraine
— **terminal,** terminal (o frontal)
  moraine
morfología, morphology
morro del subsuelo, buried hill
morsa, vise
morsa-yunque, anvil vise
mortero, (la) mortar
mosaico, mosaic
— **aerofotográfico,** mosaic,
  photomosaic
moscovita, muscovite
moteado, mottled

motita, speck
motobomba para lodo, power-driven mud pump
motogasolina, motor fuel
motón, block, pulley
— de combinación, snatch block
— de gancho, hoisting block
— de seguridad para tubería, safety tubing block
motonave, motor ship
motonería, pulley blocks
motoniveladora, motor grader, elevating grader
motor, motor, engine
— a combustóleo, fuel-oil engine
— a gas, gas engine,
— a gasolina, gasoline engine
— a nafta, gasoline engine
— auxiliar, donkey (o auxiliary) engine, servomotor
— convertible, convertible engine
— de aire, air motor
— de anillos conductores, slip-ring motor
— de arranque, starter, starting motor
— de arranque del tipo de acople a pedal, manual-shift-type starting motor
— de butano para perforación, butane drilling engine
— de combustión interna para equipo perforador, internal combustion drilling engine
— de devanado compuesto, (el) compound engine
— de explosión, explosion engine
— de gasolina, gasoline motor
— de inducción, induction motor
— de perforación, drilling engine
— diesel, diesel engine
— eléctrico, electric motor
— enfriado por aire, air-cooled engine
— enfriado por agua, water-cooled engine

— marino, marine engine
— multicilíndrico, multicylinder engine
— primario, prime mover
— primordial, prime mover
— vertical, vertical engine
mover con corriente de agua, v. sluice
movible, movable
móvil, movable
movimiento, motion, movement
— alternativo, reciprocating motion, alternating motion
— armónico, (gf) harmonic motion
— austático, (g) austatic movement
— bascular, oscillation
— epirogenético, epirogenetic movement
— eustático, eustatic movement
— paulatino del terreno, creep
— periódico, periodic motion
— retrógrado, regression
muelle, wharf, dock, quay, mole, pier; loading platform; spring
— de carga, loading dock
— de hojas, flat spring
— igualador, equalizing spring
— libre, (shipping) free dock
muerto, (nt) deadman, anchorage
muesca, notch, mortise, groove, dap, gain
— de chaveta, keyway
— de engrane, engaging scarf
— de tornillo, chap
muestra, sample, specimen; (prf) core
— compuesta, (prf) all levels sample
— de acero, coupon, steel sample
— de gasolina sin tetraetilo de plomo, unleaded sample
— de horadación, borings
muestrear con ladrón, thieving
muestreador, oil thief, sampling thief

mufla, *n.* muffle
multiplaje, multiplexing
mútiple, (tu) (mo) manifold; (mt)
multiple
— **de admisión,** intake manifold
— **de agua,** water intake
— **de doble admisión,** dual-inlet
manifold
— **de escape,** exhaust manifold
— **para distribución de vapor,**
steam manifold
multiplexor, multiplexor
multiplicación, multiplication
multiplicador, multiplier
muñequita del cigüeñal, crankpin
muñón, gudgeon, journal, pivot,
trunion
— **de brida,** flanged gudgeon
— **del cigüeñal,** crankpin
— **del malacate de herramientas,**
bull-wheel gudgeon
— **del malacate de la tubería de
producción,** calf-wheel gudgeon
— **esférico,** ball gudgeon
muñonera, journal box, journal
bearing
muralla, wall
muriato, muriate
muro, (g) sole; wall, (mn) footwall
— **colgante,** (fault) footwall;
hanging wall
— **contra incendio,** fire wall
— **de base,** foot wall
— **de detención,** safety earth wall
— **de sostén,** retaining wall
musgo, moss

N

nafta, naphtha
— **bruta,** crude naphtha
— **de alta gravedad,** light naphtha
— **de punto seco,** end-point
gasoline

naftaleno, naphthalene
nafténico, naphthenic
nafteno, methylene, naphthene
nanosegundo, nanosecond
napa de agua subterránea, (g)
water plane
napa freática, water table
nariz, (g) nose; nozzle
— **arqueada anticlinal,** anticlinal
bowing nose
natrolita, natrolite
natural, natural
navegación, navigation
neblina, mist, fog
nebraskiense, Nebraskan
nefelina, (g) nepheline, nephelite
nefelinita, nephelinite (q.v.
lencitite)
negativo, negative
negro, black
— **de humo,** carbon black,
lampblack
negrohumo, lampblack, carbon
black
neis, gneiss
neocomiense, Neocomian
neohexano, neohexane
neolítico, neolithic
neopentano, neopentane
neozoico, Neozoic
neptunio, neptunium
nerítico, neritic
nervadura, rib, counterfort; purlin;
(mn) leader
nervio, rib, counterfort; purlin; stay;
web
neto, (cm) net
neumática, *n.* pneumatics;
neumático, *a.* pneumatic
neumatólogeno, (g) pneumatolytic
neumatolítico, (g) pneumatolytic
neutralizar, neutralize
neutrón, neutron
nevadita, nevadite
nevasca, snowstorm, blizzard
niagarense, Niagaran

nicolita, niccolite
niebla, mist
nieve, snow
— **penitente,** snow pinnacles
nife, (g) nife
niple, (p) nipple
— **corto,** short nipple
— **cuello de botella,** swedge (o
   swage) nipple
— **de asiento,** seating nipple
— **de botella,** bell (o swage) nipple
— **de campana,** bell nipple, swage
   nipple
— **de largo mínimo,** close nipple
— **de varilla,** (bm rods) sub
— **elevador,** (prf) lifting nipple
— **largo,** long nipple
— **para tubería de revestimiento,**
   casing nipple
— **reductor,** reducing nipple
níquel, nickel
nitrato, nitrate
— **de plata,** silver nitrate
nitroalgodón, nitrocotton, gun
   cotton
nitrobencina, nitrobenzene
nitrocelulosa, nitrocellulose
nitrogelatina, nitrogelatin
nitrogenado, nitrided
nitrógeno, nitrogen
nitroglicerina, nitroglycerin
nitronaftalina, nitronaphthalene
nitroparafina, nitroparaffin
nivel, (in) level; grade, elevation,
   level
— **de agua,** water level
— **de agua freática,** (g) water table
— **de banco,** bench level
— **de burbuja,** spirit level
— **de burbuja de aire,** air level
— **de a caballo,** striding level
— **de caldera,** (cl) gage glass
— **de comparación,** datum
— **de cuerda,** line level
— **de erosión local,** local base level
— **de mano,** hand level

— **del mar,** sea level
— **de referencia,** (gravim) base (o
   reference) level, datum plane (o
   level)
— **de ruidos,** noise level
— **freático,** water table
— **hidrostático,** piezometric level
— **piezométrico,** piezometric level
nivelada de atrás, backsight
nivelador, levelman, levelling man;
   (ma) grader
niveladora, (rd) grader, road
   scraper
— **de empuje angular,** angle-dozer,
   bulldozer
niveladora-elevadora, elevating
   grader
nivelar, level, grade; (tp) run levels
no amortiguado, undampened
no calcáreo, noncalcareous
no consolidado, (g) unconsolidated
no metálico, nonmetallic
no poroso, nonporous
no selectivo, nonselective
no tóxico, nontoxic
nodular, nodular
nódulo, nodule
noduloso, spotted
nogal, walnut
nómina de pago, payroll
nomograma, nomograph
nonacosano, nonacosane
nonadecano, nonadecane
nonadeceno, nonadecene
nonatriacontano, nonatriacontane
noneno, nonene
nonio, vernier
nordeste (NE), northeast
**nordeste cuarto al norte (NE 1/4
   al N),** northeast by north
norma, standard, pattern, norm
normal, normal
— **óptica,** optic normal
normalización, normalization
nornordeste (NNE), north-
   northeast

361

nornoroeste (NNO), north-
northwest
noroeste cuarto de este (NO 1/4
E), northeast by east
nororiente (NE), northeast
norte, north
— geográfico, true north
— magnético, magnetic north
— verdadero, true north
notario, notary public
novaculita, novaculite
nube, cloud
nublado, cloudy
núcleo, (prf) nucleus, core
— continental, continental shield
(o core)
— de cáñamo, hemp center
— del inducido, (el) armature core
— de pasta, (ca) wire rope filler
— de un tornillo, nucleus of a
screw
— independiente de cable de
acero, independent wire rope
center
— laterales, wall core
— orientado, oriented core
— en el cable de acero, wire-rope
kink (q.v. torcedura)
nudo, knot; (nt) velocity equivalent
to 1 nautical mile per hour
número, number
— atómico, atomic number
— autoverificador, self-checking
number
— cetano, cetane number
— de emulsificación a vapor, SE
number (steam emulsification
number), steam emulsification,
demulsification test
— octano, octane number
nunatak, (g) nunatak

O

oasis, oasis
objetivo del microscopio,
microscope objective
oblicuo, skew, oblique
oblongo, oblong
observación, observation
— gravimétrica, gravity
observation
— pendiente abajo, (gf) shot
downdip
— pendiente arriba, (gf) shot updip
observatorio sismológico,
seismological observatory
obsidiana, (g) obsidian
obturador, shutter; plug, stopper;
(a) choke
— cronográfico, (gf) timing line
shutter
— de aceite, oil seal
— de empaque, (prf) packer
— de expansión que se agarra a la
pared, hook-wall packer
— de flujo, flow packer
— de pared, wall packer
— de tubería, line blind
— del tubo revestidor, casing
packer
— para pozos a dos zonas, (prf)
dual-completion packer
— para sellar las paredes del
estrato, wall packer
— para tubería de producción,
(prf) tubing packer
obturar la formación, (g)
formation plugging, plug a
formation
océano, n. ocean; oceánico, a.
marine
ocre, (g) ocher, ochre
octacosano, octacosane
octadecadieno, octadecadiene
octadecano, octadecane
octadeceno, octadecene
octadieno, octadiene
octadiino, octadiyne
octaedrita, anatase

octaedro, octahedron
octágono, octagon
octanaje de carretera, road octane number
octanaje mecánico, mechanical octane number
octano, octane
octatriacontano, octatriacontane
octeno, octene
octilbenceno, octylbenzene
ocular, ocular, eyepiece
— micrométrico, ocular micrometer
ocurrencia, occurrence
odómetro, odometer
oesnoreste (ONO), west-east northwest
oessudoeste (OSO), west-east southwest
oeste, west
oeste cuarta al norte (O 1/4 N), west by north
oeste cuarta al sudoeste (O 1/4 SO), west-east by south
oeste del norte (O del N), west-east of north
oersted, oersted
oficalcita, ophicalcite
ofician, office
ofítico, ophitic
ohmímetro, ohmmeter
ohmio, ohm
ojal, eye, eyelet, grommet
— para cable de acero, wire-rope thimble
ojiva, (g) ogive
ojo, eye
— de agua, spring
ola de fango, mud wave
ola de mar producida por un temblor submarino, tsunami
oleaginosidad, oiliness
oleaje, surge
olefina, olefin
— gaseosas, gaseous olefin

— no convertidas, unconverted olefin
oleoducto, crude oil pipeline, pipeline
— móvil de servicio, swing line
— tributario, feeder line
— troncal, trunk pipeline
— troncales malladas, loop-gathering system
oligisto, oligist
oligoceno, Oligocene
oligoclasa, oligoclase
olivina, (g) olivine, peridot
olor, odor, odour
omisión, omission
— de estratos, (g) omission of beds
onda, (gf) wave
— acústica, acoustic wave
— aérea, air wave
— central, core wave
— compresional, compressional (o primary) wave
— de amplitud máxima, maximum amplitude wave
— de compresión incidente, incident compressional wave
— de condensación, condensation wave
— de dilatación, dilatational wave, longitudinal wave
— de la explosión, blast wave
— de largo período, long wave
— de propagación, propagation wave
— de rarefacción, condensation wave
— elástica, elastic wave
— explosiva, explosion wave
— limítrofe, boundary wave
— plana de dilatación, plane dilatational wave
— primaria, primary wave
— reflejada, reflected wave
— secundaria, secondary wave
— sísmica, earthquake wave, (gf) seismic wave

— **sonora,** sound wave
— **superficial,** surface wave
— **superficial de largo período y poca velocidad,** ground roll
— **terrestre elástica,** elastic earth wave
— **transversal,** transverse (o shear) wave
— **transversal (o de cizallamiento),** incident shear wave
onice, onyx
ónix, onyx
ontogónesis, ontogenesis
ontogenia, ontogenesis
onza, ounce
oolita, oolite
opacidad, cloudiness
opaco, opaque
ópalo, opal
operación, operation
— **de mezclar,** (rf) compounding operation
— **de refinar, purificar o someter el petróleo a cualquier tratamiento,** processing operation
— **fluido-líquida,** fluid flow operation
operador, operario, (oc) operator, workman, laborer; engine runner
óptico, optic
óptimo, optimum
orden, order
— **del encendido,** (mo) firing order
— **de entrega,** delivery order
— **de sucesión,** sequence
— **estratigráfico,** stratigraphic sequence
ordenada, ordinate
ordenador, (dp) computer, data processor
— **analógico,** analog computer
— **asíncrono,** asynchronous computer

— **digital,** digital computer
— **mixto,** hybrid computer
ordinograma, (dp) flow chart
ordoviciano, Ordovician
oreja, (ma) lug, flange; fluke of an anchor; claw of a hammer; (el) ear
oreómetro, weatherometer
orgánico, organic
organismo, organism
organógeno, organogenic
orientación, orientation
— **del desviador (o guíasondas),** whipstock orientation
— **del epicentro,** bearing of epicenter
— **paralela,** parallel orientation
orificio, orifice
— **blindado,** grommet
— **de alivio,** (mc) relief fitting
— **de escape,** exhaust (relief) port
— **de limpieza a mano,** hand hole
— **de purga,** drain opening
origen, origin
— **del tiempo,** time datum
orilla, bank, shore
Orimulsión, trademark of Petroleos de Venezuela
orín, rust
orla, orle, fringe
— **continental,** continental fringe
— **freática,** capillary fringe
orogénesis, orogenesis
orogenia, orogeny
orogénico, orogenic
ortoclasa, orthoclase
ortoclástica, orthoclastic
ortófiro, orthophyre
ortofosforoso, orthophosphorous
ortogneis, orthogneiss
ortorrómbico, orthorhombic
ortosa, orthose
oruga, (tractor) track; caterpillar mounting, crawler tread
oscilación, oscillation

— **amortiguada,** damped oscillation
oscilador, oscillator
oscilar, oscillate, wabble, wobble
oscilógrafo, oscillograph
osciloscopio, oscilloscope
ostracoides, ostracoids
otorgante, (cm) grantor
oxiacetileno, oxyacetylene
oxidación, oxidation
oxidar, oxidize
óxido, oxide
— **carbónico,** carbon monoxide
— **de difenilo,** diphenyl oxide
— **de hierro,** iron oxide
— **silíceo,** siliceous oxide
oxígeno, oxygen
ozocerita, ozokerite
ozono, ozone
ozoquerita cruda, ader wax

P

pabilo, wick; packing
pago, payment
— **al contado,** cash with order
— **contra documentos,** (cm) documents against payment
pago en efectivo, (cm) cash payment
paila, small boiler
— **enchaquetada,** jacketed kettle
pala, spade, shovel
— **cuadrada de mango de asa,** D-handle square-point shovel
— **cuadrada de mango largo,** long-handle square-point shovel
— **de arrastre,** (rd) scraper, drag scraper
— **lengua de buey,** drain spade
— **mecánica,** back hoe, power shovel
— **redonda de mango de asa,** D-handle round-point shovel

— **redonda de mango largo,** long-handle round-point shovel
— **zanjadora de mango de asa,** D-handle ditching spade
palanca, lever, crowbar; arm of a couple; steel billet
— **de contramarcha,** reverse lever
— **de la chispa,** spark lever
— **de desacople de embrague,** clutch-release lever
— **de embrague,** clutch lever
— **de leva,** cam lever
— **del freno,** brake lever
— **de manejo del malacate de la cuchara,** sand-reel handle
— **de presión del malacate de la cuchara,** sand-reel lever
— **de válvula,** valve lever
— **óptica,** optical lever
palastro, plate steel; sheet metal; steel slab
paleobiología, paleobiology
paleobotánica, paleobotany
paleoceno, Paleocene
paleofitología, paleophytology
paleogeografía, paleogeography
paleontología, paleontology
— **microscópica,** microscopic paleontology
paleontólogo, paleontologist
paleozoico, Paleozoic
paleozoología, paleozoology
paleta, trowel; blade tamper; paddle; small shovel; (tr) wicket, vane
— **de ventilador,** fan blade
— **directriz,** (tr) gate
palomilla, wall bracket; bearing, journal box
palúdico, paludal
pampa, pampa
panel, panel; bay of a window
pantalla, screen; (el) shield; (in) sunshade, (hd) core wall, cutoff wall, face slab
— **de tiro,** draft hood

pantano, swamp, marsh, bog; everglades

pantoque, (nt) flat bilge

paño de cristal, glass pane

paño de filtro, filter cloth

papel, paper

— cuadriculado, profile paper, coordinate paper

— cuadriculado para escala logarítmica, log-log paper

— de estraza, kraft paper

— de lija, sand paper, emergy paper

— de tornasol, litmus paper

— esmeril, emergy paper

— heliográfico, ferro-prussiate paper

papilla, slurry

paquete, package

— de estratos, sedimentary

— de mantos sobreescurrido, overthrust mass

par, (el) cell; (cn) rafter; (mt) couple; (cm) par; pair

— térmico, thermocouple

parabrisas, windshield

paraclasa, (g) paraclase

parada, (rr) stop

parado, (ma) shut; steep, standing

parafina, paraffin, wax

— amorfa, amorphous wax

— bruta, slack wax

— cruda, slack wax

— para fósforos, match wax

— semirefinada, scale wax

— sólida, paraffin wax

parafuegos, fire stops

paragénesis, paragenesis

paragolpes, bumper, buffer

— del capó, hood bumper

— esquineros (o laterales), side bumpers

paralaje, parallax

paralelas de cruceta, crosshead guides

paralelo, parallel

— de latitud, parallel of latitude

paralelogramo, parallelogram

parálico, (g) parallic

parallamas, flame arrester

paramagnético, paramagnetic

paramorfismo, paramorphism

pararrayos, lightning arrestor

paratipo, (paleo) paratype

parcela, n. lot, plot, parcel

parche, patch; (tu) boot

pared, wall

— de material refractario, refractory wall

— desviadora, baffle wall

paredón, cliff

parejo, even, flush; uniform

paro completo, complete shutoff

paro de revisión, turnaround

paroxismo, (vlc) paroxysm

parte, part

— posterior, back

— partes contratantes, (cm) contracting parties

parteaguas, (g) divide

partícula, particle

— alfa, alpha particle

— beta, beta particle

— gamma, gamma particle

— elemental, (gf) elemental particle

partida, (cm) lot

pasador, pin, cotter; door bolt; track bolt; tie rod; driftbolt

— cónico, swedged pin

— de aldaba, latch pin

— de aletas, (ma) split pin

— de anclaje, anchor pin

— de articulación, wrist pin

— de la barra de tiro, drawbar pin

— de bisagra, hinge pin

— de brazo, wrist pin

— del brazo trabador, locking arm pin

— de cabo, marlinespike

— de cruceta, crosshead pin

— de eje, axle pin

— de émbolo, piston pin

— **de eslabón complementario,** offset link pin
— **del gancho,** hook pin
— **de manivela,** crank pin
— **de la roldana,** sheave pin
— **guía del casquete,** bonnet guide pin
— **hendido,** cotter pin
pasar el cable por las poleas, reeve
pasillo, catwalk, walk
pasivo, (cm) liability
paso, step, pace; passage; stair tread, run; (tp) pass; ford; (mc) pitch, lead
— **alternado,** chordal pitch
— **del engranaje,** pitch, circle gear
— **de rosca,** thread pitch
— **de cadena,** chain pitch
pasta, paste
— **mineral,** (g) groundmass, matrix
— **(o líquido) de relleno de rosca,** thread filler
— **para pulir (o esmerilar) válvulas,** valve-grinding compound
— **vítrea,** (g) glass paste
— **para correa de transmisión,** belt dressing
pasteca, snatch block
pata, leg
patas delanteras, front-end legs
patente, patent; grant; permit, license; concession
patín, shoe; brake shoe; contact shoe; skid; slide; runner; base of a rail; flange
— **de cruceta,** crosshead shoe
— **de tubos,** pipe skid
patio, yard
— **de tanques,** tank farm (o station)
patrón, standard; template, pattern, jig
pauta, norm
pavimentadora, paving machine
pavimento, pavement

pechblenda, (g) pitchblende, uraninite
pectolita, pectolite
pedal, pedal
— **del acelerador,** accelerator pedal
— **de embrague,** clutch pedal
— **del freno,** brake pedal
pedernal, chert; flint
pedido, (cm) order
pedregullo, gravel
pedriscal, bouldery ground
pegado, stuck
pegajoso, gummy, tacky
pegmatita, (g) pegmatite
peladura, (g) window
película, pellicle; film
— **de aceite,** oil film
— **fluida,** fluid film
— **interfacial,** interfacial film
— **iridiscente,** iridescent film
pelita, (g) pelite
pelotilla, pellet
pendiente, (g) *n.* slope, grade, gradient; downgrade; (mn) hanging wall; *a.* hanging; (cm) pending
— **del buzamiento,** dip slope
— **estructural,** dip slope
— **magnética,** magnetic slope
péndulo, pendulum
— **astático,** astatic pendulum
— **de trípode,** tripod pendulum
— **horizontal,** horizontal pendulum
— **invertido,** inverted pendulum
— **mínimo,** minimum pendulum
penetración, penetration
penillanura, (g) peneplain
— **encañada,** dissected peneplain
península, peninsula
pensilvaniano, *n.* Pennsylvanian;
pensilvaniense, *a.* Pennsylvanian
pentacíclico, pentacyclic
pentacontano, pentacontane
pentadecadiino, pentadecadiyne
pentadecano, pentadecane
pentadeceno, pentadecene

pentágono, pentagon
pentametileno, pentamethylene
pentano, pentane
pentanol, pentanol
pentatetracontano,
  pentatetracontane
pentriacontano, pentriacontane
peña, cobble
peñascal, cobble gravel
peñasco, cliff, large rock
peñón, boulder; mass of rock
peñonal, boulder graben
percha, rack
percolación, percolation, seep,
  seepage, creep, filtration
— de agua, water leaching
percusor, jar
— de carrera corta, short stroke
  drilling jar
— de perforación, jar, drilling jar
— de pesca, lifting jar
— para equipo de cable, cable-tool
  jar
— para pesca, (rot eq) rotary jar
pérdida, loss
— de remolino, eddy loss
— por evaporación, evaporation
  loss
— por fricción, friction loss
— por salpicadura, (sd) splatter
  loss
perfil, profile, section; a rolled steel
  shape; (g) (gf) log
— de equilibrio, (gravim) base-
  level profile
— de gradientes, gradient profile
— de perforación, well log
— de refracción, (gf) refraction
  profile
— eléctrico, (prf) electric log
— geológico de pozo, well log
— gravimétrico, gravity profile
— magnético, magnetic profile
— sismográfico, seismograph
  profile
— T, T-iron

perfiles,
— completos de refracción, (gf)
  reversed profiles
— de acero, structural steel
— invertidos, (gf) reversed profiles
perfilado, streamlined
perfilaje continuo, continuous
  profiling
perfilaje eléctrico, electric logging,
  electric survey
perfilaje electrónico, electron
  logging
perforable, drillable
perforación, perforation, well, hole
— a múltiples zonas, multizone
  completion
— a percusión, percussion (o cable)
  drilling
— bajo agua, submarine drilling
— con contrapresión del lodo,
  pressure drilling
— de arrastre, (dp) feed hole
— de código, (dp) code hole
— de cateo, boring, exploratory
  hole
— de correlación, structural
  drilling
— de desviación controlada,
  controlled directional drilling
— de dirección controlada,
  directional drilling
— de ensayo, wildcat
— de estudio estructural,
  structural drilling
— de poca profundidad, shallow
  hole
— de reconocimiento, boring,
  exploratory hole
— guiada, controlled directional
  drilling
— para prueba estratigráfica,
  stratigraphic test
— para voladura, blast hole
— significativa, (dp) code hole
— sin líneas guía, (mar)
  guidelineless drilling

— **submarina,** submarine drilling
perforacorchos, cork borer
perforador a bala, (prf) perforating
  gun
perforadora, drilling rig
— **de hoyo para explosivo,** shot
  hole drill
— **de hoyos para trabajos de
  sismógrafo,** seismograph driller
— **de tubería de revestimiento,**
  casing perforator
— **inicial,** spudder
— **para exploración,** prospecting
  drill
— **para pozos de agua,** water-well
  drill
— **rotatoria de propulsión directa,**
  direct-driven rotary
**perforar a bala un tubo de
  revestimiento,** gun perforating
periodotita, peridotite
peridoto, peridot, olivine
periférico, peripheral
perilla, knob
perímetro, perimeter
período, (ma) (el) period; cycle;
  stage
— **amortiguado,** damped period
— **de admisión,** (bm) admission
  stroke
— **de asentamiento,** settling period
— **de contacto,** time of contact
— **de funcionamiento,** operating
  cycle, operating period
— **del gravímetro,** gravimeter
  period
— **de inducción,** induction period
— **del péndulo,** pendulum period
— **de traslado,** transfer period
— **geocrático,** (g) geocratic period
perlita, pearlite
permeabilidad, permeability
— **magnética,** magnetic
  permeability
permeable, permeable
permiano, pérmico, Permian

permiso, permit
permocarbonífero, Permo-
  Carboniferous
permonofosforoso,
  permonophosphorous
perno, bolt, stud, spike, pin
— **arponado,** jag bolt, ragged bolt
— **cabeza de cuña,** wedge bolt
— **ciego,** blank bolt
— **común,** machine bolt
— **de anclaje,** anchor bolt
— **de anclaje de los cimientos,**
  foundation bolt
— **de argolla con pasador,** eyebolt
  and key
— **de brida,** flange bolt
— **de cabeza esférica,** ball bolt
— **de cierre,** locking pin
— **de cuello cuadrado,** carriage
  bolt
— **de expansión,** bolt expansion
— **de gancho,** hook bolt
— **de montaje,** mounting bolt
— **de pivote,** king pin
— **de precisión,** cap screw
— **de seguridad,** linch pin
— **de seguridad de la mesa
  rotatoria,** table lock pin
— **maestro,** bolster bolt
— **ordinario,** machine bolt
— **prisionero,** stud bolt, anchor bolt
— **remachado,** anchor bolt
— **rompible de seguridad,** shear
  pin
— **U,** U bolt
— **vertical de charnela de
  dirección,** knuckle pin
peróxido, peroxide
perpendicular, (tp) normal,
  perpendicular
perro, (mc) dog, pawl; cable clip;
  standing valve
persiana, (window) shutter
— **de radiator,** radiator shutter
perspectiva, *n.* prospect;
  perspective; outlook

— **en paralelo,** parallel perspective

pértiga, perch

perturbación, (g) disturbance

— **de la brújula por la presencia de hierro,** local attraction

— **magnética,** magnetic storm

— **ocasionada por la explosión,** shot-hole disturbance

— **regional,** (g) regional disturbance

pesa, *n.* weight; counterweight

— **de balanza de precisión,** weight for analytical balance

— **de contrapeso,** counterbalance weight

pesado, heavy, dense

pesca, (prf) fishing, recovery of lost tools in the hole

pescabarrena de media vuelta, half-turn socket

pescacable, rope spear

pescacuchara, (fishing tl) latch (o boot jack), boot socket

pescadespojos, mousetrap

pescado, (prf) fish, recovered tool or item

pescador, fishing tool

— **de caimán,** alligator grab

— **de cuello,** overshot

— **de cuña,** slip socket

— **de cuña para tubos,** trip spear

— **de rosca,** tapered tap

— **de gancho,** center spear

— **de pasador,** (fish tl) latch (o boot jack), boot socket

— **de tubo revestidor,** liner catcher

pescaespigas, pin socket

pescaherramientas abocinado, horn socket

pescante, boom, jib; crane; davit; the cab of a truck; driver's seat

pescar, *v.* (prf) fish

pescasondas, overshot; socket

— **de enchufe,** slip socket

— **de fricción corrugado,** corrugated friction socket

pesebre, stall, stable

peso, weight; (monetary unit of Argentina, Bolivia, Colombia, Cuba, Chile, Mexico, Dominican Republic, and Uruguay)

— **atómico,** atomic weight

— **bruto,** gross weight

— **de báscula,** scale weight

— **de joyería,** troy weight

— **molecular,** molecular weight

— **muerto,** deadweight

— **sobre la unión giratoria del cable de las varillas de succión,** (bm) watermelon

pestaña, flange, rib, shoulder; fluke of an anchor; (a) tire rim; lip

pestañadora, flanging machine, flanger

pestillo, latch, catch; bolt of a lock

— **de cerradura,** hasp

— **de fricción de la palanca del freno,** brake-lever friction latch

petrificado, lithified, petrified

petrogénesis, petrogenesis

petrografía, petrography

petrográfico, petrographic

petrolato, petrolatum

petróleo, petroleum, oil, crude

— **agrio,** sour crude

— **con base asfáltica,** asphalt-base petroleum

— **crudo,** crude oil

— **crudo intemperizado,** weathered crude petroleum

— **crudo oreado,** weathered crude petroleum

— **crudo sulfuroso,** sour crude

— **de base nafténica,** asphalt-base petroleum

— **de desperdicio,** slop oil

— **de horno,** furnace oil

— **de primera extracción,** primary oil recovery

— **de repaso,** recycle stock

— **de segunda extracción,** secondary oil recovery

— **desasfaltado,** deasphalted oil
— **descabezado,** (rf) tops, topped (o reduced) crude
— **despojado de fracciones livianas,** denuded (o stripped) oil
— **desparafinado,** dewaxed oil
— **húmedo,** wet oil
— **limpio,** pipeline oil
— **muerto,** dead oil
— **parafínico,** paraffin-base oil
— **recuperado,** recovered oil
— **reducido,** reduced (o topped) crude
— **sin gas,** dead oil
— **virgen,** raw crude
petrolero, (oc) oil operator (o producer)
petrolífero, petroliferous, oil bearing
petrolina, petroline
petrolizar, petrolize
petrología, petrology
pez, pitchstone, pitch, tar; fish
picacho, peak
picadura, (mu) pitting; bite, sting
picar, pick; break; chop; (rust) pit
piceno, picene
picnómetro, pycnometer, pyknometer
pico, pick, pickax; peak; spout; nozzle; tip; beak; (mn) sledge
— **de punta y pala,** pick mattock
— **de reflexion,** (gf) peak of observed reflection
— **regador,** spray nozzle
picosegundo, picosecond
picota, pick
pie, foot; (measure) foot: 12 inches
— **de cabra,** crowbar
— **de monte,** piedmont
— **de rey,** foot rule, gauge, slide gauge
— **de tabla,** board foot
— **derecho de la torre de perforación,** derrick leg

— **difusor,** (pr) footpiece
pie-acre, acre-foot
piedra, stone, rock
— **angular,** quoin
— **asfáltica,** asphaltic rock, albertite
— **azul,** bluestone
— **de alumbre,** alum stone
— **de amolar,** grindstone
— **esmeril,** emery stone
— **guijarrosa,** cobblestone
— **imán,** magnetite, lodestone
— **pez,** pitchstone, cantalite
— **pómez,** pumice stone
pieza, (in) (tl) part, piece, member
— **de acero en U,** steel channel
— **de aleación fundida,** alloy casting
— **de hierro en U,** U iron
— **de inserción,** (mc) insert
— **de recambio,** repart part
— **de repuesto,** repair (o spare) part
— **forjada,** forging
— **soldada,** weldment
piezas accesorias, attachments
— **de acero fundido para enroscar,** cast-steel screwed fittings
— **fundidas de metal maleable,** malleable castings
— **móviles,** working parts
— **para tanques,** tank fittings
piezoclasa, (g) compression joint
piezoelectricidad, piezoelectricity
pija, lag screw
pila, fountain, trough, basin; water tap; pile, heap; trestle bent; (cn) pier; (el) battery, cell; (g) pothole; electric column; (nucl phys) pile
— **combustible,** fuel cell
— **termoeléctrica,** thermocouple
pilar tectónico, horst fault, heaved block
pilares de la torre de perforación, derrick legs

Español - Inglés

pilón a vapor, steam hammer
pilote, (cn) pile
— de base de la torre de
perforación, derrick foundation
post
piloto, pilot
pinacoide, (g) pinacoid
pineno alfa, a-pinene
pinta, pint
pintura, paint
pínula, sight of an instrument
pinzas, pincers, nippers, pliers, tongs
— de lagarto, alligator grab
piñón, pinion
— de eje, axle pinion
— de mando, drive pinion
— loco, idler pinion
— y cremallera, rack and pinion
pipeta, (la) pipette
— medidora, measuring pipette
— volumétrica, volumetric pipette
piqueta, pick
pirámide, pyramid
pireno, pyrene
pirita, pyrite
— de cobre, copper pyrite
pirítico, pyritic
pirobitumen, pyrobitumen
— asfáltico, asphaltic pyrobitumen
piroclástico, (g) pyroclastic
piroelectricidad, pyroelectricity
pirofilita, pyrophyllite
pirofosforoso, pyrophosphorous
pirogénico, pirógeno, pyrogenic
pirólisis, pyrolysis
— drástica, drastic pyrolysis
pirolítico, pyrolytic
pirolusita, pyrolusite, bog
manganese
pirómetro, pyrometer
piroxena, pyroxene
piroxenita, pyroxenite
pirrotina, (g) pyrrhotite
pisaempaque, packing gland
piso, floor; (g) age;
— de la torre, derrick floor

pisolita, pisolite
pisón, runner, tamper; ran, stamp;
beetle
pista interior, inner race
pistola, gun, pistol
— de chorro, jet gun
— de engrasar (o de engrase),
grease gun
— de perforación, gun perforator
— de pintar, paint sprayer
— perforadora, perforator,
perforating gun
— pulverizadora, spray gun,
sprayer
pistón de achique, (well) swab
pitman, pitman
pivote, pivot
pizarra, slate
placa, plate, sheet, slab
— de agua, bootleg, water leg
— de asbesto, asbestos board
— de cimiento, ground plate
— de cuña, slip liner
— de desconexión, (prf) breakout
plate
— de desgaste, impingement plate
— de desviación, (rf) baffle plate
— de extremo, end plate
— de inspección, inspection plate
— de perno, bolt plate
— de presión de embrague, clutch
pressure plate
— de respaldo de embrague,
clutch-back plate
— de tubos, tube sheet
— de tubos de caldera, flue plate
— de tubos fija, stationary tube
sheet
— de tubos flotante, floating tube
sheet
— deflectora, baffle plate
— delantal, apron, (cl) skirt
— desconectadora para barrena
cola de pescado, breakout plate
for fish-tail bits
— desviadora, (rf) baffle plate

— **friccional del embrague,** clutch friction ring
— **giratoria,** turntable
— **portatubos,** tube sheet
— **portatubos enteriza,** integral tube sheet
— **portatubos fija,** stationary tube sheet
— **portatubos flotante,** floating tube sheet
— **tubular fija,** stationary tube sheet
placer, (mn) placer
plagioclasa, plagioclase
plagioclásica, (g) plagioclastic
plan, plan (q.v. **proyecto**)
plancha, plate, sheet; slab; smoothing iron; (nt) g angplank; (prf) pipe rack
— **acodada de eslabón,** offset link plate
— **de acero,** steel sheet
— **de apoyo,** mat
— **de asbesto,** asbestos board
— **de coronamiento,** (derrick) cap plate
— **de enfriamiento,** cooling plate
— **de eslabón común,** connecting link
— **de eslabón interior,** inside link
— **de hierro,** iron plate
— **de los pasadores de eslabón,** pin-link plate
— **de relleno,** (mc) shim
— **enfriadora,** chilling plate
plancheta, plane table
planchón, barge
planchuela de contacto a tierra, (el) ground strap
planicie estuarina, (g) estuarine flat
planimetría, survey, mapping
planimetro, planimeter
plano, *n.* plane, drawing; *a.* plane, flat, level
— **axial,** axial plane

— **de contacto de dos capas,** (g) plane boundary
— **de cota cero,** datum plane (o level)
— **de estratificación,** bedding plane
— **de nivel,** datum plane (o level)
— **de referencia,** (g) datum plane (o level)
— **horizontal,** horizontal plane
— **horizontal semiinfinito,** semi-infinite horizontal plane
— **óptico,** optic plane
planta, plant (q.v. **fábrica**)
— **atmosférica,** skimming plant
— **de absorción,** absorption plant
— **de aceites lubricantes,** lube oil plant
— **de acondicionamiento de agua,** water conditioning plant
— **de acondicionamiento de aire,** air conditioning unit
— **de almacenamiento a granel,** bulk storage plant
— **de crácking,** cracking plant (o unit)
— **de desalación,** desalting plant
— **de destilaicón,** distillation plant
— **de extracción,** (rf) extraction plant
— **de extracción de gasolina natural,** natural gas extraction plant
— **de filtración por contacto para lubricantes,** lube-contact filtering unit
— **de gas,** gas plant
— **de gasolina natural,** natural gas extraction plant
— **de isomerización,** isomerization plant
— **de parafina,** wax plant
— **de productos livianos,** light oil plant
— **de productos pesados,** heavy oil plant
— **de recirculación,** cycle plant

— de la recuperación de ácido, acid recovery plant

— de recuperación de vapor, vapor recovery plant

— de redestilación de crácking, cracked distillate rerun plant

— de refinación de aceites lubricantes mediante furfural, furfural lube oil plant

— de tratamiento, treating plant

— de tratamiento de emulsiones, emulsion treating plant

— de tratamiento doctor, doctor plant

— exhaustadora, natural gas extraction plant

— eléctrica, electric plant

— hidroformadora, hydroforming plant

— piloto, pilot plant

— poliformadora, polyform plant

— regeneradora de ácidos, acid restoring plant

— restauradora de ácidos, acid restoring plant

— semicomercial, semiplant scale

plantilla, template, pattern, jig; screed; subgrade; invert standard gage

plasticidad, plasticity

plástico, plastic

plastotipo, (paleo) plastotype

plata, silver

plataforma, (prf) platform; roadbed; (rr) flatcar

— astillero, monkey (o fourble, finger, thribble) board

— astillero para el entubamiento, tubing board

— autoelevadiza, jackup

— autoelevadiza de volada con plancha de apoyo, contilever mat jackup

— colgante, safety cage

— de acero de apoyo por gravedad, steel gravity platform

— de cables en tensión, tension leg platform

— de corona, crow's nest

— de gravedad, gravity platform (o structure), pileless platform

— de hormigón, concrete platform

— del encuellador, finger (o fourble, thribble) board

— del torrero, finger (o fourble, thribble, monkey) board

— (de perforación) con plancha de apoyo, mat supported platform

— de pilotes (hincados), piled platform

— de seguridad, (prf) crow's nest, safety platform

— epicontinental, (g) shelf, continental shelf

— fija, jackup

platea, (hd) apron

platillo de burbujeo, bubble plate

platino, platinum

plato, plate, disk; web of a wheel

— de burbujeo, (rf) bubble plate (o deck,tray)

— calentador, heating plate

playa, beach, playa

— antigua, (g) abandoned beach

pleamar, flood tide

plegable, folding

plegadizo, folding; collapsible

plegamiento, (g) fold, folding; plication

— anticlinal, anticlinal fold

— entrecruzado, crossfolding

— imbricado, imbricate folding

pleistocénico, pleistoceno, Pleistocene

plena presión, full pressure

pleocroísmo, pleochroism

pleocromatismo, pleochroism

pletina, (steel) a flat; flange; tie plate

pliegue, (g) fold; ply, sheet; bend, fold

— abovedado, dome fold

Glossary of the Petroleum Industry

— **acostado,** recumbent fold
— **anticlinal,** anticlinal fold
— **armónico,** competent fold
— **asimétrico,** asymmetrical fold
— **buzante,** dip fold
— **cerrado,** closed fold
— **competente,** competent fold
— **concéntrico,** concentric fold
— **de arrastre,** drag fold
— **de falla,** drag fold
— **de flujo,** flowage fold
— **diapiro,** intrusive fold
— **en abanico,** fan fold
— **inclinado,** inclined fold
— **incompetente,** incompetent fold
— **isoclinal,** isoclinal fold
— **monoclinal,** footfold
— **normal,** normal (o upright) fold
— **parado,** normal (o upright) fold
— **perforante,** intrusive fold
— **profundo,** deep-seated fold
— **recto,** symmetrical fold
— **recumbente,** recumbent fold
— **simétrico,** symmetrical fold
— **terraplenado o monoclinal,** foot fold
— **tumbado,** overfold
— **yacente,** recumbent fold
pliegues
— **escalonados,** en echelon folds
— **infratenuados,** similar folds
— **paralelos,** parallel folds
— **supratenuados,** suprateneous folds
— **semejantes,** similar folds
plioceno, Pliocene
plisamiento, minute folding
plomada, plumb bob
plomobagina, graphite
plomo, lead
— **en láminas,** sheet lead
— **laminado,** sheet lead
— **tetraetílico,** tetraethyl lead
— **tetraetilo,** tetraethyl lead
pluma, feather; pen; (crane) boom; derrick gin pole

— **de agua artesiana,** area of artesian flow
— **de corona,** gin pole
plushexanos, hexanes plus
pluspentano, pentane plus
plutónico, plutonic
plutonio, plutonium
plutonismo, vulcanism
poceta, sump, pool
poder, *n.* power of attorney; *v.* be able, capable
— **calorífico,** calorific power (o value)
podsol, podsol
poise, (measurement) poise
polaridad magnética, magnetic polarity
polarización, polarization
— **de electrodo,** electrode polarization
— **elíptica,** elliptic polarization
— **espontánea,** spontaneous polarization
polarizador, polarizer
polea, pulley, sheave
— **acanalada,** grooved pulley
— **de arrastre,** tug pulley
— **de la cuchara,** sand-pump pulley
— **de diámetro regulable,** expanding (o expansion) pulley
— **de guía,** idler pulley
— **de las herramientas,** crown pulley
— **del malacate de herramientas,** bull wheel tug
— **de maniobra,** snatch block
— **de remolque,** tug pulley
— **de transmisión,** band wheel
— **de la tubería de revestimiento,** casing pulley
— **de ventilador,** fan pulley
— **lateral de la rueda motora,** tug pulley
— **loca,** loose pulley, idler
— **loca de cadena,** chain idler
— **móvil,** traveling block

375

— **muerta,** idler pulley
— **para el cable de las tenazas (** o
    llaves), tong-line pulley
— **tensora,** idler pulley
— **viajera,** traveling block
policíclico, polycyclic
poligonal, polygonal
polígono, polygon
polimerización, polymerization
polimerizado, polymerized
polímero, polymer
polimetileno, polymethylene
polimorfismo, polymorphism
polín, roller, skid
— **de tubos,** pipe skid
polipasto, tackle, block and fall,
    rigging, block and tackle
— **de cadena,** chain hoisting block
polisintético, polysynthetic
polisulfuro, polysulphide
póliza de seguro, insurance policy
polo, pole
— **geográfico,** geographic pole
— **magnético,** magnetic pole
— **magnético atraído al norte,**
    magnetic north-seeking pole
— **magnético atraído al sur,**
    magnetic south-seeking pole
— **norte magnético,** magnetic
    north pole
— **positivo,** anode
— **sur magnético,** magnetic south
    pole
polvo, dust
— **blanqueador,** bleaching powder
— **de roca,** rock meat
— **impalpable,** impalpable powder
— **suelto,** free flowing powder
pólvora, gunpowder, powder
— **negra,** black powder
— **para voladura,** blasting powder
— **sin humo,** smokeless powder,
    ballistite
poner a cero, (dp) reset
pontazgo, (cm) bridge toll
pontear, bridge

pontón, pontoon
porcelana, procelain
porcentaje, percentage
— **del mol,** mol percent
por ciento, percent
porfídico, porphyritic
pórfido, porphyry
— **augítico,** augitophyre
porfirita, (g) porphyrite
porfirítico, prophyritic
por hora, per hour
por minuto, per minute
poro, pore
poros de esponja, sponge spiculae
porosidad, porosity
— **efectiva,** effective porosity
poroso, porous
portaacumulador, battery carrier
portabarrenas, drill chuck, bit
    holder
portabroca, drill chuck, pad
portabureta, burette clamp
— **doble,** double burette clamp
portacable fijo, stiff-neck socket
portaconos, bit head
portachuchillas, (bit) cutter head
portador, (cm) carrier; bearer,
    porter; holder
portaelectrodo, welding electrode
    holder, electrode holder
portafresas, bit head
portaherramientas, tool holder
— **de perforadora,** boring chuck
portal, (g) rock arch; portal; gate
portamecha, drill holder
portamira, (tp) rodman
portamuestras cerrado, closed-type
    sample container
portaobjetos, nosepiece
portapoleas, (prf) crown block
portaprobeta, test-tube holder
portátil, portable
portatrépano, drill holder
portavástago, (small drill) chuck
portezuela de limpieza, cleanout
    door

portezuela del muestreador, thief
hatch
portillo de aforo, thief hatch
portlandiense, (g) Portlandian
portón, gate
— **de glaciar,** glacier outlet
posición neutral, neutral position
positivo, positive
poste, post
— **aguantatubos,** jack board (o
post)
— **amortiguador,** bumper post
— **de ancla,** (ca) tailpost
— **de desenganche,** (bm) knockoff
post
— **de la barra de desenganche,**
(bm) bar-type knockoff post
— **del malacate de herramientas,**
bull wheel post
— **del malacate de las tuberías de
producción,** calf wheel post
— **de retención,** (prf) backup post
— **de rodillos,** (bm) rolling post
— **de la rueda motora,** jack post
— **de tope,** (prf) headache post
— **grúa,** gin pole
— **maestro,** samson post
— **posterior de apoyo,** (prf) tailpost
postor, (cm) bidder
postpaís, (g) back land
postrefrigerador, (rf) aftercooler
potasa, potash
potasio, potassium
potencia, (mc) (mt) power
— **al freno,** brake horsepower
— **asignada,** rating power
— **calorífera,** calorific power (o
value)
— **de inflamación,** ignition
quantity
— **de régimen,** rated horsepower
— **efectiva,** (mc) effective output,
brake horsepower
— **eléctrica,** electric power
— **teórica,** nominal horsepower
potencial, potential

— **de electrofiltración,** (gf)
electrofiltration potential
— **de gravitación,** (gf)
gravitational potential
— **limítrofe,** boundary potential
potenciómetro, potentiometer
pozo, well; pit; shaft
— **a alta presión,** high pressure well
— **a bomba,** pumping well
— **a dos zonas simultáneamente,**
dual-zone well
— **ahogado,** drowned well
— **artesiano,** artesian well
— **brontante,** flowing well, gusher
— **casi agotado,** stripper well
— **contrarrestante** (o
compensador), offset well
— **de acceso,** manhole
— **de agua,** water well
— **de alivio,** relief well
— **de avanzada,** outpost well,
extension wave
— **de cateo,** wildcat
— **del compensador,** (mo)
accelerating well
— **de explotación,** development
well
— **de extensión,** extension well
— **de gas,** gas well
— **de inyección,** input well
— **de inyección de gas,** gas input
well
— **de petróleo,** oil well
— **de recogida,** sump
— **de surgencia natural,** flowing
well
— **de visita,** manhole
— **descubridor,** discovery well
— **exploratorio,** wildcat well
— **franco,** open hole
— **fuera de control,** wild well
— **marginal,** edge well
— **mermado,** stripper well
— **muerto,** dead well
— **petrolífero,** oil well
— **productivo,** producing well

Español - Inglés

— **productor de gas,** gasser
— **seco,** dry well (o hole)
— **semiexploratorio,** semiwildcat, outpost well
— **somero,** shallow hole, shallow well
— **surgente,** flowing well, gusher
— **(o hoyo) de la explosión,** (gf) shot hole
práctico, *n.* (nt) (oc) port pilot; *a.* practical
precalentador, preheater
— **de agua para caldera,** feedwater heater
precámbrico, pre-Cambrian
precio, price
— **corriente,** standard price
— **normal,** standard price
precipitación, precipitation
precipitador eléctrico, electric precipitator
precipitante, precipitant
precipitar, precipitate
precisión, precision, accuracy
precursor, preliminary seismic wave
prefiltro, prefilter
prensa, press
— **de contacto,** (sd) contact jaw
— **de tornillo,** vise
— **hidráulica,** hydraulic press
prensa-guarnición, (ma) gland follower
prensado en frío, (mu) cold pressing
prensaestopas, stuffing box
presa, weir; dam; reservoir
— **de lodo,** sump hole
preservación, preservation
preservativo, preservative
presión, pressure
— **absoluta,** absolute pressure
— **atmosférica,** atomospheric pressure
— **crítica,** critical pressure
— **de bombeo,** pumping pressure

— **del flujo,** flowing pressure
— **de fondo,** (prf) bottom-hole pressure
— **de roca,** rock pressure
— **de trabajo,** operating pressure
— **de la tubería de producción,** tubing pressure
— **de vapor,** vapor pressure
— **diferencial,** differential pressure
— **dirigida,** directed pressure
— **efectiva,** working pressure, operating pressure
— **encerrada,** shut-in pressure
— **en el interior de la tubería de revestimiento,** casing pressure
— **estática de fondo,** static bottom-hole pressure
— **fluctuante,** fluctuating pressure
— **hermética,** shut-in pressure
— **hidráulica efectiva,** effective head
— **hidrostática,** hydrostatic pressure
— **interior de la tubería de revestimiento,** casing pressure
— **manométrica,** gauge pressure
— **normal,** normal pressure
— **osmótica,** osmotic pressure
— **radial,** radial thrust
— **real,** effective pressure
— **subterránea,** field pressure
— **superatmosférica,** superatmospheric pressure
primario, primary
primer impulso sísmico, preliminary seismic wave
primer separador, first-stage separator
primera tubería de revestimiento, surface casing, conductor (o drive, surface) pipe
primeros auxilios, first aid
prioridad, priority
prisionero, screw-set
prisma, prism
— **de cuarzo,** quartz wedge

prismático, prismatic
probador, (in) tester, sampler
— **cerrado,** closed tester
— **con cubeta descubierta,** open-
cup tester
— **de absorción,** absorption tester
— **de acumuladores,** battery tester
— **de bujías,** spark plug tester
— **de fondo,** bottom sampler
— **de orificio para pozos de gas,**
orifice well tester
— **de tubería de revestimiento,**
casing tester
probeta, (la) test tube
— **con pico,** plain cylinder with
spout
— **graduada,** graduate
— **graduada con pico,** graduated
cylinder with spout
— **graduada con tapón,** graduated
cylinder, stoppered
— **sin pico,** plain cylinder without
spout
procedimiento, process, method,
procedure
— **de crácking,** cracking process
— **de desulfuración con cloruro
de cobre,** (rf) copper sweetening
process
— **poliforme,** (rf) polyform process
— **para formar cristales gemelos,**
twinning
proceso, process, processing
— **aleatorio,** (dp) in-line processing
— **autónomo,** (dp) off-line
processing
— **ácido,** (steel) acid process
— **con fenolato,** phenolate process
— **de absorción,** absorption process
— **de aromatización,**
aromatization process
— **de asentamiento rápido,** quick-
settling process
— **de datos,** data processing
— **de descomposición térmica,** (rf)
cracking process

— **de deshidratación de gas,** gas
dehydration process
— **de extracción,** extraction process
— **de fase mixta,** mixed-phase
process
— **en serie,** serial processing
— **en tiempo real,** real time
processing
— **lineal,** (dp) in-line processing
— **para extraer aceite de parafina
emulsionándola con agua,**
emulsion wax deoiling
process
— **para purificación del gas,** gas
purification process
— **por lotes,** batch processing
— **Siemens-Martin,** open-hearth
process
producción, production; yield
— **a toda la capacidad del tubo,**
(oil) open flow production
— **acumulada,** accumulated (o
cumulative) production
— **afluente,** (oil) flush production
— **de coque por calentamiento
externo de la cámara,** external
coking method
— **de zona múltiple,** multizone
production
— **diaria inicial,** initial daily
production
— **en bruto,** gross production
— **final,** ultimate production,
ultimate recovery
— **intermitente por gas,**
intermittent gas lift
— **neta,** effective output, net
production
— **por acre,** per-acre yield
— **potencial,** potential production
— **regular,** settled production
— **secundaria,** (pr) secondary
recovery
productividad, productivity
productos, products
— **de alta pureza,** fine products

— **de evaporación,** overhead products

— **petrolíferos sensibles,** sensitive stocks

profundidad, depth

— **de la explosión,** (gf) shot depth

— **en pies,** (prf) footage

— **focal,** focal depth

profundo, deep

programa, schedule

programación, (dp) programming

— **de acceso al azar,** random-access programming

— **de tiempo mínimo de acceso,** minimum-access programming

promediar, average

promedio, average

— **general,** general average

promontorio, promontory, headland, foreland

promover, promote

propadieno, propadiene

propagación, propagation; (gf) diffusion

propano, propane

propeno, propene, propylene

propiedad, (qm) property; (cm) property, ownership

— **antidetonante,** antiknock property

— **nacional,** property of the state

— **particular,** private property

propiedades electroquímicas, electrochemical properties

propilacetileno, propylacetylene, pentyne

propildiacetileno, propyldiacetylene, heptadiyne

propileno, propene, propylene

propiletileno, propylethylene

propilitización, (g) propylitization

propino, propyne, methylacetylene

proporcional, proportional

propuesta, (cm) proposal, application

propulsión directa, (mc) direct drive

propulsor, impeller, thruster

prorrateo, proration

prórroga, (cm) *n.* time extension, renewal; **prorrogar,** *v.* renew, extend

prospección eléctrica, electric prospecting

prospección sísmica, seismic prospecting

prospección radioactiva, radioactive prospection

protección catódica, cathodic protection

protector, protector

— **de asiento de válvula,** seat protector

— **de indicador,** gauge protector

— **de radiador,** radiator protector

— **de la rosca de unión de la tubería vástago,** (prf) tool-joint protector

— **del tornillo de la empaquetadura,** (prf) packing screw protector

— **de la tubería de revestimiento,** (prf) casing protector

proterozoico, proterozoic, agnotozoic

protomilonita, protomylonite

protón, proton

protuberancia, (mc) boss; protuberance

— **anticlinal,** anticlinal bulge

proveeduría, commissary

provincia geológica, province

proyección, projection

— **exométrica,** cabinet projection

— **isométrica,** isometric projection

— **policónicas,** polyconic projection

— **poliédricas,** polyhedral projection

— **vertical,** vertical projection

proyecto, project

— (o **plan**) **de disparos para estudios sismográficos,** (gf) shooting program

prueba, *n.* test; test piece

— **ácida en caliente,** acid heat test

— **a la ebullición,** boiling point test

— **alcalina,** alkali test

— **al freno,** (mc) break test

— **a punto de mercurio,** mercury freezing test

— **con tira de cobre,** (qm) copper strip test

— **de acidez,** acidity test

— **de anticorrosión,** rust-prevention test

— **de la aislación del agua,** water shut-off test

— **de antidetonancia,** antiknock test

— **de asentamiento,** slump test

— **de choque,** impact test

— **de colorido,** color test

— **de combustión,** burning test

— **de congelación,** cold (o freezing) test

— **de consistencia,** viscosity test, softening point test, dropping point test, penetration test, consistency test

— **de contenido de ceniza,** ash content test

— **de corrosión,** corrosion test

— **de corrosión al cobre,** copper corrosion test

— **de deflagración,** flash point test

— **de destilación,** distillation test

— **de detonación,** (gasoline) knock-rating test

— **de detonancia,** (fuel) detonation test

— **de desemulsibilidad,** demulsibility test

— **de doblez,** bend test

— **de ductilidad,** ductility proof

— **de emulsificación a vapor,** steam emulsion test, SE number, demulsification test

— **de envejecimiento,** aging test

— **de envejecimiento acelerado,** accelerated aging test

— **de evaporación,** evaporation test

— **de flexión,** (sd) bend test

— **de flexión con plantilla,** (sd) guided bend test

— **de flotabilidad,** float test

— **de fluidez,** pour point test

— **de fluidez a baja temperatura,** (la) pour test

— **de fusión,** melting point test

— **de gomosidad,** gum test

— **de intemperismo,** weathering test

— **de mella,** nick-break test

— **de mercurio,** (rf) mercury test

— **de opacidad,** cloud point test

— **de plegado,** (mu) bending test

— **de pliegue en frío,** (mu) cold-bending test

— **del punto de combustión,** fire point test

— **de sulfonación,** sulfonation test

— **de viscosidad,** viscosity test

— **doctor,** (rf) doctor test

— **en platillo de cobre,** copper-dish test

— **media,** middle sample test

— **negativa,** negative test

— **no destructiva,** nondestructive test

— **para determinar la calidad de la ignición,** ignition quality test

— **para determinar el contenido de azufre,** sulphur test

— **para determinar el contenido de plomo tetraetílico,** tetraethyl lead test

— **para determinar el contenido de sedimentos,** sediment test

— **para determinar la gravedad,** gravity test

— **para determinar el índice de saponificación,** saponification number test
— **para determinar la presencia y contenido de azufre en el petróleo,** sulfur test
— **para determinar residuos de carbón,** carbon residue test
— **para determinar los residuos no sulfonados,** unsulfonated residue test
— **para determinar la temperatura de combustión,** fire test
— **para los puntos de opacidad y fluidez ASTM,** ASTM cloud and pour point
— **positiva,** positive test
— **Saybolt de viscosidad,** Saybolt viscosity test
pruebatubos, (prf) casing tester
psamitas, (g) psammites
psefita, (g) psephite
psicrómetro, psychrometer
— **giratorio,** sling psychrometer
psilomelano, psilomelane
pueblo, village, town
puente, bridge
— **colgante,** aerial bridge
— **de trabajo,** safety cage
— **grúa,** traveling crane
— **natural,** natural bridge
puerta, door, gate
— **de horno de caldera,** fire door
puerto, port, harbor
— **libre,** free port
pulgada, inch
— **cuadrada,** square inch
pulido, slickensided
pulidor, buffer, polisher
pulir, polish, grind, burnish
pulpa de aceite, oil pulp
pulsador, pulsator, push botton
pulso, (g) pulse
pulverizador, pulverizer; (paint) sprayer; atomizer

pulverizar, pulverize
púmice, pumice
punta de la aguja, needle point
puntal, shore, strut, prop, spur; dredge spud; (nt) depth of hold
puntero, (gage) hand; stonecutter's chisel; bullpoint
— **de vapor,** steam-jet blower
punto, point
— **arcifínico,** arcifinial point
— **brillante,** (gf) bright spot
— **cedente,** yield point
— **crítico,** critical point
— **de anilina,** aniline point
— **de apoyo de la palanca,** bearance
— **de atadura,** deadman
— **de bifurcación,** (dp) branch point
— **de burbujeo,** (rf) bubble point
— **de cambio,** turning point
— **de comprobación,** (tp) control point
— **de congelación,** freezing point
— **de control,** (tp) control point
— **de deflagración,** (rf) flash point
— **de deformación,** yield point
— **de derretimiento,** melting point
— **de ebullición verdadero (PEV),** true boiling point (TBP)
— **de escurrimiento,** melting point
— **de la explosión,** (gf) shot point
— **de fusión,** melting point
— **de goteo,** drop point
— **de humo,** smoke point
— **de imagen,** image point
— **de inflamación,** q.v. **punto de deflagración**
— **de inflexión,** inflection point
— **de opacidad,** (la) cloud point
— **de origen,** focus, focal point
— **de purga,** bleed point
— **de reblandecimiento,** softening point
— **de referencia,** (tp) bench mark; (dp) benchmark

— **de rocío,** dew point
— **de vaporización,** vaporizing point
— **inicial de ebullición,** initial boiling point
— **medio,** median; middle point
— **medio de ebullición,** mid-boiling point, fifty-percent point
— **medio de un tiempo,** mid stroke
— **mínimo de fluidez,** setting point, pour point
— **muerto,** neutral point, (mo) dead center
— **muerto inferior,** bottom dead center
— **nodal,** nodal point
— **nulo,** null point
— **plano,** (gf) flat spot
— **promedio de ebullición,** average boiling point
— **seco,** (temp) end point, dry point
— **verdadero de ebullición,** true boiling point
puntos de concentración del esfuerzo, stress concentration points
punzado selectivo, (prf) gun perforating
punzón, punch, bullpoint; gadding pin; (va) needle; pile spud; stylus
— **para correas,** belt punch
— **botador,** pin punch
— **centrador,** center punch
— **mandril,** drift punch
— **romo,** solid punch
punzonador, perforator, perforating gun
— **de tubería de revestimiento,** casing perforator
punzonar, *v.* (prf) perforate pipe, punch)
purga, draining; venting; blowoff
purgador, blowoff, drain cock, mud valve, petcock, bleeding valve, drain plug, drainator, steam trap
— **de vapor,** steam drain

purificación, *n.* purification;
purificado, *a.* purified
purificador, purifier
— **centrífugo,** centrifugal purifier
— **de aire,** air cleaner; (o purifier); air filter
purificar, purify
puro, pure
putrido, putrid
PV (presión de vapor), SP (steam pressure)

Q

quebrada, water gap; brook; gully, ravine, draw; gorge
queja, (cm) complaint
quemadero, burning pit
quemador, burner, plumber's torch
— **de aceite,** oil burner (o heater)
— **de acetileno,** acetylene burner
— **de arcilla,** clay burner
— **de boquilla sopladora,** blast tip burner
— **de gas,** gas burner
— **de gas y petróleo,** combination oil and gas burner
— **multichorro,** multijet burner
— **piloto,** pilot burner
quemar, *v.* burn
quicionera, (mc) step bearing; socket; (derrick) foot-block casting
quiebra, crack, fracture; gaping fissure; loss, damage; (cm) bankruptcy; (gf) time break
quijada, jaw
— **con aldaba,** (wrench) latch jaw
— **con uña de cierre,** (wrench) latch lug jaw
quijadas de tornillo, chaps
quilla, (nt) keel
química, chemistry
quinolina, quinoline

— **alquílica,** alkyl quinoline
quintal, hundredweight: 100 pounds
    ó 454 kilograms
quitacostra, scale remover
quitaherrumbre, rust remover

R

racha (de viento), gust
radiación, (cl) radiation
— **electromagnética,**
    electromagnetic radiation
radiador, radiator
radián, radian
radiante, radiant
radical, (mt) (qm) radical
— **alcohilo,** alkyl radical
— **libre,** free radical
radio, radio; radius
— **de viraje,** turning radius
— **ecuatorial,** equatorial radius
— **polar,** polar radius
— **receptores transmisores**
    portátiles, walkie-talkie
radiofaro, radio beacon
radiograma, radiogram
radiolarios, radiolaria
radiolarita, radiolarite
radón, radon
raedura, scraping
raer, *v.* abrade
raigón, (tu) dutchman: a piece of
    threaded pipe caught inside a
    joint
rajatubos, (fishing tl) casing
    splitter; splitter
ralo, thin, sparse, not dense
ramal, branch, arm; strand of rope;
    (p) lateral line
— **de falla,** branch fault
rampa, ramp
rangua, socket; step bearing, pivot
    bearing; (derrick) foot-block
    casting

ranura, spline
— **de alivio,** relief groove
— **de estator,** stator slot
— **de válvula,** valve groove
— **falsa para chaveta,** dummy
    keyway
— **para la circulación del aceite**
    lubricante, oil groove
ranurado, grooved, slotted
rápidos, (r) rapids
rasgador, ripper
raspa de dos caras, (fishing tl) two-
    way rasp
raspador, paint scraper
— **de la parafina,** paraffin scraper
— **de media caña,** fluted scraper
raspadura, scraping
— **ligera,** scratch
raspatubos, casing scraper, (cl)
    scraper
rasqueta, (carp) scraper
rastreador, tracer
rastros de petróleo, show of oil
ratonera, (prf) rathole
raudas, (r) rapids
rayado, scored; fluted, ribbed
rayadura ligera, scratch
rayo, ray, beam; spoke of a sheel;
    thunderbolt, stroke of lightning;
    radius
— **alfa,** alpha ray
— **catódico,** cathode ray
— **de rueda,** spoke
— **sísmico,** seismic ray
rayos
— **beta,** beta rays
— **de la rueda del malacate de las**
    tuberías, calf wheel arms
— **gamma,** gamma rays
rayos X, X-ray
razón social, corporate name;
    company address
reacción, reaction; response
— **al esfuerzo aplicado,** strain
— **de cadena,** (qm) chain reaction
— **elástica,** elastic rebound

— **por combinación,** (qm) reaction by combination
— **por substitución,** reaction by substitution
— **química,** chemical reaction
reacondicionar, *v.* recondition, overhaul
reactancia, reactance
reactivo, reagent; (qm) reactive
reactor, (rf) reactor, reaction chamber
reafilar, resharpen
reajuste, overhaul
reanudar, renew, resume, restart
rearmar, reassemble
rearranque, restart
rebaba, (sd) flash, fin; beard
rebaja, diminution, deduction, reduction; (cm) discount, rebate
rebajar, reduce, lower, cut down; abate, lessen, diminish
rebajo, offset, groove, recess, rabbet; bearding
— **para cuñas,** recess slip
rebarbadura, fettling
rebatido, (sd) peening
rebobinado, rewinding
reborde, flange; edge; dike
— **de llanta,** dish
— **de tambor,** (draw works) spooling flange
— **(o brida) de orificio,** orifice flange
rebosadero, weir
rebosamiento, overflow
rebosar, *v.* overflow; puking
rebote, rebound, resilience
recalcado exterior, banding metal
recalentamiento, overheating, superheat
recalentar, *v.* superheat
recargo de precio, (cm) overcharge
recebo, (rd) road gravel, screenings, hoggin, binder
receptáculo de enchufe a golpes, jar socket

rechinamiento, squeak
recipiente, container, vessel
— **a presión,** pressure vessel
recirculación de gas, (pr) cycling, recycling
recobro secundario, secondary recovery
recocer, *v.* (mu) annealed; **recocido,** *n.* annealing
recogederrumbes, cave catcher
recogemuestras del contenido del fondo del pozo, rathole formation tester
recogemuestras de estrato, drillstem (o rathole) formation tester
reconocimiento, reconnaissance; inspection, survey; (cm) recognition, acknowledgment
— **geológico,** geological survey
reconstrucción, reconstruction; (oil well) recompletion
recopilador de trabajos de sismógrafo, seismograph recorder
recopilacion de datos, data gathering
recorrer el afloramiento de un estrato y cartografiarlo, (g) *v.* walk a bed
recorrido, route, path, travel, run (q.v. **carrera**)
— **de una válvula,** valve travel
recortadora, (saw mill) trimmer
recorte, (sd) kerf
recristalización, recrystallization
rectángulo, rectangle
rectificador, (rf) stripper tower; (mc) (el) rectifier; (tl) tool dresser, grinder
— **de tubería de revestimiento,** casing roller
rectificador, rectifier; grinder, honing machine, hone
— **de válvulas,** valve grinder

rectificar, rectify; (cylinder) rebore; true up
recto, straight
recuesto, (mn) dip
reculada, (nt) back way
recuperación, recovery
— **primaria de petróleo,** primary oil recovery
— **secundaria de petróleo,** secondary oil recovery
recuperador de aceite, oil reclaimer
recuperar, retrieve, (pr) recover
recurso, resource
rechazar, reject
rechazo horizontal, (g) shift
rechazo vertical, throw
red, network
— **de teleproceso,** (dp) teleprocessing network
— **de triángulos,** triangulation net
redestilación, rerunning
rédito, (cm) interest
redoma, beaker
redondo, round
reducción, reduction; reducer; step down
— **del diámetro de una tubería,** bottlenecking
— **de doble engranaje,** double gear reduction
— **de engranajes,** gear reduction
— **doble,** double reduction
— **macho y hembra,** (tu) box and pin substitute
reducir, reduce
reductor, reducer, choker
— **ahusado,** tapered reducer
— **concéntrico,** concentric reducer
— **cónico excéntrico,** eccentric tapered reducer
— **de viscosidad,** visbreaker
— **de presión,** pressure reducer
— **de presión en dos etapas,** two-stage pressure reducer
— **excéntrico,** eccentric reducer

reembolso, (cm) reimbursement
reemplazable, removable
reemplazo, replacement
refinación, refining
— **a base de disolventes,** solvent extraction process
— **a tubo y tanque,** tube-and-tank refining process
— **ácida,** acid refining
— **con ácido,** acid refining
— **con furfural,** furfural refining
— **de petróleo,** petroleum refining
— **de residuo de petróleo,** sludge conversion process
— **por el método de fase de vapor,** vapor-phase refining
— **por lotes,** batch distillation
refinado, raffinate
refinar, refine
refinería, refinery
reflujo, ebb, ebb tide
reformar, reform; mend, amend, improve; reorganize, reconstruct
reforzador, (mc) booster
refracción, refraction
refracción doble, (gf) double refraction
refractario, apyrous, refractory, fire-resisting
refractividad, refractivity
refractómetro, refractometer
refrentado duro, hardfacing
refrentador de válvulas, valve grinder
refrigerador, cooler
refrigerante, refrigerant, cooling mixture
refringencia, refringence, refringency, refractivity
refuerzo, reinforcement; (tp) abutment; backing, bracing; assistance, aid
— **de las patas de la torre de perforación,** rig legs
regalía, royalty
regar, spray, irrigate

regeneración, regeneration

regenerador, regenerator

régimen, rate

— de carga, rate of charge

— de entrada, input rate

— de reposición, reset rate

— de fogueo, firing rate

— estacionario, steady state

región, region, area

— con yacimientos de petróleo comprobados, proven area

— frontera, foreland

— petrolífera, oil zone

regional, regional

registrar, (prf) logging; register; record; enroll

registrador, (mc) recorder

— de flujo, flow recorder

— de gravedad, gravity recorder

— de oxígeno, oxygen recorder

— de tiempo, timer

— de tiro, furnace damper, draft recorder

registro, search, inspection, examination; registry, census, registration; record, enrollment, entry; log; (mc) air hole, furnace register

— de anotación de errores, (dp) log

— de cabecera, (dp) header record

— de instrucción en curso, (dp) current instruction register

— de mano, handhole

— de tiro, draft damper

— de válvula, valve box

— eléctrico, (prf) electric log

— electrográfico de un pozo, electric well survey

— electrónico, electron logging

— fotográfico, photographic recording

— galvanométrico, galvanometric registration

— gráfico del subsuelo, well log

— (o informe diario) de perforación, well log

— sísmico, seismic recording

— sismográfico, seismograph log, seismic recording

regla, rule, scale; straightedge, level board, screed board

— de cálculos, slide rule

— de las fases, phase rule

— de medir, measuring rule

regleta, dip stick

regresión, (g) regression

regresivo, retrogressive

regulación de las válvulas, valve timing

regulador, regulator, governor, controller; throttle valve

— automático, automatic controller

— centrífugo, ball governor, centrifugal regulator (o governor)

— de agua de alimentación, boiler feedwater regulator

— de alimentación de combustible, fuel control

— de bolas, ball governor

— de combustible, fuel regulator

— de contrapesos esféricos, ball governor

— de contrapresión, back-pressure regulator

— de flujo, flow controller

— de intensidad de luz, dimmer switch

— de la llama de prueba, test flame regulator

— de la presión, pressure regulator (o controller)

— de la presión del gas, gas-pressure regulator

— de nivel para líquidos, liquid-level controller

— de temperatura, temperature regulator

— **de tiro,** (frn) damper, draft
damper; draft regulator (o
stabilizer)
— **de la velocidad de la bomba,**
pump governor
— **de velocidad del motor,** engine
speed governor
— **de voltaje,** voltage regulator
— **de volante,** flywheel governor
— **del enfriamiento,** cooling
control
— **del oxígeno,** oxygen regulator
— **hidráulico,** hydraulic regulator
— **reductor de la presión,** pressure
reducing regulator
— **registrador neumático,** air-
operated recording regulator
regular, *v.* adjust, regulate, govern;
a. regular, methodical, orderly;
ordinary
rehabilitar, recondition, overhaul
rehervidor, reboiler
rejilla, grid; grill; grating; rack; bar
screen
— **protectora de radiador,** radiator
screen
rejuvenecimiento, (g) rejuvenation
relación, ratio, relation; report
— **ácido-petróleo,** acid-oil ratio
— **de amplitudes,** amplitude ratio
— **de la caída de potencial,**
potential drop ratio
— **de carbono,** carbon ratio
— **de compresión,** compression
ratio
— **de engranaje,** gear ratio
— **de expansión,** expansion ratio
— **de flujo,** (va) rangeability
— **de repaso,** recycle ratio
— **de utilidad a capital,** (cm)
profit-worth rate
— **de velocidades del eje trasero,**
rear axle ratio
— **del reciclo,** recycle ratio
— **gas-petróleo,** oil-gas ratio
relai, relay, electric relay

relaves, (mn) tailings
relevador, electric relay
relevamiento, survey
— **de mapas (o planos),** mapping
relevo, relief, shift; relief man
relieve, (mc) relief
**rellenamiento de huecos
redondeados en una roca,**
segregation
relleno, *n.* backfill; (sd) pad, filling,
— **de cascajo,** (prf) gravel packing
rellenar, backfill
reloj de segundos muertos, stop
watch
reluctancia, (gf) reluctance
— **magnética,** magnetic reluctance
remachado en caliente, hot
riveting
remache, rivet
remanente, remnant
remanso, backwater
remate de la torre, masthead
remate de la perforación, tailing-in
remendar, patch, repair
remesa, (cm) remittance
remoción de la tubería, (derrick)
laying down pipe
remolcador, tow (o tug boat)
remolcar, *v.* tow
remolino, eddy, whirlpool;
whirlwind; (mn) pocket of ore;
swirl
remolque, towing
— **de cuatro ruedas,** four-wheel
trailer
— **de plataforma baja,** lowboy
truck
— **de tirante,** pole trailer
— **en tándem,** tandem trailer
— **para tubería,** pipe trailer
— **tipo oruga,** track-type trailer
removible, removable
rendimiento, yield, duty, output,
efficiency; revenue, earnings
— **de calor,** heat duty
— **de viscosidad,** viscosity yield

— **térmico,** thermal efficiency
— **total,** overall efficiency
renovable, renewable
renovación, renewal replacement
renovar, renew
renta, rent, income
reóstato, rheostat
reparación, repair; reparation
reparar, rework, repair
repartible, distributable
repasar, recondition, overhaul
repaso, (rf) recycle, recycling; revision, reexamination
reperforación, workover
— **correctiva,** remedial workover
repetición, repeatability
— **de las capas,** (g) repetition of beds
— **de pasada,** rerun
reposición, replacement
represa, reservoir
representación visual, (dp) display
representante, representative
representar, represent
represión, repressuring
reproducción, reproduction; (la) reproducibility
repuesto, spare part
repulsión magnética, magnetic repulsion
resaca, surf
resalto, projection, salient; offset; (hd) deflector sill; (gf) offset, (mc) (carp) shoulder
resaturar, resaturate
resbalamiento, (pulley) slippage
resbalar, slip
reserva, reserve
— **de pasivo,** (cm) liability reserve
— **para participación de utilidades,** profit sharing reserve
resguardo, (in) guard; shelter; (cm) collateral, clearance
resguardado del aceite, oiltight
residual, residual

residuo, residue, sludge; residuum, residue bottoms; remains
— **corto,** (rf) short residuum
— **de fondo,** bottom product
— **de resudación,** sweat residue
— **surtido,** (rf) long residuum
resina, resin
resinoso, resinous, gummy
resistencia, resistance, strength; (el) resistance, resistor, ballast; (mc) endurance
— **al cizallamiento,** shearing strength
— **al corte,** shearing strength
— **al flujo,** (steel) creep strength resistance
— **a la compresión,** (g) crushing strength
— **a la presión en frío,** (va) cold working pressure CWP
— **a la rotura,** breaking strength
— **a la tensión,** tensile strength
— **a la transmisión de calor causada por la suciedad,** fouling resistance
— **al viento,** (derrick) wind load capacity
— **de electrodo,** electrode resistance
— **eléctrica,** electric resistance
— **específica,** specific resistance
— **magnética,** magnetic resistance
— **temprana,** early strength
— **tensora,** tensile strength
— **térmica,** thermistor; thermal resistivity
resistente, strong, resistant
resistividad, resistivity
— **de la tierra,** soil resistivity
— **eléctrica,** electric resistivity
resolución, resolution, decree
resorte, (steel) spring
— **de embrague,** clutch spring
— **de válvula,** valve spring
respiradero, vent valve, breather, air inlet, air valve

389

— **de tanques,** tank vent
respirador, respirator
responsabilidad ilimitada, (cm)
    unlimited liability
restaurar la presión en un
    yacimiento, repressuring
restitución, replacement
restos, remains
— **orgánicos,** organic remains
resudamiento de la parafina, (rf)
    wax sweating
resumidero, sump
retardo, retardation
retén, retainer, pawl, catch, dog,
    fasterner; (magnet) keeper
— **de aceite,** oil seal
— **de cojinetes,** bearing retainer
— **de grasa,** grease retainer
retención, retention
retenedor de aceite, oil retainer
retenedor de cemento, (prf)
    cement retainer, cementer,
    cementing packer (o tool)
retenida, *n.* guy
retículo, (tp in) cross hairs
retinita, retinite
retiro de la tubería, (derrick)
    laying down pipe
retorta, retort
retractable, retractable
retranca, brake
retraso, retardation
— **de fase,** phase lag
retratar, *v.* photograph
retroactivo, retroactive
retrobombeo, pumparound
retroceso y atasco, cock and bind
retrolavado, backwash
retrolectura, (tp) backsight
retrotaponamiento, the plugging
    back of an oil well; backplug
retrotaponar, (well) plug back
retrovisual, (tp) backsight
reventón, (prf) blowout; explosion;
    (g) (mn) outcrop
reversible, reversible

revestido, lined
— **de metal,** metallized, metal lined
— (o **cubierto) de acero,** steel clad
— **con cemento,** cement lined
revestidor, (prf) casing, liner
— **auxiliar,** liner
— **auxiliar ciego,** blank liner
revestimiento, facing
— **de cuero,** leather facing
— **de embrague,** clutch lining,
    clutch facing
— **de fricción,** friction facing
— **de gunita,** gunite lining
— **del freno,** brake facing, brake
    lining
revestimiento, laggins
revestir, *v.* line, face, surface, coat
— **la punta de una barra,** *v.* tip
revolución, (g) (mc) revolution
revoque, (prf) filter (o mud) cake
rezumadero de petróleo, oil seep
ría, (g) ria
ribera, shore beach; riverbank
riesgo, risk
— **de incendio,** fire hazard
rigidez, rigidity
rigolina, rhigolene
río, river, stream
— **antecedente,** antecedent stream
— **abajo,** downstream
riolita, rhyolite
ripio, drill cuttings
risco, cliff, crag, bluff
roca, rock, stone
— **ácida,** acid rock
— **alterada,** altered rock
— **apartada,** outlier
— **asfáltica,** asphaltic rock,
    albertite
— **atrapada,** (g) horse
— **autoclástica,** autoclastic rock
— **clástica,** clastic rock
— **cristalina,** crystalline rock
— **de basamento,** (g) basement
    rock
— **de concha,** shell rock

— **determinante,** key rock
— **efusiva,** extrusive rock
— **eólica,** aeolian rock
— **esquística,** aschistic rock
— **esquistosa,** aschistic rock
— **extraña,** outlier
— **filoniana,** dike rock
— **fresca,** ledge
— **ígnea,** igneous rock
— **intermediaria,** mesosilicic rock
— **intrusiva,** intrusive rock
— **madre,** parent (o country) rock
— **metasedimentaria,** metasedimentary rock
— **plutónica,** plutonic (o abyssal) rock
— **productive,** reservoir rock
— **sedimentaria,** sedimentary rock
— **superficial,** extrusive rock
— **trapeana,** trap rock
— **virgen,** ledge
— **viva,** ledge
— **volcánica,** volcanic rock
rocas
— **abisales,** abyssal rocks, plutonic rocks
— **de orígen eólico,** aeolian rocks
— **extrusivas,** extrusive rocks
— **mesosilícicas,** mesosilicic rocks
— **metaígneas,** metaigneous rocks
— **metamórficas,** metamorphic rocks
— **petrolíferas,** source rocks
— **productivas de petróleo,** source rocks
— **protogénicas,** protogenic rocks
— **vecinas,** adjoining rocks, country (o wall) rock
rocalla, straited pebbles
rociada, spray
rociador, sprayer, sprinkler
rocío, *n.* spray; dew
rodados, gravel
rodaja, caster; sheave
rodilla, knee; ball joint
rodillo, roller

— **sin costura,** seamless roller
— **tensor de cadena,** chain idler
rodillos
— **laminadores,** laminating rollers
— **para tubería de revestimiento,** casing dollies
— **transportadores,** carrying rollers
rodocrusita, rhodochrosite
rodonita, rhodonite
rojo, red
— **de pulir,** crocus
rol, dolly
roldana, pulley, sheave; washer; spool insulator; tackle block
— **aisladora,** (el) insulator spool
— **a polea de acanalado múltiple en V,** multiple V-belt sheaves
— **de maniobra,** snatch block
— **de poleas de corona,** (derrick) crown sheave
— **libre,** dangling sheave
— **para correa trapezoidal,** V-belt heave
rombohedro, rhombohedral
rompecollares, rompecuellos, collar buster
rompehielos, ice breaker
rompeolas, breakwater, jetty
romper, *v.* break
— **en pedazos,** shatter
rosca, thread; nipple; nut; arch ring
— **cruzada,** crossthreading
— **de ángulo agudo,** sharp thread
— **de paso izquierdo,** left-hand thread
— **de tubería,** pipe thread
— **derecha,** right-hand thread
— **en dos series,** (tu) two-step thread
— **redonda,** round thread
roscado, threaded
roscador de tubos, pipe threader
roscadora, pipe and bolt machine
— **de tubos,** pipe-threading machine

rotación, rotation
— de inventarios, turnover of
inventories
rotor, rotor (q.v. inducido)
— en circuito corto, (el) squirrel
cage
— de jaula, (el) squirrel cage
rotura, breaking, fracture, rupture
— por fatiga, (mu) fatigue break (o
failure)
— por tensión, tension failure
— por torsión, twistoff, twistoff
failure
— espiral, spiral tear
rubí, ruby
rueda, wheel
— cabilla del tambor de
maniobras, calf wheel sprocket
— de cadena, sprocket
— de disco, disc wheel
— de enfrenamiento del malacate
de herramientas, bull wheel
brake
— de enfrenamiento del malacate
de las tuberías de producción,
calf wheel brake
— de mano, hand wheel
— de pestaña, flanged wheel
— dentada, sprocket, sprocket
wheel, gear wheel
— dentada del malacate de las
tuberías de producción, calf
wheel sprocket
— directriz, steering wheel
— esmeril, emery wheel
— hiperbólica, skew bevel
— motora, band wheel
— motriz, leader, band wheel
— motriz dentada, drive sprocket
— secundaria, follower
ruginoso, (g) aeruginous
rumbo, direction, route, course;
compass bearing; (g) strike
— del estrato, strike
— verdadero, true course
ruptor, (a) breaker

ruta, route
— de invasión marina, (g) seaway
rutilo, rutile
rutina, routine
— de descarga a disco, (dp) rollout
routine
— de reincorporación a la
memoria, (dp) roll-in routine

S

sacabarrena, drill ejector, drill
extractor
sacacuñas, key puller
sacada (de la tubería), tripping out
sacaengranajes, gear puller
sacamuestras, (prf) core barrel
— de pared, sidewall sampler
sacanúcleos, (prf) core barrel
— para formaciones duras, hard-
formation corehead
sacaróideo, saccharoidal
sacatestigos, (prf) core barrel
sacatornillos, screw extractor
saco, sack, bag
sacudida, shock, jarring
sacudidora, shaker
saetín de tanque, tank flume
sal, salt
— ácida, acid salt
— gema, rock salt
— haloidea, haloid salt
— neutra, neutral salt
sala, room
— de bombas, pump room
— de control, control room
— de gobierno, control room
— de máquinas, engine room
— de máquinas, engine room
salbanda, (g) salband, vein wall
saldar, v. (cm) balance; settle
saldo, (cm) balance
— acreedor, credit balance
— deudor, debit balance

Glossary of the Petroleum Industry

— **líquido,** net balance
salida del gas, gas outlet
saliente, *n.* (mc) projection, lug, finger, salient; *a.* projecting, salient
salino, saline
salinidad, salinity
salitre, niter, saltpeter
salmuera, salt water, brine
salobre, brackish
salón refrigerador, cold room
salteado, staggered
salto horizontal, (g) shift
salto vertical, throw
salvamento, salvage
salvo error u omisión, (cm) errors excepted, EE
saneamiento, drainage
saponificación, *n.* saponification; **saponificar,** *v.* saponify
sargento, vise
sarmatiense, Sarmatian
sarta, line, series; string
— **conductora,** foundation (o conductor) pipe
— **de lavado,** (fishing tl) washover string
— **de tubería de revestimiento,** casing string
— **de varillas,** rod string
saturación, saturation
— **insuficiente,** undersaturation
saturado, saturated
saxoniense, Saxonian
scheelita, scheelite
secadal, geest
secar, *v.* dry
sección, (tu) section
— **de convección de tiro hacia abajo,** downdraft convection section
— **de convección de tiro hacia arriba,** updraft convection section
— **geológica,** (map) geologic column (o section)

— **transversal,** transverse section
— **vertical,** (gf) vertical section
seccionar, *v.* section, cross section
seco, barren, dry
secreción, (g) segregation
sector dentado del freno, brake quadrant
sector oscilante, (mc) quadrant
secuencia, sequence
— **de intercalación,** (dp) collating sequence
secundario, secondary
sedimentación, sedimentation
— **playera,** shoreline deposition
sedimentario, sedimentary
sedimento, sediment; bottom settlings
— **corrido,** creeping sediment
— **en movimiento,** creeping sediment
sedimentos
— **anemógenos,** colic sediments
— **clásticos,** clastic sediments, mechanical sediments
— **consolidados,** consolidated sediments
— **eólicos,** aeolic sediments, aeolic deposits
— **escurridizos,** creeping sediments
— **mecánicos,** clastic sediments, mechanical sediments
segmentos dentados de las cuñas, slip inserts
segregación, segregation
segregador de gas, gas anchor
segregador de gas y lodo, mud-gas anchor
segregar por medio de lodo, *v.* mud off
segueta, hacksaw
segunda potencia, (mt) square
segunda recuperación, (pr) secondary recovery
segundo, *n. a.* second
— **de arco,** second of arc

393

— **separador,** second-stage separator
— **superintendente,** assitant superintendent
seguridad de funcionamiento, reliability
seguro, insurance; (mc) lock
— **aéreo,** air insurance
— **contra incendio,** fire
— **del buje maestro,** master bushing lock
— **de crédito,** credit insurance
— **marítimo,** marine insurance
seleccionar, *v.* sort
sello, seal
— **de aceite,** oil seal
— **guardapolvo,** dust seal
selva, jungle
semestre, semester
semiacoplado, semitrailer
semiárido, semiarid
semicontemporáneo, penecontemporaneous
semicristalino, semicrystalline
semieje, axle shaft
semiflotante, semifloating
semi-ionización, semi-ionization
semiremolque, semitrailer
sencillo, single, simple
senda, trail, track
sendero, path, footpath, trail
senectud, old age
senoniense, Senonian
sensibilidad, sensibility
— **de instrumentos,** sensitivity of instruments
sensibilizar, (gf) astatize
sentido de rotación, direction of rotation
señal de olas, ripple mark
señalizador, flag
separación, spacing, separation; (g) separation, segregation
— **del agua del petróleo,** water knockout

separador, separator, spreader, spacer, packing block; (petrol) trap
— **ciclonal,** (rf) cyclone separator
— **de aceite y gas,** oil and gas separator
— **de aceite y vapor,** steam and oil separator
— **de agua,** steam scrubber, steam trap
— **de gas,** gas separator
— **de gas y petróleo,** gas-oil separator
— **de las placas de un acumulador,** battery plate separator
— **de viscosidad,** (rf) viscosity breaker
septa, (g) septum
sequero, (g) geest
séquito de filón, (g) vein accompaniments
sericita, sericite
serie, serial, series; suite
— **aromática,** aromatic series
— **cílica de hidrocarburos,** cyclic series of hydrocarbons
— **de disparos buzamiento arriba,** updip shooting
— **dileofínica,** diolefin series
— **homóloga,** homologous series
— **nafténica,** naphthene series
— **olefínica,** olefin series, ethylene series
— **parafínica,** paraffin series
serpenteo, (p) slack
serpentín, (tu) coil
— **calentador provisto de camisa de agua,** water-jacketed coil heater
— **de enfriamiento,** chilling coil
— **de expansión,** expansion coil
serpentina, serpentine
serranía, ridge
serrucho, saw
— **calador,** coping saw

394

— **común,** hand saw
— **de punta,** compass saw
— **para ojo de cerradura,** keyhole saw
servicio, service; duty
— **de barco volandero,** (cm) tramp service
— **de conservación, preparación o mezcla del lodo,** mud handling service
— **de transporte por expreso,** express service
servidumbre de paso, right-of-way
servomotor, servomotor
sesgado, skew
sesgo, obliqueness, slope, skew
seudocódigo, (dp) pseudocode
seudocumeno, pseudocumene (q.v. trimetilbenceno)
seudofenocristales, pseudophenocrysts
seudoestratificación, pseudostratification
seudomorfismo, (g) pseudomorphism
shonkinita, shonkinite
sial, (g) sial
siciliense, (g) Sicilian
siderita, siderite
sienita, (g) syenite
— **nefelina,** nepheline syenite
sierra, (tl) saw; mountain range
— **caladora,** jig saw
— **circular,** circular saw
— **circular de torno,** bench saw
— **de calados,** fret saw
— **de contornear,** sweep saw
— **para metales,** hacksaw
— **sin fin,** band saw; belt saw
sifón, siphon (tu) trap
— **cuello de cisne,** gooseneck siphon
— **de purga,** siphon bleeder
sigilaria, sigillaria
signo óptico, optic sign

signos convencionales, (map) legend, conventional signs
silenciador, sound damper, muffler
— **de motor,** exhaust arrester, engine muffler
— **de la válvula de escape,** exhaust silencer
silenciar el escape, muffle
silicato, silicate
sílice, silica
silíceo, siliceous
silicio, silicon
silmanita, sillimanite
silla, (va) valve seat; (p) welding saddle
— **para mantener a nivel instrumentos medidores,** meter levelling saddle
— **soldable,** welding saddle
silleta para tubos, pipe saddle
siluriano, silúrico, Silurian
símbolo, symbol
simétrico, symmetric
simple, simplex, single
simulador, simulator
simultaneidad, synchronism
sinclinal, *n.* syncline; *a.* synclinal
— **compuesto,** synclinorium
sinclinorio, synclinorium
sincrónico, synchronous
sincronismo, synchronism
sincronización, synchronization, timing
— **de las válvulas,** valve timing
sincronizador, timer
singenético, (g) syngenetic
singonía cristalográfica, crystallization systems
síntesis, synthesis
— **orgánica,** organic synthesis
sintético, synthetic
sin variación, (gf) zero shift
sísmica aplicada, seismic recording
sísmico, seismic
sismo, earthquake

— **de dislocación,** tectonic earthquake
— **de foco somero,** shallow focus earthquake
— **final,** aftershock
— **preliminar,** (gf) foreshock
— **precursor,** preliminary seismic wave
— **tectónico,** tectonic earthquake
sismógrafo, seismograph
— **de dos componentes,** two-point seismograph
— **eléctrico,** electric seismograph
— **electromagnético,** electromagnetic seismograph
— **para movimientos fuertes,** s trong-motion seismograph
— **sismométrico,** seismometer seismograph
sismograma, seismograph log, seismogram, seismographic record
sismología, seismology
sismólogo, (oc) seismologist
sismómetro, seismometer
sistema, system
— **astático,** astatic system
— **Batten,** (dp) peek-a-boo system
— **de cable,** (prf) cable system
— **de circulación,** circulation system
— **de cloración,** chlorination system
— **de conexión,** hookup, linkage
— **de disolvente para la extracción de parafina,** oil-wax-solvent system
— **de electrodo de expansión,** expanding electrode system
— **de empalme del freno,** brake linkage
— **de enfriamiento,** cooling system
— **de falla,** fault system
— **de inyección de agua a cuatro pozos por medio de un quinto,** (pr) five-spot flooding system

— **de mecanismo móvil en un gravímetro,** moving system
— **de oleoductos recolectores,** loop-gathering system
— **de regeneración del catalizador,** catalyst regenerating system
— **de tubería que recoge en serie la producción de un grupo de pozos,** loop-gathering system
— **hidrográfico,** river system
— **métrico,** metric system
— **múltiple de bombeo de pozos,** multiple well pumping system
— **para descarte del cieno,** sludge disposal process
— **ternario,** (mt) ternary system
situar, *v.* locate
smithsonita, smithsonite
sobrecalentamiento, overheating
sobrecalentar, *v.* superheat
sobrecarga, overcharge, overburden, overload; surcharge; live load
— **de un acumulador,** battery overcharge
sobrecebado, overprimed
sobremango de llave, (tu) mope
sobremedida, oversize
sobrepeso, excess weight
sobresaturado, supersaturated
sobrestante, boss, foreman
socavamiento, (g) undermining, washout
socavar, undercut, undermine
socavón, adit, gallery; cavern
socio, member, partner
soda, soda
— **cáustica,** caustic soda
sodalita, sodalite
sodio, sodium
— **plúmbico,** sodium plumbite
solapado, (g) overlapped
solapadura, lap
solar, *n.* lot, plot
soldador, welder; soldering iron

— **eléctrico,** electric welder
— **de cobre,** soldering copper
soldadura, welding; soldering; solder; welding compound, a weld; (g) coalescence
— **a estilo de tubo de estufa,** (p) stove piping
— **a giratubo,** roll welding
— **a presión,** pressure welding
— **a puntos,** tack welding
— **a ras,** flush weld
— **a solapa,** lapweld
— **a tope,** butt weld
— **a tope de resistencia y por recalentamiento,** resistance flash butt welding
— **al arco,** arc welding
— **al arco con corriente continua,** direct current arc welding
— **al arco de carbón,** carbon arc welding
— **al arco de carbón protegido,** shielded carbon arc welding
— **al arco metálico,** metal arc welding
— **al arco metálico protegido,** shielded metal arc welding
— **al martillo,** hammer welding
— **al sesgo,** scarf weld
— **autógena,** autogenic soldering, oxyacetylene welding
— **automática,** automatic welding
— **con acetileno,** acetylene welding
— **con latón,** braze, brazing
— **cóncava,** concave fillet weld, convex fillet weld
— **continua,** continuous weld
— **convexa,** convex fillet weld
— **de acetileno,** gas welding
— **de aluminio,** aluminum solder
— **de bisel,** bevel weld
— **con oxiacetileno,** oxyacetylene welding, gas welding
— **de chaflán,** bevel weld
— **de chaflán cuadrado,** square groove weld

— **de chaflán en J,** J-groove weld
— **de chaflán en U,** U-groove weld
— **de costura,** seam weld
— **de cuña,** plug weld
— **de fusión,** fusion weld
— **de impacto,** percussive welding
— **de obturación,** seal (o bead) weld
— **de puntada,** tack weld
— **de puntos,** spot weld
— **de ranura doble,** double-groove weld
— **de ranura sencilla,** single-groove weld
— **de recalentamiento,** flash weld
— **de resalto,** projection weld
— **de resistencia,** resistance welding
— **de retroceso,** back-step welding
— **de rodeo,** bell-hole welding
— **de sello,** poke welding
— **de tapón,** plug welding
— **de tejido,** weaving
— **de termita,** thermit welding
— **de tope,** jam weld
— **de tubería en secciones de dos juntas,** double jointing
— **de tubería junta a junta,** (p) stove piping
— **de un solo cordón,** stringer bead, bead weld
— **de vaivén,** weaving
— **eléctrica,** electric welding
— **en ángulo,** concave (o convex) fillet weld
— **en ángulo intermitente y alternada,** staggered intermittent fillet weld
— **fuerte,** brazing
— **fuerte al arco,** arc brazing
— **fuerte eléctrica,** electric brazing
— **intermitente,** intermittent weld
— **manual,** manual welding
— **oblonga,** slot weld
— **oxiacetilénica,** acetylene welding
— **oxhídrica al arco,** atomic hydrogen welding

— **por puntos,** spot welding
— **preliminar en la que se suelda la unión en varios puntos para completar la soldadura más tarde,** tack welding
— **punteada,** tack weld
— **semiautomática al arco metálico,** semi-automatic metal arc weld
— **sin presión,** nonpressure welding
soldar, *v.* weld, solder, braze, sweat
— **a puntos,** spot welding
— **con latón,** braze
— **en fuerte,** braze
solera, sill, solepiece; (carp) wall plate; (hd) invert; a steel flat; (rd) curb
— **de frente,** nose still
— **del caballete portapoleas,** crown block beam
— **inferior,** (cn) sill, soleplate
solicitación, (mc) stress
solicitud, (cm) application
solidez, solidity
sólido, solid
solidificación, solidification
solifluxión, solifluction
sollado, (nt) spider (o hurricane) deck
soltar, *v.* release, loosen, let go
solubilidad, solubility
soluble, soluble
solución, solution
— **a mínimos cuadrados,** least square solution
— **coloidal,** colloidal solution
— **de aceite para cilindro,** cylinder stock solution
— **de almidón para indicador,** starch indicator solution
— **de iodato potásico,** potassium iodate solution
— **de jabón,** soap solution
— **doctor,** (rf) doctor solution
— **jabonosa,** soap solution
— **normal,** normal solution

soluto, *n.* solute
solvente, (qm) q.v. disolvente
— **neutral,** neutral solvent
sombreado, *n.* (drawing) hatching, shading; hachures; **sombrear,** *v.* shade
sombrerete, (mc) bearing cap; (va) bonnet; hood; cap; coping; cowl; driving cap for piles
somero, shallow
sonda, (tp) sound; (prf) drill, bit; sounding rod (o line)
sondeo, *n.* boring; sounding; drilling; well
— **acústico,** (gf) echo sounding
sonógrafo, sonograph
soplador, blower
— **centrífugo,** centrifugal blower
— **de chorro,** jet blower
— **de fragua,** forge blower
soplete, blowtorch, welding torch, blowpipe
— **cortador,** cutting torch
— **de aire,** blowtorch
— **de pintura,** paint gun
— **eléctrico,** electric blowpipe
— **oxiacetilénico,** oxyacetylene blowpipe, acetylene torch
— **para soldar,** welding torch
soplo inverso, blow-back
soporte, stand; support, bearing, standard
— **colgante,** shaft hanger
— **del tambor de maniobras,** calf wheel post
— **lógico,** (dp) software
— **para tubos,** tube support
— **universal,** (la) ring stand
soportes del balancín, center irons
sordina, sound damper
sosa, soda
sostén, support
— **de barra de desenganche,** (bm rods) bar-type knockoff post
— **de cojinete,** bearing bracket
— **de fricción,** (bm rods) rub post

— de oscilación graduable, adjustable swing
— de pared, wall hook
— de rodillo, roller-type rod line carrier
— de varillas de tracción, pull-rod carrier
— de ventilador, fan bracket
— del termómetro, thermometer clamp
— oscilante, swing
— suspendido para varillas de tracción, pull-rod hold-down
sótano, basement; (well) basement
sotavento, leeward
standard, standard
suavear, (well) swab
suavizador, (ca) dope
— de agua, water softener
sub amortiguador, travel sub
sub ponderado, bent sub
sub sacrificable, wear sub
subcapilar, subcapillary
subestrato, sole
subestructura, substructure
subgerente, assistant manager
subida del metal al enfriarse, scattering
sublimación, sublimation
submarino, submarine
— de una atmósfera, dry submersible
subproducto, byproduct
subrayar, underline
subsecuente, subsequent
subsolera, subsill
subsuelo, subsoil, subsurface
substancia química para regenerar el agua, water-treating chemical
substancias no saturadas, unsaturates
substitución, substitution, replacement
substitución metasomática, (g) metasomatism

subyacente, underlying
succión, suction
sucursal, (cm) branch office
sudeste (SE), southeast
sudeste cuarta al este (SE 1/4 al E), southeast by east
sudeste cuarta al sur (SE 1/4 al S), southeast by south
sudoeste (SO), southwest
sudoeste cuarta al oeste (SO 1/4 al O), southwest by west
sudoeste cuarta al sur (SO 1/4 al S), southwest by south
sufridera, dolly
suiche, electric switch (q.v. interruptor)
sujetador, fastener, clip, clamp, anchor
— de la bomba de inserción, insert-pump anchor
— de cable aflajable, slack holder
— de cable de acero al balancín, wire-line-type beam hanger
— de guía para soldar collares en tubos, collar welding jig
— del tipo eslabón (o anillo), link-type beam hanger
— de tubería auxiliar de revestimiento, liner hanger
— de las varillas de bombeo al balancín, (bm jack) beam hanger
— hecho de cable de acero, (bm jack) wire-line hanger
sulfato, sulphate
— de cobre, copper sulphate, bluestone
— de dialcohilo, dialkyl sulfate
— de sodio, sodium sulphate
— dimetilo, dimethyl sulfate
sulfonación, sulfonation
sulfuración, sulfuration
sulfúrico, sulfuric
sulfuro, sulfide
— alquílico, alkyl sulfide
— de butilo normal, n-butyl sulfide

— **de propilo normal,** n-propyl sulfide

sulfuroso, sulfurous

suma, sum, total

— **total,** total amount

sumario, summary

sumergible inundado, swimmer vehicle

sumergido, underwater, submerged

sumersión, submergence, immersion

sumidero, sink hole; sump, catch basin; cesspool

suministro, supply

superalimentador, supercharger

superávit, surplus

supercalor, superheat

supercapilar, supercapillary

supercarburantes, antiknock fuels

supercompresor, supercharger

superficial, superficial

superficie, surface, face, area

— **de caldeo,** heating surface

— **de cojinete,** bearing surface

— **de desgaste,** wearing surface

— **de deslizamiento**, slickenside

— **de dislocación,** fault plant

— **de fracturación,** (g) fracture plane

— **del émbolo,** piston area

— **de nivel,** niveau surface

— **de resudación,** sweating surface

— **equipotencial,** equipotential surface

— **isoterma,** isothermal surface

— **terrestre,** earth's surface

superfraccionamiento, superfractionation

superfraccionador, superfractionator

supergás, liquefied petroleum gas, LPG

superintendente, superintendent

superior, upper

superposición, superposition, (g) overlap

— **de estratos,** superposition of strata

superpuesto, superimposed, imbricated

supersaturación, supersaturation

suplemento, shims

— **para llave de herramientas,** tool wrench liner

supresor, suppressor

— **de ácido,** acid inhibitor

sur, south

surcamiento, (g) furrowing

surco, furrow

surcos, (g) rills

sur cuarta al sudeste (S 1/4 al SE), south of east

sur cuarta al sudoeste (S 1/4 al SE), south by west

surgencia imprevista de presión, (prf) kick

sur-oriente, southeast

sursudeste (SSE), south southeast

sursudoeste (SSO), south southwest

surtidor, jet, spray, nozzle, spout; filling station

— **auxiliar del carburador,** (mo) accelerating well

— **de gasolina,** service station, gas pump

susceptibilidad, susceptibility

susceptibilidad magnética, magnetic susceptibility

susexita, sussexite

suspensión, suspension

— **en tres puntos,** three-point suspension

— **macroscópica,** macroscopic suspension, coarse suspension

suspensor, hanger; beam hanger (q.v. **colgadero**)

— **de tubería de revestimiento,** casing suspender, casing support

— **de tubos,** tube hanger

— **de varillas de bombeo,** sucker-rod hanger

Glossary of the Petroleum Industry

— **para varillas asido a la cabeza
del balancín,** mule-head hanger
**suspe nsores del tubo de
producción,** tubing hangers
sutura, (g) suture

T

T con salida lateral, side-outlet T
T con toma auxiliar lateral, side-
inlet T
T de reducción, reducing tee,
reducing T
T para soldar, welding tee
tabique, partition
— **de baldosa para desviación,** tile
baffle
— **desviador para calderas,** boiler
baffle
— **interceptor,** baffle wall
tabla, a board; table, tabulation
— **ajustadora del vástago pulido,**
adjuster board
— **de conversión,** conversion table
tablazón, lumber
tablero, (in) board; switchboard;
(carp) panel
— **de avisos,** bulletin board
— **de control,** control board
— **de instrumentos,** instrument
panel, panel board, dashboard
tabular, a. v. tabulate
tachuela, tack
taco, wad; plug, bung; chock; (expl)
stemming, tamping
— **de limpiar,** pig, pigging
— **de rienda,** deadman
tacómetro, tachometer
tajamar, breakwater, jetty; sea wall;
basin
tajatubos, casing ripper
taladrar, v. tap
taladro, drill, auger, bit; drilled hole,
bore; rig

— **de pecho,** breast drill
— **eléctrico,** electric drill
— **para explosivos,** blast hole
talcita, talcite
talco, talc
talego de gas, gas bag
taller, shop, mill, workshop
— **de laminación,** rolling mill
— **mecánico,** machine shop
talud, slope, batter; talus
— **de corte,** (rd) back slope
— **exterior de la cuneta,** (rd) back
slope
tambaleo, wobble
tambor, barrel; drum, reel
— **de frenaje,** (mc) snubber
— **de la cinta de registro gráfico,**
chart drum
— **de maniobra,** calf wheel
— **de perforación,** bull wheel
— **del cable de perforación,** bull
reel
— **del cable del sacatestigos,** (prf)
coring reel
— **del cable de la tubería de
producción,** calf reel
— **del cable de la tubería de
revestimiento,** casing reel
— **del cable para medir
profundidades,** measuring reel
— **del freno,** brake drum
— **del malacate de herramientas,**
bull wheel spool
— **doble,** double drum
— **para el cable de la cuchara,**
sand-bailing reel, sand-line reel
(o spool)
— **sencillo,** single drum unit
tamiz molecular, molecular sieve
tanda, (rf) batch; turn, rotation;
task, gang of men
tangencial, tangential
tanque, tank, reservoir
— **asentador,** settling tank
— **compensador,** volume (o surge)
tank

401

— **con heno,** (pr) hay tank
— **con techo de expansión,** expansion roof tank
— **con techo de pontones,** pontoon roof tank
— **con techo flotante,** breather roof tank
— **de acero empernado,** bolted steel tank
— **de acero remachado,** riveted steel tank
— **de aire comprimido,** air receiver, tank for compressed air
— **de almacenamiento,** storage tank
— **de almacenamiento de presión,** pressure storage tank
— **de asentamiento,** gum barrel
— **de captación,** flow tank
— **de compensación,** floating (o surge, balance) tank
— **de equilibrio,** surge tank
— **de flotación,** buoyancy tank
— **de fondo cóncavo,** dish-bottom tank
— **de lodo devuelto,** mud return tank
— **de medición de petróleo,** oil gage tank
— **de orear,** (rf) flash drum
— **de prueba,** test tank
— **de radiador,** radiator tank
— **de techo flotante,** pontoon roof tank
— **de tratamiento,** treating tank
— **de purador de aire,** scrubber
— **igualador,** balance (o floating, surge) tank
— **inyector de ácido,** (rf) acid tank, acid blow case
— **medidor,** gauge tank
— **ovalado para almacenar ácidos,** acid egg
— **para gas,** gas holder, gasometer
— **receptor de aire,** air receiver, tank for compressed air

— **séptico,** septic tank
tantalita, tantalite
tapa, lid, cover, gap, cylinder head; (tu) cap (q.v. **cubierta**)
— **de cojinete,** bearing cover, bearing shell
— **de depósito,** tank cap
— **de embrague,** clutch cover
— **de gollete,** filler gap
— **de gollete de radiador,** radiator filler cap
— **de la cabeza flotante,** (heat exchanger) floating head cover
— **de radiador,** (a) radiator cap
— **de resorte de válvula,** valve spring cover
— **de seguridad,** safety cover
— **flotante,** floating head
— **guardapolvo,** dust cup
tapadero, plug, stopper
tapar, *v.* cover, plug
— **un pozo,** cap a well
tapón, stopper, plug; bulkhead, stopple
— **ciego,** bull plug
— **de cementación,** cementing plug
— **de dardo insertado por medio del fluido,** pump-down dart plug
— **de drenaje,** drain plug
— **de elevadores,** elevator plug
— **de evacuación,** drain plug
— **de huevo,** bull plug
— **de purga,** drain plug
— **de retención para tubería de revestimiento,** casing bridge plug
— **de seguridad,** safety plug
— **de tubería de revestimiento,** casing plug
— **flotante,** floating plug
— **fundible de seguridad,** fusible (o soft) plug
— **fusible,** fuse plug
— **hexagonal cuadrado,** hexagon head plug
— **intermedio,** bridge plug

Glossary of the Petroleum Industry

— **obturador,** blanking plug
— **para pozo improductivo,** dry-hole plug
— **puente inferior,** lower bridging plug
— **puente superior,** upper bridging plug
taponar, *v.* clog; plug
taquímetro, speed indicator, speed recorder, stadia
tarifa, tariff; rate
— **aérea,** air rate
— **de flete marítimo,** ocean rates
— **de fletes,** freight rates
— **de oleoductos,** pipeline rates
tarima, rack
— **para tuberías,** pipe rack
tarrajadora de dado, pipe thread die
tasa, valuation; rate; rating
— **de flujo,** rate of flow
tasación, (cm) appraisal
taxitas, (g) taxites
taza de enchufe, socket bowl
tazón, bowl
— **de agarre,** (fishing tl) catch bowl
— **de combustible,** (rf) fuel bowl
— **de cuñas,** spider, slip (o insert) bowl
— **de mordaza,** (fishing tl) catch bowl
— **de pesca,** catch bowl
tea, flare
teclado, keyboard
técnico, technician
tectitas, (g) tektites
tectónico, tectonic
techo, roof
— **en arco suspendido,** suspended arch roof
— **flotante,** floating roof
— **levadizo,** (tk) lifting roof
tefrita, tephrite
teja, roof tile
tejido de alambre, screen wire
tejuelo, pillow block

tela, cloth, fabric
— **de asbesto,** asbestos cloth
— **esmeril,** emery cloth
— **metálica,** screen wire, wire cloth
— **metálica del colador sacudidor,** shaker screen
teleclinómetro, teleclinometer
teleindicador, telegage,
telémetro, telemeter; range finder
teleregistrador, remote recorder
— **neumático,** air-actuated remote recorder
telescopio, telescope
telúrico, telluric
telurio, tellurium
temblor, earthquake
— **a poca profundidad,** shallow earthquake
— **cercano,** nearby shock
— **de tierra,** tremor
— **local,** shallow earthquake
— **previo,** (gf) foreshock
— **tectónico,** tectonic earthquake
témpano de hielo, iceberg, ice float
temperatura, temperature
— **absoluta,** absolute temperature
— **crítica,** critical temeprature
— **de ampolleta mojada,** wet bulb temperature
— **del vapor,** vapor temperature
— **de reacción,** (qm) reaction temperature
— **de salida,** outlet temperature
— **de vaporización,** vaporization temperature
— **final de destilación,** end point
— **límite,** end point
— **media,** mean temperature
— **normal,** normal temperature
— **pulsatoria,** pulsating temperature
tempestad magnética, magnetic storm (q.v. **perturbación**)
templa, batch
templado al aceite, oil tempering

403

templado de barrenas, hardening
of bits
templar, *v.* temper, quench
temple, temper, tempering,
hardening
temple superficial, case-hardening
tenacillas para cápsulas, (la)
crucible tongs (q.v. **pinzas)**
tenacillas para vasos, (la) beaker
tongs
tenazas, tongs, pliers, cutters,
nippers, pincers (q.v. **llaves)**
— **a cadena,** boll-weevil (o chain)
tongs
— **de montaje,** makeup wrench
— **para desconectar,** break-out
tongs
— **para entubamiento,** tubing
tongs
— **para perforación rotatoria,**
rotary tongs
— **para transportar tubería,**
carrying tongs
— **para tubería,** pipe tongs; pipe
hooks
— **para tubería de producción,**
tubing tongs
tendel, chalk line; bed of mortar,
mortar joint
tendencia, tendency; trend, drift
— **directiva horizontal,** (gf)
horizontal directive tendency
tender, (rr) tender
teneduría de libros, bookkeeping
tensión, tension
— **de vapor,** vapor pressure
— **electroestática,** electrostatic
stress
— **electromagnética,**
electromagnetic stress
— **interfacial,** interfacial tension
— **mecánica,** mechanical stress
— **superficial,** surface tension
tensor, turnbuckle
teñir, *v.* tinge, dye; stain
teodolito, theodolite, transit

teorema, theorem
teoría del rebote, elastic rebound
theory (q.v. **reacción elástica)**
terciario, tertiary
termal, thermal
térmico, thermal
terminación, completion
— **a dos zonas,** (prf) dual
completion
— **a presión,** pressure completion
— **con cámara impermeable,**
(mar) caisson completion
system
**terminación de pozos en varias
zonas,** multiple-zone well
completion
terminal, terminal
termita simple, (sd) plain thermit
termoclinal, thermocline
termocupla, thermocouple
termodinámica, *n.* t
hermodynamics
termófono, thermophone
termómetro, thermometer
— **a resistencia eléctrica,** electric
resistance thermometer
— **con tubo de vidrio graduado,**
etched stem glass thermometer
— **de máxima,** maximum
thermometer
— **de mínima,** minimum
thermometer
— **de prueba,** test thermometer
— **eléctrico,** electrothermometer
— **máximo,** maximum
thermometer
— **mínimo,** minimum thermometer
— **para bajas temperaturas,** low-
range thermometer
— **para el aceite,** oil thermometer
— **para el baño,** bath thermometer
termopermutador, (rf) heat
exchanger
termosifón, thermosyphon
termóstato, thermostat
termoregulador, thermo-regulator

terraja, pipe and bolt machine, threader
— **de trinquete,** ratchet stock and die
— **manual,** hand-operated threader
— **mecánica,** threading machine
— **para roscar madera,** devil
— **y dados,** tap and dies, stock and dies
— **y hembras de roscar,** tap and dies
terraplén, (g) terreplain, terrace; mound; embankment; earth fill, earthwork
— **aluvial,** alluvial terrace
terraza, (g) terrace
— **cortada por la acción desgastante de las olas del mar,** wavecut terrace
— **formada por la acumulación de sedimentos traídos por las olas del mar,** wave-built terrace
terremoto de foco profundo, deep focus earthquake
terreno, land, ground, soil, terrain
— **con posibilidades de petróleo,** prospective area
— **con yacimientos de petróleo comprobados,** proved area
— **desigual,** unlevelled land (o terrain)
— **desnivelado,** unlevelled land (o terrain)
terrestre, terrestrial
territorio, territory
teschemacherita, techermacherite
teschenita, teschenite
tesorería, treasury
— **nacional,** national treasury
tesorero, treasurer
testigo, (g) sample, specimen; (tp) a reference point
— **lateral,** (prf) wall core
testracíclicos, tetracyclic
tetracloruro de carbono, carbon tetrachloride

tetracosano, tetracosane
tetradecano, tetradecane
tetradeceno, tetradecene
tetraetilo, tetraethyl
— **de plomo,** tetraethyl lead
tetragonal, tetragonal
tetrahexacontano, tetrahexacontane
tetrahidrobenceno, tetrahydrobenzene, cyclohexene
tetrámero, tetramer
tetrametilo de plomo, tetramethyl lead
tetrametileno, tetramethylene
tetrametiletileno, tetramethylethylene
tetrapentacontano, tetrapentacontane
tetratetracontano, tetratetracontane
tetratriacontano, tetratriacontane
tetravalencia, tetravalence
tetravalente, tetravalent
textura, (mu) grain; (g) texture
— **petmatita,** pegmatite texture
— **fluidal,** flow structure
tiempo, time; (atmos) weather; (mo) cycle
— **activo,** uptime
— **consumido en la extracción de testigos,** (prf) coring time
— **de acceso,** (dp) access time
— **de aceleración,** acceleration time
— **de contacto,** residence time
— **de intercepción,** (gf) intercept time
— **de origen en el foco,** (gf) focal out time
— **de propagación,** (gf) propagation time, running time, (gf) travel time
— **de propagación calculado,** calculated travel time

— **de propagación de las ondas sísmicas,** time of transmission (o propogation) of earth waves
— **de reacción,** (rf) soaking time
— **de respuesta,** (dp) turnaround
— **de retardo,** time delay
— **de viraje,** (nt) turnaround time
— **extra,** overtime
— **observado,** observed time
— **pasivo,** idle time
— **vertical,** (gf) vertical time
— **vertical en el punto de disparo,** (gf) uphole time
tienda de campaña, canvas house, tent
tiento, belt lacing
tierra, ground, earth, soil, land, dirt; (el) ground
— **absorbente,** absorbent earth
— **adámica,** (g) adamic earth
— **baja,** lowland
— **de aluvión,** buttom land, alluvia, (g) estuarine deposit
— **de batán (o de Fuller),** Fuller's earth
— **de la soldadura,** welding ground
— **diatomácea,** (g) diatomaceous earth, diatomite
— **firme,** (g) land mass
— **floja,** loose earth
— **pantanosa,** fen land
tieso, (ca) tight, taut, stiff
tijeras, (prf) jar; shear; sawbuck; small ditch
— **de pesca,** lifting jar
— **de hojalatero,** snips
— **golpeadora,** jar bumper
tilita, (g) tilite, boulder clay
timbre fiscal, fiscal stamps, government stamps
timón, steering wheel; (nt) rudder
tinguaitas, tinguaite
tinolita, tinolite
tinte, dye
tiofano, thiophane
tiofeno, thiophene

tionizador, thionizer
tiosulfato, thiosulphate solution
tipo, type
— **de descuento,** (cm) discount rate
— **de pulverizador,** nodulizer
tirabuzón, corkscrew
tirafondo, lag screw
tiraje, (mc) draft
tirante, *n.* (mc) brace, stay, tie rod, truss rod; *a.* drawing, pulling; drawn, taut, stretched; strained; urgent, pressing
tiro, (mc) draft; (tp) course; (expl) shot
— **de aspiración,** exhaust drive
— **de chimenea,** stack draft
— **forzado,** forced draft
— **hacia abajo,** down-draft convection
— **inducido,** induced draft
titanita, titanite
titración, titer test
titulación, titration; titer test
título, title to property; professional degree; (cm) certificate, bond; headline, caption; title
— **de propiedad,** title to property
tixotropía, thixotropy
tiza, chalk
toba, tuff; sinter
— **calcárea,** travertine
— **de cenizas,** vitric tuff
tolano, tolane, diphenylacetylene
tolerancia, (mc) allowance, clearance, permissible discrepancy; tolerance
tolueno, toluene, methylbenzene
— **crudo,** toluol
— **sin refinar,** toluol
tolva, hopper, bin
toma, (el) outlet; water tap; intake
— **de fuerza,** power takeoff
tomacorrientes, (dp) jack
tomafuerza, power takeoff
tomamuestras, oil thief
tómbolo, (g) tombolo

tonelada, ton
— **bruta,** gross ton
— **larga,** long ton, gross ton
— **métrica,** metric ton
toneladas de peso muerto, (dwt)
  deadweight tons
tonelaje, tonnage
topacio, topaz
tope, *n.* (mc) stop; butt; lug; bumper,
  buffer; butt end
— **de producción,** production
  ceiling
topografía, topography
topográfico, topographic
topotipo, (paleo) topotype
torca, (g) sand gall
torcedura, twist
— **(o nudo) en el cable de acero,**
  wire-rope kink
— **de un cable,** kink
torcido, *n.* strand; lay; *a.* twisted;
  warped
torcimiento, warp
tormenta magnética, magnetic
  storm
tornado, tornado
tornallamas, bridge wall
tornapunta, spreader, brace, strut,
  spur
— **de los postes de la rueda
  motora,** jack braces
— **del poste del malacate,** bull
  wheel brace
tornillo, screw, bolt; vise
— **afianzador del ariete,** ram
  locking screw
— **alimentador,** temper (o feeding)
  screw
— **cabeza cónica,** flat head screw
— **de ajuste,** adjusting screw; setscrew
— **de anclaje,** anchor bolt
— **de Arquímedes,** Archimedean
  screw
— **de avance,** temper screw
— **de banco,** vise

— **de banco para tubos,** pipe vice
— **de cabeza,** capscrew
— **de cabeza cilíndrica,** fillister
  head screw
— **de cabeza embutida,**
  countersunk head screw
— **de cabeza fresada,** countersunk
  head screw
— **de cabeza redonda,** round head
  screw
— **de empaquetadura,** packing
  screw
— **de flijación,** holder clamp; lock
  screw, staybolt, setscrew
— **de mano,** thumbscrew
— **de máquina,** machine bolt
— **de mariposa,** wing-screw
— **de orejas,** thumbscrew
— **de presión,** lock screw
— **de retén,** setscrew
— **de separación y refuerzo,**
  staybolt
— **del compás de nivelar,**
  gradienter screw
— **graduador,** setscrew
— **para madera,** wood screw
— **para metales,** machine screw
— **regulador,** temper (o feeding)
  screw
— **remachado,** anchor bolt
— **sin fin,** screw conveyor, endless
  screw, worm
— **tangente de alidada,** tangent
  screw
— **tirafondo,** lag screw
— **transportador,** screw conveyor
torniquete, turnbuckle; turnstile
torno, (prf) cathead; drum, reel;
  lathe, hoist, hoisting engine; vise
— **auxiliar,** cathead
— **auxiliar automático,** automatic
  cathead
— **auxiliar de enrosque y
  desenrosque,** spinning cathead
— **del cable del achicador,** bailing
  reel, sand reel

— **de las llaves,** breakout cathead
— **de las tuberías de producción,** calf wheel
— **mecánico,** engine lathe
torpedeamiento, (gf) (prf) torpedoing; dynamiting, shooting
— **de un pozo,** shooting a well
torre, (rf) tower, column; (prf) derrick
— **de absorción,** absorption tower (o column)
— **de burbujeo,** bubble tower (o column)
— **de contacto,** contactor column
— **de destilación empacada,** packed tower
— **de destilación fraccionaria,** fractionating column (o tower), stabilizing column
— **de destilación por expansión instánea,** flash chamber (o drum, tower)
— **de destilación primaria preliminar,** (rf) preliminary charge stablizer, preflash tower
— **de destilación relámpago,** (rf) flash tower, (o drum, chamber)
— **de desviadores,** baffle tower
— **de enfriamiento,** cooling tower
— **de expansión primaria,** primary flash tower
— **de extensión,** telescoping derrick
— **de extensiones enchufadas,** telescoping derrick
— **de fraccionación,** stabilizing (o fractionating) column
— **de fraccionamiento,** fractionating tower
— **de lavado con agua,** water wash tower
— **del separador,** separator tower
— **depuradora,** wash tower
— **desgasificadora,** degasser tower
— **desisobutanizadora,** diesobutanizer tower
— **desmetanizadora,** demethanizer tower
— **empacada,** packed tower
— **enfriadora,** cooling tower
— **estabilizadora,** stabilizing column, fractionating column
— **evaporadora,** evaporator tower
— **plegadiza,** telescoping derrick
— **portátil de perforación,** portable drilling rig (o derrick)
— **rectificadora,** stripper tower
— **retenida,** guyed tower
torrecilla, turret
torrero, derrickman
torsión, torsion, twist, torque
tortoniense, Tortonian
tosca, (g) hardpan
total, total, sum
total de averías en tránsito, (cm) general average
tóxico, toxic
toxina, toxin
traba de vapor, vapor lock
trabajadero, (derrick) finger board
trabajo, work
— **pesado,** heavy duty
trabar, lock
trabazón, the weld of a truss; (masonry) bond
tracción, *n.* traction, pull; hauling; (mc) tension, tensile stress
tractóleo, tractor oil
tractor, tractor
— **de remolcador,** tow tractor
— **grúa,** pipe layer, boom tractor
— **guinche,** boom tractor
— **oruga,** caterpillar tractor
tiendetubos, (tractor) pipe layer, boom tractor
tractorina, tractor oil
tráfico, traffic
tragante, (frn) flue; smoke breeching
traílla, (rd) scraper
— **acarreadora,** carryall scraper
— **de arrastre,** drag scraper

— **volcadora de arrastre,** (rd ma)
roll-over scraper
tramo, bay, span, panel; (stairs)
flight; (belt) strand; (rr) block; a
length, stretch
— **suplementario,** (p) loop
trampa, (g) (tu) trap
— **conflotador de bola,** ball float
trap
— **de agua,** steam trap, drainator
— **de agua de expansión,**
expansion steam trap
— **de arena,** sand trap
— **de gas,** gas trap
— **de llamas,** engine arrester, flame
arrester
— **del raspatubos,** (p) pig-
launching trap, scraper trap
— **de vapor,** steam scrubber, steam
trap
— **depuradora de gases de horno,**
blast trap
— **estratigráfica,** (g) stratigraphic
trap
— **tipo cubeta,** bucket trap
transductor, transducer
transferencia de calor, heat
transfer
transformación anaclástica, (g)
deformation without shearing
transformador, transformer
— **de corriente alterna,** rectifier
— **eléctrico,** electric transformer
transgresión, (g) transgression
transgresivo, (g) overlapping
transistorizado, solid state
tránsito, transit, traffic
translúcido, translucent
transmisión, transmission
— **de contramarcha,** reverse drive
— **de contramarcha (o retroceso),**
reversing transmission
— **de engranaje interno,** internal
gear transmission
— **de inversión,** reversing
transmission

— **de marcha atrás,** reversing
transmission
— **en ángulo recto,** right-angle
drive
— **por cadena,** chain drive
— **por correa en V,** V-belt drive
— **sin multiplicación,** even-step
transmission
transmisiones, shafting
transmisor, (el) transmitter
— **del momento de torsión,** torque
converter
— **de torsión,** torque converter
transmitir, transmit
**transmutador de la fuerza que
causa el movimiento de
torcedura,** torque converter
transparente, transparent
transportador mecánico, conveyor
transporte, transportation
transversal, transverse
transverso, transverse
tranvía, tramway, street car
— **aéreo,** aerial tramway
traquilita, trachylyte
traquita, trachyte
trass, (g) trass
tratado al calor, heat treated
tratado con un disolvente, solvent
treated
tratamiento, treatment
— **ácido-amoniacal de la madera,**
aczolling
— **al calor,** heat treating
— **con ácido,** acid treatment
— **doctor,** (rf) doctor treating
— **hipoclorítico,** hypochlorite
treatment
— **por el método de fase de vapor,**
vapor-phase treating process
— **térmico,** heat treating
— **térmico para reducir los
esfuerzos,** stress relief heat
treatment
tratar, *v.* treat
travertino, (g) travertine

travesaño, cap, header, spreader,
batten, crosspiece, bolster;
crosstie; crossrail of a planer,
floor beam of a bridge;
(chain) stud bolt
— **de cadenas,** stud bolt
travesero alzapoleas, gin pole
traviesa, crosstie; batten, cap,
header, sill; crossarm, crossbar
trayectoria, trajectory path
— **de la onda sísmica,** path of
seismic ray
— **de tiempo mínimo,** minimum
time path
— **braquistocrónica, (gf)**
brachistochronic path
— **lineal,** linear travel
trazado, line, route, location;
traverse
— **de un poligonal,** traverse survey
trazadora de curvas, plotter
trazar, *v.* plan, locate, lay out,
design, draw
trazo, *n.* (drawing) trace
trébedes, (la) ring tripod
tremolita, tremolite
tren, train
— **de aterrizaje,** landing gear
— **rodante,** running gear
trenzado, (ca) lay
trepadera, climber
trépano, bit
— **de extensión,** extension bit
triacontano, triacontane, myricyl
triaconteno, triacontene
triangulación, triangulation
triangular, triangular
triángulo, triangle; (el) mesh
triásico, Triassic
triaxial, triaxial
tributario, (g) tributary
tricíclico, tricyclic
triclínico, (crystallog) anorthic;
triclinic
tricosano, tricosane
tricoseno, tricosene

tridecano, tridecane
trideceno, tridecene
trimestre, quarter
trimetilbenceno, trimethylbenzene,
pseudocumene (q.v.
hemimetileno)
trinquete, pawl; dog; ratchet; trip
finger
triple, triplex
trípode, tripod
triptano, triptane
tritetracontano, tritetracontane
tritriacontano, tritriacontane
trituradora, crusher, shredder
trocha, tread
trompo, (tu) swedge nipple
tronador, squib
troquel, die
truncamiento, (g) truncation
tsunami, tsunami
tubería, pipe; piping; tubing (q.v.
tubo)
— **acodada en la fábrica,** factory
bend pipe
— **adaptada,** fabricated piping
— **de ademe,** casing
— **de barro vitrificado,** vitrified
glazed clay pipe
— **de la bomba a los tanques,** lead
line
— **de carga,** penstock
— **de costura espiral,** spiral-welded
casing
— **de disparo,** tubing, flow pipe
— **de expansión,** expansion line
— **de extremidad cónica,** tapered
tubing
— **de flujo,** flow pipe
— **de perforación para enroscar
en caliente,** shrink thread drillpipe
— **de producción,** tubing; flow line
— **de revestimiento,** casing
— **de revestimiento de acero sin
costura,** seamless-steel casing

— de revestimiento de junta lisa, flush-joint casing

— de revestimiento de junta tipo Boston, Boston inserted-joint casing

— de revestimiento del hoyo inicial de un pozo, surface pipe

— de revestimiento final, water string, oil string

— de revestimiento intermedia, intermediate casing, water casing

— de revestimiento sin rosca, plain-end casing

— de transporte, pipeline

— estirada en frío, cold expanded pipe

— extrapesada, extra-heavy pipe

— intermedia de revestimiento, intermediate casing string

— para gas, gas line

— para productos refinados, products pipeline

— plástica, plastic pipe

— preformada, prefabricated piping

— revestida, coated pipe

— sin costura, seamless tubing

— soldada, welded pipe

— triturable, drillable casing, drillable liner

— usada, used pipe, reclaimed pipe

— vástago, drillpipe, grief stem

tubo, pipe, tube (q.v. tubería)

— abollado por el uso impropio de las cuñas de agarre, slip-crushed pipe

— acodado, elbow pipe

— aislante para alambres eléctricos, electric wiring conduit

— aletado, finned tube

— alimentador de gas, gas feeding line

— al vacío, vacuum tube

— ascendente, ascending pipe, riser

— ascendente del respiradero, vent riser

— a tanque, rundown line

— cacarañado, pitted pipe

— caído, collapsed pipe

— calado, perforated liner, perforated pipe, screen (o slotted) pipe; sand screen

— colador, screen (o slotted, perforated) pipe, liner; sand screen

— colador revestidor de fondo, perforated liner

— colador rodeado de grava para evitar que la arena se filtre en el pozo, gravel-packed liner

— colector, drip raiser

— condensador, condenser tube

— conducto, electric conduit

— conductor, conductor pipe

— conductor del aceite lubricante, oil line

— con extremos exteriores de mayor espesor, (tu) external upset ends, external upset pipe

— del aceite, oil-line tube

— de admisión, intake pipe

— de agua, water pipe

— de aleación, alloy pipe

— de alimentación, feed inlet

— de alimentación de combustible, fuel feed pipe

— de aspiración, (frn) draft tube; (bm) suction pipe

— de bajada, down pipe, downspout

— del colector de gas, boot vent

— del combustible, fuel line

— de convección, convection tube

— de cuarzo, quartz tube

— de descarga, eduction pipe

— de ensayo, test tube

— de entrada, penstock

— de escape, exhaust line, eduction pipe

— de estufa, stovepipe

— de expulsión, eduction pipe

411

— de extremos lisos, plain-end pipe
— de fondo, tail pipe
— de fuego, boiler tube
— del gas, gas line
— de inmersión, dip pipe
— de la manguera, stand-pipe
— de lavado, wash pipe
— del lodo, mud line (o conveyor)
— de perforación orientado, oriented drill pipe
— de procelana, procelain tube
— de rayos catódicos, (dp) display tube; CRT
— de rebose, overflow duct
— de recalcado interior, internal upset pipe
— de resalto interior, internal upset pipe
— de seguridad, thistle tube
— de sobrealimentación, supercharging pipe
— de subida, riser
— de succión, suction pipe
— de vapor, steam line
— distribuidor, distribution line, manifold
— embudado, thistle tube
— empalmado con soldadura al tope, butt-welded pipe
— en S, gooseneck
— en U, U tube
— flexible, flexible pipe
— indicador, gage glass
— macarrón, macaroni tubing
— múltiple, manifold
— múltiple de la bomba del lodo, slush pump manifold
— mutilado por las tenazas (o llaves), tong-crushed pipe
— perforado en el taller, (prf) shop-perforated pipe
— productor, tubing
— rayado, rifled pipe
— rectangular de ventilación, air box
— reductor de inserción, bean

— reforzado con nervaduras, finned tube
— revestidor, liner
— revestidor auxiliar perforado, perforated liner
— revestidor de fondo, liner
— revestidor de la ratonera, rathole pipe
— revestidor sin perforaciones, blank liner
— separador de gas, flume
— sin costura, seamless pipe
— sin perforaciones laterales, blank pipe
— sin punzonar, blank pipe
— sin soldadura, seamless pipe
— soldado en espiral, spiral pipe, spiral-welded pipe
— subiente, riser
— venturi, Venturi tube
— vertical, standpipe
tubos radiantes, radiant tubes
tuboscopio, tubescope
tubular, tubular
tuerca, nut; lock nut
— castillo, castellated nut
— ciega, acorn nut
— con salientes, horned nut
— cuadrada, square nut
— de ajuste de cojinete, bearing-adjustment nut
— de ajuste del vástago, stem-adjusting nut
— de aletas, wing nut
— de corona, castellated nut
— de eje, axle nut
— de la espiga, shank nut
— de orejas, wing nut
— de seguridad, jam nut, lock nut
— estriada, knurled nut
— hexagonal, hexagonal nut
— mariposa, wing nut, butterfly nut
— ovalada, acorn nut
tufa, tuff
tumor, (g) dome
túnel, tunnel

tungsteno, tungsten, wolframite
— **fundido,** cast tungsten
turba, (g) turf, peat
turbera, (g) peat bog
— **emergida,** upland moon
— **en forma de domo,** upland moon
turbieza, turbidity
turbina, turbine
— **de engranaje,** gear turbine
— **de vapor,** steam turbine
turbión, shower
turboaereador, turboaerator
turbocompresor, turbocompressor
turbogenerador, turbogenerator
turbonita, turbonite, oil shale
turbosoplador, turboblower
turbulencia, turbulence
turingiense, Thuringian
turmalina, tourmaline
turno, shift
— **de día,** day shift
— **de noche,** night shift

U

ubicación, location
ubicar, locate
último filete de una rosca, last-engaged thread
ultramicrómetro, ultramicrometer
umbral continental, (g) swell
undecano, undecane
undecadieno, undecadiene
undecadiino, undecadiyne
undeceno, undecene
uniaxial, uniaxial
unidad, a unit
— **CFR,** CFR fuel-testing unit
— **combinada,** (mo) compounding unit
— **de bombeo a motor,** power pumping unit
— **de bombeo con balancín,** beam pumping unit

— **de bombeo con cadenas reductoras de la velocidad,** chain-reduction pumping unit
— **de bombeo contrapesada neumáticamente,** air-balanced unit
— **de bombeo con poleas reductoras de la velocidad,** belt-reduction pumping unit
— **de conversión,** conversion unit
— **de cuadrante,** dial unit
— **de destilación al vacío,** vacuum distilling unit
— **de enfriamiento,** cooling unit
— **de fuerza,** power unit
— **de perforación de control automático,** automatic drilling-control unit
— **de potencia,** power unit
— **de repaso a presión para destilados,** pressure distillate rerun unit
— **Eötvös,** Eötvös unit
— **gravimétrica,** gravity unit
— **para redestilación,** (rf) rerun unit, rerun plant
— **térmica,** thermal unit
— **térmica británica,** British thermal unit (Btu)
unificación, *n.* unification; unitization; **unificar,** *v.* unify; (mc) (pr) unitize
uniformar, *v.* standardize
uniforme, uniform
uniformidad, uniformity
unión, joint, coupling, connection; (tu) union
— **abocardada de tubería vástago,** counterbored tool joint
— **a bridas,** flanged union
— **acodada,** elbow
— **acodillada,** toggle joint
— **articulada,** knuckle joint
— **con borde de bronce,** bronze-flanged fitting
— **de brida,** flange union

413

— **de calor,** heat union
— **de charnela,** hinged joint
— **de circulación,** circulating joint
— **de diámetro exterior a ras para tubería de perforación,** external flush tool joint
— **de diámetro interior a ras para tubería de perforación,** internal flush tool joint
— **de espiga y caja,** tongue-and-groove-joint union
— **de instalación rápida,** quickchange union
— **de lavado,** wash joint
— **de quitapón,** cutoff coupling
— **de reducción,** reducing coupling
— **de rosca,** threaded joint
— **de rosca para tubería de revestimiento,** casing coupling
— **de tubería vástago,** tool joint
— **de tubería vástago de diámetro exterior a ras,** external flush tool joint
— **de tubería vástago de diámetro interior a ras,** internal flush tool joint
— **de tubería vástago de diámetro interior uniforme,** full hole tool joint
— **de tubería vástago de doble conexión macho,** double pin tool joint
— **de tubería vástago emplamada en caliente,** shrunk on tool joint
— **de tubos,** pipe coupling (q.v. **acoplamiento**)
— **desprendible,** release couple, backoff joint
— **embridada,** flanged union
— **empernada,** bolted coupling
— **esférica,** ball union
— **en T,** T-joint
— **flexible,** flexible coupling
— **giratoria,** swivel
— **giratoria para perforadora rotatoria,** rotary swivel

— **piloto,** pilot joint
— **provista de orejas para ajuste a martillazos,** hammer-lug union
— **pulimentada,** ground-in joint, ground joint
— **rectificada,** ground-in joint, ground joint
— **roscada,** threaded joint
— **soldada,** welded joint
— **substituta,** sub
— **substituta para tubería de producción,** tubing sub
— **substituta para vástago de válulas,** valve rod sub
— **T,** T-joint
— **universal,** universal joint
uña, claw, paw, grouser, lug; fluke of an anchor; fang
útil, *n.* tool; *a.* useful
utilidad, profit
utilidades probables, estimated profits

V

vaciadero, (foundry) gate; sluiceway; dump; weir; slop sink
vaciar, *v.* empty; cast, pour; dump
vacío, void, vacuum, empty
vacuo, vacuum
vacuómetro, vacuum gauge
vagón, car, freight car
— **tanque,** tank car
vagonada, car load, truckload
vaguada, (r) waterway; channel, watercourse
valencia, valence
valía, valuation, value, worth
válido, valid
valor, value
— **asegurable,** (cm) insurable value
— **asiento inserto de,** valve insert
— **de gravedad en la estación de base,** (gravim) base value

Glossary of the Petroleum Industry

— de la referencia a la base, (tp)
base tie
— neutralizador, neutralization
value
válvula, valve
— accionada por un flotator,
float-operated valve
— acodillada, angle valve
— a la culata, valve in head
— amortiguadora, damping valve
— angular, angle valve
— apagadora de sonido, muffler
— a prueba de fallo, fail-safe valve
— a prueba de sabotaje, tamper-proof valve
— atornillada, screwed valve
— con camisa de vapor, steam-jacketed valve
— con guías de tope y fondo, top-and-bottom guided valve
— controladora de la circulación, circulating head
— de abajo, standing valve
— de abertura retardada, slow-opening valve
— de acción rápida, quick-opening valve
— de admisión, admission (o intake) valve
— de aguja, needle valve
— de aire, air valve
— de aletas, butterfly valve
— de alivio, pressure relief valve, safety valve (o relief) valve
— de alivio a resorte, spring-loaded relief valve
— de alivio de la presión, pressure relief valve
— de altas presiones, extra-heavy valve
— de arranque, (gas lift) kickoff valve
— de arriba, traveling valve
— de asiento chato, flat seat valve
— de asiento plano, poppet valve
— de aspiración, foot valve

— de bloqueo, block valve
— de bola y asiento, ball-and-seat valve
— de boya, float valve
— de caída, drop valve
— de campana, cup valve
— de ceba, (bm) priming valve
— de cierre, stop-check valve, shutoff valve
— de cierre automático, cutoff valve
— de cierre para emergencia, emergency stop valve
— de codo, angle valve
— de compoundaje, compounding valve
— de compuerta, (prf) cellar control gate, sluice gate valve
— de contrapresión, back pressure valve
— de control, control valve, blowout preventer, master gate, control head
— de control tipo de diafragma, diaphragm control valve
— de copa, cup valve
— de corona, crown valve
— de corredera, piston (o slide) valve
— de curz, cross valve
— de charnela, swing check (o flap, hanging) valve
— de dardo, dart valve
— de derivación, bypass valve
— de desagüe, sluice gate valve, drawoff valve
— de desahogo, relief valve
— de descarga, discharge (o flow, exhaust, blowoff, drawoff) valve
— de descarga con pasador rompible, shear-relief valve
— de desviación, bypass valve
— de diafragma, diaphragm valve
— de disco con movimiento vertical, poppet valve
— de disparo, pop valve

415

Español - Inglés

— **de doble asiento,** double-seat valve
— **de dos vías,** two-way valve
— **de escape,** exhaust relief valve, blowoff (o relief) valve
— **de esclusa,** gate valve
— **de estrangulación,** throttle valve; pinch valve
— **de expansión,** expansion valve
— **de globo,** globe valve
— **de gozne,** hanging valve
— **de hierro de barras,** bar stock valve
— **de jaula,** crown valve
— **de junta kelly,** kelly valve
— **de lengüeta,** feather valve
— **de macho,** stem valve
— **de maniobra,** pilot-operated valve
— **de manómetro,** gauge valve
— **de mariposa,** butterfly valve
— **de movimiento vertical,** lift valve
— **de obturador de manguito,** mushroom (o poppet) valve
— **de paso,** line (o shutoff, flow) valve
— **del pito,** whistle valve
— **de prellenado,** prefill valve
— **de punta de aguja,** needlepoint valve
— **de purga,** blowoff valve
— **de purga de la bomba del lodo,** mud pump release valve
— **de purga para la tubería de producción,** tubing bleeder
— **de reducción,** reducing valve
— **de relevo,** compounding valve
— **de respiradero,** vent valve
— **de retención,** check valve; stop-check valve
— **de retención a bisagra,** swing-check valve
— **de retención a bola,** ball-check valve

— **de retención acodillada,** angle-check valve
— **de retención de la empaquetadura,** packing-check valve
— **de rosca,** screwed valve
— **de salida,** outlet valve
— **de seguridad,** pressure relief valve, safety (o relief) valve
— **de seguridad con resorte descubierto,** exposed spring-pop safety valve
— **de seguridad enterrada,** subsurface safety valve
— **de solenoide,** solenoid valve
— **de tapón,** plug valve, kelly cock
— **de tapón suelto,** drop valve
— **de tres pasos,** three-way valve
— **de vástago hueco,** hollow stem valve
— **de la zapata de cementación,** bridging ball
— **embridada,** flanged valve
— **en la culata,** valve-in-head
— **en el fondo del achicador,** bailer valve
— **esclusa,** sluice gate valve
— **esclusa de emergencia,** emergency gate valve
— **esclusa de vástago estacionario,** nonrising stem gate valve
— **esférica,** globe valve
— **excitadora,** kickoff valve
— **excitadora de presión,** actuating pressure valve
— **fija,** standing valve
— **flotadora para tubería de perforación,** drillpipe float
— **giratoria,** butterfly valve
— **intermitente,** intermitter valve
— **intermitente de la bomba de fondo de pozo,** bottom intermitter
— **intermitente de control,** surface-controlled intermitter
— **maestra,** master valve

Glossary of the Petroleum Industry

— **matriz,** control valve, blowout preventer, master gate, control head

— **mezcladora,** blending valve

— **móvil,** traveling valve

— **para combinación de bombas en serie,** compounding valve

— **para soldar,** welding rod

— **piloto,** pilot valve

— **plana de cuchara,** flat valve bailer

— **reductora,** reducing valve

— **reductora de la presión,** pressure reducing valve

— **reguladora de flujo,** flow valve

— **reguladora de vacío,** vacuum relief valve

— **soltadora de la empaquetadura,** packing release valve

— **tipo lanzadera,** shuttle valve

— **viajera,** traveling valve

valla, fence, barricade; hurdle; barrier

valle, valley

— **aluvial,** outwash plain

— **antecedente,** epigenetic valley

— **colgante,** hanging valley

— **de drenaje,** water gap

— **de fractura,** tectonic valley

— **en el desierto,** desert valley

— **epigenético,** epigenetic valley

— **senil,** old-age valley

— **subsecuente,** subsequent valley

— **tectónico,** tectonic valley

— **transversal,** transverse valley

vanadio, vanadium

vano, opening

vapor, steam, vapor

— **de agua,** water vapor

— **de cima,** top steam

— **de escape,** exhaust steam

— **despetrolizante,** (rf) stripping vapor

— **recalentado,** superheated steam

— **saturado,** saturated steam

— **vivo,** live steam

vaporímetro, vaporimeter

vaporización, vaporization

— **en el instante de equilibrio,** equilibrium flash vaporization

— **instantánea,** flash vaporization

— **por cochadas,** batch vaporization

— **relámpago,** flash vaporization

vaporizador, vaporizer

vara, a rod, pole, staff

— **de medir la profundidad penetrada por la barrena,** measuring stick

varar, (nt) take ground

variable, variable

variación, variation

— **lateral,** (g) lateral variation

— **magnética,** magnetic variation

— **normal,** normal variation

— **secular,** (gf) secular variation

— **textural,** textural variation

variaciones

— **admisibles,** (tp) permissible variations

— **diurnas,** (gf) diurnal variations

— **proporcionadas,** proportionate variations

variador, variator

varilla, rod, bar, stem

— **arrastraválvulas,** Garbutt rod

— **corta,** pony rod

— **del acelerador,** accelerator rod

— **de bombeo,** sucker rod. (q.v. varilla de succión)

— **de bombeo substituta,** sucker-rod sub

— **de succión,** (bm) sucker rod

— **de empuje,** push rod

— **del freno,** brake rod

— **de mando,** operating rod

— **de mando del freno,** brake-actuating rod

— **de succión,** sucker rod

— **de tracción,** (bm) pull rod

— **de válvula,** valve rod

— **excéntrica,** eccentric rod
— **Garbutt,** Garbutt rod
— **graduada,** gaging pole
— **medidora,** (tk) gaging pole
varve, varve
vaselina, Vaseline, petroleum jelly
vasija, receptacle, vessel
— **de combustión,** (la) combustion
  boat
— **de filtro,** (rf) filter bowl
vaso, basin, reservoir; vessel,
  receptacle
— **abierto,** (la) open cup
— **cónico con vertedero y pico,**
  conical beaker with lip and
  spout
— **de precipitados graduado,** con
  dos vertedores, graduated beaker
  with lip and double
  spout
vástago, stem, shank, rod, spindle
— **de barrena,** auger stem, drillstem
— **de émbolo,** piston rod
— **del malacate de la cuchara,**
  sand-reel reach
— **de orificio en V,** (va) port plug
— **de válvula,** valve stem
— **pulido,** (bm) polished rod
vatímetro, watt meter
vatio, watt
vector magnético, magnetic vector
vector principal de gravedad,
  gravity gradient
vega, (g) oxbow lake
vegetación, vegetation
vejez, old age
velocidad, speed, velocity
— **aparente,** apparent velocity
— **aparente buzamiento abajo,**
  (gf) downdip apparent velocity
— **baja sin carga,** idle speed
— **crítica,** critical velocity
— **de agitación,** stirring speed
— **de intervalo,** (gf) interval
  velocity
— **del cable,** line speed

— **del flujo,** flow rate
— **de penetración,** rate of
  penetration
— **de perforación de la barrena,**
  cutting rate
— **de progagación,** (gf)
  propagation velocity
— **instantánea,** instantaneous
  velocity
— **intermedia,** intermediate speed,
  intermediate gear
— **lineal,** linear velocity
— **media,** average velocity
— **periférica,** peripheral speed
— **promedio,** mean velocity
— **sísmica,** seismic velocity
— **verdadera,** true velocity
velocímetro, speed indicator,
  speedometer
vencerse, (cm) to become due
vencimiento, (cm) expiration
vendedor, seller, salesman
veneno, poison
venenoso, poisonous
venero, (mn) pay seam
venilacetileno, vinylacetylene (q.v.
  butenino)
venta, (cm) sale; selling; marketing;
  roadside inn
ventana, (g) inlier; window
ventanilla, window
— **de inspección,** inspection port
ventilación, ventilation
ventilador, fan; blower; ventilator
— **a fuerza motriz,** power blower
— **aspirador,** exhaust fan
— **de radiador,** radiator fan
— **eductor,** exhauster
— **eléctrico,** electric fan
— **extractor,** exhaust fan
ventisquero, glacier, snow-capped
  mountain, wind gap
ventosa al vacío, vacuum relief
  valve
venturímetro, Venturi meter
verdadero, true

vereda, path, footpath, trail; sidewalk; (rr) platform
verificación de validez, (dp) validity check
verificador del contenido de una formación geológica, formation tester
verificador de pared, side hole cutter
vermiculita, vermiculite
vernier, vernier
vertebrado, vertebrate
vertedero, (hd) apron, spillway, wear; dump; slop sink; moldboard
verter, *v.* pour
vertical, vertical
vértice, vertex, crest, peak
— **de una curva,** summit of a curve
vertiente de un dique, fall of a dike
vesicular, vesicular
vesículos, vesicles
vestigios de hidrocarburos, show of oil
vesuvianita, vesuvianite
veta, (mn) streak; vein, seam; grain of wood
vía de pestaña, flangeway
viaducto de caballetes, trestle
viaje, trip, voyage; bevel, chamfer, skew
— **de ida y vuelta,** round trip
vibración, vibration; shimmy
— **forzada,** forced vibration
vibrar, oscillate
vidrio, glass
— **de nivel,** (cl) gage glass
— **poroso,** sintered glass plate
— **pyrex,** Pyrex glass
— **volcánico,** volcanic glass, obsidian
viento, wind; a guy
viga, beam, girder, joist
— **acartelada,** cantilever beam
— **angular,** angle beam

— **de asiento del motor,** engine mud sill
— **de separación,** (frame) spreader
— **en forma de caja,** box beam
— **en T,** T beam
— **en U,** structural channel
— **I de eje,** I-beam axle
— **voladiza,** cantilever beam
vigía, watch, watchman
vigilancia, watch
vigilia, watch
vigueta, beam, joist, purlin; rafter
— **de canal,** channel iron
— **de sección en I,** I beam
— **en T,** T beam
vinilacetileno, vinyl acetylene
vinilbenceno, vinylbenzene (q.v. feniletileno)
virgación, (g) virgation
virola, collar, hook, rim, ferrule, burr
viruta de hierro, iron borings
viruta de perforación, drill cuttings, borings
visa consular, (cm) consular visa
viscorreductora, visbreaker
viscosidad, viscosity
— **absoluta,** absolute viscosity
— **cinética,** kinematic viscosity
— **dinámica,** dynamic viscosity
— **relativa,** relative viscosity
viscosímetro, viscosimeter, viscosity meter
viscoso, viscous
visera, visor
visibilidad, visibility
vista adelante, foresight
vista lateral, (prf) side elevation
visto bueno, approval
visual, *n.* (tp) sight; *a.* visual
— **adelante,** foresight
— **inversa,** backsight
vitriolo azul, blue vitrol
voladura, a blast, blasting; shot
— **en el fondo del pozo para crear hendiduras,** (pr) well shooting

Español - Inglés

volante, steering wheel, flywheel;
   (a) driving wheel
— **manubrio,** hand wheel
volar, *v.* blast; project; fly
volátil, volatile
volcán, volcano
— **apagado,** extinct volcano
— **de lodo,** mud volcano
— **en embrión,** embryonic volcano
volcánico, volcanic
volframita, wolframite
voltaje, voltage
— **del flujo del arco,** (sd) arc-
   stream voltage
voltamperio, volt-ampere
**volteador de la tubería de
   producción,** tubing rotator
voltímetro, voltmeter
voltio, volt
volumen, volume
— **de crácking por recorrido,**
   crack-per-pass
— **de materia prima tratada,**
   throughput
— **de producción,** output
— **medido por contadores,** meter
   runs
volumétrico, volumetric
vórtice, vortex
vuelco de la memoria, (dp) dump
vulcanismo, vulcanism
vulcanización, vulcanization
vulcanizar, vulcanize
vuelta, (ca) bight; turn

waca, (g) wacke
winche, hoisting engine
wurzilita, wurtzilite

xenolita, xenolith
xerofítica, xerophytic
xenomorfo, xenomorphic (q.v.
   alotriomorfo)
xileno, xylene (q.v.
   dimetilbenceno)

Y

yacente, (g) hanging wall, sole
yacimiento, reservoir bed, deposit
— **petrolífero,** oil reservoir, oil
   deposit, oil bearing formation,
   oil pool, oil field
yesita, gibbsite
yeso, gypsum, plaster of Paris
yesoide, gypsite
yodo, iodine
yoduro, iodide
yugo, yoke
yugo de cuello de ganso, gooseneck
   yoke
yungas, humid valleys of the Andes
yunque, anvil
— **con sujeción para afilar
barrenas,** anvil block for dressing
   bits
— **de tornillo,** anvil vise
— **tipo puente,** bridge anvil
yute, jute
yuxtaponer, *v.* juxtapose
yuxtaposición, juxtaposition; (g)
   accretion; superposition

Z

zafiro, sapphire
zampeado, (hd) apron
zanja, trench, ditch (q.v. canal)
— del lodo, mud ditch
zanjadora, ditching machine
zapadora, excavator
zapapico, pick mattock
zapata, shoe; brake shoe, brake block; tread; (well), set shoe; (mn) head timber; (carp) foot block
— cortatubos, rotary milling shoe
— de cementación, cementing shoe, set shoe, casing shoe
— de cementación de la tubería de revestimiento, casing (o cementing) shoe
— de contrapeso, counterbalance shoe
— de la cruceta, crosshead shoe
— de flotación para cementar, cement float shoe
— del freno, brake shoe
— de hincar, drive shoe
— de la tubería de revestimiento, casing shoe
— flotadora, float shoe
— fresadora, milling shoe
— giratoria, whirler shoe
— guía para cementar, cement guide shoe
zapatilla, washer, gasket; (carp) foot block
— de cuero, leather gasket
zapatos de seguridad, safety shoes
zaranda, mud screen
— vibratoria, vibrating screen
zeolita, zeolite
zinc, zinc
zócalo, base
— de motor, engine base
zoicita, zoisite
zona, zone
— batial, (g) bathyal zone
— de aereación, zone of aeration, zone of suspended water
— de agua en suspensión, zone of aeration, zone of suspended water
— de calor, (rf) hot spot
— de cementación, (prf) belt of cementation
— de desgaste, (g) belt of weathering
— de deslizamiento cortante, (g) shear zone
— de fallas, fault zone
— de metamorfismo por contacto, (g) contact metamorphic zone
— de reacción, reaction zone
— de saturación, zone of saturation
— gasífera, gas zone
— herítica, (g) action zone
— múltiple, (g) multizone
— petrolífera, oil zone
— porosa, porous zone
— sombreada, (gf) shadow zone
zubia, channel; pool; swamp
zulaque, mortar (o mastic) for filling pipejoints
zumbador, buzzer
zumbador eléctrico, electric buzzer
zunchar, v. strap, bond, hoop
zuncho, band, hoop, iron strap